Guide to the Materials for American History, to 1783, in the Public Record Office of Great Britain

VOLUME II
DEPARTMENTAL AND MISCELLANEOUS PAPERS

BY

CHARLES M. ANDREWS
Farnam Professor of American History in Yale University

WASHINGTON, D. C.
PUBLISHED BY THE CARNEGIE INSTITUTION OF WASHINGTON
1914

Guide to the Materials for American History, to 1783, in the Public Record Office of Great Britain

VOLUME II
DEPARTMENTAL AND MISCELLANEOUS PAPERS

BY

CHARLES M. ANDREWS
Farnam Professor of American History in Yale University

WASHINGTON, D. C.
PUBLISHED BY THE CARNEGIE INSTITUTION OF WASHINGTON
1914

CARNEGIE INSTITUTION OF WASHINGTON

PUBLICATION No. 90A, VOLUME II

PAPERS OF THE DEPARTMENT OF HISTORICAL RESEARCH

J. FRANKLIN JAMESON, EDITOR

The Lord Baltimore Press

BALTIMORE, MD., U. S. A.

PREFACE.

In addition to those, mentioned in the previous volume, to whom I am indebted for courteous and helpful co-operation in the preparation of the work as a whole, there are others, who have aided me especially in connection with this volume, to whom I wish to extend my thanks. My largest debt is to Mr. R. G. Marsden, well known as an expert upon all matters pertaining to the history of the High Court of Admiralty, who has given me generously of his time and learning and has placed at my disposal lists and notes without which certain sections, duly noted in the proper place in the text, could not have been rendered even approximately complete within the time available to me. To Mr. Henry Atton, librarian of the Custom House library, I am under obligation for courtesies extended to me at the Custom House and for other favors, while to the Board of Customs Commissioners I am indebted for permission to examine Custom House papers and to Lord Dysart for permission to inspect those of the Treasurer Solicitor. To Mr. Victor H. Paltsits I owe many thanks for the data here printed regarding the transcripts of Loyalist Papers in the New York Public Library; and to Mr. Robert W. Neeser, secretary of the Naval History Society, and Mr. Edward E. Curtis, instructor in Yale College, friends and former students, I am grateful for helpful notes on the Admiralty and War Office material respectively. I wish to thank Miss Davenport also for the initial report on the Cornwallis, Chatham, and Rodney papers, and Mr. J. W. Chapman, of the Public Record Office, for his answers to my many queries regarding the rearrangement of the Treasury Papers.

CHARLES M. ANDREWS.

TABLE OF CONTENTS.

ADMIRALTY PAPERS.

INTRODUCTION.

The civil administration of the navy begins with King John, when there appears a " Keeper of the King's Ships ", who controlled naval organization before the accession of the Tudors. In the reign of Henry VIII. a great revival of interest took place in the navy; Trinity House was incorporated, the Ordnance Office remodelled, and the great docks at Deptford and Woolwich were constructed. But the navy was still the personal property of the sovereign, and during the greater part of the period was managed by the old keeper under the title of " Clerk of the Ships ", with such subordinates as were needed. Not until the end of Henry's reign was the navy placed under the charge of a separate department. Then the Navy Office was founded, and on April 24, 1546, certain officers were appointed known as the principal officers of the navy to administer the civil business under direction of the Lord High Admiral.

Thus by the middle of the sixteenth century the Admiralty had separated into three distinct parts: the Lord High Admiral, later the Admiralty Board, exercising executive and deliberative functions; the Navy Board, exercising civil and administrative functions; and the High Court of Admiralty, possessing judicial functions. In 1560, under Queen Elizabeth, a set of regulations was issued for the " Office of Admiralty and Marine Causes ", providing for definite officers to manage the affairs of the Navy Office—the vice-admiral of the fleet, the master of ordnance, the surveyor of marine causes, the treasurer, comptroller, and surveyor general of the victualling, clerk of the ships, and clerk of the stores. This board met once a week, reporting monthly to the Lord High Admiral. No departmental records exist for this early period.

After 1596, unfortunate appointments led to a decline in the efficiency of the board. In 1618, the administration was entrusted to the Duke of Buckingham, who established a board of commissioners known as the Council of the Sea, which continued to sit either at Wallingford House or, after Buckingham's death in 1628, in the Council Chamber at Whitehall. The principal officers met in Mark Lane in 1628 and in 1630 in Mincing Lane. After Warwick's tenure as Lord High Admiral by authority of Parliament (1643) had come to an end in 1649, the Commonwealth established an admiralty committee of the Council of State, and a board of commissioners of the navy, upon which the brunt of the work fell, but these boards were combined after 1654 as Commissioners of the Admiralty and the Navy. During this period the navy was brought to a degree of excellence never attained before.

The beginnings of the modern admiralty system date from the years 1660-1673, when James, duke of York, was Lord High Admiral, and Samuel Pepys was clerk of the accounts of the Navy Board. James reconstituted the Navy Board, by commission under the great seal,[1] establishing three principal officers—treasurer, comptroller, and surveyor—and three commissioners. A

---

[1] *Cal. St. Pap. Dom.*, 1660-1661, p. 110.

fourth commissioner was added in 1662.[1] Pepys as clerk of the accounts recorded all orders, contracts, bills, warrants, and other business transacted by
the principal officers and by the commissioners.[2] He was at the head of the
office work, attended the meetings of the board, and was of equal standing
with the other members. His range of interest was very wide, from ship-
building and the preservation of the forests to the discipline and actual management of the service. He was also a member of the corporation of Trinity
House, and on October 27, 1665, became surveyor general of the victualling
service. In 1673 the office of Lord High Admiral was put in commission and
Pepys was appointed to the newly created post of secretary to the Admiralty
Board. He was a member of Parliament, and his influence, as well as that
of the Duke of York, continued to be exercised until 1679, when he was sent
to the Tower and the Duke of York left England. A new commission was
appointed which took the place of both the Admiralty and Navy boards, but
it was composed of men without experience, and as a result the navy steadily
deteriorated until in five years the ships in commission sank from 76 to 24.
With the revival, in part, of the Navy Board in 1684 and a return to the system
of 1673, conditions improved. Pepys was restored as secretary, and the Duke
of York, coming back to England in 1684, exercised as king an informal
control over naval affairs, particularly in matters of ship-building and
patronage.[3] Pepys finally retired in 1689.

The existence of two boards—Admiralty and Navy, one executive and
military, the other civil and administrative, one nominally superior, the other
with the prestige of age and seniority—inevitably led to a divided control and
consequent antagonism. Though a few frigates were sent to Jamaica after
1660, the government proved incompetent to protect the island against pirates,
when, in the eighties, the latter became a serious menace. Expeditions to
America were badly managed. Those of 1676-1677 to Virginia, 1690-1691
to New York, and 1695 to Jamaica started months too late and accom-
plished little in consequence. Except for the period from 1684 to 1689, when
Charles II. and James II. acted each in his prerogative capacity as Lord High
Admiral, the office remained in commission until 1701, when the Earl of
Pembroke became Lord High Admiral, followed by Prince George of Denmark, who held the office with a board of commissioners as his council. In
1708 Pembroke served again, but the next year the office again went into
commission, and with the exception of the year 1827, when William, duke of
Clarence, afterward William IV., was Lord High Admiral, has remained so
ever since.

From 1689 to 1782, with the exceptions noted, the admiralty system consisted of an Admiralty Board with its secretary, a Navy Board with its four
principal officers, and a series of lesser boards and offices, nearly all of which,
as business increased, had been thrown off from the principal offices. The
subordinate branches were: the Treasurer's Office, the Navy Pay Office, the
Victualling Board, the Board of Transport Service, the Board for Sick and
Wounded Seamen, the Prize Office, the Rendezvous Office, the Marine Pay
Office, the Chest at Chatham, the Sixpenny Receiver's Office, the Board of
Longitude, the Royal Naval Academy at Portsmouth, and Greenwich Hospital. As the comptroller and surveyor formed different departments, the
system before the end of our period was made up of seventeen separate parts,

[1] Sir G. F. Duckett, *Naval Commissioners*, 1660-1760 (privately printed, 1889).
[2] See Instructions of 1649. Wheatley, *Pepys*, preface, p. xxiii.
[3] Tanner, *Catalogue of the Pepysian Manuscripts*, III. ix.

scattered about, as will be seen later, in Whitehall and the City. Nearly all of these offices have left records of their business, which show that the leading branches were organized as subdepartmental boards, with correspondence, minutes, registers, and accounts.

The directive branch of the Admiralty consisted of the Lord High Admiral, with commissioners under him, or later the Lords Commissioners of the Admiralty with their secretary. The board met daily, and in times of urgency twice daily, and carried on the routine work of directing the business of the navy. It shaped the policy of the government, generally under the direction of the king, as expressed in orders in Council, or in instructions from the Secretary of State, controlled the movement of the ships, determined the times of sailing, and kept a watch upon the execution of its orders. It corresponded with the admirals, vice-admirals, captains, commanders, and lieutenants of the squadrons, and after 1762 kept elaborate digests of the contents of letters received from them. It made appointments and signed warrants, not only for the higher officers but for carpenters, gunners, pursers, boatswains and their deputies, and even cooks. It administered to naval officers the oath and the test, generally by deputations sent to Chatham or Portsmouth, granted protection from impress, and furnished passes required by the merchant vessels for trading in the Mediterranean. Regarding convoys, imprests, transport, and supplies, it was in constant communication with the four principal branches of the administration—Navy Board, Victualling Board, Board for Sick and Wounded, and Transport Office—and it issued orders and instructions either directly or, as was frequently the case with the Victualling Board, indirectly through the Navy House. It kept in touch with other subordinate officers, rendezvous lieutenants, prize commissioners, and paymasters of marines, and watched over Chatham Chest and Greenwich Hospital. It received recommendations, reports, and representations from the subordinate boards, and in its turn drafted memorials and representations to the Privy Council and the Treasury. It requested the Bishop of London to name suitable persons as chaplains of the fleet, and authorized all issues of money for the upkeep of the navy and the payment of its members, civil and naval. Having control over vice-admiralty jurisdiction, it was in very close touch with the High Court of Admiralty, issuing commissions for vice-admiralty officials and taking cognizance of all difficulties that arose in the exercise of vice-admiralty jurisdiction. It issued warrants for letters of marque, controlled the holding of courts-martial, and had immediate supervision of the marines in all parts of the world.

The Admiralty and the Navy Board had a regular counsellor whose business it was to give advice in matters of law, and a solicitor who conducted prosecutions against " pirates, embezzlers of the queen's stores, and other offenders ".[1] In the early years one solicitor acted for all the principal offices, but later, as admiralty law business increased, the Navy and Victualling boards were allowed solicitors of their own. The Admiralty called for reports on cases from the judges and advocates of the High Court of Admiralty, and from the attorney general and solicitor general, chiefly concerning questions relating to vice-admiralty courts and jurisdiction, prize cases, droits of admiralty, letters of marque, and the like.[2] It also corresponded with the

---

[1] *House of Lords Manuscripts,* new series, V. 209-215.

[2] The functions of the Admiralty as officially defined may be found in the statutes, 2 William and Mary, sess. 2, c. 2 (1690), and George II., c. 33 (1749), and in the many commissions entered on the Patent Rolls. See also *Collection of Statutes relating to the Admiralty, Navy, Ships of War,* etc. (London, 1768). Though consulting these sources, I have in the main depended on the records of the Admiralty itself.

Secretary of State, the Treasury, the Commissioners of the Customs, the Ordnance Board, the General Post Office, and the Secretary at War.

Though at first the Admiralty refused to have any direct communication with the Board of Trade and demanded that all business be done through the intermediation of the Privy Council, yet in time a less formal procedure was followed and the two boards became mutually co-operative. The Board of Trade sent to the Admiralty a great amount of information regarding illicit trade, fisheries, naval stores, convoys, privateers, pirates, and vice-admiralty courts, and aided the Admiralty in the enforcement of trade laws and embargoes. It called on the Admiralty to assist in all matters involving the welfare of trade and plantations, such as convoys for merchant vessels, the transportation of governors and other royal officials, the furnishing of frigates and small craft for the protection of the colonies, the carrying of packets and letters, and other similar matters. The Admiralty, in conjunction with the law officers of the crown or the High Court of Admiralty, prepared the clauses in the governors' instructions that concerned Admiralty jurisdiction, and transmitted them to the board for recommendation to the Privy Council. It corresponded directly with colonial governors, and the latter wrote letters to the Admiralty that are often quite as important as are those written to the board itself.

The Navy Board had direct charge of the management of the navy. It built, equipped, and repaired the ships, fitted them for sea and paid the bills; it reported on their general condition, prepared estimates, hired extra boats, and had some control over the impressment of seamen; it looked after the building of docks and yards, took charge of prizes at the great stations, fitted up hospital ships, reported on the personnel of those employed in the land service, and had the care of lighters and tenders and their equipment. In the main the board was held accountable for the general condition of docks, yards, and ships, for the conduct and efficiency of all seamen and employees, who were not ranked as fighting men, and for all contracts connected with the building, repairing, or stocking the ships of the navy. On certain days the Navy Board attended the Admiralty and took part in its proceedings; at other times it submitted reports on questions referred to it, or sent in representations on its own account. It had no authority over the other subordinate boards; it could issue requests or express desires, but it could not order or require. To other departments, such as the Ordnance Office, with which it had dealings, it generally expressed its wishes through the Admiralty.

The Victualling Board consisted of five, and later seven, members and was appointed by commission under the great seal, after warrants had been issued by the Admiralty to the attorney general who prepared the bill. It was first instituted in 1683, victualling before that time having been done by contract. The board took its orders only from the Admiralty, though such orders might actually be delivered through the Navy Board; and in turn it made all its reports and representations to the Admiralty only. The functions of the Victualling Board need no description here.

The Transport Board, or Commissioners for Transportation, was first established in 1688 and was abolished and reorganized several times afterward. No records of its activities exist for the colonial period, and exact knowledge of its functions can be obtained only from the records of other departments. The office had charge of the transport service to Holland, Spain, Portugal, Gibraltar, and to the colonies, or in general to any point to which soldiers, supplies, clothing, ammunition, and the like needed to be carried.

The Board for Sick and Wounded Seamen, later known as the Medical Board, had its origin in the period of the Commonwealth, but was permanently established in 1740 to take care of sick and wounded seamen, superintend medical stores supplied by the apothecary general for the use of the navy,[1] manage naval hospitals, ashore and afloat, examine and appoint naval surgeons, and maintain and exchange prisoners of war. The Sick and Wounded Board attended the Admiralty whenever requested, and like the Victualling Board and the Transport Board took its orders only from the higher authority.[2]

The multiplication of boards and offices and the absence of any efficient and responsible central authority—for the Admiralty Board itself can hardly claim to have exercised a co-ordinating control over the unwieldy system of which it was in a sense the centre and head—must have had a disastrous effect upon the despatch of business. Procedure was clumsy and complicated and functions were badly defined and frequently overlapped. In the execution of any project so many authorities were involved that responsibility was dissipated and effective action rendered difficult. On one occasion when certain persons wished to be transported to Gibraltar and Minorca, the matter was brought to the attention of the lieutenant general of ordnance; he informed the Secretary of State, the secretary acquainted the Admiralty, the Admiralty sent its orders to the Navy Board, and the Navy Board wrote to the Victualling Board. Business was hampered not only by such roundabout methods but also by the difficulty of determining exactly the relations of one board to another, and of all to outside boards and officials. When in 1775 Generals Howe, Clinton, and Burgoyne were to proceed to North America, the king, probably through the Secretary of State, informed the Secretary at War, who made a representation to the Admiralty desiring that a vessel be provided. The Admiralty ordered the Navy Board to provide a vessel and to victual it; the Navy Board ordered its officers at Deptford to fit out a vessel and desired the Victualling Board to stock it. The Victualling Board ordered that notice be given to the proper officer to carry out the desires of the Navy Board.

The difficulties of administration were enhanced by the scattered location of the various offices.

In early times the Admiralty had no fixed place of abode, but met wherever most convenient, sometimes in the residence of the Lord High Admiral and sometimes at sea. Upon the appointment of the Duke of Buckingham in 1619 the Admiralty first settled at Wallingford House, on the site of Mrs. Kirke's lodgings, which adjoined Horse Guards Yard on the north. Here Buckingham lived during the remainder of his life and here after his death the board continued to meet till 1649. After the Restoration, when Wallingford House was resigned into the hands of the second duke, the board met in various places—from 1660 to 1674 in the Council Chamber and Robes Chamber of the old palace of Whitehall, except during the plague when it removed to Greenwich; from 1674 to 1684 in Derby House in Channel Row, Westminster; from 1684 to 1689 in Secretary Pepys's rooms in York Build-

---

[1] Apothecaries Hall was on the east side of Blackfriars. " There were prepared vast quantities of medicines for the apothecaries and others and particularly the surgeons of the fleet do here make up their chests." Hatton, *New View of London*, II. 593-594, and *Regulations and Instructions relating to His Majesty's Service at Sea* (9th ed., 1767), pp. 212-213. See below, pp. 195, 227, 247, 274, where the apothecary general's service for the army is noted, and, on the subject as a whole, Barrett, *History of the Society of Apothecaries of London* (1905).

[2] The names of many of the officials of these boards can be found readily in the *List of Declared Accounts from the Pipe Office and Audit Office* (1893). The rolls there listed contain a great deal of valuable information.

ings; and from March until May, 1689, in Admiral Herbert's lodgings in Channel Row. But finding these last quarters very inconvenient and " an unfit place " for carrying on business, the board moved again to York Buildings, but not to the house in which Pepys had lived, and later occupied part of a house built for Lord Jeffreys in 1685, at the south end of Duke Street facing St. James Park.[1] A few years afterward when Wallingford House was acquired by the crown, the board returned to its earlier place of meeting and since that time, except for a period of six years, it has remained on the same site. In 1720 Wallingford House was pulled down and the older portion of the present Admiralty building was erected in 1725. During the period of construction the board had offices in a house in St. James Square belonging to the Marquis of Halifax, but in a few years it returned to its old location, and the building then occupied, greatly enlarged and improved since that time, has remained the home of the Admiralty to the present day.[2]

The principal officers of the navy, constituting the Navy Board, were established on Tower Hill, east of the Tower, in Queen Elizabeth's reign. As early as 1628 they removed into the City proper, renting a house in Mincing Lane for £30 a year.[3] Here apparently they remained until, in 1654, the government purchased for £2400 the house of Sir John Wolstenholme,[4] standing on the grounds of the old friary of the Crutched Friars, which in the preceeding century had been employed as a storehouse for merchant goods by Sir William Winter, " surveyor of the queen's ships " under Elizabeth. Here was established the Navy Office, consisting of one large structure and a group of smaller detached buildings, where the commissioners sat and the clerks had residence or kept their papers. Pepys had his apartments and office here from 1660 to 1669. On the morning of January 29, 1673, the Navy Office " and other housen " were destroyed by fire.[5] For a month the board occupied quarters at Trinity House in Water Lane,[6] but at the end of February it moved to the Prize Office in Mark Lane[7] and remained there till the new building was finished in 1682 on a piece of ground near the old site purchased for £8500. The new quarters were suited to the business of the navy at that time, but as the years passed and the activities of the navy increased three adjacent houses were bought for £1150, and later two others were hired at a rent of £100 a year in order to extend the office quarters and to provide a place for depositing books and papers.[8]

[1] In Wheatley, *Round about Piccadilly,* p. 261, is a plan showing this location of the Admiralty, and in *The London Topographical Record,* II. 40, is a photograph of Jeffreys' house which was not pulled down till 1874. For York Buildings see Thornton, *Survey of London,* p. 455.

[2] For the Admiralty building see Sheppard, *Old Palace of Whitehall,* p. 176, and for much the same view, Maitland, *History of London,* and Dodsley, *London and its Environs.* For a picture of the Admiralty Board Room see *Microcosm of London,* I. 11 ff.

[3] Hollond, *Discourses of the Navy, 1638 and 1658,* Navy Records Society, VII. 337.

[4] *S. P. Dom.,* Apr. 11, 1654, and p. 88.

[5] *S. P. Dom.,* 1672-1673, pp. 498, 499, 508, 517, 541, 606, 622; *Commons Journal,* IX. 309.

[6] The first Trinity House in Water Lane was destroyed in the great fire. The second building on the same site, and the one referred to in the text, was destroyed in 1718. The third, also on the same site, was occupied by the corporation till 1793, when the present building on Tower Hill was erected.

[7] Maitland's plan of Tower Street Ward shows the location of Trinity House and of the Old Navy Office at the head of a court running west. In 1675 Pepys ordered the victualling contractors " to attend the lords at the navy office in Mark Lane ".

[8] Maitland shows the location. There are many illustrations of the Navy Office in Wheatley, *Pepys,* I. 178-179, Maitland, *London,* etc. Robinson, *The British Fleet,* gives the location as in Broad Street, but wrongly. There was an entrance into Navy Office Yard from Tower Hill.

In 1774 the Navy Board petitioned the Treasury, complaining of the ruinous state of the buildings, the great want of room, and the serious risks which the department ran from the dangers of fire. It laid stress upon the inconveniences that arose because of the scattered location of the subordinate offices, for the treasurer was in Leadenhall Street, the Navy Pay Office in old Broad Street, and the Sick and Wounded Board on Tower Hill, and it called the attention of the Admiralty to the distance which separated its office from Whitehall, and to the delays which ensued in the despatch of public business. It recommended the erection of a new building which should bring the subordinate offices under one roof and draw them all into closer touch with the Admiralty itself.

The request of the Navy Board simply voiced a general complaint—that for many years the administrative departments of the British government had been so badly located as seriously to hamper the execution of orders. In an age when transit was largely by water and communication was wholly by messenger, even the distance from Whitehall to the City meant prolonged delays and sometimes led to misunderstanding and confusion. Instead of asking for a new building, however, the Admiralty decided to make use of the new Somerset House begun in 1776 and finished in 1786. There the Navy Office was housed in the latter year, occupying the central and southeastern sides of the quadrangle.[1]

To Somerset House was also removed the Treasurer's Office, which had been in Leadenhall Street, and the Navy Pay Office, which had previously been in old Broad Street, corner of Great Winchester Street, in an old and plain building, part of the Marquis of Winchester's mansion, known as Winchester Place, and rented for £275 a year.[2] Near it had stood the Pay Office Coffee-house, a place of resort for all persons who had any concern or dealings in affairs relating to the navy.[3] To Somerset House was also removed the office of the Board of Sick and Wounded Seamen, which at one time had been in Princes Court, off Coleman Street, behind Lothbury, and afterward in a building at the northeast corner of Tower Hill, at the corner of Postern Row. Should the Navy Office, to which the board had ready access by means of an entrance from Tower Hill, move farther to the west, it would be necessary for this board to remove also. On September 29, 1775, it informed the Admiralty that its office must follow that of the Navy Board, and consequently provision was made for it in the new quarters contiguous to the Navy Office and at a small distance from the Pay Office. No room, however, could be found for the residence of the commissioners and they were obliged to seek quarters elsewhere.

The Victualling Office was first established in 1683 at Deptford. Before 1689 the office was removed to a site northeast of the Tower, at the end of East Smithfield Street, about where the Mint is today. Thornton says: " This is a very large building situated on the upper part of Tower Hill, from whence it is separated by a wall and gates. It contains houses for the accommodation of certain officers, separate apartments for offices, store-rooms, slaughter-houses for oxen and hogs, a brew house, and a house for salting and barrelling provisions." The building stood near Coopers' Yard, Bakers' Yard, and Pound Yard, and the board utilized these industries as adjuncts to its business. Once when the coopers' workhouses were burned down and not rebuilt, the Victualling Board complained that it suffered a great impediment to its ser-

---

[1] *Treas.* 1 : **508**, ff. 188-191; *Adm.* 3 : **80**, June 17, 1774.
[2] *Treas.* 1 : **508**, ff. 188-191.
[3] *Adm.* 1 : **5115**, f. 857.

vice. At the Victualling Office " all pursers of ships, and others entrusted with the public stores of provisions, or who contract for them ", passed their accounts.[1]

The lesser offices were scattered about in very haphazard fashion. The Transport Office, which was removed with the Navy Office to Somerset House, was in Black Raven Court, a court not far from the Navy Office, running east from Seething Lane. The Prize Office was in York Buildings early in the century but was afterward transferred to Mark Lane. At first no central Rendezvous Office existed, as the Admiralty had its agents or lieutenants in most of the outports engaged in recruiting men for sea-service, but after 1745 an office was established in London, though where it stood is not clear. The marine paymaster at first had no special office of his own. In the years before 1725, marine business was probably carried on at the house of the deputy paymaster in Charles Street, Westminster, at least while Arthur Swift was deputy to Walter Whitfield (1702-1711) and to his successor, Col. Sir Roger Mostyn (1711-1725). After the Admiralty was housed in its present building, the work of the marine service was done there by a special secretary, set apart for the purpose. With the appointment of Charles Hanbury Williams in 1739, a new office was set up (March-April, 1740) in Killigrew Court near Scotland Yard, and remained until 1751, when apparently it was removed to Deputy Paymaster Herbert's chambers in Gray's Inn. Eventually it got established permanently at the Admiralty. The muster-master general of marines also had his quarters at the War Office. The Sixpenny Receiver's Office was at first in Tower Street and after 1729 on Tower Hill. The dock-yards were at Deptford and Woolwich,[2] the three great stations were at Portsmouth, Southampton, and Chatham, the chest was at Chatham, the royal naval academy at Portsmouth, and the hospital at Greenwich. The admiralty solic-itors had their offices in various places, Clement's Inn, Piccadilly, etc.

No departmental records of the Admiralty of date prior to the Restoration exist in official custody. Such records of earlier date as are extant will be found among the state papers or in private collections. The Admiralty as a regularly organized department dates only from the period of Charles II., and even for that time but few papers now remain. The greater part of the series herein described begins after 1689 ; only a few of the papers go back as far as 1665.

Before 1840 the Admiralty papers were located in four chief places of deposit: the Admiralty Office, Whitehall (original correspondence, letter-books, ships' logs, etc.), Somerset House (papers of the Accountant General's Department), the " Pavilion " and other buildings at the royal dockyard at Deptford (letter-books, despatches, surveys, warrants, muster-books, log-books, Navy Board papers, journals, pay-books, treasurers' accounts, vict-ualling accounts, transport and medical books, etc.), and Greenwich Hospital (minutes, accounts, ledgers, registers, etc., but not the correspondence, which was at Whitehall).

The Lords of the Admiralty, wishing to demolish the " Pavilion " at Dept-ford, requested the Master of the Rolls to take its papers into his custody. In 1841 the first installment of volumes and chests of papers was removed and deposited in the northeast turret of the White Tower; other papers in very

---

[1] Thornton, *Survey of London*, p. 430. For conditions in the victualling service before 1703, see *House of Lords Manuscripts*, new series, vol. V., § 1935.

[2] Hughson, *London*, V. 78-79, 125 ff., and for a description of Greenwich, *ibid.*, pp. 85-109.

large quantities were removed in 1846 and 1847; and in 1848 the last boat loads, consisting of a great number of boxes of loose papers and nearly 9000 volumes, were towed up the Thames. The next year a beginning was made of transferring the papers from Whitehall to the Tower and the work was continued in 1850, until the Council Chamber and the Match Room were well filled. When in 1855 the War Office demanded these rooms for the use of the Ordnance Department, the papers were removed to certain houses in Chancery Lane, which were handed over by the Board of Works for this purpose. There the papers remained until removed in 1857, 1859, and 1860, in part to the newly finished Public Record Office and in part to the State Paper Branch Office. In 1859 the remaining records were taken from Somerset House; in 1856 and 1862 the contents of Carlton Ride and the State Paper Branch Office were transferred; and in 1867 a great mass of papers was brought from the Admiralty Office. With these transfers the main body of Admiralty Papers, containing material for American colonial history, was at last housed in the central repository.

SECRETARY'S DEPARTMENT.

ORIGINAL CORRESPONDENCE OR IN-LETTERS.[1]

Adm. 1.

230-243. 1713-1789. Admirals' Despatches from Stations in Jamaica.

230. 1713-1729. Admirals Walker and Hosier and Commander St. Lo.

231. 1729-1732. Admiral Stewart and Commodore Lestock.

232. 1738-1742. Admiral Vernon and Commodore Brown.

233. 1740-1746. Admirals Vernon, Ogle, and Davers.

234. 1746-1758. Admirals Knowles and Townshend.

235. 1752-1761. Admiral Cotes.

236. 1759-1761. Admiral Holmes.

237. 1762-1765. Admirals Pocock and Keppel.

238. 1763-1772. Admirals Burnaby and Parry, Commodores Forrest and Mackenzie.

239. 1771-1774. Admiral Rodney.

240. 1774-1778. Admiral Gayton.

241. 1778-1779. Admiral Parker.

242. 1779-1786. Admirals Parker, Tunes, and Rowley.

243. 1782-1789. Admiral Gambier, Commodores Pakenham and Gardner.

305-314. *Id.* Leeward Islands.

305. 1745-1747. Admiral Tounsend, Commodores Lee and Legge.

306. 1747-1759. Admirals Osborn and Frankland, Commodores Holburne and Pye.

307. 1757-1765. Admirals Douglas and Rodney, and Commodore Moore.

[1] Attention may be called to the Digests of Secretary's In-Letters, prepared annually after 1762. These digests are huge volumes, conveniently arranged for use, and are a guide to the in-letters of each year. They are listed under *Adm.* 10, 11, and 12, and the important volumes are *Adm.* 12: **52, 53, 54.** Other volumes of indexes for the period may be found in the *List of Admiralty Records*, pp. 88-89. See also the introduction, pp. iii-v, of the same list.

308. 1761-1769. Admirals Swanton, Tyrrell, and Pye.
309. 1769-1777. Admirals Man, Parry, and Young.
310. 1776-1781. Admirals Young and Barrington, and Commodore Hotham.
311. 1779-1780. Admiral Rodney.
312. 1779-1787. Admirals Byron, Hughes, Drake, and Hyde Parker, Commodores Walsingham and Affleck.
313. 1780-1787. Admirals Hood and Pigot.
314. 1781-1788. Admiral Rodney.

470-471. 1766-1783. *Id.* Newfoundland.

470. 1766-1776. Admiral Duff, Commodores Palliser, Byron, and Shuldham.
471. 1776-1783. Admirals Montague and Edwards.

480-489. 1745-1781. *Id.* North America. From Stations north of Carolina.

480. 1745-1763. Admirals Warren, Tounsend, Savage, Mostyn, and Watson, Commodores Spry and Keppel.
Warren's letters (1745-1746) are from Louisburg and Boston, and elsewhere in Canada and New England. They relate to the expedition of 1745 against Canada, to dealings with Shirley, and to affairs in Nova Scotia. Keppel's letters (1754-1755) concern the war with the French and Indians, Braddock's expedition, and contain lists, states, and reports on officers, ships, appointments, etc. Mostyn's letters (1755) and Spry's letters (1755-1763) deal with the movements of the squadrons and contain lists, orders, and other enclosures, original and copies, such as letters to the admirals from Oswego, Halifax, Boston, New York, Hampton Roads, South Carolina, and elsewhere.
481. 1755-1760. Admirals Boscawen, Hardy, Holburne, Holmes, and Durell.
Boscawen's letters (1755-1758) are from Spithead, Portsmouth, Torbay, and Off Louisburg, and they contain news from points farther south, together with many enclosures, officers' and ships' lists, and the like. Holmes's letters (1756-1759) are from New York, Halifax, and Portsmouth, and contain many copies of letters from Gen. Loudoun. Holburne's letters (1757) are from Spithead, Cork, Kinsale, At Sea, Newfoundland, and Halifax, and concern land and naval movements against the French. Hardy's letters (1757-1759) are from New York, Halifax, Portsmouth, and Plymouth. Durel's letters (1758-1760) are from the same ports and deal with land and naval movements at Halifax and Louisburg.
482. 1759-1766. Admirals Saunders and Colville.
Saunders's letters (1759-1760) are from Off Lizard and from Halifax, and give elaborate information regarding the Canadian campaign. Colville's letters (1759-1766) are from Off English Coast, Halifax, and Quebec, and are of especial interest in that they cover the results of the order in Council of June 1, 1763, entrusting the admirals with power to seize ships for illicit trading. They also give accounts in considerable detail of the Stamp Act disorders.

483. 1767-1772. Commodores Hood and Gambier.

Hood's letters (1767-1770) are from Halifax and are chiefly concerned with naval matters. A few are from Boston (Oct.-Nov., 1768) and narrate events there; others (1769) concern the attack on Capt. Reid at Newport. In the British Museum, *Add. MSS.* **35193,** are letters from Adm. Hood to Lord Bridport (1772-1783). Gambier's letters (1770-1772) deal chiefly with events taking place at Boston.

484. 1771-1777. Admirals Montague and Shuldham.

Montague's letters (1771-1776) are from Boston and its neighborhood, and the most important among them concern illicit trade in Rhode Island and the burning of the *Gaspee.* Shuldham's letters (1775-1776) are from Boston, New York, and Philadelphia, and are so detailed as to become journals of events. They are interspersed with copies of colonial papers, letters of intelligence, and reports on naval and other matters in Rhode Island, Pennsylvania, and elsewhere. Near the end is " A Journal of a Cruise in the brig *Andrew Doria,* Nicholas Biddle, commander, from the port of Philadelphia. Begun, January 4, 1776 "; interesting as the first log extant of an American privateer in the war against England. This journal is printed in Neeser, *The Despatches of Molyneux Shuldham,* Publications of the Naval History Society, III. 275-305.

485. 1774-1777. Admiral Graves.

Graves's letters are from Boston, About Cape Cod, Rhode Island, New Hampshire, New York, and deal with the weak state of the squadron, the prevalence of smuggling, the proceedings in vice-admiralty courts, the early activities of the Americans, and the growing spirit of rebellion. Adm. Graves was very assiduous in collecting information, and this volume contains not only full details of events but also great numbers of newspapers of the period, such as, the Massachusetts *Spy and Gazette,* the Boston *Gazette and Country Journal,* the *New England Chronicle or Essex Gazette,* many printed broadsides, and copies of local documents. Note Washington's letter (L. S.), Dec. 5, 1775, seized in the brig *Washington.*

486. 1775-1784. Admirals Byron and Arbuthnot, and Commodore Parker.

Byron's letters (two groups, 1775, 1778) are chiefly from northern American waters. One letter encloses a report from Maj. Tupper on the " battle of Charlestown Heights " (see below p. 41). The letters of 1778 describe the movements of the squadron and the operation of the naval hospital in Rhode Island. Parker's letters (1775-1777) are from Cape Fear River, New York, Rhode Island, and Charleston; some of them will be found in the first group of the Byron letters. Arbuthnot's letters (1778-1784) are from Halifax, New York, Jamaica, Savannah, Charleston, and Virginia. They narrate events connected with the activities of D'Estaing in the West Indies, with the movement of the fleets leading to the capture of Charleston, and with the engagement of the British with the French fleet off the capes of Virginia, Mar. 16, 1781. The enclosures include a drawing of a part of East New Jersey,

showing Lord Howe's line, a copy of the articles of capitulation
of Charleston, tales of sea fights, lists of captures and recaptures,
copies of letters from Rodney and Gen. Clinton to Arbuthnot, etc.

487. 1776-1777. Admiral Howe.

Howe's letters are from Halifax, Staten Island, Rhode Island, and
Elk River. They give important information regarding the events
of May-July, 1776, and contain many enclosures, such as, newspapers, broadsides, copies of Commodore Parker's narration of
proceedings at Charleston, a copy of a journal by the same, July
13–Aug. 18, 1776, copies of letters from inferior officers, and
extracts of letters and orders from Graves, Shuldham, and others,
lists of ships, descriptions of ships, accounts of captures, etc.

488. 1777-1779. Admiral Howe.

The letters in this second group of Howe's correspondence are from
the Delaware, Philadelphia, New York, Rhode Island, Sandy
Hook, and London. The enclosures consist of lists and tables,
intercepted letters, and letters and reports from inferior officers,
tales of operations, account of rebel armed vessels, lists, and
intelligences.

489. 1778-1783. Admirals Gambier, Ogle, and Graves.

Gambier's letters (1778-1784) are from New York, New Jersey,
Cape Cod, Philadelphia, Savannah, and give important details of
the naval aspects of the war. Ogle's letters (1780) number but
four in all. Graves's letters (1779-1781) are from Sandy Hook,
and deal with the Yorktown campaign. Among the enclosures
are copies of letters from Cornwallis. The general contents are
essentially the same as in the preceding volumes.

1435-2733. 1698-1792. Captains' Letters, arranged alphabetically.

A. 1698-1792, **1435-1447**; B. 1698-1785, **1462-1504**; C. 1698-1783, **1588-
1615**; D. 1698-1784, **1692-1710**; E. 1698-1783, **1754-1762**; F. 1698-1783, **1776-
1791**; G. 1698-1792, **1822-1840**; H. 1698-1783, **1871-1907**; I. J. 1698-1792,
1979-1988; K. 1698-1792, **2004-2015**; L. 1698-1785, **2033-2057**; M. 1698-1785,
2090-2124; N. 1698-1792, **2215-2223**; O. 1698-1792, **2241-2250**; P. 1698-1784,
2277-2307; R. 1698-1787, **2374-2394**; S. 1698-1786, **2438-2486**; T. 1698-1783,
2568-2593; U. V. 1698-1792, **2624-2628**; W. 1698-1783, **2636-2676**; Y. 1717-
1792, **2732-2733**.

A few letters from this series are in Stevens, *Facsimiles*: **1497**, letter
from Capt. Bazely, Sept. 24, 1777; **1761**, letters from Capt. John Elliot, Sept.
25, 1777, Sept. 26, Mar. 15, 1778, Apr. 14, 1779; Mar. 24, Apr. 13, Apr. 20,
another of Apr. 20 with an enclosure, Nov. 27, 1780; **2305**, letter of Hyde
Parker, Jan. 14, 1779, and enclosure of secret instructions from Adm. Gambier, Parker's letter of Apr. 17.

As showing the kind of information that one will occasionally meet with in
the captains' letters the following may be quoted. "On my passage from
Rhode Island to New York the 6th at half past two, Rhode Island then bearing about N b E distant 14 or 15 leagues, I fell in with a rebel squadron, consisting of one ship of thirty guns, another of twenty eight, two brigs, one of
sixteen, the other fourteen guns, and a sloop of twelve, and all full of men,
and continued engaging them broadside and broadside an hour and a half,
when my masts, sails, and rigging being very much shattered and an

attempt made to board us, I bore away for Rhode Island, and continued a close running fight until half past six when they left us." From Capt. Tyringham Howe of the *Glasgow,* 1776, regarding his encounter with Esek Hopkins's fleet, **1902,** § *22.*

There are no separate collections of letters from lieutenants or other inferior officers of date earlier than 1791.

3545-3652. 1673-1738. Letters from the Navy Board.

This collection of 108 volumes, the continuation of which will be found in *Adm., Navy Board, Out-Letters,* **2178-2210,** are of comparatively slight importance for colonial history, as they concern a period when the navy had but little to do with the colonies. A few items from selected volumes will show the nature of the material. Many of the volumes contain no colonial references whatever.

3545. 1673-1674. A few documents relating to the West Indies.

3547. 1676-1677. Information regarding ships for Virginia and the transportation of troops for the suppression of Bacon's Rebellion. Sir John Berry was authorized to impress ships, boats, and men if he should need to do so. *Cf.* Tanner, *Catalogue of the Pepysian Manuscripts,* III. §§ 3439, 3455, 3468.

3548. 1677-1678. Convoy for Virginia; the return of 400 troops from Virginia, Mar. 4, 1678; naval stores from New England.

3549. 1678-1679. Provisions for Virginia, Sept. 14, 1678; ketch for Virginia.

3553. 1682-1684. Naval stores.

3554. 1684-1685. Naval officers in Jamaica; things necessary for a West India voyage.

3555. 1685-1686. Vessels to Barbadoes and Jamaica; contracts for New England masts with Shorter and Warren, Mason and Randolph to assist. 1686.

3558. 1689. Packets for the West Indies, Virginia, Maryland, and Pennsylvania, 1687; naval stores, 1689.

3559. 1689. Victualling convoys to America and elsewhere, in conjunction with the Victualling and Transport offices.

3562. 1690-1691. The ship *Archangel* to go to New York; furnishing clothes for the *Deptford* ketch by William Byrd of Virginia, 1690; report on Edward Randolph's petition, with details of Randolph's negotiations with Sheafe, accompanied by the original petition, by the order of the Privy Council thereon (*Acts Privy Council, Colonial,* vol. II., § 380), and by Randolph's statement of account.

3661-3662. 1694-1708. Letters from the Prize Office.

Letters from the prize commissioners that occasionally refer to the condemnation of prizes in America, particularly in the West Indies (Jamaica). In **3662,** ff. 174, 176, 257, there are references to seizure of the ship *St. Paul* of Rochelle, taken in the West Indies and condemned and sold in the Maryland court of vice-admiralty. On f. 191 is a letter to Cullen Campbell, agent for prizes, sent to Newfoundland (1705).

3663. 1743-1745.   Letters from the Rendezvous Office.

From the lieutenants appointed by the Admiralty to raise men for the navy. Such men were raised either by voluntary enlistment or by impress.   The officers, with their headquarters at the outports, travelled along the coast beating up recruits.   They also rounded up enlisted men and deserters and saw that both were in good health and physically sound.   Their pay was five shillings a day and expenses, and ten shillings was paid for every good seaman procured by the impress gang, a sum divided among the members of the gang. The service was of considerable concern to colonial merchant ships as the following extract will show: "Yesterday I pressd three seamen from out the William and Sarah, Jno Glegg, master, from So Carolina for London, and put them on board his Maj. ship Exeter, Capt Cornwallis."   Dec. 9, 1744.

3665-3681. 1680-1783.   Letters relating to the Solicitor's Department.

3666. 1700-1704.   Papers relating to Capt. Kidd (ff. 14, 39, 53, 66, 67, 68, 78, 81, 85, 103).

Report of George Oxenden, dean of arches, who also served as judge of the High Court, on the dispute between Penn and Quary about the admiralty and common-law jurisdiction (ff. 56-58, 212). *Cf. House of Lords Manuscripts,* new series, IV. 331, 341.

Draft of the commission to vice-admirals in the West Indies, Dr. George Bramston's report (f. 183).   1703.

Bramston to vice-admirals in the plantations, stating that they have no power to try prizes under commission from the Lord High Admiral, " for he hath none in that patent which constitutes him Lord Admiral of England.   The power proceeds from commission particularly granted for that purpose under the great seal of England to His Royal Highness.   The vice-admirals must have a warrant under that great seal."   Nov. 27, 1702.

3667. 1704-1711.   Letter from Bramston.   Nov. 30, 1705.   Says that he has inquired what was done with prizes in the last war in the western plantations and has learned that all prizes taken in the West Indies were brought into admiralty courts here, except what were embezzled, that is, never condemned; and that commanders frequently bought up their company's shares or gave them nothing.   " I do not find any attempt during that whole war made by any judge or officer of vice-admiralty in the western plantations to adjudge or condemn any ship or merchandize seized or taken by the men of war or privateers there, and I am humbly of the opinion that if any authority be granted for the condemning of prizes taken abroad there will be but a small account given thereof."   He advises strongly against the granting of authority to condemn abroad (f. 38).

Bramston further advises that instructions be sent to governors and others in the plantations not to meddle with prizes (f. 39) ; says that the governor of Maryland had no power to condemn prizes to Her Majesty, and that if he had had power he should have condemned to the Lord Admiral, captors having no commission (f. 40).   Oct. 30, 1705.

Warrant to Quary to recover all concealed prizes in America (f. 84). 1707.

Appeal admitted in case of a vessel carried to Jamaica and there condemned as a prize (f. 106). Mar. 10, 1707.

Regarding the erection of a vice-admiralty court in Newfoundland (f. 129). 1708.

Right of appointment of officers in colonial vice-admiralty courts belongs to the Lord High Admiral (f. 155). 1709.

Admiralty has no power to try murder beyond the sea (f. 157, Hedges).

Appeal from Jamaica (f. 189).

Various documents about the right to impress seamen in New York; effect of the act of Parliament for the encouragement of the trade with America (f. 207), 1709; Montaigne's opinion on same; Eyre's opinion that governors, but not vice-admirals, may press from ships in America (ff. 228, 229, also 305).

3668. 1711-1715. Same subject (f. 57).

Sir Charles Hedges's opinion on the method of appeal from colonial vice-admiralty courts (f. 49). 1711.

Various opinions on the complaints of Byfield (judge of vice-admiralty in New England) about the interference on the part of the Massachusetts superior court concerning a whale (ff. 49, 116, 117, 122). 1711-1712.

Hedges's report on admiralty jurisdiction in the colonies, especially in connection with penalties and prizes (ff. 143, 159-165, 167, 169-172, 180). 1712.

Opinion of Sir Henry Newton on Byfield's memorial about inadequate compensation, and his quarrel with the Dudleys (ff. 231, 233, also 255).

3669. 1716-1719. Opinion of Sir Henry Penrice on the complaints of Judge Menzies of the vice-admiralty court in New England regarding the reservation of vice-admiralty jurisdiction in the Massachusetts Bay charter. Nov. 10, 1716; May 8, 1717. See also Sept. 12, Oct. 21, 1717; Jan. 1, 1719.

Prohibition to the vice-admiralty court in New Hampshire. May 1, 1717.

Penrice on prize jurisdiction of vice-admiralty courts in America. Nov. 29, 1718.

Regarding the power of the Admiralty Commissioners to empower governors of the plantations to use letters of marque. Dec. 31, 1718.

As to how vice-admirals abroad are to account for droits, etc. Jan. 12, 1718.

Regarding the new *Mayflower,* bound for South Carolina and cast away on her return; suit in the Exchequer against Thomas Randall, surety for Robert Ferry, master, for not returning his pass. Apr. 27, 1719.

On the vice-admiralty court in New York. Oct. 16, 1719.

3670. 1720-1722. Details about perquisites of the admiralty in the colonies, and references and letters from Archibald Cummings, agent for receiving and taking care of the rights and perquisites of the admiralty in New England, New York, and Rhode Island. Aug. 5, Nov. 19, 1720; Sept. 13, 1721; Apr. 8, 1722.

Pirate goods and droits in Barbadoes. Nov. 15, 1720.

Clauses in the commission to the Admiralty Commissioners authorizing them to give discharges for droits; condemnation of goods in the vice-admiralty court of New York; on Jan. 3, 1719, the Admiralty issued a warrant to the vice-admiralty court of New York authorizing the trial of a prize.

According to the opinion of the attorney general and solicitor general the right of His Majesty's ships to take prizes in America, under act of 6 Anne for the encouragement of trade to America, was to last during the war only. July 30, 1722.

Penrice on the dispute between Gov. Shute and Judge Menzies concerning the jurisdiction of admiralty and common-law courts. June 12 and 13, 1722.

Admiralty's perquisites in the West Indies. Oct. 4, 1722.

3671. 1722-1726. Penrice on the admiralty court dispute in South Carolina, Judge Smith *vs.* Gov. Nicholson. He advises better emoluments to the vice-admiralty judge there, for " the profits of his place will scarcely keep him out of prison. The judges at c[ommon] l[aw] take all advantages of the admiralty jurisdiction in distress, they ply it hard in prohibitions, and seem resolved to sink it quite unless their lordships come timely in with their powerful assistance ", Aug. 30, 1723. Nicholson's answer, Sept. 20, 1723.

Disputes between the vice-admiralty and common-law courts in the colonies, notably between Gov. Shute and the vice-admiralty court of Massachusetts regarding the *Elton Galley*. Apr. 16, 23, June 18, 1724; May 17, 1726.

Penrice on the question whether any admiralty court abroad is one of His Majesty's courts (7 and 8 William III., " Courts of Admiralty in the Plantations "). June 18, 1724.

3672. 1726-1730. Philip Yorke on admiralty jurisdiction in the colonies; Menzies case—legality of a seizure in New England. Aug. 10, 1726.

Penrice on the same case, with details about Menzies's quarrel with the Massachusetts common-law courts and his expulsion from the Massachusetts assembly (a long paper). Penrice decides that admiralty jurisdiction in Massachusetts is reserved to the king and is not subject to the provincial courts. May 2, 1727; June 20, 1728.

Menzies's letter regarding the seizure of the snow *Esther* at Salem, and other documents bearing on the case. Jan. 2, 1727.

Penrice declares that no instructions have been issued to governors in the plantations touching fees for the condemnation of prizes. Oct. 7, 1727.

Warrant to the High Court of Admiralty and to the admiralty courts within His Majesty's dominions to hear prize cases. Mar. 30, 1727.

Instructions to Gov. Montgomerie of New Jersey to account to Byng. Feb. 1, 1727.

Penrice on admiralty jurisdiction in North Carolina; advises that
jurisdictions be kept distinct by order in Council. June 6, 1729.

Id., Pennsylvania. Sept. 11, 1729; June 10, 1730.

Regarding sixpenny dues in the colonies. Apr. 5, 1729.

3673. 1730-1736. Details regarding the reservation of mast trees in
New Hampshire. Dec. 6, 1730.

Regarding the vice-admiralty court in South Carolina. Mar. 15,
1732.

William Browne on the vice-admiralty court in Newfoundland.
May 1, 1736.

3674. 1737-1740. Various opinions on Col. Dunbar's difficulties in en-
forcing the laws for preserving mast trees.

Proceedings in the admiralty court of Massachusetts and Dunbar's
quarrel with Belcher. Dec. 23, 1737; Jan. 28, 1738.

Penrice on the act of Parliament authorizing the Lord High Admiral, the Commissioners of the Admiralty, and persons empowered by them in America to issue letters of marque. Apr. 26,
1740.

Definite instructions to governors to issue letters of marque. Apr.
26, 1740.

Paul's opinion as to a prize seized in New York harbor. Dec. 23,
1741.

3675. 1741-1746. A number of documents regarding the claims of the
common-law courts to try prizes.

3676. 1747-1753. Reference in a letter of Feb. 17, 1748, to a sloop on a
voyage from Carolina to Providence being lost, Dec. 23, 1744,
about four miles from land; with details.

Regarding the suit brought because of the detention of the *Neptune*
at Louisburg for the purpose of taking to England naval and
victualling stores. Oct. 31, 1749; Apr. 6, 1750. See *Adm., Accountant General, Miscellanea, Various,* **64,** for defense of this
suit. The admiral was Watson.

Regarding the appeal of Capt. Innes of H. M. S. *Aldborough,* for
impressing three seamen belonging to trading vessels, from the
judgment of the court of common pleas, Charleston, Dec. 16, 1749.
Appeal not allowed.

Combination of the judge of vice-admiralty and the attorney general in one person in Barbadoes deemed inconvenient and unwise.
Sept. 11, 1751.

Many papers concerning a South Carolina case, June 3, 1752, with
a copy of the vice-admiralty court proceedings.

Suit against Capt. Smelt of H. M. sloop *Viper* by Ferdinando Clark
of the *Warren* snow for detaining said vessel in Nantasket Road,
New England, July 26, 1750.

Case of a boat, from out of " South River ", New York, flying a
pennant " in contempt of the king's colors ", which was fired on by
H. M. S. *Greyhound* and a maid-servant killed. Was Lieut. How
of the *Greyhound* liable to court-martial? Yes. Aug. 8, Oct. 18,
1750; *cf.* Aug. 28, 1751, Feb. 25, 1752 (acquitted). *N. Y. Col.
Docs.,* VI. 584-585.

Action brought by Roger Passmore against Capt. Lloyd of H. M. S.
Winchester for impressing him in New England in 1744. Oct.
18, 1750.

3679. 1767-1775. A number of cases concerning murders and other offenses committed on board ships and vessels voyaging from England or Ireland to the plantations. The events themselves sometimes took place in colonial ports.

Case of one Thomas Austin sent from Boston by Lieut.-Gov. Hutchinson on suspicion of piracy. Feb. 12, 1770.

Regarding a negro purchased in Maryland by the master of a ship. Jan. 1, Mar. 1, 1771.

Regarding commissions for the trying of pirates in America, with a list dated Jan. 14, 1762. Aug. 26, 1772.

Case of deserters from the 31st Regiment of Foot, stationed in [New?] Providence. Mar. 31, 1774.

Case of a murder on the high seas, on board a ship bound for Carolina. Aug. 17, 1775.

In this volume is a copy of the patent empowering the Lords of the Admiralty to cause four vice-admiralty courts to be established in America. To be settled by Dr. Harris's advice to the Admiralty. Aug. 11, 1768.

3680. 1776-1778. Decided in case of British ships recaptured from the Americans that one-eighth value belonged to non-commissioned recaptors and was not to be droits of admiralty. Query, shall it be appealed? Nov. 17, 1777. Another similar case, Dec., 1777. *Cf.* Apr. 23, 1776.

Dr. Marriott, advocate general, appointed extraordinary commissioner for proceedings in admiralty on the American rebellion. July 11, 1776.

Letter from America, with remarks about the course of the war. June 9, 1777.

Ships condemned in the vice-admiralty court of North Carolina— Prohibitory Act forbids taking ships in rebel colonies—appeal. July 23, 1777.

3681. 1779-1783. Case of recapture from American captors—salvage, droits of admiralty, owner's title. Dec. 13, 1779.

This series of volumes is of great importance for an understanding of the working of the vice-admiralty jurisdiction in America and of the conflict between the common-law courts and the admiralty courts in the colonies. The documents throw light also on the system of appeals from colonial vice-admiralty courts. In addition to the main subjects treated, there are others of a minor character that find elucidation here—Mediterranean passes, piracy, penalties, prizes, and the like. Many illustrations of life on shipboard are given, which present in detail naval practices and experiences in the eighteenth century. In the main, the series is composed of reports from the solicitors and judges of the High Court of Admiralty to the Admiralty on complaints, memorials, and other documents submitted to them. The supplemental papers are often interesting and informing.

3729. 1704-1706. Letters from the Transport Department.

This single volume of letters from the Transport Office relates almost entirely to other countries than America. It contains one extract of a private letter from Arnold Brown, agent of prizes at Jamaica, concerning an embezzlement in 1704. Sent from the Transport Office, Feb. 23, 1705.

3814-3816. 1697-1756. Letters from the Board of Trade.

3814 is labelled " Letters from the Board of Trade, 30 Oct. 1697–6 Dec. 1706 ", and on the title-page has this entry: " This is the first book wherein the Letters from the Board of Trade are kept entire, July 17, 1731." A few earlier letters are preserved in vols. **4080-4085,** " Letters from the Secretary of State ", a series which as a rule contains in-letters of a more general official character.

3815, 1707-1723, covers the period from Feb. 20, 1707, to Apr. 1, 1723 ; and **3816,** from May, 1723, to 1756. The volumes have tables of contents of enclosures, but these tables do not always represent the actual contents of the volumes, as many of the extracts and enclosures seem to be missing.

It is doubtful if there is anything here that is not to be found in the Board of Trade series, though the presence of original papers among the enclosures, relating to trade, fisheries, naval stores, convoys, privateers, pirates, protection of woods, and especially colonial vice-admiralty courts and cases, renders the matter uncertain.

3817-3820. 1728-1790. Letters from the Governors of Plantations.

This series contains original letters from the colonial governors and others to the Lords of the Admiralty, beginning Aug. 5, 1728.

> **3817.** 1728-1745. Hunter of Jamaica regarding admiralty matters. Aug. 5, 1728.
>
> > Council minutes of New Hampshire, Apr. 26, 1734, with many letters and depositions covering Dunbar's case.
> >
> > A. Popple of Bermuda, with enclosures. May 10, 1739; Nov. 10, 1740.
> >
> > New York and Massachusetts regarding passes. 1739.
> >
> > Trelawny of Jamaica, witnessing to the oath taken by the marshal of the admiralty and enclosing the text of the oath signed. *Cf.* Dec. 21, 1743.
> >
> > Deposition before Popple. Feb. 27, 1739.
> >
> > Belcher of Massachusetts regarding merchant ships having letters of marque. Mar. 6, 1740 ; also Jan. 19, 27, Oct. 26, 1741 ; Jan. 31, 1742.
> >
> > A. Popple and Byng of Barbadoes regarding the same.
> >
> > Dunbar, surveyor general, regarding naval stores. Mar. 29, 1740.
> >
> > Johnston of North Carolina. June 11, 1741.
> >
> > Glen of South Carolina. Aug. 18, Oct. 20, 1741 ; Oct. 9, 1743 ; Feb. 6, Sept. 17, 22, 1744.
> >
> > Shirley of Massachusetts regarding appointments in vice-admiralty courts. Feb. 1, 1741 ; Sept. 24, Oct. 19, 1742. Also from Bollan and Auchmuty.
> >
> > Shirley, with memorial of merchants. May 5, 1743.
> >
> > Various Shirley letters, Oct. 1, 3, 11, Nov. 14, 1743, regarding woods, etc., Sept. 22, Nov. 14, Dec. 17, 1744, Jan. 29, Apr. 4, 11, 16, 18, 30, May 1, 12, 1745, chiefly regarding the Louisburg expedition, with enclosures (some in duplicate), such as a copy of a letter from Pepperrell to Shirley concerning the state of the army, and other documents from Louisburg.

Shirley, Mar. 27, June 1, July 10, 31 (to the Duke of Bedford), Oct. 31 (introducing Agent Bollan to the duke and extolling his efficiency), same date (regarding future policy of Great Britain toward the French).

Mathew of Leeward Islands. Apr. 13, 1743.

B. Wentworth of New Hampshire. Oct. 17, 1743.

Thomas of Pennsylvania. July 8, 1743.

Bull of South Carolina. Nov. 22, 1743.

J. Gledhill of Newfoundland (Placentia). Aug. 15, 1744.

Gooch of Virginia. Dec. 1, 1744.

Robinson of Barbadoes. Apr. 23, May 8, 28, Aug. 24, 1745; Jan. 13, 1746.

Tinker of Bahamas. Nov. 23, 1745; Ma[y?] 25, [1746?].

3818. 1746-1758. Tinker of Bahamas. June 29, Sept. 23, 1746; Aug. 30, 1747.

Mathew of Leeward Islands. Aug. 26, 28, 1746.

Shirley, Warren, Pepperrell. 1746. Various copies.

Shirley. Nov. 1, 1746; Jan. 10, Nov. 28 (2), Dec. 1, 31, 1747; Nov. 30, 1748–Dec. 27, 1755 (from Braddock's camp); June 23, Sept. 7, 1756.

J. Gledhill. Oct. 9, 1746.

Robinson. Oct. 11, 1746; May 30, 1747.

Glen, with copy of his letter to Warren. Oct. 14, Dec. 29, 1746; Jan. 19, 1748 (on trade in South Carolina); Sept. 23, 1752.

G. Clinton of New York. Dec., 1746; May 23, 1747 (2); Nov. 23, 1748; June 11, 1749; Dec. 30, 1750; June 20, July 16, 1751; Dec. 14, 1753.

J. Belcher of New Jersey. May 6, Sept. 16, 28, 1747.

W. Popple of Bermuda. Mar. 7, 1750; Sept. 7, 1756.

Cornwallis of Nova Scotia regarding the murder of Capt. Howe; enclosures. Dec. 2, 1750.

Fleming of Tortola. Dec. 13, 1750.

Dinwiddie of Virginia. Dec. 10, 1752; Feb. 1, 1754.

Hopson of Nova Scotia. Apr. 14, 1753.

Willard, secretary of Massachusetts. Sept. 13, Nov. 6, 1754 (passes); Jan. 30, 1755.

Lyttelton of South Carolina. July 19 (trade, *cf.* letter from Glen), Nov. 20, 1756.

Fauquier of Virginia. Sept. 23, 1758.

Adm. Hardy. 1756; Jan., 1757.

Dobbs and council of North Carolina. Mar. 3, 1757.

Pinfold of Barbadoes. July 13, 1757.

Pownall of Massachusetts. Sept. 12, 1757 (duties); Jan. 12 (enclosing Wheelwright's narrative of a trip down the St. Lawrence), July 11, 1758.

Andrew Oliver. Jan. 10, 1758 (passes).

List of persons (300 names of Massachusetts men) taken in captivity, 1756-1757.

3819. 1759-1770. Stephen Hopkins of Rhode Island, about the courts of vice-admiralty, written to Joseph Sherwood, agent of the colony, who petitioned the Admiralty. Jan. 15, 1759.

Pownall. Mar. 30, 1760.

Andrew Oliver. Oct. 8, 1760 (passes).

Bull. June 15, 1761.

Moore of Jamaica. Oct. 29, 1761.

Lyttelton. Oct. 17, 1761.

Pinfold. Dec. 28, 1761 ; May 28, Dec. 24, 1763.

Gen. Amherst (from New York). May 11 (enclosing Colville's letter), June 15, July 20, Aug. 15, Sept. 21, Nov. 29, Dec. 22, 1762 ; Jan. 27, Apr. 6, May 1, 6, July 23, Aug. 13, Sept. 17, 1763.

Fauquier. Dec. 26, 1761 ; May 1, 1762 ; Sept. 22, 1763 ; June 22, 1764.

W. Popple. Nov. 3, 1762 (admiralty case, smuggling) ; ——— 6, 1763 (dispute with the collector, enclosures).

Andrew Oliver. June 4, 1763 ; Feb. 8, 1764 ; Nov. 19, 1767 (three letters about passes) ; May 26, Dec. 22, 1770.

Thomas Penn, proprietary of Pennsylvania. London, Mar. 6, 1769.

Gen. Gage (New York). Jan. 25, 1764.

Johnstone of East Florida. Mar. 3, 18, 30, 1764.

Charles Williams (New York). Feb. 22, July 12, 1764 (passes and stamps) ; Apr. 19, 1768 (passes).

Wentworth. Sept. 3, 1767.

John Penn of Pennsylvania. Nov. 4, 1768 (passes) ; Jan. 3, 1770 (*id.*).

Hutchinson of Massachusetts. Jan. 1, 13, Aug. 4, Sept. 4, 1770.

William Nelson (Virginia). Dec. 20, 1770 (passes).

3820. 1771-1790. Lists of French, Dutch, and Spanish vessels brought into Jamaica in the course of the war ; *id.,* belonging to the colonies.

Hutchinson. Nov. 12, Dec. 8, 1772 (admiralty court).

Richard Penn. Oct. 17, 1772.

Wentworth. Jan. 13, 1773 (state of the king's woods).

Arbuthnot of Nova Scotia. Nov. 20, 1776.

Charles Williams (New York). Aug. 20, 1776.

Burt of Leeward Islands. June 20, 1778 ; May 3, Nov. 8, 1779 ; Mar. 14, 1780 (admiralty case).

Gen. Haldimand. Oct. 25, 1780.

Bull. May 1, 1781.

A few documents of the years 1783-1790 have been placed in **3820**. In **3821-3823** are various documents relating to the West Indies and Canada of dates ranging from 1791 to 1839.

3825-3838. 1719-1784. Letters from British Consuls.

A series of letters (accompanied frequently by enclosures) of some value for the history of colonial trade. Among the most important of these enclosures are the registers of Mediterranean passes, recording the names of vessels bound for colonial ports, with the dates of passes and when endorsed. Were these registers in any sense complete, they would be of great interest, but they are so few and so infrequent that the information which they furnish is meagre. Such registers as exist are chiefly from consuls in Italian, Spanish, and Portuguese ports—Venice, Zante, Cagliari, Alicante, Lisbon, Oporto. The largest number of registers is from Lisbon, but the list is imperfect. The original registers were kept in the consular offices in the ports named and may still be in existence. The information furnished is as follows:

No.	Nature of ship	Name	Of what place	Tons burden	Guns	Master's name	No. of men	Where bound	What build	Dates of pass	When endorsed

Some of the lists have a column for "Lading", and others have similar variations. In many of the bundles are original passes returned, endorsed by the consuls of the various ports. Thirteen may be found in **3837**, though many others are mentioned.

The correspondence is from all parts of the world, and in the letters are allusions and statements showing the state of the trade and the working of the pass system. James Shaftoe, consul at Cagliari, wrote: "The island [of St. Peters] is more and more become the rendezvous of illicit traders under English colors, who refuse to produce their passes or own my consular authority at all." There are also occasional references to pirates, slave-traders, French trade with the West Indies; and there are letters of intelligence which deal with political and military matters, and, during the Seven Years' War, with naval movements. In **3825** are a few entries of ships going to America as early as 1723. In **3829** is a letter from Joseph Gledhill from Placentia, Oct. 31, 1745. In **3837** is a letter of Aug. 23, 1777, from Alicante with information about an American-built schooner flying French colors but believed to be furnished with credentials from Congress to cruise against British ships; others from Alicante, Nov. 26, 1776, and Lisbon, May 3, 1776, referring to American privateers; and one which mentions a vessel from Philadelphia at Leghorn, Apr. 10, 1767. The Alicante letter of Nov. 26 says that a French vessel arrived on the 25th, reporting that it had met off the Rock of Lisbon a North American armed vessel, which forcibly seized eleven sailors, part of the crews belonging to two English vessels which it had taken on Nov. 12 about twenty-five leagues west of the Rock. The privateer was a sloop called the *Union,* belonging to Cape Ann, of ten carriage-guns, eight swivels, and forty men commanded by Isaac Soams.

3863-3867. 1694-1799. Letters from the Custom House.

Only three of the bundles contain material relating to America.

> **3863.** 1694-1703. Memorial of Sir Thomas Lawrence, secretary of Maryland, on trade and navigation there and in the neighboring colonies. June 15, 1695.
>
> Memorial from the merchants trading to Virginia regarding Lawrence's statement, and a comment on both memorials by the Commissioners of the Customs.
>
> Regarding the officials sent over by the Commissioners of the Customs to administer the navigation acts after 1696. Feb. 11, 1697.
>
> Letter from the Commissioners of the Customs to the secretary of the Admiralty Board, asking for a vessel to convey Edward Randolph from plantation to plantation, in the discharge of his duties as surveyor general. Oct. 3, 1697.
>
> **3865.** 1720-1756. Letter from the Commissioners of the Customs to the secretary of the Admiralty Board, concerning the deputy judge of the vice-admiralty court in Rhode Island, being a Frenchman born. Order of the board thereon. Sept. 22, 1721.

Id. concerning a pirate ship, with an enclosure stating that the captain who rescued from the pirates the commander of a small sloop trading in fish between Newfoundland and Spain, was master of a New England-built ship of about 150 tons. Jan. 16, 1725.

Id. concerning the cases of the ships *Mary Ann* and *Esther,* brought by Robinson, collector of customs at Salem and Marblehead, in the Massachusetts court of admiralty. Mar. 16, 1727.

Draft instruction from the Admiralty to captains of men-of-war ordered to guard the English coasts against smugglers and other illegal traders. 1741.

Papers relating to a ship from Barbadoes bound for Cork and Bristol, and seized in Ireland for carrying " rum and other contraband goods ". Oct. 14, 1745.

3866. 1757-1780. Contains a certain amount of information about passes, convoys, smuggling, and other matters in which the Custom House and the Admiralty co-operated. Many of the references are to vessels engaged in the colonial trade or from the colonies. There is a list of officers of the navy to whom deputations had been granted by the Customs Commissioners. Three extracts, June 20, 1771, Aug. 15, 1771, May 4, 1774, concern the Board of Commissioners at Boston. One letter, with comments by the British Customs Commissioners, is from the custom officials at Falmouth, Oct. 5, 1771. Other papers concern vessels taken by the Americans, and contain important instructions regarding transport ships.[1]

3878-3887. 1740-1782. Letters from Doctors' Commons.

Letters with enclosures from various officers of the High Court of Admiralty in England, judge, advocates, proctors, marshal, deputy marshal, register, deputy register, etc. The corresponding out-letters are in *Adm.* 2: **1045-1061,** *q. v.,* as supplementing the following lists.

3878. 1740-1744. Letter from Andrew Belcher regarding the desire of Robert Auchmuty, judge of vice-admiralty, to remove him and to appoint his own son in his place. Oct. 21, 1742.

Letter from Robert Auchmuty. London, Jan. 14, 1742.

Representation (an original) from Nathaniel Byfield, regarding his office as judge and the extorting of fees. Feb. 2, 1731.

Letter from Leonard Lockman who acted as deputy judge for Robert Auchmuty, desiring a commission as judge. London, July 21, 1742.

Another letter from Auchmuty about his career and the various vice-admiralty offices which he had held for twenty years. n. d.

Two letters from Lockman. May 18, 20, 1743.

---

[1] From the collector and comptroller, Boston, to the Customs Board at home. " But as the military alone will not fully answer the purpose of stopping the great evil, we therefore most humbly conceive it highly necessary that a cutter of superior force to ours be ordered to cruize as much as possible on our coast, with Capt. Wharfe and who might occasionally assist him (whose vessel is a prime sailor) with three or four hands in order to chase any large suspected smuggling cutter in view, that when he comes up with her he may be able to take her, as otherwise she may prove too strong for him and set him at defiance (they being generally manned by a set of desperate outlawed villains) which has several times been the case, and that for want of more hands, which renders many of his attempts vain and fruitless."

Letter (duplicate) from Andrew Belcher. Boston, Oct. 21, 1742.

Id. from Auchmuty. London, July 4, 1743. Farther on in the bundle are other letters bearing on the same question.

William Bollan, appointed advocate general of New England. Boston, June 2, 1743.

George Cradock, deputy judge of the vice-admiralty court. Boston, Oct. 18, 1743.

Various proceedings in the vice-admiralty court of Newfoundland. William Keen was appointed judge of the vice-admiralty court at St. John's, May 19, 1736.

E. Howe, commissary of Nova Scotia. Canso, Sept. 8, 1743.

Joseph Anderson, appointed by the governor to succeed Porter, the late judge. Edenton, N. C., Nov. 16, 1743.

Lockman. Rhode Island, Nov. 9, 1743.

Joseph Anderson, with an account of prizes. Nov. 12, 1744.

W. Keen. St. John's, Nov. 5, 1744.

Jonathan Blenman. Barbadoes, May 16, 17, Oct. 18, 1744 (enclosures).

Robert Auchmuty. London, June 11, 1744.

Copy of a letter of marque.

Ja: Grame (list of ships). Charleston, June 23, 1744.

Benjamin King, reporting that his commission as judge had lain on the *Deptford* eight months before being delivered. Antigua, June 13, 1744.

Lockman (list of prizes). Rhode Island, Sept. 17, 1744.

In a list of prizes proceeded against in the High Court of Admiralty, 1739-1743, are entries of one prize taken into the port of Charleston and two to Jamaica. In a similar list, to be found in the next bundle, there are no such entries.

3879. 1745. Robert Auchmuty (list of prizes and the expedition to Cape Breton). Boston Mar. 25, 1745.

Jonathan Blenham (long account of the proceedings in the vice-admiralty court of Barbadoes), May 7, 1745; also Mar. 24, 1744, regarding the same.

Ja: Grame (list). May 17, 1745.

Lockman (list). May 28, 1745.

3880. 1746. Similar lists from Grame and Lockman.

Proceedings in the vice-admiralty court in Jamaica, 1740. Sent, 1745-1746. For the accompanying letter, Aug. 12, 1746, see next bundle.

The remaining papers in this bundle are chiefly from the proctors and marshals of the High Court of Admiralty or their deputies.

3881. 1747. Letter from William Faris concerning prizes. North Carolina, Nov. 27, 1747.

Letters from Keen, Newfoundland, and Huske, N. H.

Robert Auchmuty regarding trade under cover of flags of truce between Rhode Island and the French. June 8, 1747. An important letter.

Benjamin King, St. Christopher, Dec. 4, 1746, regarding the capture of the island of St. Bartholomew by English ships, with enclosures. A second letter speaks of St. Bartholomew as an island

which has been a great nuisance to trade, because there numbers
of British vessels bound to the West Indies have been made prizes
by the enemy, thus causing scarcity and famine as well as loss.
The island lay "directly in the jaws of all our trade to Europe and
North America as well as the American trade to us, most vessels
from thence chosing to fall in between St. Bartholomew and Barbuda where most constantly taken ", Mar. 29, 1747. King's letters
are from Antigua, except one from St. Christopher, and all are
interesting. The remainder are as follows: Nov. 12, 17, 1745
(endorsed) ; May 20, 1746 (on trade with St. Eustatius, with
a valuable list of prizes).

Lockman. Boston, Oct. 21, 1746.
Andrew Belcher regarding Lockman. Boston, Nov. 22, 1746.
Blenham. Barbadoes, July 10, 1746.
Robert Auchmuty. Nov. 29, [1746?].
Ja: Grame (list). Oct., 1746.
James Morse. Jamaica, Aug. 12, 1746.
John Burke. Jamaica, Aug. 10, 1746.

3882. 1748-1757. Letter from the custom house, Boston, complaining
of Andrew Belcher as " never giving his attendance or appearing
at court notwithstanding I have had several cases there tried of
consequence on the acts of trade relating to the plantations ; the
fees of his office chiefly arise from the seizures we make which to
him are a trifle so I suppose he thinks it not worth his attendance,
being allowed no sterling salary from your board ". The writer,
[Charles] H[enry] Frankland, the collector, recommends William Sheaffe. In a postscript Frankland adds, " Mr. Belcher was
dismissed by their lordships a few years ago but reinstated by a
petition of a few merchants here. Such petitions, I assure you,
are very easy to be obtain'd, as the merchants here are generally
smuglers ", Feb. 5, 1749. The Admiralty in commenting on this
letter wishes " To see when Mr. Belcher was dismissed and when
restored and why ". Answer, " Sir, Appointed 13 July, 1743, and
does not appear to have been dismissed ". This statement regarding his appointment is confirmed by *Adm.* 2: **1054,** 138. Belcher
took the place of Samuel Auchmuty.

Letter from Belcher, Aug. 13, 1750, contains a memorial of Boston
merchants, written in his behalf and dated Aug. 10, 1750. This
original document is signed by 53 men, well known in the mercantile annals of Boston. Among the signatures are those of William Bowdoin, James Bowdoin, Andrew Oliver, Ezekiel Cheever,
Edmund Quincy, John Osborne, Thomas Hancock, Benjamin
Faneuil, Nicholas Boylston, Thomas Hutchinson, Thomas Lech-
mere, Joseph Green, John Boylston, W. Read, and Benjamin
Hallowell.

Letters from St. John's, Annapolis Royal, Jamaica, Halifax, Barbadoes, etc., relating to admiralty business. One is from William
Smith, jr., New York, Apr. 8, 1757, and concerns the French
snow *Bon Rencontre,* laden with sugar and indigo and bound for
New York.

3884. 1768-1777. Important set of papers regarding the court of vice-
admiralty at Halifax ; drafts, with alterations in red ink, and other
papers. 1768.

Regarding the conviction of David Ferguson for murder on board the merchant ship *Betsey* near Cape Charles off the coast of Virginia.

Statement of the case of William Story, deputy register of the court of vice-admiralty, Massachusetts. Speaks of a " mob that broke into his office and dwelling house, Aug. 26, 1765, destroyed the greater part of his household furniture, greatly damaged the house, rifled, burnt, and destroyed many of the court records and files and most of his own private papers ". An allowance of £50 was made him by the General Court. The petition is dated Jan., 1772, and mentions Story's wish to return to Boston, his native country.

John Andrews, judge of the vice-admiralty, Rhode Island, regarding admiralty proceedings there and a dispute between the admiralty court and the superior court of the colony. Apr. 20, 1773. The chief justices of the latter issued a writ of prohibition.

Correspondence with judges of the vice-admiralty courts of Charleston, St. John's, Barbadoes and other West India islands, New York, Boston (Robert Auchmuty, from which we learn that Auchmuty was an Irishman), Virginia (list of seizures) ; also memorial and other papers from Richard Starke. Mar. 12, 1771.

Many papers regarding American vessels seized and condemned. Various questions put to the king's advocate and king's proctor on a great variety of subjects, particularly with reference to seizures and sales.

Papers regarding the powers of Antigua to fit out vessels against the Americans, with the opinions of the king's advocate and king's proctor thereon.

Copy of a warrant authorizing West India governors to seize American ships.

Robert Bayard, judge of vice-admiralty. New York, Nov. 4, 1777.

Gov. Morris of St. Vincent and Gov. Burt of Leeward Islands.

Dr. Marriott regarding a new set of interrogatories for American seizures. Old set is not sufficient.

A list of all captures which have been condemned in the vice-admiralty court of Dominica since the breaking out of the rebellion. Wilson, judge of vice-admiralty there, in sending this list, writes, Dec. 19, 1777, " I take the liberty to mention to you a circumstance which struck me as a remarkable instance of their impudence and folly, that on board each of the two [American] vessels, which have been condemned since I presided in that court, there have been found certificates that bond had been given that no subject of the King of Great Britain had any interest in either ship or cargo."

Alexander Stewart, judge of the vice-admiralty court of Dominica, in a letter dated Apr. 10, 1777, speaks of " the almost daily depredations which were made with impunity by a number of rebel or piratical vessels, which infest these seas, on the properties of the inhabitants of this and the other neighboring islands to the great interruption also of the trade between the islands ". A valuable letter.

A. Symson, judge of the vice-admiralty courts, Grenada. Oct. 20, 1777.

Instructions for " commanders of private ships or vessels employed in trade or retained in His Majesty's service, who shall pursuant to 17 George III., c. 7, take out commissions for the seizing and taking all ships and vessels belonging to the inhabitants of the colonies now in rebellion, in order that said instructions may remain on record in the High Court of Admiralty ". Apr. 2, 1777.

3885. 1778-1779. Lists of captures and condemnations of colonial vessels in various West India islands, sent in pursuance of instructions from the Admiralty in 1777. These lists and accompanying papers are from Barbadoes, Antigua (longest list of captures),[1] Grenada, Jamaica, Tortola, the Bahamas, and St. Vincent. Also from New York, East Florida, Halifax, and Georgia (memorial of James Edward Powell).

Papers regarding the ship *May* or *George,* which sailed from Charleston, S. C., with a cargo of rice and indigo for Bordeaux in France. The crew seized the ship and took it into Lamlash in Arran (Firth of Clyde), Apr. 13, 1777. Question of the admiralty jurisdiction of the courts of the two countries, Scotland and England.

Set of standing interrogatories to be administered to persons found on board French prizes. Dec. 3, 1778.

Dr. Marriott's report on the petition of Patrick Byrne, who in 1777 went as a trader to South Carolina (two petitions giving details of experiences in Philadelphia and New York).

Case of the ship *Molly* condemned in the vice-admiralty court of New York. 1779.

3930-3969. 1697-1785. Letters of Intelligence. 1st Series.
3970-3974. 1738-1800. *Id.* 2d Series.

These letters of intelligence are usually written in French, chiefly from the Continent—Dunkirk, Paris, Rochelle, Marseilles, Rochefort, Toulon, Brussels, Brest, Rotterdam, Madrid, St. Ildefonso, Genoa, and other places. A few are from Ireland, Bristol, Southampton, Topsham, Alderney, and other places in the United Kingdom. Some are from Lloyds, by whom all letters of intelligence received were forwarded to the Admiralty.

The information contained in the earlier volumes is only indirectly of service to the student of American history, though much of it has diplomatic interest and is of importance to any one dealing with Anglo-French commercial rivalry in the eighteenth century, particularly in the West Indies. The letters frequently furnish intelligence of the movements of French ships and of various phases of the trade and commerce of France and other European countries. Occasionally the letters are accompanied by lists, such as, " État de Force de Mer et de Terre de l'expédition ", or " État des Vaisseaux en armament à Brest ", etc.

Bundle **3963** and the bundles that follow in the first series are of more importance because they deal with events leading up to the alliance between France and the colonies and treat of French activities in America as seen

---

[1] In the Leeward Islands there were six courts of vice-admiralty, one in each of the islands of Antigua, St. Christopher, Montserrat, Nevis, Tortola, and Anguilla, each of which courts had a distinct and separate jurisdiction. 1779.

through French eyes. "Nous commençons à croire un peu à la guerre", wrote one correspondent, Dec. 18, 1776. An intelligence of Nov. 21, 1781, speaking of the battle of Yorktown says, "Il ne reste plus dans le sud de l'Amérique que Charles-Town et Savannah, qui tomberont d'eux mêmes après quoi toutes les forces réunies, de France et des Américains, tomberont sur New York."

3977-3981. 1750-1810.   Intercepted Letters.

Nearly all the papers in these bundles are of date 1795-1807. In some of the lists dates as early as 1751 are entered, but there are no papers or letters dated earlier than 1793.

> **3978,** 1801-1806, contains a number of letters sent to Baltimore and Washington by Rear-Admiral Willaumez, commander of the French fleet. One is addressed to His Excellency Gen. Thurreau, ambassador from the Emperor of the French to the President of the United States of America.
>
> **3979,** 1793-1809, contains a series of letters and papers relative to Cuba, the Floridas, and Mexico.
>
> **3980,** 1794-1803, contains a few letters in French, unsigned, from Philadelphia and New York.   1795.
>
> > Others are from "Les membres du Comité des colons de St. Domingue réfugiés à Philadelphie chargés de l'organisation de la fête du 21ᵉ Janvier (v. s.) aux Citoyens composans la municipalité de Paris". Many papers.
>
> **3981.** 1797-1798.   Spanish despatches from Havana concerning commercial, naval, and administrative affairs.

3988-3991. 1691-1700.   Letters relating to Ireland.

These papers chiefly concern the movements of the British army in Ireland. They contain, however, occasional references to ships going to America or to the arrival of American ships at Kinsale or Cork. Also a few references to Mediterranean passes. Many of the letters contain enclosures.

3999-4013. 1703-1783.   Letters from the Ordnance Office.

Bound volumes of letters from the Ordnance Office generally in reply to instructions or recommendations from the Admiralty. They concern guns and ordnance for the navy, equipment of store-ships and convoys for the same, shipment of ordnance to the naval stations, and supplies of small arms, locks, powder, mortars, bombs, waist belts, slings, cartouch boxes, and leather accoutrements for marines. Many letters relate to the sending of ordnance stores to the colonies, notably the West Indies, and to places under attack, such as Louisburg.

4071. 1694-1704.   Letters from the Post-Office.

From the General Post-Office to the Admiralty regarding the postal and packet service, notably regarding the installation of new packet boats in 1703 between Falmouth and Lisbon, by contract with Edmund Dummer. Dummer's sloop *Prince* carried mail from Falmouth to the West Indies May 22, 1703. *Cf.* Hist. MSS. Commission, *15 Rept., Portland Manuscripts,* VIII.

4080-4151. 1689-1785.   Letters from the Secretaries of State.

The volumes of this series vary greatly in importance. Some (**4092, 4096, 4100, 4103,** etc.) contain practically nothing relating to the colonies; others

(**4086, 4087, 4088, 4090, 4091, 4093, 4094, 4095**) but few papers, of which only an occasional one is of value. On the other hand some of the earlier volumes are worth examining. The first six volumes (**4080-4085**) contain letters from the Secretary at War, William Blathwayt, and, during his absence in Holland with the king, Apr.-Sept., 1697, from George Clarke, who acted as his deputy. For such letters after 1697 see **4316-4330**. The same volumes contain also a few letters from the Board of Trade, continued after 1697 in **3314-3316**. The letters are all arranged chronologically, so that a search covering a known period is comparatively easy.

The subjects dealt with are: convoys; naval stores (**4080**, 903, 1015, 1131, 1135, **4089**, 14); victualling and transports (**4081**, 1003, 1015, 1027, 1039, 1067, 1069); troops, New York (**4081**, 217, 281, **4082**, 59); trade, pirates, passes, Lutherans and Palatines (**4093**, 18, 119, 137-138, 199, **4104**, 29); and scattering letters and petitions from governors and others in the colonies: Quary, 1703 (**4089**, 15, 52), Dudley (**4090**, 26), Gale, South Carolina, 1718 (**4101**, 53), Drysdale, Virginia, 1722 (**4104**, 24), Andros, 1708 (**4091**, 260). **4081**, 1694, contains many original letters from John Povey, secretary of the Lords of Trade, to the Admiralty. **4085** has " The Humble Proposal of Richard Long ", asking for the loan of a ship for the purpose of discovering gold and wrecks in America, May, 1697; an extract of a letter from William Randolph, justice of the peace, Maidstone, Kent, to Edward Randolph, London, June 29, 1697, regarding the French design upon New England, an extract that was sent by the Secretary of State to the Admiralty (p. 641); and (p. 1103) instructions to commanders employed by Gov. Nicholson of Maryland for preventing frauds on that coast, in pursuance of the order in Council of Aug. 9, 1694. *Cf. Acts Privy Council, Colonial,* II. 272-273.

Later volumes seem equally important. **4121**, 1756-1757, contains many orders and instructions from the secretary to the Admiralty dealing with many phases of the war in America.

The secretary instructs the Admiralty to give directions to the Victualling Board to agree with Kilby and Baker, contractors, to supply 1500 barrels of beef, etc., for the troops in North America. May 3, 1756.

To provide a man-of-war to carry Lord Loudoun to North America.

To give positive orders to the commanders-in-chief of the king's ships to co-operate with Lord Loudoun and to prevent the pernicious trade carried on between the English and French subjects. May 5.

To provide vessels for transporting 4000 stand of arms to North America. May 15.

To order the transports bound to America to proceed to New York. May 31.

Encloses a copy of a letter from Thomas, governor of the Leeward Islands, giving an account of the capture of the man-of-war *Warwick*. Antigua, June 8.

States that directions will be sent to His Majesty's governors in North America and the West Indies concerning the reception and treatment of French prisoners. June 16.

Instructs the Admiralty to acquaint Messrs. Van Neck that the Acadian neutrals have proper care taken of them. June 16.

To cause 80 German planters at Portsmouth to be embarked on board the ships going to Nova Scotia; and to release as many of the Protestant prisoners at Bristol as may be willing to enlist with Col. Prévost. Sept. 15.

To send the transports with the troops from Cork for North America to
  New York instead of to Nova Scotia.   Oct. 2.

To permit the ship *Seaflower* to proceed from Dublin to Barbadoes and
  the Leeward Islands with provisions for His Majesty's fleet there.
  Jan. 4, 1757.

To direct the proper officers to land in America with the troops such part
  of their sea bedding as shall be required.

To despatch, by a sloop to New York, an enclosed packet to the Earl
  of Loudoun and His Majesty's governors in North America.

To cause the store-ships, taken up to carry a number of engineers, etc.,
  to North America, to be supplied with a sufficient quantity of
  provisions.   Jan. 6.

To cause 12 ships of the line, with a proper number of frigates, to be
  got ready for immediate service, and to proceed under the command of Rear-Adm. Holburne to Cork, and from thence to North
  America.   Jan. 7.

Encloses a letter to be forwarded to Gen. Lawrence by the sloop going
  to Halifax.   Jan. 12.

Instructs the Admiralty to grant the usual powers to Thomas Pownall,
  appointed governor of Massachusetts.   Feb. 21.

To order the transports going to North America to be furnished with
  1200 lines, hooks, etc.

To provide transports for carrying two Highland battalions to North
  America and to provide a convoy for them.

This list of the contents of a single volume so far as American affairs are
concerned will give an idea of what may be found in other volumes.   The
letters are often short and perfunctory, though some are elaborate and informing.   The enclosures are generally copies of papers in the Secretary of
State's Office, though some are originals.   The instructions noted above are
signed by H. Fox (May 1–Nov. 12, 1756), Holdernesse (May 27, 1756–Jan.
5, 1757), W. Pitt (Dec. 9, 1756–Mar. 26, 1757).   After Dec. 26 Pitt signs
nearly all the despatches.

4283-4289. 1698-1789. Letters from the Treasury.

These papers are of considerable importance though how far duplicating
the corresponding out-letters among the Treasury papers it is difficult to say.
See *Treas.* 27.

4283. 1698-1714.   Regarding an advice boat sent to Maryland against
  illegal traders.   Aug. 24, 1699.

Petition from William Penn and Col. John French, naval officer,
  against Quary.   Apr. 14, 1712.

Petition of Thomas Coram, " who hath lived ten years in New England wholly employed in the management of building ships ",
  regarding naval stores.   Jan. 13, 1710.

Extract of the report of the Transport Board about the Palatines.
  July 6, 1710.

4284. 1714-1744.   Memorial from the merchants and traders to New
  York regarding the surveyor of the woods.   Aug. 24, 1715.

Regarding Bridger, salary and instructions.   Nov. 29, 1716.

Regarding French smugglers, who land brandy by force near Boston.   Sept. 19, 1729.

4285. 1744-1756. Various bills of exchange drawn by Gov. Shirley.
Oct. 29, 1745; Mar. 20, 26, 1746; Jan. 23, 1747; Mar. 31, May 5,
Sept. 21, 1749.

Papers relating to convoys, smuggling, and transportation of
marines, and queries about provisions, expenses, prisoners, and
protection of men from impressment.[1]

4286. 1757-1770. Extract of a letter from Dinwiddie asking for protection. Jan. 4, 1757.

Papers regarding provisions for troops in North America and
money for the same.

Memorials of the Customs Commissioners regarding smuggling in
Rhode Island. May 24, Nov. 28, 1763.

Papers regarding smuggling in the West Indies and the distribution
of forfeitures. Dec. 17, 1764.

Extract of a letter from Colden of New York to the Earl of Halifax
regarding smuggling and illicit trade. Oct. 9, Nov. 27, 1764.

Extract of a letter from Sharpe, Maryland, to Halifax. Oct. 20,
1764.

Id. regarding smuggling. Jan. 18, 1765.

Case of Capt. Brown in New York, letter from the Customs Commissioners. Feb. 4, 1765.

4287. 1771-1777. Paper on smuggling. Jan. 16, 1771.

Paper on the prosecution of Capt. Keeler in Rhode Island courts.
Aug. 19, 1773.

Regarding Scammell and Ruggles, surveyors of white pines in
America, expenses. Oct. 29, 1772; July 6, 1773; Apr. 12, 1774.

Pay of troops in Boston. May 2, 1774.

Paper on the prevention of illicit trade on the Mississippi, followed
by a large number of papers on trade, smuggling, military and
naval matters, ammunition, etc.

4288. 1778-1782. Many papers relating to movements of American
privateers (*e. g.*, the *Ranger*), troops, prizes, convoys, the transporting of money and provisions, surveyors of white pines and
their pay, intelligence about Paul Jones, Mar. 7, Sept. 25, 1779,
and the like. Most of the papers are departmental, but they
supplement other and more important papers and are useful and
necessary for a study of the system of administration. The
volume closes with Dec. 19, 1782.

4316-4330. 1697-1794. Letters from the War Office.

These letters are from the Secretary at War or the deputy secretary.
Haydn's list of the secretaries (*Book of Dignities,* p. 233) needs correcting
in some particulars. George Clarke was never Secretary at War, but only a
deputy acting in Blathwayt's absence. On Blathwayt's return Clarke retired
and became second secretary to the Admiralty in 1702, Blathwayt continuing
as Secretary at War until 1704. He was followed by St. John, 1704-1709,
Walpole, 1709-1710, Granville, 1710-1712, Wyndham, 1712, Gwyn, 1713, Pulteney, 1714-1717, Craggs, 1717–May, 1718, Pringle, May-Dec., 1718, Treby,
Dec., 1718–July, 1722, Pelham, Aug., 1724–June, 1730, Yonge, 1735–1746,
Fox, June, 1746–Nov., 1755. There is no indication in this correspondence of

[1] There is a Register of protection from being pressed. *Adm.* 7: **313-373.**

Wandesford, Trevor, or Winnington, as given in Haydn. From 1722 to 1740 the office seems to have been conducted largely by the deputy secretary, Richard Arnold, who retired in 1741, with Edward Lloyd as assistant, 1740.

The letters relate to the convoy of transports with forces for the West Indies, Newfoundland, Nova Scotia, and other places in America, and to the Continent—Flanders, Holland, Gibraltar, Minorca, Dunkirk; to the despatching of arms and accoutrements to various places in Great Britain and elsewhere; to the conveyance of passengers, or commissioned officers, surgeons, chaplains, and others going to their regimental posts with servants and equipage;[1] to the shipment of money, medicines, clothing, etc. The information is valuable for dates and for the movements of the various companies that went to America before 1746. There are references here to the companies in New York, South Carolina, Jamaica, an establishment list of the regiment of foot commanded by Oglethorpe, and a list of officers of the six independent companies "now gone to Jamaica", Mar., 1739. There is also a reference to George Gould, appointed surveyor general of North Carolina and collector of customs at Bath Town, Feb. 29, 1740.

The later volumes contain but little that has any direct bearing upon colonial history, yet they are important as showing the part that the Admiralty played in the affairs of the army. In **4321** is a request from the Secretary at War to the secretary to the Admiralty that he move the Lords Commissioners for an order to a captain of a man-of-war going to South Carolina to receive John Hall, surgeon's mate to the three independent companies in that province, with his baggage on board, as he is repairing to his duty. In **4324** and the following volumes there are many orders regarding prisoners of war. A letter of Aug. 2, 1758, mentions certain provincials, released from French prisons, trying to work their way back to America.

4352. 1756-1800. Secret Letters.

One paper only, a memorial from George Walker, agent for Barbadoes, regarding the cultivation of the mango tree and the breadfruit tree in the West Indies. Speaks of the former "now growing on the lands of your memorialist" in Barbadoes, and of the latter as better than plantain. He says that when the Ceded Islands were occupied (after 1763), it was provided that part of the land should always be wooded to prevent the denudation that had injured the other islands, and that cultivation of the breadfruit tree would be a benefit to Barbadoes in that respect. June 28, 1772.

5114-5118. 1686-1790. Miscellaneous Letters, Reports, etc.

A very miscellaneous collection. A number of registers of passes, with entries of plantation vessels and many copies of passes. One of the latter, a fine example that had seen many years service, 1768-1777, gives the movements of a New England vessel, as follows: sailed from Falmouth (Portland), arrived Genoa, July 12, 1770, and remained till the 20th; was again at Genoa, May 14, 1773, June 5, 1774, Feb. 9, 1775; at Carthagena, Mar. 6, 1775,

---

[1] Col. Phillips went to his command in America by way of Boston in a merchant ship and was taken from there, with his servants and equipage, to Annapolis Royal in a British man-of-war some time after July, 1719. He was again in London in 1725, raising recruits, and wrote the Admiralty regarding them to this effect: "In case they arrive safe at Boston they must there be disembarked and another hyred to proceed with them, during which time a great part of them may desert, that country being ever remarkable for incouraging such practices." He wanted a small ship of war to go direct to Annapolis. **4318**, letters of July 7, 1719, Feb. 10, 1725.

returned to Genoa the same year, and again in May, 1776; was at Carthagena again, June 21, sailing July 12, 1776; again at Genoa, Aug. 21, 1776, and June, 1777 (**5116**). In the same bundle is an abstract of His Majesty's ships in commission, mentioning those that were in the West Indies, in the harbors of North America, and on Lake Ontario.

In **5117** are Rodney papers, 1771; general account of the fishery at New-foundland, 1774; scheme of the English fishery, Newfoundland, 1774, from Commodore Shuldham; career of William Pullen, 1777; commissions of marque, standing interrogatories, printed instructions, with blank forms, licenses to carry coals and oats for use of troops in North America; papers regarding American prisoners (pp. 217-231, 1778); extract of intelligence regarding D'Estaing's fleet, Oct.-Dec., 1778; papers regarding piracy in Grenada, interesting for questions of jurisdiction and trial, 1772-1775.

5138-5176. 1673-1783. Orders in Council.

These volumes contain the original orders in Council sent to the Admiralty, beginning July 25, 1673. This collection, the contents of which are not neces-sarily duplicated in the Privy Council Register, is in very convenient form to use in searching for the policy of the King in Council on all matters which came under the cognizance of the Lords of the Admiralty. Each order is signed and sealed by the secretary of the Council. To each order is attached a copy of the paper—petition, memorial, report, or representation—upon which it is based, and some of these attached papers are not to be found elsewhere, particularly for the earlier period. The volumes after 1776 contain practically nothing of value for colonial history. In **5138** (pp. 516, 520, 528, 540, 544, 566, 570, 574, 594, 598, 1275) are documents relating to the expedition under Sir John Berry sent to suppress Bacon's Rebellion in Virginia; and in **5138** and **5139** are documents relating to Sloughter's departure for New York. Copies of earlier orders in Council can be found in **5246**.

5253-5323. 1680-1783. Reports of Courts-Martial.

These volumes contain the minutes of proceedings of courts-martial held on board ships of His Majesty's navy, some of which were lying at the time in colonial waters. Where the inquiry concerned losses incurred during wars in America, the evidence is often very valuable. This is particularly true of courts-martial held during the Revolutionary War, but it is also true of the earlier period. Answers, depositions, letters, etc., often at great length, may be found (*i. e.*, **5309-5319**), which contain information in detail of important sea fights. The court-martial for the loss of the *Serapis* is in **5315**. See p. 46, below.

OUT-LETTERS.

1-115. 1665-1679, 1689-1783. Orders and Instructions from the Lords of the Admiralty.

Adm. 2.

All the entry books of out-letters are bulky volumes that show signs of frequent use. The contents are listed by years, not by names or places. Though the first vol-ume is not indexed or paged, later volumes are indexed alphabetically by names, and the documents are arranged chronologically. Some of the indexes have subject entries, such as "Convoys and Cruisers", "No. America", "Foreign Voyages", including the colonies, "Passengers", "Prisoners", etc. The orders and instructions are issued to admirals and other naval officials, to the Navy Board, Victualling Board, and other departments, to the officials of the High Court, and to sundry officials in the colonies. Many of the volumes are unimportant for colonial history, but others are full of matter showing the Admiralty's share in colonial business. For example, **48** contains the usual orders to councillors in the royal colonies to administer the oaths and test; the same to the proprietaries to be administered in their respective colonies " to such persons, whose commissions, warrants, or letters of mart shall be sent unto you ". Also to captains of His Majesty's ships employed in the plantations to attend on this colony or that, New York, South Carolina, or New England, for the service of the government there, to carry boxes directed to the governors, to follow their orders, to avoid impressing men there, and to send accounts of their proceedings to the Admiralty. The captain of the *Rose* was to aid and assist the inhabitants of South Carolina against the Indians; the captain of the *Roebuck* to proceed to Tobago with such persons as shall be sent to cut timber for building a college, and to carry them with the same to Barbadoes; others were to prevent foreigners, Spaniards, and others from fishing on the banks of Newfoundland, to take out royal officials, to convoy home such ships as wished to come, to bring despatches from the governors, to meet the expenses of sick seamen put ashore at Boston, or to carry out money. Capt. St. Lo of the *Valeur* was ordered to return home from Maryland as the province required no attendance. In **78** Spry was " to proceed directly with several packets to New York and to return with the trade ". In general this series and those that follow contain the record of the share which the Admiralty took in the administering of England's policy toward the colonies. They are therefore of importance to every student of colonial history.

169-259. 1689-1783. Letters from the Lords of the Admiralty to the Secretary of State and to other Departments.

After 1694 the letters to the secretary were separately entered. See **363-374** of the out-letters. The above volumes, constituting the Lords' letter-books, contain entries of all letters written to the Navy Board, the Ordnance Office, and other departments, to the Privy Council, Board of Trade, Trinity House, to governors of stations in England, mayors of port towns, commissioners, officials, and law officers. In the periods when the navy was active in North American and West Indian waters all these volumes are worthy of attention. If dates are known and names of captains and admirals have been ascertained, information can be easily acquired, or if a given naval movement is involved, the details can be readily discovered.

377-501. 1689-1746. Secretary's Letters in General.

502-581. 1746-1783. Secretary's Letters to Public Offices and Admirals.

In general, the secretary's letters are more informing than are those signed by the board. They are more informal, though relating to the lesser business of the board which was turned over to the secretary to deal with. They were written under orders from the board and contain the board's wishes and instructions, but they have a more personal flavor and, because sent frequently in answer to letters received, contain details and expressions of opinion not found in the more formal correspondence. They are addressed to boards and to individuals, to the Navy Board and Ordnance Board, to governors of colonies about forwarding packets, and to naval officers regarding their duties. According to his own statement the secretary was a hard-worked official, burdened with long hours of service and a heavy correspondence.

1045-1061. 1689-1783. Letters relating to Admiralty and Vice-Admiralty Courts.

These letters are addressed to the Board of Trade and the Navy Board, and to the judge, king's or queen's advocate general, king's or queen's proctor or procurator general, register, deputy register, and marshal of the High Court of Admiralty, to the council for the Admiralty, solicitor of the Admiralty, receiver general of the rights and perquisites of the Admiralty, receiver and deputy receiver of the High Court of Appeals for Prizes, and sometimes to the crown lawyers, the attorney general and solicitor general.

These books contain copies of the warrants for vice-admiralty commissions, but not the commissions themselves. They contain copies of warrants for letters of marque, and for appointments of various officers of vice-admiralty courts in England and the colonies. They contain instructions and orders of various kinds, touching wrecks, embargoes, convoys, and fees (see below). The volumes are generally indexed and paged.

In the case of a vice-admiralty commission the procedure was as follows. The petition or request was sent to the Commissioners of the Admiralty, who instructed the judge of the High Court of Admiralty to cause letters patent to be issued out of the High Court in the king's name to the person desiring the office (see *Acts Privy Council, Colonial*, vol. III., § 207). The commissions themselves were made out by the solicitor of the Admiralty. Warrants for inferior officers, judges, advocates, marshals, and registers, either authorizing or confirming their appointments, were issued in the same way at the request of the governor or vice-admiral of a colony. The letters patent were not issued out of Chancery and so copies will not be found on the Patent Rolls. The originals should be among the records of the colony or among the papers of the appointee. The formal enrollment was in the muniment books of the register of the High Court, and copies were entered in the entry books of the Admiralty and sometimes in the entry books of the Lords of Trade or Board of Trade. Copies ought to be found also among the privy seal warrants. The vice-admiralty commission did not bear the great seal. As the warrants are entered also in *Admiralty Court, Miscellanea*, **752-763**, it should be possible to make out a complete list of vice-admiralty officials in the colonies. A list of commissions is printed in the *Report* of the American Historical Association for 1911 and the Massachusetts commissions are printed in full (with translations when in Latin) in volume II. of the *Publications* of the Colonial Society of Massachusetts.

Though there appears to have been a vice-admiralty court in Jamaica as early as 1658 and we hear of one frequently after 1660, and though in Barbadoes mention is made of such a court as early as 1662, the earliest commissions here entered are: New York, from the Duke of York, Andros, 1678, Dongan, 1682, from the king, Fletcher, 1692, including East and West New Jersey, Pennsylvania, and Newcastle, Cornbury, 1701, Lovelace, 1708; Dominion of New England, Dudley, 1685, Andros, 1686; Massachusetts, Phips, 1691; New Hampshire, Allen, 1692; Maryland, Copley, 1691; Virginia, Andros, 1692; South Carolina, from the proprietors, Trott, 1716, from the king, Nicholson, 1720; North Carolina, Burrington, 1730.

From these and later commissions certain conclusions may be reached regarding the erection of vice-admiralty courts and the appointment of vice-admiralty officials in the colonies. Until 1696 a separate commission was, or might have been, issued to each governor possessing vice-admiralty powers and all inferior officers were appointed by the Admiralty at home; in 1696 the Privy Council, on representation from the Board of Trade, agreed that in case of the death of a governor vice-admiralty powers might devolve upon his successor in the office; after 1697, when the general system of vice-admiralty courts in the colonies was projected and in part set up, the royal governors were empowered to appoint inferior officers in case of a vacancy, the Admiralty retaining the right to confirm or disallow; after 1702, royal governors were authorized " to erect court or courts admiral for the determining of all marine and other causes and matters proper therein to be heard, with all necessary powers, authority and fees " (**1047**, 53-54, 101-102, 104; **1049**, 7, 59). According to their commissions as vice-admirals, the governors had also power to appoint all the officers of the vice-admiralty courts in the colonies, saving the right of the judge and register of the High Court of Admiralty in England. The procedure above described continued until 1764 and 1768 when important changes were effected (**1057**, 267, 397, 403, 409, and see below). Vice-admiralty officials received their letters patent after they had taken oath and subscribed to the test.

The volumes are fairly well indexed, and entries appear under the name of the colony and the name of the individual. The following statements show the character of individual entries.

1054. 1741-1747. Leonard Lockman, judge of the vice-admiralty court, Rhode Island, regarding his being obstructed in the exercise of his office.

Privateers in America breaking the marine treaty.

Letters to judges of vice-admiralty courts in America. One to Samuel Auchmuty of New England, then in London.

Cases of murder, whether to be tried in the court in the colonies or in the Admiralty Court in England.

Lists of letters of marque, together with full instructions and additional instructions to private men-of-war, and instructions arising out of letters of marque.

Embargoes laid and taken off.

General orders from the judge of the High Court to all vice-admirals abroad and to vice-admirals and judges in America.

Letters sent directly to vice-admiralty officials in America, as to Shirley, owning " the receipt of several of his letters in relation to the preservation of the white pine trees and of irregularities in the vice-admiralty courts ", and desiring him " to continue his correspondence "; to the judge of the vice-admiralty court in Barbadoes, instructing him to send copies of all proceedings in prize cases to the judge of the High Court of Admiralty at Doctors' Commons to remain a record.

Letters to admirals, captains, etc., of the fleet regarding admiralty matters. For example, to Capt. Collins, Dover, Downs, Aug. 15, 1745. " Herewith you will receive six packets, vizt., for the vice-admirals of New York, New Jersey, New Hampshire, Massachusetts Bay, South Carolina, and Rhode Island, which, being of consequence, I am commanded by my Lords Commissioners of

the Admiralty to signify their direction to you to deliver the said
packets to the senior captains of the convoy bound with the transports from Gibraltar to Louisburgh to convey them as opportunity
offers to the persons they are directed to, on his arrival at Louisburgh."

Entries regarding the transportation of felons to America. Andrew
Reid was contractor at this time (1740-1744). Some of the
masters of his ships were charged with murder and other felonies
on the high seas, and the instructions were that such masters (if
evidence were sufficient) be tried at the court of Oyer and Terminer, which the judge of the High Court would hold for the
purpose. *Cf.* Penrice's letter, Mar. 31, 1744, *Adm.* 1 : **3878**.

1057. 1762-1770. Warrants and other documents relating to the vice-
admiralty court for all America, vice-admiral, the Earl of Northumberland (p. 213), judge, William Spry (p. 183), surrogate,
Joseph Gerrish, one of the council of Nova Scotia, to act as Spry's
deputy while the latter was governor of Barbadoes (p. 427), register, Spencer Perceval (p. 194), marshal, Charles Howard (p.
191). There was no advocate. See also pp. 183, 335, 402-409,
and for the revocation, p. 427, and *Adm. Court, Miscellanea,* **943**.

Appointment of Samuel Fitch as advocate general of Massachusetts
and New England in the place of Jonathan Sewall, resigned.
Nov., 1769.

Egerton Leigh of South Carolina and Peyton Randolph of Virginia,
each of whom held at the same time the offices of judge of admiralty and attorney general, were ordered to resign one of the offices.

Regulations governing the four courts erected in 1768, instead of
the single court of 1764 (pp. 409-414).

1. Halifax, to have original jurisdiction in all cases within the limits
of Quebec, Newfoundland, Nova Scotia. Jonathan Sewall was
to be judge and Alexander Chorley register.

2. Boston, *id.* within the limits of New Hampshire, Massachusetts,
Rhode Island, Connecticut. Robert Auchmuty, judge, Charles
Howard, marshal.

3. Philadelphia, *id.* within the limits of New Jersey, New York,
Pennsylvania, Delaware, Maryland, Virginia. Jared Ingersoll,
judge, Arodi Thayer, marshal, Richard Peters, register.

4. Charleston, *id.* within the limits of North Carolina, South Carolina, Georgia, and the Floridas. Augustus Johnston, judge,
Andrew Dummer, register.

Probably each court was designed to have its full complement of officials,
but those named above are all that I can find recorded. The judge, judge
advocate, deputy judge advocate, register, and marshal of these courts were
all appointed by the Admiralty.

In **1048** are many papers relating to Capt. Kidd and other pirates brought
from New York and Virginia, with names, court judgments, warrants of
execution, fees, etc. See also *Adm. Court, Oyer and Terminer,* **15, 16, 48**.

1116. 1781-1789. Letters relating to Courts-Martial.

This volume contains a few references to losses at the hands of American
privateers and other colonial happenings, pp. 56-57, 59, 84, 170-172, 179, 309.

1147-1174. 1703-1721, 1745-1783. Letters relating to Marines.[1]

The marines were regular regiments on marine service, and colonels of marine regiments were called marine colonels. They took their orders only from the Lord High Admiral (Prince George of Denmark, **1147**, May 20–Oct. 25, 1708) or the Admiralty, having been formally placed under the former's direction, Mar. 23, 1703 (*Treas.* 64: **5**).[2] Rules were drawn up in May, 1740 (**1151**, duplicates in *Adm.* 1: **4318**, and *Adm., Marine Office,* **3**) ; new regulations were issued in 1748 (**1151**, 323-358) and in Mar., 1755 (**1152**, 1-5) ; and many acts of Parliament regulating the marine forces while on shore were passed between 1755 (28 Geo. II., c. 11) and 1785 (25 Geo. III., c. 3).

By royal sign manual, Feb. 28, 1747, the king placed all the marine regiments under the command of the Admiralty, authorizing the commissioners to draft all rules and regulations and to direct all payments of money. Hitherto the business had been done partly by the Admiralty and partly by the Navy Board. From this time forward the whole was managed by one of the Admiralty's secretaries aided by two clerks, with a clerk from the Navy Office to examine the marine clothing. If the War Office wished to instruct the marines, it could do so only through the Admiralty.

The marines were raised and mustered in the same manner as the land forces, and there were always appointed a muster-master general and a commissary-general of marine forces. They were likewise reduced and disbanded at the end of a war, as in 1713 and 1748, under direction of a regular " commission for disbanding the marine regiments ". A number of those disbanded in 1713 were restored by George I. as regiments of foot, and such act of restoration shows the interchangeability of the land and sea forces. A marine corps could at any time be incorporated with the regiments of infantry of the line or could be constituted a regular regiment of foot, and a regiment of foot could be constituted temporarily a regiment of marines.

The earliest regiment of marines appears to have been raised in Oct., 1672, for service on board the fleet and to have been disbanded at the close of the Dutch War. Two regiments were raised in 1690, and six regiments in 1702 ; and in succeeding years marine forces were regularly provided for by Parliament, " to be employed on board our ships or on shore as there shall be occasion ".[3] When raised, the marines were dispersed by detachments on board the ships of the royal navy and scattered over the world.[4] Marines served at the taking of Annapolis Royal in 1710,[5] and detachments from a marine regiment remained in Nova Scotia during 1710-1711. There were marines in garrison at St. John's in Newfoundland, 1740; marines went with Lord Cathcart in

---

[1] There are no marine entry books from 1721 to 1745. That there have been such is evident from the index to **1151** which does not belong to that volume but to one of earlier date, 1740 to 1744.

[2] Instructions for the paymaster of marines in 1702 may be found in *Treas.* 64: **197**.

[3] *Adm.* 1: **4318**. *Cf.* in this series, vol. **1151**, letter from Sir William Yonge, May 8, 1740.

[4] The detachment assigned to a ship consisted of a captain, three subalterns, and one hundred men. Colonels, lieutenant-colonels, and majors of marines were not allowed to accompany their battalions. Marine chaplains went with the marine regiments, though they were sometimes served by deputy at half-pay. For a case of actual numbers, see *House of Lords MSS.,* new series, VI. 13.

[5] For the history of the marines consult Edge, *The Historical Records of the Royal Marines* (1893) ; Dalton, *English Army Lists and Commission Registers,* to 1714 (5 vols. published, 1892-1902) ; Cannon, *Historical Records of the Marine Corps, 1664-1748,* afterwards the *Present Corps of Royal Marines from 1755* (1848).

1740-1741; and others were on board the *Princess Mary,* which was sent in 1745 to assist in the expedition against Louisburg. From that time forward marine regiments played some part in the history of the colonies.

The marines were paid in like manner with the land forces, being provided for by Parliament exclusive of the money granted for the service of the navy. The money furnished for their maintenance did not go, however, through the hands of any officer of the navy, but through the hands of the paymaster-general of the forces. The accounts were made up at first apparently in the Admiralty Office, but very early a marine office was established, under a paymaster-general of marine forces (see under *Adm., Marine Office,* below). The system of payment, in this case as elsewhere, was fitful and uncertain. Pay was frequently in arrears and the troops were discontented and mutinous. As early as 1706 Prince George endeavored to find a remedy but without success. In 1712 pay was three and a half years in arrears. The marines on shore were left without subsistence; marine widows could not get their pensions; the clothiers were not paid. The Admiralty complained to the paymaster, but he seems to have been helpless because of the failure of the paymaster-general of the forces to issue the money.

But the fault did not lie entirely with the Pay Office. Bad as the conditions were in that " subordinate but opulent " post, they found their counterpart in the Marine Pay Office itself. When in 1745 the House of Commons made an investigation into the abuses of the army, the committee summoned before it, among others, Edmund Herbert and Edmond Jones, deputies. The latter made a sorry appearance. " Being examined ", says the report,[1] " he stated that he had been in the office ever since its establishment and was allowed a salary of *about* 300l. a year and that he gave no security. That he always received the money issued from the Exchequer and sometimes deposited it in the bank, with whom he kept a book in his own name; in which book were entered the several sums paid into, and received from the bank; and that he had then upwards of 100,000l. in his hands belonging to the marines, which sum he, at first, declared was cash and bank notes, but upon further examination he confessed, after numberless prevarications, that part of it was placed at interest, without the paymaster's knowledge." Herbert gave additional evidence to the effect that for technical reasons a certain warrant for pay had not been complied with and certain regiments of marines had consequently been left unpaid. To which a contemporary critic replies, " We shall soon see why the objection was made to this particular warrant. Sixty-four thousand pounds was too great a sum to be called in by Mr. Edmond Jones, the Paymaster's Deputy's Deputy, who had so carefully *lent* out that and other large sums for the trifling consideration of a little paltry Interest Money." [2]

The matter was complicated by the fact that the marines when on shore were placed on the regular establishment and their sea pay became land pay which was looked after by the War Office. The pay of the marines suffered the same deductions and stoppages as did that of the land forces, including the allowance for Chelsea Hospital, a day's pay once a year from officers and soldiers. The marines, when on board, had the same leaves of absence as the regular seamen, and when sick were given the benefit of the hospitals provided for sick and wounded sailors.

[1] *Report of a Committee of the House of Commons relating to the Army* (1746), pp. 51-52; *Commons Journal,* XXV. 124.
[2] *National Oeconomy Recommended* (London, 1746), p. 49.

Marine uniforms were provided in 1747, though not for the first time. In that year it was proposed to furnish a very good cloth coat, well lined, a good but inferior waistcoat, strong kersey breeches, two pairs of strong yarn stockings, one pair of shoes, two good linen shirts, two neck-cloths, and a cloth cap. But this outfit proved too expensive for the marine off-reckonings, so the waistcoat was omitted, except with the first clothing, and each man was allowed a shilling with which to convert his old coat into a waistcoat; cloth breeches were provided for the sergeants, but kersey breeches for the privates, corporals, and drummers; while the double supply of shirts, stockings, shoes, and neck-cloths or rollers was reduced by half. The coats were to be red, breasted in lapel fashion, and the sleeves to be closed. The lapels were faced and turned up with bright, full yellow, the button holes and lining to be of the same color, with white or yellow (brass) buttons. The waistcoat and breeches were to be of the same color and buttoned as the coat, and the caps to have an anchor and cable on the forepart instead of a crest, as formerly. The drummers were to wear yellow coats with proper lace on them, and the corporals to have a white shoulder knot. In 1755 hats were substituted for caps and gaiters were introduced. Sword belts with frogs, cartouch boxes with nine holes, slings for muskets, and drum belts were also provided. The Navy Board furnished the clothing and the Ordnance Board the arms, under directions from the Admiralty. The contractors were no better than they should have been, and supplies were not infrequently rejected.

The letters in these entry books are addressed to vice-admirals, commanders, and captains of the royal navy, to colonels and lieutenants of marines, to the Navy Board and Secretary at War, to recruiting officers, mayors, justices of the peace, governors of Portsmouth, Chatham, and Southampton, to the muster-masters general, the paymasters-general of marines, auditors, governors of the Chatham Chest, judge advocate, and others. The subjects of the correspondence are of great variety, the largest number concerning the marines in England or on board ships in other waters than American. Much attention was devoted to the position of the marines on board, their rank, treatment, duties, provisions, arms, and sea pay. In regard to courts-martial, the question arose whether the marines, who were appointed to serve on board the fleet and were borne as part of the complement of the ships on which they served, could be tried at a naval court-martial for offenses which they committed while serving on board or while carried on the ships' books as part of their complements, by virtue of 13 Charles II., c. 9, or any other law. The question was answered in the affirmative. At first the marines seem to have been tried at courts-martial provided by the Secretary at War under recommendation from the Admiralty, but later, at marine regimental courts-martial held on board, and the Admiralty was not disposed to take any orders from the Secretary at War in regard to such trial or the sentence that followed.

Many of the later volumes of this series are full of interest for colonial history, as may be seen from an analysis of one of them.

1168. 1773-1775. Chatham division of marines, 460 strong, embarked for America under Maj. John Pitcairn between Oct. and Nov., 1774. The Navy Board had ordered 800 white shirts and 1400 pairs of white worsted stockings for the use of the marines in North America. The knapsacks, haversacks, and pioneer utensils were sent Dec., 1774. The marine detachments were transported by the *Boyne* and the *Somerset,* while Maj. Pitcairn went in the *Asia.* Apparently there was no intention of landing the marines at Boston unless it should be found absolutely necessary. On Jan. 25, 1775, a reinforcement was despatched, with tents for 24 officers and 150 privates, with 10 bell tents, 10 camp colors, and 2000 gun flints, showing that a landing had been decided on. Important letters follow from the Admiralty to Maj. Pitcairn regarding the marines at Boston, and referring to Pitcairn's letter of Dec. 10 (pp. 323-325) ; also letters to Adm. Graves. These letters and the entries that follow are of great interest, pp. 373, 375, 379, 390, 393, 400, 420, 421-423, 436, 458, 461, 500, 544, 546, 548, 549. They refer to the position and equipment of the troops, to the knapsacks as worn and bad, to the fact, which the Admiralty regrets, that Pitcairn had lost so many men by excessive drinking, and to the sending of a sufficient number of marines to replace those killed in the battles of Lexington and Concord. A letter of July 25, 1775, refers to the deaths of Majs. Pitcairn and Short, who died of wounds received at Bunker Hill, and speaks of a letter from the former, dated June 1, to Maj. Tupper. A letter to Tupper, Aug. 3, 1775, refers to his letters of June 21 and 24 (*Adm.* 1 : **486**, first four papers), giving an account of the battle of Bunker Hill and enclosing a return of the marines killed and wounded. The Admiralty through the secretary expresses satisfaction " at the gallant behaviour of the marine corps and the honour they have acquired in the defeat of the rebels on that day ". It repeats Tupper's statement that the marines had lost by their tents being plundered while they were engaged in action, and instructs the secretary to express to Tupper their astonishment that such an event could have happened, " as the greatest part of the army as well as one of the battalions of marines remained in camp ", and at the same time to acquaint him that " they cannot consent to the introducing a precedent for charging the public with the expence of making good such losses." Lieut. Collins was despatched to Boston by the *Cerberus* to take the place of Maj. Pitcairn.

Unfortunately the letters mentioned from Pitcairn cannot be found. A few letters from Capt. Hartwell of the *Boyne* are in *Adm.* 1 : **1902**, § 18, where mention is made of fifteen marines that were sent on July 23, by order of Adm. Graves, to guard the lighthouse at Boston and were taken by the Americans on July 31, 1776. The log-book of the *Boyne* is also extant and furnishes a small amount of information.

1319-1323. 1730-1786. Letters relating to Passes or Pass Letter-Books.

Passes were required for trade in the Mediterranean and for protection against Barbary cruisers, the most menacing of whom were the Algerine pirates ; and these volumes contain full information about their issue and use. A new system was established by order in Council of Dec. 18, 1729, superseding the older order of June 14, 1722. Rules for the use of passes and instructions to the governors of the colonies may be found in **1319**, 2, and **1321**, 336-339.[1] Letters follow regarding passes for colonial merchants or

[1] *Cf. Commons Journal,* XXI. 733, 735, Oct., 1732. The gist of these regulations was as follows :

No pass was to be granted to the master of any ship or vessel until a certificate had been obtained by the governor of a plantation from the naval officer, giving the number of men and guns and stating that such ship or vessel had been built either in Great Britain or Ireland or the islands of Guernsey or Jersey or one of the plantations or that it was a foreign ship made free ; and further that the master and all the owners of her were the king's natural-born subjects or foreign Protestants made denizens.

Oath was to be taken by masters of ships and vessels as to the property of them, and a bond was to be entered into by the master and one of the owners, or if an owner

for merchants trading with America, some of which are answers to letters received in "Letters from the Governors" (*Adm.* 1: **3817-3820**). These answers give considerable information, not about the actual use made of the passes, but about the conditions under which they were to be used—fees, registers, unused passes, exceptions, stamps on bonds, etc.

Note the letters of instruction to Rhode Island (**1319**, 427-429, Sept. 12, 1733, **1321**, 336-338, Oct. 8, 1754) and Connecticut (**1322**, 375, 377) ; also the case of foreigners navigating British ships [1] (**1320**, 144-145, **1323**, 13), bags of money sent from Boston, 1753-1754 (**1321**, 63, 106, 168, 243, 331), stamps on bonds (**1322**, 211, 231, **1323**). For further information regarding passes see *Adm.* 7 (*Miscellanea*) : **75-103**, " Register of Passes ".

Instructions were sent to the consuls at Alicante, Barcelona, Cadiz, Carthagena, Cagliari, Coruña, Faro, Genoa, Leghorn, Lisbon, Malaga, Naples, Oporto, Seville, Venice, Messina, Malta, bidding them to demand passes of all masters of ships or vessels that might come into their ports, in order to endorse the same and to compare them with the specimens sent out by the Admiralty, and to discover whether they were forged or not. The Admiralty sent out two blank forms, one for the use of inhabitants of Great Britain and the plantations, and the other for the use of inhabitants of Minorca and Gibraltar only.

The colonial ship-owners and captains must have made use of large numbers of these passes, which were sent out to America in batches of thirty to fifty at a time. There was hardly a colony that did not make application for them. Sec. Willard of Massachusetts received, between 1749 and 1760, nearly 650 passes, though not all were issued out to captains. This number seems large when we realize that one pass did service for many voyages. Probably both Connecticut and Rhode Island obtained their passes from Massachusetts, but not New Hampshire, which received its own supply.

1331-1341. 1745-1782. Secret Orders and Letters.

A very valuable series of secret despatches, that is not duplicated elsewhere, as far as a comparison has been made. In only one instance, that of a secretary's covering letter, was a document of this series found to have been

---

were not present by some substantial and responsible person, in conjunction with the master, who was to give bond for the return of the pass.

Before the pass was delivered, it was to be endorsed in words at length and not in figures, the time when delivered, at what place, and to whom, and to the endorsement the governor was to put his hand and affix his seal.

An act of Parliament was passed (4 George II., c. 17, 1731) to prevent counterfeiting or erasing of passes, and an advertisement was published in the *Gazette* of Jan. 7, 1734, relating to masters who refused to produce their passes to His Majesty's ministers or consuls abroad, and the governors were to show the law and the advertisement to masters that they might not plead ignorance.

By the order in Council a register was to be kept by the Admiralty of all passes issued out, therefore the governor and secretary of a colony were to transmit to the Admiralty Board a register of such as were issued in the colony. Also by order in Council a fee of twenty-five shillings was to be paid for each pass for the benefit of the secretary to the Admiralty and his clerks, and the governors were to receive this sum from the masters before they issued a pass, and to transmit it to England by the first convenient opportunity. All passes returned by the masters were to be cancelled and transmitted to the Admiralty, together with the bonds and oaths that should be given for new ones. All passes not issued out were also to be returned.

[1] From other sources we learn that there were many abuses in the matter of Mediterranean passes. In 1760 the British consul at Gibraltar informed the Secretary of State that false passes were in use and that sometimes masters after obtaining passes would discharge their English sailors and take on Italians.

entered in any other Admiralty volume. These entry books may be the " Private Order Book " mentioned in the Admiralty minutes (*Adm.* 3 : **70**, Aug. 3, 1762).

1331. 1745-1761. Admiralty orders in connection with the Louisburg expedition, 1745, and the Braddock expedition, 1754.

Instructions to Boscawen, 1755, Byng, 1756, Hawke, 1756, Hardy, 1757, Cotes, 1757, Holburne, 1757, Frankland, 1757, Moore, 1757, Palliser, 1757, Gordon, 1757, Wheelock, 1757, Saunders, 1759, Holmes, 1759, Cotes, 1759, Colville, 1760 (June 20, sent the same night at half-past twelve by a messenger to Portsmouth to go by the *Vengeance*—important because concerning operations against Canada), Swanton, 1760, Colville, 1761, Douglas, 1761, Rodney, 1761 (reduction of Martinique, etc.). This series relates to the movements of the squadrons in connection with the war in America, and is extremely important for the naval side of the war.

1332. 1762-1768. Continuation of **1331.** Instructions to Houlton, 1762, Colville, 1762, Rodney, 1762, Holmes, 1762, Pocock, 1762, Keppel, 1762, Richards, 1762, and Spry, 1762. On account of the peace, the instructions to Burnaby and others, 1764, were returned and cancelled.

Instructions to Byron to make discoveries in the south seas (Falkland Islands) ; *id.* to Capt. Cook, 1772; instructions to aid the Royal Society in its expedition to observe the transit of Venus, 1768 ; to Graves, 1775 ; to Shuldham, 1775 ; to Bellew and Cooper, 1775 (rebellion in New England). The remainder of the orders concern the movements of the navy in North America and the West Indies.

In **1331** is a " List of ships at present stationed in North America ". In **1332** are " A List of His Majesty's Ships and Vessels in North America and of such as are under orders or intended to proceed thither forthwith ", " Schedule of copies of instructions and orders from the Admiralty to Admirals Graves and Shuldham sent to Ld Viscount Howe, with his lordships instructions " (May 4, 1776), " A Schedule of copies of Letters from the Secretary of the Admiralty to Vice-Admirals Graves and Shuldham " (same date).

Further instructions to Capt. Cook, 1776; to various captains regarding American privateers, 1777-1778.

1333. 1770-1779. A smaller volume of secretary's letters, supplemental to those noted above, with additional instructions informally couched. Important for the Revolutionary War.

1334-1341. A set of volumes, numbered 1 to 8, of which 3, 4, and 5, **1336, 1337, 1338,** were (at the time of examination, July, 1912) in the hands of the Admiralty. They are of the same character as **1333,** secretary's letter-books.

1334. 1776, Oct.–1778, Apr. Letter to Sir John Hamilton of the *Hector* and other captains, Mar. 8, 1777, describing Capt. Hynson (Brit. Mus. *Add. MSS.* **34414**) as " a lusty, black looking man, who will as it is expected endeavor to pass for a passenger ". Hynson was the real owner of the boat on which he expected to sail, an English-built cutter sloop about 90 tons. From this letter one would not judge that Hynson was a spy in England's employ, as he is shown to be in the Auckland Papers. Another letter, Mar. 28, 1777, speaks of one Hammond, "a little man who wears a green uniform with red lapels and anchor buttons, lately arrived at Nantz from Baltimore in Maryland with dispatches from the Congress, and is to return with other dispatches when cleaned and new fitted". Other letters have to do with the interception by the Admiralty of American and French correspondence. "My Lords Commrs of the Admiralty having received intelligence that two French ships were fitting out on the 21st (of May, 1777), either at Marseilles or Toulon", and "that they were to be purchased or at least freighted by Mr. Deane to be laden with different sorts of goods for the use of the rebels", have discovered "that one Hynson is to have the direction of the expedition [and] to receive his instructions from Mr. Deane". Letters follow of a similar character, furnishing the admirals with information about suspected vessels sailing for America with cargoes of warlike stores. For example, "The ships going out will be loaded with fusils, pistols, accoutrements for cavelry, saddles for one squadron, clothing for troops, and other military stores." "The *Hippopotame,* sold by the court of France to Mr. Beaumarchois, is to carry a very principal cargo, a quantity of large brass cannon, about 60 field pieces, 14000 fusils, and other stores. Mr. Carmichael, a gentn in much confidence with the rebel agents is to go on board the ship." "The rebel agents have settled an agreement for a packet boat to be dispatched once a month to the Congress from Nantz." "One Nicholson is set out for Nantz to command the *Lyon,* an American frigate of 36 guns. He is to sail with the fleet and it is supposed carries dispatches for the Congress. A Mr. Carmichael goes with him. Several people lately picked up who escaped from prison in England are going on the fleet as pilots for the coast of America. Their rendezvous is about Nantz, L'Orient, perhaps Belle Isle. Mr. Deane's brother is going with dispatches and embarks on board a frigate of 36 guns, which has been sometime laying in the river of Bourdeaux."

Secret instructions for Lord Howe, Mar. 21, 1778; additional secret instructions, Mar. 22. Then follow instructions to admirals, in other waters, to guard against the French. Secret instructions for Adm. Keppel, Apr. 25, 1778, with a list of vessels under his command.

1335. 1778, May-Dec. Secret instructions to Adm. Montague, governor of Newfoundland, May 2, 1778, Barrington in the West Indies, May 3, Young, *id.,* May 3, informing them of the declaration of war against France; to Byron, Keppel, and others regarding the movements of the French, particularly the sailing of D'Estaing's fleet, May-July, 1778; and to Barrington and others calling on them to co-operate; to Capt. Peyton to intercept French ships with stores for America, Nov., 1778; to Byron, Nov. 6; to Gambier, Nov. 6; to Barrington, Dec. 15; to Shuldham, Dec. 15; to Parker, Dec. 15, 18, regarding D'Estaing and the French.

1339. 1781, Jan.-June. Instructions to Elphinstone of the *Warwick,* Jan. 13, 1781; to Arbuthnot, *id.* The next few letters relate to the defense of Gibraltar. To Capt. Bazely of the *Amphion* regarding the transportation of Hessians from Bremer Lehe to New York, Mar. 21, 1781, with original drafts. To Arbuthnot, May 22, 1781, speaking of " having received intelligence from Paris dated the 13 inst. that large supplies of money, clothing, and military stores were preparing to be sent from France (part of them with young Laurens) for the use of the rebel army in North America ". *Cf.* letters to Darby, June 7, 8. Letters also relate to the defense of St. Helena, Brazil, East India, and the Cape, and to protection of convoys from the East and West Indies.

1340. 1781, July-Dec. Instructions to Adm. Digby, mentioning an extract of a letter from Sir Henry Clinton, with extracts of two intercepted letters from Washington to Lafayette and Gen. Sullivan; also a copy of a letter from the commander of the French fleet at Rhode Island to Luzerne at Philadelphia, regarding the movements of De Grasse's fleet, July 14, 1781; instructions to Rodney, July 14, 1781; to Arbuthnot, Digby, July 24, regarding the Dutch fleet laden in part with cloths and linens for the Americans, and bound, it was believed, for Rhode Island; to Digby, Aug. 31, protection of Florida and the West Indies, and to co-operate with Clinton; to Shuldham and others, Sept. 4, to guard against the attack of the combined fleets of France and Spain, which were cruising in the chops of the English channel; to Digby, Dec. 3, most secret, regarding his future movements; to Rodney, Dec. 3, to go to the West Indies; Dec. 6, most secret, same as to Digby above, with important variations; Capt. Onslow of the *Bellona* and three other captains, to go to the West Indies, Dec. 18.

1341. 1782. Instructions to J. Rowley, Jan. 11, 1782, to join the force assembled under Rodney for the defense of Jamaica; to others, captains, to join Rodney; to Hood, Jan. 15, statement of plans; to Rowley, Feb. 9, defense of Jamaica; to Barrington, most secret, Apr. 5, to intercept the French fleet preparing at Brest for a secret expedition; to Digby, Apr. 17, German recruits for Halifax. Letters to Lord Howe, Apr. 29–July 17, and to others, regarding movements of the combined French, Dutch, and Spanish fleet, W. S. W. from the Lizard in July, 1782, which had captured Adm. Campbell's convoy, " 18 sail of inconsiderable burthen and loaded with Salt provisions ", in May; secret, to Pigot, Aug. 8, to take the garrison of New York on board and go to Barbadoes and land the troops there; to the same, Dec. 28, defense of Jamaica.

MINUTES.

1-98. 1689-1783. Board's Minutes.

Adm. 3.

In 1689 the Admiralty Board sat in Adm. Herbert's lodgings, Channel Row. It met frequently and the secretary wrote that " For some time past this office has been and is in such a continual hurry of business, by continually setting twice a day from morning till neere 2 and some times longer and from afternoon till midnight, that it is always morning ere I can get to my bedd." This practice was maintained, the board continuing to meet daily, Sundays included.

The first seventy-five volumes of this series, although they contain many references to the plantations, are of little importance for colonial history.

The minutes are as a rule meagre, more so than are those of the Treasury Board, and rarely contain record of debate or discussion. The entries in most cases take the form of directions, resolutions, and orders. We read much of the location and movement of ships, of transfers, wages, stores, victualling, building, supernumeraries, superannuation, appointments, exchanges, leaves of absence, and so on, but almost nothing of naval policy, naval programmes, or the larger aspects of sea-power in its relation to the territory overseas. If debate on such questions was entered on at the board, it was not recorded in the minutes. Sometimes orders and additional orders are inserted, but always very briefly; sometimes an important change is commented upon, and in such case the proper directions follow.

Undoubtedly many orders came from the king, as head of the navy, through the Secretary of State, and in all such cases debate was not likely to take place, the Admiralty acting as the intermediary, issuing the orders, confidential, secret, and most secret, to the admirals and captains.

After 1770, and particularly after 1773, the minutes become fuller and the references to American affairs more frequent. After 1780 the volumes become still more full and affairs in America bulk more largely. Yet even in these volumes, the evidence is not very satisfactory, and there is reason to believe that the minutes as a whole are incomplete, inasmuch as business known to have been transacted at the board is not mentioned in them. Vols. **89-90** contain a certain amount of information regarding the movements of Paul Jones, and we find it stated under dates Mar. 6 and 13, 1780, that the officers and companies of the *Serapis* and *Countess of Scarborough* were acquitted at a court-martial, which was held at Sheerness, of any misconduct on that occasion and their wages were paid to the day the court-martial was held. *Cf. Adm.* 12: **21-26**, Digests of Courts-Martial, 1755-1806, and *Adm.* 1: **5315**, for the court-martial proceedings, beginning Mar. 10, 1780.

ORIGINAL PATENTS.

VICE-ADMIRALTY AND SUBORDINATE OFFICES.

33. 1749. Governor of Newfoundland.

Adm. 5.

Original parchment commission to Rodney, as governor of Newfoundland. In a box, with seal (broken), accompanied by instructions on paper, May 2, 1749, with a copy of 15 Charles II., c. 16.

38. 1746. Vice-Admiralty Court, Cape Breton.

39. 1763. *Id.*, Quebec, Florida, etc.

40. 1763. All America.

Bundle **40** contains a single letters patent empowering the Lords of the Admiralty to constitute a vice-admiral " for all America ", and also " proper officers for a court of vice-admiralty for all America ". See *C. O.* 5: **216**. The Treasury had sent a memorial to the Privy Council saying that there ought to be such a court. The Privy Council approved in order of Oct. 5, 1763, and referred the matter to the Admiralty. The latter replied, Mar. 14, 1764, defining conditions—powers, salaries, etc. Consequently letters patent were issued: the Earl of Northumberland was appointed vice-admiral (*Adm.* 2: **1057**) and William Spry, judge, June 15, 1764 (*Treas.* 28: **1**, 16, 17).

Spry gave up his business and actually entered upon the appointment;[1] but on Sept. 7, 1768, the commissions were revoked and instead of one court four courts were set up at Halifax, Boston, Philadelphia, and Charleston. See further, Brit. Mus. *Add. MSS.* **35910,** ff. 224, 225, *Acts Privy Council, Colonial,* III. 663-665, V. 151-153, VI., §§ 591, 803; *Treas.* 1, 1763-1768; *House of Lords MSS.,* nos. 226, 229; *Adm.* 1 : **3679,** *id.*: **3884,** separate parcel tied up with red tape. Also above, pp. 18, 37.

REGISTERS, RETURNS, AND CERTIFICATES.

VARIOUS.

Adm. 6.

3-23. 1695-1789. Commissions and Warrant Books.

Arranged chronologically as the warrants were issued. Of little value.

LIST BOOKS.

Adm. 8.

1-59. 1673-1783. List Books.

Entry books showing the disposition of ships, and containing the names of officers, etc.

MISCELLANEA.

Adm. 7.

61-63. 1745-1748. Lists of Convoys.

Chiefly convoys in English waters or north of Cadiz. Occasional references to colonial convoys. The lists show the disposition of the ships in the years named and sometimes indicate the ships that were despatched to American waters.

75-103. 1683-1783. Register of Passes.

These volumes are a register of all ships to which passes were issued, whether British or colonial, arranged chronologically by days, beginning Wednesday, Jan. 16, 1683. The information given covers the date of the certificate, ship's name, of what place, nature of vessel (whether ship, pink, ketch, etc.), tons burden, guns carried, dock, master's name, men (whether English or foreign-born), built (whether English or foreign), date of return, date of pass, and by whom signed. The Indexes (**79, 81, 85, 93, 95, 97, 99, 101**) enter the ships alphabetically by names. At the opening of vol. **76** are " the several rules now in force for the granting passes made since the peace with Algiers in April, 1682, and authorized by order of council, May 11, 1682 ". See 4 George II., c. 18, and above, p. 41.

These volumes furnish a considerable amount of statistical information regarding American shipping, and make it possible to follow the expansion of American trade. For example in the years 1684-1686 plantation ships are mentioned from New York (2 pinks, 80 and 90 tons, 2 ships, 100, ketch, 60), New England (4 ships, 200, 190, 140, 120, pink, 80), Barbadoes (ketch, 80).

---

[1] William Spry, LL. D., was commissioned governor of Barbadoes, Feb. 11, 1768. He had married the daughter of Thomas Pitt, brother of William Pitt, and his wife died in Barbadoes, Oct. 3, 1769. Spry married again and died in office, 1772.

134-140. 1729-1784. Register of Foreign Passes.

Large square volumes with the information tabulated as follows:

No. of pass	Ship's name	Of what place	Master's name	Whither bound	Whither bound from thence	Date of pass	By whom signed	To whom sent or delivered	When returned
916	Sheffield	Boston	John Reed	Lisbon	Cadiz	30 Mar.	A. D. W. E.	To Josiah Willard, Esq. at Boston	March 31 1756

A study of these volumes will give a good idea of colonial trade with Portugal, Spain, the Straits, and the Mediterranean. The vessels from the colonies usually went to Portugal, Spain, or the Western Islands and back; some entered the Mediterranean; others followed more varied routes as, from Falmouth to Oporto, Quebec, Falmouth; New England or New York, Africa, West Indies, and back; New York, Cork, the Mediterranean, and back; New York, Newfoundland, Madeira, and back; New York, Holland, Africa, and back; New York, Africa, South Carolina, and back; New York, Bermuda, Fayal, and back; New England, Lisbon, Barcelona, and back; New England, West Indies, Great Britain. One New York ship (the snow *Johnson*, 70 tons, John McConnell, master, 11 British men, no foreigners, plantation build) went to Venice and back to New York. Others went to Leghorn, Seville, Benecarlos [?], Alicante, Senegal, and Goree. The lists also furnish some information regarding Irish trade to the plantations and to the Mediterranean (Naples), for many passes were sent to the lieutenant general of Ireland.[1]

201-205. 1746, 1747, 1766, 1781. Naval Instructions.

Various sailing and fighting instructions for His Majesty's fleet, generally printed. In **205** is Adm. Parker's copy, showing ample evidences of use, with many changes and additions, including flags on the margin, hand-drawn and colored.

298-300. 1733-1783. Law Officers' Opinions.

Decisions by the advocate of the Admiralty, constituting a large body of reports concerning impressment, privateering, courts-martial and their procedure, vice-admiralty cases and appeals, and other admiralty questions, as follows.

298. 1733-1756.

3. Jan. 20, 1740. Case of wrecks and droits and flags in the West Indies.

12. Apr. 23, 1742. Clause of an act to secure the importation of provisions from the colonies for the use of the fleet in America.

13. May 8, 1742. *Id.* touching the jurisdiction of the Admiralty in the colonies.

---

[1] In the India Office, Whitehall, are a few papers relating to colonial trade, reference to which can be found in the printed *List of General Records, 1599-1879,* issued in 1902. For example, in India Office, *Home Series, Miscellanies,* **124,** are papers dealing with American vessels at St. Helena (1776); *ibid.,* **337,** American trade with India; *ibid.,* **439,** American and Portuguese trade with the Indies; *ibid.,* **494,** trade with the northwestern coast of America, 1785-1791. The same series contains four volumes relating to England and the Philippines.

17. Aug. 11, 1742. Interpretation of a clause of the Navigation Act.

22. Feb. 1, 1744. Regarding a judge of the vice-admiralty court in Rhode Island, against the governor and company there.

24. Feb. 18, 1744. Regarding Hops's complaint against privateers in America.

36. Dec. 22, 1744. Proceedings in the court of vice-admiralty, Barbadoes.

39. Feb. 20, 1744 [5 ?]. Negro laws of Antigua.

49. Aug. 6, 1745. How were convicts, captured while being transported and then recaptured, to be disposed of? Spoken of as a " new case ". Opinion rendered that convicts were still liable to be transported (see no. 62).

50. Aug. 10, 1745. Redress in case of an unjust sentence in a vice-admiralty court is by appeal to the King in Council.

59. May 10, 1746. Interpretation of an act regarding naval stores.

68. May 4, 1747. Case of salvage—ship *Matilda,* from Maryland to London.

84. Jan. 23, 1750. Complaint from Ireland of interference of common-law courts.

299. 1756-1777.

108. Dec. 29, 1757. Have Lords of the Admiralty power to erect vice-admiralty courts in the East Indies?

122. Nov. 1, 1760. Vessel from Philadelphia and New York to Jamaica carrying provisions, confiscated.

128. Mar., 1764. Murder on a king's ship at Jamaica—question of trial by court-martial or civil court.

131. May, 1764. Can Lords of the Admiralty appoint a vice-admiral for all America, with a court, judge, and officers, and leave the existing vice-admiralty courts to continue exercising their jurisdiction? Answer to first query, Yes; to second, that such single court cannot " entertain any jurisdiction in cases where particular acts of Parliament have confined the recovery of penalties and forfeitures to local jurisdictions ".

137. Dec. 29, 1768. Case of seaman's wages—copy of a letter from James Simpson of Charleston, S. C., to Capt. Robinson of the *Fowey* (Aug. 11, 1768).

138. Dec. 29, 1768. Case of the *Resolution* of Philadelphia, bound for Amsterdam, wrecked off the coast of France—long story of the wilful destruction of a ship.

152. Apr. 18, 1776. Can an American vessel, seized by its crew for His Majesty's use, be condemned as prize, after the passage of the Prohibitory Act—the snow *Dickinson* of Philadelphia?

153. Aug. 8, 1776. Case of the sloop *Peter,* from Santa Cruz to Amsterdam—all mariners English but the owner, one Codwise of New York; can the vessel captured be considered a droit of admiralty? That is, does the vessel belong to the Americans? Difference of opinion among the lawyers. Marriott, the king's advocate, believes that the ship should be condemned; Wynne, his successor as king's advocate, the same but less positively; Harris, advocate of the Admiralty, doubtful, though inclining to the same opinion.

154. Oct. 26, 1776. Regarding a ship in the Thames, supposed to belong to the rebels.

155. Nov. 2, 1776. Similar case.

158. No date. As to the operation of a proposed clause in a bill;
would it or would it not revoke that part of the Prohibitory Act
regarding appeals from vice-admiralty courts to commissioners
appointed or about to be appointed?

160. Jan., 1777. Case of a vessel manned by " Savages ", except the
master, a New Englander, and bound for Nantucket—shall it be
proceeded against in a court of vice-admiralty?

162. Mar. 20, 1777. Case of a ship under convoy from Jamaica—
commander separated and arrived without ship or convoy—can
he be proceeded against?

163. Mar. 26, 1777. Can Lords of the Admiralty, consistently with
the Prohibitory Act, authorize the judge of vice-admiralty, New
York, to proceed to the adjudication of a prize?

164. Apr. 2, 1777. Case of the brigantine *Betsey,* sailed from Leghorn—master put a boy, supercargo, and seamen (Tuscans)
adrift, and steered westward instead of to Alexandria.

166. Aug. 3, 1777. Regarding the powers of the deputy judge of
vice-admiralty at Halifax.

167. Aug. 7, 1777. Brig *Dinah,* Halifax to New York, taken
by American privateer, retaken by H. M. S. *Juno.* Question of
salvage.

168. Aug. 22, 1777. Regarding the granting of a letter of marque
to the owner of a ship, who is not a merchant, to be used against
American privateers.

169. Oct., 1777. English vessel captured by an American privateer
—prize-master carries the vessel to Ireland. Question of salvage.

300. 1778-1783.

193. June 21, 1780. Are two Americans found on board a French
privateer guilty of treason or piracy?

225. Mar. 15, 1783. Regarding appeals from the vice-admiralty
court of Newfoundland.

317-318. 1777-1783. Registers of Letters of Marque, America.
See acts 17 George III., cc. 7, 40.

319. 1812-1815. *Id.*

333-342. 1695-1787. Memorials and Reports.

413-439. 1741-1784. Muster Books.

Contains the names of ships, their stations, etc. The volumes are not ships'
muster books and do not give lists of crews.

566. 1776-1780. Lists of Transports licensed to go to America.

By the Prohibitory Act all intercourse and trade with the rebellious colonies
was forbidden. Accordingly the Admiralty issued instructions requiring that
all transports going to America should be licensed. Such licenses were addressed to all flag officers—captains, commanders, etc.—and a list of them is
preserved in this volume. The list gives the ship's name, master's name,
tonnage, date, and time to be in force. Some of the earlier entries omit the
last item, or simply insert " till her return ". Later a specific date of expiry
is given.

569. 1736-1740. Abstracts of Ships' Logs.

Begins with the ship *Greenwich,* bound for the coast of Guinea, Barbadoes, Antigua, and Lisbon, 1736-1738, and ends with the sloop *Alderney,* 1739-1740. As many of the voyages were to the colonies, the abstracts, which give dates, places, number of days in port, time when sailed, number of days at sea or cruising, remarkable observations and accidents, are of value.

592. 1768-1769. Tabular Statements of Exports and Imports from Colonial Ports.

From Jan. 5, 1768, to Jan. 5, 1769, the following ports are given: St. John's, Quebec, Halifax, Piscataqua, Falmouth, Salem, Marblehead, Boston, Rhode Island, New London, New Haven, New York, Perth Amboy, Salem, Cohensy (Cohansey, N. J.), Burlington, Philadelphia, Newcastle, Lewis, Pocomoke, Chester, Patuxent, North Potomac, Accomac, South Potomac, Rappahannock, York River, James River (lower district), James River (upper district), Currituck, Roanoke, Bath Town, Beaufort, Brunswick, Winyaw, Charles Town, Port Royal, Savannah, Sunbury, St. Augustine, Pensacola, Mobile, Bermuda, Bahamas.

The tables of exports take up the first half of the volume and give information as follows:

To	Great Britain	Ireland	Southern parts of Europe, Africa, etc.	British and foreign West Indies	Total
Entry of species of merchandise	Entry of quantity	*Id.*	*Id.*	*Id.*	*Id.*

The tables of imports are in the last half of the volume, as follows:

From	British and foreign West Indies	Southern parts of Europe, Africa, and the Azores
Entry of species of merchandise	Entry of quantity	*Id.*

The information here given is supplemental to the naval office lists. Unfortunately, it covers but a single year and omits all mention of importation of goods from England.

ACCOUNTANT GENERAL'S DEPARTMENT.

ACCOUNTS.

Adm.
A. G. Department.
Accounts,
Treasurer.

1-116. 1681-1783. Treasurer.

Volumes of bills paid, tabulated accounts, itemized.

2-7. 1742-1795. Admiralty Officers' Contingent Account, Bundles.

Adm.
A. G. Department.
Accounts,
Various.

2. State of the account of William Green, secretary to Adm. Arbuthnot, for disbursement at Savannah and Charleston, 1780, with " observations " of value.

4. I. Admiral's account current with Navy Board, chiefly of expenses incurred at Halifax and Quebec.

Expense account of transportation agent, Joshua Loring, containing interesting items of expenses incurred in New York, Lake George, etc.

Letters from Samuel Shipton to the board from Boston and Louisburg. 1746-1748.

Capt. Shackerling's accounts. 1756-1757.

II. Expense account of the British fleet at New York, as disbursed by William Fowler, storekeeper at New York. 1776-1780.

III. Expense account of the British fleet in the Delaware River, as disbursed by William Fowler at New York. 1777-1778.

Fowler's account with the Navy Board. 1776-1781. Many papers; *cf.* **220.**

Vouchers of bills drawn and sales made.

Expense account of British fleet at Boston. 1775-1777.

5. Admiral's contingent fund, general expenses current unless otherwise stated: East Florida; Shuldham (1777); Edwards (Newfoundland, 1779, 1780); Gambier (1779); Rodney, (Jamaica, 1762-1763, 1771-1774); Colville (St. Lawrence, 1760); Cotes (Jamaica, 1757-1760); Knowles (West Indies, 1747-1749); Saunders (St. Lawrence, 1759-1763); Lee (Leeward Islands, 1744-1747); Edwards (Newfoundland, 1781); Capt. Pearson (Quebec, 1777); Keppel (Virginia, just before Braddock's march, with expenses of his attendance on meeting at Alexandria and Annapolis with Braddock, £95 (=£76 stg.)—general disbursements, 1754-1755. This paper contains such items as were not regularly allowed by the Navy Board; Warren (North America, 1745-1746); Commander Wallace (Florida and Bahamas, port orders, 1779); Capt. Henry (Savannah, 1779-1780); Commander Douglass (Barbadoes and Leeward Islands, Carolina, 1745-1746); Howe (North America, interesting items, May 6, 1776–Sept. 20, 1778); Commander Holburne (Barbadoes, 1749-1752); Duff (Newfoundland, purchase of vessels, 1775); Parker (Jamaica, 1780, 1782).

6. State of the account of William Cole. Charleston, 1780.

In addition there are a few documents in these volumes relating to the purchase of vessels during the American war, with tables of prices.

111-112. 1655-1658.   Victualling Accounts.

150. 1757-1808.   Yards and Stations.   Accounts of Naval Storekeeper, Halifax.

174-176. 1747-1783.   *Id.,* Jamaica.

220. 1775-1783. *Id.,* New York.   William Fowler's Accounts, etc., of Disbursements as Naval Storekeeper at New York.

Four parts: I., similar in form to William Green's account (*Adm., A. G. Accounts, Various,* **2**) and containing interesting "observations"; II., III., different in form and content; IV., similar to I.   Fowler had been storekeeper at Boston also.   See *Adm., A. G. Accounts, Various,* **4** (III.) and *Adm., A. G. Miscellanea, Various,* **7**.

REGISTERS, VARIOUS.

45. 1779-1782. Pay-Lists of Ships engaged in America.

Adm.
A. G. Department.
Registers,
Various.

From the Imprest Office. " Payments to Crews of Armed Ships ", under Adm. Digby. These lists are regular payment sheets, of little importance in themselves, but in one case (the *Comet Galley* pay book, 1780-1782, Lieut. Andrew Law, commander), of value as showing how many of the sailors on the British ships were American born. Twenty-three out of 117 seamen were born in the colonies. Unfortunately the place of birth is omitted in the others.

MISCELLANEA, VARIOUS.

1. 1756-1766. Documents relating to Expenses in America and the West Indies.

Adm.
A. G. Department.
Miscellanea,
Various.

" An account of the expense of the wear and tear of His Majesty's Ships employed in America and the West Indies, according to the time of service of each respective ship, from the 1st Jan'y, 1756, to the 31st Decemr. 1766; with the value of such as were lost, etc.: from the most exact estimate that can be made thereof "; prefaced by a large table giving " a particular state of the expenses " covering all the items. Following these statements are tables of one kind or another, giving the names of flag officers and commodores, pay and table money, estimates of wages, victualling of land forces, expenses of sick and wounded, charge of transports, freight of transports, etc., value of stores with cost of transportation, amounts of bills of exchange, by whom and from what place (colonial) drawn, etc., with the correspondence connected therewith.

2. 1775-1782. Documents relating to Transports and Tenders employed during the American War.

Letters, tables, and other documents. Some of the letters are from Carolina, Virginia, New York, and the West Indies, and occasionally deal with the details of important military operations. The second part of the volume is almost entirely taken up with letters from the colonies.

3-6. 1776-1782. Muster Books of Transports.

3. Muster book of transports sent home. 1779.
Id., transport seamen. 1779.
Index to the musters, by Lieut. Evans, agent to the transports.
Muster book of 49 transports, Staten Island in New York Harbor, Oct. 30, 1776.
4-6. Rolls of muster books of transports with indexes, volumes of blanks filled in. 1776-1782.

7. 1776-1784. Letters of William Fowler, Naval Stores Keeper, New York.

Dated " New York ", but labelled " Imprest Office, Boston ", Jan., Sept., Nov., 1776; Dec., 1778, 1780, 1784. Also letters to Fowler from the Navy Board, and enclosures—admiral's proclamations and orders, ship surveys and valuations, inventories, and sales—with comments by the Commissioners of the Admiralty.

8. 1783-1794. Surveys in North America.

Bundle of papers relating to surveys in Canada; and containing a statement of disbursements by Sir John Wentworth, appointed surveyor of the woods in 1766, in making surveys of pine trees in Nova Scotia, 1783-1784. Also maps of Stewiac and Lahave rivers.

9. 1783-1786. Papers and Letters respecting Loyalists put on board Transport Ships.

Bundle of expense accounts of Loyalists removed from various parts of America to Nova Scotia, Quebec, Jamaica, Dominica, and the Bahamas; including cost of victualling, names of ships, their starting place and destination, date of departure, with correspondence regarding the settling of the Loyalists in the places mentioned. The papers give no clue to either names or numbers of the Loyalists, and the bundle is labelled on the back " not giving the information wanted ".

10. 1814-1820. Bundle of Papers relating to the American Schooners, *Tigress* and *Scorpion,* captured on Lake Huron in 1814.

Some of the papers are of date as late as 1820.

119. 1697-1720. Prices of Naval Stores.

Drawn up pursuant to a vote of the House of Commons that an account be laid before the House of all timber, planks, wood, and lumber, delivered into the several yards for the use of His Majesty's navy from Christmas, 1712, to Christmas, 1720, distinguishing the prices and sorts and the countries from which they were brought:

(a). An account of the prices given for each species and size of foreign stores, bought for the service of the royal navy, in each year, between 1697 and 1716; and from what places they have been respectively imported.

(b). An account of all foreign timber, planks, wood, and lumber delivered into the several yards for the use of His Majesty's navy from Christmas, 1712, to Christmas, 1720, distinguishing the prices and sorts and the countries from which they were brought. This account was prepared by order from the Lords of the Admiralty, signified by letter from the secretary, Nov. 27, 1721, and grounded on an address from the House of Commons to the king.

(c). Prices and sizes of naval stores. 1717-1720. This table and the last (d), which is a duplicate, repeat the figures for foreign timber mentioned in the second (b) for the years in question, but add figures for other naval stores than timber, such as canvas, hemp, oil, pitch, rosin, tar, turpentine, and tallow.

121. 1777-1800. Prices of Naval Stores.

Covering everything used on board ship from augur bits to varnish. Large numbers of documents relating to contracts and prices have been placed in the volume, which is indirectly of value for colonial history, as giving an opportunity for comparison of prices. Subject-index.

122. 1704-1736. Warrants upon Standing Contracts.

Itemized account covering iron work, ironmongers' ware, platerers' ware, stone ground glass, masons' work colors, painters' works, oars, plumbers' ware, etc., with prices.

123. 1686-1724. Returns of Stores.

The only documents of any particular value in this volume are lists of ships (1709-1724) containing mention of a few ships built in New England such as: 4th class, *Falkland*, 1695, New England, rebuilt 1702, Chatham ; 6th class, *Bedford Gally*, 1697, New England, rebuilt, 1709, Portsmouth ; etc.

124. 1771-1822. *Id.*

Sundry accounts of foreign stores and oak timber, prepared at different periods for the use of the House of Commons, Admiralty, and Navy Board, commencing Feb. 27, 1771, and ending Dec. 31, 1774. Of some consequence as showing the amounts of stores produced in America at this time.

125. 1744-1800. Transports : Orders received from Mr. Greg-ton.

Contains one or two letters from America (Boston and New York) regarding transports (1780), and a collection of documents labelled " North America and West Indies, Transports ", consisting of letters from the colonies of some importance.

126. 1754-1773. Register of Hired Transports.

Contains date of contract, owners' name, ships' name, burden, time of service, rate per ton, amount of freight, when the bills were passed, where the ships were employed, etc. Many of these transports were engaged in carrying troops to America. The names of the vessels are arranged alphabetically. At the end of the volume is a document entitled " Promiscuous allowances made to owners of transports, exclusive of their freight ", with descriptions of extra services. The statements are often of considerable interest.

127. 1773-1794. *Id.*

NAVY BOARD.

1-69. 1660-1688. Letters from the Admiralty.

| Adm. |
| Navy Board. |
| — |

The Navy Board in-letters from the Admiralty begin with 1660 and extend only to 1688. After that date all such letters must be sought for among the Admiralty out-letters. There is nothing of importance for colonial history in these volumes. **242-271** are bundles of letters from transport agents in England, 1742-1784 (chiefly 1746-1763). **272, 273,** are bundles from the Victualling Board, Sick and Wounded Board, and Ordnance Board, 1744-1765. They contain many references to the activities of these departments in equipping vessels of the navy during the period of the war in America. The letters from the Victualling Board are practically covered by *Adm., Victualling Department, Out-Letters,* but no out-letters of the Board of Sick and Wounded to the Navy Board are extant.

274. 1741-1759. Letters relating to American Transports.

Contains a list of transport ships and vessels that were employed in carrying troops from North America under the command of Col. Gooch, followed by letters from James Wallace, transport agent, with tables, lists, and supplemental papers from Port Royal harbor, Jamaica, 1741-1742. Also the cash account of James Randall, transport agent, for carrying troops to North America, etc., 1757-1759, an interesting document.

275-280. 1746-1779. Promiscuous Letters as to Transports.

From both boards and individuals, official and private. Scattered among papers relating to transportation elsewhere are letters, lists, and correspondence relating to transportation to North America and the West Indies. They are all of minor importance, though some of the lists are interesting and bits of useful information appear here and there. For instance, " The Navy transports, named in the enclosed list, I send to England under convoy of his Majesty's Ship *Grampus* (Capt. Reddall having my directions for that purpose), They being the same that were intended to convoy General Burgoin's army, but the Convention being broke by the Congress, they were in consequence remanded back to this port."

281-1299. 1673-1789. Miscellaneous.

This long series of miscellaneous correspondence contains chiefly letters from all whose communications were not filed elsewhere. The writers were captains, masters, clerks of the cheque and other officials at the naval stations, who sent information regarding matters of routine—repairs, transfers, payments, tickets, pay books, complaints, leaves of absence, etc., in great variety. The letters for 1673 (**281-293**) are arranged chronologically, the remainder alphabetically for each year. The bundles average about nine to a year, and the letters are carefully endorsed.

2178-2210. 1738-1783. Out-Letters to the Admiralty.
2544-2614. 1729-1783. Minutes of the Navy Board.

These two voluminous series of volumes contain the out-letters and minutes of the Navy Board. The letters are entered chronologically, and all the volumes are easy to use, if the date be known. The character of the business that came before the Navy Board has already been explained in the introduction (p. 4).

PASSING CERTIFICATES.

1-9. 1691-1785. Lieutenants' Passing Certificates.

Adm.
Navy Board.
Passing Certificates.
—

The Navy Board examined the qualifications of lieutenants for the navy on direction from the Admiralty. These volumes of certificates contain the records of such examinations, and are well indexed.

VICTUALLING DEPARTMENT.
OUT-LETTERS.

1-31. 1683-1783. Letter-Books of Out-Letters.

Adm.
Victualling
Out-Letters.
—

Chiefly to the Admiralty, the Navy Board, treasurer of the navy, the Treasury, contractors, transport and commissary agents, and others with whom the Victualling Board carried on its business. The volumes, particularly after 1739 (**12**), are important for all questions touching the provisioning of the fleets that had to do with American affairs.

MINUTES.

1-96. 1702-1783. Minutes of Board and Committees.

Essential to an understanding of the work of the board. The entries are on the whole full and satisfactory.

ACCOUNTS.

1-5. 1776-1783. Accounts of Agents at Yards and Stations in North America.

1. 1776-1778. Account of George Cherry, agent at New York, covering bills of exchange drawn, on one side, and provisions purchased and sundry disbursements, on the other. The account is rendered quarterly; prices and salaries and values are given in New York currency and in sterling. The accounts of provisions purchased are elaborate.

2. 1778-1779. Account of John Marry, Cherry's successor, covering provisions, labor, wages, and other services.

3. 1779-1780. Account of William Green.

4. 1780-1782. *Id.,* Henry Davis.

5. 1782-1783. *Id.,* John Delafons. Davis and Delafons got into trouble because "of want of vouchers, irregularities of various description, and suspicious circumstances attending many of the transactions". See the documents at the end of volumes **4** and **5.**

REGISTERS.

1. 1779-1783. Pay Lists, North America.

Payments to coopers, brewers, bakers, etc., New York and Savannah. For similar lists, Leeward Islands, 1782-1783, see **124,** at the end.

MARINE OFFICE.

1-4. 1690-1790. In-Letters.

The papers in this series are accounts and vouchers, with a small number of letters from the Admiralty and others, particularly marine officials, and a few petitions and memorials. There is very little here of any importance for colonial history. The regimental accounts generally concern England only. Items that concern America and the West Indies are not of much value, as, for example, a list of camp necessaries for Jamaica, July 18, 1740; mention of eight chests of medicines prepared for the land forces in the West Indies, Sept. 16, 1742; list of marine officers who were killed or who died abroad on the expedition to America, 1739-1740; "a list of paymasters appointed by letters of attorney to the undermentioned regiments of marines", with dates and names of colonels of marine regiments, 1740-1741 (endorsed "America").

By far the most important document in this collection is the journal of Edmund Herbert, deputy paymaster of marines, extending from 1739 to 1769, and furnishing an almost daily record of his movements. Though the entries are often very brief and perfunctory, they give an impressive picture of the way much departmental business was done at this time. Herbert led a dreary life, making up accounts, waiting on his superiors, attending various offices in Whitehall and the City in the performance of his routine duties, and suffering great delays in getting desired information or having warrants signed. We come into close touch with the working of the deputy system, as is seen in Herbert's relations with his chief, Charles Hanbury Williams (afterward Sir Charles), and with the prevailing official attitude of irresponsibility, as when Francis, earl of Godolphin, went off to Newmarket for a week with the privy seal and thus brought the issue of money to a standstill. This journal should be compared with the itemized account of the services which Ferdinand John Paris, colonial agent and agent of the Treasury, performed in connection with the Fairfax claim in Virginia. *Treas.* 1 : **335**, 1739-1742. For the charges brought against Herbert and his colleague Jones see below, p. 39.

13. 1778-1784. Out-Letters.

A few references to marines in America—notably the Marine Grenadier Company, stationed in Philadelphia and New York. A part of this company, with its lieutenant (afterward captain), Ragg, was made prisoners and carried to France (see below, **153**). From this volume we learn that there was a deputy paymaster of the marine battalions in North America.

125-154. 1739-1790. Effective and Subsistence Lists. Muster Rolls, and Returns of Marine Regiments.

A useful collection of lists, showing the whereabouts of marines in North America and the West Indies, as well as elsewhere.

   153, 1772-1780, contains the effective list of the Grenadier Company named above, at Philadelphia, New York, and Halifax, with names, qualities, etc., of non-commissioned officers and privates. Also lists of marine battalions at Halifax under captains Elliott, Johnston, McDonald, Griffith, and Pitcairn.

512. 1740-1742. American Expedition. Entry Book.

Edmund Herbert's entry book of letters kept by himself and his fellow deputy, Edmond Jones. The letters are signed by Herbert and Jones, and annotated by Herbert. They are from Capt. John Chambre, paymaster of marine forces in America, Colebrooke, the contractor, and others, and concern the subsistence of the marine forces on the Carthagena expedition. Many of the letters are from Carthagena and other places in the Caribbean, and relate to finances, bills, drafts, etc. They have little interest, though occasionally furnishing information.

MEDICAL DEPARTMENT.

IN-LETTERS.

85-87. 1709-1754, 1766-1779. Letters from Surgeons and Agents and from Officers in Command in all Waters.

Adm. Medical In-Letters.

   85. 1709-1754. Packets of original letters from surgeons and agents for sick and wounded seamen, from Virginia, North and South Carolina, Georgia, Massachusetts, New York, Cape Breton, Nova

Scotia, containing monthly abstracts, sick tickets, and accounts. Occasionally a bit of information, as in a letter from J. Cusick, New York, July 1, 1740, " I am told the Troops cannot assemble together at New York before the middle of September, they say they are like to meet with great success in their levyes, the people of these Provinces being very desirous to goe to fight the Spaniards."

86. 1766-1775. Chiefly requests for food and medicines; reports on hospitals, details relating to the care of the sick and to accounts. Sometimes dates and places mentioned are important and occasionally full descriptions are given of situations and circumstances that are useful: note Gambier's letters from Boston, Oct. 30, 1770, Apr. 9, Nov. 9, 1771, and Nov. 27, 1771, from London; Montague, Boston, Aug. 30, 1772; Man, Antigua and Barbadoes, Dec. 20, 1770, Mar. 18, June 24, 1771, Apr. 21, 1772; Parry, Antigua, Sept. 19, 1772.

87. 1776-1779. Letters from Capt. Wallace of H. M. S. *Rose,* Halifax and Rhode Island; Parker of the *Bristol,* New York Harbor; Hammond of the *Fletcher,* Delaware; Young from the West Indies; Howe of the *Eagle,* New York, Philadelphia, Rhode Island, Jan. 25, 31, June 15, 1777, and accompanying papers, July 19, Dec. 25, Mar. 20, 1778, etc. Many other letters from American waters. Vols. **102-130** relate almost entirely to French and occasionally Spanish prisoners.

OUT-LETTERS.

1-14. 1742-1745. Letters from the Board of Commissioners for Sick and Wounded Prisoners and Exchange of Prisoners of War to the Admiralty.

> Adm.
> Medical
> Out-Letters.

These volumes, often large and bulky, well filled and indexed, are a continuation of *Adm.* 1: **3528** and **3529.** They should be used in connection with *S. P. Dom., Naval.* The commissioners for the period of the Revolutionary War were J. Bell and Dr. Farquharson; their office lay on Tower Hill and in Broad St. Many of the volumes contain material of considerable importance, relating to American prisoners for the period 1775 to 1781. In *Minutes,* **49,** Apr. 8, 1778, there is an entry of a hearing before the board regarding the work of the committee of subscribers for clothing American prisoners. **226-229** of the letter-books relate to the War of 1812.

MINUTES.

1-49. 1701-1781. General Minutes of the Board of Commissioners for Sick and Wounded Prisoners and Exchange of Prisoners of War.

> Adm.
> Medical
> Minutes.

These minutes seem very meagre, considering the amount of business done by the board, particularly in times of war. So far as examined they seem unimportant, though they should always be used in connection with the in-letters and out-letters.

MISCELLANEA.

43. 1756-1764. Legal Opinions.

7. Case of two ships with cargoes to Louisburg intending to go to Virginia for freight home, detained at Louisburg and impressed by the governor. Is payment for the four months sufficient, or should further claim be made? Answer, that they are legally and justly entitled to such freight as they would have made, and that the terms on which one was actually chartered for Virginia should be the measure of payment for both. 1760.

8. Case of the *Peggy*, Boston, bound from Newcastle-on-Tyne for Boston, taken Oct., 1756, by a French privateer, ransomed by the master, James Freeman, for 5000 livres and the mate left as hostage. Ship afterward lost and captain dead. Sitwell of London, on whom the bill for 5000 livres was drawn, received the insurance money but not the ransom, and the mate was kept a prisoner. Opinion, that the case was unusual and a gross breach of public faith. The only way was for Sitwell to sue the owners in New England. 1761.

Solicitor General Yorke, expressing his opinion, stated that the proper method of procedure was to carry the ransom bill to a proper admiralty jurisdiction in France for sentence of condemnation as lawful prize, and then an action was obtainable in England against the owners, as they were bound by the act of the master.

Similar opinion rendered by George Hay, king's advocate.

12. Case of a contract (1758) between the Board of Sick and Wounded Seamen and Robert Patterson to supply surgeons' stores, etc., in Antigua and Barbadoes. Patterson died, and the business was continued by others. Question as to payment of creditors.

15. Case of a French inhabitant of Guadeloupe, who signed the capitulation and had lately arrived in London under a pass from the governor. As this pass did not give special permission to come to England, was such inhabitant a prisoner of war? Opinion, that under the circumstances such person may be so considered. 1762.

21. Case of Coverdale Richardson, master of the *Prince Frederick,* merchant ship, who when at New York applied to the agent for taking care of prisoners of war for three men to assist in working the ship home. On arrival one Gautier apparently aided the men, who were Frenchmen, to escape. The board wishes to punish Gautier but how? Opinion, that Gautier's behavior was unwarrantable but not criminal and no prosecution could be carried on. 1757.

Other opinions in this volume relate to French prisoners.

GREENWICH HOSPITAL.

ACCOUNTS, VARIOUS.

89-143. 1732-1783. Annual Account of the Receiver of Sixpences.

The Registered Seamen's Act of 1696 (7-8 William III., c. 21, § 10) obliged all mariners in " Great Britain, Ireland, and the Dominions thereunto belonging " to contribute from their wages sixpence a month toward the maintenance of Greenwich Hospital, created out of the royal palace of

Greenwich by William III. in 1694. A committee was appointed under the act to register seamen for the purpose of collecting the sixpences, and this committee sat from 1696 to 1699 and kept a journal of its proceedings (*Adm., Medical, Miscellanea,* **41**). The early operation of the act was very ineffectual and new acts were passed in 1697 (8-9 William III., c. 23) and 1711 (10 Anne, c. 17). By the act of 1711, the Admiralty was empowered to appoint a receiver or receivers of the duty, who in turn were to make use of the customs collectors at the outports or others as deputies. Consequently an office was set up in Tower Street and John Clarke appears to have been its first incumbent, serving till 1725. In that year Clarke's place was taken by three receivers or commissioners, Thomas Hawes, M. Owen, and William Young. The earliest accounts date from 1716, and from that time to 1727 the receipts averaged about £5500 a year.

As the colonies were not specifically mentioned in the earlier acts, no effort was made during these years to collect the duty in America. Therefore, in order to remedy this defect and to carry out the intent of the original statute, a new act was passed in 1729 (2 George II., c. 7), extending the duty not only to the Channel Islands and the Isle of Man, but also to " all and every his Majesty's Colonies, Islands, and Dominions in America ", and the receiver was authorized to call on the collectors of customs in the various colonial ports to " deduct and detain " from the wages of seamen in the merchant marine the amount named, in sterling money or its equivalent in colonial currency. To aid in the enforcement of the act, an order in Council was issued, Jan. 22, 1730, and instructions were drafted to the governors, Feb. 2, 1730, with printed orders " to be observed by Mr. ————, Receiver of the sixpence a month out of the seamen's wages at the port of ———— in America ",[1] and by the term " seamen " was meant, not only able-bodied seamen, but also masters and commanders, servants, apprentices, and boys, from whose services their masters received any profit. The deputy receiver's commission was half a crown in the pound.

The office of the receivers in England was removed to Tower Hill in 1729, and William Young and William Allix became the new appointees. They immediately sent letters to all the colonial governors, Feb. 14, 1730, enclosing the royal instructions, and calling on the governors for aid and assistance.[2] Colby took the place of Young and served with Allix till 1731, when the latter became sole receiver. He lived in the house on Tower Hill, which he rented of the Mercers Company for £50 a year, and had at first one assistant or clerk, afterward two. In 1750 he had seventy-seven deputies in England, one in Scotland, one in Jersey, and forty-two in America. His successor in 1765 was Thomas Hicks, who served for the remainder of the colonial period. The disbursements of the office included a ten per cent. commission paid to the plantation clerk or inspector of the American account in the London Custom House, on all sums received from America, and among those who held this office was Henry Hulton (1763), who, afterward, in 1767, was appointed one of the American Board of Customs Commissioners, and became principal deputy receiver of the sixpenny duty in America (see below). The duty was finally abolished in 1834.

The volumes in this series contain the accounts of the receipts and payments of William Allix, 1732-1765, and Thomas Hicks, his successor. At the be-

[1] *C. O.* 324: **36**, 168-170; *Acts Privy Council, Colonial,* III. 257, 814. In the Plantation Registers of the Privy Council Office the date of the instructions is given as Oct. 28, 1731, but a first instruction was issued as stated, on Feb. 2, 1730.
[2] *Conn. Hist. Soc. Coll.,* IV. 193-194.

ginning of vol. **89** will be found a summary of receipts, 1716-1752. In this summary the annual receipts range from £4800 in 1727 to £8563 in 1731. The amount received in 1716 was £5886, in 1720, £4961, in 1730, £7330, in 1740, £5846, in 1750, £7802, and in 1752, £7666, with an average for the thirty-seven years of £6598. From the receiver's itemized accounts we learn that in 1732, out of a total of £8016, America contributed £636; in 1754, out of a total of £9403, America contributed £947; in 1764, out of a total of £11,455, the American sixpences came to £1931; and in 1765, out of a total of £10,435, they came to £977. These figures refute Mr. Beer's statement that before 1768 " this law had not been executed ".[1] It is nevertheless true that after 1768 the amounts received from America increased from those ports directly under Hulton's charge. In 1775 the amount was £1554, and this did not include what was received from Barbadoes, Dominica, Grenada, Jamaica, Montserrat, St. Christopher, and St. Lucia, colonies that remained under the control of the Commissioners of the Customs in England and from which the sixpences were collected in the old way. In view of this diminution in the business done at the Custom House, London, it is not surprising that the assistant plantation clerk should have been no longer required.[2] In 1783, out of a total of £11,500, only £147 came from America, collected at Jamaica, Bermuda, Halifax, Pensacola, and Quebec.

That in 1764 the collection was made at all the ports in America is evident from the lists. From January to February, the sixpences were taken at Bath, Falmouth, Perth Amboy, Philadelphia, Piscataqua, Pocomoke, and the Rappahannock; from March to December, at Antigua, Beaufort, Boston, Barbadoes, Brunswick, Charleston, James River, Montserrat, New London, New Providence, New York, Nova Scotia, Philadelphia, Potomac, Patuxent (Oxford), Quebec, Rappahannock, Savannah, Salem and Marblehead, Winyaw Bay or Georgetown, and York River. As a rule the largest amount came from Philadelphia and the smallest from Halifax. Newfoundland was apparently not included at first, though in 1768 it was placed under Hulton's charge. It is uncertain whether or not collections were made there before that date. After 1775 the sixpences were taken under the direction of the admiral-governors. See *Greenwich Hospital, Miscellaneous, Various,* **121**, 73, order of the governor, Adm. Duff, July 12, 1775.

A study of the figures in these accounts is important in determining the commercial position and activity of the various colonial ports.

194-204. 1725-1784. Names of Ships and Amounts paid for Six-pences.

This series is not only of great value for the commercial history of the colonies but is also unique among colonial records. Its large, square ledgers (twenty-five to 1834) contain itemized statements of the payments of six-pences from every vessel that came to the port of London. The arrangement is strictly chronological, by days, months, and years, and the information was entered by the clerks in the receiver's office as it was sent up each day from the Custom House by the plantation clerk or his assistant. From these entries a complete list of all colonial vessels that entered or cleared at the port could be made up. The information covers the name of the last port, date of arrival, ship's name, of what place, tons burden, number of men, master's name, time of first man's entry on the ship's books, time of last man's discharge or

---

[1] *British Colonial Policy,* 1754-1765, p. 288, note.
[2] Brit. Mus. *Add. MSS.* **8133 C**, f. 131.

end of the voyage, number of months' service per man, and amount of money received. The lists indicate further whether or not the ship was new and on its first voyage, and whether the sixpenny duty had or had not been paid before. From this record can be learned what plantation-built vessels crossed the ocean to London and what English vessels from the port of London did the carrying trade to America. Similar ledgers must have been kept at the outports, as considerable sums were forwarded thence to the receiver's office in London, but no trace of them can now be discovered. The letter-books at the outport customs houses contain few references to the matter. Mr. Atton informs me that in his inspection of these books he has found very little about the Greenwich Hospital dues. At Whitehaven, the chief traffic of which was with Ireland, the mariners preferred to pay the sixpences in that country as the rate of exchange favored them. Virginia ships generally went to Scotland first and paid their dues there. A few entries of such payments may be found, but no books specially kept for the purpose.

Mr. Atton further says, " Thus it seems that the Greenwich Hospital accounts, if found, may not give any accurate information as to the shipping, etc., of particular ports. It should be borne in mind that the maritime trade of old was often a kind of huckstering, the masters taking their cargoes from port to port to find market." He further adds, " I find, however, that there are certain books at the Dublin Record Office that may furnish better information. In the catalogue, entitled ' Custom House, Vol. I.' pp. 198-199, is entered ' Naval Books, Greenwich Hospital 1790-1832 ' ", but the date is too late for our purpose.

The payments in the Public Record Office volumes range from one shilling to £150, the amount dependent on the number of men and the length of the voyage. The average payment seems to run from £2 to £5. The volumes also contain the totals given in the preceding series, including itemized statements of bills and cash remitted from America. To every master who paid the duty a receipt was duly given on a blank supplied for the purpose.

MISCELLANEA.

NEWS-LETTERS, ORIGINAL.

Adm. Greenwich Hospital. Miscellanea, News-Letters, Original. —	**1-4.** 1673-1696. News-Letters, Original. A series of news-letters from London forming a sort of running account of events happening there, political, judicial, personal. The information is chiefly domestic or foreign, rarely colonial. The letters are valuable for the student of contemporary English history, and have been in part calendared for the Domestic Series.

VARIOUS.

Adm. Greenwich Hospital. Miscellanea, Various. —	**116.** 1806-1807. Papers relating to Negotiations between Great Britain and America. **121.** 1749-1805. Book of Orders and Proclamations by Governors of Newfoundland.

Entry book of orders issued by the admirals as governors of Newfoundland, from Aug. 14, 1749, to Oct. 4, 1805. A valuable series for the early history of Newfoundland and the fishery, that is manifestly only a selection from some larger collection of original entry books. Not only are orders and proclamations referred to here that are not entered in this volume, but on the margin are references to volumes 1 to 18 of some other series, and to " Books of Remarks ", " Observations ", and " Order Book of Remarks ", all of which may be different names for the same thing. Of these volumes I have been unable to obtain a trace, and they are not known to Canadian archivists.

The orders are directed from various places—court-house, St. John's, Trinity, " Croque ", on board ship—to the justices of the peace, the high sheriff, and sundry individuals. They concern rioters, strong liquors, debtors, gallows, Roman Catholics, churches, marriages, wrecks, the " Esquimeaux " in Labrador,[1] lands, fishing, the carrying off of handicraftsmen, seamen, and fishermen by American traders (Capt. Byron, 1769), rinding fir trees, fish flakes, illicit fishing, French rights, Moravians in Labrador, bait, firewood, public houses, etc. References may be found to the admirals' court, abolished 32 George III., c. 46. In the volume is an inserted paper on " Illicit Trade ", commenting on 10-11 William III., c. 25, 26 George III., c. 26, and 15 George III., c. 31, and another headed " Sunday School ", without date, except " Tuesday, Feb. 11, Revd Thomas Ewer in the chair ".

131. 1768-1777. Book of Letters sent by H. Hulton, deputy receiver of the Sixpenny or Greenwich Hospital Duty in America.

132. 1768-1783. Book of Letters received by the Same.

These two volumes constitute the record of Hulton's experiences as principal deputy receiver of the sixpenny duty in America. The colonial ports under Hulton's charge were Accomac, Bermuda, Boston, Beaufort, Brunswick, Chester and Patapsco, Charleston, Halifax, James River, upper and lower, Mobile, Nantucket, New York, New Haven, Newfoundland till 1775, New London, North Potomac, Philadelphia, Patuxent, Pensacola, Piscataqua, Plymouth, Pocomoke, Rhode Island, Rappahannock, Sunbury, Salem and Marblehead, Savannah, Salem and Cohenzie (Cohansey), York River.

LOG BOOKS.

The great collection of captains' and masters' logs in the Public Record Office is rendered readily accessible by means of a typewritten index in which the names of ships are arranged alphabetically. This index, copies of which may be found in both the Literary Search Room and the Government Search

---

[1] " Whereas many and great advantages would arise to his Majesty's trading subjects, if a friendly intercourse could be established with the Esquimeaux Indians inhabiting the coast of Labrador, and as all attempts hitherto made for that purpose have proved ineffectual owing in a great measure to the imprudent, treacherous, or cruel conduct of some people who have resorted to that coast, by plundering and killing several of them, from which they have entertained an opinion of our disposition and intentions being the same with respect to them, as theirs are toward us, that is, to circumvent and kill them. And whereas such wicked practice is most contrary to his Majesty's sentiments of humanity, to his desire of conciliating their affection and his endeavors to induce them to trade with his subjects, in conformity to these his Majesty's sentiments, I hereby strictly forbid such wicked practices for the future and declare that all such as are found offending herein shall be punished with the utmost severity of the law." Adm. Palliser to Mr. Hans Haven " to be dispersed among the Indians on the coast of Labrador ". St. John's 1st July, 1764, p. 30. *Cf.* pp. 56-57, 62, for treatment of the Indians of Newfoundland.

Room, is in five volumes as follows: Admiralty, Captains' Logs, 4, A-F, 5, G-P, 6, Q-Z; Admiralty, Masters' Logs, 7, A-K, 8, L-Z. The index gives the ship's name, the dates of the log, and the press-mark. When the latter is obtained, the log may be called out by the description *Adm., Captains' Logs,* ———, and *Adm., Masters' Logs,* ———. No indication is given of the direction of the voyage, so that the searcher will need to know the names of the British men-of-war in American or West India waters before being able to make use of the lists. Such names can be found in the various lists of ships, *Adm.* 8: **1-59**, 1673-1783, and *Adm.* 1: **230-243, 305-314, 470-472, 480-490.** Much information can also be obtained from the out-letters, *Adm.* 2: **1-114,** where the names of ships appointed to attend the colonies can be found. See also Deputy Keeper's *Report,* vol. 8, app. 1, § 8.

The earliest logs are of date 1669, 1671, 1672, 1673, and the series continues through the colonial period. One must not, however, expect to find logs of all ships that had to do with American affairs. Quite as frequently as otherwise the log of a particular ship will be missing, for the collection is incomplete. The series of captains' logs is much longer than the other and is more likely to contain the desired book; often, however, the logs of captain and master of the same ship have been preserved. Though the contents of such logs are likely to be identical, variations occur that are sometimes important. The master was the log keeper and his version is therefore the more authoritative of the two.

The log books are not inspiring reading, but they are valuable for dates and as an itinerary of the voyage. Though the weather is the chief " remarkable observation and accident ", yet certain voyages were full of incident and the " remarks ", though always brief, are occasionally informing, particularly in war times. We read of encounters with pirates, of colonial governors and other colonial officials, of ships spoken and passed, of other ships of the navy, of captures of merchant ships, and, once in a while, of sea fights. As examples of logs containing valuable information of events taking place in American waters, we may refer to *Captains' Logs,* **23, 51, 60, 118, 156, 157, 293, 331, 360, 420, 548, 607, 630, 675, 749, 762, 875, 895, 906, 931, 1017, 1091, 1100, 4141, 4172,** and *Masters' Logs,* **1633, 1865.** On the *Rose,* when in harbor (*Captains' Logs,* **801**), guns were fired and colors spread on King William's birthday, King George's birthday, Gunpowder Day, Coronation Day, the Day of the Martyrdom of Charles I., on the day of the restoration of Charles II. (Anniversary Day), and on Proclamation Day. When the *Solebay* (*id.,* **4345**) was in American waters in 1780-1781, it was used as a prison ship, and when in Charleston harbor, Oct. 28, 1781, " received a Rebel govr and seven other Rebel officers at ¼ before 4 ".

Though the information furnished varies greatly in character and is more often nautical than historical, yet the logs can often be used with great profit in settling difficult questions of dates and naval movements.

AUDIT OFFICE PAPERS.

The Audit Office was in New Palace Yard, Westminster, and in 3 White-hall Yard before it was removed to Somerset House, whence its papers were transferred to the Public Record Office in December, 1859. In addition to the general series of " Declared Accounts ", a printed list of which was issued in 1893 and which are here entered separately, the Audit Office records include the following volumes and bundles containing material for colonial history. In a number of instances the accounts are but duplicates of the Declared Accounts.

ACCOUNTS, VARIOUS.

<table>
<tr><td rowspan="5">

A. O.
Accounts, etc.,
Various.
—
</td><td>

10-11. Admiralty Court; Accounts of Prize Proceeds: American. 1813-1816.
</td></tr>
<tr><td>

55. 1776-1784. Accounts of Payments to Foreign Troops, with Musters, Pay-Lists, and other subsidiary documents: Hessians.
</td></tr>
</table>

An account of the extraordinary expenses, to be made good by the British government, for the corps of Hessian troops from 1776 to 1784. The claim appears to have been presented in 1790 by P. and C. Van Notten, and amounted to £163,926 5s. 6d. The letter of the comptroller of the army is dated 1794. The reports, letters, and itemized accounts, all in English, deal with a great variety of interesting and valuable details, touching extraordinary expenses, including sickness and hospital charges, cost of repairs to guns, travelling expenses, postage, and the like. One of the most important schedules contains lists of the losses of the officers and others at the battle of Trenton, money, baggage, and personal effects.

126-128. 1711-1819. Miscellaneous Accounts of Governors and others in America, Nova Scotia, New Brunswick, etc., with subsidiary documents.

126. (1). The Account of James Oglethorpe, general and commander-in-chief of His Majesty's forces in South Carolina and Georgia, for extraordinary expenses incurred in His Majesty's service in Georgia and Florida from September 22, 1738, to July 22, 1743, when Gen. Oglethorpe sailed for England. And of money paid and set apart for the said services to Michaelmas, 1743, or consequent thereupon. Received Aug. 2, 1745. This is the original account.
(See *Declared Accounts, Audit Office,* **162.** 441.)

(2). 1764-1767. The account of George Johnstone, governor of West Florida, for Indian presents between Oct., 1764, and Jan., 1767.
(This account is not among the *Declared Accounts.*)

(3). 1764-1767. Gov. Johnstone's contingent account for West Florida.
(*Decl. Acc., A. O.,* **1261.** 152.)

(4). 1785. The account of Col. William Taylor, commanding in East and West Florida.

(5). 1776-1781. Account of Peter Chester, late governor of the province of West Florida, for contingencies and other expenses for the defense of the province. This account is dated Feb. 6, 1792.

(6). 1782. Account of Brig.-Gen. Alured Clarke of military contingencies incurred in the province of Georgia and East Florida between May 26, 1780, and June 30, 1782.
(*Decl. Acc., A. O.,* **166.** 462.)

(7). 1765-1767. Abstract of cash paid by Gen. Gage, commander-in-chief of all His Majesty's forces in North America, on account of the public services carrying on under his command from Apr. 1, 1765, to June 30, 1767, both days included, in which is included the amount of an account transmitted to the Lords of the Treasury, June 30, 1766.
(*Decl. Acc., A. O.,* **163.** 446.)

(8). 1767. An account of the bills of exchange drawn on the Lords of the Treasury by Maj.-Gen. Thomas Gage, commander-in-chief at New York, payable to Brig.-Gen. Guy Carleton, for defraying the contingent expenses incurred in the northern district.

(9). 1763-1773. Debit and credit account kept by the secretary's office of Gen. Gage followed by accounts of expenses for expresses, clerks in the office, office rent, stationery, extraordinaries, postage, etc.

(10). General statement of John Smith, secretary to Sir Henry Clinton. Account current with the public. 1776-1778.
(*Decl. Acc., A. O.,* **164.** 452.)
Id., expenditures in the secretary's office. 1778-1782.
(*Decl. Acc., A. O.,* **165.** 455.)

Account by Sir William Howe of money received by him of Robert Mackenzie, his late secretary and paymaster, ending June 30, 1778.
(*Decl. Acc., A. O.,* **164.** 450.)

Account current of Lieut. Donald Stewart of the 74th Regiment. 1781-1782.
Id. 1782.
(*Decl. Acc., A. O.,* **2533.** 674.)

Account of the Canada expedition as made out by Auditor Varley. This was the expedition organized in 1711 by Gov. Hunter of New York.
(*Cf. Decl. Acc., A. O.,* **217.** 730.)

Account of Lieut. Andrew Durnford, assistant deputy quartermaster-general in Georgia and East Florida. 1780.

Abstract of the account of Sir William Erskine, quartermaster-general of the forces in North America. Dec. 25, 1776–June 30, 1779.
(*Decl. Acc., A. O.,* **337.** 1348.)

Account of James Murray, governor of Quebec. 1766.

Account of Robert Mackenzie. Oct. 1, 1775–June 30, 1778.
(*Decl. Acc., A. O.,* **164.** 449.)

Account of Enoch Storey for monies paid and services done by direction of Sir William Howe, with vouchers and receipts (wanting). 1777.
(*Decl. Acc., A. O.,* **165.** 454.)

(11). 1777-1782. Account of Col. Alexander Inness, Capt. Rooke, inspectors-general of provincial forces, department at New York, Philadelphia, Nova Scotia, and Pensacola, from Jan. 29, 1777, to Sept. 30, 1782, inclusive. Including Capt. Staws's account while deputy inspector in Georgia, and clothing purchased in Virginia for negroes.

(12). Account of Capt. William Wood, paymaster of incidental expenses, Quebec. 1784.

Account of Sir Thomas Mills, receiver general of Quebec. 1778-1789.

Account of William Grant, deputy receiver of the province of Quebec. 1779-1785.

Id. 1779-1783.

Account of Josiah Martin, governor of North Carolina. 1776-1779.
(*Decl. Acc., A. O.,* **1259.** 139.)

Account current of the late Gov. George Johnstone of West Florida. 1787.

Abstract of the account of Lieut. Henry Haldane, secretary and aide-de-camp to Gen. Cornwallis in the Southern District of North America. June 1, 1780–Dec. 31, 1781.
(*Decl. Acc., A. O.,* **166.** 463.)

Account of Maj.-Gen. Prevost. May, 1776–May, 1780.
(*Decl. Acc., A. O.,* **166.** 451.)

Account of Lieut.-Col. John Campbell. 1777-1780.

Account of John Smith. May 25, 1778–June 30, 1782.
(*Cf. Decl. Acc., A. O.,* **165.** 455.)

Various abstracts of Drummond, Franks, and Nesbitt's account for victualling the soldiers in America for 52 weeks per contract stated. 1779-1783.
(*Cf. Decl. Acc., A. O.,* **197-205.**)

Id. 1766-1778.

Id. 1776-1777.

Id. containing an interesting account of procedure by Maj. Franks.

Id. 1764-1768.

Account of George Brown of provisions for 4000 men for 52 weeks, delivered at Cork and Cowes. 1781.

Id. 1782.
(*Cf. Decl. Acc., A. O.,* **202, 204.**)

Accounts of Sir John Henniker. 1776, 1778, 1779, 1782.

Account of John Durand for provisions. 1776-1777.
(*Decl. Acc., A. O.,* **199-203.**)

Account of Potter, Dearman, and Shaw for provisions. 1782.
(*Decl. Acc., A. O.,* **205.** 668.)

Account of Smith, FitzHugh, and Peacock for provisions. 1781, 1782.
(*Decl. Acc., A. O.,* **203, 205.**)

Account of Stephenson and Blackburn for provisions. 1775-1782, 1779.
(*Decl. Acc., A. O.,* **194-196.**)

Account of Sir James Cockburn, 1776, 1779, 1781, 1782, Edward
Lewis, 1781, for provisions at Cork and Cowes.
(*Cf. Decl. Acc., A. O.,* **194, 203.**)

Account of James, Smith, Baynes, and Atkinson. 1776, 1777-1779.
(*Decl. Acc., A. O.,* **205, 206.**)

Accounts of William Devaynes, Canada, 1781-1782, Harley and
Drummond, 1782-1783, Kender Mason, 1777-1785.
(*Decl. Acc., A. O.,* **194, 195.**)

Accounts of Jonathan Mallet and Charles Morriss, purveyor and
deputy purveyor, Carolina, 1779-1785, 1775-1783, and of Edward
Codrington, West Florida, 1767-1771, 1771-1775.
(*Decl. Acc., A. O.,* **1518.** 261; **194.** 609, 610.)

Account of John Blackburn for rum furnished. 1776.
(*Decl. Acc., A. O.,* **199.** 636.)

Various barrack-master's accounts: George Clark, 1776-1780; Gen.
James Robertson, 1765-1776.
(*Decl. Acc., A. O.,* **147.** 355, 356.)

(13). Account of Maj.-Gen. Christie. 1757-1777.
127. Various papers and books.
(1). Hospital, Charlestown. 1781.
Dr. Hayes. Canada, 1776-1783.
(*Cf. Decl. Acc., A. O.,* **1519.** 265.)

(2). Gen. Burton. Three Rivers, 1760-1763.
(*Decl. Acc., A. O.,* **1324.** 624.)

Maj. T. Brown. South Carolina, 1781.
Maj.-Gen. J. Campbell. West Florida, 1779-1781.
(*Decl. Acc., A. O.,* **325.** 1290.)

Guy Johnson. Indian Dept., 1774-1783.
Brig.-Gen. J. Campbell. Indian Dept., 1775-1785.
(*Decl. Acc., A. O.,* **1530.** 6.)

H. T. Cramahé. Quebec, 1774-1780.
(*Decl. Acc., A. O.,* **324.** 1285.)

Edward Lewis, payment of troops. West Florida, 1767-1781.
(*Decl. Acc., A. O.,* **194.** 611.)

Richard Murray, disbursements for American prisoners. June 25,
1778–Dec., 1782.
(*Decl. Acc., A. O.,* **573.** 480.)

James Fraser. Engineer's Dept., New York, 1782.
(*Decl. Acc., A. O.,* **2534.** 675.)

George James Williams, deputy paymaster-general. Nova Scotia,
1783.
Lieut.-Col. A. S. De Peyster. Upper Canada, 1775-1784.
(*Decl. Acc., A. O.,* **376.** 1.)

Col. Matthew Dixon, engineer. New York, 1776-1777.
(*Decl. Acc., A. O.,* **2532.** 667.)

Lieut.-Gen. Jones. New York, 1778-1779.
Col. James Moncrief, engineer. 1778-1782.
(*Decl. Acc., A. O.,* **2532.** 668.)

John Montrésor, engineer. 1768-1774, 1770, 1775.
(*Decl. Acc., A. O.,* **2531.** 663.)

Maj. A. D'Aubant. 1776-1782.
(*Decl. Acc., A. O.,* **2532.** 665.)

Lieut.-Gen. John Campbell. Pensacola, 1781-1782.
   (*Decl. Acc., A. O.,* **325.** 1290.)
Maj. Richard Bailey, necessaries. 1777.
   (*Decl. Acc., A. O.,* **199.** 638.)
Josiah Paul Collins, militia. Charleston, 1781-1782.
   (*Decl. Acc., A. O.,* **326.** 1292.)
John Stuart, Indian affairs. 1776.
John Smith, provincial forces. 1778-1782.
James Simpson, intendant-general of police, South Carolina, and
   secretary to the Commission to Restore Peace. 1780-1781.
   (*Decl. Acc., A. O.,* **1949.** 2.)
Thomas Aston Coffin, paymaster of contingencies. New York,
   1783-1784.
   (*Decl. Acc., A. O.,* **326.** 1294.)
(3). Dunn's accounts: of bills drawn for His Majesty's service by
   commanding officers and lieutenant-governors in the upper
   country by order of Gen. Haldimand, 1778-1784, and paid by
   Thomas Dunn, paymaster of Quebec; *id.,* by order of Gen. Carleton, 1778; *id.,* 1786, marine department; *id.,* 1776-1784; pay-list
   of officers and seamen serving on lakes Erie, Huron, and Michi-
   gan, July 1, 1780–June 30, 1781; *id.* of seamen missing or taken
   prisoners at the Convention of Saratoga and at other periods,
   1777 and 1778.
   (*Cf. Decl. Acc., A. O.,* **324.** 1286; **1827.** 530.)
(4). Capt. George Benson, 74 Regt. 1780-1784.
   (*Decl. Acc., A. O.,* **167.** 464.)
Robert Mackenzie, provincial forces. 1778.
   (*Decl. Acc., A. O.* **164.** 449; **325.** 1287.)
Samuel Bean, deputy commissioner of accounts and commissary of
   musters to the southern army. 1782-1785.
   (*Cf. Decl. Acc., A. O.,* **113.** 191.)
James Hughes, who furnished carriage train for Burgoyne's army.
   1777.
John Macomb, provincial forces under Burgoyne's command. 1777.
   (*Decl. Acc., A. O.,* **325.** 1289.)
Robert Mathews, military secretary to Gen. Haldimand. Quebec,
   1779-1784.
Lieut. Twiss, comptroller of works, Canada. Mar. 1, 1779.
   (*Cf. Decl. Acc., A. O.,* **2532.** 666.)
Robert Jones, provisions. 1770-1774.
Capt. George Forster, 8th Regiment of Foot at Oswagatchie, on
   expedition. 1776.
   (*Decl. Acc., A. O.,* **218.** 736.)
Peter Paumier, commissary-general. 1781-1783.
   (*Decl. Acc., A. O.,* **495.** 104.)
H. C. Litchfield, East Florida Claims. 1786-1789.
   (*Decl. Acc., A. O.,* **861.** 4.)
John Forster, secretary American Loyalist Claims Commission, ex-
   penses, 1783-1785, 1785-1791; *id.,* expenses of the commissioners
   to Nova Scotia, 1786-1791.
   (*Decl. Acc., A. O.,* **458.** 4, 5, 6.)

Francis Moore, payments under the seventh article of the treaty, salaries of British commissioners, etc. 1797-1799, 1803.
(*Decl. Acc., A. O.,* **12.** 35.)

James W. Hay, secretary to the commission. 1802-1804.
(*Decl. Acc., A. O.,* **467.** 52.)

David Skene, secretary to the commission. 1805-1806, 1807.
(*Decl. Acc., A. O.,* **467.** 54, 55.)

James MacDonald, secretary to the commission. 1807-1810, 1812. An item here records the purchase for £3 10s. of four large deal boxes to hold the official books and papers for the purpose of depositing them under the direction of the Treasury.
(*Decl. Acc., A. O.,* **468.** 55-59.)

Joseph Alcock, payments to Loyalists. 1803.
(*Cf. Decl. Acc., A. O.,* **12.** 37.)

John Martin Leake, agent for the American Board of Customs Commissioners. 1768-1786.
(*Decl. Acc., A. O.,* **844.** 1140.)

John Ellis, agent for West Florida. 1772-1776.
(*Decl. Acc., A. O.,* **1262.** 157.)

John Craigie, payments to Loyalists. 1785, 1786.

Account of monies received by Viscount Howe, one of the Commissioners for Restoring Peace in America, for defraying expenses, etc. 1777-1782.

Daniel Claus, expenses incurred. 1777-1782.
(*Cf. Decl. Acc., A. O.,* **1531.** 8.)

Account of money paid by Sec. Scott to British soldiers, prisoners of war, who escaped from the enemy, 1782. Auditor's Office, Charleston.
(*Decl. Acc., A. O.,* **167.** 467.)

Id. for contingencies of public service. Camp near Charleston, 1782.

George Hay and James Fraser, commissaries of captures, Charleston.

Account of expenses of remitting money to North America by S. Fludyer and John Drummond. 1767-1769.
(*Decl. Acc., A. O.,* **190.** 594.)

Peter Chester, governor of West Florida, contingent and Indian expenses, Aug. 10, 1770, to the surrender of the province, May, 1781.
(*Decl. Acc., A. O.,* **1262.** 155.)

Account of expenses, Indian Department, western division, Southern District, by John Graham. 1782.

Capt. Alexander Fraser, superintendent of Indian Affairs. Quebec, 1776-1777.

Brig.-Gen. John Campbell, expenses at Penobscot. 1779-1781.

John Moultrie, expenses of building the state house and making roads in East Florida. 1772-1774.
(*Decl. Acc., A. O.,* **1261.** 147.)

Col. Roger Morris, money to refugees. 1779-1782.
(*Decl. Acc., A. O.,* **850.** 1.)

Sir Archibald Campbell, expenses at Savannah. 1779.

John Campbell, agent for Georgia. 1774, 1775.

Sir James Wright, expenditure in Georgia. 1781-1782.

Nathaniel Hall, militia and refugees (many names of Loyalists). 1781.

Capt. Alexander Fraser, superintendent of Indian Affairs. 1778-1781.

Sir James Colebrooke, for remitting money for the garrison at Louisburg. 1759-1762.

(*Decl. Acc., A. O.*, **192**. 601.)

128. Ledger containing an account of the cost of engineering works in North America. 1667-1774. On p. 114 begin particular accounts of assistant engineers.

American correspondence book, an entry book of letters written from the Treasury Chambers by John Robinson, secretary, to Howe, Adm. Shuldham, Cornwallis, Burgoyne; instructions to Nathaniel Day, commissary; list and description of ships; letters to Carleton, Day, Chamier, Stephens, Gordon; copies of requisitions on contractors, 1775-1779. The letters, extracts, and documents chiefly relate to provisions, accounts, etc.

Marriott's account as agent and paymaster to the troops of rangers, etc., in Georgia. 1743.

Account of the pay of the staff of the army in Quebec by James Murray. 1760.

Crosby, barrack-master. 1780-1783.

(*Decl. Acc., A. O.*, **148**. 359.)

Henry Savage, deputy quartermaster-general " in Rhode and Connanicut Islands ". Dec. 25, 1776, and Oct. 25, 1779.

(*Decl. Acc., A. O.*, **337**. 1349.)

Simon Fraser, deputy quartermaster-general. 1779-1782.

(*Decl. Acc., A. O.*, **337**. 1352.)

Brig.-Gen. H. Watson Powell. 1780-1782.

(*Decl. Acc., A. O.*, **376**. 4.)

Lieut. Thomas Gamble, assistant quartermaster-general. 1773, 1775-1779.

(*Decl. Acc., A. O.*, **335**. 1342; **336**. 1347.)

Lord Cathcart, acting quartermaster-general, Georgia, South Carolina. 1780.

(*Decl. Acc., A. O.*, **338**. 1353, 1354.)

Maj.-Gen. William Dalrymple, quartermaster-general. 1780-1782.

(*Decl. Acc., A. O.*, **338**. 1355.)

Maj. Richard England, deputy quartermaster-general. 1781.

(*Decl. Acc., A. O.*, **338**. 1357.)

Gen. Carleton, contingencies. 1766-1770.

(*Decl. Acc., A. O.*, **163**. 448.)

Col. Thomas Carleton, quartermaster-general. July 11, 1778-1782.

(*Decl. Acc., A. O.*, **337**. 1351.)

Maj. John Carden, assistant deputy quartermaster-general. Montreal, 1775-1777.

(*Decl. Acc., A. O.*, **336**. 1346.)

Charles Stedman and Benjamin Booth Boote, commissaries of captures. 1780-1782.

(*Decl, Acc., A. O.*, **514**. 193.)

Christopher Kilby, settling emigrants in Nova Scotia. 1749-1758.
(*Decl. Acc., A. O.,* **1301.** 482, 483.)

Nova Scotia accounts. 1750-1760, 1775-1778, 1776-1777, 1781 (chiefly Halifax).

129. 1775-1778. Entry Book of Letters and Reports: America.

Contains extracts of letters from commanders-in-chief in North America relating to provisions and subsistence, transport, tonnage, effectives, horses, cattle and sheep, forage, wagons, state of barracks, etc. Nov. 1, 1775–Dec., 1777. Only an examination can show how far these letters are duplicates of papers in the Treasury series. They are valuable in showing the difficulties of provisioning the army in America, and furnish what amounts to a history of the commissariat there. The copies of letters are supplemented by copies of letters and enclosures from the commissaries, paymasters, and others.

130-132. *Id.* 1780-1781, 1782, 1783.

396. 1764-1788. Colonies and Dependencies, North America. Papers relating to Accounts of the Survey.

Small packet of papers. The Board of Trade, acting under a suggestion contained in a memorial from Capt. Samuel Holland, recommended that accurate surveys should be made of North America or certain parts of it and proposed that a division be effected into northern and southern districts with a surveyor general for each district acting under instructions from the board. The Privy Council referred the matter to the committee of the whole Council and that committee reported favorably. The Privy Council then directed the Lords of the Treasury to cause the proposal to be carried out, which was done. The order is dated Feb. 10, 1764. *Acts Privy Council, Colonial,* IV. 619-623.

The representation of the Board of Trade and Holland's memorial are given in full. Holland was appointed surveyor general for the Northern Department (Mar. 6, 1764) and Wright for the Southern. The papers that follow are Holland documents and deal with Holland's career as surveyor in America (1764-1776). One document contains a list of the plans, mostly Canada and New England, 27 in all, sent to the government. Holland's account of his service and his career (1776-1786), with lists of plans, closes the series.

The papers were evidently collected by Holland to meet the demands of the Audit Office for an auditing of his accounts in 1789, and might be called " Papers relating to the Appointment, Career, and Expenses of Samuel Holland, surveyor of the Northern District in North America ".

400. 1754-1835. Accounts and Subsidiary Documents: Cape Breton, Prince Edward Island (St. John), West Florida, Georgia, Bahamas, Barbadoes.

Packets:

King's warrant authorizing the expenses of the establishment of East Florida, 1775-1782, Nova Scotia, 1777-1830, St. John, 1777-1835 (commission for Samuel Smith to be agent for the island of St. John from Jan. 1, 1777).

Account of the agent of Georgia for silk culture (purchase of cocoons and reeling silk, etc.). 1754.

6

Commission for Samuel Hannay, provost marshal of West Florida.
1766.

Narrative of the motives of Gov. Des Barres's appointment to Cape
Breton and the circumstances of the expenditures for the public
service there, with remarks. Des Barres had served under Wolfe
and afterward, as engineer and surveyor, in America. This account covers his career to 1787.

401. 1764-1776.   East Florida: General Record Book.

Entry book of council proceedings, with instructions, commission, and other
documents—fees, warrants, petitions, land grants, king's orders relating to
land grants, letters written by the governments, etc. A valuable volume.

441. (4). 1775-1777.   Virginia.

Account of the Earl of Dunmore of expenses in raising regiments and
equipping them, with clothing, arms, accoutrements, and other necessaries;
also for the purchase of three vessels for the service of the government, etc.,
Nov. 1, 1775–May 2, 1777.

    (*Decl. Acc., A. O.,* **1324.** 627.)

481-482. 1777-1783.   Commissariat Accounts, etc., America.

  481. Daniel Wier, store account current—provisions, rum, molasses, oil,
porter. May 22, 1777–Nov. 11, 1781.

    Id. May 25, 1777–Nov., 1781.

    (*Decl. Acc., A. O.,* **494.** 100.)

A summary account of public cash received, disbursed, and paid by
Frederick William Hecht, assistant commissary-general in North
America. June 28, 1779–Aug. 16, 1786.

    (*Decl. Acc., A. O.,* **495.** 103.)

George Alsop, deputy commissary-general of stores and provisions
for the province of Quebec, 1770-1778, with affidavits sworn at
Quebec, Oct. 22, 1787.

    (*Decl. Acc., A. O.,* **573.** 479.)

George Brinley, deputy commissary-general under Brook Watson.
1783.

    (*Decl. Acc., A. O.,* **496.** 106.)

Maj. John Morrison, deputy commissary-general. May 25, 1777–
Feb. 12, 1785.

    (*Decl. Acc., A. O.,* **494.** 99.)

Daniel Wier, general account current. May 25, 1777–May 25, 1779.

    (*Cf. Decl. Acc., A. O.,* **494.** 100.)

Brook Watson, balance of general account. Sept. 17, 1783; sworn
Nov. 26, 1787.

Id., account general. May 31, 1782–Mar. 13, 1783.

Entry book containing minutes of meetings of the board appointed
by the commander-in-chief to examine the public accounts of the
army. May 23, 1782–Nov. 22, 1783.

  482. Account of assistant commissary-general with Brook Watson. June
25–Dec. 5, 1783.

A general account, Brook Watson. June 25–Dec. 26, 1783.

Various particular accounts—provisions, rum, horses, scows, boats, fuel, etc. Jan.-June 30, 1783.
> *Id.* July 1–Dec. 5, 1783.

These returns of Brook Watson are similar in appearance and form to those in the *Commissariat Office Papers.* Some of them are on huge sheets, pasted together and backed with linen.

500. 1751-1769. Commissariat: Newfoundland. Receipts for stores and lists of garrisons.

Lists of garrisons, with rosters of the men, amounts of food furnished, etc.

581-588. 1638-1672. Customs Accounts of the Receiver General.

> **581.** 1639-1641. Entries of defalcation of sundry parcels of tobacco, from Barbadoes, St. Christopher, and Virginia, for which the merchants " did not only refuse to pay custom but did violently take the same away, without paying any duty for the said goods " (pp. 31-33). The other volumes contain a few similar items. In **587** there is mention of West India hides brought in as prize (1654) among payments made by the Commissioner of the Customs. 1672, " Pd John Jeffries Esqr for Edward Digges, Esq, surveyor of the customs in Virginia "; " Jamaica goods custom free by virtue of his Majesty's privy signet and signe manuel dated September 23, 1664, and Lord Treasurers Warrant dated June 13, 1666 "; " Collector of the duties on the Act of Navigation, Sr. John Shaw ". Such are the items, of little importance, but occasionally valuable.

589. (1). 1677-1678. Customs Receipts at American Plantations.

> (2). 1681-1682. *Id.*
> (3). 1685-1686. *Id.*
> (4). 1777-1786. North America.
> (5). 1786-1787. *Id.*

The state of the accounts of His Majesty's customs in the American plantations, stated with the accounts of His Majesty's customs in England, etc., for the year 1678.

Plantation duties, with the name of the collector and the disposition of the amount collected. The list of collectors is as follows:

Antigua, William Thomas, 1674-1675, Philip Everden, 1675-1677, William Barnes, 1677-1678.

Nevis, St. Christopher, 1674-1675.

Jamaica, Richard Butler, 1676-1677.

Barbadoes, Edwyn Stede, 1674-1675.

Carolina, Charles Town, Maurice Mathews, to Sept. 2, 1676.

Virginia, lower precinct of the James River, Joseph Bridger, 1676-1677.

> Upper precinct of the James River, Thomas Ballard, 1677-1678.
> Potomac River, Nicholas Spencer, 1677-1678.
> Rappahannock, Ralph Wormely, 1677-1678.
> Eastern Shore, Col. John Stringer, 1677-1678.

Maryland, Christopher Rousby, 1677-1678.
New Jersey, Col. Philip Carteret, 1676-1677.
Nevis, St. Christopher, Joseph Martin, 1681-1682.
Antigua, William Barnes, 1681-1682.
Barbadoes, Edwyn Stede, 1680-1682.
Montserrat, John Syms, 1680-1682.
Virginia, Rappahannock, Ralph Wormely, 1681-1682.
   Lower James, Joseph Bridger, 1681-1682.
Maryland, Christopher Rousby, 1681-1682.
Jamaica, Thomas Lamb, 1683-1684.
Barbadoes, Edwyn Stede, 1683-1684.
Nevis, St. Christopher, Joseph Martin, 1684-1685.
Virginia, Lower James, Joseph Bridger, 1684-1686.
   Upper James, William Cole, 1685-1686.
   Rappahannock, Ralph Wormely, 1685-1686.
   Potomac, Nicholas Spencer, 1684-1686.
   Eastern Shore, John Stringer, 1684-1686.
   York River, Philip Ludwell, 1684-1686.
Maryland, Nicholas Sewall, 1685-1686.

An Account of the Receipts and Payments by the Cashier and Paymaster of His Majesty's Customs in North America. Jan. 5, 1777–Apr. 5, 1786.

Statistical table including ports, collectors' names, duties by 25 Charles II., 6 George II., 4 George III., 6 George III., 7 George III., seizures by officers, seizures by ships of war, total. Signed, Chas. Stewart. Also payments: to whom paid, salaries by establishments in America to July 5, 1776 (valuable). Belongs to the papers of the American Board of Customs Commissioners.

1786-1787. Supplemental Account. Deals with the winding up of the affairs of the board, Apr. 5, 1786–Jan. 5, 1787.

912. 1754-1780. Hospitals.

Receipts for pay, various hospital officials in America. 1762-1763.

Two warrants authorizing payment, 1762-1763, 1779-1780, with names of the general and staff officers and officials of the hospitals " attending our forces in North America ".

Account current of His Majesty's hospitals in North America, signed by James Napier. 1754-1764.

Account of the deductions of 12*d.* per £ and one day's pay in the year for one year, Dec. 25, 1779–Dec. 24, 1780, covering the entire army, with sections devoted to the officers and garrisons in North America. These deductions were for the benefit of the paymaster-general of the forces (see p. 131 and note 2).

1255-1280. 1703-1783. Stamp Duties, General Account.

These accounts are valuable in that they contain lists of the newspapers of the period and the names of their proprietors. The papers are British and the volumes contain nothing regarding colonial stamp duties. See next item.

1391. 1765-1772.   American Stamp Duties.

The general account of American stamp duties, by virtue of an act passed 5 George III. and repealed 6 George III.; a paper book containing:

Distributors' abstract, with names of distributors, districts, consignments, transfers, totals, cash, returns, and balances.

Account of Tonson and Company, stationers; warehouse-keeper of stamped goods; warehouse-keeper of unstamped goods; the charge and the discharge, and the net produce.

Statement of the account of Gov. John Wentworth of New Hampshire, directed to be paid to him by Richard Rigby, paymaster-general, by warrant under the royal sign manual, July 4, 1780.

(Parchment, much damaged, out of place in this bundle. *Cf. Decl. Acc., A. O.,* **1295.** 432.)

1398-1399. 1689-1786.   Treasurer Solicitor's Accounts.

The earliest references to colonial matters are of date 1700:

Pirate cases.

Law charges.

Expenses paid about pirate goods.

Then, 1732-1733:

Regarding an agent for an independent company on the Island of Providence.

Quit-rents in South Carolina.

Murder at Placentia.

Seignory and quit-rents at Annapolis Royal.

Treasonable practices in Jamaica.   1743.

For publishing the charts of Merryland, king against Torbuck.   1745.

In **1399** are a few items:

Regarding passing the patent for the surrender of Georgia.   1752.

Patent, Georgia, South Carolina.   1752.

Earl and Countess of Cardigan's claim to St. Lucia.   1763-1764.

Wilkes and Almon cases.   1764-1765.

Fraser and forage contract.   1780.

A few other items.

The series is less satisfactory than that in the *Declared Accounts.*

1590-1591. 1570-1830.   Warrants, etc.; 1651-1703, Treasury Orders to Auditors.

1590. Among the many accounts in this bundle is one for the wages of laborers employed at Louisburg, unloading wood for the garrison at Louisburg.   1745.

Among the warrants are:

Placing Worseley of the 2d battalion of the 60th or Royal American Regiment on half-pay.

Messrs. Baker, Kilby, and Baker for victualling.

Oglethorpe, for £40,000 (part of £66,109 granted by Parliament for extraordinary expenses incurred in the service in Georgia from Sept. 22, 1738, to Sept. 29, 1743).

Gen. Burgoyne, £1890, to enable him to replace 126 horses belonging to the 16th or Queen's Regiment of Light Dragoons, which were lost or killed in service during 1776-1777.

Civil establishment of East Florida.   1782-1783.   Four papers.

1591. Entry book of letters received by auditors of the imprests or receipts and by other officers of the Exchequer, 1651-1702, though
some early entries go back as far as 1643-1650.

1594. 1560-1820.   Miscellaneous States of Accounts.

No. 23. Account of the Commissioners of Transportation, including hire
of ships transporting soldiers to Jamaica, 1694, and to Newfoundland, 1697.

1609-1667. 1670-1783.   Enrollment Books of Warrants.

Contain copies of patents, warrants, letters of attorney, assignments, indentures, etc., many of which concern colonial appointments and interests.
For example:

Patent to Charles Stewart, cashier and paymaster of the customs in
America.

Warrant allowing Jared Ingersoll, judge of vice-admiralty in America,
£238 16s. 8½d., out of the sale of old naval stores.

Letters of attorney from Ingersoll to Thomas Life of London to receive
this money.

Many half-pay warrants, off-reckoning assignments, etc.

DECLARED ACCOUNTS.

The declaration of accounts meant the final settlement of accounts with the government on the part of those who were entrusted with funds for disbursement or to meet their contingent and extraordinary expenses.

" The practice of declaring accounts before the Lord High Treasurer of England or before the Chancellor of the Exchequer and two or more of the other Commissioners of the Treasury seems to have been introduced in the sixteenth century and established in the seventeenth.

" When the system was in full operation, the practice was as follows :—Two copies of a particular account were prepared in the Audit Office, the one written on paper, and the other on parchment. Both were sent to the Treasury and there declared before the Lord High Treasurer, or before the Chancellor of the Exchequer and two or more of the other Commissioners of the Treasury, and both were alike signed by the proper Auditor, or, in later times, by the Commissioners for Auditing Public Accounts, and by the Lord High Treasurer, or the Commissioners of the Treasury as above. The account was at this stage registered at the Treasury in volumes known as ' Declared Accounts ' and ' Auditors' States of Accounts ', which are now preserved in the Public Record Office. The copy on paper was then returned to the Audit Office, and the copy on parchment was sent to the office of the King's Remembrancer of the Exchequer, where it was enrolled in a series known as ' Enrolments of Public Accounts (Exchequer Q. R.) '. Thence it was forwarded to the office of the Lord Treasurer's Remembrancer, where a brief abstract of it was entered among the ' States and Views of Public Accounts '. Finally it was forwarded to the Clerk of the Pipe, who, until the practice was abolished, enrolled an abridgment of it, and retained the original. Thus the Audit Office series should consist of documents on paper, and the Pipe Office series should consist of duplicates on parchment. In some cases, however, accounts on parchment have found their way into the Audit Office " (preface to *List and Index of the Declared Accounts from the Pipe Office and Audit Office* (1893). Also *D. K. Rept. 55,* 16-17).

The following statement from P. R. O., *Chatham Papers,* **231,** shows the practice at the end of the colonial period.

" Every person receiving public money passes an account for the same before the proper auditors. In ordinary accounts, after having passed the examination of the auditor and been signed by him, the account is presented to the Chancellor of the Exchequer for declaration. In extraordinary accounts, a state of the charge and discharge, together with such articles as may not be regularly vouched, and cravings for fees or otherwise, with the auditor's observations thereon, is previously laid before the Treasury Board ; the Lords allowing those articles in whole, or in part as they think fit, and a warrant is granted to the auditors, authorizing them to state the account for declaration accordingly.

" The chancellor usually appoints two days in a year for the declaration of Public Accounts, one at Midsummer, the other at Christmas ; tho' other days are sometimes appointed for particular accounts."

Except for the receipts from customs, the accounts here listed are entirely of monies issued out of the British Exchequer. That the Treasury intended the royal revenues from the colonies to be similarly declared is clear from the instructions issued in 1703. Godolphin ordered that all accounts of Her Majesty's revenues in the plantations should be kept more systematically than before, and should be properly prepared for declaration every year by the auditor general, at that time Blathwayt. The deputy auditors in the colonies were to put their accounts into suitable form for declaration, have them examined before the governor and council, sworn to by an accomptant, in this case the collectors and receivers general in the colonies, attested by the governors, and signed by themselves. The colonial deputies were furthermore instructed to give an authority or letter of attorney to an agent in England in order to procure their quietus. Should any deputy auditor fail in his duty he was liable to a process issued out against him to compel him to obey the Treasury's orders.

Blathwayt made strenuous efforts to have these instructions carried out, and his own books and the minutes of the Treasury show that his accounts were more or less regularly declared. But his successors, Walpole and Cholmondeley, seem to have neglected this part of their duties, if we may judge from the absence of such accounts in this series or elsewhere. No declaration of royal receipts from America is to be found among these papers.

For a statement of the fees taken at the Exchequer when an account was declared see *Treas.* 1 : **337**. 83-84. The Declared Accounts, with other similar papers, were removed to the Public Record Office in 1859.

In the following lists selected rolls are described in full; others are entered by title only.

Inasmuch as all parchment rolls of date later than 1714 that duplicate the paper rolls of the Audit Office have been transferred to the Bodleian Library, the Pipe Office rolls in the Public Record Office are but few in number as compared with those of the Audit Office. In the printed list they are entered by rolls only, **1-3616**, while the Audit Office rolls are entered by bundles, **1-2541**, within which are the rolls, separately numbered. Therefore, when a given subject covers more than one roll, the numbering is continued through the series of rolls, thus: "Indians", bundle **1530**, rolls 1-6; **1531**, rolls 7-11. To obtain an Audit Office roll both bundle number and roll number must be given; for a Pipe Office roll the roll number is sufficient, as follows:

P. O. Declared Accounts. Roll —.	A. O. Declared Accounts. Bundle —, Roll —.

PIPE OFFICE, DECLARED ACCOUNTS.

CUSTOMS.

Roll.

1249. Declaration of the account of W. Mellish, receiver general and cashier, Barbadoes, Leeward Islands, and Caribbees. 1775-1779.

1250. *Id.* 1779-1786.

1254. *Id.*, J. Strode, farmer of the four-and-a-half per cent., Leeward Islands. 1670-1677.

1255. *Id.*, Spencer Wheeler and Strode, farmers of the four-and-a-half per cent., Barbadoes. 1670-1677.

1256. *Id.* 1670-1677.

1257. *Id.,* J. Selwyn, receiver general and cashier of the four-and-a-half per cent., Barbadoes. 1721-1726.

1258. *Id.,* J. Selwyn. 1726-1727.

1259. *Id.,* H. Selwyn, Barbadoes and Caribbee Islands. 1727-1732.

1260. *Id.,* H. Selwyn. 1732-1734.

1261. *Id.,* J. Eckersall, Barbadoes, Leeward and Caribbee Islands. 1734-1739.

1262. *Id.* 1739-1744.

1263. *Id.* 1744-1748.

1264. *Id.,* W. Mellish. 1765-1766.

1265. *Id.* 1766-1770.

GOVERNORS, AGENTS, ETC.

1556. Declaration of the account of C. Codrington, of the produce of the customs duty on sugar, etc., to be employed for the payment of troops in Barbadoes and the Leeward Islands. 1690-1694.

1566. *Id.,* Mathew, Fleming, and Mann, commissioners to contract for the purchase of that part of the island of St. Christopher yielded by France to Great Britain by the treaty of Utrecht. 1726-1728.

1567. *Id.,* G. Fleming, commissioner. 1728-1737.

AUDIT OFFICE, DECLARED ACCOUNTS.

Bundle. Roll.   AMBASSADORS.

12. 34. The declaration of the account of Richard, Lord Viscount Howe, one of the Commissioners for Restoring Peace in North America, from Apr. 30, 1777, to June 6, 1778. Contingent expenses chiefly.

ARMY.

PAYMASTERS-GENERAL.

66-92. 84-123. The declared accounts of W. Pitt, H. Fox, Richard Rigby, Edmund Burke, Isaac Barré, and others who were paymasters-general of the forces from 1746 to 1783.

These accounts fill forty rolls in all and contain items of importance for the financial history of the various wars in America.

COMMISSARY OF ACCOUNTS.

113. 191. The Declaration of the Account of Samuel Bean, Esquire, as Commissary of Accounts and Commissary of Musters to the Southern Army in North America, Dec. 15, 1781, to Sept. 30, 1783, of the money by him received of the Paymaster-General of His Majesty's forces by the hands of the Deputy Paymaster in South Carolina, and of the expenditure thereof for the pay of Clerks, Office Rent, sundry necessaries for the use of the Spanish sick officers at Charlestown, and other expenses in the Commissary of Accounts and Musters Department. See also " Commissariat, Abroad ", **493-496**, rolls 97-106.

BARRACK-MASTERS (ABROAD).

147. 355. The Declaration of the Account of Lieut.-Gen. James Robertson, Barrack-master General in North America, from May 1, 1765, to June 30, 1776, of the money by him received of the Paymaster-General and of the expenditure thereof, purchasing barrack furniture, wood, candles, repairs at the several ports by warrant of Maj.-Gen. Gage, fuel, candles, rent of houses, supplying officers and soldiers with lodgings.

Bills were drawn on Gen. Robertson by commanding officers and barrack-masters at Fort Pitt, Pensacola, Newfoundland, and other forts in Canada and Florida. The accounts contain some interesting details but in general are rather juiceless. At the end is, " Barrack expenses at the several Posts : Quebec, Three Rivers, Montreal, Oswegatchie, Michilimakinac, Fort George, Halifax, Mobile, Pensacola, St. Augustine, Fort Chartres, Crown Point, Fort Frederic, Fort Pitt, New York, Boston, Boston (Castle William), Providence ". Then follows an abstract of each year's expenses.

356. *Id.,* Lieut.-Col. George Clark. Apr. 1, 1776–June 30, 1780.

The arrangement of the accounts is quite different from that noted above, but the items given are about the same.

357. *Id.,* R. Murray, deputy, Quebec. 1776-1779.

148. 358. *Id.,* D. Brehm, deputy, Quebec. 1779-1783.

359. *Id.,* Lieut.-Col. W. Crosbie, North America. 1780-1783.

360. *Id.,* J. Putnam, Nova Scotia. Jan., 1783–Dec., 1784.

BRIDGE-MASTERS.

157. 410. Declaration of the Account of money paid for the salaries and wages of the several persons in the Bridgemaster's department, by Robert Fenwick, Bridgemaster in North America, together with an account of money received from the Paymaster-General from Sept. 26, 1776, to Mar. 31, 1779.

The account covers :

Salaries to bridge-master, assistant bridge-master, sergeants.

Wages to carpenters, boatmen, sawyers, pontoonmen.

Expenses for pontoons, planks, cordage, anchors, canvas, foraging bags, scantling, white paint, paint brushes, hammers.

Rents of various kinds.

411. *Id.,* Capt. Robert Lawson, bridge-master. Apr. 1, 1779–Nov. 8, 1782.

The lists of expenses are more elaborate than in the previous case, including in addition to those given above such items as bar-iron, hinges, files, padlocks, chest handles, small cables, pitch, calking-irons, chains, staples, hooks, anchors, ring bolts, stanchions, staples, and " Scaw for the use of the Ferry over Herlean Creek ".

COMMANDERS-IN-CHIEF, MILITARY GOVERNORS, ETC.

162. 441. Declaration of the Account of James Oglethorpe, Esq., Genl. and Commander-in-Chief of his Majesty's forces employed and to be employed in the Province of South Carolina and Georgia in America, from Sept. 22, 1738, to Michaelmas, 1743.

This account covers :

Expenses of stores, provisions, arms, ammunition, and other necessities of war.

Presents to the Indians.
Pay of rangers or cattle hunters, Highland Independent Company.
Wages of boatmen.
Hire of sloops and other vessels.
Charges of garrisons and fortifications.
Cost of building barracks and other military works.
Subsistence of sick and wounded, prisoners of war, etc.
Charges for letters of intelligence.
It is of value for its detailed exactness, both as to items and dates, and to the movements of individuals and troops.

444. *Id.*, Lieut.-Gen. Haldimand, governor at Three Rivers. 1762-1765.
163. 446. *Id.*, Lieut.-Gen. Thomas Gage, commander-in-chief, North America. 1765-1767.
447. *Id.*, Lieut.-Gen. E. Massey, commander in the Northern District, North America. 1766-1767.
448. *Id.*, Lieut.-Gen. Carleton, commander in the Northern District, North America. 1766-1770.
164. 449. *Id.*, R. Mackenzie, secretary and paymaster to Sir William Howe, army in North America. 1775-1778.
450. *Id.*, Sir William Howe, commander-in-chief in North America. 1775-1778.
451. *Id.*, Maj.-Gen. Prevost, commander-in-chief of the Southern District, North America. 1776-1780.
452. *Id.*, J. Smith, secretary to Sir Henry Clinton, commander-in-chief of the Southern Provinces in North America. 1776-1778.
165. 453. *Id.*, Lieut.-Gen. E. Massey, commanding officer in Nova Scotia. 1776-1778.
454. *Id.*, Enoch Storey, various disbursements, chiefly for clerk hire and stationery, pursuant to the directions of the commander-in-chief, Sir William Howe. 1777.
455. Declaration of the account of John Smith, secretary and paymaster to Gen. Sir Henry Clinton, of the money received of the paymaster-general, from May 25, 1778, to June 30, 1782, and sundry contingent disbursements in the secretary's office.
Many interesting items in addition to those covering contingent expenses, such as :
Cost of a " map of the road in the country between the Delaware and the Susquhanna, delivered in June, 1778 ".
Charges " for extraordinary duty and trouble in going to Virginia with clothing for the army of the Convention ".
" Geo. Wallaner, a refugee from Baltimore, for an allowance to enable him to subsist at £50 per ann."
Pay for Maj. John André, deputy adjutant-general, for certain services, etc.
456. *Id.*, Lieut. Thomas Trollope, secretary to Maj.-Gen. Eyre Massey, Nova Scotia. Mar. 5–June 30, 1778.
Contains a few interesting details, such as £5 Halifax money equivalent to £4 13s. 4d. stg. ; but chiefly concerns stationery, etc.
166. 458. *Id.*, Lieut.-Col. Pringle, commanding officer at Newfoundland. 1778-1782.
459-461. *Id.*, Sir H. Colder, Gen. Vaughan, and Maj.-Gen. Christie, commanding officers in the West Indies. 1779-1781.

462. *Id.*, Lieut.-Col. Clarke, commander in Georgia and East Florida. 1780-1782.
463. *Id.*, Lieut. Haldane, secretary and aide-de-camp to Lieut.-Gen. Cornwallis, commander in North and South Carolina and Virginia. 1780-1781.
167. 464. *Id.*, Capt. Benson, secretary to Lieut.-Col. Balfour, commandant at Charleston. 1780-1781.
465. *Id.*, Lieut.-Col. Pringle, commanding officer at Newfoundland. 1780-1782.
466. *Id.*, Lieut.-Col. Leslie, commander-in-chief in Virginia. 1780-1782.
467. *Id.*, Lieut. Scott, secretary to Maj.-Gen. Leslie. 1782.
468. *Id.*, Maj. Lewis, commandant of the Provincial Regiment of Jamaica Rangers. 1783.
168. 469. *Id.*, Lieut.-Col. Huddlestone, commandant at St. John's, Newfoundland. 1783-1786.

CONTRACTORS, PURVEYORS, ETC. (ABROAD).

187-188. 575-584. Declaration of the accounts of T. Missing and M. Woodford, victual contractors for Placentia, Canso, and Annapolis, Nova Scotia. 1720-1768.
189. 585. *Id.*, Thomas Revell, contractor for victualling the regiment of foot under the command of Gen. James Oglethorpe, in the province of Georgia. 1738-1744. Brief but valuable.
586-588. *Id.*, purveyors for Rattan (1744-1749), Nova Scotia (1745-1752), Louisburg (1746-1749).
190. 590-591. *Id.*, Halifax (1750-1760), St. John's, Newfoundland (1752-1760).
592. *Id.*, John Thomlinson and John Hanbury of London, merchants, contractors for providing money for the subsistence and payment of the land forces sent from Great Britain and Ireland to Virginia and other parts of North America, and for such other forces as may be raised there for the service of the expedition under the command of Maj.-Gen. Braddock, according to the terms and conditions of their contract with the Treasury, dated Dec. 29, 1754. Which said accountants do yield and make this their account of all the monies received and had from the respective paymasters-general of his Majesty's forces between Dec. 24, 1754, and May 27, 1757, and of their investing the same in the purchasing Spanish milled dollars and other Spanish coined silver and Spanish and Portuguese coined gold either in England or in the colonies and shipping the same to North America, and for their commission, brokerage in purchasing gold and silver consigned to America, for insurance, freight, and sundry other disbursements. This account covers also the valuations, by what vessels shipped, and to whom consigned.
592-594. *Id.*, contractors for remitting money for the forces in North America: Thomlinson and Hanbury (1754-1765), Fludyer and J. Drummond (1767-1769).
191. 595-597. *Id.*, Harley and J. Drummond (1769-1770, 1770-1778), Harley and H. Drummond (1770-1778).

598. *Id.*, W. Baker, Kilby, and R. Baker, purveyors for North America. 1756-1760.
192. 601. *Id.*, J. Colebrooke and Nesbit, contractors for remitting money to the garrison at Louisburg. 1759-1767.
193. 605. *Id.*, J. Kennion, victuals for the expedition against Havana.
606. *Id.*, A. Bacon, victuals for Tobago, Dominica, and St. Vincent. 1764-1770.
607. *Id.*, Cuming and Mason, victuals for East Florida. 1764-1776.
608. *Id.*, Major and Henniker, victuals for West Florida. 1765-1767.
194. 609-610. *Id.*, E. Codrington, victuals for West Florida. 1767-1775.
611. *Id.*, E. Lewis, contractor for remitting money for the garrisons of Pensacola and Mobile. 1767-1781.
612. *Id.*, Stephenson and Blackburn, victuals for West Florida. 1775-1778.
613. *Id.*, Mason and Jones, victuals for East Florida. 1776-1778.
195. 614. *Id.*, Mason, victuals for East Florida. 1778-1780.
615. *Id.*, Stephenson and Blackburn, victuals for West Florida. 1781.
616-618. ⎱ *Id.*, purveyors for Nova Scotia, Newfoundland, Penobscot.
196. 619-623. ⎰   1768-1782.
624. *Id.*, J. Durand, victuals for the " Ceded Islands " in the West Indies. 1770.
197. 627-631. *Id.*, various purveyors of rum and victuals for North America. 1776-1777. As for example:
631. Declaration of the Account of Anthony Bacon, Esq., of the money by him received of a late Paymaster General of the forces pursuant to warrants under the royal sign manual, and of sundry quantities and species of provisions by him delivered into store for the supply of a body of his Majesty's forces serving in North America pursuant to five contracts with the Lords Commissioners of his Majesty's Treasury dated, etc., 1780.
From this and other similar accounts it is possible to determine the price and character of the provisions furnished, the allowance per capita to a given number of soldiers for a given length of time, together with (in some instances) the procedure employed in conveying the provisions to America, and the various fees and allowances. Rum from St. Vincent, Grenada, Tobago, and elsewhere bulks large in these accounts.
198. 632-635. ⎱ *Id.*, various purveyors of rum and victuals for North Amer-
199. 636.   ⎰   ica. 1776-1777. As for example:
633. The declaration of the account of Sir James Cockburn, contractor for delivering 100,000 gallons of rum for the use of the forces in North America.
The contract is dated May 2, 1776; the rum came from Grenada.
637. *Id.*, Jacob Jordan, contractor for furnishing a carriage train for the service of the army under the command of Lieut.-Gen. Burgoyne in the year 1777.
Covering horses, carts, harness, and drivers. The declaration mentions 970 horses, 528 carts, 970 sets of harness, as having been taken or destroyed by the enemy. The contract is dated June 10, 1777.

638. *Id.*, stores for North America. 1777.

639-640. *Id.*, various contractors, victuals for North America. 1777-1778.

200. 641-643. *Id.* 1778-1779.

644. *Id.*, Harley and Drummond, contractors for remitting money for the forces in North America; also expenses of the forces in the West Indies. 1778-1781.[1]

201. 645. 646-649. } *Id.*, various contractors, victuals for North America and the
202. 652. } West Indies. 1778-1782.

201. 650. } *Id.*, contractors for victuals for New York, Georgia, and
202. 651, 653. } Florida. 1779-1781.

202. 654. *Id.*, contractor for victuals for the Carolinas. 1781.

655. *Id.*, contractor for victuals for the Carolinas, Georgia, Florida, Bermuda, and the Bahamas. 1781.

203. 656, 658. } *Id.*, various contractors for victuals for America and North
204. 662-665. } America. 1781-1782.
205. 666-667. }

203. 657, 659, 660. *Id.*, various contractors, victuals for New York. 1781.

204. 661. *Id.*, Harley and Drummond, contractors for remitting money for the forces in North America. 1782-1783.

205. 668. *Id.*, purveyors of victuals for South Carolina, Georgia, and Florida. 1782.

205. 669, 670. }
206. 671-675. } *Id.*, various purveyors of victuals for Canada. 1776-1782.
207. 676, 677. }

207. 679, 680. } *Id.*, various purveyors of victuals for the West Indies.
208. 681-685. }

Leeward Islands, Jamaica, West Indies in general, roll 684 including also Nova Scotia.

EXPEDITIONS.

217. 730. Declaration of the account of J. Arnott, paymaster of the forces on the expedition to Canada in 1711.

731. *Id.*, D. Campbell, commissary on the expedition to the West Indies. 1740.

218. 734. *Id.*, Lieut.-Col. J. Hale, secretary to the Earl of Albemarle, commander-in-chief of the expedition against Havana in 1762.

735. *Id.*, Maj.-Gen. Dalrymple, commander-in-chief on the expedition against the Caribs in the Isle of St. Vincent. 1772-1773.

736. *Id.*, Col. Foster, commander of the expedition to the Cedres. Bills of exchange drawn for the same, and for the government at Oswagatchie in North America. 1776.

219. 737. *Id.*, Col. Barry St. Leger, commander of an expedition against Fort Stanwix, of the money by him received from the Paymaster-General of his Majesty's forces by the hand of the Deputy Pay-

---

[1] The contract with Harley and Drummond was made June 17, 1778, and expired June 17, 1783. The specie thus remitted was sent in ships of war, without insurance, and for the carriage the commanders of the ships were allowed one per cent. freight. (See below, p. 247.)

master of Quebec and of the issue and expenditure thereof for
the pay of the military artificers, guides, batteau-men, conductors,
horses, wagons, fresh beef and sundry contingent expenses, also
for stands of arms and for cattle lost or destroyed. 1777.

Gives equivalents of colonial currency in sterling.

738. *Id.,* Sir Archibald Campbell, of the money received and expended
in commanding an expedition against the province of Georgia.
1778-1779.

Many interesting details, including such items as " gratuities to
distressed Loyalists ".

739. *Id.,* J. Christie, commissary-general on the expedition in the West
Indies. 1778-1779.

740-741. *Id.,* Capt. Goldfrap, secretary to Maj.-Gen. Grant, commander-
in-chief on the expedition to the West Indies, 1779; also money
for secret service.

PAYMASTERS AND TREASURERS OF THE FORCES, ETC.

These rolls, small at first but of great size during the period of the Revolution, contain the allowances made to the deputy paymasters in America for
salaries and expenditures there, from 1700 to 1783. The pay and allowance
lists include inspectors-general, superintendents of hospitals, deputy commissaries, superintendents of forage, quartermasters-general, and colonial
governors; the expenditures include the pay and entertainment of officers and
privates of the regiments, and chaplains and surgeons of the garrisons; cost
of provisions for the garrisons in Nova Scotia, Newfoundland, and elsewhere,
of trains of horses and wagons, of mustering foreign troops (in Germany for
service in America), of postage, stationery, etc.

In the early rolls we find the expenses of the few troops in America, at
New York, Newfoundland, and New England; these expenses in constantly
increasing bulk can be traced through the campaigns of 1745-1748,1754-1763,
and 1775-1783, covering all general items and allowances and furnishing the
names of every official—general staff, military officers, officers of hospitals,
etc.—in the pay and service of the British government. The rolls furnish many
valuable bits of information regarding dates, movements of officers, messengers, and envoys, number of dead (killed in battle), sick and wounded, and
other matters in connection with which indebtedness was incurred. The accounts are, of course, strictly military and have nothing to do with naval
matters, convoys, or customs, except incidentally. A more particular account
of a selected number of rolls is given below.

312. 1236. Declaration of the account of Gov. Stapleton of the Leeward
Islands. 1672-1686.

316. 1257. *Id.,* T. Fotherby, paymaster of troops, commissary-general of
provisions and stores of war, and deputy judge advocate on an
expedition to the West Indies. 1692.

324. 1285. *Id.,* H. T. Cramahé, paymaster of military contingencies in the
Northern District of North America. 1774-1780.

1286. *Id.,* T. Dunn, Quebec. 1775-1784.

325. 1287. *Id.,* Robert Mackenzie, Paymaster-General of the Provincial
Forces raised for his Majesty's service in North America, to

which office he was appointed by Commission from Gen. Sir William Howe, K. B., Commander-in-Chief there, bearing date, Aug. 14, 1776, of the monies by him received of the Paymaster General of the forces by the hands of his deputies in North America. 1776-1782.

This account is concerned with the following provincial regiments: Royal Highland Emigrants, Royal Fencible American Regiment of Foot, New York Provincials, Royal Nova Scotia Volunteers, 5th Battalion, New Jersey Volunteers, Company of Black Pioneers, Company of Guides, 1st Company of Dutchess County Troops, North Carolina Troops, Queen's Rangers, King's American Regiment, Loyal American Regiment, New York Volunteers (three companies), New York Volunteers (six battalions), Maj. William Stark's Corps, Four Independent Companies, Pennsylvania Loyalists, Maryland Loyalists, Loyal New Englanders, Roman Catholic Volunteers, Philadelphia Dragoons, Capt. Emmerick's Company of the American Chasseurs, West Jersey Volunteers, Loyal Rhode Islanders, Skinner's Brigade. Continued in roll 1288, containing the declaration of J. Smith, secretary to Sir Henry Clinton (1778-1782).

1288. The British Legion, Volunteers of Ireland, Garrison Battalion, Bucks County Light Dragoons, Diemar's Troop of Hussars (mention of Chaplain Seabury receiving £20 for 60 days' service), the Batteaux Company, Royal Georgia Volunteers, Gov. Wentworth's Volunteers, the Nassau Blues, South Carolina Royalists, Georgia Light Dragoons, Georgia Loyalists, Rogers's Rangers, the United Corps of Pennsylvania and Maryland, West Florida Foresters, Carolina Dragoons, Stewart's Dragoons, the Light Infantry Company, Wilmington Light Dragoons, North Carolina Highlanders, North Carolina Independent Company, Loyal Foresters, and several special companies. See below, pp. 302-303.

The data furnished regarding these provincial companies, though varying in the different instances, generally consist of names of commanding officers, periods of service, and pay of special officers and the rank and file. 1776-1782.

1289. *Id.,* John Macomb, Paymaster of the Provincial Forces with Gen. Burgoyne, of the monies by him received in pursuance of warrants of the said general and of the expenditure thereof. 1777-1778. Of little importance.

1290. *Id.,* Maj.-Gen. J. Campbell, expenses in West Florida, and pay of the staff of the late garrison at Pensacola.

326. 1291. *Id.,* Robert Grey as deputy paymaster and paymaster successively to the militia and distressed refugees in South Carolina in 1781 and 1782.

The account furnishes no names, simply recording payments " To Sundry Refugees ", and to the militia.

1292. *Id.,* J. P. Collins, Charleston. 1781-1782.

This account is much more valuable than the last because it gives the names of individual refugees from South Carolina—Col. Thomas Fletchall, William Elfe, John Doak, Capt. Paris, John Gibson, Mary Crowther, widow of a distressed refugee, etc.

1293. *Id.,* Capt. Charles Handfield, appointed paymaster to men of absent corps by order of his Excellency Sir Henry Clinton [. . . of monies issued and disbursed] to sundry soldiers drafted from the Convention army, being the intermediate pay due them from the days they were settled with by their former regiments to the days they commenced pay in the corps to which they were drafted and for Bounty Money to sundry soldiers who had been prisoners with the rebels and made their escape into New York. Jan. 1, 1782–Dec. 24, 1783. Of little value.

1294. *Id.,* Thomas Aston Coffin of the Money by him received of the Paymaster-General of his Majesty's Forces and of the expenditure thereof as storekeeper at New York, Feb. 1–24, 1783, and as paymaster of contingencies and extraordinaries not payable by the Deputy Paymaster-General at the same place, Feb. 25–Dec. 5, 1783. Also at Halifax, Dec., 1783–Apr. 24, 1784.

This account contains many interesting items—payments to refugees, allowances for widows of provincial officers, allowances to distressed Loyalists, as well as salaries, etc., paid in course.

327. 1298. *Id.,* Col. Edward Winslow as Deputy Paymaster of Contingencies for New Brunswick, between Oct. 19, 1785, and Nov. 9, 1787 ; and as Muster-Master-General of the forces in North America from Aug. 1, 1776, to Aug. 24, 1777, of the money by him received of the Paymaster-General of the forces and of the issue and expenditure thereof for his pay for mustering the loyalists in New Brunswick, for pay to officers, artificers, and laborers, and for expenses incurred in the engineer and barrack departments, for pay to clerks, storekeepers, and others employed in the commissariat for freight, wood, cartage, etc. The account is very detailed.

INSPECTOR OF PROVINCIAL FORCES.

335. 1338. Declaration of the account of Lieut.-Col. A. James, inspector of provincial forces. 1777-1782.

QUARTERMASTERS.

1339-1342. Declaration of the accounts of Lieut.-Col. Bradstreet (1756-1760), Lieut.-Col. Robertson (1757-1765), and Lieut. T. Gamble (1765-1773), North America, and of Lieut.-Col. Irving (1760-1765), Quebec.

336. 1343. *Id.,* Maj. William Shirreff, Deputy Quartermaster-General of his Majesty's forces in North America, of the money by him received of the several deputy paymasters there in pursuance of warrants of Lieut.-Gen. Thomas Gage, Commander-in-Chief, and of the several sums of money by him issued and paid for freight of vessels, marching of troops, transporting of stores and provisions, payments to artificers and laborers and sundry other contingent disbursements. 1768-1773.

1344. *Id.,* Lieut.-Col. William Shirreff. 1773-1776, 1777-1778.

1345. *Id.,* Maj. J. Maxwell, Montreal. 1770-1772.

1346. *Id.,* Maj. J. Carden, Montreal. 1775-1777.

1347. *Id.,* Maj. T. Campbell, Canada. 1775-1779.

337. 1348. *Id.*, Sir W. Erskine, North America. 1776-1779.
1349. *Id.*, Maj. H. Savage, Rhode Island and Conanicut Island. 1776-1779.
1350. *Id.*, Lieut.-Col. W. Handfield, Nova Scotia. 1776-1783.
1351. *Id.*, Col. T. Carleton, Canada. 1778-1782.
1352. *Id.*, Lieut.-Gen. S. Fraser, North America. 1779-1782.
338. 1353. *Id.*, W. Lord Cathcart, North America. 1779-1780.
1354. *Id.* 1780.
1355. *Id.*, Gen. W. Dalrymple, North America. 1780-1782.
1356. *Id.*, Capt. A. Durnford, Georgia and East Florida. 1780-1783.
1357. *Id.*, Maj. R. England, Carolina and Virginia. 1781.
339. 1359-1360. *Id.*, Lieut.-Col. Moneypenny, expedition to Martinique and Havana. 1762-1763.
340. 1361-1362. 1363-1364. } *Id.*, various quartermasters in the West Indies. 1779-1784.

CANADA AND NOVA SCOTIA.

376. 1. Declared account of Col. A. S. De Peyster of expenses incurred in the public service at the upper posts of Canada. 1775-1784.
2. *Id.*, Sir J. H. Craig, public expenditure at Halifax. 1779.
3. *Id.*, Brig.-Gen. J. Campbell, public expenses at Penobscot. 1779-1781.
4. *Id.*, Maj.-Gen. H. W. Powell, public expenses in Canada. 1780-1782.

CLAIMS FOR COMPENSATION, ETC.

458. 1. Declaration of the Account of John Thomlinson and John Hanbury, merchants of London, of the sum impressed to them out of the Receipt of his Majesty's Exchequer by virtue of a warrant under the royal sign manual dated March 3, 1756. Which sum was granted to his Majesty pursuant to a resolution of the Hon. House of Commons out of the supplies for the year 1756 to be distributed to the colonies of New England, New York, and New Jersey in such proportion as his Majesty should think fit, as a free gift and reward for their past services and an encouragement to them to continue to exert themselves with vigor in defense of his Majesty's just rights and possessions. Which said accountants do yield and make this their account of the said sum of money by them received as aforesaid and of the payment of the same into the hands of the governors of the said colonies in the several proportions and agreeable to the directions mentioned in the said warrant.
This account gives in exact detail the sums paid to the northern colonies for the expenses incurred by them in the expedition of 1756, of which one may find a full discussion in *C. O.* 323 and *C. O.* 391, in volumes of that date.
4. *Id.*, J. Forster, secretary to the commissioners appointed to inquire into the claims of American Loyalists, 1783-1785, based upon their losses and services in consequence of their attachment to the British government.
5. *Id.* 1785-1791.
6. *Id.* of Loyalists in Nova Scotia and Canada. 1786-1791.
These accounts contain little of importance regarding the Loyalists.

459-465. 7-43. Accounts of T. Cotton (1788-1810), A. Rosenhagen (1810-1815), T. Crafer (1815-1827), paymasters of pensions to American Loyalists. 1788-1827.

466. 47. Account of the payment of demands of American claimants of ships and cargoes captured at Martinique by the forces under Sir John Jervis and Sir Charles Grey. 1794.

467. 52. Account of the secretary to the commissioners appointed for distributing the money to be paid to the United States as claims for compensation. 1802-1804.

COMMISSARIAT (ABROAD).

493. 97. Declaration of the account of Daniel Chamier, commissary-general in North America. 1774-1777.

494. 98. *Id.*, Joshua Loring, Commissary-General of the Prisoners in North America, of the money by him received of the Paymaster-General of his Majesty's forces and of his issuing and paying the same for sundry expenses as commissary-general between Aug. 27, 1776, and Sept. 30, 1782. And also an account of the money received for the subsistence of French prisoners between July 24 and Oct. 31, 1780.

This account contains a few interesting items regarding the quarters of the French prisoners on Long Island and elsewhere; and regarding the rebel prisoners taken at the battle of the Brandywine, with detail of their duties and employments and attempts to escape. Important for a study of the treatment of prisoners in the hands of the British. 1774-1783.

99. *Id.*, J. Morrison, deputy commissary-general in North America. 1776-1782.

100. *Id.*, Daniel Wier, Commissary-General in North America, of the money by him received of the Paymaster-General of his Majesty's forces . . . and of the expenditure thereof for provisions, forage, vessel hire, rent of stores, cartage, pay of assistants, clerks, carpenters, coopers, laborers, and repairs of magazines, etc. 1777-1782.

A very detailed list; among the items is a valuation of a number of vessels (names given) taken by the Americans.

495. 101. *Id.*, J. Crawford, commissary-general in North America. 1778-1782.

102. *Id.*, Maj.-Gen. Roy, commissary-general for the sale of stores remaining (after the march of the troops into winter quarters) in the camp magazines of the five campaigns of the late war in America. 1778-1782.

103. *Id.*, F. W. Hecht, assistant commissary-general in North America. 1779-1786.

104. *Id.*, P. Paumier, acting commissary-general in North America. 1781-1783.

105. *Id.*, Brook Watson, commissary-general in North America (from Nova Scotia to West Florida). 1782.

496. 106. *Id.*, G. Brinley, deputy commissary-general in North America. 1783.

514. 192. *Id.,* J. Fraser, commissary of captures in South Carolina. 1780.

193. *Id.,* Stedman and Boote, commissaries of captures in North and South Carolina and Virginia. 1780-1782.

579. 514. *Id.,* M. Forster, commissary-general in the Leeward and Caribbee Islands. 1780-1782.

CUSTOMS.

FARMERS, COMMISSIONERS, AND COMPTROLLERS GENERAL (VARIOUS).

This series of 791 rolls contains very little of importance for colonial trade. **607**, 65, is " Money recd for the Navigation Duty ", 1660-1662 ; **607**, 67, is " The Declared Account of the Farm of Logwood or Blockwood for twenty years, imported into England, Wales, or Berwick on Tweed ", 1662 ; **607**, 68, contains an elaborate introductory statement of the nature of the farm (*cf. Treas.* 64 : **137** for a copy of an agreement for farming the revenues) ; **611**, 93, **612**, 98, are separate accounts of the tobacco receipts, but as these receipts are combined with the sugar receipts and are given in lump sums they are of little use. The first separate account of tobacco receipts is **644**, 244, 1714-1715, but is likewise of no value in determining the colonial output. More important than these rolls in the Audit Office series are those from the Pipe Office, entitled " Farmers of Duties on Tobacco ", **667-672**, 1632-1639, and " Collectors of New Impositions on Tobacco ", **911-917**, 1615-1628. Though these rolls cover but a brief period of time they are of considerable value, and the use to which they can be put can be seen in Beer's *Origins of British Colonial System,* pp. 87, 109, 110, 112, 117, 126, 127, 134, 141, 147, 148, 160, 168, 170, 171.

RECEIVERS GENERAL AND CASHIERS (VARIOUS).

Certain rolls of this series are of first importance for the history of colonial customs. Those containing the tobacco and sugar accounts (separated after 1698), and those containing the coinage, wine and vinegar, and silks, linen, and calicoes accounts furnish nothing of value. From the early rolls (described below) we learn that Michael Wicks was the first receiver of the duty on plantation goods (" Tobacco and other Merchandize from the Plantations ") and of the duty on wine and vinegar. The most important rolls are those containing the general accounts of the customs, which begin (for our purpose) with **759**, 808. These rolls, often bulky and frequently in bad condition, contain the full customs establishment for England and the plantations, and record the amounts of receipts, allowances, salaries, and sometimes money remaining in the hands of the collector. A complete list of all these entries beginning with **756**, 792, 1671-1672, has been prepared, and is now to be found in the Library of Congress. It is desirable that some day this list should be printed.

The contents of the early rolls, as far as they concern the colonies, are as follows :

756. 792. Sept. 30, 1671–Sept. 29, 1672. Includes money accounted for by Michael Wicks, receiver of the duty and customs payable on goods brought from the plantations. Also his payments of half subsidy, additional duty, and abatement of x *li. p. c.* (ten pounds in the hundred) to those who paid ready money " in discharge of the new imposition layd upon linnen, Tobaccoes, or any other comodities imported from the said Plantacons ".

793. Sept. 30, 1671–Mar. 25, 1672. Money had of Michael Wicks; salaries to Wicks, receiver, Elton, surveyor of the Act of Navigation, and two watermen.

795. Sept. 30, 1672–Sept. 29, 1673. Items as in 792.

796. Sept. 30, 1672–Mar. 25, 1673. Money had of Wicks; salaries to Digges, surveyor for Virginia, Calvert, Maryland, Wicks, Elton, and watermen.

797. Mar. 26, 1673–Sept. 29, 1673. *Id.*

757. 798. Sept. 29, 1673–Sept. 29, 1674. Items as in 792 and 795.

801. Sept. 30, 1674–Sept. 29, 1675. Money from Wicks, and from the collectors at Antigua and Barbadoes; salaries paid to Wicks, Elton, and to Shaw as collector of the Act of Navigation.

802, same dates. Money from Wicks; from the plantations remitted by the collectors ("though they have not transmitted account of particulars "), *viz.*, Barbadoes and Antigua, payment by Wicks of half subsidy and additional duty, as in 792.

758. 803. Sept. 30, 1675–Sept. 29, 1676. Money from Wicks; from the collectors at Antigua, Barbadoes, Nevis, and Virginia.

804. Sept. 30, 1675–Sept. 29, 1676. *Id.* with the addition of salaries paid to Wicks, Elton, Shaw, and Molesworth, clerk for the plantation business.

806. Sept. 29, 1676–June 24, 1677. *Id.*, except Nevis.

807. June 24, 1677–Sept. 29, 1677. Money from Wicks; from Bridger, collector at Virginia.

The contents of the rolls from this time on (**759**, 808, to **829**, 1086) may be briefly summarized. They contain the English and colonial establishments for all the ports, and enter the names of collectors, surveyors, riding surveyors of various kinds, searchers, tidesmen, waiters, weighing porters, and boatmen. On the English establishment will be found the names of those who had to do with the plantation receipts, such as, plantation and western clerk and (later) his assistant, husband of the four-and-a-half per cent.; surveyors of the Act of Navigation and attending watermen; and surveyor of the plantation trade in Ireland. The colonial establishment includes all the customs officials from Halifax to Barbadoes, from 1676-1677, to the close of the colonial period. For the establishment in America, 1767-1783, see *Custom House, Registers, Series I., Establishments,* **310-410,** and the Custom House Establishment Books now in the Custom House, London, below pp. 118-119. For the years 1697, 1717, and 1720, see *Treas.* 38 : **346-348,** *Treas.* 42 : **2, 3,** and for 1744, Brit. Mus. *Add. MSS.* **8831.**

The colonial establishment begins in 1676-1677 with four collectors; in 1685 we find surveyors and collectors; in 1716, nine surveyors, one riding officer, one preventive officer, and collectors; in 1730-1731 appear two surveyors general, one for the northern and one for the southern part of America, and a comptroller in addition to the other officials; in 1761, surveyors general, surveyors and searchers, surveyors, comptrollers, collectors, and land-waiters; in 1763, the offices of collector, surveyor, and searcher, surveyor and searcher, and waiter and searcher are occasionally held by single men; in 1767, three surveyors general, one for the northern, one for the eastern middle, and one for the southern part of America. At this time boats and boatmen are included. With the names of the officials and the amounts of receipts, salaries, etc., are sometimes found additional information (as for extra charges and losses), incidental details of their experiences, and the names and charges of special officials. The receipts cover enumerated commodities or plantation duty, prize duties (from Jamaica), fines and forfeitures (Philadelphia), and duties from 6 George II. and 4 George III. (rum, sugar, etc.). Charges against both the four-and-a-half per cent. and the plantation duty will also be found. The customs officials received their authority from the Commissioners of the Customs and Treasury establishment warrants (see *Treas.* 11 : **1-32**), and we learn that in 1761 before receiving their pay, they were obliged to furnish certificates that they were " living at their respective times " (**818,** 1064), a suggestive commentary on previous practices.

COMPTROLLERS AND CASHIERS.

(West Indies and America.)

843. 1132. Declaration of the Account of the Duties and Impositions of the Four-and-a-half per cent. Duty, payable to his Majesty in the Island of Barbadoes and also in the Leeward Islands, *viz.*; Nevis, St. Christopher, Montserrat, and Antigua. 1684-1685.

1133. *Id.* 1684-1685.

1134, 1135. Declaration of the General Account of the Customs and other Duties in his Majesty's plantations and provinces in America, exhibited by James Porter, Comptroller of the Customs, 1767-1777; containing an account of the customs and duties on sundry goods or merchandize imported into or carried from any of his Majesty's colonies, plantations, or provinces lying or being on the Continent of America, from Davis Straits to the Capes of Florida, and islands and territories thereto belonging or adjoining, together with Bermuda and the Bahamas.

Roll 1135 carries the account from Jan. 5, 1777, to Apr. 5, 1786, but is much smaller than roll 1134 and much less complete. There is also charged in the general account (roll 1134) the money received by Charles Stewart, cashier and paymaster of the revenues of customs and other duties in America.

Porter was appointed by letters patent under the great seal, Sept. 11, 1767, and he calls his account " the first general account of these revenues ". It records the money received from the collectors of customs in the colonies, in pursuance of several acts of Parliament (25 Charles II., 6 George II., 4 George III., 6 George III., 7 George III.), by them received from duties on sundry goods imported, from seizures made by officers of the customs, and from pecuniary penalties imposed in the colonies. The account, which runs from Sept. 8, 1767, to Jan. 5, 1777, contains an enumeration by years, and the figures are given for every port of entry or clearance. These rolls are of great importance for the revenue history of the period and deserve careful attention.

844. 1136. *Id.* 1691-1697.

See also *Pipe Office,* **1249-1252,** where will be found the accounts of the receiver general and cashier of the four-and-a-half per cent. for 1775-1797; **1254-1265,** *id.,* for 1670-1677, 1721-1748, 1765-1770. Also *Audit Office,* under " Receivers General and Cashiers (Various)", **756-829.** Other references are given below, p. 217.

1137. *Id.,* Charles Stewart, Cashier and Paymaster of his Majesty's revenues of customs and other duties imposed by several acts of Parliament, etc., to which office he was appointed by letters patent under the great seal, Sept. 11, 1767.

The account shows the revenues received by Stewart or his agents from the several collectors within the years 1767-1776, and records his issuing and paying the same for salaries of the commissioners and other officers of the said customs, and for incidental charges attending the management thereof, and the money remitted to the receiver general.

1138. *Id.* to 1781.

1139. *Id.* to 1788.

These accounts are also of the utmost importance for the history of customs in America during the years named.

1140. *Id.,* John Martin Leake, agent for the commissioners of his Majesty's customs in America, of the monies imprested to him to pay sundry contingent expenses in England respecting the said commission, Nov. 5, 1768, to Apr. 5, 1786.

Contains a few items of interest. Leake received the money from Stewart, and certain additional sums from Nuthall, solicitor of the Treasury, to reimburse money advanced and expenses incurred by the solicitor for the American Board of Customs on account of the appeal relative to the Mohegan Indians (£22), by the collector of Rhode Island to defray the expense of appeals from that colony (£430), and by the same in the case of Dudley *vs.* Clark and Nightingale, and of Dudley *vs.* Shaw (£310).

EMIGRANTS AND REFUGEES.

(PENSIONS AND ALLOWANCES TO.)

850. 1. The Declaration of the Accounts of Col. Robert Morris, Inspector of the claims of refugees in North America, of the money by him received of the Paymaster-General of the Forces by the hands of their deputies abroad. Jan. 1, 1779–Mar. 31, 1783.

Contains no names; merely a record of the money, £23,848, paid for allowances.

ENQUIRY COMMISSION.

861. 4. Declaration of the account of H. C. Litchfield, secretary to the commissioners to enquire into losses by the cession of East Florida to Spain. 1787-1789. See *Treas., Expired Commissions, East Florida Claims*; *C. O.* 5 : **562**; *Treas. Solicitor*, **3662**; *A. O. Accounts, Various*, **127** (4).

GOVERNORS, AGENTS, ETC.

1255. 100. Declaration of the account of Gov. Knowles of Cape Breton and the town and fortress of Louisburg. 1746-1747. See **1282**, 314.

1259. 139. *Id.,* Josiah Martin, Governor of North Carolina, of money received from the Paymaster-General of his Majesty's Forces, by the hands of the deputy paymaster there . . . and of the expenditure thereof in disbursements for necessaries to distressed refugees and other expenses in North Carolina; as also for the pay and subsistence of several officers and soldiers in a corps of provincial forces raised in North Carolina pursuant to authority, from January 10, 1776, to October 24, 1779.

£300 were spent to supply the necessities " of divers persons well affected to the government who have been obliged by the persecution of the rebels to take refuge on board the shipping in Cape Fear River "; also other items regarding prisoners and provincial officers, medicine, attendance, provisions, etc. The names of individuals are given and a large amount of detailed information of interest for North Carolina. 1776-1779.

140. *Id.,* Gov. Melville of St. Vincent, Dominica, Grenada, and Tobago. 1765-1772.

1261. 147-151. *Id.,* East Florida, Gov. J. Moultrie and Lieut.-Gen. Patrick Tonyn, and Agents W. Knox and J. Cowan. 1772-1786.

Roll 147 contains Moultrie's account of the expense of building the state house at St. Augustine (£3283 19s. 2½d.) and the costs incurred in making roads in East Florida. Roll 148 contains an account of contingent and extraordinary expenses, in which the object of the expenditure is stated. Alexander Skinner was the keeper of " Indian presents " and many unitemized entries of such presents may be found. This roll furnishes an elaborate and interesting account, in form different from the usual declaration. Roll 149 mentions money spent for presents and for the expenses of the Indian congress. Roll 150 mentions the salary of William Gerard de Brahm as £150 a year with £30 for an assistant. Roll 151 is valuable for the names and official titles given; it shows that Florida was not actually handed back to Spain until 1786.

152-155. *Id.,* West and East Florida, Govs. Johnstone, Grant, and Chester. 1767-1781.

Roll 152 covers presents to the Indians, sundry expenses in settling the various trade treaties, in determining boundary lines of possession with the various tribes of Indians surrounding West Florida, and for attending congresses held with the Choctaw, Chickasaw, Cusatee, and all the Creek Indians. The items furnish many interesting details, including references to congresses with the Indians and other forms of intercourse. Roll 153 mentions a congress held at Pensacola with the Creeks, May 24–June 7, 1765. Roll 154 contains an account of money received and expended for the " Distrest Greek Settlement at Smyrna in East Florida ", 1769-1770. Total £2000, spent for provisions, tools, implements, and necessaries. Andrew Turnbull had the matter in charge. In all these rolls are references to Elias Durnford. Roll 155 (in bundle **1261** not in **1262** as *List* says) contains interesting items of expense, many details with dates of payments for the Indian Department.

1262. 156-159. *Id.,* Agents Ellis and Leake.

1263. 162-170. *Id.,* Georgia, Agents B. Martyn, C. Garth, J. Campbell, J. B. West. 1752-1783. For example:

162. Declaration of the Account of Benjamin Martyn, Esq. Agent on behalf of the Publick for the Colony of Georgia in America, to

which office he was appointed by warrant under his Majesty's royal sign manual, dated February 14, 1753, of money imprested to him out of the Receipt of his Majesty's Exchequer for the use of the said colony and of his issuing and paying the same for salaries and incident charges paid by the President and Assistants of said colony in Georgia; as also for the charges attending the silk culture and other disbursements and allowances from the surrender of the Charter by the late Trustees, etc. 1752-1773.

This account records not only the financial history of the colony but also its official organization; among the items are such as these: " for cleaning the council room ", " for medicine and provisions and necessaries for sick people and Indians ", " for wine supplied on rejoicing days and for firing the cannon and other disbursements ", " for gunpowder, paint, and other goods for presents to the Indians ". The entries contain considerable information regarding the culture of silk, and mention is made of parcels of raw Georgia silk sold at public auction in London. This series of Georgia accounts extends to 1783.

1273. 242. *Id.,* Lieut.-Gen. Keppel, governor and commander-in-chief of Havana. 1762-1763.

1274. 248A-253. *Id.,* various accounts relating to Jamaica. 1661-1675.

Rolls 248A, 248E, 249, contain statements of Sir James Draxe and Thomas Povey, members of the Council for Plantations, and of the committee appointed on the affairs of Jamaica and New England, as to certain expenditures for brandy and the maintenance of ministers incurred in behalf of that island. The other rolls contain declarations by Governors Windsor, Lyttelton, Modyford, and Lynch of various charges and expenses.

1275. 254-256. *Id.,* Gov. Keith of Jamaica, Lieut.-Gen. Dalling, governor and commander-in-chief, Gen. A. Campbell, governor and commander-in-chief. 1774-1784.

1282. 314. *Id.,* Gov. Hopson of Louisburg. 1747-1749.

1295. 432. *Id.,* John Wentworth, governor of New Hampshire, of the money received for the value of bills drawn by him on the Lords Commissioners of the Treasury, which were paid at the Bank of England; also for money received at the Treasury by Paul Wentworth, for his use, and of the several sums of money by him issued and paid for the support of himself and family, and to aid and succour sundry refugees, etc.; for the hire of a vessel for their passage from Boston to Halifax and New York; for sundry stores and necessaries, etc. 1775-1777.

From the record it would appear that Gov. Wentworth did not hesitate to charge the British government with whatever he wanted in the way of luxuries—wine, walnuts, rum, porter, etc.

1300. 473. *Id.,* Maj.-Gen. W. Tryon, Captain General and Governor of New York, also late Gov. of North Carolina, of the money (received Nov. 26, 1776–Apr. 26, 1779) and of disbursements between Jan. 19, 1775 (" the time the Rebellion broke out in those Parts ") and Mar. 22, 1780 (" when he was superseded in the said government "), including extra services and expenditures occasioned by the said Rebellion, and his loss by fire when the governor's house at Fort George was destroyed.

Every item in this account is of interest and value.

477-479. *Id.,* Governors Hopson, Arbuthnot, and Parr of Nova Scotia. 1752-1753, 1776-1779, 1782-1792.

1301. 482-483. ⎫
1302. 484-487. ⎬ *Id.,* Agents Kilby (1749-1758) and Cumberland (1758-
1303. 488-489. ⎭ 1785) of Nova Scotia.

1311. 532. *Id.,* Gov. W. Patterson of Prince Edward Island (St. John). 1780-1787.

1316. 579. *Id.,* Gov. Valentine Morris of St. Vincent. 1776-1779.

1324. 624. *Id.,* Gen. R. Burton, governor of Three Rivers. 1760-1763.

626. *Id.,* Robert Dinwiddie, late Lieut.-Governor of Virginia, for the sum impressed to him by the Paymaster General of his Majesty's Forces . . . and the application thereof for defraying the charges and expenses for clothing, provisions, and necessaries supplied the independent companies of several provinces, employed in the expedition to the Ohio, for presents made to the different tribes of Indians, for the charge in building a fort in the Cherokee Nation, etc. 1755.

This roll contains the expense account of the Braddock expedition, rendered by Gov. Dinwiddie. It shows the character of the equipment and the expenses en route.

627. *Id.,* The Right Hon. John, Earl of Dunmore, governor of Virginia, of the money received from the Paymaster General of his Majesty's Forces . . . and of the expenditure thereof in raising several regiments in North America, between Nov. 1, 1775, and May 2, 1777, including bounty money to recruits.

This account mentions the Ethiopian Regiment, Queen's Own Loyal Virginia Regiment, Troop of Light Horse; and among the many items has the following: " This accountant for keeping open table for the officers of the army and navy and for persons coming for protection or on business on board the fleet in Virginia, £861."

HANAPER.

KEEPER OR CLERKS.

The accounts of the clerks of the Hanaper, extending from 1605 to 1783, are in bundles **1363-1412** of the Audit Office series, and in rolls **1640-1722**, 1605-1715, of the Pipe Office series.

The clerk of the Hanaper received all the sixpences (23 George II., c. 25) due the crown for affixing the great seal upon charters, letters patent, commissions and writs. Either he or his deputy was obliged to attend the keeper of the great seal, usually the Lord Chancellor, every day in term time and at all times when the seal was to be affixed, with hampers in ancient times but later with leather bags, wherein were put all sealed charters, patents, etc., which were afterward delivered to the comptroller of the hamper. He paid a regular allowance to the Lord Chancellor for diet, liveries, robes, wax, wine, etc. One of his duties was to take account of all grants that passed the great seal and to register the same in his office (see *Guide,* I. 272, note 1). The name " Hanaper " arose from the custom of keeping the papers " in hanaperio ". For payments from the Hanaper Office see *Treas.* 1 : **382,** f. 194, and for the fees paid on passing a patent through the seals, *id.* : **340,** ff. 42-52, **391,** ff. 128-133. The office was abolished in 1845, 8-9 Victoria, c. 34.

The hanaper accounts are occasionally of value for colonial history. See, for example, the *Report* of the Connecticut Historical Society, 1899, pp. 17-20. They show the money received on sealing writs and commissions and on granting various kinds of patents. The names of persons in whose favor the patents were granted are given and historical notes are frequently added.

HOSPITALS AND INFIRMARIES.

1504. 206. Declaration of the account of J. Cathcart, director and purveyor of the hospital for the sick and wounded in the expedition to the West Indies under Lord Cathcart. 1740-1742.

1505. 211. *Id.*, J. Cathcart, director and purveyor of the hospital for the sick and wounded in the expedition to North America under Lieut.-Gen. St. Clair. 1746-1747.

1506. 213. *Id.*, J. Napier, director of the hospitals for the forces employed on an expedition to North America under Maj.-Gen. Braddock. Also inspector general of the regimental infirmaries and chief director of the hospitals there. 1755-1763.

215. *Id.*, G. Corryn, purveyor to hospitals on an expedition against Guadeloupe under Gen. P. T. Hopson and Gen. Barrington. 1758-1760.

217. *Id.*, J. A. F. Hesse, appointed to issue money to several officers of hospitals in (among others) Jamaica, Guadeloupe, and Havana. 1758-1764.

1518. 261. *Id.*, J. Mallet, purveyor to the hospitals in North America. 1775-1783.

262. *Id.*, J. M. Nooth. 1775-1778.

263. *Id.*, W. Barr. 1776-1784.

1519. 264. *Id.*, Dr. G. Young, surgeon to the hospital in St. Vincent. 1777-1779.

265. *Id.*, J. McNamara Hayes, physician to the hospital with the army in North America. 1777-1778.

266. *Id.*, R. Roberts, director and purveyor to the hospital for prisoners in America. 1778-1779.

267. *Id.*, Dr. J. Jeffries, purveyor to the hospitals at Halifax in Nova Scotia. 1778-1779.

268. *Id.*, J. Stewart, Leeward Islands. 1782-1784.

1522. 278. *Id.*, Andrew Turnbull, purveyor to the General Hospital in the West Indies. 1795-1798.

INDIANS (NORTH AMERICA).

1530. 1. Declaration of Account of Benjamin Martyn, Esq., late agent for the Province of Georgia in America . . . of money imprested to him by the Paymaster General of his Majesty's Forces, for purchasing of presents to be sent to the Indians bordering on the Province of Georgia, and of his issuing and expending the same to sundry tradesmen for goods, wares, and merchandize bought for presents sent to the said Indians and sundry expenses in the insuring of said goods and in the lading and carriage thereof, in the years 1755, 1756, 1758, 1760, 1761, 1763.

This account gives detailed statement of the character of the presents, the value of which amounted to £9322.

2. *Id.*, Sir John Johnson, legal representative of Sir William Johnson, Bart., later sole agent and Superintendent of Indian affairs in the northern district of North America, of the sum of £146,545 expended between the years 1755 and 1774. " Which said accountant stated to the Court of Exchequer the impossibility of rendering any vouchers in support thereof, his father's property and papers having been plundered and destroyed by the Rebels, owing to the active part which he took in favor of the British Government."

The items, which were allowed by the Exchequer, included salaries, expenses of negotiations with the Indians, presents, and contingent and incidental expenses. The destruction mentioned occurred when Johnson Hall in Tryon County, New York, was plundered and burned in May, 1776. The account contains no detailed statement of the nature of the presents, but is full of information regarding the working of the Department of Indian Affairs.

3. *Id.*, John Pownall of £4000 expended in procuring presents for the Indians bordering on the colonies. 1756.

The presents were sent from London to New York and a long detailed list of them is here given. No particular Indian tribes are mentioned.

4. *Id.*, James Wright, late agent of the province of South Carolina, of expenditure of £2000 for purchasing " an assortment of goods, such as should be thought proper by the Lords Commissioners of Trade and Plantations to be provided and consigned by him to the governor of the province of South Carolina and distributed as presents in order to preserve and strengthen the friendship of other Indians and for the more effectually establishing and securing the British power and dominion in the southern portion of North America ". 1758.

Lists of articles sent, which differ somewhat from the presents mentioned in other lists.

5. *Id.*, Col. Guy Johnson, late superintendent of Indian Affairs in the Northern District. 1774-1783.

This account contains no detailed lists of presents, but mentions in many instances the Indians to whom the presents were sent. It refers also to numerous expeditions and gives many important and interesting bits of information.

6. *Id.*, Lieut.-Col. John Campbell, deceased, superintendent of Indian Affairs in North America, from Oct. 8, 1775, to June 25, 1785.

Unimportant except for detailed information of the presents.

1531. 7. *Id.*, Capt. Alexander Fraser, superintendent of Indian Affairs in the Northern District. 1776-1783.

Many interesting and peculiar items such as " a cow for a war feast, £5 "; also information regarding Indians in the service of the British government.

8. *Id.*, Daniel Claus, agent of the Indian Department of Six Nations in Canada from 1777 to 1802.

Such items as " Hogs for war feasts ", pay of an Indian schoolmaster and clerk of the Indian church; reference to " Gen. Ross' Expedition to the Rebel Country ".

9. *Id.*, Lieut.-Col. Thomas Brown, as superintendent of Indian Affairs in the Atlantic Department of the Southern District of North America, of money received and spent for salaries of assistants, interpreters, and others, for rations, rum, and sundries. 1779-1784.

Interesting and valuable; references to presents, etc., chiefly for Creeks and Cherokees. For Johnstone's account, 1764-1767, see *A. O. Accounts, Various,* **126** (2).

10. *Id.*, Lieut.-Col. John Graham, Superintendent of the Affairs of the Choctaws, Chickasaws, and other nations of Indians in the southern district of North America, lying on the Mississippi. 1782-1783.

Longer and fuller than the other rolls and of value, as are all the accounts, for a study of the British policy toward the Indians in America. Items concern salaries, presents, provisions, carriage, etc.

11. *Id.*, John Douglass, of the money by him received and expended as Deputy Superintendent of Indian Affairs for the western division of the Southern District in North America. July 1, 1783–Dec. 31, 1784.

Deals with Choctaws and Chickesaws.

NAVY: PAYMASTER OF MARINES.

1827. 530. Declaration of the account of T. Dunn, Quebec. 1775-1786.

POLICE.

1949. 1. Declaration of Account of Andrew Elliot, Esq., Superintendent General of the Port and Police of New York, appointed by proclamation of Maj.-Gen. William Howe, of money received and of the issuing and expenditure of the same for salaries and sundry necessary disbursements, between July 18, 1777, and Nov. 1, 1782.

The disbursements covered printing proclamations, stationery, office furniture, repairs, etc. But no clear idea of the functions of the department in question can be obtained from this document.

2. *Id.*, James Simpson, Intendant General of the Police of South Carolina and Secretary to the Commission to restore peace to the revolted colonies of North America, of money received and of the issue and expenditure thereof, for salaries, expressage, stationery, printing, etc.

Two items refer to the proclamations issued by the commissioners: " For the use of the Rev. Mr. Leydecker for translating into the German language a long manifesto and Declaration, £21..15..6⅔ "; " For the use of Mr. Sowers for translating the Declaration of the Commissioners into the German language, £6..10..8 ". There are also included Simpson's expenses in travelling as secretary of the commission from Georgia to New York and thence to South Carolina and back to New York.

SECRET SERVICE.

2122. 1, 2. Declaration of Account of Maj. Robert Mathews, as military secretary to Gen. Haldimand, of the money received by him from the Paymaster General through the deputy paymaster at Quebec, and of the expenditure thereof for sundry private and particular services, gratuities, procuring intelligence, fitting out Indian scouts, expresses, stationery, etc., from June 24, 1779, to Nov. 11, 1784.

The information furnished by these accounts is meagre. The fact is mentioned that the office of commissary of prisoners was discontinued in Dec., 1782.

3. *Id.,* Maj.-Gen. Edward Mathews, of the money by him received of the Paymaster General, whilst on service in the West Indies, for pay, secret service or otherwise, from Oct. 26, 1781, to July 24, 1784, and from Oct. 20, 1787, to Dec. 24, 1792.

Of little importance. No suggestion as to the character of the secret service.

4. *Id.,* Brevet Maj. George Beckwith, of the money received by him of the Paymaster General by the hands of the deputy paymaster at New York and of the expenditure thereof for secret services by order of his excellency Sir Guy Carleton, from July 19, 1782, to Nov. 18, 1783.

Total amount £4495; no mention of the character of the service.

SETTLERS IN NOVA SCOTIA.

2131. 1, 2. Declarations of the accounts of various persons charged with the business of settling emigrants in the colony of Nova Scotia; and of transporting foreign Protestants to the same colony in 1751, 1752, 1753, pursuant to an agreement with the Board of Trade.

Roll 1 is of no particular importance except for the subject in question; 2 is of considerable value.

STAMP DUTIES.

2192. 207. The Comptroller General's Declaration of the General Account of the several duties arising on stamped vellum, parchment, and paper in the British colonies and plantations in America. 1765.

This account is of great interest and value. It shows that the total amount received by the government for the stamped paper sent to America was £224,119 0s. 4d.; that of this sum the government paid to the three warehouse-keepers of stamped goods, who acted as intermediaries and took the paper from the government, £160-043 7s. 10½d., for salaries, incident charges, and allowances for stamps and goods returned from North America; and that there remained in the hands of distributors in America unaccounted for (destroyed ?), at the time the account was made up, goods and stamps to the value of £64,155 12s. 5½d. The account further states that the government was enabled to sell damaged parchment paper returned from America to the amount of £1481. It contains also a complete list of all the colonial receivers of stamps with the arrears due in goods, money, or bonds, as, (Name) Jared Ingersoll, (Colony) Connecticut, (Amount) £1909 10s. 11d., from Canada to the West Indies, including Florida.

TRADE.

2303. 1. The Declaration of the Account of William Popple for the sum of £450 by him received and laid out of the Receipt of Exchequer upon account to be by him expended and laid out for incidental charges relating to the Commission for Trade and Plantations; being in part an order for £1000 payable to him for that service, the tenour whereof ensueth [recital of warrants follows], and of the issuing and expending thereof between Mar. 25, 1696, and Mar. 25, 1701.

A few items of interest for the history of the Board of Trade and the establishment of the Plantation Office.

2. The Declaration of the Account of John Lock[e], secretary and treasurer for the late Council for Trade and Plantations, *viz.*: of the money by himself or his agents received and had (whereas his Majesty by his commission under the Great Seal bearing date 27 September, 1672, hath for the better carrying on of his service been pleased to grant to this council the yearly sum of £1000).

This account itemizes the expenses of the council during its period of service.

TRANSPORT SERVICE.

2305. 12. Declaration of the account of Atkinson and Roope for transporting troops from England to Spain and the West Indies. 1702-1703.

TREASURY SOLICITOR.

2311. 1-6.
2312-2337. 7-128.
} This long series of rolls beginning as early as 1657 continues in an almost unbroken sequence to 1827. Each roll is entered in the printed list by the name of the solicitor for the year, and the same name, as for example that of Joshua Sharpe,[1] colonial agent and brother of Gov. Horatio Sharpe of Maryland, will be found recurring regularly for many years. The rolls before 1660 are of no importance for colonial history, but after that date they contain a great many references to colonial matters, particularly to the costs and charges attending suits and causes. The business of the treasury solicitor was to prosecute law-suits in the Exchequer Court and elsewhere. The expenses incurred, which are itemized in these rolls in detail, include the cost of searching records, drawing and carrying documents, attendance on the suit, fees to council and witnesses, obtaining information, employing messengers, passing patents, deeds, warrants, etc. The rolls vary considerably as to the amount of information furnished; they tend to grow more elaborate as they increase in number.

In order to show the character of the data given in these rolls of value for colonial history a few selected items are here printed:

2311. 5. " To several officers and other clerks for their fees in passing a patent under the Great Seal of England with several instructions thereby empowering Mr. Randolph to be Customer and Comptroller of his Mats Customes in New England."

2312. 8. " For drawing and engrossing a surrender of the Vt. parte of the province of New Hampshire in New England in America . . . xxx sh."

" To the Attorney Genl for perusal thereof . . . xliii sh iiii d."

" To the Master in Chancery for acknowledgement and enrolling thereof in Chancery . . . xxxv sh. vi d."

---

[1] There was another brother John Sharpe, who was also a solicitor and colonial agent. For Sharpe correspondence, see *B. M. Add. MSS., Catal. Index,* 1882-1887.

9. " For the charges and expenses in the prosecuting a quo warranto against the corporation of Massachusetts Bay in New England and for obtaining judgment and seizing the liberties thereof . . . £181..9..10."

" For charges in the proceedings made for avoyding the Lord Culpeper's Commission as governor of Jamaica . . . £82..2..10."

" For charges upon a quo warranto against the Barmudus Company a judgment being recovered and an exemplification sent over . . . £79..18..2."

10. " Expenditure in the cause between Mr. Atty. Genl Plf. and Capt. Shales and others Defts, for receiving of money twice pd upon tallies struck on the Barbados revenue for pay of Col. Stapleton, kgt. etc."

" To Mr. Jowle for carrying on the prosecution against planters of tobacco in England, by order of the treasury." July 30, 1684.

2313. 12. " In the cause between Mr. Culmer, Plt. and Mr Randall [Randolph] Def. for money due on the defendent's bond, defended by order of their Lordships Commrs of the Treasury hee being in the King's service in New England [three items] vi li xii s vi d."

" In the cause between Mr. Atty Genl, Plt. and Massachusetts Bay Defd., upon an information for several misdemeanors in the King's Bench."

" To Councell for drawing the Informačon and for a copy thereof and filing the same . . . lvi sh viii d."

" To the sheriffe for serving the processe and returns thereof . . . xxx sh."

" To Mr. Atty Genl and others of his Maj. Council for moving the Court that the Def. should appear . . . vii li xi sh viii d. And for drawing the Rule thereupon . . . vi sh viii d."

16. " Proceedings on a quo warranto agt Connectucote Island to reduce them to obedience, viz :

Ffor prparing Instručcons for a Quo Warrto : and to the Sheriffe for his summons thereupon and to Mr Normandsell for returning a sumons on the Quo Warrto : and to Mr. Jones for moving the court for Judgmt thereupon . . . iii li xxl sh viii d.

And for drawing the Rule for Judgmt and Letters to and from the Island etc. . . . xviii sh vi d (total . . . v li x sh ii d)." The account was from Mich. Term, 1686–Mich. Term, 1687. " Mr Jones " was " his Maties Councell ".

2315. 24. " For fees paid to the Atty Genl and his Clerks on his attending thrice on the Commrs of Trade by order of the Lords of the Treasury about the Conduct of Col. Fletcher, late govr of New York."

25. " To Jno. Towers for ix cases, for ix commissions under the Great Seal of England for trying pyrates in America . . . iii li xv sh.

" And for sevll expenses about a pretended discovery of a treasure in England and about Pirates goods taken and sent from America . . . xx li xv sh vi d.

" For the remaining part of £1218..5..6 by Sd Atty paid for ix commissions under the Great Seal of England directed to ix of his Maj. Governors in America for trying of pirates there, the charges of each commission coming to £79..16..2, for which the accountant hath produced no acquittance " (1702).

2320. 45. " To John Watt in full of all claims and demands and in recompense to him for his service in the transportation of several families of Palatines to Germany."

" To John Grubb, Clerk of the Patents, for the fees and charges of passing at the several offices xxty commissions for pardons to Pyrates in the Plantations."

47. " Against the Proprietors of the Bahamas Is. to maintain the King's Rights to the Civil and Military Governt there [fees in great detail] . . . lviii li xvii sh vi d."

" Against the proprietors of Carolina for abuse of their charter."

" The Attorney General for fees with a Brief and attending a Committee of the Council twice, as also with a draught of Scire Facias and for a Consultation xxxiii sh xv d ; Sergt Pengelly for perusing the Draught of the Scire Facias, viii sh, viii d. Edward Salter for fees for Council attending committees of the Privy Council at the Cock Pit, xxx sh ; William Rook, Clerk of the Rolls Chapel for a copy of Carolina Charter, vi li iii sh ix d ; and to the Atty Genl, the Solic. Genl, and Sergt Pengelly, their Clerks xxv sh vi d." The total charges were £84 8s. 3d.

2328. 81. " The Honble Charles Yorke, his Majesty's Attorney Genl, for 17 Reports and Draughts prepared by him for the Lords of the Committee of the Council for Trade and Plantations (1767) . . . lxv li xv d."

WORKS AND FORTIFICATIONS.

2531. 662. The declaration of the account of Lieut.-Col. Harry Gordon, as engineer employed in building and repairing several forts and places in North America, from Aug. 18, 1756, to Nov. 26, 1761 ; and as chief engineer from Sept. 16, 1764, to Nov. 25, 1767.

Valuable as disclosing the activities and movements of this British engineer, who was constantly travelling westward and southward repairing forts, making discoveries, draughting maps, etc.

663. *Id.,* John Montrésor. Oct. 1, 1768–Sept. 30, 1778.

The money was spent in erecting and repairing forts and batteries, barracks, magazines, and other public works.

664. *Id.,* Col. William Spry. 1774-1782.

2532. 665. *Id.,* Abraham D'Aubant, commanding engineer in North America. May 6, 1776–May 31, 1782.

666. *Id.,* Col. William Zwiss, comptroller of the works in Canada, July 1, 1776–June 30, 1778 ; and as commanding engineer in the same province, July 1, 1778–June 30, 1784.

667. *Id.,* Col. Mathew Dixon, commanding engineer. Aug. 13, 1776–May 20, 1777.

668. *Id.,* Lieut.-Col. James Moncrief, commanding engineer in the Southern District. July 1, 1778–Dec. 31, 1782.

669. *Id.,* Capt. M. Pitts, commanding engineer at St. Lucia. 1778-1781.

2533. 670. *Id.,* Lieut.-Col. A. Mercer, commanding engineer in North America. 1778-1781.

671. *Id.*, Maj. J. Cambel, commanding engineer in North America. 1779-1780.
672. *Id.*, Capt. T. Hartcup, commanding engineer at Penobscot, 1779-1784; at Halifax, 1783.
673. *Id.*, Lieut. C. Shipley, commanding engineer at St. Lucia, Antigua, and Grenada. 1781-1784.
674. *Id.*, Lieut. D. Stewart, deputy paymaster at Penobscot. 1781-1782.

Interesting as showing the method of distributing the money received.

2534. 675. *Id.*, James Fraser, acting paymaster in the Engineer's Department at New York. June 1–Dec. 31, 1782.

Taken as a whole these rolls furnish little information of value.

LORD CHAMBERLAIN'S PAPERS.

On warrants issued by the Lord Chamberlain to the master of the Jewel House or Office, orders were given to the goldsmiths to make silver communion plate for use in the churches and chapels of the colonies. When completed, such plate was received from the goldsmiths into the Jewel House and a receipt given therefor. From the Jewel House it was handed over to the governor of the colony or to some one authorized to receive it, and transmitted to North America or the West Indies. In but few instances was it an outright gift. Generally it was a loan to the governor for the use of the chapel or church in the colony, designed to be handed on from governor to governor, or, on demand, or when no longer needed, returned to the Jewel House. In all such cases the plate remained the property of the crown.

The plate consisted of two flagons, one chalice, one or two patens, and a receiver or basin. Though the warrant generally limited the value to £80, the actual cost ranged from £56 to £87, and the weight from 180 to 205 oz. In the volumes noted below entries are made of plate loaned to the following colonies: East Florida, West Florida, Barbadoes, Jamaica, Bahamas, Dominica, Leeward Islands, St. Vincent, Bermuda, Quebec, Nova Scotia, St. John, New Hampshire, Massachusetts, New York, North Carolina, South Carolina, Gibraltar, Minorca, and Senegambia. Gifts are recorded to Christ Church, Boston, to the Indian chapels of the Mohawks and Onondagas, and to Trinity Church, New York. The plate to the Mohawk chapel was valued at £140 11s. 0d., and that for the chapel of the Onondagas at the same amount. In a few instances a marginal entry, "Returned into this office", appears in the delivery books; once or twice only part of the plate was returned, and in a few cases a newly commissioned governor found that the plate in the colony had disappeared altogether.

In the same volumes will be found entries of the receipt and delivery of silver plate to the various members of the peace commission sent to America in 1778 and of the peace commission of 1776 and 1779—the Howes, Clinton, Arbuthnot, Digby, Carleton, Eden, Carlisle, and Johnstone. This plate covered a great variety of table silver—knives, forks, spoons, dishes, tureens, covers, ladles, platters, sauceboats, vases, épergnes, coffee-pots, etc., and in each instance weighed 1200 oz. It is receipted for in the delivery books by each commissioner or his agent. In the same volumes are entries of collars of the Order of the Bath for Clinton, Carleton, Ligonier, and Rodney.

The Jewel Office was situated on the ground floor of the building in Whitehall north of Whitehall Court and northeast of the Banqueting Hall, in which were the Privy Seal and Privy Signet offices. The quarters were in bad condition, but the Jewel Office was still there in 1772, though the other offices had been removed in 1760. The silver itself was kept in the Jewel Office or House in the Tower, a dark, strong room to the eastward of the grand storehouse or new armory. For a plan of the room in the Tower see *Treas.* 1: **343. 74.** The Jewel Office was in part suppressed in 1782, *Treas.* 1: **338.**

<table>
<tr><td>Lord
Chamberlain's
Books.
Series I.</td><td>The proper order of the volumes is, 1, Warrant Books,
2, Receipt Books, 3, Delivery Books.</td></tr>
</table>

WARRANT BOOKS.

601-608. 1618-1793. Entry Books of Warrants.

Issued by the Lord Chamberlain to the master of the Jewel House. No warrants for colonial plate appear in the first three volumes. Partly indexed.

RECEIPT BOOKS.

595-599. 1685-1811. Goldsmiths' Books. Plate Books.

Contain entries of plate received from the goldsmiths with details and costs. The volumes are not indexed but marginal headings show the purposes for which the plate was received.

DELIVERY BOOKS.

440, 441, 610. 1700-1796. Delivery Books.

Vol. **440** is rather a day book of deliveries than a classified entry book and is of no importance here. **441** and **610** belong together and are filled with interesting entries of the nature recorded above. The entries furnish date of delivery, the particular pieces of plate, and the weight in ounces, but not the cost.

COMMISSARIAT PAPERS.

At first all supplies for the army were obtained by contract, but later a regular commissariat was established as a department of the Treasury. The head of this department was the commissary-general, who looked after the providing of supplies and of transports, forage, food, drink, etc. The office was not regularly commissioned, as it was called into existence only in time of war and a commissary-general and his deputies were appointed only as part of the customary preparations for war. During the eighteenth century, a constantly increasing number of duties was added to the commissary-general's original functions.

At the time of the American Revolution there existed but three species of contracts—for victualling the land forces abroad; for remitting money for the pay of the troops abroad, and for supplying bread, wood, and forage for the troops at home. In victualling the forces abroad information was first obtained from the Victualling Board of the prices of the several articles of provision that formed the ration;[1] then the Treasury made its proposals to the contractors, received from them proposals in return, and finally struck a bargain in the form of a compromise between them. Victualling contracts were made annually, the provisions were delivered at Cowes or Cork to agents appointed by the Navy Board, and then transported to America by the Commissioners of the Navy. The agents granted certificates to the contractors, which the latter produced at the Treasury. The Treasury referred them to the comptroller of army accounts for review, on whose endorsement the money was paid. The commissary-general in England does not appear to have had supervision of provisions sent to America, but to have been concerned only with the bread, wood, and forage for home encampments, the contracts for which were often "very fallaciously stated". Provisions shipped to America were received by the commissaries-general there.

The accounts here listed are Treasury papers, but are collected separately under their own title. Other commissariat accounts will be found in the Treasury and War Office series. The numbers here described are the reports of Brook Watson, commissary-general in New York at the end of the Revolution. They consist of long rolls mounted on linen.

Brook Watson, afterward Sir Brook, was known as "the wooden-legged commissary", having lost a leg in 1749. He came to America before the French and Indian War and remained here, residing at Halifax, Quebec, Montreal, Boston, and New York, until after the peace of 1783. He travelled widely and acquired an intimate knowledge of colonial conditions, so that after his return to England he was frequently called upon by the government for information. His experiences as commissary began as early as 1755, when he served under Monckton at Beauséjour and later under Wolfe at Quebec, and were continued during his tenure as commissary-general under Carleton in 1782 (*W. O. 28: 9*). There is a brief life of him in the *Dictionary*

---

[1] The ration remained about the same for army and navy (*Treas.* 1: **380**). In 1781 the commissary at Charleston recommended an alteration but the Treasury refused to consider it.

of National Biography, but it is very deficient in all that concerns his American career. Watson went to England in 1774, in the same ship with John Singleton Copley, who painted his portrait, and again in 1775, in the ship that carried Ethan Allen, who had been captured at Montreal shortly before. He was a man of character, integrity, and ability.

Commissariat Accounts. —

11. 1782. Table of Clothing, Provisions, etc., received and issued in North America. 1782. Contains a general account of clothing, blankets, stores, horses, wagons, provisions, rum, vessels, hulks, scows, boats and stores thereunto belonging, fuel, candles, forage, from June 30 to Dec. 31, 1782. From Brook Watson, commissary-general.

12. 1782. " Account General with the Crown, being for receipt and expenditure of £248,594..0..10[4] stg. received and expended by him in the district of New York, between the 22d day of May, 1782, when he took charge of the Department, to the 31st day of December, following, when with the approbation of the Commander in Chief he delivered over the King's Stores to officers appointed to different departments under his direction and control, the said Commissary General continuing no longer a Public Accountant, but for the purpose of closing and finally passing his accounts being all composed in this general state."

13. 1782-1783. " A General Account of all provisions and rum—fuel and candles—forage—horses, waggons, etc.—clothing, blankets, stores, and materials—vessels, hulks, scows, boats, etc.—Received, issued, etc., in the district of New York, Under the direction and comptrol of Brook Watson, Esq, Commissary General to the army in North America, serving under the Command of his Excellency General Sir Guy Carleton, Knight of the Bath, Commander in Chief, etc., Commencing on the twenty seventh day of May, anno 1782, when he took charge of this commissariat and ending on the fifth day of December, anno 1783, when the army sailed from the port of New York and the said commissary general's charge terminated."

A very large manuscript roll, mounted. The length of the roll is about fifteen feet, its height six.

For supplemental papers see *A. O. Accounts, Various,* **481**, and *W. O.* 57: **24-33**.

CUSTOM HOUSE PAPERS.

INTRODUCTION.

Until 1671 the customs duties of England were let out to farm, but in September of that year the king appointed a board of commissioners to manage the customs revenue, though some of the farms were not wound up till 1676. The appointees were Sir George Downing, Sir William Lowther, Sir William Thompson, William Garway, Francis Millington, and John Upton, each at £2000 a year, and they had a secretary and a solicitor. The board served for England and Wales only, until 1723, when Scotland was added and the number of commissioners was raised to fourteen, seven of whom were to reside in London, five in Edinburgh, and two, travelling commissioners, were to take charge of the outports. In 1742 the commission was divided, nine for England and Wales and five for Scotland. This arrangement continued until 1823.

The duties of the commission were to collect the revenue, to appoint or remove inferior officers under warrant from the Treasury, and in general to administer the whole customs service. Some time later a receiver general was appointed to keep separate accounts of the standing customs and temporary imposts, and surveyors general, to visit and inspect " all ports and creeks throughout the realm ". Goods could be landed in London at some twenty specified wharves between the Tower and Blackfriars Station, from Tower dock to Puddle dock, while certain commodities could be discharged or laden in midstream. For the collection of the duty enjoined by the act of 25 Charles II., special collectors of customs were appointed in America and the West Indies, and such officials were directly under the control of the commissioners in England until 1767, when a board of American commissioners was created with headquarters at Boston. The collectors of Bridgetown (Barbadoes), Roseau (Dominica), Grenville Bay (Grenada), Kingston and Montego Bay (Jamaica), Sandy Point (St. Christopher), and the ports of Montserrat and other Leeward Islands remained subject to the old board, but those of Accomac, Bermuda, Boston, Beaufort, Brunswick, Chester and Patapsco, Charleston, Halifax, James River, upper and lower, Mobile, Nantucket, New York, New Haven, Newfoundland, New London, Potomac, Philadelphia, Patuxent, Pensacola, Piscataqua, Plymouth, Pocomoke, Rhode Island, Rappahannock, Sunbury, Salem and Marblehead, Savannah, Salem and Cohenzie (Cohansey), and York River were transferred to the establishment books of the board in America.

Certain officials and clerks were appointed in the London Custom House to have charge and supervision of the revenues from the plantations. These were the " western and plantation clerk " (£250), " the solicitor of debts standing out in the plantation receipts " or the " examiner of officers' security and the solicitor of the payment of debts standing out in the plantation receipts " (£100), with a clerk (£20), the " viewer and examiner of tobacco, inward and outward " (£250), and the " surveyor of the acts of navigation " (£100), an assistant (£30), and two watermen (£60). From 1663 to 1684 the four-and-a-half per cent. duty was farmed, first for £7000 and then for £5000 a year, and managers were appointed in Barbadoes and the Leeward

Islands to collect the duty and render an accounting to the farmers.[1] In 1684 the control of the duty was taken over by the commissioners, who appointed a " husband of the four-and-a-half per cent " (£100), a clerk (£50), and a " check to the husband " (£40). In the islands the duty was generally paid in sugar, which was sent to London and stored in a separate warehouse, where three times a year it was put up at auction and sold.[2] This duty, according to a conservative estimate, produced about twice as much as all the other plantation duties put together. After 1768 the staff of clerks in the Custom House, that had to do with American revenues, was reduced by the discontinuation of the offices of the assistant plantation clerk and the assistant to the husband of the four-and-a-half per cent.[3]

The Board of Customs in England had to do largely with the enforcement of the acts of trade, and with the collection of the plantation duty imposed by the act of 1672. This duty was established not so much as a source of revenue as to prevent trade with Europe, and the collections in the earlier years, particularly from Virginia and Maryland, where the large rivers and the great distances rendered the work of the collectors difficult, were very meagre, the whole produce of the imposition being little more than sufficient to defray the officers' salaries and the incident charges for boat hire.[4] After 1696, with the increased number of collectors and the improved condition of the service, the amount became larger and the net returns sufficient to constitute an item in the commissioners' states of the revenue.[5]

The Commissioners of the Customs had no power of appointment, but they were able to control the personnel of the establishment through their right to nominate and approve. They named the leading customs officials in America and approved or disapproved of the minor officials selected by the surveyors general there, but in all cases the actual appointment lay in the hands of the Treasury.[6] Apparently all the officials on the colonial establishment received their authority, pay, leaves of absence, instructions, and power to

---

[1] Blathwayt's Journal, Library of Congress transcript, I. 75, 183, 378.

[2] Atton and Holland, *The King's Customs*, I. 102-104, 146; *Treas.* 38: **255**. " Four and a half per cent. is remitted from the West Indies in sugar, etc, to the husband of the 4½ per cent., and by him sold, and the nett produce brought to account. There are pensions, salaries, etc., payable out of the fund by patent, by privy seal, and by king's warrant. Some of these are payable by the hands of the husband, who having satisfied the same, as they become due, pays the surplus into the Exchequer, which is applied to satisfy the charges upon it payable at the Exchequer. The payments by the husband are made without any further instrument than that originally granting them. Those at the Exchequer are paid pursuant to warrant and order, as there is money to satisfy the same; except the Treasury think fit to grant a preference. This revenue is under the management of the Commissioners of the Customs." *Chatham Papers,* **231** (1782-1783).

[3] Brit. Mus. *Add. MSS.* **8133 C.**

[4] Blathwayt's Journal, Library of Congress transcript, I. 354.

[5] For references, see below, *Treas.* 38: **346-348.**

[6] " Appointments to all places on the establishment of the Customs are by instruments arising at the Treasury. Some hold by patent, some by commission under the hands of the Lords of the Treasury, and others, by much the major part, are by warrant to the Commissioners of the Customs to issue their deputation to the person therein named.

" Incident officers are appointed by the commissioners themselves and deputies to patent officers by the principals, when the Treasury does not interfere; but the person is more frequently recommended to the commissioners and to the patent officers by a letter from the secretary of the Treasury.

" When the commissioners find any incidental officers necessary to be continued, they by memorial recommend the establishment of such officers, which is done by warrant on the commissioners memorial." *Chatham Papers,* **231** (1782-1783).

hire boats and boatmen by means of Treasury warrants. From 1767 to October 16, 1783, this method of procedure was changed by the creation of the American board. During those years, some of the incidental officers, but not those on the establishment, were appointed by the board in England, others by the surveyors general in the colonies, with the approval of the American board, and still others by the American board itself. The commissioners in England not only drew up special instructions for the colonial officials, but also wrote the general instructions to the governors, as far as these instructions concerned the part which the governors were to play in upholding the collectors and surveyors in the performance of their duties. The same was true of all colonial laws that affected trade. Such laws were sent by the Board of Trade to the Customs Commissioners for approval and ratification.

Before the end of the colonial period the British customs organization and administration had become hopelessly complicated and inefficient, involving great losses of revenue through smuggling, corruption of officials, and sinecures. The systems of collection and account were " preposterous ", and bookkeeping at the Custom House itself was a " hopeless muddle ".[1] The figures given for the plantation revenues must always be used with caution, as the accounts were invariably in arrears, and it is far from clear that the sums recorded actually represent the net produce for each year. In fact, it is evident that in many years the collection charges exceeded the gross revenue.

There have been five custom houses in London, all on the same or approximately the same site. Three of these houses were destroyed by fire. The first was built in 1385, on the site occupied by its immediate successors. The second was built in Queen Elizabeth's reign and burned in 1666. The third, designed by Sir Christopher Wren, was built in 1668, at an expense of £10,000, and was destroyed by fire in 1711. This building was principally of brick, but the lower story, which was of the Tuscan order, had stone columns. The upper story was in the Ionic style, with pilasters and pediments. While the new quarters were in preparation, the commissioners had offices in the house of Lord Bayninge in Mark Lane. The fourth structure, a much larger and more commodious building, designed by Ripley, was erected a short distance west of the old site, and it too, somewhat altered later, was burned down on January 12, 1814. At this time the papers, which seem to have been saved in 1711, were in large part destroyed. The fifth and present building was erected in 1817.[2]

Congreve, Rowe, and Prior, the poets, Sir Dudley North, and Adam Smith all served either as officials or commissioners of customs.

---

[1] For an elaborate statement of conditions at this time, see Atton and Holland, *op. cit.*, pp. 356-370.

[2] An illustration of the second building is given in Allen, *London*, III. 744, but a better print is the frontispiece to Chester's *Chronicles of the Custom Department*. Many illustrations of the third building may be found, Besant, *London in the Seventeenth Century*, p. 191, Lambert, *History of London*, III. 385, Chester, *Chronicles*, p. 75. For references to the fire of 1711 see *A. O., Decl. Acc.*, **788**, 988, and 1 George II., c. 2 (private acts). See also Hatton, *New View*, II. 601. For illustrations of the fourth building see *Microcosm of London*, I. 217, Dodsley, *London and its Environs*, II. 212, Chester, *Chronicles*, p. 76 (both original design and alteration) ; and for the building burned, Pennant, *London*, II. 64. For the present structure, see Shepherd, *Views of London*, Chester, *Chronicles*, p. 78 (original buildings).

Bundles and volumes containing Custom House accounts may be found among the Colonial Office Papers, the Treasury Papers, and the series described below, which is composed of original Custom House documents, the greater part of which appear to have been deposited at the time in the Treasury. Some 565 volumes were transferred thence to the Custom House in 1835 and of these 438 were removed to the Rolls House in 1848 and the remainder in 1851. Many volumes were brought directly from the Treasury Chambers in 1846, 1847, and 1853. A number of volumes were returned to the Custom House in 1853 and 1854.

Except for certain volumes, hereafter to be described, there are in the Custom House today no volumes of correspondence, minutes, or accounts of date earlier than 1814. There are, however, in the Custom House library nineteen volumes of minutes of the Scottish board, 1723-1783 (described below), a calendar of outport records (Greenock), letters to the commissioners of the port of Whitehaven, 1775-1785, and a collection of " Customs Papers, Seizures after 1814 ", which contain many documents relating to smuggling in the Canadian provinces and the seizure of American vessels trading contrary to the navigation acts.[1]

The bundles in the Treasury series that contain customs accounts will be found in *Treasury, Classes* 38 and 64, to which the searcher may be referred (pp. 215-220, 237, 238) ; those of the Board of Trade series may be found among the *Colonial Office Papers, Class* 390 : **5-12**, already described in the preceding volume (pp. 262-265), but of which a supplementary account is given here, together with a brief entry of a few volumes now in the Modern Board of Trade series.

BOARD OF TRADE SERIES.

C. O. 390.	**6.** 1677-1731. Custom House Accounts, Exports and Imports. AP.
	7. 1670-1729. Custom House Accounts. AD.
	8. 1712-1717. Custom House Accounts. AK.
	9. 1725-1771. Custom House Accounts.

10. 1750-1765. *Id.*

11. 1714-1757. Index to Custom House Accounts.

The significance of the letters AP, AD, and AK is not apparent. All of these volumes belonged to the regular Board of Trade series and are those referred to in other Board of Trade volumes and the calendars, as " Custom House Accounts " (see preceding volume, p. 105). But the calendar (**11**) omits many of the documents here bound up and lists others which are not here. Some of the latter can be found in the old Plantation General series (*C. O.* 323 : **1-29**) or in the old Trade series (*C. O.* 388 : **2-58**). The calendar enters documents for the period, June 17, 1726, to about Feb., 1732, only. Some other arrangement of the Custom House accounts that were sent to the Board of Trade must have been in vogue when the calendar was made, since

---

[1] On this subject see *Reports of the Commissioners on Special Revenue Inquiry during the Years 1812, 1813, 1814* (London), a report on the Canadian and West Indian colonies.

we find references to volumes that cannot now be identified, as " A, 1743-1745 ", and " Large Books of Custom House Accounts ".

6 is an entry book of the Board of Trade, containing tables of exports and imports, arranged under the name of colony or subject—Newfoundland (fishery and inhabitants), Jamaica (goods), Barbadoes (goods), Leeward Islands (goods), Virginia (goods exported and shipping), Maryland (goods exported), Italy, Spain, Portugal (" State of the Trade "), East India (goods and ships), Coinage, Naval Stores (from all countries, including the plantations, 1701-1723). Also a " Scheme of the Fishery of Newfoundland ", 1720, 1722-1727, 1729-1731, by Capt. Percy. Also tables of goods imported and exported, Jamaica, 1718-1722. Also " Account of all Gold and Silver coined in the Tower, from the last day of December, 1689, to 1710 ".

9 is also a Board of Trade volume, containing the original reports sent from the Custom House at the request of the board in the years 1760-1772. There would seem to be some duplicating of information in the lists. Early returns are of hemp and rice imported, 1752-1762; hats exported, 1735-1738, 1750-1753, 1759-1762; beaver skins, imported and exported, 1735-1738, 1750-1753, 1759-1762; beaver wool, exported, 1735-1738, 1750-1753, 1759-1763; beaver skins, imported, 1749-1763.

(From the former *B. T. Commercial,* series II.)

83-88. 1780-1786. Commercial Intercourse.

B. T. 6.

These bundles contain many Custom House accounts, chiefly of date after 1783. They concern commercial intercourse with America and the West Indies, American intercourse with Great Britain, and American intercourse with Newfoundland and Nova Scotia. They are of considerable value for a history of American commercial relations after the attainment of independence by the colonies.

(From the former *B. T. Commercial,* series II.)

CUSTOM HOUSE SERIES.

ACCOUNTS.

INSPECTOR GENERAL'S ACCOUNTS.

Custom House. Accounts. Inspector General's Accounts.

1-10. 1696-1702. Imports and Exports.

Each volume contains summaries of imports and exports from London and the outports to and from the English plantations. Also, an abstract of the amount of the several estimates of the goods imported and exported into or out of London and the outports for each half year, reckoned from Lady Day to Michaelmas and from Michaelmas to Lady Day. The dates and contents of each volume are as follows:

1, Imports, 1696-1697; **2**, Exports, 1696-1697; **3**, Imports, 1697-1698; **4**, Exports, 1697-1698; **5**, Imports and Exports, Michaelmas to Christmas, 1698; **6**, Imports and Exports, Christmas, 1698–Christmas, 1699; **7**, Imports, 1699-1700; **8**, Exports, 1699-1700; **9**, Imports and Exports, 1700-1701; **10**, Imports and Exports, 1701-1702.

IMPORTS AND EXPORTS.

<table>
<tr><td>Custom House.
Accounts.
Ledgers of
Imports and
Exports.
—</td><td>

1-80. 1697-1780. Ledgers of Imports and Exports.

These volumes contain statistics not only for foreign countries (including Newfoundland under that title) but for the plantations also, under the headings given below.

</td></tr>
</table>

Although the order differs in the various volumes and the headings are not always the same, the information here recorded covers essentially the entire series of volumes. The period is sometimes Michaelmas to Michaelmas; sometimes Christmas to Christmas. This series and the inspector general's accounts contain practically the same information for the brief period covered by the latter volumes.

I. London. Importation of English manufactures from Michaelmas to Michaelmas, with an estimate of the values and the subsidy payable thereon.

II. Outports. *Id.*

Where imported and from whence	Goods imported	In English ships	In foreign ships	Estimate of the original cost or value	The amount of that value	Subsidy	New subsidy	Add'l duty	Old import and importation on tobacco, wine, and vinegar	New additional import

III. London. Exportation of English manufactures from Michaelmas to Michaelmas, with an estimate of the values and of the subsidy payable thereon.

Whence exported and where	Goods exported	Quantity	Estimate of the original cost or value	The amount of the value	Subsidy

IV. London. Exportations of foreign goods by certificate (in time [1]) from Michaelmas to Michaelmas, with an estimate of the values, the amount of the subsidies and other duties drawn back by debenture thereon.

V. London. Exportations of foreign goods by certificate (out of time) from Michaelmas to Michaelmas, with an estimate of the values and the amount of the subsidy and other duties payable thereon and left in England.

VI. Outports. Exportations of English manufacture from Michaelmas to Michaelmas, with an estimate of the values and the subsidy payable thereon.

VII. Outports. Exportations of foreign goods by certificate (in time), etc.

VIII. Outports. Exportation of foreign goods by certificate (out of time), etc.

[1] Goods bought on the Continent for exportation had to be re-exported within a given time or lose the drawback. Hence the terms " In Time " and " Out of Time ".

Vol. **28A** in this series contains an account of imports and exports, London and outports, 1728. It has been transferred from the Treasury series and was formerly *Miscellaneous, Various,* **195**. The present numbering is subject to alteration.

IMPORTS AND EXPORTS: AMERICA.

<table>
<tr><td>
Custom House.
Accounts.
Ledgers of
Imports and
Exports.
America.
—
</td></tr>
</table>

1. 1768-1773. America.

    I. An account of the number of vessels which have entered inwards at the several ports in North America, distinguishing the kind of vessels, their tonnage, and voyages.

    II. An account of the number of vessels that have cleared outwards at the several ports in North America.

    III. An account of the imports into the several ports of North America from the British and Foreign West Indies, southern parts of Europe, and the Wine Islands.

    IV. An account of the articles subject to duty imported into the several ports of North America and also the articles that are dutiable upon exportation exported.

    V. An account of the exports from the several ports in North America to Great Britain.

    VI. *Id.* to Ireland.

    VII. *Id.* to the southern parts of Europe, Africa, and the Wine Islands.

    VIII. *Id.* to the British and Foreign West Indies.

    IX. An account of the imports coastwise.

    X. An account of the exports coastwise.

    XI. An account of the imports from the British and Foreign West Indies, parts southward of Cape Finisterre, in Europe, Africa, and the Wine Islands . . . distinguishing the goods which have paid duty at the port of importation from such as are free or have paid duty at ports not under the management of the American Board of Customs.

    XII. An account of the articles on which duty has been paid on importation from the British and Foreign West Indies and on exportation at the several ports in North America.

    XIII. An account of the produce or manufacture of Great Britain and Ireland imported into the several ports of North America from Great Britain and Ireland.

    XIV. An account of the foreign goods and produce imported into the several ports of North America from Great Britain and Ireland.

This list contains but a few of the titles of the documents included in this bulky volume. The statistics are based on the reports sent home by the American Board of Customs Commissioners. Each table covers but one year, and the tables as a whole vary considerably in form and often in content. In some cases the accounts are combined, in others they are rendered as separate tables. The volume is of great value.

IMPORTS AND EXPORTS: IRELAND.

Custom House.
Accounts.
Ledgers of
Imports and
Exports.
Ireland.

1-87. 1698-1783. Ireland.

STATES OF NAVIGATION.

1-8. 1772-1784. States of Navigation.

Custom House.
Accounts.
States of
Navigation.

Contains, among other statistical tables, the following:
I. Accounts of the total number of British and
foreign ships and their tonnage including
their repeated voyages that have entered inwards or cleared outwards in Great Britain,
from or to foreign kingdoms or states or British colonies or settlements in foreign states . . . distinguishing England from Scotland.
II. Accounts of goods, wares, and merchandize imported into England
from British and foreign America . . . distinguishing the species,
quantity, and value of each article and the particular colony or
island from whence imported.
III. *Id.*, goods, etc., exported.
IV. Accounts of the goods, wares, and merchandize imported into Scotland from British and foreign America, distinguishing the species,
quantity, and value of each article and the particular colony or
island from whence imported.
V. *Id.*, goods, etc., exported.
VI. General Abstracts.

REGISTERS.

1-410. 1675-1783. Custom House Establishments.

Custom House.
Registers,
Series I.
Establishments.

This series, of which many volumes are missing,
relates as a whole to the customs establishment in England only. Vols. **310, 312,** however, contain in addition,
as follows:

310. " The Establishment of the officers of his Majesty's customs in the
Plantations for the half year ending the 5th July, 1767 " (not
including Jamaica).
312. " The Establishment of the officers of his Majesty's customs in the
Plantations from the 5th day of July to the 8th day of September
following, exclusive, the date of the patent appointing commissioners of the Customs in America " (*Treas.* 1: **465**).

The two lists are nearly identical, except that **312** has a few additions and
an extra column of " Sums due ". In **314, 316, 320,** etc., the list of officers
for Jamaica appears.

A series of 29 volumes of American Custom House Establishment Books,
now in the Custom House, London, containing a full record of the quarterly
accounts of officers employed and salaries paid in North America from Sept.

8, 1767, to Jan. 5, 1776. These accounts were sent to the Lords of the Treasury from the Custom House, Boston. The dates of the volumes are as follows:

> **1**, Quarter ending, Jan. 5, 1768; **2**, Apr. 5, 1768; **3**, July 5, 1768; **4**, Oct. 10, 1768; **5**, Jan. 5, 1769; **6**, Apr. 5, 1769; **7**, July 5, 1769; **8**, Oct. 10, 1769; **9**, Jan. 5, 1770; **10**, Apr. 5, 1770; **11**, July 5, 1770; **12**, Oct. 10, 1770; **13**, Jan. 5, 1771; **14**, Apr. 5, 1771; **15**, July 5, 1771; **16**, Oct. 10, 1771; **17**, Jan. 5, 1772; **18**, Apr. 5, 1772; **19**, July 5, 1772; **20**, Oct. 10, 1772; **21**, Jan. 5, 1773; **22**, Apr. 5, 1772; **23**, July 5, 1773; **24**, Oct. 10, 1773; **25**, Jan. 5, 1774; (the accounts for the quarters ending, Apr. 5, July 5, Oct. 10, 1774, are missing) ; **26**, Jan. 5, 1775; **27**, Apr. 5, 1775; **28**, July 5, 1775; (the account for the quarter ending, Oct. 10, 1775, is missing) ; **29**, Jan. 5, 1776.

These volumes can be inspected by permission of the Commissioners of the Customs, Custom House, Lower Thames Street, London.

In the Custom House is another volume containing the customs establishment in America just prior to Sept. 8, 1767. The information given is of the same character as that in the 29 volumes noted above and in the main duplicates **312** of the Public Record Office volumes. From the salary lists, the headings of which are given below, we are able to discover the manner of appointment of the incidental officers. The established officers were appointed as before by Treasury warrant.

Name and Rank	Salary			
	Established Officers	Incidental Officers appointed by the Commissioners in England	Incidental Officers appointed by the Surveyor General and confirmed by the Commissioners in America	Incidental Officers appointed by the Commissioners in America
	£ s d	£ s d	£ s d	£ s d

As we have already said (above, p. 92), a complete list of American customs officials has been prepared from the rolls of Declared Accounts in the Audit Office and is to be found in the Library of Congress. Similar information can be obtained from the out-letters of the Treasury Board (*Treas.* 11 : **1-32**). See also references, above, p. 93. An establishment list for 1723 is in *Acts of the Privy Council, Colonial,* VI. 632; and other lists are in *Treas.* 42.

MISCELLANEA.

16. 1768-1775. Register of Letters Outward, beginning, Jan. 5, 1768.

> Custom House.
> Miscellanea.
> ———

This volume is an entry book of letters sent by the register general of shipping of the American Board of Customs Commissioners to the various collectors and comptrollers of customs at the different ports in the colonies, from Halifax to Savannah, under the management of the board. The letters are dated Boston, chiefly before 1771, and are signed J. W. Malcolm and James Murray. From these letters it appears that the board was trying to bring order into the customs system in America, and the writers are constantly finding fault with the returns sent in to the board. They instruct the American officials—collectors and others—to send no more accounts to England, because " the general accounts in this office originate with the commencement of the American Board and those in England terminate at the same time ".

SUPPLEMENTARY CUSTOM HOUSE PAPERS.

1. SCOTLAND.

1-19. 1723-1783. Minutes of the Scottish Board of Customs Commissioners.

These bulky volumes are in the library of the Custom House, London. They are not indexed before 1776, and, because large and completely filled with the minutes of proceedings and other matter, are not easy to use unless a given date be known. At best the series is of but slight value to students of colonial history, except perhaps for the period of the Revolution, and even for that period the entries relating to American affairs are relatively few in number.

The earlier volumes contain some references to plantation trade, particularly to that of tobacco from Virginia and Maryland, rum from New England, and coffee from the West Indies. They give information about passes issued by the Privy Council for the re-exportation of tobacco, and something about tobacco raised in Scotland. In the volume dated 1755-1759 is a mention of the deportation to South Carolina of three men sentenced for " deforcing " [1] the customs officers, Sept., 1755. The volume for 1762-1767 contains entries showing the existence of a considerable plantation trade in tobacco ; that for 1768-1775 has " An Account of British Plantation Tobacco imported into Scotland, 1760-1775 ", which was sent to the House of Commons and a duplicate to the Commissioners of the Treasury.

The volumes for 1776-1778 and 1778-1781 list cases of seizures of prizes from the Americans ; entries regarding trade with South Carolina, Georgia, and New York, the despatch of provisions to New York under certain conditions, copies of orders in Council permitting ships to proceed to the plantations without convoy, and taking off the embargo. On pp. 196-197 of the volume for 1778-1781 are entries relating to John Paul Jones, Sept. 20, 1779, and a record of measures taken for defense.

2. OUTPORTS.

The following notes on the material to be found in the English, Scottish, and Irish outports are based on the report made by Mr. Henry Atton, librarian of the Custom House, to the Royal Commission on the Public Records, and are here presented with the permission of the commission and of Mr. Atton, to whom thanks are due. The original report contains a survey of only a few of the many volumes preserved in the various custom houses, so that this précis can indicate only in general terms the nature of their contents. The Greenock records, for example, number 200 volumes altogether, some of which are very bulky.

The value of this outport material is not confined to the volumes antedating the year 1783. The volumes of later date are important for the War of 1812 and for the trade of the United States as late as the period of the Civil War.

---

[1] In Scottish law " deforce " meant to resist an officer.

ENGLAND.

Liverpool.

Letter-Books. Collectors to the Board. 1712-1863. 264 vols. One break
    in the series, 1827-1828.
Order Books. The Board to the Collectors. 1711-1863. 117 vols. Vols. for
    1761-1771, 1780-1782, are missing.
Shipping Registers. 1785-1911.
Book of Seizures. 1702-1734.

Liverpool had a good plantation trade and the volumes record the arrival
of plantation vessels, with names, occasional seizures of prizes, suggestions
as to seasons for trade, especially with the West Indies, statements about reshipped tobacco smuggled into Scotland and about the tobacco duty, references to the operation of the Stamp Act in connection with the stamping of
clearances in America and the question as to whether or not vessels whose
clearances were not stamped should be entered at Liverpool.

The year 1769 shows extensive export trade in wheat from America to Leghorn, Lisbon, etc., and the volumes for that and following years contain references to trade with Newfoundland, to tea returned from Hampton, Virginia,
because the colonists there would not allow it to be landed, to the extent of
trade with the colonies in 1775, with many interesting items relating thereto.
Beginning with 1776-1777 we get many references to privateers brought to
Liverpool as prizes (*Aurora,* Capt. Hutchinson, of Virginia, for example),
many vessels taken and retaken, Paul Jones's squadron, ships captured by
Kelly and Dowlin, American privateersmen. The series is valuable for the
War of 1812 and the Civil War, particularly as to the fitting out of Con-
federate cruisers.

In the shipping registers are certain particulars of Confederate cruisers,
and in the book of seizures a few entries of colonial vessels.

Bristol.

The Bristol Custom House was burned in 1831 and the records destroyed.

Letter-Books of the Port of Barnstaple. 1727-1835, 1847-1878. 29 vols.

With the decline of the Barnstaple trade in woollens (1722), the trade in
tobacco came to the front and continued to be conspicuous until 1732. Until
the rise of the tobacco trade, except for a small amount of oil from Newfoundland, Barnstaple did no import business. An account is given, with names
of ships and number of hogsheads, of the tobacco trade with Maryland and
Virginia for these ten years. Between 1753 and 1772 ships from Barnstaple
went to Piscataqua, Massachusetts, New York, and Virginia. In the volumes of the Revolutionary period there are many entries concerning pirates
and privateers, including probably Kelly and Dowlin.

Dover.

Letter-Books. The Board to the Collectors.
Id. The Collectors to the Board.

Both series begin with about 1750, but as the trade was chiefly with France,
the volumes are of little importance here.

9

Portsmouth.

Letter-Books. The Board to the Collectors. 1726-1731, 1740-1819. 80 vols. *Id.* The Collectors to the Board. 1748-1750, 1760-1761, 1764-1814. 143 vols. Account of Incidents. Portsmouth. 1689-1702.

These volumes contain very little relating to American affairs. There are a few items regarding stamps returned from Nova Scotia because of the repeal of the Stamp Act; Palatines from Rotterdam, via Portsmouth for Philadelphia, 1774; arrival of passengers via East Indiamen; smuggling and quarantine. Beginning with 1776, there are a few references to America, such as to the attack by Americans on Parker's fleet in Charleston harbor, with a list of casualties. The second series is the more important of the two.

Exeter.

Letter-Books. The Board to the Collectors. 1676-1805. *Id.* The Collectors to the Board. 1743-1860. 49 vols.

Exeter at the end of the seventeenth and the beginning of the eighteenth centuries had an extensive traffic with Europe and the plantations. We meet with items regarding convoys, and information that East India goods were concealed in casks of Barbadoes sugar which the officers were instructed to split open. The tobacco trade was large, much tobacco being exported from Virginia and repacked at Exeter for export. After 1744 this trade declined. In 1738, 400,000 lbs. were imported and 398,000 exported, but in 1744 the figures had dropped to 6094, and in 1745 to "Nil". Trade with Newfoundland kept up the prosperity and life of the city. The volumes contain a great deal about smuggling.

Dartmouth.

Letter-Books. The Board to the Collectors. 1675-1731. *Id.* The Collectors to the Board. 1775-1779, 1782-1860. 36 vols.

Not particularly important for colonial history, though of some value during the period of the Revolutionary War. The volumes contain items relating to shipping, smuggling, and American privateers.

Falmouth.

The older letter-books of Falmouth have disappeared. There are no volumes for the colonial period.

Penzance.

Letter-Books. The Board to the Collectors. 1722-1761. *Id.* The Collectors to the Board. 1738-1741, 1748-1750.

Of value chiefly for smuggling.

Scilly.

Goods Landed and Shipped. 1736-1752.

A few references to colonial ships, but apparently the islands had no direct foreign trade.

Newcastle.

Letter-Books. The Board to the Collectors. 1706—.
Id. The Collectors to the Board. 1724—.

Exact statements regarding the number of volumes at Newcastle are not possible, as the series need to be reorganized. Tobacco from Maryland and Virginia was entered at Newcastle as early as 1727-1734. In 1777 the entries show no vessels inward from the plantations and but four vessels outward, to Newfoundland, Senegal, Montserrat, and Jamaica. The volume for 1778-1780, which might contain entries regarding Paul Jones, is missing.

Stockton.

Letter-Books. The Board to the Collectors. 1675-1819. 31 vols.
Id. The Collectors to the Board. 1763-1863. 25 vols.
Additional Letter-Book. 1709-1794.
Licenses, Passes, Declarations. 1763-1854. 4 vols.
Miscellaneous Letter-Books. 1763-1854. 4 vols.

Many references to plantation trade, beginning as early as 1675 (train oil). Such trade seems to have been extensive and is frequently mentioned. In a letter from the Admiralty, 1676, reference is made to the proclamations of Dec. 22, 1675, and Jan. 28, 1676, defining the time of endurance of " sea briefs ", granted in pursuance of the treaty with Algiers and warning the collectors that they are not to grant such briefs under the treaties with Algiers, Tunis, and Tripoli, as the power to do this rested only with the Admiralty. Under date June 22, 1714, we find a definition of such goods as were deemed at that time contraband of war.

Whitby.

Letter-Books. The Collectors to the Board. 1721-1724.

Many volumes apparently are missing. Those examined disclose no references to colonial trade.

Whitehaven.

Letter-Books. The Collectors to the Board. 1775-1785.

These volumes are of considerable value for colonial trade during the war. The trade was with Ireland, North America, and the West Indies, and not with the Continent. Items refer to a vessel from North America with timber and lumber; to the *Molly* of Virginia, laden with British dry goods for Canada, which tried to carry its cargo to Virginia, June 24, 1775, and to many vessels from Virginia to England, showing the working of the Prohibitory Act. Vessels going to American ports were not permitted to load any goods or provisions whatever. Seven American vessels were seized and brought to port, Apr. 16, 1778. Under date Apr. 20 there is a reference to Paul Jones: " At 4 o'clock a privateer of eighteen guns and one hundred and twenty men landed about thirty men in our harbour and set a vessel on fire and distributed combustibles in several others. The privateer is yet standing on and off and as we just now hear is stretching with wind at east to the WNW " (p. 96). There is a reference to the arrival of the *George,* belonging to this coast, from Rhode Island, with the *Grampus,* on board which was

Gen. Burgoyne (May 15, 1778). In the latter part of the volume are entries of interest relating to the transport service.

Hull.

Letter-Books. The Collectors to the Board. 1748-1862. 92 vols.
Id. The Board to the Collectors. 1744-1761, 1766-1811, 1812-1817, 1827-1828, 1848-1851, 1854-1861. 31 vols.
Board's Order Books. 1726-1754, 1727-1795, 1786-1790. 3 vols.
Board's Order Books for Landing Surveyors. 1741-1749, 1799-1816, 1825-1841. 6 vols.
Daily Receipt Book. Cash. 1757-1760.

The letter-books seem to contain very little relating to American affairs. Under date July 28, 1777, there is a reference to a brigantine of Lynn (England), " the captain of which stated that on the 21 he was taken by an American privateer 30 leagues NE by E from the Spurn " (mouth of the Humber) ; the privateersman robbed him of all his provisions and stores and put on board him the crews of four other captured English vessels, and these the brigantine, at the time of making statement, was conveying to Lynn. The American ship carried 16 carriage guns, 24 swivels, and 100 men, and had " sent away " the four captured English vessels. In a letter of Sept. 23, 1779, from the collector to the board, we are given information regarding Paul Jones, to the effect that there were three ships in his squadron. The trade of Hull was almost entirely coastwise or with the northern part of Europe. Few if any colonial vessels entered at that port.

Plymouth.

Letter-Books. The Board to the Collectors. 1791-1795, 1799-1808, 1820-1860. 118 vols.
Id. The Collectors to the Board. 1799-1860. 60 vols.

Of interest for the War of 1812. Voluminous entries with regard to prizes. Many American ships detained as prize, possibly on the suspicion of infringing neutral privileges, but with the result of greatly annoying the Americans, to as great an extent indeed as the more famous impressment of seamen. Apr., 1808, case of American East Indiaman, *General Clarkson,* and others. Also entries showing that American ships landed tobacco in Guernsey contrary to the navigation acts. Twenty vessels engaged in this trade were seized in 1791. Many of the volumes for Plymouth, Truro, and Looe have disappeared.

SCOTLAND.

Greenock (Port Glasgow).

Letter-Books. The Collectors to the Scottish Board.
Id. The Scottish Board to the Collectors.
Id. Deputies at Greenock to the Scottish Board via Port Glascow.

About 200 volumes in all, dating from as early as 1736. As the collection is in process of reclassification, it is possible that earlier volumes may be recovered.

The books show that from early times there was an extensive tobacco trade with Maryland and Virginia, and that much of the tobacco was re-exported. Items concern this trade and re-exportation, discrepancies between cargoes and manifests, violations at the time of the Revolution of the Prohibitory Act, vessels being licensed in Great Britain and certificated by British commanders and others in the colonies. Passengers suspected of being Americans were carefully watched; many historical and semi-historical allusions may be found as to the work of the Continental Congress. References to the appearance of John Paul Jones so near the land as to be identified; to an American privateer plundering the house of St. Mary's Isle, seat of the Earl of Selkirk (in a letter from Kirkcudbright, Apr. 23, 1781, from John Murdach to the provost or any of the magistrates of Dumfries); to the 70th Foot, proceeding from Glasgow to America, their shoes and linen; to Wexford, an American privateer, Apr. 11, 1778, and an engagement in which Capt. Innes struck to the American; to D'Estaing in the West Indies, May 28, 1779; and to other privateer cases. In these records one can find references to the careers of many vessels which throw light on American trade after 1775 and the working of the license system.

The books have many entries relating to the activities of American privateers off the English coast, to prizes brought into port, to Paul Jones as expected to sail from France " shortly ", Aug. 20, 1778, to vessels waiting for letters of marque against the French and the Americans. There is evidence here and in the Liverpool records that the American privateers sometimes cruised in squadrons.

Ayr.

Letter-Books. The Collectors to the Scottish Board. 1729-1741, 1751-1781, 1786-1821. 28 vols.
Order Books. The Scottish Board. 1740-1745.
Letter-Books. The Scottish Board to the Officers. 1746-1764.
Id. The Scottish Board to the Collectors. 1764-1767, 1793-1796. 3 vols.

Some foreign trade and much friction between traders and subordinate officers, many references to smuggling, particularly from 1776 to 1780, when something like a state of war existed. Evidence of considerable colonial trade in tobacco, reshipped to France and Norway, the French farmers generally being the chief customers (1752); also trade in rum with the West Indies, the rum being sometimes shipped from Ayr ostensibly to Ireland, but run back from Ireland to Scotland by the Manxmen, who smuggled rum to a large extent before England acquired control of the island. Instructions from the Admiralty regarding Paul Jones, the Prohibitory Act, and licenses, 1778-1779; other interesting references to Jones and other privateers, with a copy of a letter from the Dublin custom house to the provost of Ayr.

Dumfries.

Letter-Books. The Scottish Board to the Collectors. 1708-1735. 2 vols.
Id. The Collectors to the Scottish Board. 1727-1749, 1776-1784, 1791-1794. 4 vols.
Id. 1759-1771, 1779-1788, 1794-1797, 1802-1807. 5 vols.
Id. The Scottish Board to the Officers. 1764-1776, 1784-1788, 1794-1803, 1806-1811. 10 vols.

Much tobacco, probably colonial, smuggled in by way of the Isle of Man. A reference or two to Paul Jones. On the whole there is very little in these volumes.

Troon.

Letter-Books. The Collectors to the Scottish Board. 1757-1760, 1765-1767, 1772-1776, 1791-1793, 1801-1808, 1810-1834, 1846-1863. 15 vols.
Id. The Scottish Board to the Collectors. 1763-1771, 1797-1801, 1804-1805, 1809-1811, 1815-1824. 7 vols.

Chiefly of value for smuggling. Some time in the middle of the nineteenth century about a dozen volumes disappeared, which may yet be discovered. As these volumes mainly covered the period 1777-1791 it is possible that they contained references of interest. It is known that in them there was at least one item regarding Paul Jones.

Leith.

Order Books. The Scottish Board. 1750-1776, 1792-1829. 98 vols.
Id. Sent to the Custom House, London. 1777-1787, 1790-1791. 5 vols.

Many signatures of Adam Smith. The older orders were to the port of Dunbar. The items concern chiefly the tobacco and rum trade with New York, Georgia, and other colonies. Reference to Paul Jones's squadron, Sept. 16, 1779, and to Loyalists from New York, Oct. 22, 1783.

Alloa.

Letter-Books. The Scottish Board to the Officers. 1718-1772, 1778-1795, 1810-1821. 13 vols.

Considerable trade with the West Indies, 1752, 1757-1758. A great deal about smuggling, and of legal trade in tobacco, though the latter seems to have been designed for " pretended exportation ". Goods were often relanded after clearance outward, and wholesale frauds committed. Direction of trade chiefly to northern Europe. Of little interest for colonial commerce.

IRELAND.

Londonderry.

Letter-Books. The Collectors to the Board. 1773-1829, with many volumes wanting.
        These books concern also Letterkenny and Ballyraine.
Id. The Board to the Collectors. 1774-1800, with many volumes wanting.
Precedent Book. 1699-1819.

The Londonderry books contain material of considerable interest concerning smuggled tobacco, the fisheries, privateers, convoys, prizes, prisoners, captures and recaptures, and the like. Under date Apr. 20, 1776, mention is made of a vessel from America carrying the goods of J. Crawford, a Loyalist, who had been compelled to convert his property into cargo and to leave by stealth. There are many references to American privateering during the Revolutionary War, to the experiences of convoys with the privateers, and to mistakes and misunderstandings. Paul Jones's squadron is mentioned under date Apr. 28, 1778, and again in 1779; mention is also made of Kelly and Dowlin, who did a great deal of damage to British commerce at this time. Mr. Atton comments upon these records as follows, " It may be possible to secure from Custom records a complete journal of his [Paul Jones] cruises on the coasts of the United Kingdom ", and he adds, " the Customs department acted in an energetic and creditable manner on the occasion in question and it appears that the frustration of some of Jones' plans may have been due to this fact."

In the same series mention is made of seizures of American privateers and ships during the War of 1812, and of detentions and seizures of American vessels prior to 1812. In the precedent book is a copy of a register of a prize ship (Philadelphia), 1746, and an account of the quit-rents of Derry, 1753.

WALES.

Cardiff.

Letter-Books. The Board to the Collectors. 1689-1861. 17 vols.
Id. the Collectors to the Board. 1746-1861. 24 vols.
Salaries and Incidents. 1733-1756.

A few items relating to colonial goods and shipping, particularly in connection with the " wrecking " of ships cast ashore. Apparently Cardiff had very little foreign trade.

Swansea.

Letter-Books. The Collectors to the Board. 1730-1734, 1740-1864. 41 vols.
    No colonial trade ; many references to smuggling.

3. PORT BOOKS (IN THE PUBLIC RECORD OFFICE).

Exchequer K. R. Port Books. —	**1-160.** London. 1588-1697. **161-184.** Berwick. 1606-1784. **185-302.** Newcastle. 1579-1798. **303-386.** Hull, including Scarborough and Grimsby. 1565-1644, 1654-1787.

387-424. Boston. 1565-1773.
425-470. Lynn. 1565-1794.
471-586. Yarmouth, with Blakeney, Dunwich, Walberswick, Southwold, Aldborough, and Woodbridge. 1565-1780.
587-637. Ipswich, including Colchester and Malden. 1565-1736.
638-736. Sandwich and Deal, with Rochester, Milton, Faversham, and Dover. 1565-1756.
737-813. Chichester, with Folkestone, Hythe, Romney, Rye, Winchelsea, Hastings, Pevensey, Matching (Meeching, now Newhaven ?), Lewes, New Shoreham, Arundel, and Littlehampton. 1565-1731.
814-863. Southampton and Portsmouth. 1565-1758.
864-924. Poole, including Lyme and Weymouth. 1565-1759.
925-1009. Exeter, with Dartmouth, Barnstaple, Bideford, and Ilfracombe. 1565-1788.
1010-1080. Plymouth, with Looe, Fowey, Penryn, Truro, Helston, Mount's Bay, St. Ives, and Padstow. 1565-1758.
1081-1127. Bridgewater and Minehead. 1566-1776.

1128-1240. Bristol. 1565-1788.
1241-1269. Gloucester. 1581-1776.
1270-1297. Cardiff, including Chepstow, Neath, and Swansea.
1298-1322. Milford, including Bury, Carmarthen, and Cardigan.
　　　　1565-1784.
1323-1447. Chester, including Beaman's, Conway, Carnarvon,
　　　　Liverpool, and Lancaster. 1565-1789.
1448-1461. Carlisle, with Whitehaven. 1611-1743.
1462-1464. Uncertain Ports.

This series of 1464 bundles contains altogether between fourteen and fifteen thousand parchment books of varying size and thickness, each bundle including on the average eight to twelve books. The latter vary greatly in condition, some being well preserved, others little injured except for the adhering of the leaves, while a few, especially those of Bristol, are so badly damaged by damp and mildew as to be almost illegible.

The great value of the books for colonial history lies in the record they contain of the nature and distribution of colonial staple products and of goods exported from the English outports to America. This record is not confined to the direct trade between Great Britain and America, but includes also a very large body of material showing the reshipment and re-exportation of colonial staples to other parts of Great Britain and Ireland and to the Continent, and the transportation of such commodities inland as well as by water. For the British coastwise trade the books are indispensable, and of this traffic American staples formed an important part. Furthermore, in these lists are hundreds of names of vessels, either colonial or English-built or taken as prize, that were concerned in the trade and passenger traffic between England and America, and these lists date back to the beginning of our history. So far as observed the earliest recorded names are the *John* from the West Indies (1614) and the *Treasurer* with the tobacco of Sir Thomas Dale from Virginia (Southampton, 1616). . The *Charity* (1624) is the earliest from New England. A list of such vessels, with the data furnished by these entries, would be unique among the sources for the history of colonial commerce.

Regarding the importance of the Port Books for our early history, Mr. R. G. Marsden says, " I have examined many of those for James' reign and am fairly well acquainted with the character of their contents during that period. The ship that chiefly interested me was the Pilgrim Fathers' *Mayflower,* and, if my attempt to identify her was successful, the Port Books contain at least a dozen references to her and her master, the ' Mr. Jones ' of Bradford's narrative, showing her career between 1610 and 1621, the voyages she made, the cargoes she carried, and who paid customs duties on them. To the historic voyage no reference has been found in the Port Books, possibly because of the decayed condition of some of them, but more probably because of the secrecy and hurry of the ship's sailing. One entry, however, relating to the sailing of a *Mayflower* to New England in 1624 will have to be explained by New England historians ; there is reason to think that the ship referred to is the Pilgrims' ship of 1620 (which returned to England in 1621), but no *Mayflower* is known to have arrived in New England, or to have sailed for New England, in 1624, and the puzzle is complicated by another entry in another of the Port Books referring to the same ship, but describing her as bound, not for New England, but for Ireland.

" Apart from the *Mayflower* the Port Books give a good deal of information as to the sailing of ships to and from America and the West Indies, which probably is not to be found elsewhere. In 1634, for example, full details of the cargoes of 19 ships, with their masters' names, are given, with the statement that the New England ships ' per licentiam Regis ' paid no customs duty ; so in 1625 particulars are given of 14 ships and cargoes bound for America and the West Indies. Similar information may be collected as to the Baltic, Mediterranean, African, and East Indian trades. In most cases the destination, in outward voyages, and the port of sailing, in homeward voyages, is given ; and where it is not given the character of the cargo—Virginian tobacco, elephants' teeth, whale oil, or logwood—indicates where the ship had been." [1]

If we omit the books containing entries of duties on wine, as relating in no way to colonial history, the remainder may be classified under three heads : those that record imports and entrances, those that record exports and clearances, and those that concern the coasting trade. The outports differed greatly as far as their activities in these three directions were concerned. Some of them, such as Chester, had no ocean-going commerce, confining themselves to coast ports in England, Ireland, Wales, and Scotland, and handling a considerable amount of colonial produce in this way. Chester received plantation and colonial products from London, Liverpool, Lancaster, Bristol or Dublin in small vessels, and redistributed these products either inland or to the smaller coast towns by water. The invoices of vessels clearing for Ireland, the Continent, or other British ports are sufficiently detailed to give an excellent idea of the goods transhipped and their destination.

The books are not specially easy to use. The number is very large, the entries are scattered, and the form of the entry is such as to require a certain amount of experience in reading it. The following specimen entries show the character of the information given.

London. 1696. " In the Margarett Robert Kelly per New York Robert Hackshaw pro als 120 Stuffes, 35l English wrot silk 5 thrown ditto 4 lb wrot brasses one north: Kersey 30 yards Freez."
" In the Johana Rot Griffing per New York Rot Hackshaw pro als 3 double Dozen of Kerseys 180l Goads Cotten."
" In the Speedwell Jam. Moulton per Nevis Isaac Gomes als $\frac{1}{2}$ lb wrot brass 18 doz plane Leather Gloves 4l wrot silk, 1 haberdashery 1 wrot iron One piece English lace att 12l 18s 0."
Chester. 1761. " In the Kildare Daniel Briscoe Mr for Dublin Jas Folliott for Hanson and Co 3 casks qty 1357 lb Carolina Indico for wch no praemium has been allowed per Cert. from London the 6 Inst 5. 13. 1."
" The ship Susannah formerly called Le Chevase Marine Douglas Campbell now Master French built pink stern'd with two decks and three Masts burthen 150 Tons a Captive from the French King's subjects by a private Snow of War the Royal Hester of New York in America and was condemned as lawfull prize in the Court of Admiralty of the province as by sentence of Condemnat. dated 12 Octr 1758. Valued on oath by Jas Folliott at £687. 13. 8$\frac{1}{2}$."

[1] *First Report of the Royal Commission on Public Records* (1912), vol. I., part II., p. 49. See also the memorandum and evidence of Mr. N. S. B. Gras, *ibid.*, pp. 47-49, and part III., pp. 160-161. Mr. Albert Cook Myers tells me that he has found the Port Books very useful and informing in his work on Penn and the settlement of Pennsylvania.

"Cocketts Inward in Michaelmas Quarter 1761."

Aug. 21. Liverpoole No. 25.	In the Chester trader John Anderton Mr from Richd Savage 23 hhds 15 tierces 9 barrells cont. 403l. 2s. 3d. muscovado sugar, 1 barrell Indico, 12 hhd 1 cask 1 barrell oil, 18 hhd mollasses, 10 cwt Logwood, 16 barrells Tar, 2 cart-loads old ships timber, 3 tons hemp, 2 tons iron, 12 hhd qty 12343 lbs british plantation tobacco. Dated the 18 August 1761.	Cert. 23d Nov. 1761.

Exportations in Midsummer Quarter 1761.	Sums.
May 21. John Hincks for Light and Hutchinson one cask contg 353. lb. Carolina Indico for wch no praemium has been allowed p Certe from London.	1. 9. 5.

Bristol. The Bristol books show a large plantation trade, as was to be expected, and from the entries of goods exported a good idea can be obtained of the manufacturing activities of the port.

"In the Polly Chas Thomson Mr per Antigua Jamaica and Honduras Permit Thos Frank $61\frac{1}{10}$ Wheat flour Imported by himself 24 Oct. 1775 per Betty and Hellen warehoused under the joint stocks of king and proprietor agreeable to an act of 13 Geo. 3 ", etc.

"Betty of and for Milford Jas Morris Mr (among other commodities) muscovado sugar, train oil, melasses, refined sugar tobacco, snuff, June 21, 1775."

Many similar detailed invoices of goods laden for the coastwise traffic, such as tar, pitch, flour, deal boards, salt, redwood, mahogany, logwood, ginger, potash, pimento, lignum-vitae, rice, Madeira wine, balls of tobacco clay (also in boxes, baskets, pails, casks, and bundles), and tobacco and snuff in boxes, hogsheads, baskets, casks, trusses, and rolls.

In the export books will frequently be found references to goods that were part of a prize cargo, and in this case the name of the prize is always given. Such cargoes were brought in by the merchants and reshipped to America and the West Indies.

"Part of a cargo of the Margaretha Dorothea a prize taken by the Eagle and Charlestown privateers and condemned 7 March 1757." Scores of such entries may be found during the war periods. Only half subsidy was paid.

For an official report on the Port Books see the Deputy Keeper's *Report* for 1912, pp. 14-16, where it is stated that the books of the Port of London, 1697-1799, " were destroyed years ago ".

PAYMASTER-GENERAL OF THE FORCES.

INTRODUCTION.

The paymaster-general of the forces was the banker of the army. The office originated early in the reign of Charles II., as a device for meeting the expenses of the troops raised to check Venner's uprising.[1] So successful was the first appointee, Sir Stephen Fox, grandfather of Charles James Fox, that in 1661 the office was enlarged and Fox was constituted paymaster in general of all the troops. The position proved an exceedingly lucrative one, as large amounts of money passed through the paymaster's hands and he received as one of his perquisites a stoppage of five per cent. (one shilling in the pound) of the pay of all ranks of the army.[2] The refusal of Pitt to receive this iniquitous allowance, when holding the paymastership in the years from 1746 to 1755, gave him a wide reputation for probity. On the other hand Lord Ranelagh, paymaster from 1691 to 1702, was convicted of defalcation to the amount of £72,000 and turned out of Parliament, and later the situation became so notorious[3] that the House of Commons appointed a committee to investigate the affairs of the army. While in the main the report exculpated the paymaster-general, it brought to light the peculations of Edmond Jones, deputy and cashier to the paymaster of marines, who had lent £90,000 of public money and divided the interest money (£1000) with his fellow deputy Herbert[4] (see above, p. 39). There is ample justification for Lord Rosebery's characterization of the office when he speaks of the gilded subordination of the paymastership, with its vast profits and safe obscurity, and when he

[1] The idea was probably borrowed from the practices under the Commonwealth and Protectorate, the first treasurer or paymaster-general being J. Blackwell, whom Penn sent over as governor of Pennsylvania in 1685. The earliest accounts date from 1652 and 1653.

[2] The paymaster's establishment cost £3000 a year, which came out of deductions of 12d. in the pound and one day's pay in the year and not out of any revenue of the crown. The paymaster was also treasurer of Chelsea Hospital and had a salary of £365 a year and £365 established pay.

[3] "Sir, I don't know what the Method of the Treasury is at present, but I humbly imagine, that if you approve the Reduction of the Pay of the Officers and order proper and distinct Advertisements to be put upon the Doors of the Treasury and Pay Office as often as Money is issued for the service of the Army, and throw of[f] the Jargon of Poundage, Hospital, Agency, Offreckonings, Warrant, and several other articles altogether unintelligible, it will be of great Ease to the Army and of vast Service to the Public. The Pay-Office, then, will neither be perplexed itself nor perplex others, as in the time of some Pay-Masters; every Officer will know when his money is in the Pay-Office to a minute, and will not be sent away with a *There's no Money*, as has been done formerly, when there was really Money, but confounded under such different Heads of Service, that the Officer could not get at it, *and perhaps some Clerk was then making a Hand of it in the Alley*. A great many gallant men will not then be obliged, as heretofore, to dance Attendance at the Door of the Pay-Office, as I have often seen them do in the most uncomfortable Seasons of the Year, and pay more Court to a little Clerk there than a Sub-lieutenant or Ensign here would to a Mareschal of France." Foreman, *A Letter to Walpole* (1732), pp. 32-33.

[4] *Report of the House of Commons relating to the Army* (1746). For a trenchant criticism of this report see a contemporary pamphlet, *National Oeconomy Recommended*, addressed to a member of the committee (London, 1746). Also *Commons Journal*, XXV. 57, 60-61, 77, 79-80, 124 (Jones), 166 (report).

calls to mind the habitual practice of the paymaster " to take poundage of all subsidies paid to foreign princes and to use the great balances at his credit for his own purposes of speculation ".[1]   Yet under the Hanoverians the pay-master became a cabinet officer and a member of the Privy Council, and the office was deemed, and naturally, one of the most desirable in the gift of the crown.   It was held by such men as Walpole, Cornwallis, Spencer Compton, Henry Pelham, Pitt, Henry Fox, Charles Townshend, North, Burke, and Barré.

The functions of the paymaster-general were first regulated by statute in 1782 and again in 1783. Complaint having been made of the financial conduct of the war in America, commissioners were appointed to examine the accounts of the kingdom. The commission reported that the paymaster—Richard Rigby was the official especially referred to—had been accustomed to accumulate large sums of public money in his hands, beyond what was necessary for carrying on the service of the department, and to take and carry out of office with him, upon his resignation or removal, large balances of public money, which he had retained and kept in his hands many years after being out of office.   Therefore it was ordered that henceforth all fees of the paymaster's office should be abolished, that all money voted by Parliament should be deposited in the Bank of England, that the Secretary at War should take charge of all the estimates, and that the paymaster, the Secretary at War, the judge advocate general, and other officials should be placed upon a salary.[2] This act entirely altered the position of the paymaster and the Secretary at War, though both offices were continued, one until 1836, when it was merged in that of the paymaster-general, the other until 1854, when it was assumed by the Secretary of State for War until abolished entirely in 1863.

Under the paymaster were the deputy paymasters in America and through them the troops were paid, works and barracks erected, and all other ordinary and extraordinary expenses met.   The paymaster received the money fur-nished him by writ of privy seal,[3] and accompanying such writ were instruc-tions from the Treasury, though disbursements were controlled by the pay-master alone.   Books containing the off-reckonings, or clothing accounts of the regiments, are to be found among the paymaster's papers.   Twenty-five per cent. of a soldier's pay, that is, during our Revolutionary War, two pence per man per day, was stopped for his clothing, and this stoppage was paid to the colonel who arranged for the supply, though the records of the allowance were kept in the paymaster's office.   A fuller discussion of the off-reckonings is given below.   The subject is important as the manipulation of the off-reckonings was little short of scandalous.

[1] Rosebery, *Chatham*, pp. 234, 432, 433.
[2] 22 George III., c. 81, 23 George III., c. 50.
[3] " The monies granted by parliament in each year for military services are issued from the Exchequer to the Paymaster General, in pursuance of a sign manual warrant and order, founded on the general letter of privy seal, which sign manuals, etc., have been of late for £1,000,000 each ; and by virtue thereof the Paymaster General has a credit at the Exchequer to receive any sum not exceeding that sum.   The money is afterwards issued as occasion requires by the secretary's letter to the auditor, which letter states the sum, the fund in the Exchequer out of which it is to be satisfied, and the service for which it is to be applied by the Paymaster.

" When this credit is exhausted, another is given, till the whole amount of the year's grants for military services is nearly issued, and then particular letters of privy seal are made out, directing the payment of the remainder, and completing the authority for the payment of the whole.   When the money is thus in the Paymaster's hands, he must have the authority of the king's sign manual, countersigned by the Treasury, to author-ize him to pay it." *Chatham Papers*, **231** (1782-1783).

The Pay Office was located at one time in Golden Square and at another in one of the houses west of Wallingford House, facing St. James Park. After the completion of the new Horse Guards in 1756, the office was removed to the southeast corner room on the second (first) floor. The records, covering the period from 1721 to 1835, were transferred about twenty-five years ago to the Public Record Office. Volumes from this series are important for the history of the wars in America, as they furnish information regarding the services of British officers there.

PAYMASTER-GENERAL'S PAPERS.

LEDGERS.

Paymaster-General.
Army Ledgers.

1-33. 1757-1783. Army Ledgers.

HALF-PAY.

Paymaster-General.
Army Establishment Books.
Half-Pay and Retired Pay.

1-34. 1737-1782. Half-Pay and Retired Pay.

MISCELLANEOUS.

1-5. 1751-1773. Deputy Paymaster's Accounts, etc.: America.

Paymaster-General.
Army Miscellaneous Books.

These volumes include various accounts of the deputy paymasters in America during the period named. Vol. 4 begins with 1769—an account of Abraham Mortier of New York with Richard Rigby (paymaster-general, 1768-1782), covering a great variety of expenses, and extends to 1772-1773. In the same volume is Gen. Maturin's account of extraordinaries, 1772. Vol. 5 contains the account of Maj.-Gen. Wrightson, deputy paymaster of the forces at Martinique, of the expenses of the expedition under Maj.-Gen. Monckton, 1761-1763. These volumes contain little information except of a financial character, *i. e.*, ordinary and extraordinary expenses, but they do give details regarding works, barracks, the movement of troops, and the like, and are quite likely to be useful in furnishing exact information not otherwise obtainable.

70-72. 1753-1777. Extraordinaries in North America.

Huge volumes containing notes, warrants and by whom drawn, objects of warrants, and dates. Many of the items of expense are interesting, and many of the statements here made are of historical importance. For example, among the items are payments to Loyalists with names and dates. The accounts are by years.

    70. 1755-1764. Braddock, Shirley, Dunbar, Abercrombie, Loudoun, Webb, Hopson, Howe, Forbes, Stanwix, Amherst, Gage, Monckton, Murray, etc.

    71. 1765-1777. Gage, Carleton, William Howe, Clinton, Pigot, Earl Percy, Prescott, Smith, Burgoyne.

72. Massey, Carleton, Haldimand, Howe, Clinton, Pigot, Prescott, Burgoyne, Phillips, Hamilton, Vaughan, Robertson, Bruce, McLean, Balfour, Campbell.

86-102. 1749-1780. Cash Books.

These volumes contain the king's account current with the Bank of England and the record of the disbursement of money received by virtue of letters of privy seal and Treasury directions. They concern only such payments—to contractors, agents, staff officers and others—as were made directly from the king's account.

104-111. 1759-1783. Entry Books of Letters and Powers of Attorney.

These entry books contain copies of letters, signed, sealed, witnessed, and delivered in America, conferring powers of attorney on some one in England to receive from the Treasury the pay or emolument due, or to contract for clothing for the regiments, or to make over the off-reckonings or clothing money to such person as the one empowered should see fit. The volumes contain also copies of letters given by persons leaving England for an extended stay in the colonies empowering some one to manage their affairs in England; and authorizations from the colonies instructing the Treasury to make payments to agents, as in the case of the money voted by Parliament to Massachusetts, Connecticut, Virginia, New Jersey, New Hampshire, Rhode Island, New York, and Pennsylvania. Among the entries are letters of administration, king's sign manuals, bonds, instructions from the paymaster-general to deputies, articles of agreement with contractors and others, etc.

138-141. 1721-1741. Entry Book. Off-Reckonings.

The off-reckonings consisted of an allowance for the colonel in command of a regiment, marine or other, to maintain the uniforms of his men, which consisted of coat, waistcoat, breeches, shoes, stockings, and gaiters. The money thus allowed was not specifically appropriated for the purpose, but was obtained by a twenty-five per cent. stoppage on the soldier's pay, taken half yearly at midsummer and Christmas. Hence the off-reckonings were sometimes defined as "pay stopt from the poorer part of the army for their clothing". Abuses arose in the manipulation of these allowances, the most serious of which was the prevailing practice of receiving off-reckonings according to the number of men that should be in a regiment and paying out according to the number that was actually there, and the regiments rarely if ever had their full complement of men. The colonel pocketed the difference. No attempt seems ever to have been made by the paymaster-general to ascertain whether or not the actual men in the regiment conformed to the muster-rolls, and the fault lay of course with the commissary of musters, who, it is said, was frequently bribed by the colonel and other officers.[1] When the regiments

[1] "Ought these colonels to put so much of the nation's money in their pockets, when they do so little service and run so little danger for it; at a time when England is so much in debt; and it is self demonstrable, the clothing service can be performed for so much less, as the clothiers give for presents. No doubt but those clothiers have also a round profit by the bargain they take in hand, or they would hardly bid so high for them." Foreman, *A Letter to Walpole* (1732). Foreman recommends that the off-reckonings be abolished and that "a fund be fixed in lieu of them, no more than sufficient for clothing the army", pp. 29, 34. The reference to "little service" and "little danger" is

were in North America or the West Indies, the colonels profited by the difference in exchange, and it was not difficult for them, when so far away, to increase that profit by the insertion in the rolls of fictitious names or the retention there of the names of officers and soldiers that were dead.

The assignments took the form of authorizations to the regimental agent in England to supply clothing or to contract for its supply. They are of very little importance.

142-146. 1756-1784. Register of Letters of Attorney.

The entries are in the following tabulated form:

Pepperrell's Foot. Lieutenant Benjamin White.	To Mr. Richard Partridge of Mason's Court, Brick Lane, Spitalfields.	Dated. 12 Jan'y 1758.

Few names of American officers or soldiers appear in these volumes. Both Pepperrell and Shirley had the distinction of serving as colonels of regiments, which though raised in America were entered upon the English establishment.

169. 1759-1765. Off-Reckonings or Clothing Accounts: Entered as follows:

(On the lefthand page:)

44th Regiment of Foot, Dr.

1764						
26 Jan'y	172	Nett Offreck's paid Mr. Calcraft to 24 Dec. 1762		1023	19	10
17 Dec.	182	" " paid him more to 24 June 1763		1083	10	6
1765						
5 Mar.	11	" " paid him more to 5 July 1763		65	9	9

(On the righthand page:)

Per Contra.

1761

Nov. 17 Abercrombie, Lieutenant General assigns his Offreckonings of this Regiment, commencing the 6 July, 1762, and ending the 5 July, 1763, Amounting to Two Thousand, One hundred Seventy three pounds and one penny to John Calcraft of St. Margaret's Westminster, Esq., His Exõrs, etc.

£   s   d

2173   1

The assignee, in this case Calcraft, was the regimental agent in England. The entries cover all troops serving in America—regiments of foot, four companies at New York, three companies in South Carolina, one company at New Providence (Shirley's), and one at Bermuda (Popple's).

There are no in-letters or out-letters among the paymaster's papers. That such must have existed is not only likely from the nature of the business of the office but is demonstrated from references in other correspondence to letters so written.

---

to the fact that marine colonels, lieutenant-colonels, and majors did not accompany their detachments to sea.

The practice of signing muster-rolls by commissaries, without seeing the troops, was well known and is supported by ample evidence. *Report* (1746), pp. 73-78. The same report brings out the laxity of the comptrollers of the army, whose business it was to be a check upon the commissaries of musters, but who had never, according to the witness of their secretary, made any attempt (in twenty-six years) to obviate frauds in musters. *Ibid.*, pp. 84-85.

TREASURY PAPERS.

INTRODUCTION.

The Exchequer in Norman days was one aspect of the *curia regis,* and though in the twelfth century it had begun to have a distinct organization, it did not separate from the *curia regis* until after the time of the *Dialogus de Scaccario*. This document does show, however, a distinct departmental exchequer, that is, the court in session dealing with questions of finance. At its head, as president, sat the Justiciar, with the Chancellor on his left. On his right, once removed, sat the Treasurer and with him were grouped those who had strictly to do with matters of account. The Chancellor seems to have been present as a control or check upon the Treasurer,[1] and when in the reign of Henry III. he severed his connections with the Exchequer, he turned over his duties to a special exchequer chancellor, to whom the Treasurer was instructed to deliver the seal of the department.

The court of Exchequer, as a distinct financial body dealing with the king's revenue and debts, consisted of two branches, the administrative and the judicial. The administrative branch had (1) its exchequer of account, of which the King's Remembrancer and the Lord Treasurer's Remembrancer were the most important officials, the duties of whom were to recover the king's occasional debts and regular duties, such as rents, fines, amercements, issues, etc.; and (2) its exchequer of receipt, comprising the auditors and the treasury of receipt where the money was received and paid out. The judicial branch consisted of the Lord Treasurer, the Chancellor of the Exchequer, and three or four lords, who sat as a court of revenue and a court of equity to adjust and recover the king's revenue or any goods or chattels belonging to the crown. Though designed as a court dealing with cases in which only the king's debtors were concerned, it came by process of legal fiction to consider all sorts of personal actions, a result which transformed it from a court of equity into a court of common law held before the Treasurer and the lords only. Any person might file a bill there, though technically he had to be construed as a king's debtor in order to do so.

After the fourteenth century, when the separation between the administrative and judicial branches was effected, the Exchequer formed a definite financial department at the head of which was the Treasurer. This official was the King's Treasurer, without control over expenditure, either of the king himself or of any of the royal officials. He was responsible to the king for the revenues due and for the smooth working of the Exchequer machinery. The king, by virtue of his prerogative, controlled the revenue, the administration, the army and navy, and the judicial system, and the Treasurer was simply his servant to do his bidding. Parliament alone could restrain the royal will. Such was the position of the Treasurer until after the revolution of 1688, not the head of a department, but the financial servant of the king.

After 1500 the Treasurer's office increased steadily in importance, until in Elizabeth's reign he who had been known only as the King's Treasurer was

---

[1] Madox, *History of the Exchequer* (1 vol. ed.), p. 580; Poole, *The Exchequer in the Twelfth Century,* ch. V. In the time of the *Dialogus,* the Chancellor did not always attend, but nothing of importance could be done without his consent. Poole, p. 104.

transformed into the Lord High Treasurer, just as the King's Secretary had developed into the principal Secretary of State. In rank the Treasurer stood next to the Lord Chancellor. He and the lords under him, all of whom were appointed by the king, constituted the department exercising financial control, as contrasted with the Exchequer proper which was the department of account and receipt. These two departments, which were not departments at all in the modern sense of the word, remained united until 1612 when, the office of Lord Treasurer being for the first time put in commission, they were separated. This separation became complete after the Restoration, when the Treasurer was given an office in the Cockpit, Whitehall, while the Exchequer remained at Westminster, where the records and the money were kept. From this period, therefore, the Treasury as distinct from the Exchequer began its separate existence.

Before 1714, the head of the Treasury was the Lord High Treasurer, although several times in the Stuart period the office was put in commission (placed in the hands of a group of commissioners), notably after the death of the Earl of Southampton in 1667, when the Treasury as an independently organized department takes it origin and the minutes of the Treasury Board as a regular series begin. The last acting Lord High Treasurer was Robert Harley, earl of Oxford, who retired from office on July 30, 1714. His place, filled for two days only by the Duke of Shrewsbury, was, on the accession of George I., taken permanently by a board, consisting of a First Lord of the Treasury, the Chancellor of the Exchequer, and three junior lords. These five men met generally on four days in the week, frequently sitting twice on the same day, and under them was a secretary, generally known as the Secretary to the Treasury.

Before 1680 the King in Council had entire control over estimates and apportionments. This control it exercised in various ways.

    I. It ordered the Lord High Treasurer
        to carry out certain instructions;
        to prepare a privy seal for the payment of certain money;
        to prepare a warrant for the king's signature.
    II. It referred business to the Lord High Treasurer
        for consideration and report;
        for action without report;
        for reference to other departments and report, or for action without
          report;
        for a hearing of the petitioner with report or action without report;
        or with instructions to do as he thought fit.
    III. It received original recommendations from the Lord High Treasurer, of which it approved or disapproved or to which it consented with the approval of the Lord High Treasurer.

After 1680 the Treasury was again put in commission and the Privy Council issued fewer orders and more instructions. It is evident that in its commission the board had received powers rendering it partly independent of the Council. This independent position was definitely established after 1714.

Until the period of the Commonwealth taxes were granted to the king and added to his own revenues, forming a fund or group of funds that he controlled as he would his private purse. The king, without interference from any one, met both the royal and the national expenses. After 1660, the same practice was continued, though occasional efforts were made by Parliament to define the object for which a specified appropriation was made. After 1689

Parliament took into its own hands the control of the finances and in 1694 established the Bank of England as the depository of funds. Thus it took from the Exchequer the duty of guarding the actual money, and eventually reduced that office to an impotent and useless organ of financial administration. By the middle of the eighteenth century the auditorship of the Exchequer had become a sinecure office worth £8000 a year. As a result of this differentiation of function, three interdependent but separate branches were created: the Treasury, the board of control, in the Cockpit; the Exchequer, the department of audit and receipt, in New Palace Yard and later in Whitehall Yard; and the Bank of England, the place of deposit, first in Grocer's Hall till 1734 and afterward in Leadenhall Street. All receipts were kept as separate funds against which charges were made, involving an enormous amount of complicated clerical machinery. The financial methods prevailing during the colonial period were antiquated and cumbersome, but it was not until after 1787 that a single consolidated fund was established, into which all receipts from every source were turned. The Exchequer was abolished in 1834.

Under Charles II., when the modern treasury system was evolved, the Treasury Board sat in two capacities, executive and administrative, and it continued to exercise these functions throughout the colonial period.

In its executive capacity, the board considered questions of finance, debts, loans, petitions, requests, approvals, appointments, etc. Its activities in these particulars gave rise to the minute books and the original correspondence. The first, at the beginning, are fairly full and informing, but later they become meagre and perfunctory. The second are of great value throughout our entire period. The meagreness of the minute books forces the student to search elsewhere for information. The board kept a series of registers and reference books that contain lists of documents read, and frequently bear, as endorsements, the resolutions of the board. These books are valuable as supplementing the minute books and as giving a key to the contents of the original correspondence.

In its administrative capacity, the board kept a series of books, in which were entered the warrants or orders by means of which expenditure was controlled. The money books contain orders emanating from the Lords of the Treasury and addressed to the auditor of the receipt of the Exchequer, authorizing that official to draw an order for the payment of a certain amount of money to a certain person. Though privy seals for money always began in the Treasury, whence the first warrant issued, countersigned by the board, all Treasury warrants theoretically rested upon a royal order, either a letter of privy seal, a letter of privy seal dormant, a general letters patent dormant, or a royal sign manual. These warrants, which concern every branch and species of Treasury payment, begin with 1660, though the regular series dates from 1676. The order books contain the entries of the orders drawn by the auditor on receipt of the Treasury warrants and returned to the board for verification and signature. Such orders always recited the authority by which they were paid. After the order was entered in the Treasury book it was forwarded to one of the tellers of the Exchequer on whom it was drawn. The order was also entered in the books of the Pells Office. Of the three series of order books thus established, that of the Treasury is the most valuable historically, though it does not begin until the inauguration of the new system of Treasury bookkeeping in 1667. The disposition books contain entries of the letters drawn by the board, before sending the final order to the teller, stating from which fund the money was to be paid. There existed a bewildering variety of separate funds, and these books are difficult to use and are of relatively less importance historically than are the others.[1]

Of all the departments constituting the British system from 1660 to 1783, none was so imperious and dictatorial and none so intimately connected with the routine of government as was the Treasury. Its correspondence included the Privy Council, the Secretary of State, the Commissioners of the Customs, the Ordnance Office, the Admiralty, the Commissioners of the Navy, the paymaster of the forces, the excise commissioners, office for taxes, the procurator general and other legal officers, the various auditors and receivers of accounts at the Exchequer, the auditor general of plantation revenues, the commissary of prisoners, the commander-in-chief in America, the commissary-general, colonial agents, many contractors and purveyors, and a miscellaneous body of correspondents in America, particularly those connected with royal revenues and expenditures there, such as the surveyor of customs and the surveyor of the woods. The board made up elaborate reports from its records and sent them to Parliament, the Privy Council, and the Board of Trade, and it took into consideration any matters that might be referred to it from one or other of these bodies. It received a great many petitions, memorials, and proposals from the colonies on its own account, and dealt with them either directly or after consultation with the Board of Trade, the auditor general, or the Commissioners of the Customs. It shared with the latter the control of the customs establishment in America, had general oversight of the acts of navigation, and was in communication with governors and other officials in America regarding matters of trade and revenue. It drafted, or had the Commissioners of the Customs draft, that part of the governor's instructions which related to the due execution of the acts of Parliament. It wrote to the collectors of customs in America, and after 1767, when the American Board of Customs Commissioners was established in Boston, it received directly from that board information regarding the customs affairs of all the colonies except Jamaica and other West India islands, which continued to correspond with the authorities in England. It received shipping returns from the naval officers, and reports, when it could get them, from the collectors. It drafted warrants and commissions, and the former, which were sometimes prepared as a preliminary step to the issue of a letters patent or a privy seal, concerned salaries, contracts, money grants, and remittances, allowances for civil establishments, expenses of all kinds, distribution of prize money, and the like. It received great numbers of accounts from the Commissioners of the Customs, not only in England but in Ireland also.

The Treasury had under its charge not only the Board of Customs, but also the commissariat and the transport service, the Post-Office, the auditor general of the plantations revenues,[2] the Registry Office,[3] and such occasional commissions as those appointed to investigate the Royal African Company, American Loyalist claims, and East Florida compensation claims,[4] and it made all payments resulting from the work of these commissions. It received reports from Blathwayt, Walpole, and Cholmondeley, auditors of the plantation revenues; it came into touch with the Bishop of London regarding the

---

[1] For the powers under which the Treasury was enabled to direct money to be issued from the Exchequer at the end of the colonial period see a manuscript in the *Chatham Papers,* bundle **231**, which deals with the establishment of the Treasury, its powers, and the distribution of its business. The date is 1782-1783. *Cf. Treas.* 1 : **526**, 344.

[2] See below, p. 142.

[3] See *Guide,* I. 58, note 2.

[4] See below, pp. 255-265.

allowance of £20 made to clergymen going to the plantations, and with the Lord Chamberlain in connection with communion plate given to Anglican churches in the colonies or loaned to them from the royal Jewel House. All accounts of money spent were settled by declaration before the Lord High Treasurer, the First Lord, or the Chancellor of the Exchequer, and were duly registered in the series of Declared Accounts.[1] The formal declaration, engrossed at the Audit Office from the statement sent in by the person responsible for the expenditure, was returned from the Treasury after declaration and preserved in the Audit Office. A parchment copy went to the Exchequer for enrollment and for preservation in the Pipe Office in Gray's Inn Lane. The Treasury had its own solicitor, whose office was in Whitehall and whose business it was to prosecute law-suits in the Exchequer Court or elsewhere.

The relations between the Treasury and the Board of Trade were always intimate. The Treasury frequently called on the board for information, and received from the board many appeals from colonial officials regarding their claims, a persistent source of trouble, for the Treasury was constantly in arrears of payment. In time of war it was confronted with that most difficult of colonial questions, the question of protection, and it was accustomed to call for all the information it could obtain regarding the state of the colonies, the number of troops needed, the kind and quantity of arms and ammunition, and the time necessary to supply adequate forces for an expedition. It obtained such information chiefly from the Board of Trade, and handed on the information thus obtained to the Ordnance Board or the Secretary at War with suitable recommendations. It played a large part in the business of apportioning the various Parliamentary allowances to those colonies that took part in colonial military undertakings, though it left to the board the general control of disbursements, carrying out such recommendations as the board saw fit to make.

The relations between the Custom House and the Board of Trade were equally close. At the request of the latter the Board of Customs sent in reports of all kinds, furnishing information regarding exports and imports—of hemp, beaver, hats, rice, etc.—often going back many years for its data. These customs reports have a special value owing to the scarcity of custom house material, large masses of which were destroyed when the Custom House was burned in 1814. Inasmuch as the Customs Board in England was responsible for the enforcement of the navigation acts, having a special official on its establishment for that purpose, and inasmuch as it had under its control the appointment of customs officials in America, it was inevitable that its relations with the Board of Trade should be frequent and regular. The Treasury, the Board of Customs Commissioners, and the Board of Trade shared, therefore, the management of the customs system in America. As the governors acted the part of colonial agents in the enforcement of the navigation acts, their instructions on this point and on all matters relating to trade and commerce, though drafted by the Board of Trade and issued by the King in Council, were either written in the first instance by the Commissioners of the Customs or revised by them at the request of the board. Sometimes the two boards met and considered important details, each board giving the other valuable and helpful information. At the same time the Board of Trade used many of the customs officials in America as agents for the obtaining of direct information. Quary, Randolph, Fitzwilliam, and others, though in no way responsible to the Board of Trade, sent it long letters, frequently biassed and exaggerated, but always valuable.

[1] See p. 79.

Of equal importance, though in a different way, were the relations of the Treasury with the Post-Office. The Treasury appointed the post-office officials, such as the deputy postmasters in America, though probably lesser postmasters, commanders of packet boats, etc., were commissioned by the postmasters general,[1] who also issued all necessary orders and instructions. The postmasters general sent many letters, reports, and memorials to the Treasury and received from it warrants, instructions, and orders in return. They also received any petitions or other similar papers that came into the hands of the Treasury bearing on postal business, and were required to make reports or representations thereon. With other departments the postmasters stood in equally close business relations, for the general Post-Office had under its charge all that concerned communication with the colonies, as far as letters and transmissions were involved.[2] The Post-Office building, during the eighteenth century, was in Lombard Street on the south side.[3]

Outside the Treasury, but in close connection with it, was the office of the paymaster-general of the forces, a post of ministerial rank and political importance.[4]

Before the destruction of the palace of Whitehall in 1698, the Treasury had its chambers in the building that lay between the Banqueting Hall and the privy garden, though the Lord High Treasurer seems to have had an office in Wallingford House during the reign of Charles I., and again after the Restoration when Clifford was Lord Treasurer. After 1700, the Treasury Chambers were located in the Cockpit, but in 1733 a handsome stone building was erected, from designs by Kent, one of the surveyors of the Board of Works, facing St. James Park and the Horse Guards Parade, and adjoining the Cockpit, which lay between it and the street leading from Charing Cross to Westminster.[5] To this building, which still remains, the Treasury Chambers were confined until the completion, in 1846-1847, of the present structure facing Whitehall and stretching from Dover House to Downing Street, the southern wing of which, erected in 1824-1825, was already occupied by the Privy Council and the modern Board of Trade. At the western end of Downing Street, connected with the Treasury by a passageway, was the home of the First Lord of the Treasury, occupied by Walpole in 1731 and probably by his successors. This residence was remodelled about 1750 and continuous occupancy by the First Lord can be proved from 1772 (Lord North) to the present time.[6]

The books and papers of the Treasury date chiefly from the first years of the Restoration, but it was not until the reorganization of the office in 1667

[1] There were two postmasters general from 1690 to 1824.

[2] Dodsley, *London and its Environs*, V. 208-222. Dodsley gives the rates as follows (1781): to the West Indies, 1s. 6d.; New York, 1s.; West Indies to New York, 4d.; New York to Perth Amboy, or to any town within 100 miles, 6d.; Perth Amboy to Burlington, 4d., etc.; pp. 215-218.

[3] Maitland's plan of Langborn Ward and Candlewick Ward shows the location of the Post-Office in Lombard Street.

[4] See pp. 131-132.

[5] The Chancellor of the Exchequer, though he afterward lived in a house adjoining the new Treasury, had at this time a house in Arlington Street, and there the Treasury Board met for a while in 1732. During the remainder of the time, when the new building was in process of erection, the board used the State Lottery Office next to the Banqueting Hall on the south. Views of the building of 1733 are in Shepherd, *Views of London*, vol. II., plate 173; Knight, *London*, V. 289; Britton, *Public Buildings of London*, vol. II., facing p. 420; Dodsley, *London and its Environs*, VI. 196, and elsewhere.

[6] Pascoe, *No. 10, Downing Street*; and *Crown Lease Book*, VIII. 146, 168, XVI. 457-458.

that orders were issued for a more regular keeping of papers and a more efficient despatch of business. A keeper of the papers was first established in 1726, and the latter were described at that time as being in bags and presses, in a disordered condition for want of a proper place wherein to deposit them, and a fit and able person to collect, sort, digest, and put them in order.[1] New rooms were assigned at that time as a repository for the papers. After the erection of the new Treasury building, the books and papers lay for years neglected and uncared for in the cellars, vaults, and lofts of the Cockpit and the structure facing St. James Park. When at the request of the Lords of the Treasury an assistant keeper of the Public Record Office was sent to examine them in 1842, he found them in a condition discouraging in the extreme. " Many of them had received every injury ", says the deputy keeper in his report, " to which papers could be exposed. They were found deposited in lofts and garrets, in vaults and cellars, in dust holes and coal holes ", where they were exposed " to dust, dirt, and filth of every description, to damp and rain, and more than all to foul water from the common sewer ". Operations upon the worst of these papers afterward were sometimes of " a most tedious and dangerous character, the documents having a peculiarly offensive and fetid odour and being agglutinated or adhering one to another and page by page in such manner as to render the use of a paper knife indispensable in separating them, while the gritty deposit or dust found universally on their surfaces was of a saline, pungent, and irritating character ".

The papers and books thus examined from 1842 to 1846 included a large number of the records herein described, many Custom House papers (though 565 volumes of establishment books had been sent to the Custom House in 1835), and the papers of the Royal African Company and the East Florida Claims Commission, which had suffered greatly from the inflow of foul water. All these papers were transferred to the Rolls House in 1846 and 1847, a few of those most offensive and decayed being stored in the loft of the engine house in Rolls Yard. The great mass of Treasury Board papers or original correspondence was removed from the Treasury Chambers in 1846 and 1856 and weeded out by order of the Treasury, pursuant to a report of committee, in September, 1863. Additional papers, of date later than 1783, were transferred in 1851 ; and in 1852 and 1853 was removed a collection of 850 volumes of Treasury books, which having lain for years in the lofts over the Treasury Chambers had been cleaned and sorted in 1842-1843 by the Treasury clerks, who thought that the books might be of value to the department. These volumes consisted of customs and commissariat books, docket books, various money and warrant books, quarterly and yearly revenue ledgers, and registers of declared accounts. In the collection were a few papers relating to Loyalist and East Florida claims.

With the removal of the last of the papers and accounts of the Treasury solicitor in 1855 and of the original correspondence in 1856, all the volumes and bundles originating with the department of the Treasury and containing material for American colonial history had been placed in the custody of the Master of the Rolls.

AUDITOR GENERAL OF THE PLANTATION REVENUES.

Almost the only administrative official, whose office was called into existence because of England's interest in her colonies, was the surveyor and auditor general of the king's revenues in America, whose duties were much

[1] Thomas, *The Ancient Exchequer of England,* p. 139.

the same as those of the auditors of the Exchequer in England. This office was established in 1680 for the purpose of bringing the royal revenues in the plantations " under a more certain method of account ", and for other reasons which may be found stated in the commission [1] to William Blathwayt, who was the first incumbent. Before that date the method of securing the royal revenues, such as they were, had been very haphazard. In England an office of receiver general of plantation revenues had been erected as early as 1663, granted to Chiffinch and Brown, and sublet to Thomas Povey.[2] The revenues aimed at were chiefly those from the West Indies, and at most probably never amounted to much, as the four-and-a-half per cent. was farmed and the returns from other sources were meagre. Still the office was filled and the fees were paid. The question of establishing a more efficient system of collecting the royal revenues in the colonies had been debated in the plantation council in 1663, and the larger question of the enforcement of the navigation acts had been considered by the Council of Trade in 1668, with the result that the Privy Council ordered the farmers of the revenue to send over and make choice in the colony and from time to time commissionate and maintain one or more persons in each plantation, to be approved by the king, to take care that the navigation acts be enforced.[3]

Virginia had had a registrar of casks as early as 1639,[4] and we read of Claiborne as commissioned by royal patent to receive the quit-rents as early as 1643. Henry Norwood had been made escheator and treasurer by Charles II., while the latter was at Ft. Johnstone in Scotland, Sept., 1650, and by the same patent had been made receiver of the quit-rents.[5] Norwood probably exercised none of these functions till after 1660 when he held the office for many years. There was also in Virginia an auditor, Thomas Stegg, jr.,[6] followed in 1670 by John Lightfoot. In 1669 the farmers in England commissioned Edward Digges, a former governor of Virginia, to carry out the instructions from the Privy Council, and Digges, after a struggle, supplanted Lightfoot and held the office until 1675, when he was succeeded by Giles Bland. After 1680 the office came under Blathwayt's control. With the auditorship, Digges seems to have combined the functions of treasurer, escheator, and collector.[7] There were in the West Indies escheators and receivers of quit-rents and managers of the four-and-a-half per cent. serving under the farmers in England.

The royal revenues in the plantations consisted of the four-and-a-half per cent., the quit-rents, returns from fines, forfeitures,[8] and escheats,[9] shares in

[1] Printed in *Mass. Col. Rec.*, V. 521. Many copies exist, Brit. Mus. *Add. MSS.* **12429, 22357,** and in Blathwayt's Journal, *Treas.* 64: **88,** at the beginning of the volume.
[2] *Cal. St. Pap. Col.*, 1661-1668, §§ 99, 100, 376, 435, 486, 487, 488, 644, 1527.
[3] *N. Y. Col. Docs.*, III. 48-49; *Cal. Col.*, 1661-1668, §§ 444, 1884, 1669-1674, § 104, p. 169.
[4] *Cal. Col.*, 1574-1660, p. 305.
[5] Blathwayt's Journal, I. 10, 46, 68, 94-95.
[6] Bruce, *Institutional History of Virginia,* II. 598. Bassett, in the *Report* of the Am. Hist. Assoc. (1901), I. 556-557.
[7] *Cal. Col.*, 1669-1674, §§ 104, 192, 696; Brit. Mus. *Egerton* **2395,** f. 147.
[8] A case of forfeiture arose when John Holt of Lownescreek, Va., committed suicide. His personal estate accrued to the king as a forfeiture. In this case the forfeiture was remitted because the deceased had five children. Blathwayt's Journal, II. 323-324.
[9] Escheats arose on the failure of an heir to the property which was declared a seigniory though held in free and common socage, or on a failure to fulfill conditions of a grant, or for felony or treason. In Jamaica escheats when they happened were valued by a jury of twelve men on oath and the amount was paid into the Treasury. Escheats could not be granted away. *C. O.* 33: **27.**

prizes and prize goods, the king's third share of ships seized for illicit trading, imports on strong liquors and export dues on tobacco, sugar, cocoa, etc., in Jamaica, port dues in Virginia, certain customs dues and receipts at the king's weigh-house in New York, land returns and whale licenses in Bermuda, licenses on wine and ale houses, though of the former probably there were few if any among the continental colonies—Virginia saying that there were no wine houses in that colony—halves of wrecks, treasure trove, and other droits of the crown, not claimed by the Admiralty, the two shillings a hogshead from Virginia and Maryland, all mines, and tribute beaver from Indian tribes owing beaver, a revenue that the governor of Virginia claimed as a perquisite of office. The auditor also accounted for proprietary payments from the Jerseys and the Carolinas, which were due the crown under the terms of the charters, and which seem to have been always in arrears. In 1703 the New Jersey proprietaries were still owing £260, the payment of which had to be shared by some fifty persons, and in 1704 the Carolina proprietaries owed the crown £93. As in time many of these revenues came to an end or diminished almost to the vanishing point, new activities were discovered by the auditor. He audited, or claimed the right to audit, the revenue accounts of territories in America and the West Indies that had been taken by the enemy and held for a short time or acquired and annexed permanently to the crown. He claimed the right to audit all prize money from prizes taken by His Majesty's ships in time of war, and the accounts of the commissioners appointed to take charge of prizes captured from the French previous to the declaration of war in 1756. Many of these revenues became in time a negligible quantity, and by 1774 had ceased altogether from the thirteen colonies, but in the early years most of them in one form or another appeared in the reports which the auditor sent to the Treasury.

Before 1680 all financial relations with the colonies had been very loosely conducted and the revenues due from the colonies were heavily in arrears. Blathwayt took vigorous hold of the situation. He called the colonial receivers to a sharp accounting, demanded regular statements and the payment of all arrears, stirred up the proprietaries, and forced from Culpeper a surrender of the quit-rents that he claimed from the southern part of Virginia. Then in October, 1681, he appointed his own deputy auditors and drafted rigid instructions for their guidance. From this time forward all deputies were to audit the revenues and render an account twice a year. Their appointment had to be approved by the Treasury, and in the case of a vacancy occurring in the colony, the governor was authorized to appoint a successor, as Gov. Martin appointed Archibald Neilson in North Carolina, who could exercise full powers until the approval or disapproval of the auditor general in England was received. All such appointments in America were only during the pleasure of the higher official in England, and, beginning as early as 1689, service by deputy was allowed, the principal officer remaining in England.[1] From the accounts of his deputies the auditor general made up his report to the Treasury. Occasionally he sent his accounts to the commissioner of public accounts, and, as in the case of all officials handling money, he made the usual declaration before the Lord High Treasurer, or the Chancellor of the Exchequer, through the Audit Office.[2] He received from the Privy Council

[1] *Acts Privy Council, Col.*, vol. III., § 303.
[2] Henry McCulloh, who had had an unpleasant experience as receiver of quit-rents in the Carolinas, wrote in 1755 of the duties incumbent on the auditor or his deputies in the plantations as follows:

through the Treasury or directly from the Treasury itself all petitions from America relating to revenue and financial questions, and he reported on these petitions in writing to the board. He was occasionally called upon to attend the meetings of the board, to answer questions and to furnish information. The office was no sinecure in Blathwayt's day; his reports display an intimate knowledge of colonial affairs, as far as such knowledge could be obtained from the sources at his command, and he corresponded extensively with governors and other officials in all parts of the colonial world. His successor, Walpole, seems to have confined his activities to his reports, of which many are extant, while the last auditor, Cholmondeley, certainly drew a revenue from the office out of all proportion to the work he performed.

Blathwayt belonged to an office-holding family. His uncle was Thomas Povey,[1] who had been a member of the plantation council of 1660, treasurer to the Duke of York, receiver general of plantation revenues in 1663, and receiver general and treasurer of the affairs of Tangier. He was a cousin of John Povey, secretary of the Lords of Trade until 1696. He himself held many offices. He was auditor general from 1680 to 1717, secretary of the Privy Council and the Lords of Trade, Secretary at War, and member of the Board of Trade. Before his death, a reversionary grant of the auditor's office was made to Horatio Walpole, younger brother of Robert Walpole. After Blathwayt's death in August, 1717, a patent was issued to Walpole, October 16, and a commission the next day, conferring on him the office of auditor which he held until his own death in 1757. During that time he served in many important diplomatic capacities, was for a while secretary to the Treasury Board and cofferer of the household, but it cannot be said that he allowed his duties as auditor to interfere with his manifold other activities.

The value of the auditorship as a post of light duties and large pay appears from the fact that as soon as Walpole entered upon the office a reversionary

---

"They ought to give in charge to the receivers of his Majesty's revenues in the colonies respectively, a schedule or rent roll of all the money to be collected by them.

"And then it becomes the duty of the receiver or receivers to return to the auditor or his deputy a specifick account, not only of the persons from whom they receive any money, for the use of the crown, but also in what proportion they have paid, whether in whole or in part, and what remains due; and further to return a list of all such persons as have not paid any part or proportion of the chief rents, or any other revenues arising to the crown, distinguishing the places of their abode. And when such persons as are upon the receiver's list are non residents or not to be found, from the defects which have been in the records, in such case they are to be marked or dotted accordingly, that proper steps may be taken thereupon to enforce the payment of his Majesty's revenues. And unless this method is observed, the receiver's accounts cannot be properly checked.

"And after the receivers have observed the said rules or methods of proceeding, then it becomes the duty of the auditor to make a brief declaration of every [one] of his receivers accounts, and to shew the last year's arrearages, for the allowance or disallowance of the Lords Commissioners of his Majesty's Treasury on that head; and if this is omitted, the auditors or the receivers, as either are in fault, are liable to be prosecuted, and to forfeit their commissions.

"How far the above regulations have been complied with or whether the receivers of his Majesty's revenue in *America* have acted agreeably to their duty, in regularly transmitting their accounts home to the auditor, will appear by the dates, and likewise by their accounts. And whether the auditor general hath had any objection to the said receivers accounts, or endeavored to correct the same, or laid the said receivers accounts before the Lords Commissioners of the Treasury, for their lordships allowance or disallowance of them, may be known to those who have the power to examine into this matter." *A Miscellaneous Essay concerning the Courses pursued by Great Britain in the Affairs of her Colonies* (London, 1755), pp. 104-117.

[1] See *British Commissions*, etc., Johns Hopkins Univ. Studies, XXVI. 55, 79.

grant of it was obtained by George, Lord Newburgh, poet and general, later George, second earl of Cholmondeley, to take effect on Walpole's death. Cholmondeley himself died in 1733, but already on August 14, 1732, he had willed the office to his youthful grandchildren, Frederick, afterward Lord Viscount Malpas, and Robert, passing over their father George, the third earl, who became lord privy seal in 1735 and was still living in 1760. The bequest, which was secured by letters patent September 6, 1732, was designed as a provision sufficient to render all further assistance to the grandchildren unnecessary. Lord Malpas died in 1751, and his brother, who had become the Hon. and Rev. Robert Cholmondeley, surrendered the office on October 14 of that year, receiving it back by letters patent bearing date November 20 (*Patent Rolls,* 5 George II., pt. II., p. 20). When Walpole died in 1757 Cholmondeley became possessed of the office, after waiting for it twenty-five years, and he held it largely as a sinecure throughout the remainder of the colonial period. In 1770 one Bradshaw received a patent in reversion of the auditorship for his own life and the lives of his two sons, but he died before Cholmondeley, and the extinction of the office deprived his sons of their expected emoluments.

Robert Cholmondeley had a chequered financial career. He does not appear to have possessed means of his own, and until 1755 seems to have been dependent on his income as a clergyman. But he had influential friends and relatives. His father was chancellor of the court of the duchy of Lancaster, and after retiring in 1742 obtained for his son the reversion of the office of clerk or prothonotary of the court, to go into effect on the death of two incumbents, one of them also a Cholmondeley. Unhappily for Robert Cholmondeley's expectations, this event did not take place until after 1783, so that until 1757 Cholmondeley lived under the hope, long deferred, of two reversions. The situation was relieved in 1755, when Lord Edgcumbe, who had succeeded the elder Cholmondeley in the chancellorship, presented Robert Cholmondeley with two rectories or livings in Herefordshire. The revenues from the glebe lands, tithes, rights, and appurtenances of these livings, added to the income from the auditorship, placed Cholmondeley in affluent circumstances, but he maintained a scale of expenditure which after 1774, when the troubles in America deprived him of most of the advantages of the auditorship, brought him to bankruptcy. Hoping that the suppression of the rebellion would restore to him the emoluments of the office, he continued his usual mode of living, until in 1780 he had incurred debts to such an extent as to compel him to leave the country. To meet his obligations he made over the reversion of his office of prothonotary, the rectory and livings, and the office of surveyor and auditor for the benefit of his creditors, and did not return to England till 1784. He promptly laid a claim for losses due to the American Revolution before the Commission on American Loyalist Claims, and received at the hands of the commission compensation at the rate of £400 a year. He died June 5, 1804, in his seventy-seventh year.

In 1711 Blathwayt reported that his own salary amounted to £600, made up of £150 paid from Barbadoes, £100 from the Leeward Islands, £150 from Jamaica, £100 from Virginia, and five per cent. of the New York revenues, apparently valued at the same sum. He complained, however, that the amounts were in arrears and that he had little expectation of payment from

Barbadoes, Leeward Islands, or Virginia.[1] In Walpole's time the amount was not less than £800, as after 1730 each of the Carolinas paid £100, and there were contingent receipts in the form of fees. But according to Cholmondeley's statement, made to the claims commission in 1787, the salary during his incumbency amounted to £950, the Virginia fees (averaging the years from 1750 to 1759) to £636, those from Carolina, New York, and Georgia to £300, the Jamaica allowance to £100, and the whole to £1836, of which less than £500 went for clerk hire. Probably Cholmondeley exaggerated the total, as it was to his advantage to make his losses appear as serious as possible, but even at best the value of the office was very great when compared with the work which the incumbent performed. There are very few reports from Cholmondeley among the Treasury papers and little evidence that he had much work to do.[2]

Mention is made in various places of the " auditor general's office ", of the various clerks of that office, and of the books and papers thereto belonging. Though Blathwayt had his private house in the country, he occupied, when in town, quarters in the neighborhood of Wallingford House (on the site of which the present Admiralty is built), and, it may be, held a lease of Little Wallingford House, which George I. in 1724 granted to his son, Lieut.-Col. Blathwayt. If so, probably the Auditor's Office was located there. Blathwayt accumulated large quantities of papers, some of which are in the British Museum, others in the Public Record Office, while the bulk of the collection was taken to Dyrham House, Gloucestershire, probably on his retirement from active life in 1710.[3]

Walpole in 1727 acquired a lease of the property on the corner of Downing Street and the " Great Area ", which had been the western part of Lord Rochester's house, of which King's Gate till 1723 and the part later occupied by the Board of Trade had formed the remaining portions. On this site Walpole built a house, which must have been used for an office also, for he had a deputy and clerks, and kept books, the present whereabouts of which are unknown. There are no Walpole papers of value for colonial history except such as exist among the Treasury series. Cholmondeley, likewise, has left no papers, except the reports, comparatively few in number, among the Treasury in-letters. An explanation of this fact may be found in the statement made in 1787 that " his papers relating to his receipts and payments [were] in his distress mislaid and lost ", and again that " the greatest part of his papers had been lost when a sudden necessity of quitting the country threw all his property into confusion." We know that Walpole kept books of the four-and-a-half per cent. and of the entries for the affairs of New York, and it is probable that both Walpole and Cholmondeley kept a record of all the

[1] Blathwayt's Journal, III. 52-53, *cf.* 61-68. In 1737 the New York assembly flatly refused to pay the 5 per cent. allowance, though Governor Clarke in his letter to the Board of Trade said that the amount had been regularly paid for forty years. *N. Y. Col. Docs.*, VI. 94. Later the payment was changed to a salary of £100 stg., but it is doubtful if this sum was regularly paid as a whole. *Ibid.*, VIII. 454.

[2] Cholmondeley gave in his statement the figures covering the fees from the 2s. per hhd. and the quit-rents for each year from 1749 to 1758. He estimated the corresponding fees from the Carolinas, New York, and Georgia at £400 but " to avoid all possibility of an overcharge " he placed them at £300. The fees from other places he deemed inconsiderable.

[3] The Blathwayt correspondence preserved at Dyrham Park was sold at Sotheby's in April, 1910. An additional lot, from the Phillipps Collection, was sold by the same firm in May, 1913. The descriptions of these papers contained in Sotheby's catalogues of the sales give an excellent idea of their value.

revenues, and entry books of reports, petitions, and letters. Of such books no trace remains. There is some reason to believe that Cholmondeley had an office at or near the Plantation Office in the Treasury, as he speaks of himself in one report as the " auditor of the Plantation Office " and he dates one of his reports from the " Plantation Office ". His payments of deputies' salaries shows that he had clerks.

IN-LETTERS.

319-623. 1746-1785. Original Correspondence or Treasury Board Papers.

Treas. 1.

The Treasury Board papers have been calendared through the year 1745,[1] therefore the description of these papers here begins with the year 1746.

At present the arrangement of the papers in the bundles is partly chronological and partly by subject, while a rough form of classification by geographical sections, Scotland, Ireland, the colonies, has been introduced, but not very strictly adhered to. The present distribution of papers is in a measure haphazard, as many documents that belong together have become scattered, and enclosures are mentioned that are either lost or separated from the enclosing letter. Furthermore the dates of the documents do not always correspond to the dates of the bundles, though in the main the chronological grouping can be relied on. The average number of bundles to a year is between seven and eight and because of the system of classification adopted documents relating to the colonies are apt to be found somewhat grouped together in given bundles. But this grouping is incomplete, as all the bundles contain one or more documents of importance. The total number of documents that bear directly or indirectly upon American history is very great as the following lists will show. The Minute Book, which stands to the In-Letters as does the Journal to the papers of the Board of Trade, should always be consulted, not only for the discussions that took place at the meetings, but also for decisions that have sometimes failed to be endorsed on the original documents.

The documents are of so varied a character as to render a general description of little value. Therefore the plan has been adopted of listing in detail the contents of each bundle, as far as they concern our subject, by means of rapid summaries of the subject-matter. The numbers in parentheses, accompanying the present numbers of the bundles, represent the former arrangement, which remains unchanged except in this particular.

1746.

320 (246). Papers on the four-and-a-half per cent. Memorial of Robert Dinwiddie. Nov. 23.

Report of H. Walpole, auditor general, on the Fairfax claim, with petition annexed.

Papers regarding the provisioning of Rattan.

Memorial of Edward Lascelles, collector of Barbadoes.

[1] *Calendar of Treasury Papers,* 1557-1728, ed. J. Redington (six vols., 1868-1889) ; *Calendar of Treasury Books and Papers,* 1729-1745, ed. W. A. Shaw (five vols., 1887-1903, see vol. I. of this *Guide,* p. 15).

321 (247). Petition of laborers for the Board of Works, stating that they had had " no sort of subsistence but from their daily labor and being now seven months in arrears have exhausted their credit as well as substance, which has reduced them and their families to the lowest circumstances and are become real objects of compassion ". June.

Petition of Capt. William Thomson, commander and owner of the *Success,* in His Majesty's service in Georgia.

Bundle of papers relating to Canso and Annapolis Royal.

Extracts from the minutes of the board of Georgia trustees.

Account of expenses of Capt. John Gorham and his company in Nova Scotia.

322 (248). Papers relating to the case of Charles Dunbar, receiver of His Majesty's casual account in the Leeward Islands, with a letter from H. Walpole, auditor general.

Petition from the widow of Samuel Clarke, late chamber keeper of the Plantation Office.

323 (249). Account of His Majesty's revenue of two shillings per hogshead, arising within the colony of Virginia. Apr. 25–Oct.

Petition regarding the independent companies formed for the service of South Carolina.

Walpole's report on the case of John Hammerton, receiver general of quit-rents in South Carolina.

Account of revenues from quit-rents and from the two shillings a hogshead levy in Virginia. 1745-1746.

1747.

325 (251). Memorial of Gov. Bladen of Maryland.

Samuel Smith on the transportation of the rebels of 1745, showing their distribution among the colonies.

Virginia revenue statistics.

Id., four-and-a-half per cent. in Barbadoes.

Question submitted to the attorney general—a vessel re-exporting tobacco started from London and was wrecked at Portsmouth; was the drawback due as if it had been wrecked in the open sea? Answer, yes.

Papers concerning the South Sea Company.

326 (252). With the exception of a few papers at the end this bundle is made up of documents relating to the tobacco trade.

327 (253). Report by H. Walpole. June 26.

328 (254). Proposals regarding the tobacco duties.

Letter from Charles Dunbar. Antigua.

Demand by Gov. Clinton for payment of expenses incurred in the expedition against Canada, with explanations in red ink.

Petition of Thomas Marriott, agent and paymaster of two troops of rangers serving in Georgia.

Petition of John Grymes, receiver general of revenues in Virginia.

Formal demand of Richard Partridge, agent for Rhode Island, that the sum allotted to that colony be paid.

Account of services incurred during the war in behalf of the intended expedition against Canada.

Report by H. Walpole on the petition of George Clark of New York, with other papers, including Clark's petition.

Petition of Gov. Wanton of Rhode Island regarding military expenses.

Memorial of Richard Gildart, who transported rebel prisoners to Maryland and Virginia (names given).

1748.

329 (255). Duplicate of proposals regarding tobacco duties.
Some statistics of tobacco exported and imported.
Papers regarding customs disputes in Barbadoes (at the end).
Memorial of Richard Partridge regarding bills of credit of Rhode Island.

330 (256). Petition of Henry McCulloh regarding quit-rents, and other papers.
Letter from Gov. Trelawny of Jamaica regarding money expended for the Mosquito Shore (also **333**).
Gov. Shirley's affidavit regarding deposition of Moses Bennet of the brigantine *Boston Packet,* with muster-roll of men under his command.
Group of Massachusetts papers concerning the money granted by Parliament (four Shirley letters, Sept. 13, Nov. 23, Dec. 10, Dec. 20, abstract of others, letter from Sec. Willard).
Walpole's report on Grymes's memorial.
Report of the attorney and solicitor general on the payment of money to the colonies.
Petition to the Treasury in behalf of the inhabitants of Annapolis Royal, with many accompanying papers.
Account of merchandise paid for the support of New England troops by the inhabitants of Nova Scotia.
Walpole's report on McCulloh's petition.
Petitions of McCulloh to the Treasury and to Walpole.

331 (257). A few papers relating to the sugar plantations and to the duty on molasses, etc.

332 (258). Memorial from the creditors of the Royal African Company.
Opinion of the attorney and solicitor general on payments to the colonies; question of the powers of the agents to receive the money.
Tobacco papers; proposals for the prevention of frauds.

333 (259). A number of papers regarding the money for Massachusetts and New Hampshire.
" Copie de l'arret du Conseil concernant la perception des Droits sur les Liqueures fortes en Canada."
Rhode Island's account.
Regarding the pay of Hugh Whitefoord, commissary of musters, on the West Indian expedition of Lord Cathcart.
Shirley to Sec. Pelham. Jan. 25.
Letter from the War Office regarding regiments in America.
Memorial of Adm. Peter Warren, with an accompanying account of expenses at Louisburg.

Some tobacco papers, one on " Instances of fraud in the tobacco and
other goods outward ".
Regarding the garrison at Rattan.
Memorial of Thomas Marriott.
Memorial of John Catherwood, secretary to troops in New York,
for intended expedition against Canada.

1749.

334 (260). Only a few tobacco papers.
335 (261). Letter from John Catherwood regarding Clinton's bills and
certificates in connection with the intended Canadian expedition.
Apr. 11.
Letter from Gov. B. Wentworth. June 12.
Id., John Thomlinson, agent of New Hampshire, regarding bills
drawn on the navy by Gov. Shirley; and many other papers relat-
ing to the claims of Massachusetts and New Hampshire.
Letter from Shirley to the Duke of Bedford regarding paper
currency in Massachusetts.
Paymaster H. Fox on Clinton's claim.
Copies of Col. Joseph Dwight's oath and bond (sent by Shirley).
Walpole's report on Eleazer Allen's accounts. Allen was receiver
of North Carolina.
Virginia statistics. 1748-1749.
Georgia and Nova Scotia papers.
Bedford to Capt. Hodgson appointing him governor of the Mos-
quito Shore.
Letter from Shirley. Boston, May 10.
Copies of the *New Hampshire Gazette and Historical Chronicle,*
Jan. 17, 1766.
336 (262). Victualling list for Chebucto.
337 (263). Draft of orders regarding droits of admiralty.
" The State of the Case of The Connecticut Regiment."
Letter from Shirley. Jan. 31, 1748. (Duplicate.)
Memorial regarding a ship taken by the French belonging to Joshua
Pierce of Portsmouth.

UNDATED MEMORIALS AND PETITIONS. 1750-1800.

338 (264). " Extraordinary Depredations committed in the River
Thames on ships arriving in that River from the West Indies,
particularly in the article of Sugar ", stating that 100,000 hhds.
are imported a year, but that all does not reach the custom house
because plundered by the " lumpers ", who shift from ship to
lighter, by lightermen, while the sugar is on the lighter, and by the
journeymen coopers, sent on board to repair the casks. *Id.,* rum,
indigo, and other West India products.
Petition of A. Frazer for the right to trade at Tadousac, Chicoutimi,
etc.
Petition of Capt. John Savage of Quebec for promotion and relief.
Petition of the planters and merchants trading to the sugar colonies,
against the practice of importing French sugar as British to
British ports from colonial ports, and desiring that importation

from any other place than the British sugar islands should be forbidden.

Observations on a scheme for the sale of the late French lands in St. Christopher, signed by William Mathew, Gilbert Fleming, Edward Mann.

Entry of passengers for Wilmington, N. C., by the *Industry,* John Alexander, master. Belongs to the same series as *Treas.* 47: **9-11.**

Petition of Craister Greatheed regarding escheated lands in St. Christopher; speaks of Gilbert Fleming as opposing him. After 1756.

Instructions to the agents for prisoners of war in the West India islands, by the commissioners for taking care of sick and wounded seamen. On f. 180 are similar instructions for surgeons.

Abstract of pay of the commissioned officers of all His Majesty's forces and garrisons. Other military charges and estimates.

Observations on sugar production and refining, with an argument against sugar refining in the West Indies, as involving loss to British navigation (because of less freights) and to manufactures (because an injury to refining and distilling in England).

Memorial of the representatives of the island of St. Vincent to Gov. Morris, in behalf of themselves and their constituents, against Archibald Ingram, receiver general of quit-rents. *Cf.* **339,** f. 114.

List of compensations granted to persons whose offices have been suppressed. 1782. A complete list of the offices, their incumbents, and the annuities allowed. The list includes the Secretary of State for the Colonies, the Board of Trade, and the staff of the Plantation Office, consisting of the secretary, deputy secretary, clerk of the reports, eleven writing clerks, chamber keeper, office keeper, and necessary woman.

339 (265). Sir Henry Clinton's observations upon certain returns—a valuable commentary on the careers and services of officers, Loyalists, and others during the Revolutionary War. After 1783.

Commissioners appointed for the sale of French ships taken before the declaration of war.

Quit-rents of the Island of St. John, with arrears.

Memorial of Christopher Codrington and other trustees of the will of Sir William Codrington, Bart., deceased. After 1792.

The remaining papers are all after 1783.

1750.

340 (266). Charges incurred by transporting to Nova Scotia officers and men dismissed from His Majesty's sea-service, 1749, and other expenses. *Cf.* ff. 163-167; **341,** ff. 83-96; **342,** f. 163.

Proposals for a colony in South America.

Kilby papers. Christopher Kilby was agent for Nova Scotia, and his statements to the Treasury are to be found in many of the bundles that follow. They will not be referred to again.

Order in Council, Aug. 2, on the report of the auditor general regarding the memorial of John Roberts, joint receiver general of Virginia, and reciting the report.

Accounts of the late intended expedition against Canada, showing the claims of the colonies.

Letters from John Thomlinson and Gov. Wentworth, and memorial of William Shirley, with other papers regarding these claims.

Instructions to David Dunbar, surveyor of the woods, with changes in pencil.

Letter from Sec. Harrington to the Treasury regarding additional military forces for Nova Scotia.

Certificates for the transportation of criminals. Many such in the bundles that follow. They will not be referred to again.

Coffee from St. Christopher, with a report from the excise office. *Id.*, tea from Philadelphia.

Letter from Gov. Cornwallis, Halifax, regarding the appointment of a customs officer there, stating that such officer is not needed as the naval officer is sufficient. Commissioners of the Customs say that the officer at Canso (Newton since 1724) can reside at Halifax and keep watch over Annapolis and Canso.

341 (267). An account of the several quantities of tobacco seized and prosecuted from Christmas, 1732, to Christmas, 1748. British ports only. Other papers follow concerning tobacco frauds. *Cf.* **345**, ff. 1-45; **347**, ff. 42-43. These papers lead up to the bill passed by Parliament for regulating the tobacco trade.

War Office establishment for the year 1750.

Report from the Secretary at War upon Col. Hopson's memorial on Louisburg accounts. *Cf.* ff. 119-156; **343**, f. 148.

Regarding tobacco frauds, ff. 162-184.

342 (268). Two reports of the attorney general on Henry McCulloh's memorial. Oct. 28, 1749, July 17, 1750.

343 (269). Concerning Col. Alexander Heron's Georgia accounts. Heron was lieutenant-colonel of foot stationed in Georgia.

Memorial of John Catherwood in behalf of Gov. George Clinton, with documents.

Memorial of William Shirley. May 5.

William Pitt to the Treasury regarding the claims of the colonies. Pay Office, Aug. 30. *Cf.* f. 192.

Memorial of Richard Partridge, agent for Rhode Island. Apr. 9. *Cf.* 142.

1751.

344 (270). Victualling lists, Halifax. 1751-1752. Four paper books.

345 (271). Establishment of St. John's and Placentia.

Various war estimates.

Report of the Board of Trade to the Treasury on the claims of Rhode Island.

Id., Nova Scotia victualling.

346 (272). Memorial of Lieut.-Col. John Caulfield, commander of the late garrison of Rattan.

347 (273). Memorial of Samuel Venner, late secretary to the Commissioners of the Customs in America. Oct. 29, 1770. Venner was appointed in 1767 and superseded Jan. 23, 1769.

Account of quit-rents in South Carolina, 1746-1751, with warrants of various dates, 1731-1746, for salaries paid out of the quit-rents.

Letter from Louis Burwell, president of the council, Virginia, regarding the revenue of 2 shillings a hhd., and the statute of Champerty (32 Henry VIII., c. 9, The Bill of Bracery and Buying of Tithes), " which was not known till very lately to extend to this colony ".

Mosquito Shore accounts. Such accounts may be found in succeeding volumes and will not be referred to again. The Mosquito Shore was directly under the control of the Secretary of State and the Treasury and of the Board of Trade.

Letter from Shirley regarding his warrants and accounts (not 1751 as endorsed). Upper Brook St., June 8, 1757.

Memorial of Edward Holland, agent of Indian affairs. New York, Dec. 21.

1752.

348 (274). Minutes relative to the case of Charles MacNaire of South Carolina.

Petition of Peter Wraxall, town clerk, clerk of peace, clerk of common pleas for the county and city of Albany, and secretary or agent of Indian affairs; appointed Nov. 5, 1750.

Georgia accounts, *cf.* ff. 216-219, silk culture. Report of the Board of Trade on the same. Dec. 20.

Grant of Cornwallis Island, Nova Scotia, by Gov. Cornwallis to his sons.

Letter and memorial of Harman Verelst for payment of claims. Also Oglethorpe's letter denying that Verelst was his agent (Feb. 10) ; answer to Verelst on the Treasury minute of Feb. 4, 1752.

Letter from Gov. Dinwiddie, with an account of quit-rents and 2 shillings a hhd. duty (ff. 230-233, 252-258). Dec. 10.

Papers regarding the Mohegan case, including the affidavit and statement of Moses Park, and petition of Samuel Mason, with statement of expenses and request for payment out of the four-and-a-half per cent. (ff. 234-247).

Case of John Roberts, joint receiver of Virginia.

Extract of a letter from Gov. Lyttelton, South Carolina, to the Board of Trade. Oct. 2.

349 (275). Extract of an act passed in Pennsylvania, Aug. 22, 1752, for regulating and establishing fees.

Copy of a letter from Gilbert Fleming, with papers relating to an escheated land case, and the petition from Craister Greatheed. St. Christopher, Sept. 21.

Petition of merchants trading to Virginia regarding the Spanish prize, *St. Juan Baptista,* condemned in 1744, which they bought and made free.

Regarding ships stranded on the coast of Ireland, having enumerated goods on board from the plantations. Report from the Commissioners of Customs.

350 (276). Petition of Gov. Trelawny, with Solicitor Sharpe's report thereon.

Letter from the Board of Trade about dispute between William Baker and Chauncey Townsend regarding a bill drawn by Gov. Cornwallis.

A state of the account of Francis Moore with the Trustees of Georgia, 1735-1736, signed Harman Verelst, accountant. Feb. 8. See also ff. 113, 115, 116b, Georgia papers, ff. 131, 133.

Memorial of Charles MacNaire, employed on an expedition to the " Chactow Nation ". Dec. 20.

Warrant for payment of Henry McCulloh.

Memorial and claim of the widow of Gabriel Johnston, deceased, late governor of North Carolina, in behalf of herself and her children. Johnston died July 17, 1752.

1753.

351 (277). Memorial of merchants and others concerned in the whale fishery, refers to the plantations. *Cf.* f. 180; **353**, ff. 50, 66, 217-224; **359**, f. 20; **361**, f. 172.

Petition of Benjamin Goldthwait to the House of Commons, who under commission from Gen. Shirley, Feb. 8, 1744, raised a company and commanded it at Louisburg and performed other services, with an account, 1744-1749; asks for recompense.

Report by Walpole on Greatheed's petition regarding land in St. Christopher. *Cf.* **356**, f. 138.

Report of the Ordnance Office on Cecilius Calvert's request that arms and accoutrements for 300 men raised in Maryland in 1746 for the intended expedition to Canada, " may be replaced in the magazine there ". With petition, and extract from the journal of the lower house, address of the house to Gov. Ogle, and extract of report of the Board of Trade.

Memorial of Charles MacNaire for money expended in furnishing the Choctaws with arms, ammunition, clothes, etc., to promote their revolt from the French to the British interests. Sept. 10. *Cf.* **353**, f. 3; **348**, f. 21.

Order in Council regarding the pay of judges in Virginia. Mar. 7.

352 (278). Smuggling of tobacco at Lundy, report from the custom house.

Request by the Board of Trade for Treasury report on Pennsylvania act regarding fees and customs, grants of land, and quit-rents, Georgia.

353 (279). Ordnance for Nova Scotia.

Petition of Benjamin Martyn, asking that the £2632 granted by Parliament for the civil list of Georgia may be issued without the deduction of 6*d.* in the pound, charged for the civil list, as all the sums granted to the late trustees were thus issued. June 20. *Cf.* **356**, ff. 119, 121.

Regarding account of Thomas Marriott.

Extract of Virginia act regulating the governor's fee for signing and sealing patents for land.

Statement of W. Horseley, " at the desire of the Carolina merchants ", regarding the converting of tar into pitch in England and consequent loss to the revenue.

Report from the Board of Trade upon the memorial of Gov. Osborn of New York regarding the policy of giving presents to the Indians. The memorial is f. 180 and is accompanied by an itemized estimate.

Quit-rents in Nova Scotia, Treasury to the Board of Trade.

Letter from Gov. Dinwiddie regarding fees for grants of land. Dec. 29. Speaks of having written to Walpole about it and says, " What situation is a govr in if he acts up to his instructions, with the advice of the council and approbation of the Lords of Trade? If a House of Burgesses, influenced by a few hot headed people, making a strong party in their house to address his Majesty against the govr in unjust terms and for a trifling fee, received by all other governors on this continent. . . . The above is a just detail of the whole affair; if your Lordships think me in the right I flatter myself with your interest and protection " (f. 241). A long and interesting letter.

354 (280). Memorial of Richard, freeholder of Frederica in Georgia and appointed tithingman of that town, Oct. 3, 1740, serving from 1741 to 1747, with certificate of Thomas Marriott, who served as second magistrate, asking for salary of £5 per year, or £35 for the seven years.

Order in Council regarding the charge that Andrew Stone, secretary to the lords justices, had drunk the Pretender's health. Many papers concerning this matter. Feb. 26.

From the Bishop of London regarding an allowance for the commissary of Virginia, and speaking of Thomas Dawson as appointed in place of his brother, deceased.

1754.

355 (281). A list of all ships and vessels which have entered inwards in the port of Annapolis in Maryland, Apr. 5–July 5, 1754. Benj. Tasker, naval officer. *Id.*, Jan. 5–Apr. 5. *Id.*, outwards. Other Maryland naval office lists follow in later bundles.

Memorial of Arthur Dobbs, governor of North Carolina, regarding the need of small coin; says that there is scarcely any gold or silver bullion in the colony, and wishes a copper coinage to be struck off at the mint for the use of the colony. The reply of the Mint follows, Oct. 1. Dobbs gives the number of white persons in the colony as 80,000.

356 (282). Copy of a letter from Oglethorpe to Harman Verelst, denying that Verelst was his agent or had any claims on him. Feb. 10, 1752.

Letter from Gov. Charles Knowles, with account of disbursements for the Mosquito Shore, July 19, 1744. Nov. 15. *Cf.* f. 49.

Treasury Board minute regarding the pay of American regiments (part of Gov. Shirley's and Sir William Pepperrell's). Oct. 9. (Rough draft.) Also f. 104.

A state of the case and particular services of Abraham Bosomworth, reduced ensign in Gen. Oglethorpe's late regiment of foot. In **358**, ff. 357, 359, is an account of goods supplied to the Indians by Bosomworth, 1747, and of his expenses as agent. See also *id.*, ff. 349, 351, 353, 355.

Quit-rents in Virginia. 1753.

358 (283). Memorial of Gov. Lyttelton regarding the defense of the colony against the Indians and the maintenance of friendship with them. Wants appropriation for Indian presents. A useful paper.

Account of money expended in experiments made on potash, " which have produced a discovery of a method of making the commodity and of the most proper places for erecting works in America ". 1741-1753.

Papers regarding the embezzlement by Hume, deputy receiver in Jamaica, of £20,000.

Extract of a letter from Dinwiddie on the fee question. Oct. 25. *Cf.* f. 316; **363**, f. 171.

Memorial of William Bollan regarding reimbursement of Massachusetts.

In this bundle are two itemized statements of the cost of passing a patent through the seals, £68 5s. 0d. in one case, £61 6s. in the other.

Bosomworth papers (ff. 349-359).

Memorial of Christopher Kilby regarding supply of specie for payment of troops in North America.

1755.

359 (285). Annapolis naval office lists. 1754-1755. Signed William Lux, naval officer. Against one of the bonds is this note, " This bond given pursuant to an act of assembly of this province, lately made, to prevent supplying the French, or their Indian allies, with ammunition, warlike stores, or provisions of any kind."

Petition of Thomas Stephens to the House of Commons regarding encouragement for the making of potashes in the plantations.

360 (286). Halifax naval office lists.

Copy of Dinwiddie's commission to Peter Randolph and William Byrd, commissioners to the Catawba and Cherokee Indians.

An account of the warrants drawn by Gen. Shirley, 1755, with explanations. (Valuable.)

List of ships, some for America, ready to sail, the masters of which desire leave to ship gunpowder.

Petition from Harman Verelst, recently released from the Fleet, asking for bounty or employment and enclosing " a plan of utility for the public which my thoughts have put together ", entitled " A Plan for raising a Fund in America to be applied in defraying the necessary expences attending the Defence and Protection of the British Possessions there ". Verelst advocates a stamp duty in America. The plan is that already noted among the Newcastle Papers in the British Museum, where no indication is given of date or author, Andrews and Davenport *Guide,* p. 140. The scheme is very much like that eventually adopted.

Draft of a letter from the Board of Trade to Gov. Dinwiddie regarding fees for patented lands.

From Gov. Knowles regarding the Mosquito Shore and the protection of the inhabitants there against the Spaniards. *Cf.* ff. 134, 136; **361**, ff. 86, 88.

Case of importers of whale-fins.

Case of Craister Greatheed and escheated lands in St. Christopher.

Regarding ordnance for Nova Scotia.

From John Sharpe, on petition of Lord Baltimore and Maryland merchants for the privilege of importing salt from any part of Europe.

Various Kilby papers regarding supplies for expeditions furnished by Kilby and Baker.

Copy of act in North Carolina for ascertaining and securing the payment of quit-rents, with marginal comments. The papers mentioned in the accompanying Board of Trade letter are in **361**, ff. 117, 119, 149, 159, 160, 182.

Account of letters to and from the West Indies.

Petition of Thomas Bosomworth regarding lands and the services of his Indian wife.

Thomlinson and Hanbury's accounts for subsistence of forces in New England and Virginia. 1754-1755.

Prices allowed for New England masts, yards, and bowsprits.

Answer by John Rutherford, receiver general of North Carolina, to charges against him. See **372**, f. 190, for Gov. Dobbs's explanation of the case; also **376**, f. 132.

Case of Francis Dalby, whose ship was planning to go to Madeira and South Carolina for a cargo of rice. *Cf.* **376**, f. 107.

361 (287). Case of French ships seized at Jamaica by Commodore Cotes before the declaration of war. After May, 1757.

Case of Craister Greatheed, with an elaborate statement, and the attorney general's opinion.

Correspondence regarding the packet service to New York, " a branch of service altogether new ".

Memorial of James Abercrombie agent for Virginia; and an address of the council of Virginia. These and other papers were sent by the Board of Trade to the Treasury. See previous bundle.

Letter from Gov. Dinwiddie enclosing an account of the 2 shillings a hhd. duty.

Naval office lists, Savannah, with list of vessels that have cleared outwards with enumerated commodities on board.

Id., Annapolis.

Account of money paid by the deputy paymaster general pursuant to Gen. Shirley's warrants. 1755-1756.

Copy of Gen. Braddock's letter to John Hunter and the latter's letter to Thomlinson and Hanbury. Braddock complained of having received only £10,000, and said that he could not move from Fort Cumberland without at least £1500 more. May 10.

Instructions to William Shirley from Braddock. Camp at Alexandria, Apr. 16.

Prices of provisions at New York in 1755, 1756, compared with the same in 1759, 1760.

Copy of quit-rent act in North Carolina, with Child's objections to the same, and the report by Sir Matthew Lamb (ff. 149, 159, 160, 182).

362 (288). In various accounts of " Disposeable Money in the Exchequer for his Majesty's Civil Government ", here and in other bundles, will be found the costs of the establishments of Georgia, Nova Scotia, and the Royal African Company. *Cf.* **364**, ff. 106, 120.

363 (289). On the payment of forces in Nova Scotia.

1756.

364 (290). Some army estimates and many tables of expenses, some of which relate to America.

365 (291). Naval office lists, Savannah.

Report of the attorney general on Shirley's warrants, with extracts from a letter of the Earl of Loudoun, Apr. 19, 21.

Memorial of the paymaster general on the deputy paymaster's accounts relative to the Shirley warrants, a valuable itemized statement of the expenses of the colonies. Further statements of expenses follow.

Board of Trade to the Treasury regarding the distribution of the £150,000 to the colonies voted by Parliament.

Further extracts of Loudoun's letters.

Anthony Bacon's proposal for the carriage of provisions in America.

Questions and answers relative to the commercial state of Canada. Endorsed " To be carried upstairs ", that is, from the Treasury Chambers to the Plantation Office.

Many provision contracts ; one an invoice of goods furnished by Israel Pemberton of Philadelphia, Dec. 15, 1755.

Copy of act appointing an agent for South Carolina, Nov. 19.

Gov. Benning Wentworth's acknowledgment of the receipt of bounty money.

List of papers relating to lands in Bermuda. *Cf.* ff. 112, 114, 124, 131, 139, 141, where papers will be found.

Papers regarding the trade from Milford Haven to the plantations (ff. 191-203).

366 (292). Board of Trade to the Treasury regarding Indian presents.

Thomas Pownall to Gen. Loudoun regarding questions of currency and payments in America. Written from Albany, Sept. 6, and bearing marginal comments.

Contracts and estimates, various.

367 (293). Gen. John Winslow's commission from Gov. Fitch of Connecticut (copy).

Thomlinson and Hanbury to the Treasury asking for a deposit of funds. *Cf.* f. 35.

List of papers relative to Shirley's accounts.

Winslow papers. *Cf.* **368,** ff. 5, 114, 118.

Halifax to Newcastle regarding payment to Capt. Cunningham and Lieut. Loring for bringing news of success at Nova Scotia.

Georgia establishment payments. There are many others in succeeding bundles and they will not be mentioned again.

A state of the claims of several of the American colonies.

Gen. Shirley's account, no. 1, for sundries supplied for the Niagara Expedition. *Cf.* f. 99. Various other accounts follow: ff. 111-116, 131 ; **368,** f. 121 (mutilated).

Many papers here and there relative to French prizes in the West Indies (f. 101). **381,** at end.

Memorial (copy) from Gov. Ellis, Georgia, on the state of the colonies.

Order in Council regarding barracks, Antigua.

Provision contracts (ff. 124-126 ; **368,** f. 106).

From Gov. Denny, Pennsylvania, regarding Stevens's experiment with potash.

368 (294). Report of the attorney general about the pay of the foreign officers of the American regiment.

From Robert Palmer, Point Bath, N. C., regarding the seizure of a ship.

Report on ordnance and stores supplied by Massachusetts, Connecticut, New York, New Hampshire, and Rhode Island, for the intended Crown Point expedition of 1756.

Gunpowder for Virginia, and other papers regarding the carrying of gunpowder out of the kingdom.

Letters from Loudoun (Aug. 20), Abercrombie (Nov. 10), and Loudoun again (Aug. 27), to Gen. Winslow.

Petition of Gen. Winslow for his pay, which four colonies refused to give him. Shirley's instructions to Winslow (f. 116).

Greatheed case, ff. 87-97 (fragile), and other papers.

2d Regiment of Foot sent to America (f. 192).

A bundle of Hessian papers.

369 (295). Letters from Fox (paymaster general) and Barrington (Secretary at War) regarding Shirley's warrants and the payment of troops in America. Oct. 12, Dec. 7.

Memorial of Henry McCulloh regarding his salary, with an account of his case, and a request that he be exempted from paying quitrents (f. 38).

Halifax naval office lists.

370 (296). Account of money raised by South Carolina for the king's service. Aug. 25, 1756–Oct. 20, 1757.

Various pay and commissariat papers.

Account of the money received by the paymaster general of His Majesty's 50th Regiment of Foot in America. Other similar statistics, with comments.

Account of provisions sent to America (Quebec) for the use of 10,000 men for 13 months. 1758, 1759.

Bond of Samuel Waldo. June 17.

Many letters from the War Office, some of which concern recommendations.

Receipt for provisions received from Massachusetts, also copy of resolution of Massachusetts assembly regarding money for commanding officers in the intended expedition against Crown Point, etc.

Order in Council regarding petition of Henry McCulloh. Oct. 13.

Benjamin Martyn, regarding the salary of William Clifton, attorney general of Georgia, to be given to his wife.

Extracts of Dinwiddie letters, showing disbursements and cost of expedition to the Ohio. 1754-1755.

Letter from Commissary-General Abraham Hume to Lord Barrington regarding various commissariat questions, especially concerning the appointment of deputy and under deputy commissaries. Barrington's reply, making recommendations to the Treasury. Also another Barrington letter regarding the augmenting of the 48th and 51st regiments, levy money to be obtained from the colonies. But, he says, toward such levy money " nothing (as I am informed) has been or will be obtained from the colonies." John Calcraft was agent of these regiments, and a memorial from him is enclosed.

Draft of a provision contract.

Account of sundry articles furnished by Rhode Island for the Crown Point expedition.

Account of the 2 shillings a hhd. revenue in Virginia, with letter from Dinwiddie, June 11.

371 (297). Many papers relating to ordnance and supplies for America, to augmentations of regiments, and to general expense accounts.

Petition from Fountain Cooke, planning to go to Jamaica to practise law and recover his fortune. *Cf.* f. 46.

Returns of provisions in store at Albany and what have been received since June 19. Shirley quitted the command on June 25. *Cf.* ff. 44, 45, 50, 51, 52, 53-56.

Memorial of Peter Van Brugh Livingston and Lewis Morris, jr., regarding their services as commissaries.

" An account of English merchant ships taken by the French before the declaration of war by way of reprisal for the merchant ships that had been taken by English men of war, and an estimate as near as at present can be learnt of their value." " It is said that the French prizes taken by the English men of war before the declaration of war sold for about 65000 pounds, and that the value of the English merchant ships which the French took by way of reprisal amounted to about 20000 pounds." *Cf.* f. 65.

Extracts of letters from A. Mortier, deputy paymaster, Boston.

1757.

372 (298). Various War Office estimates.

Report on the unlawful practice of supplying the French American settlements with provisions from Ireland. Custom House, Jan. 11.

Review of the revenues in Virginia, showing disbursements and deficiencies. 1750-1758.

Claims of Virginia and North and South Carolina to the £50,000 granted by Parliament.

Gov. Dobbs to the Treasury on the Rutherford case. Speaks of " his Majesty's interest which has hitherto been too much neglected in this province ". *Cf.* f. 190.

Memorial of Gen. Shirley, which gives his side of the warrant difficulty and begs the Treasury to dismiss Loudoun's suit (a useful statement).

Memorial of William Byrd and Peter Randolph for allowance recompensing them for negotiating a treaty with the Indians. *Cf.* **381**, f. 24.

Report from Robert Cholmondeley, auditor general, on land grants in North Carolina. Walpole's last report was in January; this is Cholmondeley's first report. From the " Auditor of Plantations Office". *Cf.* ff. 194, 196; *Patent Rolls*, 5 George II., pt. II., 20.

Extract of letter from Loudoun to Pitt, Apr. 25, and a letter, Jan. 28, stating his side of the Shirley dispute.

Letter from Robert Cholmondeley, addressed to Adm. Frankland (Barbadoes and Leeward Islands), claiming the right to audit all the prize money, asking what prizes he has taken, and calling for an account. See also **382**, ff. 99-115.

From the Earl of Bath recommending a friend of his, Mr. Neven, as customs collector at Piscataqua. Four letters, one to New-castle.

Extract of a letter from Gov. Dobbs to the Board of Trade. Jan. 20.

373 (299). Similar to **362**.

374 (300). Annapolis naval office lists.

Memorial of Abraham Hume for allowances to his deputies.

Victualling papers, Nova Scotia, comptroller's reports, and report from the Mint " in order to ascertain rates and proportion at which foreign gold coins are proposed to be current in America ", with a table.

Many Hessian and Hanoverian papers. *Cf.* **375**, ff. 56-237.

Other military estimates, with a letter from Barrington regarding Shirley's and Pepperrell's regiments taken prisoners at Oswego.

375 (301). Qualifications of a commissary-general of stores; many commissary lists and estimates of some importance for a study of the provisioning of the army in America.

Articles of complaint to be exhibited against James St. John, sur-veyor of South Carolina. No date, but must belong to 1732 or 1733.

Hessian and Hanoverian victualling and supply papers.

376 (302). Papers relating to the case of Gen. Winslow. March.

Dimensions of the vessels to be built at Oswego, with equipment (interesting).

Letter from Samuel Waldo to Capt. Stansbury.

Various affidavits in the Shirley case, and a letter from Spencer Phips to the Treasury.

Memorial of James Wright, agent of South Carolina, relative to the colony's share of the £50,000.

Regarding the crown lands in Bermuda.

Apportionment of the £50,000 to Virginia and North and South Carolina.

Quit-rents from Virginia.

377 (303). Barrington to the Treasury (Sept. 14) enclosing a letter from Cornwallis (Aug. 15) regarding the payment of troops in Nova Scotia. At the end " to be laid before parliament ".

Memorial of the commissioners for the sale of French prizes taken before the declaration of war. *Cf.* **378**, f. 172 ; **379**, f. 31.

Loudoun to Pitt, criticising the claims of the colonies. New York, May 3.

Shirley to the Treasury in his own behalf, with an account of his conduct.

(Printed in the *Correspondence of William Shirley,* II. 581-584.)

An account of the application and disposal of £800,000, authorized by Parliament for extraordinary expenses, 1757. Many Amer-ican items.

Connecticut's claim for repayment of expenses in victualling the provincials (1757), as stated by J. Ingersoll, June 29, 1761. En-dorsed " June 30 read, reconsidered the application of Connecticut, agreed that the former minute do stand ".

Letter from Thomlinson and Hanbury regarding complaint against William Johnson.

378 (304). Expense statistics, clothing for soldiers, etc.

Printed proclamation by Gov. Dobbs against James Murray and John Rutherford for issuing notes to pass current as money, with one original printed specimen and two written copies of notes for twenty shillings. Dec. 5.

Order in Council relating to the exportation of corn from New York to St. Augustine.

Memorandum by Horatio Walpole, cited to uphold Cholmondeley's claim to audit prize money. See **372**.

Memorial of Shirley, with accompanying letter from the War Office.

379 (305). Admiralty question. The Admiralty Board does not think itself authorized to direct the payment of certain charges for transport service to New York, Boston, and Philadelphia, amounting to £9000, out of naval money, as being foreign to the navy.

Halifax naval office lists.

Various colonial claims to money granted by Parliament, 1757, 1758. *Cf.* ff. 150, 151.

Dinwiddie regarding quit-rents and 2 shillings a hhd. revenue, with lists and a state of the country.

Papers relating to currency rates in America, transportation of money, etc.

1758.

380 (306). Naval supplies contracts. The navy allowance per man was, bread seven pounds, beef four pounds, pork two pounds, peas three pints, oatmeal three pints, cheese six ounces, butter twelve ounces or oil in proportion, rum seven half pints or wine seven pints or seven gallons of beer. See another list **382**, f. 16; **389**, f. 64.

A number of custom house papers.

Extract from Gen. James Abercrombie's letter to James Abercrombie, with the latter's power of attorney as agent for the 60th Regiment, Royal Americans. In this bundle are many papers connected with the business of paying the troops in America, and with the supply of provisions for the army.

Regarding New Hampshire's share of the Parliamentary grant.

Letter from Pitt to the Treasury regarding " careening warfs " at Halifax.

Report by Privy Council committee regarding allowances out of the quit-rents for councillors in North Carolina, with accompanying papers.

381 (307). Barrington to the Treasury regarding the Indian traders who supplied rum to the garrison at Oswego; and other Secretary at War letters regarding the war in America and elsewhere.

Id., letters from the Admiralty.

Letter from the Board of Trade to the Commissioners of the Customs regarding evasion of the acts of trade, Nov., with copies of the commissioners letters, 1730-1737.

Memorial of Francis Lewis, late commissary of stores at Oswego, with a report from the paymaster general.

Petition of Edward Dismore, postmaster general of Jamaica, 1754-1758.

Letter from Gov. Moore of Jamaica, with account of presents sent to the Mosquito Indians.

382 (308). Letter to the Commissioners of the Customs regarding the charge that the Boston collectors exact illegal fees and connive at illicit trade.

Victualling and contract papers.

Collection of papers relating to Cholmondeley's claim to audit prize money, May–July. Attorney General Pratt reported favorably, as also did the deputy auditors. The citations here given from Walpole's papers (ff. 109-115) are important.

Hessian and other German papers.

Resignation of Abraham Hume as commissary of stores. Jan. 31.

Annapolis naval office lists.

South Potomac, *id.*

Petition of John Reynolds, late governor of Georgia; left Georgia, Mar. 25, 1757, captured by French privateer, who seized all his apparel (except one suit of clothes), sword, watch, £250, and sent him to Bayonne. Recovered all but the value of £150, wants reimbursement. Aug. 23.

John Rutherford's explanation to Gov. Dobbs.

Accounts and victualling papers (coals to Louisburg).

Annapolis naval office lists.

Memorial of Gov. Hopson of Nova Scotia.

Copy of instructions to Gov. William Popple of Bermuda relative to the disposal of the crown lands there.

Memorial of John MacCulloch, late storekeeper at Oswego.

Report of Privy Council committee on the case of Henry McCulloh, with a copy of the latter's petition.

Pay list of troops employed in erecting a fort in the Island of St. John, by order of Gen. Amherst and Lieut. William Spry, engineer. In **381**, f. 16, it is stated that strict orders were given to the commanders-in-chief of the army in North America that no pay should be issued but for effective men.

387 (313). Papers relating to Lieut.-Col. Burgoyne's regiment.

Various certificates and accounts.

Deposition of Joseph Caruthers in the John Rutherford case. Jan. 4.

Order in Council authorizing the payment of McCulloh. June 16.

Memorial of Richard Cumberland, agent for Nova Scotia, with endorsement of the Board of Trade.

Halifax naval office lists.

388 (314). Account from Massachusetts of expenses incurred in the king's service.

A state of the claims of the several colonies, New York, Massachusetts, New Hampshire, Rhode Island, Connecticut, and of Gen. Winslow for his pay.

Regarding the collectorship at Piscataqua.

McCulloh's receipt for £1035 paid out of the four-and-a-half per cent. The whole sum due was to have been paid out of the quit-rents, but the amount was not sufficient. July 14.

Memorial of Benjamin Martyn for £1510 spent in Indian presents.

A return of the number of men raised by the colonies for the year 1758. From Abercrombie, a valuable statement, f. 85.

Gov. Reynolds on the expenses of the rangers in Georgia, and a memorial on the same, with endorsement by the Plantation Office.

Extraordinary expenses, New York.

Warrant of William Mathew Burt as agent for prize effects.

Memorial of Benjamin Franklin, agent for Pennsylvania, and an account of expenses to the end of 1758. Valuable.

South Potomac naval office lists.

Claim of Virginia on the £200,000 granted by Parliament, from James Abercrombie, agent.

Petition of John Rutherford, praying to be restored as receiver general of quit-rents for North Carolina, with a careful statement in his own defense. Rutherford was suspended by Gov. Dobbs, Dec., 1757. Also a letter from Cholmondeley.

Gen. Winslow to Gov. Fitch of Connecticut. May.

Resolutions of the House of Commons, 1756-1758, regarding granting sums to Massachusetts, Connecticut, Newfoundland, and to various persons.

Memorial of John Rutherford.

Id., Harman Verelst.

Account of 2 shillings a hhd. revenue in Virginia.

Various papers concerning Massachusetts accounts and the state of the province. Evidently sent over by Gov. Pownall.

1759.

389 (315). Memorial of Cholmondeley, with the attorney general's report thereon; favorable to the auditor general's claim to audit prize money (f. 22 ff.). July 30. *Cf.* **108**, ff. 112-113.

Paper relating to Virginia's claim to the money granted by Parliament.

Various victualling and transport papers, a valuable series for a study of this branch of the service.

A state of the provincial debt of New Jersey.

Copy of Adm. Cotes letter regarding trade at Monte Christi, and other papers.

Letter from Gen. Amherst. Crown Point, Oct. 22.

Memorial of Brig. Forbes, commander-in-chief of the expedition to the Ohio and Fort du Quesne in 1758, with a letter from Barrington to the Treasury, Apr. 3. Forbes states " That your memorialist immediately repaired to Philadelphia the place of Rendezvouze and with the utmost expedition assembled his troops, But had the mortification to discover disagreement, constant jarring, and animosity among the troops of the different provinces, and coolness and dispondency in the Indians. He first applied himself to remove the difficulties by reconciling his men to one another and to the service they were going on. For this purpose he took a house and kept open table at Philadelphia; he had the leading men of the different provinces constantly with him; he made them acquainted with one another, and by degrees had the good fortune to introduce harmony and unanimity amongst them." Barrington's letter is an important declaration of War Office policy.

Memorial of the governor and council of Virginia desiring that the deficiencies in revenue from the 2 shillings a hhd. duty may be made up from the quit-rents (ff. 107, 110).

Board of Trade to the Treasury regarding the bond of James Hamilton, appointed governor of Pennsylvania.

390 (316). Valuable collection of Guadeloupe papers relating to the problems arising out of the capture of the island.

Memorial of the commissioners for the sale of French prizes taken before the declaration of war.

Extract of Treasury minutes relating to the case of Adms. Frankland and Cotes. May 9, 1759–Aug. 22, 1763.

391 (317). Robert Leake, commissary of stores in North America, regarding provisions at Albany.

Many military estimates, including the plantations (ff. 89-130).

Memorial regarding Maj. Rutherford killed at Ticonderoga.

Annapolis naval office lists.

Roster of the garrison at St. John.

Victualling lists, Cape Breton.

392 (318). Instructions for stamp distributors in England, interesting with respect to the method of distributing stamps in America.

Representation from the Commissioners of the Customs on abuses in the plantation trade. " It being the custom and practice of this board in matters of revenue only to receive directions from and to make reports to the Lords Commissioners of the Treasury or his Majesty in Council." A letter from the Board of Trade to the Customs Board follows, and then a longer representation from the latter naming three forms of illicit trade: (1) importing rum and molasses from the French islands; (2) importing goods direct from the Continent (Hamburg and Holland) to America and carrying enumerated commodities to the same places and elsewhere; (3) supplying the French colonies with provisions from the American colonies or Ireland. Accompanying this report is the joint opinion of the solicitors of the Customs Board on certain law proceedings, to which reference is made in papers submitted by William Bollan and here given in copies, and a list of papers concerning illicit trade from the Board of Trade (26 in all, useful).

Memorial of Thomas Chapman, receiver general and collector of Guadeloupe, with the report of the Customs Board. July 19.

393 (319). Halifax naval office lists.

Bundle of Georgia accounts; unpaid bills held by merchants in England, drawn between Aug. 4, 1744, and May 31, 1750, for military expenses, amounting to £15,497.

Other provincial accounts, ff. 79 ff., 107-116, 161, 175.

394 (320). Claims of South Carolina for services in the prosecution of the war.

Memorial of Anne Cunninghame, widow of Lieut.-Col. William Cunninghame, late engineer to the expedition against Martinique.

Several Louisburg papers.

395 (321). Hessian papers (Germany).

396 (322). Representation of the Board of Trade on Indian presents. This paper states that since the beginning of the war the king had placed the direction of all matters relative to the North American Indians in the commander-in-chief of the forces there, and had appointed two agents to act under his orders.

Various victualling papers, mostly German but one or two American (ff. 25, 71).

Representation of the Board of Trade, Aug. 31, with copies of several depositions concerning illicit trade of the northern colonies with Monte Christi.

Gov. DeLancey to Pitt, Aug. 10, with enclosures.

397 (323). Auditor General Cholmondeley on the Rutherford case. July 21.

Guadeloupe papers.

Pay-list of the New England company of carpenters under Col. Meserve, Feb. 25–Mar. 24. Another list, Mar. 18-31. *Cf.* ff. 1-7, 112-137.

Memorial on behalf of Rhode Island by Joseph Sherwood (successor as agent to Richard Partridge, lately deceased).

Maryland's claim since 1754, signed Cecilius Calvert, secretary.

Expenses of Massachusetts, from the Board of Trade.

1760.

398 (324). Victualling and paymaster's papers. See also **399, 401, 402, 404, 405.**

400 (326). Gen. Amherst on the expenses of Forbes's expedition of 1758, with enclosures; a few memorials of colonial agents for the reimbursement of colonial expenses. A number of Amherst letters will be found in **406** (332)–**428** (354), especially **415.**

1761.

406 (332). Victualling and army estimates.

407 (333). Guadeloupe trade. See also **409** (335).

Paper from Henry McCulloh on the troubles in South Carolina, 1748-1760.

408 (334). Gov. Boone on smuggling in New Jersey.

Papers concerning the charges of corruption brought against Barons, collector of Boston, including, as enclosures, a number of letters between Barons and the Customs Commissioners, and depositions as to his alleged offense.

409 (335). Gov. Ellis of Georgia on the Creek Indians.

Bosomworth and the Georgia rangers.

Stores at Oswego.

412 (338). Military expenses in New England; references to the fire in Boston.

1762.

414 (340). Annapolis naval office lists. 1762, 1764.

Lists of officers victualled at Halifax and Quebec.

415 (341).   Compensation for Massachusetts, Rhode Island, North
          Carolina, and South Carolina, for expenses in 1760.
Memorial of Boston merchants in defense of Barons.

416 (342).   Papers relating to the affairs of the southern Indians.
Halifax naval office lists.
Plans for custom houses at Montreal and Martinique.

418 (344).   Value of exports from England to the several colonies in
          1740-1761.
Salary of Chief Justice Pratt of New York.   *Cf.* **421.**

419 (345).   New York provision contracts.
Indian relations, South Carolina.
Affairs in Manila.

421 (347).   Indian relations, South Carolina.
Customs at Quebec.

1763.

423 (349).   Quit-rents in the southern colonies.
Reimbursement of military expenses.
Civil estimates for Georgia and Florida.
Smuggling in New York and the West Indies.

424 (350).   French Protestants in South Carolina.   See also **423.**

425-426 (351-352).   Many papers on customs reforms in America.

1764.

429 (355).   Enforcement of the Molasses Act.
Projected court of vice-admiralty for all America.
Temple's charges against Cockle, the collector at Salem, and Gov.
          Bernard (*Acts Privy Council, Col.,* VI. §§ 621, 627).   Many of
          Temple's letters and memorials discuss with great detail the cus-
          toms difficulties in New England and the disagreements later
          among the members of the American Board of Customs Commis-
          sioners.

430 (356).   Papers preparatory to the Stamp Act, for which see also
          432-434.
Tables of customs receipts at each American port, covering the
          period Sept. 29, 1764–Oct. 10, 1768, and continued in **442, 452, 461.**

431 (357).   Customs and trade in the West Indies.

433 (359).   Tea smuggling from Holland and the Channel Islands.
Memoranda for a general fiscal consideration of the colonies.

434 (360).   Statistics and calculations on the molasses duty.

435 (361).   Annapolis naval office lists.

1765.

437 (363).   This bundle and the following bundles contain many papers
          describing Stamp Act riots, especially that which destroyed Dr.
          Thomas Moffatt's house at Newport.
Gov. Johnstone on the Spanish trade in West Florida.   See also
          440.
Letters from Gen. Gage.   New York.

439 (365). Stamp distributors, appointments, compensation, resignations. See also **440, 441, 442**.

441 (367). Letters on the dispute between Temple and Gov. Bernard.

442 (368). Letters from the various governors, chiefly to Halifax, on illicit trade.

Indian affairs in Canada.

443 (369). Memorials, etc., on the Spanish bullion trade.

1766.

445 (371). Scheme for a tea tax in America. Jan. 6.

Reports from the stamp distributors.

446 (372). Alleged smuggling by Daniel Malcolm at Boston.

In this bundle, ff. 134-143, are the notes of Grey Cooper, secretary to the Treasury Board, on the Stamp Act repeal debate, printed in the *American Historical Review,* Apr., 1912.

447 (373). Many papers relating to the opposition to the Stamp Act, and an unsigned draft of a stamp act. This bundle and following bundles contain many papers dealing with the Stamp Act, all of which, except the draft mentioned above, are in Grey Cooper's handwriting.

448 (374). Returns of stamped papers. *Cf.* **449**.

South Carolina Indian affairs.

449-450 (375-376). Various papers on the Indians, etc., in the Mississippi valley.

452 (378). Many reports and letters on Stamp Act riots and the issue of unstamped clearances, etc.

453 (379). On unstamped bonds, etc.

Opinion of the attorney general, De Grey, on many points in the administration of the acts of trade.

Malcolm's case.

455 (381). Opinion of Yorke and De Grey on the Spanish bullion trade.

Letters from the stamp distributors.

1767.

456 (382). This bundle and succeeding bundles contain many letters and reports from the customs boards in London and Boston.

Regarding posts on the Great Lakes—Maj. Robert Rogers, the well-known New England ranger.

West Florida papers.

458 (384). Letters from the stamp distributors.

Letters from Pensacola and Fort Cavendish.

459 (385). Plan for a board of customs in America. Apr. 16.

460 (386). Papers regarding the Ceded Islands, Tobago, St. Vincent, Dominica, and Grenada.

461 (387). Regarding the finances of the American Customs Board.

Papers relating to affairs in Quebec.

Letters from Gen. Carleton.

462 (388). An account of the gross and net produce of the duty laid upon the importation of molasses in the American colonies by an act passed in the 6 George II. Covers the years 1734-1764.

Id. by an act passed in the 4 George III. (ff. 132-134).

Some War Office estimates, especially estimates of the charge of His Majesty's plantations in the plantations and Africa, 1767-1768, compared (f. 172).

1768.

463 (389). Statement by Thomas Nuthall, solicitor of the Treasury, of cases prepared for the opinion of the attorney and solicitor general, among which is a case touching the entry of cargoes and unloading the same in America, Sept. 9, with written comments of the law officers, De Grey and Dunning.

Certificates from Gen. Haldimand regarding victualling in West Florida. Feb. 24.

Memorial of Henry Spencer, brother of John Spencer, late of Georgia. Read Apr. 14.

Extract of a letter from Mr. Roupell, searcher at Charleston, S. C., to the commissioners regarding vice-admiralty matters. Aug. 6.

A list of Gov. Carleton's warrants drawn upon Thomas Mills, receiver general of Canada, since Apr. 11, 1767, for contingent and incidental expenses (according to the *Minute Book,* **39,** 124, there should be an accompanying letter, but it is not here).

Memorial of William Graves on behalf of Lancelon Graves Berry, collector in North Carolina. Read Apr. 19.

Report on John Mason's second petition regarding the Mohegan Indians, with petition attached. Received May 18.

Case concerning the seizure of a ship at Boston—the *Liberty* case. Read July 28.

Memorial of the agent for Nova Scotia. Read May 2.

Memorial of Sir William Burnaby, late admiral and commander of H. M. S. at Jamaica and the Gulf of Mexico, " having been at great expenses in entertaining the Mortar King of the Indians, his chiefs and numerous attendance during the Congress held at Pensacola " (Brit. Mus. *Add. MSS.* **14034,** f. 227). Read June 30.

Memorial of Richard Shuckburgh, secretary for Indian affairs at New York. Read Feb. 18.

Memorial of John Ellis, agent for West Florida, regarding the year's expenses of the provincial sloop there. Received May 18.

Letter from John Robinson, one of the Commissioners of Customs in America, enclosing a copy of a paper posted up in Rhode Island on the " town house ". Boston, Feb. 22.

Two bundles of papers sent in Lieut.-Gov. Carleton's letters to Grey Cooper, Feb. 3, Aug. 4, with inventories attached, relating to the government of Quebec.

Memorial from Robert Cholmondeley praying for an allowance for his deputy at Guadeloupe. June 21.

A statement of account, containing a section on " American Revenue ". 1767.

Report by Nuthall on Lieut.-Col. Christie's memorial from the West Indies, Aug. 28, regarding the claim of Valentine Jones and Company for charges on the prizes taken before the declaration of war and carried to Barbadoes, Mar. 1, 1768, with the king's warrant for payment.

Memorial of Charles Garth on behalf of the province of South Carolina (a long detailed paper, see *Minute Book,* **39,** 105-106). Received Jan. 22.

464 (389 A). Letter from Gen. Gage regarding bills of exchange, with list enclosed. Dec. 19, 1766. Received Feb. 28, 1767.

Case of Grover, late chief justice of East Florida. Received May 13, 1767.

Memorial and annexed papers from John Uring regarding the impressment of the snow *Polly* at Quebec (1759). Feb., 1767.

Memorial of William Clifton, late attorney general of Georgia and now chief justice of West Florida. Oct. 13, 1767.

Petition of William Robinson, newly appointed comptroller of His Majesty's customs in Jamaica, for aid in paying his passage there. Apr., 1767. Endorsed " nil ".

Extracts of letters from Generals Gage and O'Hara. War Office, May 22, 1767.

Form of a bond for non-enumerated goods agreeable to 6 George III., c. 52, § 30, and 7 George III., c. 2. (Printed.)

Draft of a bill to require collectors of customs in America to inform masters of ships regarding " what they are required to do in order for the entry and clearance of their ships ".

465 (390). Certificates witnessing the transportation of convicts to the plantations, giving names but not destination. June 8.

Copy of the proceedings in a South Carolina admiralty case, George Roupell and the *Anne,* transcribed from the Registry Office, Court of Admiralty, Aug. 18.

Schedule of 21 papers enclosed in the memorial from the Commissioners of the Customs relating to the *Liberty* case. Read July 21.

An account of the gross receipts, payments, and net produce by each act, Jan. 5 to Jan. 8, 1769, " as appears by the accounts in my office ", James Porter, comptroller general. Custom House, Boston, Nov. 15, 1769.

Estimate of the civil establishment of Georgia and other incidental expenses, June 24, 1768–June 24, 1769.

Copy of a letter signed by Gov. Bernard, Lieut.-Gov. Hutchinson, Sec. Oliver, and Judge of Admiralty Auchmuty to four of the Commissioners of the Customs, Boston. Read June, 1769.

Two collections of papers relating to the *Liberty* case, sent from Boston by Samuel Venner, secretary to the American Board of Customs, to Thomas Bradshaw. 1768, 1769.

Letter from F. Mackay to the Treasury regarding a survey of part of Lake Champlain, and marking trees for the royal navy. Montreal, May 15.

Report of the committee appointed to examine accounts and claims against the government of Quebec, Dec. 27, 1767, to June 26, 1768, signed, Guy Carleton.

Case " touching what ships may pass from port to port to America ", submitted by Nuthall to the attorney and solicitor general, Aug. 12. The case originated in South Carolina and the statement covers opinions of lawyers and judges of Admiralty there and part of the vice-admiralty decree, Boston. The opinion of the attorney and solicitor general is given.

Copy of a contract of the Treasury with Edward Lewis for remitting money to pay the forces in West Florida. Dec. 10.

Letter from Gov. Bernard regarding Melchisedec Kinsman, charged with the murder of William Odgers, customs officer at Penzance, Cornwall. (See *Minute Book*, **39**, 239, and bundle **467**, f. 193.)

Statement of indebtedness of the Quebec government to Edward William Gray, deputy provost marshal of the district of Montreal, and many other similar papers.

Extract of a letter from " a Gentleman of Character ", Boston, June 14. " One of their grand objects is to spread the infection and thereby bring all the colonies to the very verge of a general revolt, if they are disappointed in this their projects will drop, of course."

Communication (27 pp.) from the collector and comptroller of the custom house, Boston, Apr. 30, with " Establishment of the Officers of his Majesty's Customs in the Northern District in America, 1716 ", and a " Table of Fees " taken by the officers of the customs at Boston since Sept. 29, 1764. This is an answer to queries, giving practically a history of the Boston custom house administration since 1707 and an account of the trade of the colony, Boston and adjacent towns, and of Martha's Vineyard and Nantucket.

Abstract of cash " paid by me on account of the public services carrying on in America, 1 April, 1765, to 30 June, 1767 ", with a letter from Gen. Gage, New York, May 13.

Representation from the speaker of the Massachusetts assembly by order of the assembly. Feb. 17.

Memorial from Andrew Brown, searcher in South Carolina, relative to an illicit trade in East India goods carried on in " Connecticut, New England, and New York ". London, Jan. 21.

Copy of minutes of council, Massachusetts Bay, regarding disturbances in Boston and insults to Commissioners of the Customs, with accompanying papers. Mar. 18.

Certificate from Temple, late surveyor general of customs in the Northern District, in favor of Folger of Nantucket. May.

Letter from David Lisle regarding the situation in Boston, indicating " a total revolt of the colony ". Boston, May 14.

Memorial of Richard Reeve and Thomas Irving to the Commissioners of the Customs regarding insults received from a mob assembled on the Long Wharf. Boston, June 25.

Copy of a memorial from Charles Garth upon the conduct of the collector of South Carolina. Jan. 20.

Extract of a letter from Gov. Bernard to Sec. Hillsborough. Boston, July 11.

Order in Council revoking the commission appointing only one vice-admiralty court and establishing four at Halifax, Boston, Philadelphia, and Charleston. Sept. 7.

Letter from the Commissioners of the Customs, and a copy of a letter from Grey Cooper to the same, relative to the suspension of Fisher, collector at Salem, with three accompanying documents about the case, Dec. 26. Boston, Oct. 4.

Memorial from the Commissioners of the Customs in America. Feb. 12. This valuable paper, which contains a reference to the

" Farmer's Letters ", does not appear to have been read before the Treasury Board and is not entered in the *Minute Book*.

Memorial from the same, with the establishment of customs officials in America, Sept. 8, 1767, to Jan. 5, 1768. Jan. 26.

Copy of a letter to Gov. Bernard from the same. Mar. 28.

Memorial, same date, from the same, supplemental to that of Feb. 12.

Memorial from the same, on the bad regulation of the post-office in America, referred to the Postmaster General. May 12.

Memorial from the same, with enclosures, chiefly concerning insults received in the prosecution of duty, with exact details from tidesmen regarding the brigantine *Lydia,* belonging to John Hancock (*Minute Book,* **39,** 161).

Memorial from the same, with copies of letters from officers in Philadelphia, Halifax, New Haven, etc., regarding writs of assistance (*Minute Book,* **39,** 179).

Case touching writs of assistance in America, sent to the attorney general, who replied, " There can be no doubt but that the superior courts of justice in America are bound by the 7 Geo. III. to issue such writs of assistance as the Court of Exchequer issues in similar cases to the officers of customs."

Memorials from the same with enclosures full of information giving the British side of the case. July 11, Aug. 25, Sept. 15, Oct. 4.

466 (391). Petition from Harford and Powell praying for the payment of £45 for freight on a cargo of stamped paper sent to Philadelphia, where the freight should have been paid " but on the ship's arrival in the river Delaware the populace were so outrageous against the Capt. of the ship that they threatened his life and destruction to his vessel ". Mincing Lane, July 16 (*Minute Book,* **39,** 195, " My Lords can give no relief ", and the document is endorsed " Nil ").

Copy of a circular from the Secretary of State to various ministers and consuls in ports of Europe warning them to look out for vessels from North America or going to North America engaged in illicit trade (based on a representation from the Treasury, which was roused to act in the matter by the memorials, etc., from the American Board of Customs). Dec. 6.

Mr. Litchfield on the case of tidesmen and the brigantine *Lydia,* June 29, with an opinion from Philip Yorke, attorney general, Sept. 28, 1731, as to the meaning of 13-14 Car. II., c. 11, § 4.

467 (392). Account of plantation goods granted on lease to the French inhabitants of Dominica according to the agreement of May 4, 1766.

Draft of instructions to commissioners in the Ceded Islands. Feb. 2.

Petition of John Brown and others, merchants of Glasgow, relative to duties taken on imported iron from America. (Referred to commissioners of the customs in Scotland, whose opinion follows. *Minute Book,* **39,** 221, Oct. 11).

Opinion of Attorney General De Grey about colonial collectors taking securities in Great Britain and the colonies from officers of customs there (*Minute Book,* **39,** 177; see f. 202 of bundle **467** for other papers).

Letter from the Admiralty regarding Burnaby's bill (*ante,* **463**).

Warrant for the appointment of James Pott, judge of the vice-admiralty, Quebec. Apr. 20.

Petition from Stephen Fuller, agent for Jamaica, regarding money raised in that island by the Stamp Act (*Minute Book,* **39,** 76, 89).

Letter from the Commissioners of the Customs in America to Gov. Wentworth of New Hampshire. June 18.

Documents in the case of a master of a vessel, the *Aurora* brig, supposed by the governor of North Carolina to be guilty of a breach of the acts of trade. Read Oct. 25.

468 (393). Mutilated letters from Sec. Hillsborough, with extracts of letters from Gov. Bernard, July 10, 11, regarding the conduct of the people of Boston in the case of a schooner seized for having 30 hhds. of uncustomed molasses on board.

Opinion of the attorney general on the question of tea—should not East India Company make good the deficiency in the revenue arising from the drawback on teas exported to Ireland and the plantations (mutilated; see *Minute Book,* **39,** 233-234).

Nuthall's report on the memorial of John Mason regarding the Mohegan Indians (memorial enclosed). Read July 4.

Letter from Walters, consul at Rotterdam, regarding ships to America (reply to the Secretary of State's circular). Dec. 13.

Opinion of John Sewall, attorney general for Massachusetts, on a clause in 7 George III., c. 46.

Memorial from Francis Noble Knipe regarding his trouble with Deputy Quartermaster Christie, who interrupted his shipbuilding at Montreal (see *ante*). Received May 3.

Instructions from Sec. Hillsborough, enclosing a copy of a letter from Gov. Moore of New York regarding the orders given by the American Board of Customs to Andrew Elliot, collector at New York, not to receive anything but silver for duties. Oct. 12.

Letter from Moore, collector of customs at Charleston, stating his case and his reasons for leaving the province. Received Mar. 5.

Memorial of William Russell, comptroller of customs in Georgia, regarding his leaving the province. Mar.

Letter from Charles Stewart, surveyor general of customs, Quebec, New York, New Jersey, Pennsylvania, 1765-1768, asking leave to return to England. June 3. (Endorsed "Nil" and in *Minute Book,* **39,** 181, "My Lords cannot in the present state of America give leave to any one of the officers of the Customs to be absent from their duty.")

1769.

469 (394). Quebec fees; West Florida accounts.

Memorial from Michael Francklin, lieutenant-governor of Nova Scotia.

Revenue statistics, payments out of the four-and-a-half per cent., 1752-1760.

Victuals for Mobile.

Scottish trade to America, 1768-1775, with names of colonies and valuation of goods.

Quebec accounts.

Letter from J. Temple to Lord Hillsborough. Boston, Oct. 25, 1768.

Letter from Dr. Moffat, New London, Conn., Nov. 14, 1768, with an estimate of the losses in the riot at Newport, R. I., Aug., 1765; also letters from the same, Nov. 27, 1767, Mar. 11, May 14, 1769.

Quebec accounts and other papers.

Affidavit of E. Davis, temporary collector at Charleston.

Virginia quit-rents.

Four-and-a-half per cent.

Papers relating to Tortola and the Virgin Islands.

Memorial of Dr. Campbell, agent for Georgia.

470 (395). Memorial from John Williams, inspector general of customs in North America. Received Mar. 25.

Memorial from John Foxcroft regarding the post-office in America.

Letter from John Michael Dwyer about Jamaica. Dec. 26.

From the Commissioners of the Customs regarding the appointment of a customs officer at Nantucket.

Memorial from William Randall, late surveyor general of the Southern District of America. Apr. 26.

Documents regarding the payment of customs officers in America.

Letter from the governor of East Florida regarding the Greek colonists lately introduced into that province by Dr. Andrew Turnbull (see **410**, f. 201 ; *Decl. Acc., A. O.,* **1261**, 154).

Copy of a petition from Thomas Walpole, T. Pownall, Benjamin Franklin, and others, for a grant of land at the back of the settlements in Virginia, with an offer to become purchasers thereof from the crown (referred to the Board of Trade).

471 (396). Letters and memorials from Samuel Venner, and other papers regarding Boston troubles, transfer of the board from Castle William to Boston, removal of Venner as secretary (see *Minute Book,* **40**, 22).

Gross receipts and payments and net produce of the customs in America (interesting table, dated Nov. 15). Jan. 5.

Account of receipts and remittances to the receiver general in London, 1769-1770, drawn up by Nathaniel Coffin for Charles Stewart, cashier and paymaster (f. 90, valuable).

Case of customs fees in Rhode Island, colony refusing to allow an appeal, opinion of Attorney General De Grey. Aug. 21, 1770.

Case of seizure, Philadelphia, collector and informer insulted by a mob. Oct. 13.

Report from Charleston, with accounts of duties.

Extracts of letters regarding pine timber on the Kennebec, sent by Wentworth.

Copy of a decree by Auchmuty, admiralty court, Boston, in case of Folger *vs.* the sloop *Cornelia,* James Otis and John Adams advocates for informer (ff. 151-199, 363-369).

Statistics from the port of Mobile.

Details regarding the destruction of the sloop *Liberty* (ff. 200-226, 289-293).

Quebec accounts.

Statistics from Maryland and Pennsylvania (ff. 241-255, 296), Halifax, Virginia, Boston, Pensacola, Newcastle, Charleston, Potomac River (ff. 256-286, 317-333, 341, 361).

Plan of the district proper to be allotted to the courts of admiralty to be erected in America.

Letter from Commissioner Temple regarding the trouble with Venner.

Petition from Moses Park, agent for the Mohegan Indians. June 27.

Various expense statements of civil and customs establishments, and papers relating to conflicts between the collectors and the colonists, Rhode Island, Philadelphia, New London (ff. 371-403), and giving results of the applications for writs of assistance to superior courts.

From the American Board of Customs Commissioners, enclosing copies of letters from Commodore Hood, the state of the coasting trade and an opinion for its better regulation, etc., many papers relating to the history and work of the board with statistics of various kinds (ff. 412-505).

472 (397). Case of Roupell of Charleston, with the opinion of the attorney general (*Minute Book,* **39,** 350).

Memorial from Stephen Fuller, agent for Jamaica, regarding the *Lawrence* (*Minute Book,* **39,** 339).

473 (398). A few papers relating to New York (f. 1), Quebec (ff. 5, 180-191, 329), Newfoundland (f. 11), Grenada (f. 154), West Florida (f. 196).

474 (399). A number of papers relating to the Floridas, Quebec, Grenada, St. Vincent, Dominica.

Rhode Island case (printed), of money due that colony, signed Joseph Sherwood (*Minute Book,* **39,** 354). Apr. 6.

Petition of John Mason (f. 152; *cf.* f. 212). Received Jan. 10.

Opinion of Attorney General Sewall of Massachusetts "upon sundry acts respecting the coasting trade".

Vice-admiralty case (ff. 184, 192-206, 230-234, 237-242). Quebec, Nov. 17.

Letter from Duncan Stewart (f. 247). New London, June 7.

1770.

475 (400). Case of vessels arriving in America with wines, etc., presented to the attorney general for his opinion.

Whalebone exported from Scotland to New England and elsewhere.

Concerning land sales, Bermuda.

Papers relating to America (ff. 230-404): Campbell's application for pay as surveyor, West Florida; Stedman's proposals regarding the carriage of stores at Niagara Falls; memorial of Jonathan Carver regarding his work of exploration "into interior and unknown parts of America"; petition of Edward Montague, agent of Virginia, regarding the petition for lands in Virginia, petitioners not named, with a quotation of the query of the Board of Trade "whether it may not be necessary to sever such lands from the said colony and erect a new and distinct government thereof" (f. 246, *cf.* ff. 57, 68; **470,** ff. 38-41, 295, 401); paper regarding timber duty.

476 (401). Papers regarding the relations between the American Board of Customs and Commodore Hood (ff. 1-40).

Civil establishment of West Florida.

Account of receipts and remittances (*cf.* **396**, f. 90).

Memorial of Thomas Walpole *et al.* for a tract of land in America, " within the late cession made to the king at Fort Stanwix by the Six Nations ", paying for the same £10,460 7s. 3d. and a quit-rent of 2s. for every 100 acres of cultivable land, payment of latter to begin after expiration of 20 years, one-fifth part of the principal to be paid immediately and the remaining four-fifths in annual installments—accompanied by an exact description of the tract in question and a *New and Accurate Map of the British Dominion in America according to the Treaty of 1763, by Thos. Kitchin, Geographer,* with the above tract laid out in pencil (ff. 38-41).

Group of papers regarding the working of the customs system at Boston and the troubles and outrages at Boston, Newport, Philadelphia, Salem, Cohansey (*cf.* **407**, f. 148), the removal of the custom house in Virginia, establishment at Norfolk, various reports from John Williams regarding the condition of things in Virginia and Maryland (a series of letters, 10 in number, ff. 117-138, 255), of value inasmuch as Williams, who went on a tour of inspection at the request of the American Board of Customs, 1769-1770, took a fair view of the situation.

Memorials from Charles Stewart (ff. 145, 151).

Monthly accounts of receipts of customs, of warrants issued for incidental expenses.

Letter from Gov. Bull of South Carolina (f. 178).

Quebec papers.

Gen. Gage's report on the memorial of Maj. Farrar touching the Greek settlement in East Florida (f. 210).

Accounts of duties received at separate ports.

Report by the American Board of Customs of affairs at Boston, and of the result of a visit to New Hampshire, Apr. 3 (ff. 233-237, important).

Bussard case in South Carolina.

Report on the quit-rent act of New York (ff. 246-247).

Map showing the entrance into the river St. Mary's (1769, W. Fuller) near St. Augustine (ff. 262, 263).

From Mr. Wegg regarding the seizure of the *Little Bob* at Mobile, Apr., 1765.

Custom house accounts (f. 287).

477 (402). Quebec accounts (f. 309).

478 (403). Quebec accounts and papers.

Case of the snow *Recovery* and the brigantine *Sea Flower,* Nova Scotia (f. 112 ff.; *cf.* ff. 273-287).

Letter from James Grant. St. Augustine, Sept. 18, 1769.

Letter from Gov. Bull of South Carolina relative to the remission of fines on German settlers (f. 198).

Papers relative to the difficulty with Sir William Johnson about the payment of bills for supplies issued to Indians of Michilimackinac.

Case of Maj. Robert Rogers, the well-known bush ranger.

Memorial of the collector of customs, Mobile (f. 235).

West Florida letters (*cf.* ff. 301, 309).

Case of the schooner *Betsey,* Quebec.

Petition of Maj. Rogers and a letter of the same (ff. 251, 253).

Copy of a letter from Gen. Carleton to the Commissioners of the Customs (f. 269). July 4, 1770.

Case of the *Sea Flower* and other ships (ff. 273-287).

Petition of Jonathan Carver (ff. 321-331).

Quebec papers.

Maj. Rogers's case (ff. 358-377).

Copies of letters from the collector of Quebec to the Commissioners of the Customs and others in Boston and Montreal (ff. 387-397).

Letter from Temple to Lord North giving an account of the proceedings of the American Board of Customs Commissioners to Nov., 1770, with enclosures from Charleston (ff. 465-470).

Memorials of John Mein of Boston, stationer to the American Board of Customs (f. 478).

Memorial of Thomas Barrow, deputy paymaster (f. 482), and of John Ellis, agent for West Florida (f. 484).

479 (404). Report of the attorney and solicitor general upon the complaint of the American Board of Customs regarding a tax act in Massachusetts (f. 13).

Quebec accounts.

Pensacola papers.

De Brahm's petition (a number of other petitions from De Brahm are in this and preceding bundles).

Letter from Gen. Gage regarding Maj. Rogers (f. 92; *cf.* f. 130). New York, Sept. 8.

Letter to Gov. Botetourt of Virginia from John Williams, enclosing " Observations on the tobacco trade in America and Scotland " (f. 166). Jan. 1, 1770.

From Sec. Hillsborough regarding the suspension of certain fines in Virginia (f. 206).

Victualling papers (ff. 219, 225, 232, 292). 1770.

Case (printed) of damage from confiscation of stamped paper carried from London to Philadelphia, 1765, signed Geo. Dickinson (f. 223). London, Dec. 31, 1769.

Pensacola and Quebec papers.

Petition of Moses Park, agent for the Mohegan Indians, desiring an advance of 2 guineas a week (f. 334).

Quit-rents in Nova Scotia (f. 344).

Grenada papers (scattered).

480 (405). Concerning the importation of rum into Ireland (f. 33).

Memorial from John Campbell, agent for Georgia (f. 54).

Letters from Gen. Gage, New York, regarding provisions (ff. 57, 80, 86, 120).

Memorial regarding the late surveyor general of Barbadoes (f. 196).

Memorial on behalf of Francis Lewis, merchant of New York, commissary of Shirley's Niagara Falls expedition, 1752, and other papers of value (f. 213).

Regarding the illegal importation of spirits and tobacco from America (f. 259).

Memorial of merchants of London trading to North and South Carolina and Georgia (f. 353) ; and of the agent of South Carolina praying for an alteration in the rating of rice, with Custom House report *contra,* Mar. 30 (f. 354).

Petition of Thomas Doten, late of Boston, a prisoner in Lancaster Gaol (f. 376).

481 (406). List of all ships and vessels which have entered inwards from the port of Hampton, Va., between July 5 and Oct. 10, 1771, with the particular quality and quantity of the loading of each vessel. On reverse, *id.,* vessels that have cleared outward (valuable ; *cf.* **488,** 100-103).

Id., clearing outward, York River, June 24–Dec. 24, 1771.

Letter from New York regarding prizes condemned there, signed T. Kempe. Nov. 10, 1779.

Extract of a letter from Gen. Gage to Sec. Hillsborough regarding the snow *Florida Pacquet.*

Regarding the smuggling of British plantation rum into Scotland (f. 27).

Petition from N. Turner, provost marshal, Quebec (f. 47).

Letter from St. Christopher regarding smuggling (f. 121).

Regarding surveys of Lake Champlain.

1771.

482 (407). Letter from Sec. Hillsborough to Gov. Tryon of North Carolina, referring to riots there (f. 96). Feb. 11.

Concerning the Mississippi peltry trade (ff. 109-110 ; *cf.* **486,** 55, 56, 67).

Customs difficulties in Newfoundland (f. 138 ; **486,** ff. 37, 256).

Regarding outrages, etc., at Salem and Cohansey (f. 148 ; *cf.* 476), Philadelphia (f. 166), East Florida (f. 174), Philadelphia and Salem (f. 178), Rhode Island (f. 200).

Letters from Samuel Venner (ff. 190-192), and further papers regarding customs establishment in America (ff. 193-199).

Reports of the American Board of Customs Commissioners on the memorial of Reid, commander of the sloop *Liberty* (f. 206), concerning illicit trade in the West Indies (f. 212), regarding John Williams's salary (f. 220), regarding incidental expenses (f. 222).

Account of receipts, payments, and remittances of the board, Jan. 5, 1771–Jan. 5, 1772 (ff. 237, 335).

Halifax and Quebec accounts, naval office lists, Rappahannock River (f. 239).

Reports on naval office fees, New York (also **484**), Philadelphia, Pensacola, Savannah, Piscataqua, New Hampshire, Quebec, Charleston (letter from Gov. Bull), Connecticut (letter from Gov. Trumbull, Lebanon), Salem (Mass.), Island of St. John (see also **483,** 240), Charlotte Town, Mobile, Boston, Philadelphia, etc., sent in answer to a Treasury letter, Nov. 7, 1770 (ff. 240-324 ; for New Hampshire, **484** ; for Jamaica, **486,** f. 306).

Copy of a letter from the collector of New York to the Commissioners of the Customs (f. 325). Jan. 16.

Reasons for establishing a British custom house on the Mississippi River, West Florida (f. 329).

Letters from Scammell, surveyor of woods (f. 331), and from Benzel, inspector of white pines (f. 333).

Quebec and other accounts.

483 (408). Memorial from Thomas Bladen, former governor of Maryland, regarding money for troops raised by him in 1746 (f. 40).

Various papers regarding lands in St. Vincent, Dominica, etc.

Collectors' accounts, Bahamas.

Estimates for Nova Scotia.

484 (409). Packet labelled " Papers relating to the steps Ld Hillsborough has taken upon the Representation of Outrages committed on officers in America ", containing copies of Hillsborough's letters to governors and proprietaries.

Letters from Agent Ellis, Gen. Gage, Gov. Wentworth (on fees at Portsmouth, N. H.), Deputy-Commissary Cunningham, East Florida, Gov. Dunmore (on fees at New York).

Petition from Robert Moreton for salary as clerk of the American Board of Customs Commissioners.

Memorial of William Randall, late surveyor general of the Southern District (f. 221, important).

Memorials from Robert Johnston about public roads in East Florida, from Zachary Hood, late distributor of stamps in Maryland (f. 300, important).

Group of Jamaica, Dominica, and West Florida papers.

Memorial from Jonathan Carver, Moses Park, Phineas Atherton, Isaac DeCosta, upholding the proposal of Maj. Rogers to find a northwest passage (f. 377), and proposing to accompany him. May 18, 1772.

Memorial from Rogers, and other interesting papers relating in general to Rogers and his affairs (ff. 378-393).

Copies of letters from Gov. Tryon regarding himself and his difficulties (ff. 401-408, mutilated).

485 (410). Memorial from John Williams (mutilated, also ff. 145, 188).

Accounts, Royal American Regiment.

Pensacola and Dominica papers.

Thurlow's opinion on a case touching the right to compel the supreme courts of America to grant writs of assistance (f. 306). Aug. 31.

Papers regarding the seizure of the *Speedwell* at Philadelphia because laden with tea from Holland (ff. 38-39). Apr. 30.

Dominica and West Florida papers.

Letter from the comptroller of the port of Philadelphia regarding leave of absence.

486 (411). Memorial of Robert Hodgson, superintendent of the Mosquito Shore.

Reports of the attorney and solicitor general on the case of the Rhode Island naval officer (f. 97) and on a Quebec case (f. 93).

Memorial of Thomas Mills, receiver general, Quebec.

Account of the application of the money received from the duties collected in America (f. 220, valuable).

Paper on the neglect of the inspector of tar at Beaufort, N. C. (f. 262).

Order in Council disallowing Pennsylvania Act, passed Feb., 1770 (f. 268).
Bundle of St. Vincent papers.
Jamaica fees.
487 (412). Martinique, Jamaica papers.
Rigby's account of extraordinary services of the army, Dec. 20, 1770–Feb. 20, 1772 (f. 58).
Letter from Surveyor Benzel (f. 70).
Account of gross receipts, payments, and net produce of all duties laid by acts of Parliament, Jan. 5, 1770, to Jan. 5, 1771 (f. 266, duplicate f. 273).
Nuthall's report on John Mason's petition (f. 278).
Id. on the petition of Francis Waldo, collector at Falmouth (ff. 318, 355).
Articles recommended for Fort Niagara by Col. Butler (f. 354).
488 (413). Benzel's remarks on Lake Champlain (f. 41).
Memorial of John Leake, agent of the American Board of Customs Commissioners, on a Rhode Island case (f. 147).
Letter from Thomas Dicey, collector of customs, Jamaica (f. 285).

1772.

489 (414). Cholmondeley's report on the memorial of Montfort Browne, late governor of West Florida.
Order in Council referring to the Treasury the address of the rector and inhabitants of New York regarding the remission of quit-rents (f. 28).
Id., address of the governors of the college of the province of New York to be constituted a university.
Report on rum exported to Ireland.
Naval office lists, Montserrat (ff. 149, 150), Nevis (ff. 151-152), St. Christopher (f. 153).
Halifax victualling lists.
490 (415). Lists of transported convicts (ff. 75, 284).
Bermuda and St. Vincent papers.
Letter from Benzel (f. 161).
Nova Scotia establishment (f. 192).
Mahogany duty (f. 232).
Regarding clandestine trade between the Mediterranean and America (f. 248).
Memorial from the proprietors of iron works in Maryland (f. 263).
491 (416). Collection of papers of the American Board of Customs Commissioners, chiefly relating to the Hatton case (ff. 1-67), outrages at Falmouth, Piscataqua, and Philadelphia (ff. 89-111), Providence, *Gaspee* (ff. 124-136), other cases (ff. 137-174), Mackay case (f. 205), writs of assistance (f. 209), etc., to the end of the volume, forming a valuable series of documents. Other papers are:
Quebec accounts, Mobile statistics.
Memorial from George Suckling, late attorney general of Quebec.
Table of warrants granted by Gen. Gage for contingent and extraordinary expenses (ff. 75-180, valuable).

Various naval office statistics; civil establishments of Georgia and West Florida (ff. 197-203).

492 (417). Map of the upper Connecticut River, showing tracts of pine timber, laid out by T. Ruggles, inspector of white pines (f. 11).

Id., from Waterchichi River to beyond White River (f. 12).

Plan for connecting Connecticut River, " near the great falls of Walpole ", by locks around the falls (f. 13).

Ruggles's report (f. 14). May 24.

Papers of the American Board of Customs Commissioners about writs of assistance (ff. 16-83), warrants issued on account of incidental expenses (ff. 98-103), outrages in Rhode Island (ff. 129-154), regarding the employment of Fleming as office printer (ff. 159-167), and on to the end of the bundle, covering the following points: permitting enumerated commodities to be exported to Gibraltar, Minorca, Senegambia, upon taking the necessary bond; controversy between collectors at Patuxent and Chester as to the limits of their respective districts; regarding Quebec difficulties, writs of assistance, and the Rhode Island trouble. Other papers are: parchment warrant of Roupell, Charleston (f. 111), and papers relating to his appointment (ff. 112-128); Halifax accounts.

Letter from Benzel regarding Lake Champlain (f. 157).

493 (418). Naval office lists, Antigua and St. Christopher (ff. 9-36, 50), Nevis (f. 48), Montserrat (f. 135).

Memorial from Agent Ellis of West Florida (f. 41, comment on envelope).

Letters from John Williams regarding the deception of Duncan Stewart, collector at New London (f. 72).

Warrants and other papers, Gen. Gage (ff. 89-104, 117).

Dominica and Grenada papers.

Adm. Gambier's accounts for extra services, Boston, 1770-1771 (f. 127).

Copies of letters from Gov. Bull regarding the memorial of Surgeon Milligan (f. 299), Gov. Wentworth, Sept. 23, 1771 (f. 295), proprietary of Pennsylvania and governor of Rhode Island concerning customs officers there (f. 288).

Receipts and payments, Sept. 8, 1767, to Apr., 1772 (f. 276).

Letter from Gen. Gage transmitting an estimate, with several plans of works proposed to be carried on in North America (f. 236), entrance to Pensacola harbor, barracks at Pensacola, etc.

494 (419). Virginia papers (ff. 1, 163) including naval office lists for 1772.

Letter from Fraser about a British vessel sailing from Amsterdam with a cargo of tea for New York (f. 6).

Regarding a schooner for West Florida (f. 24).

Memorial and many other papers, Montfort Browne (f. 49).

Extracts from Wooten's report, New London (f. 89).

From Sec. Hillsborough regarding the salaries of officers, Bahama Islands (f. 100).

Regarding Duncan Stewart (ff. 125, 172, 247, 310 ff.).

Outrage at Rhode Island, from Adm. Montague, etc. (ff. 144, 158 ff. 306, many papers).

Bills and warrants, Gen. Gage.

Memorial from A. Johnstone, deputy vice-admiral, Quebec (f. 198).

Condemnation at Pensacola (ff. 203, 240).

Memorial from De Brahm (f. 252).

Memorial from Dr. Moffatt, New London (f. 279).

495 (420). Regarding the pilotage of certain vessels employed in aiding officers in America (f. 330).

Letter from Benzel (f. 29).

Duncan Stewart case (ff. 49, 199).

Warrants, Gen. Gage.

Conflicts over timber cutting in Maine (ff. 95, 121, many papers).

496 (421). Concerning the seizure of a ship, Newfoundland (f. 5).

Quebec papers.

Extract of a letter from Gov. Martin of North Carolina regarding quit-rents (f. 18).

Petition from the Dutch Reformed Church, New York, praying relief from quit-rents (ff. 40, 44).

Letter from Scammell, collector at Falmouth, Casco Bay (f. 62, valuable). July 20.

Petition from merchants for bounty on timber (f. 134).

Memorial from the collector at Mobile (f. 142).

Account of the clothes and effects of Lieut. Dudingston, lost in the *Gaspee* (f. 167).

Memorial praying satisfaction for the loss of the schooner *Hawk*, a royal vessel with South Carolina troops (f. 170).

497 (422). Admiralty to the Treasury regarding " essence of Spruce " from Quebec, "which when brewed into beer may be of great service to the navy in preserving the seamen from scurvy". Sept. 21. In the log of the *Boyne* (*Adm., Capt. Logs,* **129**) are many entries of butts of spruce beer taken on while lying in Boston harbor, 1774-1775. The beer was sent on board from Boston in the yawl or the long boat.

Memorial from Gov. Leyborne regarding lands in the Ceded Islands, and other similar papers.

Bundle of papers from Thomas Dunn, acting receiver general of Quebec, containing accounts of charities, salaries, accounts and claims, fees, coroners' expenses (ff. 90-127).

Pensacola and Grenada victualling papers.

Letter from the proprietary of Pennsylvania to Sec. Hillsborough regarding customs troubles in Philadelphia. Dec. 24, 1771.

1773.

498 (423). Naval office lists, Montserrat (also ff. 77, 78, 81, 82), St. Christopher (also ff. 63, 69, 91, 94), Nevis (also ff. 75, 76, 84, 85), South Potomac, Hampton, James River, and Antigua (also ff. 86-87, 89-90).

An account of the gross and net produce of all duties laid by Parliament on goods imported into Nova Scotia from Sept. 7, 1767, when the American revenue was placed under the management of the board at Boston, to Jan. 5, 1773.

Halifax victualling lists.

Memorial and petition of the merchants of Liverpool trading to Africa and the West Indies, in respect of the Free Port Act.

Memorial of John Christopher Roberts for the office of secretary, register, and clerk to the council of Quebec.

499 (424). Memorial of John Robinson, one of the American Board of Custom Commissioners, for relief.

Bills drawn to pay provost marshal fees, Quebec.

Report concerning the island of Bequia.

Letter from Joseph Smith Speer regarding his chart of the West Indies. *Cf.* **506**, f. 140, and *Treas.* 62, map no. 125. Speer was a captain who served upward of 31 years in the navy and army and 21 years in the West Indies, and made a chart and many plans. He belonged to the 49th Regiment and was at one time captain of a fort at Black River on the Mosquito Shore. See also the preceding volume of the *Guide,* pp. 46, 240, where the name is wrongly printed " Speers ".

Proposal submitted to Lord North by John Robinson regarding inspectors for the Windward Islands. Aug. 21.

Grenada and St. Vincent accounts.

Petition from the inhabitants of Dominica regarding lands and tenures; quit-rents, f. 91; other papers on the same subject, ff. 93-104.

Letter from Col. Blaquiere regarding illicit trade between Ireland and the plantations.

Adolph Benzel, inspector of unappropriated lands in Canada, disbursements, 1771-1772. Interesting lists of items; Benzel travelled through the Lake Champlain region. Letter, New York, July 2, 1772.

Memorial of James Merrifield, charging Henry Bennett, customs collector at St. Christopher, with connivance at illicit trade. Feb. 5.

Papers regarding the enforcement of revenue laws in the Channel Islands.

John Robinson on the general inspection of Barbadoes and the Leeward Islands. Sept. 10.

Papers regarding indigo from America.

500 (425). Draft of a report on the proposition presented by John Norton for a copper currency in Virginia. Refers to act 10 George III.

Papers regarding land difficulties in Dominica, St. Vincent, and Antigua. June, Dec., 1774. *Cf.* ff. 109, 119, 122. Other papers touching the Ceded Islands.

Remarks of Robert Jones on the North Carolina quit-rent act (f. 111).

Letters from the custom house, Inverness, Jan. 3, 1774, and Wigtown, Jan. 5, 1774, regarding emigration from Scotland, with papers of considerable value. "The information from the northern parts strongly describe a dissolution of the old Highland attachment." The migration was from the county of Sutherland, whence four or five hundred men, women, and children embarked at Lochbroon, indented for George Town, Sassafras River, Md. Three hundred more embarked later from the same place, and other migrations followed, due to high rents and severe season. An association was formed at Wigtown to promote migration (see *Treas.* 47: **9-12**).

501 (426). Financial papers, estimates of civil establishments, making surveys, and the like are scattered through this bundle.

Various papers from the custom house, Boston, July, regarding writs of assistance, Pennsylvania, Maryland, and Virginia. *Cf.* ff. 257-318, 354-390.

Draft of a bill for regulating the coasting trade in America, 1773; comment of the American board.

Halifax port papers, duties, and seizures.

Valuable collection of papers of the American Board with enclosures.

502 (427). A number of scattered financial papers, bills, payments, etc., America and the West Indies.

Memorial of George Walker, agent of Barbadoes, in behalf of Samuel Rous, president of the council there. Apr. 20.

Gov. Martin, North Carolina, on quit-rents.

Hillsborough to the Treasury regarding judges' salary in Massachusetts. July 27, 1772.

Memorial of Dartmouth merchants trading to Newfoundland, replying to the assertions of the collector there. *Cf.* **504**, f. 165.

Naval office lists, Antigua, St. Christopher, Montserrat.

Memorial from Gov. Tonyn for annual allowance for a schooner, East Florida.

503 (428). Various financial papers.

Adm. Clinton's claim (f. 119).

Virginia royal revenues.

Letter from collector Patterson, Philadelphia.

Memorial from Jacob Blackwell, Mobile.

Papers regarding Gov. Fitzmaurice of St. Vincent, who died intestate. Also **504**, f. 103, and papers in later bundles.

Memorial of John Campbell, superintendent and inspector of Indian affairs, Quebec.

Memorial of Alexander Dunn, collector, Newfoundland.

Naval office lists, Nevis, Montserrat.

504 (429). Various contract papers, Ceded Islands.

Memorial from the officers of the 31st Regiment landed in Pensacola, in the autumn of 1765, with accounts.

Account of the gross and net produce of the customs in America from 1767 to 1773.

Various memorials.

Letter from Dr. Thomas Moffatt regarding his losses at Newport. May 26. Depositions of Capt Robert Ferguson, Thomas Robinson, and James Holmes (ff. 51, 53, 57, 59, 67).

From Gen. Gage, Indian matters. New York, Apr. 7.

Annual amount of the value of the office of receiver general, South Carolina, 1766-1773.

Letter from Brown and Welsh, Jamaica, to Brown and Birch, Liverpool, regarding the seizure of a ship.

Memorial of Capt. Samuel Hood, R. N., with an outline of his career to 1773.

Various financial papers, and accounts of West Florida, Nova Scotia, Mosquito Shore.

Petition of Esther Davis, widow of Caleb Davis, late commander of the guard schooner, the *Walker,* in service in Georgia, 1742-1747 (f. 195).

1774.

505 (430). Regarding ship *Buchanan* of Glasgow, from New York with flour for Bordeaux, lost going up the Garonne. Oct. 24. An interesting case.

Letter from the American Board of Customs Commissioners regarding the throwing overboard of tea in Boston harbor, with many enclosures. Jan. 4.

Memorials of Hezekiah Coffin, master of the brig *Beaver* with tea on board, dated Dec. 23, 1773; James Bruce, master of ship *Eleanor,* Dec. 16; Francis Rotch, part owner of the *Dartmouth,* James Hall master. The total number of chests here given is 340. Many depositions of tidesmen and others.

Extract of a letter from Gov. Martin of North Carolina regarding Fort Johnston and Capt. Collet (ff. 49, 49b). May 5.

Petition of Isaac Chorrurier of Dominica recounting a dispute and enclosing a map.

Letter from Gov. Francis Legge regarding quit-rents (f. 61). Halifax, Mar. 23.

Many papers, with interesting reports from Rhode Island and Piscataqua, from the American Board, regarding the Privy Council's order forbidding the exporting of military stores from Great Britain.

Other American Board papers, giving Boston and American affairs in detail, with tables of customs statistics (ff. 74-295, 304-307, 322-348, 349).

Petition of Henry Flower, Capt. Samuel Bayard, and Edward Chamberlain for grant of unappropriated lands in New York. Mar. 8.

Memorial of William Gerard de Brahm, who arrived in London in 1751 and brought with him a number of German Protestants, who afterward formed the colony of Bethany in Georgia, now (1774) one of the most flourishing settlements in North America. The memorial gives an outline of De Brahm's career, notes his suspension from office as provincial surveyor of East Florida (Oct. 4, 1770), and requests reinstatement and fees and profits from the time of suspension.

A number of customs papers and reports.

H. T. Cramahé to Gen. Carleton regarding an admiralty case. Quebec, Nov. 11.

From Gov. Martin regarding quit-rents and the receiver general (Rutherford) of North Carolina. July 29.

Customs duties, Pensacola (1763-1764), New London, May-Oct., 1774, signed Thomas Moffatt, comptroller.

Account of gross receipts, payments, and net produce of the customs in America, 1772-1773. Other similar sheets of tables.

Account of tea that had been imported into the several ports under the management of the American Board since the partial repeal of 7 George III., and other tables.

Order in Council on petition of Charles Dudley, collector (original petition given). Dec. 31, 1773. Action of trespass (ff. 349-403).

506 (431). Naval office lists, York River, Accomac, Hampton, South Potomac, Rappahannock, James River. 1773-1774.

Petition of George Suckling, appointed attorney general of Quebec (through Halifax's influence). In office five years when he was superseded by Francis Maseres. Accompanying papers.

Petitions of Joseph Smith Speer, with many letters and affidavits.

Memorial of merchants and manufacturers of Manchester regarding the free ports of Jamaica. *Id.*, Lancaster.

507 (432). Copy of tea bill.

Regarding Newfoundland ships and emigrants.

Regarding officers of customs absent from their stations.

Case of ship *Betsey* seized at St. John's by Capt. Elphinstone of the *Pearl*, in 1768.

From the custom house, Plymouth, England, regarding a ship bound for Philadelphia with gunpowder. Oct. 14.

Naval office lists, St. Christopher, Montserrat, Nevis.

Halifax victualling lists.

508 (433). Letter from Gov. Carleton regarding a claim of Joseph Sanguinet for goods furnished the Indians in 1767.

Letter from J. T. Kempe regarding escheated estates in New York (escheated by death of John Wenham, clerk). Oct. 4.

Expenses attending the execution of the royal commission for enquiring into the affair of the *Gaspee*, Dec. 29-31, 1772, May 28-31, 1773, with other papers.

509 (434). Petition of John Wetherhead, merchant of New York, agent to the late Sir William Johnson, regarding the bail of Benjamin Roberts, commissary for Indian affairs at Michilimackinac. Nov.

Memorial of the receiver general of Dominica regarding obstructions to payments there.

Memorial of Jacques Blancard, Dominican planter.

State of the wool-card trade to North America, from Charles Gray. Colchester, England, Aug. 19.

Naval office lists, Montserrat, Antigua, Nevis.

Petition of Peregrine Cust and others, merchants of London, who shipped tea to Boston in the *Fortune,* which arrived there Mar. 6, 1774, and on May 7 was boarded " by a great number of persons, all of whom were unknown to the captain and many of them disguised and dressed and talking like Indians armed with axes and hatchets ", who broke open " the hatches and proceded to rummage the hold and hoisted out 28 chests of tea (amongst which were the before mentioned 16 chests of tea) upon the deck of the said vessel, and then with hatchets, axes, and clubs broke open the said chests and emptied and threw the tea into the water ". The petitioner valued his tea at £472 2s. 10d. (ff. 94-95). For this " tea party " see Winsor, *Memorial History of Boston,* III. 50, note ; Newell's Diary, *Proc. Mass. Hist. Soc.,* 1st ser., IV. 219 ; *ibid.,* XIII. 173.

Letter from John Foxcroft, deputy postmaster general in America, regarding the case against Goddard, formerly postmaster, Providence. New York, Apr. 5.

Extracts of letters from Gov. Wentworth regarding the destruction of tea. July 4, 11, Sept. 15.

From the Secretary at War regarding the payment of regiments sent to America. July.

Letter of John Gregg, secretary of the commissioners for the sale of lands, Dominica. Jan.

Petition of Joseph Smith Speer, as above.

Memorial regarding coffee plantations in the British West Indies, and the reduction of duty on coffee.

510 (435). Naval office lists, St. Christopher.

Various victualling accounts and accounts of contingent expenses, West Florida, Ceded Islands, and elsewhere.

Petition of John Malcolm, customs officer in Boston, recounting his experiences and referring to his memorial of June 16. Wants recompense, but the petition is endorsed " Nil ". *Id.,* Alexander Dunn, collector, Newfoundland.

Quebec papers and accounts.

511 (436). Papers from John Ellis, agent of Dominica, regarding the declining coffee industry. *Cf.* ff. 374, 417, 418, 431.

Many contract and expense papers.

Memorial of Thomas Irving, receiver general of quit-rents, South Carolina. London, Feb. 22.

Id., Archibald Baird, collector, Winyaw, S. C., who had served 34 years as collector there and wanted leave of absence. May 5.

Id., George Ball, land waiter and searcher, port of Roseau, Dominica.

Establishment of a court of exchequer in Dominica and Grenada for the recovery of quit-rents. *Cf.* f. 278.

Representation of the proprietors of St. John against the governor's being collector and receiver of quit-rents also.

Memorial of John Temple of the American Board, superseded in 1770 and wants relief.

Id., De Brahm, praying for payment.

Id., Alexander Grant, London merchant who sold goods to the king's Indian agent in Nova Scotia. 1762.

1775.

512 (437). Naval office lists, Antigua, St. Christopher, Montserrat, Accomac, Rappahannock, James River, Nevis, South Potomac, Hampton.

Memorial of John Christopher Roberts, late register, clerk of council, and commissary-general of stores, Quebec.

Memorial of James Grant, late governor of East Florida, regarding repairs of Fort St. Marks, Appalachee ; expenses attached.

513 (438). Nova Scotia customs reports.

Papers regarding the seizure of the *Lady Gage,* importing illegally arms and ammunition into New York.

Copy of the *Massachusetts Gazette, and the Boston Post-Boy and Advertizer.* Monday, Jan. 9, to Monday, Jan. 16, 1775.

Memorial of Elizabeth Fitz Roy, relict of the Right Hon. Augustus Fitz Roy and now wife of James Jeffries, one of the American Board, regarding lands in New York. She was daughter of Gov. Cosby and sister of William Cosby, a lunatic.

Series of valuable papers remitted by the American Board, with references to the occurrences of the time (ff. 20-110). Situation distressing, business stopped, customs officers in fear of their lives, mob dominant, etc. Many enclosures.

514 (439). War Office correspondence (ff. 147, 151, 155, 180, 190).

Letter from Gen. Carleton. Quebec, Dec. 20.

Some American financial statements (ff. 140, 143).

Two letters from John Robinson, secretary to the Treasury Board, regarding New England captains of ships about to sail for America, who " are what they call high Sons of Liberty and likely to be entrusted with despatches "; also regarding the seizure of such ships as were carrying intelligence to the rebels. Nov. 28. Other papers relating to America.

Grenada accounts.

An account of the application of the monies arising from the duties collected and received in America by acts of Parliament, 1767-1771. Total, £106,708. Out of this fund, Lord Dunmore, John Tabor Kempe, Robert Auchmuty, Jonathan Sewall, and Jared Ingersoll were paid (f. 226).

Letter from Gen. Howe. Boston, Dec. 19.

Victualling and contract papers (scattered).

Regarding Palatines for North America by way of Rotterdam (f. 115).

Treasury minute relating to Duncan Campbell's losses on a contract for transporting felons.

Letters from Gov. Thomas Shirley. Dominica, July 29, Sept. 30, Nov. 23.

515 (440). List of warrants granted by Gen. Gage for extraordinary military expenses in America. July 1–Sept. 30.

Quit-rents in St. Vincent (f. 15).

Some War Office estimates and Barrington papers (scattered).

Inventory of the clothes of James Dundas, master of the *Gaspee,* which were burned.

Victualling and ordnance papers. All the bundles of the Revolutionary period contain large numbers of ordnance, victualling, and subsistence papers that are often of value as showing the condition of the army and the system of organization. Sometimes they give information that is worth while, particularly about the food and clothing furnished, character, quantity, and regularity or irregularity of the supply. They give also information as to the system of distribution, methods of payment, and the contracting business generally, and they deal with the movements of vessels, and with trade, transport, smuggling, and the like. Some of the letters from subordinate officials, such as the collectors, comptrollers, superintendents, and surveyors, in Canada and the West Indies as well as elsewhere, contain details and comments that are informing and suggestive. We have too long got our knowledge of the events of the Revolution from American sources only.

The other side should have a hearing, and all this material is deserving of an examination. These letters were written by British officials from all over the colonial territory, particularly from ports and colonies held by the British, and they show the difficulties, financial and commissarial, under which the British forces in America labored.

Thomas Ainslee, collector, Quebec, to Gov. Carleton.

Brook Watson on Joseph Sanguinet's petition. *Cf.* **508, 527.**

Memorial of William Pollock in behalf of De Brahm.

Petition of Richard A. Harrison, collector at Boston, giving an interesting review of events since 1772 (f. 163). Dec. 16.

516 (441). Memorial of George Sullivan, agent for injured British subjects on the Hudson River and counties adjacent, with a copy of a letter from Gov. Tryon, Sept. 30, 1771, regarding the sloop *Hawk* seized by the Spanish.

Memorial of Anne Leyborne, wife of Gov. Leyborne, who entered on his government, Nov. 1, 1771, and died Apr. 16, 1775, at St. Vincent.

Petition of Charles Bedford, son of Grosvenor Bedford, collector at Philadelphia.

Id., William Randall, late surveyor general of the Southern District, 1768, appointed in 1764. Some interesting statements, such as that he was from July 7 to Aug. 31 in going from Charleston to Boston.

Papers regarding the expedition of the East India Company to Manila, subsequent to the surrender of the island to the company's servants. Nov. 2, 1762.

Memorial of the Society for the Propagation of the Gospel (S. P. G.) regarding a plantation in Barbadoes.

Id., B. and C. Berwick and David Harvey, and George Apthorp, merchants, regarding shipping money to America.

Various papers regarding the conduct of the surveyor general of Barbadoes. *Cf.* f. 254.

Id., bounty on indigo from America.

Papers from the custom house concerning an illicit and clandestine trade in arms and ammunition, with a letter from John Patterson, deputy collector, Philadelphia, on the same general subject of supplies for the rebels and of letters and papers despatched by them in ships going to England (to f. 404).

517 (442). Hessian papers.

Memorial of James Glen, late governor of South Carolina (f. 145).

Petitions of George Wilmot and Ebenezer Richardson, both lately of Boston, relating to services rendered as officers of the revenue.

518 (443). An account of the tonnage of all ships and vessels employed in the trade between Scotland and the colonies, 1772-1775.

Number of hogsheads of colonial tobacco imported at Glasgow, July 5–Oct. 11.

Petition of agents of American Loyalists to Parliament, signed by Joseph Galloway and Henry Eustace McCulloh (f. 51).

Memorial of J. F. W. Des Barres, surveyor of the coast and harbors of North America. *Cf.* f. 348.

Memorial of Peter Livius, judge of vice-admiralty court, Quebec. May.

Id., Robert Rogers, referring to a former petition Oct. 25, 1774, and a proposal. Dec. 1, 1774.

Id., Richard Cumberland in behalf of Samuel Holland.

1776.

519 (444). Drafts of Treasury letters, chiefly to Robert Gordon, commissary at Cork, regarding contracts, transportation, expenses, etc. 1777.

Id. to Anthony Merry regarding shipping cattle, sheep, and hogs to Boston, and other similar victualling questions. 1776.

Letter from Guy Johnson regarding Indian expenses. Mar. 28.

Draft of instructions to the commissioners for settling land differences in the Ceded Islands.

An account of the office of Lord George Germain, chiefly expenses of under secretary and clerks.

Canadian victualling lists and schedules.

520 (445). Petition of Francis Rotch, in behalf of himself and Aaron Lopez, engaged in whale fishing in southern waters. Jan. 9. *Cf.* **524**, f. 323.

Id., Samuel Porter, lawyer of Salem, Mass., sufferer by the Revolution. Feb. 23.

Id., Alexander McAlister, planter of Dominica, regarding lands sold there.

Id., Col. Alan Maclean and other officers of the regiment of Royal Highland Emigrants, regarding the place of the regiment on the establishment. Full roster of officers and other information.

Id., James Hume, late acting attorney general of Georgia Loyalists. May 14.

Copies of applications upon which licenses had been granted by the Admiralty to carry provisions to North America. March.

Invoices of Indian presents sent to John Stuart at Pensacola and St. Augustine.

Papers of the American Board, tables and important enclosures. On f. 163 is a list of the officers of customs in North America.

Letters from Andrew Elliot, in which it is stated that all the books and papers belonging to the collector's and receiver general's office in the custom house had been consumed by fire (interesting letter). Perth Amboy, Mar. 22; New York, Nov. 30.

Many estimates and victualling papers.

Letters regarding drugs for Boston.

Papers regarding losses sustained during the siege of Quebec.

Memorial and letter from Edmund Armstrong regarding the King's Regiment (8th) at Niagara, Detroit, Michilimackinac, and Oswagotchie, desiring extra pay (ff. 240-241).

521 (446). Gen. Gage, on the petition of John Whitmore and Son respecting the *Charming Peggy* of Philadelphia, seized and sent to Boston by H. M. S. *Glasgow,* and her cargo of 2143 barrels of flour sold there. June 5.

Case of the ship *Concord* of Philadelphia, at Rotterdam, July.

List of His Majesty's ships arranged alphabetically with rates, guns, in commission, in ordinary, observations. Of some value as showing where the ships were and what others were building.

Petition from Owen Byran, late master of the merchant ship *Diana,* who served at Quebec in Nov., 1775, and seeks relief.

Warrant for pay of John Fenton as captain and commander of William and Mary castle, in Portsmouth harbor, to July, 1782.

Letter from James Marriott, king's advocate, regarding the operation of the Prohibitory Act.

Various papers from the Scottish board regarding trade with America. *Cf.* f. 119, case of the sloop *Polly,* the ship *Logan* (invoice, f. 128), the *Christian,* and the *Betsey,* to f. 147. These papers are valuable as showing the experiences of those who fled from America in 1776. " Carry Mitchell, collector of customs at Norfolk, who with the vessel in which he was and all his books and papers were taken by the rebels. The whole of the goods in the vessel were taken on board in the greatest hurry and confusion imaginable, to rescue them from the flames when Norfolk was burnt."

Report on convicts received for transportation but pardoned on condition of entering the king's service, accompanied by a draft of the articles of agreement with Duncan Campbell, showing many changes and erasures. *Cf.* f. 289.

Various letters regarding lands in Dominica.

Memorial of George Etherington, major, 60th Regiment (Royal American Regiment of Foot), stationed at St. Vincent, 1773, at the time of the Carib revolt, asking for permission to purchase Carib land. By terms of the peace with the Caribs, Feb., 1773, lands granted to them were not to be alienated.

Quit-rents, St. John, St. Vincent (ff. 253, 257, 283, 287).

Regarding land in the Ceded Islands, letters from Thomas Shirley (ff. 258, 293, 295).

Report of the attorney general on a Jamaica case.

Case of the ship *Morris* from Philadelphia, loaded at Havre de Grace, cargo of powder and pig lead, sailed about May 15, probably bound for North America.

Regarding the inability of the owners of vessels employed in the herring fishery to obtain sufficient supply of knapple or oak staves for herring barrels on account of disturbances in North America (f. 348).

522 (447). Rum contract for supplying troops in North America ; also a bundle of bills, vouchers, statements, memoranda, certificates, and petitions concerning provisions and victualling ; ordnance, Pensacola ; barracks, St. Augustine ; schooner, West Florida ; the brig *John and Elizabeth* destroyed by a rebel battery at Point Levy.

Papers here and in succeeding bundles regarding the printing press of Robert Gilmour at Norfolk, taken off by the Earl of Dunmore ; statement signed by Hugh Gaine, New York, Nov. 6.

Account of extraordinary services incurred and paid, Jan. 31, 1776– Feb. 1, 1777, by Richard Rigby, for troops in America.

Memorial of the committee of the society for relief of the soldiers serving in America, their widows and orphans.

Great mass of bills, etc., of every description and for every sort of service, barracks, hospitals, public works.

Memorial of the council and assembly of Tobago against threatened prosecutions for default of land payments. *Cf.* f. 271; **527**, f. 201.

Affidavit touching events in Savannah harbor, Feb. 1–Mar. 3, participated in by " a set of people stiling themselves the parochial committee ". Accompanying memorials (f. 386). *Cf.* f. 434; **526**, f. 377; **527**, f. 209.

Memorial of George Gregory, merchant and lieutenant of the artillery company of the British militia; had a house, barn, and other effects burned by order of Gen. Carleton.

Memorial of Lieut.-Gov. Thomas Desbrisay of St. John; has had no salary and wants arrears.

Id., John Williams, inspector general of customs in America, recounting experiences in Boston since 1768; speaks of unjust and cruel treatment from the American Board.

Id., James Chambers, late commander of the ship *London* in New York trade, telling of events in New York harbor and of the actions of the " committee of people of New York " and of " a number of rioters and disorderly people (who were called Mohawks), who destroyed 18 chests of tea on board ".

Petition of Charles Mackenzie, dealing in goods for the use of the forces at Boston.

Order in Council on the case of John Gordon, Loyalist, South Carolina. Mar. 4. (Not in *Acts Privy Council, Colonial.*)

523 (448). From the Custom House, London, (1) regarding a ship suspected of communication with the rebels, and (2) American ships taken by the navy. Two groups of papers.

Bundle of returns. (1) Vessels setting out for America, in compliance with the orders of the Commissioners of the Customs, from any of the outports; (2) returns of vessels inward at London and outports, 1775-1776, showing

1.	Ships' name and place	Masters' name	Whither bound	Owner's name and place of abode	Contents of cargo and remarks

2.	Ports	Date	Ship's name	Master's name	From whence	Lading	Owner	Observation

Collection of papers from the outports transmitted to the Custom House, and by the latter to the Treasury. Chiefly about vessels from America.

Regarding lower duty on British plantation coffee.

From the Secretary of State regarding the American brig *Betsey* (or *Elizabeth*) seized at Falmouth. Not the *Betsey* of **521**. Report also of Dr. Marriott.

Papers relating to the German auxiliaries.

Memorial of Capt. John Fenton, taken prisoner at Oswego by Montcalm, confined at Quebec and Old France, promoted to a lieutenancy in the 34th Regiment, returned to America, served in 1762, etc.

Orders for every commissary of provisions in Canada. Headquarters, Quebec, Dec. 17.

Account of William Barr, purveyor of hospitals in North America,
Jan. 1–Sept. 16.

524 (449). Expense accounts, victualling papers, and contracts for rum.

Letters from Gov. Wentworth. Jan. 16, June 3.

Petition of Henry Fleming and John Pew, merchants, late of
Norfolk in Virginia. Oct. 3.

Memorial and petition of Charles Thompson, commander of H. M. S.
Boreas.

Petition of Richard Sharwin, saddler from Boston.

Memorial of John Christopher Roberts regarding his position as
commissary-general.

Id., Sir Thomas Mills, receiver general, Quebec.

Id., Gov. Tonyn for reimbursement of expenses of a sloop.

525 (450). Invoice and particulars of the sundry ships, expenses,
cost of cargoes, etc., for conveying live stock to America. Other
victualling and contract papers.

Petition of John Schoolbred of London, merchant, engaged in trade
to Canada (f. 177).

Memorial of Richard Reeve, appointed deputy paymaster-general,
on a southern expedition.

Id., Col. John Wilkinson, late commanding as governor and chief
magistrate in the Illinois country, for repayment of advances.

Id., Francis Waldo, collector, Falmouth in the province of Massachusetts Bay. Waldo mentions the burning of the town of Falmouth, Oct. 18, 1775, under orders of Capt. Mowatt of H. M. S.
Canceaux, and the destruction of the custom house. On f. 147 we
have the answer of Waldo to John Malcolm's charges.

A return of the periods to which the several receivers of His
Majesty's quit-rents and revenues in the plantations and the West
Indies have made up their accounts, as transmitted to the auditor
general (f. 87, a valuable account, with helpful remarks, containing a statement of amounts given and where expended). Oct. 2.

Letter from John Stuart to John Thomas, deputy superintendent of
Indian Affairs. Charleston, Nov. 15.

Id., Lord George Germain, Mar. 28; and Thomas to the Treasury,
Jan. 1.

526 (451). Account showing the quantities of live stock, provisions,
lumber, etc., imported into the British islands in the West Indies
(Jamaica excepted) from Great Britain and Ireland, from the
time the rebellion in North America has prevented the importation
of these articles from thence to May 31 last. Similar tables follow. Together with considerations for permitting the Leeward
Islands on failure of their usual supplies from North America to
import from any part of Europe provisions, live cattle, and
lumber.

Petition of J. F. W. Des Barres (f. 345).

Distribution of the several branches of the business of the Treasury
to take place Mar. 1, 1776. This paper (1776) is not duplicated
by a similar paper in *Chatham Papers,* **231** (1782-1783).

527 (452). Memorial and other papers concerning Jeremiah Terry's bringing over two deputies of the Mosquito Indians.

Acting receiver general's account, Quebec, May 1, 1775–Nov. 11, 1776.

Petition of Edward James of London, merchant, owner of a transport which took a prize from the Americans.

Petition of Joseph Sanguinet, Canada.

Memorial of James Stewart, contractor, of Newfoundland.

— Petition of Dr. Thomas Moffatt (f. 346).

Bill of drugs, medicines, surgeons' instruments, and other material delivered by George Garnier, apothecary general to the army for the service of His Majesty's hospitals and forces in Africa, America, Canada, East Florida, Isle of Wight, etc., by orders from the Secretary at War (ff. 399-414; *cf. Treas.* 38: **816**).

Petition of Christopher Henderson, agent to the owners of the ship *Dunmore,* which was impressed into the king's service by the Earl of Dunmore, Aug. 22, 1775, with accompanying papers.

1777.

528 (453). Account and certificate of Col. Christie's losses in consequence of the rebellion in America (*Minute Book,* **46,** p. 424); many papers in this bundle concern losses by the Loyalists in Canada, Georgia, New York. The other papers relating to America concern accounts, receipts, and payments; estimates of civil establishments and other expenses; communications from the American Board of Customs Commissioners, with admiralty proceedings in the case of Shearjashub Bourne; Dominica papers; original letters, Howe (ff. 129, 133), Day, commissary-general (f. 174), letters and memorials from royal officials regarding salary payments; various provisions and other contracts, to f. 189.

529 (454). The last third of the bundle contains documents relating to the Ceded Islands, Grenada, St. Vincent, Dominica.

530 (455). Case of the brigantine *Nelly,* Savannah to Liverpool (ff. 53-73).

Forces in West Florida.

Memorials of merchants trading with the West Indies regarding spirits and sugar clay (f. 111).

Report of the Commissioners of the Customs on a plan for consolidating the customs, especially with reference to the plantations (valuable, f. 250).

531 (456). Victualling documents, forage money, New York. 1777, 1778, 1780, 1781, 1782.

Lists of names of British officers and soldiers.

Documents regarding clothing, private losses, copies of licenses for trading with America, establishment at Quebec, naval officers' reports, Jamaica, Barbadoes to 1782, admiralty proceedings, New York, Sept., 1777 (f. 313).

Memorial of T. M. Reid regarding raising royalist troops in North Carolina (f. 343).

532 (457). Naval office lists, Barbadoes. 1776, 1778.

533 (458). Quebec papers, with statement of losses.

Memorial of Anthony Stewart and Thomas Charles Williams regarding indemnification for the brigantine *Peggy Stewart* and her cargo, destroyed by the colonists, 1777.

Antigua and St. Vincent papers.

Papers relating to ships hired and seized by Gov. Dunmore of Virginia.

Observations on extraordinary expenses for 1777.

Regarding East Florida rangers, from the engineer in charge of the works at Pensacola.

Petition from Jared Ingersoll, judge of vice-admiralty in Philadelphia, praying for pay and arrears of salary.

Regarding the transmission and insurance of specie.

Nova Scotia documents.

534 (459). Letters from Gov. Tryon about salary.

Other letters about victualling, contracting, rum supplies, breadstuffs, peas to East Florida.

Petition of merchants, planters, and inhabitants of Dominica to Gov. Thomas Shirley regarding an American " pirate ".

Quebec accounts.

Papers regarding the ship *Boston,* licensed to trade from London to Boston, drawbacks, bounties.

Account of the quantities of British hardware exported from Scotland to the West Indies, Nova Scotia, East and West Florida.

535 (460). Papers from Gov. Dunmore regarding vessels seized and used (scattered).

Memorial of John Brown, late merchant in Norfolk, Va., a refugee, Dec., 1777, regarding a vessel of his seized at St. Christopher because it had no regular clearance, as this could not be obtained in Virginia at that time.

Invoices of provisions and naval stores for Canada and the Lakes.

Army warrants issued by Gen. Carleton.

Memorial from Lieut. Alexander Fraser, of the *Scarborough,* for compensation for losses at the hands of the rebels.

Reference to the four-and-a-half per cent. office.

Various requests for pay for work done in North America.

Various Quebec papers.

Memorial from Henry Gouch regarding the loss of a ship destroyed by the rebels at the siege of Quebec.

Extracts of letters from Stuart to Lord George Germain about the Creeks and the Cherokees. Mar. 10, 1777.

Id. to William Knox.

Expenses attending the army in Canada; list and distribution of commissaries in 1778.

Robert Auchmuty's warrant for £100 and one guinea a day for his expenses as commissioner in the affair of the schooner *Gaspee.*

536 (461). Quebec accounts.

Letter from Commissary Robert Gordon regarding the sailing of the New York fleet from Cork, Aug. 19, 1777.

Letter from Gen. Howe regarding provisions, etc. (f. 70).

Proceedings in the vice-admiralty court, Quebec.

Admiralty appeal, Newfoundland, opinion of king's advocate (f. 42).

Lists of goods suitable for presents to the Indians.

Many papers from Cork, whence ships set out with provisions for America.

Letter from Gen. Carleton to Gen. Howe regarding the seizure of three American vessels (f. 276).

Staff of the garrison in Canada.

Indians in Canada.

537 (462). Intelligence letter, Sept., 1777, says, " on the 16th an express was arrived from Gen. Burgoyne to Sir Guy Carleton, giving an account that the Rebels had abandoned the fort at Saratoga and every other place on the approach of the king's army. That Mr. Washington with his army were marching up the East side of the River Delaware and that Gen. Sir Wm. Howe was in full march after him. That Gen. Burgoyne was in possession of the Hudson's River. That none of the other armies were 25 miles distance from Albany when the express came away. That it was the general opinion at Quebec that the two generals meant to surround the Rebel Army which it was imagined must have effected in a few days " (ff. 48-52).

Petition of John Jervis, a refugee from New England, escaped to Nova Scotia in an open boat (f. 76).

Id., John Saltmarsh, refugee from Connecticut, and acting as a spy (valuable and detailed, ff. 115-118).

Papers regarding the Brunswick and Hessian troops.

Memorial of George Walker, who was carried into Newbury, Mass.

Returns, East Florida rangers.

538 (463). Letter from Gen. Howe with some information about Hessians (f. 47).

List of stores, clothing, etc., sent to America in 1776 (f. 164).

Memorial from James Burrows regarding his commission to go to England and praying for payment (f. 244).

Invoice of presents to the Indians (ff. 220-242).

Quebec accounts, and many papers relating to the Commissariat Department.

1778.

539 (464). Many lists of prizes.

English vessels taken and privateers commissioned since Oct. 13, 1778 (see **540, 541**).

Kempe's list. Jan. 17, 1778.

540 (465). Similar lists. Aug. 22, Dec. 18, 1778.

Letters between the Peace Commissioners and the Treasury as to their expenses.

Many papers and accounts relative to East and West Florida.

Thomas Skilton, victualler's agent, to Atkinson, D'Estaing off Sandy Hook. July 14, 1778.

541 (466). Dr. Thomas Moffatt, his losses at Newport.

Many Moffatt papers here and there.

542 (467). Detailed state of St. Eustatius trade.

543 (468). Patterson, deputy collector at Philadelphia, to the Treasury, complaining that Howe was missing £40,000 of duties there and much more at New York, conditions of trade, etc.

544 (469). Thomas Mills to Gen. Carleton on Canadian accounts; interesting as to Carleton's character. Aug. 24, 1777.

545 (470). Memorial of freighters and owners of the ship *Martha,* London to New York.

Petition of Philip Callbeck, attorney general of St. John and commander-in-chief in the absence of the governor, taken by two armed vessels from Massachusetts and carried into captivity. They robbed him of all his goods, stores, houses, furniture, plate, clothes, etc. Encloses an accompanying narrative.

Quit-rents, Grenada (f. 23).

Memorial of James Chambers, London, regarding tea seized at New York.

Case of the *Lovely Sally,* detained at Quebec during the siege.

Memorial of John Graham, lieutenant-governor of Georgia, for subsistence of troops and rangers, with additional papers.

Letter from Commissary Robert Gordon regarding arrivals from America, with some interesting information (f. 157). Cork, Apr. 15.

Petition of Lieut. Simonton, commander of H. M. S. *Dunmore,* and agent of all transports employed in Virginia.

Letter from Valentine Morris. St. Vincent, Apr. 8.

Return of clothing and camp equipage for provincial forces. Oct. 8. Speaks of fire, New York, Aug. 3.

Memoir of Samuel Greatheed (for Craister Greatheed), requesting salary as acting governor.

Letter of J. T. Kempe, explaining his appeal from the New York court of vice-admiralty. New York, Aug. 24.

Case of the snow *La Jeune Pauline,* cargo believed to belong to Franklin or Deane (f. 401).

Petitions of John Spiller, William Stark, James Crosby, claims.

Id., William Brown, Georgia, for damages done to his estate. States facts regarding his salary as " searcher and officiating comptroller ", and says that the customs records of Savannah were destroyed on board the ship *Inverness.* An important petition.

Id., John Coffin, a Loyalist from Boston, who fled in the summer of 1775.

Memorial of Bartlett Goodrich, son of a family in Virginia that suffered as Loyalists. *Cf.* **565,** f. 172. There are other memorials relating to prize money and Loyalist sufferings.

546 (471). Memorial of Robert Gilmour, Loyalist, printer at Norfolk, regarding his press which was seized by Dunmore.

547 (472). Memorial of Sir John Johnson as to his Loyalist brigade.

1779.

548 (473). Accounts from Gov. John Wentworth, June, 1775–Mar., 1777.

Information from the Scottish customs of a rebel squadron off the coast (Paul Jones?).

549 (474). Andrew Elliot to the Treasury regarding trade and general conditions in New York. Nov. 13. An excellent letter.

Robert McKenzie to Sir W. Howe on the management of **trade**, duties, and prize goods. New York, Dec. 26.

Paumier on conditions in Georgia, with 26 enclosures. Nov. 4.

Prevost to the Treasury regarding Loyalists and navy to be fed.

Kempe's list of New York prizes to Jan. 28.

Accounts of Alexander Ross, Dunmore's agent to Ohio, with Dunmore.

Carlisle and Eden to the Treasury on their regulation of trade at New York, while there as Peace Commissioners. Many papers also in **552**.

Robinson, late collector in Rhode Island, to be reimbursed for costs of his dispute with J. Otis in 1769, details.

Four letters from Haldimand.

Letters and accounts from Haldimand, Castleton, and Clinton. Some are originals, some copies.

550 (475). Narrative memorial of Anthony Stokes, chief justice of Georgia.

551 (476). Bundle of Custom House papers, of considerable interest for commerce during the year 1779. Chiefly West Indian.

553 (478). Papers from John Stuart, of the Southern Indian Department.

Memorial of George Leonard, late of Boston, referring to Nantucket and its trade, 1778, 1779.

554 (479). Quit-rents, Tobago, St. Vincent.

Petition of Alexander Speirs and others regarding the loss of the brigantine *Loyal Subject,* taken by the rebels (f. 35).

Memorial from Col. Lord Cathcart to Sir Henry Clinton regarding the infantry of the British Legion at Greenwich, Conn., and the stealing of £447 pay money.

Letter from Gen. Carleton on bounties for Loyalists (f. 369). Jan. 25.

1780.

556 (481). Petition of John Brooks, Loyalist.

Letters from Andrew Elliot about trade in New York, 1780, 1781. Interesting. Also in **559**.

Kempe's list of prizes, showing the activity of Bermudan privateers.

559 (484). Observation on the " enormous expense of Stuart's Indian presents ".

560 (485). Letters from Gov. Wright of Georgia.

562 (487). Duties at Halifax. Many papers in this and succeeding bundles.

1781.

565 (490). Contract and subsistence papers ; many others about military estimates and expenses. Group of papers from Haldimand, Oct., relating to expenses of Quebec.

567 (492). Andrew Elliot to Gov. Robertson of New York regarding the possibilities of reconciliation. Jan.

Chamber of Commerce to Clinton, thanking him for his attention to the mercantile interest of the city. Mar. 8.

1782.

570 (bundle 1). Cornwallis on the losses of Lyonel Bradstreat at Yorktown (f. 149).

Petition of Col. Clark regarding the rental of houses in New York,
where the troops were quartered.

Id., Capt. Henry Bellew, commander of the ship *Liverpool* at Norfolk, who entertained many Loyalist refugees (f. 145).

Memorial of Gen. Carleton against P. Livius, chief justice of Quebec
(f. 216).

Id., Elias Durnford, for his money (f. 230).

Id., Frederick William Hecht, assistant commissary, taken prisoner
by the French, with statement of losses (f. 230).

Letter from Benedict Arnold, with accompanying papers (f. 276).
Dover Street, London, Apr. 19.

Condemnation of the ship *Bird* in the New York court of vice-admiralty (ff. 324 ff.).

571 (bundle 2). Forage papers.

Narrative of services of Sir Charles Burdett, late collector of customs at St. Augustine, since Lexington.

Papers (11) from Clinton to Gage on conditions in Charleston, 1781-
1782.

572 (bundle 3). Tryon's memorandum book of expenditures at New
York, 1775-1776.

A thick bundle of papers on supplies for Fraser's expedition, before
Saratoga; referred to Burgoyne, whose report thereon follows.

573 (bundle 4). Clinton to Lord George Germain in praise of Andrew
Elliot.

578 (bundle 9). Various papers by and relating to Maurice Morgann.

1783.

580 (bundle 1). Dunmore accounts.

Letters from Brook Watson, conditions in New York, also **582** and
583.

Fox to the Treasury—outfit and pay of D. Hartley. Apr. 18, 1783.

582 (bundle 3). Loyalist papers, Bruce at Pensacola.

James Russell on the confiscation of his iron-works by Maryland.
Loyalist memorials.

586 (bundle 7). Papers on the establishment of a plantation office,
Sept., 1783, and claims of the Board of Trade for salaries to July,
1782. They deal with the history of the Board of Trade in a case
which bears Kenyon's opinion (see below, p. 247).

Long and able report, with a mass of evidence, on fluctuations in
exchange at New York, 1777-1782. Dec. 30, 1782.

589 (bundle 10). Loyalist memorials, Stair Agnew and Gov. Wright.

590 (bundle 11). Letter from Benedict Arnold, claiming a share of
prize money. July 24, 1782.

591 (bundle 12). Memorial from Kempe, attorney general of New
York.

1784.

596 (bundle 1). Services of Guy Johnson, many enclosures which were sent to the auditor of public accounts.

598 (bundle 3). Services of Charles Stedman, author of the *History of the War*.

600 (bundle 6). Thick bundle from Brown at Pensacola on Indian affairs and Spanish intrigues.

602 (bundle 8). Hartley to Carmarthen requesting that J's baggage be not opened at Dover where he plans taking a British ship to America.

Memorial and papers of Gen. DeLancey.

604 (bundle 10). Memorial with letters and papers from Burgoyne.

Dartmouth and Jonathan Trumbull in favor of Philip Skene, appointed governor of Crown Point and Ticonderoga. Jan. 28, 1775.

606 (bundle 12). Philip Dean to G. Rose regarding £1800 issued to André for secret service.

607 (bundle 13). List of officers of established provincial corps in North America, as recommended by the commander-in-chief (42 pp.).

1785.

611 (bundle 1). Personal narrative of Ann Bates, British spy in New York in 1778-1779; implies that Arnold was in treaty with the British in July, 1778.

612 (bundle 2). *Id.*, Mary McCarthy.

613 (bundle 3). Thick bundle accompanying the report of Generals Fawcett and Ray on the Loyalists.

Case of Du Calvet, accused (with Pillon) of conspiring with the Americans to invade Canada in 1780 (36 papers).

614 (bundle 4). Letter from Brown, St. Augustine, on the Indians.

618 (bundle 8). Memorial and papers of James Glenny, pilot on the lakes of Canada, 1776-1784.

621 (bundle 11). John Temple on his quarrel with the American Customs Commissioners.

622 (bundle 12). Petition of Samuel Dashwood, Boston.

East Florida Loyalists, from J. Cruden, himself a sufferer, a series of pathetic stories.

List of persons entitled to allowances as Loyalists.

Memorial of John Temple, giving an outline of his career from 1760 to date; the Commissioner of the Customs' reply.

Regarding the loss of Maj. Sheridan's baggage.

Case of the *Charming Polly,* New York court of vice-admiralty.

623 (bundle 13). Illicit trade carried on by subjects of the United States with the West Indies, 1785 (ff. 78 ff.).

Petition of councillors of Georgia for pay as commissioners of claims there.

Memorial of William Lucas, chief justice of Grenada, regarding losses, when the island was taken by D'Estaing.

Memorial of John Cooper, in the employ of the second Peace Commission.

Allowance to Daniel Coxe.
Many other claims by Loyalists.

Among the later bundles, at least as far as 1792, are many memorials dealing with the events of the Revolution, recounting services and opinions held at the beginning or during the war, from Galloway, Hill of Boston (juryman in the Preston trial, 1770), Tory privateers, George Leonard, Col. William Bayard, J. D. Smith, author of *Laws of the United States,* 1788, and many others, protesting their loyalty and the value of their services, and asking for half-pay.

REGISTER: ALPHABETICAL-NUMERICAL.

1-329. 1777-1879.   Alphabetical - Numerical Register.

Treas. 2.
—

A useful series of small square indexes to the documents. Three volumes cover the period to 1783; thirteen to 1789; forty-eight to 1803, etc. Generally two volumes are given to a year, one alphabetical, the other numerical or chronological. As a register the series is often general in the form of its entries and does not give detailed lists of documents. Each volume is indexed by proper names. The volumes from 1783 to 1803 are of value in that they record claims of Revolutionary origin that were not settled until after the peace. They are consequently well worth examining, though the references to American matters are not numerous.

INDEXES: REFERENCE BOOKS.

1-11. 1679-1680, 1684-1783; **12.** 1758-1788. Indexes, Reference Books.

Treas. 4.
—

The system of separate reference books seems to have been adopted in 1676, but the earliest volume is missing. These books contain an entry of such papers as were referred by the Treasury Board to some official or department for report and advice. Papers were referred to the Customs Commissioners, the Excise Commissioners, the Mint, the Navy Board, the Office for Taxes, the Pay Office, the Secretary at War, the solicitor, the procurator general, etc., but the official who received the greatest number of petitions from the colonies was the auditor general. Some of the petitions were sent from the Privy Council or the Board of Trade to the Treasury and by the latter sent on to the department or official interested. The dates indicate when the paper was referred. The list given below includes, it is believed, every plantation memorial or other paper contained in vols. **2-6** and **12** that was thus referred.

2. Petition, Gov. Culpeper, Virginia (p. 158). Dec. 15, 1684.
   Petition, administrator to the estate of Gov. Jeffreys, Virginia, who died Dec. 17, 1678 (p. 178).
3. Account by Randolph of £471 expended by him for the king's service in New England (p. 28). Mar. 9, 1685.
   Petition, George Muschamp, who had served as had his father in the customs service in Ireland, and prays to succeed Gibbs, who was "king's collector of Carolina and Roanoke" (p. 148). 1684.

Petition, Culpeper, containing important statement of Culpeper's relations with Virginia and of the money which that colony still owed him (pp. 314, 315, 316). 1684.

Petition, John Scott, merchant and owner of the ship *Abercorne,* bound from Londonderry to Port Royal (Carolina), where it arrived, May, 1685. Took on freight of timber for Barbadoes. Great sickness in Carolina, so ship sailed for Virginia, arrived at Pautuxent (Maryland), there seized by Col. Darnell and Maj. Sewall because it had Irish linen on board (p. 380).

Petition from " Commanders of ships using the Virginia trade " regarding allowances at the port of London, and containing details regarding the tobacco trade (p. 381).

4. Petition, Ed. Cranfield, showing " that he being bred in Barbadoes spent some time under the treasurer there, whereby he understood the account of the revenue of the Four and a half per cent.", and wishes the place lately filled by " Mr. Gasconge " (p. 4). Dec. 20, 1686.

" The Earl of Sterline's Case " from the grandson of the old earl (pp. 4-5). (See *Treas.* 64: **88**, 221.)

5. Petition, Thomas Robson, on behalf of Col. Edwyn Stede, governor of Barbadoes, a matter of salary (p. 22). Feb. 14, 1686.

Petition for a warrant for payment of £240 per annum to Sir Robert Robinson of Bermuda (p. 34).

Petition touching the property of Edwin Plowden in England—nothing to do with the grant to Plowden in America—(p. 51).

Petition, Nicholas Spencer, secretary of Virginia, for compensation for expenses incurred in that government upon the departure of Culpeper (p. 62). Apr. 25, 1687.

Petition, Culpeper, with an exact statement of his financial relations with Virginia (p. 116). July 14, 1687.

Petition, merchant adventurers of Virginia and Maryland, urging that all tobacco ought to be shipped in casks and not in bulk; accompanied by a " paper of reasons " (p. 132). Aug. 13, 1687.

Petition, commander of the ship *Dartmouth,* for payment of expenses incurred in purchasing a small sloop " that could go among the rocks and shoals ", in checking illicit trade in the Leeward Islands (p. 133). Aug. 18, 1687.

Extract of letter, Gov. Robinson, Bermuda, complaining of the inconveniences which that island undergoes in having but one ship to carry off the produce of the island (p. 165). Nov. 24, 1687.

Petition, Jane and Mary Robinson for £240 due their father, the governor of Bermuda (p. 196). Dec. 20, 1687.

Petition, Gov. Powell, Antigua, for salary, etc. (p. 203). June 26, 1688.

Petition regarding the lands of the regicides in Bermuda (p. 212). Feb. 3, 1688.

Petition, Robert Danvers, " baron and justice of pleas of the Crown " in Barbadoes, for salary (p. 233). Mar. 19, 1688.

Petition, Gov. Powell, Antigua (p. 249). Apr. 11, 1688.

Petition, sugar refiners and merchants, regarding competition of the French in sugars and molasses (p. 255, see also p. 307). May 6, 1688.

Proposal from the Lords of Trade regarding mines in New England (p. 281). June 21, 1688.

Petition, Francis Burghills, who brought the quo warranto against the charter of the Bermuda Company, regarding the lands of the regicides, etc. (p. 286). July 12, 1688.

Petition from proprietaries of East New Jersey, surrendering their government but asking for a new patent of the soil (p. 296). July 12, 1688.

Petition, Culpeper, requesting confirmation of his title to lands in Virginia (p. 298). July 10, 1688.

Petition, Patrick Mein, " being lately returned from my survey of his Majesty's plantations in the Continent of America ", and being ordered to the West Indies, etc. (p. 308). 1688.

Petition, Col. Stede, governor of Barbadoes, for collectorship of the four-and-a-half per cent. for his brother John Stede (p. 325; see also **6,** 346).

6. Petition, New England merchants and one Virginia merchant, to go to the plantations despite the embargo (p. 130). Feb. 4, 1690.

Petition, Jahleel Brenton, for the position of surveyor of the woods (p. 222). New England, Aug. 20, 1690.

Petition, " Mr Randolph ", for license for the ketch *William* of Barbadoes for two men and a boy to sail her home (p. 302). Mar. 10, 1690.

Petition, Robert Beckford, commander of the privateer *Greyhound* of Jamaica (p. 311). Apr. 16, 1691.

Petition, Edward Randolph, for position as collector and receiver general of customs and revenue in the province of New York, made vacant by the death of Chidley Brooke (p. 317). May 11, 1691.

Petition, West India merchants, and planters concerned in and trading to the plantations, regarding new duty on ginger (p. 325). July 9, 1691.

Petition, Edward Randolph, for remainder due him for masts and bowsprits supplied by him to the navy in 1689 and 1690 (p. 337). Aug. 26, 1691.

Id., to be employed as " surveyor in riding the coast of America which is nearly 2000 miles in extent ", Oct. 5, 1691 (p. 343). Referred to the Commissioners of the Customs " to consider and examine the petitioner's fitness for the office and if they have no objection to present him to their Lordships ".

Id., regarding the survey of woods in America. " For some years past I was surveyor of woods in the province of Maine and being now appointed surveyor general of their Majesties' customs in North America I have an opportunity to make particular surveys of all the woods growing upon that Continent " (p. 350). Oct. 16, 1691. Referred to Blathwayt ; and the petition and Blathwayt's report were referred to the Commissioners of the Customs to report " if it doth not interfere with what is granted to Mr. Brenton ".

Order of reference from the Lords of Trade on the case of Nicholas Lawrence *et al.* concerned in the ketch *Salisbury* appealing from judgment given in court of assistants, Boston (p. 350). Nov. 20, 1691.

Proposal of Sir William Phips and Increase Mather for coining money in New England (p. 364). Jan. 12, 1692.

Petition, Henry Rycroft, Mathew Rider, Samuel Allen, and others that their ships may go with the governor of New England (Phips) (p. 364). Jan. 18, 1691.

Proposal concerning the erection of a college in Virginia, together with a report from Blathwayt thereupon (p. 390). Apr. 21, 1692.

Petition, Jamaica merchants, to have 80 or 100 seamen allowed them for the year's trade over and above the 200 already granted (p. 427). Oct. 14, 1692. This was on account of the embargo.

This list of petitions, etc., in vols. **2-6** will give an idea of the general value of these volumes for colonial history. Vol. **12** calls for a special listing.

12. 1758-1788.

Application from Gov. Shirley, for clothing for his regiment, his public table, and his intelligence service (p. 1). Referred to the Secretary at War, Jan. 13, 1758.

Applications (very numerous) from Sir James Colebrooke or his representatives, from Kilby and Baker, and from others who had contracts for victualling the forces in America. Generally speaking these applications are of but little value; occasionally, however, one meets with an interesting bit of information, as when mention is made of the fact that " provisions issued irregularly to his Majesty's troops were destroyed and taken by the enemy in March and August, 1757 ".

Application of Gov. Reynolds of Georgia for raising a troop of rangers (p. 16).

Id., Alexander Hume, praying for the remission of quit-rents from the lands of his brother, Robert Hume of South Carolina (p. 42).

Representation of Gov. Gabriel Johnston of North Carolina regarding arrears of salary (p. 48). Oct. 10, 1760.

Id., Joseph Sherwood, agent of Rhode Island, regarding reimbursement of that colony for expenses incurred in 1756 (p. 49; *cf.* p. 127). Oct. 23, 1760. Connecticut and Massachusetts had been reimbursed but not Rhode Island.

Proposal of Benjamin Martyn, agent for Georgia, that the Earl of Shaftesbury be accepted as his security for £1500 and he himself for £1500 (p. 56; *cf.* p. 237). Apr. 10, 1761.

Proposal of John Roberts, receiver general of quit-rents in Virginia, regarding security (p. 86).

Id., Charles Garth, agent for Georgia (p. 100).

Id., George Saxby, receiver general of quit-rents, South Carolina (p. 121).

Answer of Joseph Sherwood, agent of Rhode Island, to the objections made by the Secretary at War and the paymaster of the forces to certain of Rhode Island demands (pp. 49, 127). Dec. 7, 1765.

Memorial of Peter DeLancey, inspector of stamps for Quebec, Nova Scotia, and New Hampshire, setting forth that since his appointment he had had no advantage whatever from his office and prays some relief (p. 134). July 11, 1766.

A number of similar memorials follow from British officials in Canada for pay, etc.

William Bowden offered as security for Charles Stewart, paymaster and receiver general of customs in America (p. 152). May 2, 1768.

Memorial of John Mason, trustee and agent for the Mohegan Indians, for cost of prosecuting their appeal (pp. 153, 174). May 26, 1768. *Cf., Treas.* 1 : **463**.

Memorial of bondsmen of Jared Ingersoll, distributor of stamps, that bond be delivered to them and cancelled (p. 169). May 9, 1770. See *Treas.* 54 : **41**, 120.

Security, Anthony Wheelock, son of Bryan Wheelock of the Plantation Office, agent for East Florida (pp. 174, 206, 222). Aug. 15, 1770.

Regarding the fishing trade, from settlers in Quebec and Nova Scotia (p. 210). Apr. 7, 1773.

Memorial, merchants trading to the sugar colonies, praying reduction of excise duty on plantation coffee (p. 216). Mar. 11, 1774.

Memorial of Liverpool traders to the West Indies on the failure of the African trade (pp. 249, 301). June 11, 1777.

Memorial, John Bourke, praying for payment for sundry articles sent to the Bahamas for Loyalist refugees settled there (p. 320). Jan. 28, 1784.

15-18. 1702-1711. Alphabetical Register.

These volumes are prefatory to the Registers of Papers that follow. In them few clues are given to the contents of the petitions or letters. The names of the petitioners are arranged alphabetically, the date of each petition is generally given, and a comment of the board is added by way of endorsement. If the petition was discussed before the board the decision will usually be found in the Minute Book. A list of the petitions, etc., relating to colonial affairs is here appended.

15. Order in Council continuing an allowance of £50 per annum to a minister and £30 per annum to a schoolmaster in Pennsylvania, out of the 1*d.* per hhd. paid on tobacco (plantation duty). Ordered.

Id. for preparing new seals for the plantations. Ordered.

Charles Thomas, to be receiver of the casual revenue in Barbadoes. Ordered.

Lord Culpeper, to be laid before the queen.

16. Report, Blathwayt, with several states of Her Majesty's revenue in the plantations (followed by a brief statement of revenue accounts in Massachusetts, New York, Jamaica, Virginia, Caribbee Islands, the Jerseys, and Carolina).

Report, Blathwayt, on several papers from the commissioners of prizes, regarding prizes taken to the West Indies (" Write to Mr. Burchett to move his Royal Highness to give instructions accordingly, viz.: that the commanders of ships of war bound to America do not dispose (at their own will) of the prizes they shall take but submit themselves to the courts of admiralty ", etc.; a long and important instruction).

Letter, Thomas Byerly, prays to be receiver general of New Jersey. Referred to Blathwayt.

Letter, Burchett, with a copy of Dr. Bramston's report on admiralty courts in the West Indies. To be laid before the Queen in Council. Nov., 1705.

Letter, John Bridger. All has been done that was proposed by the Board of Trade.

Letter, Col. Heathcott. Referred to Blathwayt.

Letter, Sir Jeff. Jeffrys, with a report from Mr. Howe about the subsistence of the Four Companies at New York. Agreed.

Letter, William Popple, secretary of the Board of Trade, for 40 copies of the act to encourage trade in Newfoundland, to be dispersed there. Ordered; " but Mr. Popple to be acquainted that my Lords doth not like these preceedings ".

Board of Trade for two collections of the statutes of England for the service of New York and New Jersey. Read July 12, 1705.

17. Thomas Byerly, collector and receiver general of New York, with Blathwayt's report about his salary.

Representation, Blathwayt, regarding casual revenue in Barbadoes. Read Aug. 1, 1710. Make a representation of this for the queen and Council.

Letter, Lord Lovelace, governor of New York and New Jersey, signifying his arrival in New Jersey and the restoration of Byerly suspended by Lord Cornbury as receiver; and the expense of subsisting the German Protestants till the snow be off the ground when they can distribute the lands amongst them. Read May 25, 1709.

Letter, Robert Livingstone, from New England. Read Oct. 31, 1707.

Owners of ships employed in transporting Palatines to New York, with commissioners of transports' report about their demand for demurrage. Read July 31, 1710. Payment to be made easy.

Proposal, William Penn, with report of the commissioners of victualling.

Pomroy and Mathews, with Burchett's letter. Palatines' debt to tradesmen for goods and tools furnished them on their going to New York. Read July 21, 1710. To be paid, but my Lord expects an exact and particular account of the collection.

Col. Quary, representation from the Commissioners of the Customs about his being obstructed in getting judgment on plantation bonds executed. Read July 24, 1710. To be laid before the Privy Council.

John Reyner, attorney and advocate general of New York, with the Board of Trade's report. Read June 21, 1710.

Memorial, Board of Trade, for salaries.

18. Thomas Byerly, report from Blathwayt. Agreed according to the report.

Id., draught of warrant. Approved all but the last paragraph. To be transcribed for their lordships' signing.

Letter, Bishop of London, for Williamson, chaplain to Maryland, Orr, chaplain to Leeward Islands, Dennis, schoolmaster to South Carolina, Macouchi, chaplain to Maryland. Sept. 28, Oct. 20, 1710. Her Majesty thinks these come very frequently. Respited.

19-36. 1713-1782. Register of Papers read at the Board.

This register contains chronological entries of applications to the Treasury Board, with the replies thereto. There is an index nominum in each volume. The later books are very similar to the Reference Books (*Treas.* 4).

19. Lovelace. Blathwayt's report on Lady Lovelace's petition regarding money due her late husband, governor of New York.

Earl of Orkney. Order in Council referring his memorial regarding a mine discovered in Virginia to the Board of Trade.

Report, Auditor Harley, on New England bills. Copy to be sent to the Ordnance, Navy, and Victualling boards.

Letter, Popple, desiring an account of the annual expense of the plantations; also letter, Ferne, regarding the four-and-a-half per cent. Referred to Blathwayt, to the paymaster of guards and garrisons, and to the Ordnance Board.

Order in Council concerning Pennsylvania and about temporary laws. To the attorney general, to take care that all requisites be pursued so that Her Majesty's pleasure may be complied with.

Memorial, William Byrd, receiver general of revenues in Virginia, desiring to return to England. Read Feb. 3, 1714. Granted.

Report of the Commissioners of the Customs upon a memorial of William Keith, praying to succeed Col. Quary as surveyor general. To rest till the report from Mr. Nicholson comes in.

Memorial of William Keith about the place of surveyor general in America. Write to the Commissioners of the Customs to think of some way of employing him. See the presentment made by the Commissioners of the Customs.

Letter without name from Virginia, proposing that every clergyman there should be allowed a hogshead or two custom free for augmenting his living. July 20, 1714. Read.

20. "Memorials, Petitions, and other Papers read before the Rt. Hon. the Lords Commrs of his Mats Treasury and the Directions given by their Lords thereupon." Index arranged chronologically, June 6, 1717–July 10, 1718. Entries briefer than in preceding volume.

Letter, New England, about Canada bills. July 30, 1717. My Lords will consider this.

Several accounts and papers from Col. Spotswood about the quit-rents and duty of 2s. per hhd. on tobacco. Aug. 2, 1717. Blathwayt to state the account.

Report from the Board of Trade upon the petition of Francis Kennedy. Oct. 2, 1717. Prepare a sign manual directed to the governor of Virginia to pay him £200 for his expenses in going to Carolina and £50 as a reward for his services.

Commissioners of the Customs' report on the petition of Kenneth Gordon to be collector at Philadelphia. Oct. 22, 1717. Agreed.

The items thus given will show the general character of the collection as far as it relates to colonial history. The actual documents themselves can be found, generally but not always, among the In-Letters.

OUT-LETTERS.

These entry books contain copies of letters which were written and signed by the secretary to the Treasury Board as a result of instructions or orders delivered by the board at its meetings. Many of the earlier letter-books were kept in an irregular manner, so that the dates must be taken as approximate only. The letter-books are divided into three groups, " customs ", " general letters ", and " various ", the lines of division between which do not appear to be very strictly drawn. The volumes are generally indexed, so that if name and date be known the letter sought for can be found. Though the board's replies were frequently formal, a number of details are met with that cannot be obtained elsewhere, particularly in the case of appointments, where the reasons are sometimes given. Taken as a whole, these volumes are important and supplement the In-Letters and the Minute Book.

CUSTOMS.

1-33. 1667-1784. Letters relating to Customs.

Treas. 11.
—

The first six volumes of this series, extending from 1667 to 1681, form an earlier group of which only vols. **1, 3,** and **4,** are of interest for colonial history. These volumes contain material similar to that in the later volumes, only less extensive.

6 and **7** are excise volumes. Beginning again with **8,** 1681-1683, the series contains entries relating to the breaches of the acts of navigation, employment of foreign seamen and the like, compositions for running plantation tobacco and frauds in the tobacco trade. It contains letters to the farmers of the customs, to the Commissioners of the Customs in England, and to the collectors and others in America, relating to a great variety of matters—ships, convoys, transportation of bullion, exemption from embargoes, troubles in America, illicit trade. Among the most important documents are the entries relating to the plantation customs establishment; lists of leaves of absence, instructions to collectors, and warrants appointing customs officials—comptroller of the customs, collectors, tide waiters, with place, office, and generally name of predecessor—increasing the plantation establishment by the addition of boats, boatmen, etc., and authorizing the payment of salaries and other expenses.

The entries contain information about such surveyors general as Mein, Quary, Keith, Birchfield, Fitzwilliam, etc., for the southern territory, and Randolph, Bacon, Peagrum, and others for the northern, with orders and instructions. They note the changes of 1767 and include many extracts from the letters regarding the troubles in America after that date. They contain detailed lists of the customs establishment in the plantations, so that it would be possible by means of the warrants and the lists to make out a fairly complete series of appointments, thus supplying information similar to that furnished by the customs rolls in the *Declared Accounts* series. At the beginning of **26** (1759-1762), continued on p. 456 of the same volume, is a list of the officers of customs, with titles, places, predecessors, if any, date of warrant of each officer for the plantations and England. In **27** (1762-1765) is an important body of instructions issued to the collectors, and rendered necessary by the new customs conditions created by the revenue acts (p. 318).

GENERAL.

1-34. 1668-1783. General Letters.

Treas. 27.

These volumes are of some importance for colonial history. They contain letters to a great variety of people:

Gen. Amherst regarding bills.

Colebrooke and Hanbury regarding transportation of gold and silver to New York.

John Pownall, secretary of the Board of Trade, regarding Adm. Gambier's extraordinary expenses.

Quit-rents in East Florida.

William Story, who wanted to be customs collector at Newport.

Philip Stevens, secretary to the Admiralty, regarding £36,000 to pay the army in America.

John Pownall regarding Monte Christi trade (many papers).

John Thomlinson, coin to America.

To others regarding payment of forces.

Gov. Murray (Quebec) to aid Tarrant and Cross by going to Quebec to inquire into commercial conditions there.

Other papers regarding quit-rents and appropriations therefrom.

Contraband trade, Rhode Island.

On the bill for the repeal of a part of the act of 1733 (1763) preparatory to the passage of the act of 1764.

On other acts—hemp, whale-fins, beaver hats.

On vice-admiralty. 1764.

Case of the *Gaspee.*

Complaints on illicit trade from the American Board of Customs Commissioners (1668).

Writs of assistance (English practice, 13, 14 Charles II.).

Case of the seizure of the ship *Liberty,* etc.

Also letters to the Treasury, which correspond to documents in *Treas.* 1; letters to the Board of Trade, Admiralty, Privy Council, Commissioners of the Customs, Secretary of State, solicitor of the customs, auditor and receiver of accounts, colonial agents, various American correspondents, contractors and victuallers, paymaster of the forces, army officials, auditor general of plantation revenues, surveyor of woods in America, and sundry private individuals. After 1777 the letters become quite formal.

VARIOUS.[1]

1, 2, 3. 1763-1778, 1778-1797, 1797-1823. Letters relating to America.

Treas. 28.

In the indexes to the other entry books, these three volumes are referred to as the " America Books ", and the entries in them relate solely to the colonies, from Canada to Tobago. For colonial history their importance, which is very great, ends with **2,** 185, where is entered the " revocation of the Commissioners of the Customs for America ", Oct. 16, 1783. In the main the volumes are colonial warrant and commission books; the com-

[1] The term " various " indicates that this group contains letter-books formerly belonging to series that have since been discarded.

missions and warrants, letters patent and privy seals, given in full and in form convenient to use, making up the bulk of the entries. They concern governors, captains general, judges of admiralty and other courts, chief justices, registers in chancery, agents, surveyors, naval officers (in the instances where the naval officers were named by the king though constituted under the seal of the colony), attorneys general, postmasters general, and special appointees, such as commissioners of peace and their secretary (Ferguson), in fact all officials whose appointment was in the hands of the crown. The warrants concern contracts, money grants and remittances, allowances for civil establishments, expenses of surveys and maps, grants of shares in condemned vessels, allowances for property seized or damaged, governors' salaries, and distribution of prize money (**2,** 160, 165). There are also copies of instructions sent to individuals and officials relative to many matters, such as the outrages at Newport and New London. There are also great numbers of papers relating to the American Board of Customs Commissioners, of first importance as supplementing the documents in *Treas.* 1.

MINUTE BOOKS.

1-54. 1667-1783. Treasury Minute Books.

Treas. 29.
———

These volumes, which are well indexed and easy to use, contain the minutes of the meetings of the Commissioners of the Treasury or Treasury Board. They note every important matter that came before the board and thus furnish a clue to the character of the documents in the bundles already described. They contain also occasional discussions, observations, depositions, and decisions not found elsewhere, and should always be consulted in conjunction with the original documents. Note especially the reports of the auditor general of the plantation revenues. After 1767 the minute books increase in fullness. In order to supplement the description of the board papers (*Treas.* 1), a few volumes of the minute books are here examined.

46. Jan., 1777–Feb., 1778.
> Financial accounts with America.
> Memorials for impressment and losses of vessels.
> Presents to the Indians and communications from the Superintendent of Indian Affairs.
> Contracts for provisions.
> Letter from Andrew Elliot, collector of customs, New York, giving an account of the measures taken by him while the rebels were in possession of New York. Nov. 30, 1776.
> Payments to British officials, civil and military.
> Many papers about Loyalists, convicts, the American Board of Customs Commissioners.
> Letters from Carleton, Clinton, Dunmore, Gage, Howe, Haldimand, De Brahm, Fraser, Glen.
> Papers relating to shipment and insurance of specie and issues of the paymaster-general.

47. Feb.–Nov., 1778.
> Many papers regarding Loyalists.
> Army contracts and contracts for provisions.
> Affairs of Florida, the Ceded Islands, Canada, Nova Scotia.
> Vice-admiralty matters.

48. Dec., 1778–Oct., 1779.

Many papers regarding Loyalists, with names and business and amount of the allowance made, often accompanied with comments by the members of the board.

Appointments.

Contracts.

Memorial from those concerned in the production of " British plantation cotton-wool ".

Letters regarding the Peace Commission of 1778 and communications from Dr. Adam Ferguson, the secretary.

49. Nov., 1779–Feb., 1781.

Many papers regarding the Loyalists, of whom a good list could be made up with details of their experiences.

Commissariat matters.

Convoys.

Contracts.

Requests for money from the plantations for salaries, losses, etc.

Reports from various officials.

Petitions regarding losses of provisions seized, vessels impressed or sunk (Maryland, Rhode Island, Mississippi).

Proposals, letters, bills, accounts.

Letter from De Brahm, begging not to be superseded as he cannot return home owing to age and infirmities.

Papers regarding condemned ships, New York vice-admiralty court.

Hurricane in the West Indies.

Indian presents.

Affairs of the American Board of Customs Commissioners.

Letters from Haldimand and Clinton.

In the remaining volumes we have many accounts (estimates chiefly) of losses, arrears, and the like. For extracts from the *Minute Books* see *D. K. Rept.*, 7, app. 2, pp. 65-69, and many original " Treasury Minutes " among the Treasury Board Papers.

628. 1771-1777. Copies of Minutes relating to the American War.

This volume is an entry book of the Treasury minutes laid before the House of Commons, Feb. 21, 1771, to Dec. 5, 1777. The minutes record the expenditures for carrying on the war in North America and omit all other matters that came before the board during those years. They concern the cost of provisions, clothing, transportation, camp equipage, and the like.

ACCOUNTS.

These volumes contain the elaborate financial accounts of the Treasury, made up yearly and quarterly, with various declarations, registers, customs accounts, fee accounts, prize accounts, auditor's states of accounts, military and customs establishments, and miscellanea. The number of these volumes is very great, and it is not always easy to determine the exact measure of their value for colonial history.

ACCOUNTS GENERAL: YEARLY.

1-18. 1688-1785. Revenue Accounts, Yearly. Income and Expenditure of Great Britain.

Treas. 30.
—

Of little importance for our purpose, as the entries make no separate mention of the plantation duty and other royal revenues from the plantations. The imposition on sugar and tobacco is rated and the receipts from the four-and-a-half per cent. are entered.

ACCOUNTS GENERAL: QUARTERLY.

1-328. 1701-1783. Revenue Accounts, Quarterly.

Treas. 31.
—

Of greater importance than the yearly accounts. The plantation duty is entered, also the expenses of the Board of Trade, the cost of civil establishments in America, and the salaries of British officials there, as far as they were paid salaries and were not dependent on the fees of their offices or the grants of the colonial assemblies.

ACCOUNTS GENERAL: DECLARATION, AUDITORS.

1-191. Declaration of all the sums received and paid at the receipt of the Exchequer, arranged chronologically, payments rendered at Easter and Michaelmas.

Treas. 33.
—

These volumes contain brief declarations of receipts and expenses, among which are occasional items relating to the colonies, for example:

75. *Receipts.*

Custom bonorum import' a coloniis Anglic' . . . . cxxii l. i s. iii d.
Debit' 4½% at les Leeward Is.
Denar' pro vendicione agrorum in Insula St. Christopheri.

Expenses.

Horatio Walpole Ar' supervisor et auditor genl Revenc' dmi Regis in America de annuitat' s. ad c l. et cc l. per annum . . . . cxxv l.
Jonathan Forward mercator pro transportation felon'.
R. Rogers As. Capitan Genl et Gubernator in capite de Bahama Insul' in America super allocacon.

150. *Receipts.*

Debit' super Bon' a colon'.
4½% a colon'.

Expenses.

Georgio Bisset pro transportation ad Rhode Insul' ut ministr'.
Edward Ellington pro transportation ad Georgia ut ministr'.
Roberto Cholmondeley arm', Supervisor et Auditor General Revenc' Dmi Regis in America.
Also payments to governors of various colonies and to agents of Cape Breton and Newfoundland.

151. *Expenses.*

John Tabor Kempe Attornat' General apud New York super allo-
cationem s. ad cl l. per annum.

Willo Tryon, Arm. Gubernator N. Carolinae super allocation' s. ad
m l. per annum.

There are no entries in these volumes of receipts from quit-rents; and no
declarations of plantation accounts. Among the items of expense are many
payments to clergymen, etc., for costs of transportation to the colonies.

ACCOUNTS GENERAL: DECLARATION, PELLS.

Treas. 34.	**1-131.** 1636-1783. Declaration of all Receipts and Issues of the Four Tellers of the Exchequer made by the Clerk of the Pells.

The entries in these volumes correspond to those in
the collections of auditors' declarations, and probably
duplicate them.

ACCOUNTS GENERAL: VARIOUS.

SUMMARY OF REVENUE.

Treas. 35.	**1.** 1636-1638. Summary of Revenue and Expenditure.

The only colonial commodity mentioned is tobacco,
but no clue is given to the amount furnished by the
colonies, either individually or as a whole.

ACCOUNTS DEPARTMENTAL: AUDITORS'

STATES OF ACCOUNTS.

Treas. 38.	**79-80.** 1776-1786. Auditors' States of Account Books.

These volumes contain a registration of particular
accounts, similar to the registration in the volumes
known as " Declaration of Accounts ".

(Formerly *Accounts Various, States of Accounts, 267-268.*)

225. 1721-1725. An Account of all Monies which have been issued and paid out of the Receipt of his Majesty's Exchequer to any person or persons on account of the privy
purse, secret service, pensions, bounties, or any sum or
sums of money to any person or persons whatsoever.
Mar. 25, 1721, to Mar. 25, 1725.

Under " Gifts and Bounties " are entered allowances to ministers going to
America, and royal payments to sundry colonial officials. *Id.* under " Pensions and Salaries " to governors in the West Indies. *Cf.* **226.**

(Formerly *Miscellaneous, Various, 195.*)

253. 1685-1738. Accounts of Various Duties.

Three documents only, showing the receipts from the four-and-a-half per cent. duty since 1685; from the comptroller general in England, H. Holt.
(Formerly *Accounts Various, Customs Accounts,* 69 (1).)

254. 1713-1734. Receipts of the Four and a Half Percent. Duties from the several Islands, and Payments into the Exchequer.

"An account of the gross produce, as it comes into England of the Four and a half percent. and how much thereof has been paid into the exchequer for twenty one years, distinguishing each colony and each year."
(Formerly *Miscellaneous, Various,* 208 (5).)

255. 1713-1734. Sugar taken in payment for the same.

An account of the quantity of sugar, collected in kind, and the quantity for which money has been paid and received on account of the four-and-a-half per cent. for twenty-one years, together with an account of the expense of the officers and of the other charges in collecting the said duty in Barbadoes and the Leeward Islands, distinguishing each island and each year.
(Formerly *Miscellaneous, Various,* 208 (4).)

256. 1720-1727. Instructions from the Commissioners of the Customs to the Surveyor General of the Islands and Establishment there.

A small paper book, containing instructions to the officers of the customs at Barbadoes, and explaining what were the duties of the surveyor general of customs of Barbadoes, Leeward Islands, and Bermuda. At the end is an establishment of the customs officers of these islands, with location and salary and forms of customs papers.
(Formerly *Accounts Various, Customs Accounts,* 67.)

257. 1723-1728. Accounts of Divers Duties.

An account of cash received on the half-crown levy, etc., by George Plaxton, receiver of Barbadoes.
(Formerly *Accounts Various, Customs Accounts,* 69 (2).)

258-268. 1725-1734. Journal of the Four and a Half Percent. Bridgetown, Barbadoes.

Large paper folios containing journals of receipts of the four-and-a-half per cent. duty and of the plantation duty.
(Formerly *Accounts Various, Customs Accounts,* 67, 68.)

269. 1773-1783. "An Account of the Imports and Exports between that part of Great Britain called England and the British West Indies, for the last ten years, vizt.: from Christmas, 1773, to Christmas, 1783, which is as far as the same can be made up, distinguishing each year and the several articles and the value thereof, and the amount of the duties and drawbacks thereon. Pursuant to an order of the Honorable House of Commons, dated 24 February, 1785, presented to the Honorable House of Commons, 29 April, 1785."

The separate islands are not distinguished, but the articles or commodities are listed under the following heads: Foreign Goods exported (In Time and Out of Time), Goods of English Manufacture exported to the British West Indies, British Subsidy Goods exported to the same. *Cf. Custom House, Ledgers of Imports and Exports.*

(Formerly *Accounts Various, Customs Accounts,* 65.)

270. 1775-1833. Divers Accounts of Four and a Half Percent. Duties.

Similar to **258-268.**

(Formerly *Accounts Various, Customs Accounts,* 70.)

277. 1729-1735. Accounts of Quit-Rents, Albemarle County, North Carolina.

Accounts of the receipts of one-half of the arrears of His Majesty's quit-rents for Albemarle County, from Sept. 29, 1729, to Mar., 1732, made up to 1735, and computed at the difference of 7 for £1 sterling in the currency of the province.

The figures are arranged under the following heads: By whom paid, number of years paid, number of acres, quit-rent reserved, amount in sterling money, currency at seven for one, total of currency. The names, which constitute a directory of the landed proprietors of North Carolina in 1735, number over 300, arranged by precincts in alphabetical order—Bertie, Edgecombe, Tyrrel, Currituck, Pasquotank, Perquimans, Chowan. At the end is a debit and credit account, showing the expenditures out of the quit-rents—to Gov. Johnston one-fifth of his salary, Auditor General Walpole's salary, salaries of chief justice, chief baron of exchequer, etc.

(Formerly *Miscellaneous, Various,* 34 (5).)

291. 1777-1783, 1787-1789. Account of the Receivers General, Quebec.

Two accounts: one marked A, being the account of William Grant, a deputy to Sir Thomas Mills, from May 1, 1777, to Oct. 31, 1783; the other marked B, being the account of Sir Thomas Mills, receiver general of the province of Quebec, from Oct. 31, 1787, to Oct. 31, 1789.

(Formerly *Miscellaneous, Various,* 34 (2).)

340. 1679-1761. Abstract of Yearly Receipts.

" Gross and Net Produce of all the Branches of the Revenue under the Management of the Commissioners of his Majesty's Customs in England."

This volume opens with " The Yearly payments into the Receipt of the Exchequer on all the several branches of the Customs from Michaelmas, 1679, to Christmas, 1710 ". Among the payments we find the four-and-a-half per cent., 1698-1711, and plantation duty, 1699-1711. Then follows an account of the gross and net produce, beginning with 1710 and extending to 1761. Here too will be found the gross receipts from the plantation duty entered for each year, Christmas to Christmas (no entries for 1738-1741), the salary charge, and the net returns; also the four-and-a-half per cent. for each year; and for the years, 1712-1717, 1730-1732, " Prize Duties from the Plantations ".

There are in the British Museum and the Public Record Office many lists making mention of the plantation duty or duty on enumerated commodities in the plantations. The figures do not always agree, but they can probably be reconciled by taking into account the differences in the time of reckoning, whether from Christmas, Jan. 5, Lady Day, or Michaelmas; the period of reckoning, whether yearly, half yearly, or quarterly; and the sum, whether gross or net. The following references may be found useful: *Treas.* 31, *Treas.* 38: **258-268**, Brit. Mus. *Sloane* **665**, *Add. MSS.* **8133** C, **8829, 8830, 10119, 10122, 17756-17759, 18051, 29446, 29447, 29990, 30200-30201, 36859, 36862-36865**. References to the four-and-a-half per cent. are *Sloane* **1983** B, *Add. MSS.* **8133** C, **10119, 28089, 29990, 36862**, *Treas.* 38: **253-268, 270, 340**, *Treas.* 56: **36** (warrants various, four-and-a-half per cent. duties, 1765-1832), *Treas.* 64: **50** (letters relating to the four-and-a-half per cent. duties, 1807-1829), *Treas.* 56: **36**, *Treas.* 64: **88-90** (Blathwayt's journal), *passim, A. O., Decl. Acc.,* **843**, 1132, 1133.

(Formerly *Miscellaneous, Various,* 50.)

346-348. 1691-1700. Customs Accounts.

Altogether forty-nine papers.

1. An abstract of the receipts and payments of Her Majesty's customs, new and additional impositions, Dec. 25, 1701–Mar. 25, 1702 (plantation duty).
2. Receipts and payments of His Majesty's customs in London and outports, for the year ending Michaelmas, 1695 (no mention of plantation duty).
3. Receipts and payments of His Majesty's customs for the year ending Michaelmas, 1696 (plantation duty).
4. Receipt of His Majesty's customs and new impositions (plantation goods, rendered weekly by Henry Wolstenholme). Jan. 2, 1697–Mar. 19, 1698.
5. Receipts and payments . . . of enumerated duties collected in the plantations, Michaelmas, 1696–Michaelmas, 1697 (including a schedule of debts in money and bonds owing his Majesty in money and bonds on the Plantation duty, Michaelmas, 1697, and thirty names of plantation collectors with the amounts entirely in money, for example " Xopher [Christopher] Rousby, Gent., late of Maryland . . . £146.6.5½ "; and three names, " on plantation goods in London ", amounts in bonds and money).
6. Schedule of overpayments or of money advanced to his Majesty's use by several collectors of the customs, etc., over and above their receipts, to Michaelmas, 1697 (Wolstenholme in England, Cranfield in Barbadoes, Payne in Maryland, Carpenter and Nagle in Nevis, and John Custis and William Cole in Virginia). In the same bundle is an abstract account of the debts in money and bonds at Christmas, 1698, and the receipts and payments on the customs and other impositions for the year ended at Christmas, 1699, with the debts then standing out. Enumerated commodities in the American plantations: debts in money at Christmas, 1698, £10259; receipt in money, 1699, £3025; overpayment, Christmas, 1698, £863; payment to the receiver general to Christmas, 1699, £1905; on salaries of the collectors of the outports, £498; incidentals " pr detto " allowed by the Commissioners of the Customs, incidents, £156, loss by returns, £443; debts in money at Christmas, 1699, £10282; overpayments at Christmas, 1699, £846.

(Formerly *Miscellaneous, Various,* 220.)

357. Receiver General's Annual Abstracts of Customs and New Impositions, 1746-1780, signed by Robert Townshend to 1759 and W. Mellish or deputy to 1779.

These lists are valuable as giving figures for the gross plantation duty from 1746 to 1780, with the exception of the years 1775 to 1778, reckoning from

15

Jan. 5. The gross amounts, 1746-1761, agree with the corresponding figures in **340**. The lists distinguish between London and the "outports", under which term plantation ports are included, and the figures for both the plantation duty and the four-and-a-half per cent. are given. The figures after 1766 are of particular interest, for in addition to the plantation duty, which diminishes and does not recover until after 1772 (£7378 for 1766; £3910, 1767; £517, 1768; £1075, 1769; £20, 1770; £184, 1771; none, 1772; £277, 1773; £1200, 1779) are given the amounts collected under 4 George III., 6 George III., 7 George III., "Fines and Forfeitures", and for two years, 1769, 1773, "Seizures of Ships of War" (4 George III., c. 15). The amounts collected under 4 George III. are significant, £29,685 for 1767; £14,802, 1768; £6047, 1769; £2526, 1770; £2076, 1771; £736 (+£80), 1772; £2006, 1773; £7699 (+£10026), 1774. The additions in 1772 and 1774 were received from Charles Stuart, cashier and paymaster of the revenues of customs, etc. See *A. O. Decl. Acc.*, **844**, 1137.

(Formerly *Accounts, Revenue, Miscellaneous, England,* 59.)

362-363. 1691-1784. English Customs Accounts of Imports and Exports.

Six bundles containing a great variety of papers, of which the following may be noted.

362. Account of Tonnage Duty. Sept. 29, 1694–Sept. 28, 1695. Of some value for tobacco and for the four-and-a-half per cent.

Fees of officers at the port of London. (n. d.)

H. Holt's account of debts for customs, etc., standing out at Christmas, 1698, containing a report from 37 collectors (names given) of enumerated duties in the plantations. 1698.

A schedule of tobacco bonds, due and unpaid. Mar. 25, 1702. Contains names of each merchant, his security, and the amount due.

An account of the net sums paid into the Exchequer by Henry Ferne, receiver general of customs. 1708-1710. Contains figures for the four-and-a-half per cent., and for the plantation duty before Mar., 1701, since Mar., 1701. In a later paper a special note reads as follows: "The 4½% and enumerated duties collected in his Majesty's islands and plantations in America, the produce whereof is about £7000 per annum". 1715. According to the figures in the lists, as noted above, even the gross amount never amounted to anything like this sum before 1715.

An account of the gross and net produce of several of the branches of the customs. Christmas, 1709, to Christmas, 1715.

Enclosed in this account is a letter from the Commissioner of the Customs, containing the following remark: "Through want of several accompts from the Plantations the gross produce of the enumerated duties cannot be compleated." The account itself gives the figures found in vol. **340**, but a line has been drawn through the figures for the four-and-a-half per cent., and a note added: "Through the want of the plantation accounts from Bermudas, Rhode Island, and from other places on the Continent of America the gross produce of the enumerated duties cannot be at present compleated, and by the net produce of that duty is meant only what has been returned to England."

Customs salaries under £100 per annum. The following figures here given are of interest: plantation salaries paid in England, £1005; paid in the plantations, £1890; total, £2895; corresponding total cost for England, £65,689. Plantation salaries paid by incidents (fees), in England, £330; in the plantations, £177; total, £507; corresponding cost for England, £2642.

An account of the quantities of foreign coin and bullion entered for exportation from Jan. 16, 1717, to Mar. 25, 1727, distinguishing each year, and the countries for which the said entries were made. The document is dated, Apr. 3, 1728. The only colonies receiving coin and bullion are the West Indies, New York, Virginia, and Carolina. Amounts small. See later documents, same bundle, for 1722-1727.

An account of what duties are payable for iron imported from the British colonies in America, what quantities have been imported from thence for the last ten years and how much the duties paid for the same amounted to, distinguishing each year.

An account showing the quantity of rice imported and exported from Christmas, 1705, to Christmas, 1712, Carolina showing the largest quantity, but New England, New York, Pennsylvania, Virginia, and Maryland exporting a considerable amount. See also another paper giving the figures for 1721-1723.

363. An account of the numbers of ships and names of the masters that have since Sept. 29, 1730, taken licenses and given bond for liberty to carry rice from Carolina to the southward of Cape Finisterre; and how many of the ships have returned and the masters thereof redelivered the licenses. Feb. 29, 1732.

An account of the importation and re-exportation of sugars from the British plantations for the last fourteen years, distinguishing each year. Mar. 24, 1732.

An account of the value of the exports to New England, New York, Pennsylvania, Christmas, 1714, to Christmas, 1726. Apr. 4, 1732.

An account of the exports to His Majesty's sugar colonies in America, Christmas, 1714, to Christmas, 1726, distinguishing how much by certificate-goods and how much by English manufactures. Apr. 4, 1732.

An annual account of the number of ships with their tonnage that have entered at the several ports of Great Britain from the northern colonies, Christmas, 1720, to Christmas, 1730. Apr. 4, 1732.

Id. from the sugar colonies and the northern colonies respectively.
Id. from the sugar colonies.

An account of what sugars have been imported from the plantations and exported to foreign parts for five years past. Feb. 20, 1733.

An account of the whole charge of management of the revenue under the care of the Commissioners of the Customs in England. 1721-1732. Separate lists for the plantations. Total charge for England, £2,077,558; for the plantations, £55,129; with this note added: " The several accounts of the collectors in the plantations from Christmas, 1731, to Christmas, 1732, not being yet arrived, the Incidents paid in the plantations for the year could not be completed."

An account of the value of the exports to New England, New York, and Pennsylvania, Christmas, 1714, to Christmas, 1726. Mar. 10, 1730/1.

An account of the quantities of sugar imported from Barbadoes, Jamaica, and the Leeward Islands for seven years ending 1729. (See next paper.)

The amount of the value of the exports from England to New York and Pennsylvania, 1708-1709, 1715-1716, 1720-1721, 1728, 1729, distinguishing each year, and particularly what was the amount in each year of the woolen manufacture exported to those provinces. Mar. 17, 1731.

An account of the value of the exports from England to Barbadoes, Jamaica, and the Leeward Islands. Christmas, 1714, to Christmas, 1726. A duplicate further on.

Id. for Maryland, Virginia, and Carolina. Apr. 8, 1731.

Id. for New York, New England, Pennsylvania, Virginia, Maryland, and Carolina. Apr. 21, 1731.

An account of the quantity of sugar imported into England from Barbadoes, Jamaica, and the Leeward Islands. 1714-1726. Apr. 21, 1731.

An account of what quantity of pig-iron has been imported into England from Christmas, 1720, to Christmas, 1730. Feb. 9, 1732. Figures for Virginia, Maryland, Pennsylvania, and Carolina (very little).

Id., bar-iron. Figures for Jamaica, Virginia, Maryland, Barbadoes, New England (small amount), Carolina (very small amount).

364. An Account of the Quantity of Tobacco imported into England from any of the Islands in the British West Indies. 1780-1781.

An account of the same, which appears by the clearances not to have been of the growth or produce of those islands nor prize tobacco, for the last four years, ending Jan. 5, 1781. Also *id.*, Jan.-Mar., 1781.

An account of the quantity of furs exported from Canada, 1763-1777. Feb. 12, 1783.

An account of goods and merchandise from England to the Dutch islands of St. Eustatius and St. Martin, 1776-1780.

An account of all salted beef, pork, and fish, wheat, flour, biscuit, and peas, exported from England, 1765-1784, with columns for North America and the British West Indies. Mar. 22, 1784.

(Formerly *Revenue Accounts, Miscellaneous, England,* 77, 82, 78.)

367-374. 1687-1767. Declaration of Accounts.

These volumes contain brief registrations of particular declared accounts. After an examination of about sixty declarations in vols. **368, 369, 370, 371, 372, 373, 374,** and comparison with the rolls in the Audit Office and Pipe Office series, I can say that all the entries are duplicates in briefer and less valuable form. The declarations are arranged chronologically, but the dates on the backs of the books are not to be relied on.

(Formerly *Accounts Various, Declaration of Accounts,* 74-81.)

438-457. 1711-1783. Treasury Fee Books.

These books contain only occasional entries of fees connected with colonial matters. The entries are difficult to find and of little value when found.
(Formerly *Accounts Various, Fee Books,* 83-102.)

580-610. 1673-1701. Navy Accounts.

Account books of the treasurer of the navy, containing the amounts received and paid, with the dates and the names of the persons to whom payments were made. Sometimes also the names of the ships are given.
608-610 contain imprest accounts.
(Formerly *Accounts Various, Navy,* 156-165.)

620-637. 1704-1710. Accounts of Prizes and their Cargoes.

These accounts are tabular statements, apparently from the comptroller of the navy to the Treasury, of the number of ships taken, their names, masters, burden in tons, names of ships and commanders that seized them, date of condemnation, ladings, appraised value when sold, prices realized at sale, and the total and when paid. Appended are accounts of the receiver general of prizes.
(Formerly *Accounts Various, Prizes,* 243-246.)
624-637 contain states of account of prize money, monthly receipts and payments of prize money, comptroller's account of prize cash, arrears of prizes, weekly certificates of prize money, day books of prize money (particularly **632**), accounts of prize money (no particulars), arrears of prize money, and accounts of arrears on different prizes. They need no special description here.

661. 1701-1709. "An Account of the cost of Provisions and Charges which have been furnished by the Commissioners for Victualling her Majesty's Navy." Mar., 1701, to Sept. 30, 1709.

Contains very few items relating to the colonies. This account was formerly no. 17 in *Miscellaneous, Various,* 78; the remaining papers in that bundle have been scattered among the other bundles in *Treas.* 38.

812-814. 1776-1784. Accounts of the German Auxiliary Troops engaged during the American War that were repaid by the British Government agreeable to the Treaty of Feb. 1, 1777. (In French, German, and English.)

A calendar of these and similar papers in the Public Record Office and the British Museum is in the Library of Congress. The accounts are for losses sustained, money levied, expenses incurred, soldiers' pay and stoppages, subsidies, expenses of transportation, hospital charges, money advanced by wounded Hessian officers, charges for forage, ammunition, cannon, and muskets, repairs, tents, horses and wagons, etc., together with great numbers of muster-lists, containing names of regiments, officers, soldiers, chasseurs, artillery lists of killed and wounded (arranged by years, 1776-1782). The accounts were sent in by Lieut.-Gen. Faucitt to Sec. Rose of the Treasury and some of them do not appear to have been settled until 1793. In bundle **814** are a few papers of the year 1756. Bundle **813** relates to 1793 only.
(Formerly *Miscellaneous, Various,* 248-250.)

815. 1782-1783. Paymaster-General's Accounts.

Account of extraordinary expenses incurred and paid by Richard Rigby, paymaster-general of the forces, Jan. 31–Mar. 31, 1782, Mar. 25–Dec. 6, 1782, and not provided for by Parliament. *Id.,* Isaac Barré, Edmund Burke, Apr. 19–Nov. 9, 1782, Apr.-Aug., 1782.

(Formerly *Miscellaneous, Various,* 226.)

816. 1794. Account of the Apothecary General.

Of interest when taken in connection with a similar account in *Treas.* 1: **527.** The drugs were ordered by the Secretary at War, who issued instructions from time to time to the apothecary general to forward such medicines to certain quarters. In this case the medicines were for the use of the forces and hospitals at Chelsea and Chatham, armies on the Continent and in the West Indies, and encampments in Quebec, Halifax, Jersey, etc. *Cf. Treas.* 64: **188,** 225.

REGISTERS.

The registers of military establishments, formerly among the Treasury papers, have been transferred to the War Office series.

ESTABLISHMENT LISTS.

1. 1766. Customs Establishment.

Treas. 42.
—

"A list of the officers of his Majesty's customs appointed by patent or constitution." For England only. From this list, which is dated Aug. 13, 1766, we learn that Henry Hulton was appointed plantation clerk under the commissioners, Oct. 19, 1763, at a salary of £500.

2. 1717. Customs Establishment.

A "list of all the officers employed in the Customs, with the salaries and allowances they respectively receive, distinguishing therein such as are paid out of incidents from those that are placed upon the establishment or paid by dormant warrant, as they stood at Michaelmas, 1717". Oct. 8, 1717.

Including London and all the outports, followed by a list of plantation officials. The latter is very complete, distinguishing place, name (with remarks), and salaries. The following remarks are worthy of note (f. 102 b).

"There are many persons employed by the Patent officers in London and the Outports as their deputies or clerks, who are paid by their Principals."

"The Officers at Barbadoes and the Leeward Islands are paid there out of the produce of the duty of 4½ p. cent."

"The Officers on the Continent of America and the Bahama Islands are paid in London by the Receiver General out of Old Customs, except the Incidents Allowances for Boats and Boatmen in New York and New England which are paid there."

"The Officers at Jamaica are paid there out of the Enumerated duty."

3. 1720. Customs Establishment.

"A list of such officers whose salaries or additional salaries have been paid by order of the commissioners for the last year." These entries furnish additional information regarding salary payments, for example:

South America.

South Carolina	Wm Rhett, Survr and Compr of Carolina and Bahama to maintain a yatch	150
	Richard Wigg Surveyor and Searcher	30
Pensilvania	Newcastle Sam. Lowman to maintain a boat and 2 Boatmn additional	40
	Lewis Henry Brook a boat and 2 boatmn additional	40
		260

Jamaica
- Mr Beckford Surveyor and Compr £150
- Jamaica money out of the duties there.
- Geo Dawes Collector
- Alexr Forbes Searchr
- Giles Diston Landwaiter

⅓ of the whole collection distributed in proportion among these officers for defraying charges.

North America.

West Jersey	Bridlington Jere: Bass Collr and preventive officer	30
New York	Fra. Harrison Surveyor and searcher besides £50 for a boat and 2 Boatmen	60
	Wm Chambers Landwaiter	50

The allowance for Mr. Harrison for a boat is to be paid out of the King's ⅓ fines and forfeitures, but if that falls short no allowance to be made.

New England	John Jekyle for a boat and 2 boatmen addl	50
	Archibald Cummings Survr and Searchr in lieu of the established salary of £180 which he had at Newfoundland	100
Piscataway	Robert Armstrong for a boat and 2 boatmen 50£ addl to be paid out of the King's ⅓ ds.	
Salem and Marblehead	Charles Blechynden, collector and Surveyor for a boat and two boatmen addl	40
Rhode Island	Nathaniel Key for a boat and 2 boatmen	50
	To be paid the same as Mr. Armstrong above named.	
Connecticut New London	John Shackmaple, collector and preventive officer besides 50£ for a boat and 2 boatmen.	80
	The allowance to Mr Shackmaple to be paid the same as Mr. Keys above named.	

Many of these statements, particularly about the use made of the king's thirds, are not to be found in the Declared Accounts rolls.

In this series vols. **4 A, 4 B, 6, 7**, relate to London or the outports only.

VICTUALLING LISTS.

21. 1765–1770. Halifax Victualling Lists.

Treas. 46.

This register contains lists of officers, soldiers, gunners, artificers, etc., at Halifax. Many similar lists can be found in *Treas.* 1.

(Formerly *Registers, Victualling Lists,* 19.)

MISCELLANEOUS.

9-11. 1773-1776. Emigration Lists.

Treas. 47.

These lists contain accounts of persons who booked passage on board ships or vessels going out of Great Britain in the years named, and give age, quality, occupation, employment, and former residence, to what port or place they proposed to go, by what ship or vessel they were to sail, with what master, and on what account or for what purpose they left the country.

The lists were drawn up in response to a letter from the Treasury, Dec. 8, 1773, and as here preserved are imperfect, lacking entries for Apr. 13-18, 27–May 9, 1774, and Nov. 7-12, 1775. They have been printed in part in the *New England Genealogical and Historical Register* (1911), but without adequate appreciation of their importance or significance. The largest group of names includes redemptioners and indented servants going to Virginia, Maryland, Philadelphia, New York, and (a few) North Carolina, the total number of which runs into the thousands. The servants were indented for four, five, and six years, and in certain cases the redemptioners rendered themselves liable to a seven years' service. The second largest group includes emigrants sailing from Yorkshire and other north of England ports going to Nova Scotia, Virginia, and New York. The reasons assigned for the migration are " rents being raised by their landlords ", " provisions and every necessary of life being so high ", " the small farms being absorbed into large ones ", and " they cannot support their families "; or " to settle ", " to work as clerk ", to obtain " better employment ", " to travel ", " to see friends ", etc. In these lists the port of departure for America was generally London, Bristol, or Hull. In Sept., 1775, a considerable body of Germans went to Maryland. After that date the emigration to America practically ceased; a few emigrants went to Nantucket, and in Mar., 1776, three went to Boston " to reside ". Bundle 11 covers emigration to the West Indies and the Continent only, except for the three persons going to Boston.

(Formerly *Registers, Emigration*, 1-3.)

12. *Id*.

Lists of emigrants, chiefly servants, from the ports of Greenock, Kirkaldy, Wigtown, Kirkwall, Stornaway, Stranraer, Lerwick, and Glasgow in Scotland bound for Nova Scotia, New York, Pennsylvania, North and South Carolina, Georgia, Antigua, and elsewhere. Many details are given, including such specific reasons as " high rents and oppression ", the report from Lerwick especially being an elaborate one.

(Formerly *Miscellanea, Refugees, Carolina*, 6 (1).)

Additional information can be obtained from a series of valuable letters in *Treas.* 1 : **500**, 231-235. Other material is not wanting to throw light upon this remarkable movement, which owed its origin to the rack-renting policy of the Scottish Highland proprietors, from Ayrshire to the Shetland Islands. Thousands of Highlanders were driven to America by fear of eviction due to " the avarice and folly of their thoughtless masters ". A traveller who went to America in 1774 on the same vessel with a number of them, wrote: " It is needless to make any comment on the conduct of our Highland and Island proprietors. It is self evident what consequences must be produced in time from such numbers of subjects being driven from the country. Should levies be again necessary, the recruiting drum may long be at a loss to procure such soldiers as are now aboard this vessel." The particular company to which reference is here made had been driven out of the Fair Isle, and failing to find a vessel at Greenock, had finally embarked at Leith. Another body of emigrants is noted in *Treas.* 1 : **338**. In 1776 was raised the Royal Highland Regiment from among the emigrants thus driven to America. See *W. O.* 28 : **4**, and *Acts of the Privy Council, Colonial*, V. 340–341.

MISCELLANEA.

LOYALISTS.

1-5. 1780-1782. North and South Carolina Refugees.

> Treas. 50.
> —

These volumes contain an account of disbursements for the militia and for Loyalist refugees at Charleston. 1780-1782.

1. The militia receipt book of Capt. John Cunningham, paymaster-general of militia at Charleston, 1781, containing the receipt-signature of each militia man, the amount paid to him, and the period for which it was paid.

Books of payments to several militia regiments, containing the names of the officers and men, rates, amounts, and places where each regiment served. June 14–Dec. 13, 1780.

Alphabetical index nominum to the South Carolina militia. Charleston, 1781.

Id., North Carolina militia.

Book of receipts of cash paid by Col. Robert Gray, paymaster-general of North Carolina militia, to the men of Col. Faithful Graham's regiment.

Similar documents. 1782.

Many of the papers in this bundle are damaged and difficult to read. They are valuable for the names in the lists, particularly those of Col. Graham's regiment. The book of receipts for cash paid on the South Carolina abstracts furnishes a list of royal regiments with the names of the men and in many cases interesting comments added to the names given in the lists.

2. Continuation of the second item in bundle **1.**

Indices nominum of distressed refugees who received charitable donations. 1781. No. 11 is of importance as giving names, dates, etc., in full.

Cash book of money received from the commandant of indigent refugees, with contingent expenses (interesting items). Sept. 18, 1781–Jan., 1782.

3. Small packets containing abstracts of pay of North and South Carolina militia, 1782 ; the third packet more damaged than the others.

4. Reports touching the cases of distressed refugees, with details, the names of those recommending the case, and the amounts allowed (important). 1781.

Collection of exhibits justifying the recommendation.

Militia and refugee receipts, South Carolina. 1781-1782.

5. Continuation of **4**, abstracts of pay and receipts signed by refugees receiving allowances ; also contingent expenses of the hospital for refugees in Charleston, 1781, and other similar papers.

(Formerly *Miscellanea, Refugees, Carolina*, 1-5.)

6-28, 31-48. 1782-1831. Loyalists Quarterly Pension Lists.

These valuable schedules are indispensable to the student of Loyalist claims, and furnish information supplemental to that given in the Audit Office series of bundles and volumes of American Loyalist claims.

At the beginning of the war, from a date as early as 1776, the Treasury inaugurated the policy of making payments to Loyalist refugees, who had incurred losses in America. But the methods were faulty and the results unsatisfactory, consequently in 1778 the Treasury notified Gen. Carleton that it would pay no more money on account of Loyalist losses until a further investigation had been made of the matter. Thenceforth Loyalist claims were carefully investigated, and such payments as were made took the form of temporary allowances. The pension lists contained in this series begin with 1782 and extend to 1831, and the earliest allowances entered are temporary, no pensions becoming permanent until after 1783.

These volumes, which are ledgers of actual allowances and payments, are of particular value because the entries show how long the claimants drew their pensions and whether or not the pensions lapsed at death or were continued to widows and children. They also contain other facts of historical and genealogical interest. The tables give the number of the receipt, arrears or advances, names, professions, residences, allowances per annum, entries of payments with dates, and generally the signature of the Loyalist, which served as a receipt for the allowance received. A fine series of Loyalist signatures is contained here, the same names appearing year after year, some dropping out altogether, others showing signs of feebleness and advancing years, and still others continuing in the names of children or grandchildren. When the allowance was not received by the Loyalist claimant in person, the name of the attorney is entered. Incidentally the entries give items of additional information, either as part of the original record or added later in pencil.

A few selected names are here given to show the character of the evidence. The names are entered alphabetically.

6. 1782.

Cooper, Myles, Dr of Divinity, N. Y.	200
Dulaney Lloyd, Gentn of Fortune, Md.	200
Dulaney, Eliz., widow of Lloyd Dulaney, late of Md. (added later).	200
Kempe, John Tabor, Attorney General, N. Y.	200
Little, Stephen, Surgeon and Apothecy, New Hants.	80 (60)
Martin, Jos. Govr of No. Carolina.	500
Moore, Thos, Gauger.	20
Munro, Revd Harry, of Albany, Clergyman.	100
Morison, John, Barrister, West Florida.	nil
Oliver, Peter, Chief Justice, Mass.	400 (300)
Pelham, Henry, Limner, Boston.	50 (30)
Reeve, Richard, Secy of Customs.	50 (100)
Shingle, Saml, Stucco Worker, Annapolis, Md.	40
Snowden, Myles, Brewer, Phila.	60 (40)
Sandford, Philo, Gentn and Planter, Conn.	80
Vanschaack, Peter, Lawyer, N. Y.	+100 (80)

The figures in parentheses are in pencil at the side of the original amounts. Against a number of names " nil " is written, and many names are crossed through. In each list are names added in another hand. At the end is " Payments to American Customs Officers ", evidently the members of the board at Boston, which gives the complete establishment there. On succeeding pages are the names of customs officials from other colonies.

7. 1783.

Faneuil, Benj., Merchant and Consignee, Mass.	150
Griffin, Owen, Publican, No. Carolina.	50
Galloway, Jos., Speaker of Assembly, Penn.	500
Harkey, G. H., Organist, So. Carolina.	
Love, Revd David, Rector, St. Anne's, Annapolis, Md.	
McCulloh, H. E., Gentn, No. Carolina.	300
Neilson, Arch., Deputy and Naval Officer, No. Carolina.	60
Peters, Saml, Clergyman, Conn.	200
Ryan, William, Pavior, New York.	
Ryan, Thomas, Carman, "	
Rose, Peter, Shoemaker, Mass.	
Rogers, James, Farmer, Ga.	
Wentworth, Elizabeth, Mother of the Govr, N. H.	100

8. 1784.

Byles, Revd Mather, to carry him to Nova Scotia.	30
Colden, Cadwallader.	36
Hewatt, Revd Alexander.	60
Moffatt, Dr. Thomas.	200
Robinson, Beverley.	200

11. 1789 and 1790.

Bull, Gov. William.	500
" " "	300

" By minute 31 Dec. 88 £300 in addition to his former allowance of £500 pr ann frõ 5 July 88 and £400 pr ann to Mrs Bull in case she survives him, until Gov. Bull shall either recover possn of his estate or the value thereof from Stepn Bull."

Rutherford, Jno.   50

" Until his brother Wm receives the compensation, (signed) Alex Anderson and Shaw, attys."

In **12** the note reads, " Until he and his brother Wm receive their compensation ", " To cease from 5 Jan. 1791 ".

20. 1806, 1807.

Opens with an account of allowances as they stood Jan. 5, 1806. Gov. William Franklin's name appears, also four members of the Hutchinson family, Archibald Neilson, Henry Pelham, Rev. John Vardill, Benning Wentworth, and many whose surnames indicate that they are the children of deceased Loyalists.

31. 1788-1790.

Bainbridge, Dr. Absolom, Surgeon of the New Jersy Volunrs.

Blowers, Sampson, Atty Genl of Nova Scotia.

Cholmondeley, Honble and Revd Rob. Auditor Genl of the Plantations and Prõthy of the Dutchy Ct of Lancasr granted in 1732 or 33—[Held recto] ries in the county of Hertford to which he was preseñ in [175]5   £400

DeLancey, Inspector of Loyalists.

Sewall, Jonathan, Pension for loss of office of judge of court of vice-admiralty at Halifax.

Upham, Joshua, Major of the King's Amern Dragns.

29. A Book of Payments made by Samuel Remnant to American Loyalists, by order of the Treasurer. 1783.

(Formerly *Miscellanea, Refugees, Various*, 5 (2).)

30. 1789-1795. An Account of the Principal and Interest of the Order made out at the Exchequer, pursuant to the Act, 28 Geo. III., for the Relief of American Sufferers, also for the Relief of Sufferers by the Cession of East Florida to the King of Spain.

(Formerly *Miscellaneous, Various*, 34 (1).)

49. 1815-1821, 1832-1835. Entries of Money paid as Allowances or Pensions to Loyalists.

(Formerly *Miscellanea, Refugees, Various*, 5 (3).)

50-56. 1833-1834, 1835-1836. Accounts of Thomas Crafer, Paymaster of Pensions and Allowances to American Loyalists, and Others.

A series of twenty-five paper books. **53** is a printed statement of the cases of uncompensated Loyalists, dated 1820.

(Formerly *Miscellanea, Refugees, Various*, 5 (1) and (4).)

WARRANTS EARLY.

Treas. 51.
—

1-14. 1660-1667. Entry Books of Treasurer Southampton.

These volumes contain entries of all kinds, particularly relating to lands, money, customs, excise, patents, etc.

(Formerly *Miscellanea, Warrants Early*, 1-14.)

15-29. 1667-1686. Early Warrants.

Miscellaneous warrants touching money, hearth money, lesser revenues, excise, etc. These warrants have very little to do with the colonies, though **15** and **28** contain a few entries.

(Formerly *Miscellanea, Warrants Early*, 17-22, 23, 24, 26-29, 39, 40.)

30-32. Abstracts and General Calendars.

33-40. 1667-1692. Early Warrants.

A series of eight books containing entries of early warrants, none of which relate to the colonies. **34** contains an appeal to the farmers of the customs and others to loan money to the king (pp. 29-31).

(Formerly *Miscellanea, Warrants Early*, 34-38, 41, 42, 44.)

WARRANTS: KING'S.

Treas. 52.
—

1-68. 1667-1783. King's Warrants.

A series of books containing entries of letters patent, privy seals, royal sign manuals, relating to commissions or salaries or pensions, or payments of money to ambassadors, colonial governors, etc.

1. Entry book of privy seals and king's warrants, among which is a warrant for the pay of the officers of Sir Tobias Bridges's regiment in Barbadoes, one of whom was Sir Edmund Andros. There are also a number of warrants issued to Sir George Carteret relating solely to English affairs, and a warrant for a privy seal constituting the council of trade, Dec. 18, 1668.

(Formerly *Miscellanea, Warrants Early*, 15. **2** and **9** were formerly *id.*, 15 A, 16. Former *King's Warrants* 29-36 are now *King's Warrants* **36-43**.)

5. Warrant to the governor of Barbadoes to appoint a receiver of the king's revenue there (p. 67).

To Blathwayt and the Lords of Trade (p. 91).

Instructions to the governor of Barbadoes about sending revenue returns (p. 208).

Warrant for payment of £86 to Lord Culpeper for the expense of the sloop *Katherine* (p. 159).

Letters to Lord Howard of Effingham and to the governor of Maryland about Patrick Mein, who had been appointed surveyor general for inspecting the accounts of the collectors and other officers in Virginia and Maryland, ordering them and all their officers to aid and assist him in the collecting of the plantation duty (p. 214). Nov. 18, 1685.

Warrant for the payment of £471 " to Edward Randolph (who hath ever since the year 1675 been employed in the service of our late dear Brother here and in New England in reducing that Province to the obedience of our Laws and Governors), in full satisfaction as well of his charges and disbursements in eight several voyages made by him to and from thence and in prosecuting the Quo Warranto brought against the charter granted to Massachusetts Bay, as of his great losses he sustained in his goods by storm at sea, which hath been examined by William Blathwayt, Esq. and sworn to by him the said Edward Randolph " (p. 69). Mar. 31, 1685.

Letter regarding the renewal of the office of collector, surveyor, and searcher of customs in New England erected in 1681, and Randolph's appointment to the post. Sept. 20, 1685.

Warrant for the appointment of Randolph as surveyor of woods in New England (p. 199). Oct. 13, 1685.

Letter regarding the seizure of Virginia tobacco by the Dutch and the request of the owner that he be allowed to ship more " free of the impost of the country " (p. 258).

Appointment of William Tyack, escheator of Leeward Islands (p. 407). *Cf. Cal. Col.,* 1685-1688, § 665.

6. Warrant for the payment to Andros of £1200 for his expenses to New England (p. 55). July 10, 1686.

Letters to the governors of Bermuda and New York, instructing them to assist Blathwayt and his deputies (pp. 34, 189).

Id. to the governor of the Leeward Islands regarding the four-and-a-half per cent. (pp. 115, 197).

Warrant for salary of governor of Bermuda (p. 209).

Letter to Andros regarding the *Swallow.*

The later volumes contain similar warrants addressed to the clerk of the signet bidding him prepare bills for the king's signature to pass the privy seal; and also warrants with the king's sign manual directed to the paymaster of the forces, the Commissioners of the Treasury, and others, authorizing the payment of money for civil establishments, medicines, troops, sick and wounded, hospitals, camp necessaries, salaries, special appropriations (as of £200,000 for the northern colonies, Virginia, Pennsylvania, and the Lower Counties, and £50,000 for Virginia, North and South Carolina) for services rendered, rewards (as to Col. John Hale, £500, for bringing the news of the fall of Quebec, and of £400 to Maj. Halkett for the news of the taking of

Fort Duquesne), forage money, victualling expenses, presents to the Indians, and governors' salaries. There are also a few warrants for the preparation of commissions for colonial governors. The king's warrants, bearing the king's sign manual, are signed by the secretary or the secretaries of State, " by his Majesty's command ". *Cf.* the preceding volume of this *Guide,* pp. 227-236.

WARRANTS RELATING TO MONEY.

1-56. 1676-1783. Money Books or Warrants relating to Money.

Treas. 53.

These volumes, which are well indexed, contain entries of warrants from the Treasury Board to the auditor of the receipt of the Exchequer, authorizing that official " to draw an order or to make forth and pass debentures for paying so much to such a person for such a purpose ".[1] The following is an example of such a warrant:

" After our hearty commendation By virtue of his Majesty's General Letters Patent Dormant bearing date 14 August, 1714, these are to pray and require your Lordship to draw an order for paying unto Jonathan Forward of London, merchant, or to his assigns the sum of 264 li without acct the same being paid in pursuance of certain articles of agreement bearing date the 9 day of May last, 1723,[2] and made or mentioned to be made between us on his Majesty's Behalf of the one part and the said Jonathan Forward of the other part, for the allowance of 4 li [it was 5 li later, **48, 56**] per head for and upon 66 Malefactors who were lately lying in Newgate in the city of London under sentence of transportation, which said Malefactors were received by order of the said Jonathan Forward on board the ship *Anne,* Capt. Thomas Wraugham, Comr, to be transported to his Majesty's Plantations in America, as appears by the annexed certificate expressing the names of the said Malefactors. In consideration of which allowance the said Jona. Forward agreed at his own cost and charges to transport the said Malefactors to some of his Majesty's Plantations in America without any charge to his Majesty for their transportation, carrying on board or otherwise, and hath given security pursuant to the said articles accordingly. And let the said order be satisfied out of any money in the Receipt of the Exchequer applicable to the use of his Majesty's Civil Government. For which this shall be your Lordship's warrant. Whitehall, Treasury Chambers, March 7, 1723/4 " (**31**, 76-77).

Then follows a copy of the certificate with the names of the 66 convicts, of which 28 are women, and the statement that they were to be transported to Carolina or Virginia.[3]

The warrants cover a wide range of official grants to those serving in England as well as America and include ministers whose passage to the colonies was paid out of the Exchequer. For example:

" Thos Barclay, Chapln 20 li — After, etc, By vertue of her Maj. Genl Lres Pat Dormt bearing date 19 March, 1707. These are to pray and require yor Lop to draw an Order for paying unto Thos Barclay clerke or his asses the sum of 20 li for and towards defraying the charge of his passage to New Yorke whither he is going chapln

---

[1] Dr. Shaw, preface to *Cal. Treas. Pap.,* pp. xxvii-xxxiii.
[2] See *Treas.* 54: **32**, 228-230.
[3] Forward had a monopoly of this business for many years. Certificates granted to him and others will be found in *Treas.* I.

and let the same be satisfied etca, for which this shall be yor warrt. White-hall, Treasury Chambers, 4 June, 1707. Godolphin. To Audr Rect " (**18, 476**).

WARRANTS NOT RELATING TO MONEY.

1-44. 1667-1786. Warrants not Relating to Money.

Treas. 54.

These volumes contain the full text of warrants, reports, accounts, etc., not having to do with the payment of money. The warrants or orders generally authorize or empower some one to do something or require others not to do something else, and are usually based upon some memorial, petition, statement, or account, which, often entered at great length, constitute a most important source of information. The warrants concern the renewal or exercise of offices, accepting security, making agreements and contracts (victualling, transporting, provisioning, etc.), demanding information from law officers, boards, colonial officials, and the like. The volumes also contain sundry answers or reports from legal advisors and others that are of importance as giving the reason for the warrant which follows, and they furnish lists of fees for passing accounts through the Exchequer, an expensive business.

More specifically some of the matters dealt with are as follows:

1. Regarding the working of the navigation acts.
    Case of ship going from Barbadoes to Tangier.
    Reference to petition of Lord Ashley, and to the king's debt to him as acknowledged in privy seal of Nov. 25, 1661.
    Letter to the Council for Trade and Plantations regarding claims to the Caribbee Islands.
    Regarding Thomas Povey and the affairs of Tangier.
    Appointment of Andros as inspector. Aug. 30, 1669.
    Regarding the king's affairs in Barbadoes. Dec. 20, 1670.
2. Ships coming to America not to unlade in Ireland. Mar., 1671.
    Letter to Baltimore, stating that strict care be taken that all ships trading to the English plantations for tobacco be obliged to return to England, and saying that the king hath written to that purpose and hath bidden the Treasury instruct him to order his deputy in Maryland to examine all commanders and masters of English ships arriving there. Nov. 17, 1671.
    Appointment of Robert Quary as comptroller of customs at Chichester.
    Regarding the prohibition of tobacco planting in England.
    Letters sent to justices of the peace in Worcester, Gloucester, Wilts, Hereford, and also to the governors of Barbadoes, Virginia, and Jamaica stating that the board learns that certain ships (names given), upon pretense of going on a coasting trade to some of the king's dominions in Europe, intend to sail to some of the plantations without giving bond, and ordering that such be seized if they cannot produce a certificate.
    Letter to one of the surveyors of customs bidding him see that the order to the justices of the peace is carried out.
    Regarding the *Augustine* from Virginia taking away tobacco, notwithstanding the efforts of tidesmen to prevent it.
    Payments in sugar from Lord Willoughby and Barbadoes.

31. Report from the Treasury on the proposals of the proprietaries of the Carolinas.

Directions to David Dunbar to execute the office of surveyor general in America.

Security of Gov. Ogle of Maryland.

Vice-admiralty courts in the colonies.

Appointment of Robert Byng as receiver general of the rights and perquisites of the Admiralty.

Requirement that governors settle accounts with Byng or his deputy and pay over what belongs to the king.

Directions to Gov. Shute to pay the same.

Query directed to the governor and council of Virginia regarding the payment of £600 to complete the £1600 asked by Gov. Spotswood for his journey to treat with the Indians at Albany.

Warrant authorizing Auditor General Walpole to have a deputy in the Carolinas for receiving quit-rents, with the same salary as the deputy receives in Virginia and New York, payment to begin July 25, 1729.

38-39. Warrants for transportation of coin to America.

Regarding the distribution of the parliamentary grant to New York, New England, and New Jersey.

Instructing the king's receiver in Guadeloupe.

Regarding West India and New York packet boats.

Accepting security from John Penn to enforce the navigation acts.

Approving the nomination of the deputy auditor of Jamaica by the auditor of that island.

Appointing John Morrison packer and messenger in American stamp warehouse.

Recommending extension of the four-and-a-half per cent. duty to Grenada. Jan. 10, 1764.

Deputing several persons to be distributors of stamps in America. Apr. 3, 1765. *Id.* May 1, June 13, 15.

Recommending the removal and appointment of courts of vice-admiralty, judges, etc. July 4, 1765.

Among the papers entered are also many accounts supplemental to or duplicating those in the Audit Office declarations, such as:

Account of John Cathcart, purveyor to the hospital in North America (**31**, 375; *A. O. Decl. Acc., Hospitals,* **1505**, 211).

Account of Jermyn Wright, merchant trading to South Carolina, and Harman Verelst, regarding goods purchased in 1748 as presents to Indians (**31**, 395 ff., **32**, 218 ff.; not in *Declared Accounts*).

Account of Gov. Knowles of Cape Breton and Louisburg, 1746-1747 (**31**, 399-406; *cf. A. O., Decl. Acc.,* **1255**, 100).

Id. of Lieut.-Col. John Bradstreet (*A. O., Decl. Acc.,* **335**, 1339).

Id. of French prizes carried into Boston and Virginia.

Id. of A. Heron, commanding officer in Georgia. 1747-1749.

Id. of Gen. Hopson, governor of Nova Scotia. 1752-1753.

These volumes are worthy of a careful examination, for though the number of documents entered is not great, their importance is considerable. The entries increase greatly in number after 1761. In the rearrangement of the series vols. **1** and **2** were brought from former *Early Warrants* 33 and 43, and vols. **31-34** were formerly numbered 24-27. Former vols. 31 and 32 are now **38** and **39**. **3-7** are in the possession of the Duke of Leeds.

CROWN LEASE BOOK.

1-32. 1727-1819. Warrants for Crown Leases.

Treas. 55.

Relating entirely to lands and leases in Whitehall, the royal palaces, and English counties, with two exceptions. In the first four volumes are numerous entries (I. 185, 300, etc.) touching the sale of lands in the island of St. Christopher at Cabeccaterre, Basseterre, etc., and in **2**, pp. 210-211, Sir Joseph Eyles, Jonathan Perrie, John Drummond, and Thomas Watts petition for " the equivalent land " in New York, because the same was formerly taken from Connecticut, " in lieu of a like quantity yielded to that colony by the province of New York, upon the settling of their respective boundaries." The territory was bounded on the north by the south line of Massachusetts, at about twenty miles from the Hudson River, running parallel with that river.

WARRANTS VARIOUS.

Treas. 56.

36. 1765-1832. Four and a Half Per Cent.

ORDER BOOKS.

1-25. 1667-1783. Auditor's Order Book.

Treas. 60.

" On receipt of the Treasury authorization to draw an order for a particular payment, the auditor of the receipt drew such an order in the prescribed form and remitted it to the Treasury for the signature of the Lord Treasurer or the Lords Commissioners." [1]

These volumes contain copies of such auditor's orders for the payment of money, many of which are for the salaries, etc., of colonial governors, and do not appear either in the Money Books or the King's Warrant Books. An important feature is the occasional indication of the fund against which the payment was charged. For example, the auditor general's salary and the salaries of some of the governors were paid out of the four-and-a-half per cent. Among the payments are the £20 allowances to clergymen, schoolmasters, etc., going to the colonies. The latest date of an order issued for the allowance to a clergyman going to one of the thirteen colonies is June 21, 1776 (North Carolina); the date of the last of such orders is 1779 (East Florida). These volumes are valuable for a study of the disposition of the royal revenues from the colonies and for a general understanding of the financial aspects of British control in America. A typical order is as follows:

" Charles Garth Esq, Agent for Georgia, £4,031 8sh, 8d, for the civil establishment.

Order, etc, this 17 day of March, 1764, by virtue of an act passed in the last session of parliament for raising a certain sum of money by loans or Exchequer Bills and for applying certain monies remaining in the Exchequer for the service of the year 1764 and for applications of certain savings of public monies and of monies arisen by sale of military stores and for further appropriating the supplies granted in that session of parliament and other purposes therein men-

[1] Shaw, preface to the *Cal. Treas. Pap.*, pp. xxxii-xxxviii. *Cf. Exchequer, Accounts of Receipts and Issues, Order Book (Pells)*.

16

tioned and in pursuance of a warrant under his Majesty's royal sign manual dated 15 May, 1760, that you deliver and pay of such his Majesty's treasure as remains in your charge unto Charles Garth, Esq, agent (on behalf of the publick) for the affairs of the Colony of Georgia in America or to his assigns the sum of 4031..8..8. by way of imprest and upon account for defraying the charge of the civil establishment of the said colony of Georgia and other incidental expenses attending the same, from 24 June, 1763, to 24 June, 1764, according to such warrant or warrants as he hath received or shall receive from his Majesty in that behalf and these."

Out of the aids or supplies granted for the service of the year 1764.

PUBLIC DISPOSITION BOOKS.

1-43. 1679-1785. Public Disposition Books.

Treas. 61.

These volumes show, by " letters of direction ", " letters of disposition ", or otherwise, the particular fund from which a payment was to be made or upon which it was to be charged.[1]

The " letter " corresponding to the " order " cited above is as follows:

" To the Auditor of the Receipt from C. Jenkinson, secretary to the Treasury Board.

£4031..8s..8d. North J. Turner. T. O. Hunter.

My Lord. The Lords Commissioners of his Majesty's Treasury desire your Lordship will please to issue unto the persons undermentioned the sums set against their names respectively. Pursuant to the proper warrants and orders signed in that behalf.

To Charles Garth, Esq., agent for Georgia, out of Exchequer Bills to be placed as cash and charged on the Land Tax for the year 1764

£2031..8..8.

To Charles Garth, Esq, by Exchequer Bills made forth pursuant to an act of the last session of parliament for raising a certain sum of money by Loans or Exchequer Bills for the service of the year 1764 and charged on the supplies that shall be granted

£2000..0..0.

MAPS AND PLANS.

11. Bundle of Maps and Plans.

Treas. 62.

Only three relate to the colonies.
No. 1 (formerly no. 91). British and French Dominions in North America (Mitchell). Feb. 13, 1755.

No. 125 (formerly no. 94). West Indies (Joseph Smith Speer). Aug. 31, 1771.[2] See *Treas.* 1 : **498**.

No. 98 (formerly no. 96). River St. Lawrence. Feb. 16, 1775.

---

[1] Shaw, preface to *Cal. Treas. Pap.*, pp. xxxviii-xxxix; see also the preface to the volume for 1731-1734, where the reason is given for discontinuing the calendaring of these volumes.

[2] Captain Joseph Smith Speer, *West India Pilot, containing the Latitudes of the Head Lands, Islands, Keys, Harbours in all parts of the West Indies,* with 26 folding maps and plans, including plan of Jekil Sound, Province of Georgia; also plans of the entrance into Cape Fear Harbour, North Carolina (large folio).

MISCELLANEA VARIOUS.
APPOINTMENTS.

3-4. 1705-1723. Treasury Appointments.

> **Treas. 64.**
> —

Entry books of appointments by the Treasury Board, among which is the record of a few appointments made with plantation merchants, who were summoned before the board. After 1723 such appointments were entered in the Minute Book.

ARMY.

8-11. 1690-1705. Establishments.

8. 1690. Irish Establishment.

9. 1691. Computation of muster-rolls for one year, Jan. 1, 1691–last of Dec., 1691. Entries include " Duke of Bolton's Regiment in the West Indies " (pages blank), " Two Companies of Foot at New Yorke ", " A company at the Leeward Islands ", and under " Guarrisons ", " Virginia—executors of Lord Culpeper, £600 ".

10. Apr. 10, 1704. Sign manual, defining regulations for the three regiments in the West Indies—two in Jamaica and one in Leeward Islands—each to be of 12 companies of 2 sergeants, 3 corporals, 2 drummers, and 59 private soldiers, servants included. Then follow " Rules, Methods, and Instructions ", the establishment, and form of a muster-roll.

11. *Id.,* Apr. 30, 1705. Longer and fuller regulations, especially as regards the off-reckonings for non-commissioned officers and soldiers, the deductions being stated: sergeant out of one shilling, 6*d.*; corporal out of nine pence, 3*d.*; drummer out of eight pence, 4*d.*; private soldier out of six pence, 2*d.*, " which will answer for the complete clothing, the poundage, one day's pay, and agency for the pay of the said non-commissioned officers and soldiers ".

20-22. 1759-1763. Sir Jeffrey Amherst's Accounts including Colonial Muster-Rolls.

The papers in these bundles, nearly all of which are in the form of vouchers, have been weeded out and only specimens retained.

20. Capt. Loring's accounts for the transports taken up at Boston on the expedition to Canada, 1759.

Id., accounts and disbursements, containing a choice collection of the signatures of carpenters, sawyers, blacksmiths, sailors, seamen, etc., as well as of captains and lieutenants serving chiefly on Lake Ontario, Lake George, and Lake Champlain. 1760-1762.

Muster-rolls of two troops of rangers in Georgia. 1761-1763. Four bundles.

Thomas Hancock's disbursements for supplies sent to Louisburg, to St. John for the expedition up the St. Lawrence in 1759, and to Halifax for the fortification works there. 1759-1762. Four bundles.

21. David Price's disbursements for transports and other expenses. 1763. Two bundles.

Joseph Scott's disbursements, in pursuance of Col. Forbes's warrants for the works at Halifax, to Dec. 31, 1761, containing much interesting information about construction work. Maj.-Gen. Bastide was chief engineer and Hugh Debbieg engineer in charge. *Id.* 1762.

George Croghan's accounts for Indian services. Jan.-Nov., 1761. Croghan was deputy agent of Indian affairs in the southern department.

Vouchers in support of Maj. Robert Rogers's account against the crown. 1761.

22. Muster-rolls of the Rhode Island regiment. 1758.

Billeting rolls of the Massachusetts Bay troops in 1759 and 1760. Two bundles.

Accounts and vouchers.

1. Massachusetts. Returns of the state and numbers of the different companies and parties of Brigadier Ruggles's regiment.

General list of the different companies of the two battalions of Brigadier Ruggles's regiment of Massachusetts forces, mustered, victualled, and paid at Fort No. 4 (a frontier fort on the east bank of the Connecticut River, thirty miles north of Fort Dummer, or Brattleborough). Nov. 24, 1759.

Id., Col. Willard's regiment. Dec., 1759.

2. Connecticut. General list of the different companies of Col. Worcester's regiment as mustered, victualled, and paid, at Fort No. 4. Nov. 20, 1759.

Id., Col. Fitch's company at No. 4, Dec. 2, 1759, with a return of men not mustered in Col. Fitch's company.

Id., Maj.-Gen. Lyman's company at No. 4, Dec. 3, 1759.

3. Rhode Island. General list of the different companies of Col. Babcock's regiment.

List of a party of twenty-seven men belonging to different companies of Col. Babcock's regiment, who being unable to keep up on the march from Crown Point to Fort No. 4 were left behind and not included in the general list.

General list of a detachment from different provincial regiments sent to Crown Point, under the command of Maj. John Hawke of Brig.-Gen. Ruggles's Massachusetts Regiment, to cut a road from thence to No. 4 and dismissed there by order of Maj.-Gen. Amherst.

General list of a party of sick men from the different provincial regiments at Crown Point sent by way of No. 4 under the command of Lieut.-Col. James Smedley of Col. Worcester's Connecticut regiment.

General account of disbursements. Nov.-Dec., 1759.

Billeting rolls of Col. Thwing's regiment of Massachusetts troops embarked at Boston for Halifax. 1762.

Billeting rolls of Col. Hoare's regiment of Massachusetts troops, similarly embarked. 1762.

Muster-rolls, being the vouchers for the provision money paid to the provincials of Massachusetts Bay, Connecticut, and New Hampshire, on their return home by way of Fort No. 4 in Nov., 1761.

Id., on their return home by way of Fort No. 4 in Nov., 1762.
List of warrants granted by Sir Jeffrey Amherst for public services
in North America. 1759-1763.
(Formerly *Miscellaneous, Various,* 3-5.)

23. 1783.   List of Provincial Regiments.

This paper book contains lists of provincial officers that served in North
America, Canada, and the West Indies during the war. It includes also
rosters of Canadian Indians, Six Nation Indians, and Indians of the Southern
District. See *Decl. Acc., A. O.,* **325,** 1287, 1288, *W. O.* 65 : **165.** The presence of this volume among the Treasury Papers is probably explained by the
fact that in Mar., 1788, the Treasury asked the Secretary at War for " as
accurate an account as possible of the Provincial Establishments during the
late war in North America " and the secretary in reply transmitted this book
and other papers the following June. *Treas.* 1, year 1788.
(Formerly *Miscellaneous, Various,* 179 (2).)

24. 1779-1782.   Register of Letters from the Commissaries of
    Prisoners, containing papers relating to the exchange of
    prisoners according to the conditions settled by the com-
    missioners at Amboy.

The deputy commissary was David Sproat, appointed in place of Peter
Dunant. Sproat was stationed at Staten Island to receive the prisoners of
war coming in from captivity. The returns contain lists of the prisoners
mustered at Elizabeth, South Amboy, and Staten Island from May 9, 10, and
11, to June 3, 4, and 5, 1783—British regulars, German auxiliaries, provincial
troops. Pp. 17-21 contain a general return and recapitulation. Among the
schedules is a tariff of exchanges—lieutenant-general, 1044=an admiral,
commander of a fleet; brigadier-general, 200=a commodore; colonel, 100
=captain in navy, 3 years post, etc.

Similar information follows regarding the exchange of naval prisoners,
French, Spanish, and Dutch. From these papers, which are corrected and
attested copies, a complete statement could be made up of the prisoners in
American hands at the close of the war.
(Formerly *Miscellaneous, Various,* 179 (1).)

COLONIES.

41. 1733-1735.   Imports, America.

An account of what rum or spirits, molasses, syrups, sugar, and paneles
have been imported into any of the northern colonies from any of the French,
Dutch, or other foreign colonies, since Dec. 25, 1733, with the amount of the
duty collected thereon, by virtue of an act passed in 6 George III., entitled
" An Act for the better securing and encouraging the trade of his Majesty's
sugar colonies in America " ; distinguishing each colony and each year. Mar.
4, 1735.

42. 1728-1735   An Account of the Quantity of Rum, Molasses,
    and Sugar which have been Imported into the Northern
    Colonies from Jamaica, Barbadoes, and the Leeward
    Islands, distinguishing each year and colony.

Lists of the amounts of each commodity—rum, pp. 1-8, molasses, pp. 9-16, sugar, pp. 17-24—from each West India colony to each northern port; no duties listed.

(Formerly *Miscellaneous, Various,* 208 (1) (2).)

43. 1731-1735. Shipping Returns, America.

An account of the quantity of tonnage of each ship and vessel which has entered and cleared out, 1731-1735, from any of the colonies to Jamaica, Barbadoes, Antigua, or other of the Leeward Islands, with lumber, flour, or any other goods or merchandise. *Id.,* to the French, Dutch, or other foreign plantations in America, distinguishing each year and each plantation.

(Formerly *Miscellaneous, Various,* 208 (3).)

44. 1750. Representation of the Board of Trade.

To the Treasury, giving elaborate details regarding the part taken by the colonies in the intended expedition to Canada in 1748. Feb. 28, 1750. The representation covers ninety-five pages and refers to one hundred and nineteen appendixes containing the documentary evidence. These appendixes are not here. The account of each colony is presented in turn.

(Formerly *Miscellaneous, Various,* 34 (4).)

45. 1751-1771. Two Returns of Customs Fees.

Tables of fees taken by the officers of the customs at ports from Newfoundland, Halifax, and Quebec to Bermuda and Bahamas. Altogether twenty-eight ports are named. The returns give information as to whom paid (collector, comptroller, surveyor, searcher, waiters), and in most cases " how long and by what authority taken ". The information varies with each return.

(Formerly *Miscellaneous, Various,* 216.)

47. 1710-1711. Barbadoes Shipping Returns.
48. 1737-1738, 1772-1780. *Id.*
49. 1772-1780. *Id.*

Large paper folios, unsigned, containing the usual naval office information. **48,** no. 16, has " A List of Plantation Bonds entered into at the Naval Office in Barbadoes ", Jan. 5, 1775–Jan. 5, 1776. No. 17 is an " Account of all the cash received and Sums bonded for in the Treasury Office at Barbadoes arising from the duty of liquors and negroes imported, with the quantities and qualities of the same in the vessels named ", 1737-1738. This is a brief paper mentioning two plantation vessels. The returns in **48** are of shipping inward, those in **49,** contained in thirteen books, are of shipping outward.

(Formerly *Miscellaneous, Various,* 273, 168, 169.)

71. 1765. Courts of Law, Ceded Islands.

An ordinance for establishing courts of common pleas and courts of error in the islands of Grenada, St. Vincent, and Dominica, and for the better regulating the proceedings thereof. Other documents in this bundle relate to Grenada and other West India islands after 1783.

(Formerly *Miscellaneous, Various,* 36.)

72. Jamaica and Savannah Returns.

I. 1777-1785. Jamaica Shipping Returns.

For the port of St. Antonio, made up of printed forms, filled in, and giving information as follows:

Imports, 1775-1785; number of vessels belonging to Great Britain or the British possessions in America and the West Indies, laden with the produce of the United States, that have entered this port since the king's proclamation thereto, and also of their cargoes; imports from Canada, Nova Scotia, etc.; quantity of rum exported the last year compared with the average of four foregoing years.

For the port of Kingston, with similar information.

Imports in British bottoms; *id.* in foreign bottoms; account of rum exported and cleared, 1778-1784; imports from Canada and Nova Scotia, 1783-1785; number of vessels belonging to Great Britain, etc., similar to information from St. Antonio.

For the port of Kingston, imports and exports.

Imports in British bottoms; number of vessels belonging to Great Britain.

II. 1781-1785. Account of imports and exports from the port of Savannah, showing how little trade existed between this and other continental ports in America.

(Formerly *Miscellaneous, Various,* 218.)

82. 1770. Newfoundland Shipping Returns.
Clearances and entries, St. John's.

84. 1749-1753. Halifax Shipping Returns.
Clearances and entries.

85. 1805-1806. Surinam. Accounts of Imports from the United States, and Correspondence.

88-90. 1680-1718. Entry Books of William Blathwayt, Auditor General and Surveyor of the King's Revenue in the Plantations.

These important volumes open with copies of the oath of office and the commission in full. Then follow entries of Blathwayt's reports to the Treasury Board. The earlier of these reports have to do with Virginia and the West Indies only. In the description that follows a brief indication is given of the contents of these reports. The first volume is well paged and indexed; the second, which is in two parts, contains only tables of contents.

88. Regarding quit-rents in Virginia (p. 10).
Appointment of deputies. Oct. 15, 1681. (*Cf.* p. 71.)
Rent due from the Carolina patentees (p. 96).
Lord Culpeper and his claims on Virginia (pp. 123-133, 193, 226-240, 254-256, 303-304), especially regarding the Arlington and Culpeper grant (pp. 128-133).
Petition of Robert Smith of Virginia praying payment of his arrears as " major general " in the suppression of the tobacco cutting riots in Virginia (pp. 143-144, 171-172).
Letter from Lord Howard of Effingham regarding quit-rents (pp. 178-180), with the Lord Treasurer's reply (pp. 181-182); *id.* (pp. 184, 185).
Letter from James II. to Gov. Dongan, and another to Lucas Santen, 1686 (pp. 189-192).

Order to Edmund Andros, appointing two foot companies, a surgeon, an armorer, a gunner, and a chaplain for New York (p. 200). Oct. 2, 1686.

Regarding the importation of Canary wines, whether contrary to 15 Charles II. or not (pp. 201-202, 210-211), with the attorney general's opinion thereon (pp. 203-204).

Royal letter to Andros about auditing the revenue (pp. 206-208).

Minutes of council, Virginia, regarding tribute beaver and wine licenses (pp. 212-213). Apr. 26, 1686.

Royal letter regarding Thomas Sandys (pp. 213-214) and minute of the Virginia council regarding the same, July 1, 1686 (pp. 214-215, 242).

Report on the case of the Earl of Stirling (pp. 221 ff.).

Report on compensation for Col. Spencer as president of the council of Virginia (pp. 230-234).

Commission to Randolph as deputy surveyor and auditor general of New England (p. 238).

Regarding Phips and the treasure (pp. 244-249).

Letter from Andros regarding the king's revenue in New England, followed by the king's instructions and a paper entitled " State of His Matys Revenue in New England " (pp. 250-253). Aug. 31, 1687.

Commission and instructions to Plowman (pp. 260-261, 264-266), with a letter from Dongan, May 9, 1687 (p. 270).

Santen case, New York (pp. 261-278, 289, 295).

Commission to William Byrd, sr. (p. 279).

Warrant to pay Andros £1200 (later £1400) as governor of New England (pp. 282, 296).

Establishment of two companies of foot in New York (p. 294).

Letter to Deputy Auditor Bacon, Virginia, about a ship seized for trading in negroes and elephants' teeth contrary to the Royal African Company's charter (p. 295).

Warrant to Andros to spend £200 on new fortifications (p. 300). Aug. 1, 1688.

Chidley Brooke's commission as collector and other papers (pp. 315-323).

Report on Brenton's petition to be surveyor of the woods, and on Andros's request for the same, Nov., 1691 (pp. 338-339).

Regarding the erection of a college in Virginia (pp. 346-365, 399-400—valuable series of papers).

Orders to Gov. Copley to have his part of the two shillings a hhd. from Maryland, and other Maryland entries (pp. 364-372).

Neal's petition regarding mines in America (pp. 373-375).

Brief history of the collector's office, New York (pp. 375-377).

Report on revenues in the plantations (pp. 378-381).

Report on Gov. Nicholson's query as to escheats in Virginia (p. 383).

Report on Copley's memorial (pp. 385-386, 448).

Report on Cortlandt's petition regarding foot companies in New York (pp. 387-388, 391-392).

Report on Dongan's petition for lands on Staten Island (pp. 396-398, 402-403, 438-439, 446-447).

Warrant for payment by the executors of Nathaniel Bacon of £850 to the college (p. 399).

Warrant for payment to the same of £1135 out of the quit-rents (p. 400).

Letter to the governor of Virginia to send £500 to New York (p. 403) ; to Maryland to send £250 (p. 404).

Letter to the governor of Virginia to pay Commissary Blair £100.

Commission to Randolph as deputy in Maryland (p. 412) ; other deputations (p. 417).

Warrant to the governor of Virginia to pay £765 out of the quit-rents (p. 424).

Petition of Lord Baltimore regarding Maryland revenues and Blathwayt's report (pp. 425-430).

Letter to the governors of Maryland and Virginia regarding the prevention of illegal trading (pp. 430-431, other letters, pp. 431-432).

Trever's memoir on behalf of Muschamp as receiver in Maryland (pp. 432-437).

Address of the commissioners of accounts about the king's revenues in America (pp. 444-445).

Report on petition of the Maryland assembly regarding twenty-five ships that came from that province in 1690 without paying duty (p. 448).

Volume ends Sept. 23, 1692.

89. Warrant for a chaplain for the New York companies (pp. 4-5).

Regarding Bellomont's salary (p. 5).

Petition of William Byrd, jr., for balance of his father's account (p. 11) ; report on the same (pp. 12-16).

Report on Gov. Nicholson's letter regarding Maryland's account (pp. 17-20).

Report on Andros's petition (pp. 22, 27, 31-32).

Report (by Povey in Blathwayt's absence) on memorial of Brooke, New York (pp. 26-31).

Report on Quary's petition relating to a minister and schoolmaster in Pennsylvania (p. 33).

Letter from Nicholson and report thereon (pp. 34-40).

Letter to Bellomont regarding Weaver's salary (pp. 40-41).

Letter to William Penn regarding the king's share of rents, issues, and profits from the Lower Counties (pp. 41-42, 53-54, 55, 60).

Commission to A. De Peyster (p. 43).

Various accounts of plantation revenues (pp. 44-53, 61, 63-69, 78-88, 96-97, 132-135, 138, 146, 154-159, 177-186, 213-214, 285, 286, 322-323, 331-335, 336-339).

Report on Gov. Fletcher's petition regarding his bond (pp. 55-57).

Letter to Gov. Nicholson regarding ordnance and ammunition sent to Virginia (pp. 70-71).

Weaver's accounts (pp. 73-76).

Cornbury's petition (pp. 76-77).

Commission to Clark, deputy auditor, New York (pp. 92-93).

Letter from Blathwayt to Gov. Dudley regarding New Hampshire accounts (pp. 93-94) ; other similar letters (pp. 94-95).

Instructions for William Byrd, sr. (pp. 97-98).

Letter to Gov. Nicholson about arms (pp. 99-100).
Report on Muschamp's petition (pp. 101-103, 115-116, 129-131) ; *id.*
    on a grant to Cornbury (pp. 105-106).
Dudley's account for a company of foot (pp. 107-108).
Lowndes's letter about the public accounts (pp. 117-122).
Instructions to Bladen (pp. 126-128).
Report on Culpeper's £600 a year (p. 135).
Blathwayt's memorial about lands discovered near Maryland (p.
    136).
Paper regarding a prize taken near Maryland (p. 137).
Report on the memorial of the attorney general of Virginia (pp.
    138-139).
Report on the memorial of the Bishop of London regarding lands
    for a church in New York (pp. 140-141, Jan. 27, 1704, valuable).
Muschamp's petition for salary (pp. 141-144).
Warrant for an addition of £60 out of the quit-rents to the salary of
    the attorney general of Virginia (p. 145).
Letter to Clark, New York, about church lands (pp. 159-162) ; to
    Bladen (p. 164) ; to other deputies (pp. 165-169, 176-177).
Warrant to Jennings (who had inspected and amended the laws of
    Virginia) for £200 reward out of the quit-rents (pp. 187-188).
Regarding ordnance stores sent to New England (pp. 189-195).
Blathwayt's declaration of accounts before the Lord Treasurer (pp.
    203-214, valuable).
Report on Robert Livingstone's petition for payment of salaries,
    etc., in New York (pp. 219-228, valuable).
Letter to Gov. Dudley regarding pirates' goods (pp. 228-229, 276-
    277).
Letters to Clark and Cornbury, with observations on the New York
    revenues (pp. 230-232).
Letter to Gov. Nicholson for remittance of £3000 from quit-rents,
    Virginia (pp. 234-236, also 236-238, 243).
Warrant to Livingstone for £670 (pp. 239-241).
Report to the Lord Treasurer on quit-rents in Virginia (p. 244,
    valuable).
Regarding William Byrd's accounts (pp. 245-246, 247-249).
Regarding prizes in the plantations (pp. 250-258).
Report on the office of treasurer of revenue in Virginia (pp. 264-
    266).
Warrant for Indian presents (p. 267).
Confirmation of Peter Fauconniere, New York (pp. 269-270).
Regarding allowance to the governor of Virginia for house-rent
    (pp. 270-272).
On security from plantation officials (pp. 273-276).
Deputation to William Byrd, jr., to succeed his father (pp. 277-278,
    286-289) ; *id.*, Diggs (p. 281).
Regarding the pirate Quelch and his treasure (pp. 290-291, 293-
    296).
Warrant to Livingstone for provisions for the four companies, New
    York, £252 (pp. 297-299, 300-301).
Report on the petition of Charles Lodwyck, merchant, attorney for
    Gertruyd Van Cortlandt (pp. 304-305).

Report on the petition of the widow Bridges for her husband's arrears as chief justice, New York (pp. 306-307).
Regarding Virginia quit-rents (pp. 307-309).
On pirate goods in New England (pp. 309-310).
Letter to Cornbury restoring Byerly (p. 311).
Letter to the governor of Virginia for remission of residue of Byrd's balance (pp. 311-312).
Concerning the state of the royal revenues, New York (pp. 318-320).
Regarding suicide in Virginia (pp. 284, 323-324).
Report to the Lord Treasurer upon the address of the Maryland assembly concerning the expenditures of Blakiston (pp. 348-350).
Letter to Gov. Hunter of Virginia for remission of quit-rents, £2060.
Dummer's memorial regarding postal service with the plantations and other papers (pp. 352-382, valuable).
Regarding Hunter's salary (pp. 391-396).
Report on Muschamp's petition (p. 397).
Letter to Gov. Lovelace regarding New York accounts (p. 398).
On increasing Byrd's salary (pp. 400-401).
Regarding the Fairfax estate in Northern Neck, Virginia—proposition for an exchange (pp. 401-405—a history of the Hopton grant, 1649-1688).
Regarding boundaries between Virginia and Carolina (pp. 406-413).
Report on a petition from the College of William and Mary, building burned (p. 419).
Circular letter from Blathwayt to his deputies, 1709 (p. 421).
At the end of the volume, which closes with Mar. 26, 1709, is a loose sheet containing an account of the two shillings a hhd., Apr. 25–Oct. 25, 1756, arranged by counties.

90. Report on William Byrd's lands in St. Christopher (pp. 1-2, 7-10).
Report on Hunter's memorial regarding the Palatines (pp. 15-16, 18-19, 22-23).
Report on the petition of Robert Armstrong, collector, New Hampshire, for office of surveyor of the woods (pp. 17-18).
Report on Byrd's salary (pp. 20-21).
Report on the Bishop of London's letter on behalf of the College of William and Mary (pp. 26-27, 30-31).
Report on Gov. Spotswood's memorial regarding house-rent, etc. (pp. 28-30).
On the building of a chapel in an Indian fort near New York (pp. 32-33).
Byrd's accounts (pp. 37-38).
Deputation to Philip Ludwell (pp. 39, 45).
Various accounts of plantation revenues (pp. 37-38, 39-40, 46-48, 49-58, 59, 70, 71-73).
Allowance to Byerly during his suspension (p. 40).
Virginia quit-rents (pp. 59, 71-73).
General state of the plantations (pp. 61-68).
Report on the petition of Berkeley Seymour, son of Gov. Seymour of Maryland (p. 71).
Letter regarding the accounts of New Hampshire and Massachusetts Bay (pp. 73-74).

Regarding the education of Indian children at William and Mary College and the conversion of neighboring Indian tribes, memorial by Gov. Spotswood (pp. 82-85).

Report on Lady Lovelace's papers (pp. 91-91 b, important, note underlined passages and marginal comments).

Warrant for paying Lady Lovelace £481 (p. 92).

Warrant for the expense of settling bounds between Virginia and Carolina, £250 (p. 93).

On Spotswood's house-rent (p. 95).

Commission to Roscoe, Grymer, and Dixon (pp. 100-102).

Last date Apr. 15, 1718.

(Formerly *Miscellaneous, Various*, 37, 38.)

COMMISSARIAT.

101. 1772-1776. Letter and Account Book of Commissariat Supplies to the Troops in North America.

A general account of such monies as have been required from the deputy paymaster-general, Oct. 1, 1773–June, 1774, for the carrying on the public works, services, and other contingent and extraordinary expenses. Also a half-yearly return of provisions issued to the British forces in North America, Dec. 25, 1722–June 24, 1773, sent by Haldimand to Sec. Robinson.

Id., from Gage, to Sept., 1775; the last letter, Gage to Robinson, dated Aug. 20, 1776.

Entry book of warrants, returns of provisions, general accounts with the crown, and copies of all letters to the secretary to the Admiralty Board. Valuable.

(Formerly *Miscellaneous, Various*, 42.)

102-103. 1776-1777. Copies of Letters from Nathaniel Day, Commissary General to the Army in America, to Secretary Robinson and Others, and the Answers thereto.

102. Letters from Montreal, Berthier, Quebec, St. John's, with tables of returns of provisions, general states of provisions, orders, instructions, lists of commissaries, etc., written to Sec. Robinson, Gen. Carleton, assistant commissary-general, deputy commissary-general, conductors, etc.; also a few answers.

103. As far as p. 46, this volume is identical with **102**, except that it contains a letter of Aug. 22, 1777, and certain tables not in the earlier volume, and omits certain lists of commissaries (**102**, f. 27 b) and letters from the Treasury (31-34 b). After p. 46 the volume contains letters to Sec. Robinson and a series of memoranda, orders, and instructions from Day; letters from assistant commissaries (27 letters in all), Jan. 26–Apr. 25, 1777; and a series of papers of a more general character, of some importance for the Burgoyne campaign.

(Formerly *Miscellaneous, Various*, 43, 44.)

104. 1776-1781. Copies of Letters from Secretary Robinson to Nathaniel Day.

Supplements **102-103**, extending from Mar. 30, 1776, to Aug. 22, 1781. Contains instructions, authorizations, orders, acknowledgments, warrants, etc.

(Formerly *Miscellaneous, Various*, 48.)

105. 1777-1783. Copies of Letters from Secretaries Robinson, Rose, Burke, and Sheridan of the Treasury Board, to Gen. Haldimand.

From Sept. 30, 1777, to Dec. 15, 1783. Chiefly regarding provisions, equipment, warrants, law-suits, Indian presents, appointments, revenue accounts, leaves of absence, etc.

106-107. 1774-1777, 1778-1783. Letters to and from Commanders-in-Chief in America.

Five entry books (North America, 1, 2, 3, 5, Canada 1) containing copies of the correspondence between the Treasury Board and the commanders-in-chief of the army in North America, upon all the subjects that arose in that connection.

North America, 1. Letters from the Treasury, signed by Robinson and Grey Cooper, to Gage, 1774-1775, Howe, 1775-1777, and to and from Robert Gordon, commissary at Cork, chiefly regarding the provisioning of the army.

Id., 2. Letters to Howe, Clinton, and Carleton regarding salaries, losses, American sufferers, etc. 1778-1783.

Id., 3. Letters from Howe and Clinton regarding the question of disbursement of money, of which detailed accounts are rendered, also a few other documents, such as memorials from Lord Cathcart. 1778-1779.

Id., 4. Missing.

Id., 5. Letters chiefly from subordinates to Howe and Clinton, with very elaborate accounts.

Canada, 1. Letters from Haldimand, with copies of reports and memorials from subordinates. 1778-1781. On p. 77 is an original letter from Haldimand, June 8, 1779.

This collection is important and forms a part of the series of in-letters and out-letters of the Treasury Board.

(Formerly *Miscellaneous, Various,* 35.)

108-112. 1775-1777. Entry Books of Letters from the Commanders-in-Chief in America.

113. 1783. *Id.*

114. 1778-1779. Correspondence Book and Accounts of Commissariat Supplies, touching the Army during the American War.

The principal correspondent is Daniel Wier, commissary at Philadelphia (formerly commissary at Bremen), and his letters are from Philadelphia, Rhode Island, and New York, Jan. 20, 1778–Dec. 12, 1779. They are important as showing the difficulties encountered by the British army in obtaining oats and hay, the conditions in Philadelphia during the winter of 1778, and the character of the provisions, and in furnishing abstracts of the number of men, women, and children victualled, accounts of damages and losses, sundry agreements, oaths, protests, and receipts. A useful collection.

115. 1778-1781. In-Letters from the Commander-in-Chief in Canada.

116. 1778-1782. Register of Letters from the Commissaries in North America and the West Indies.

This register covers vols. **108, 111, 114, 115,** and other books now lost. The letters thus listed are from Gens. Clinton, Haldimand, and Christie, Commissaries Wier and Day, Deputy Commissaries Morrison (Charleston), Foster, Naylor, Fraser, Glasford (West Indies), and others. Nov., 1779–Nov., 1782.
(Formerly *Miscellaneous, Various,* 179 (3).)

117. 1776. Copies of Letters from the Treasury to Anthony Merry, merchant of London, relating to the Transportation of Cattle, Sheep, Hogs, despatched from Wales.

The volume covers the period Jan. 24–May 14, 1776, and contains also instructions to George Jackson, under secretary of the Admiralty, to furnish assistance, and letters to Gen. Howe on the same subject.
(Formerly *Miscellaneous, Various,* 34 (3).)

118. 1776-1777. Copies of Letters from Daniel Chamier, Commissary General of Stores and Provisions to the Army in America, to Secretary Robinson, and copies of the Answers thereto.

Written from Halifax, Staten Island, New York, June 8, 1776–May 19, 1777, with many tables of returns of provisions, and occasional bits of general information. Robinson's letters are dated, Apr. 12, 1776–Apr. 8, 1777.
(Formerly *Miscellaneous, Various,* 45.)

119. 1777-1783. America: Out-Letters and Observations.

Copies of letters from Sec. Robinson to Daniel Wier (pp. 1-68), Peter Paumier (pp. 69-70), and Brook Watson (pp. 70-77), commissaries in America, Sept. 26, 1777–June 20, 1783; with many enclosures, tables, extracts of letters, and the like. Valuable as supplementing previous volumes.
(Formerly *Miscellaneous, Various,* 49.)

120. 1779. Correspondence and Account Book of Peter Paumier, Deputy Commissary in Georgia.

This volume is only partly filled, containing a few letters, with thirty or forty tables and other enclosures.
(Formerly *Miscellaneous, Various,* 47.)

150. 1756. Representations of the Register General of Tobacco for Scotland to the Commissioners of the Customs of Edinburgh.

Of little importance. On p. 3 b is a reference to plantation tobacco. This report was sent in obedience to clause 17 of 24 George II., c. 41, " For the more effectual securing the Duties upon Tobacco ", enjoining upon the chief customs officials at London and the outports to transmit information regarding tobacco imported from the plantations. No other representations are known to exist.
(Formerly *Accounts, Revenue Accounts, Miscellaneous, England,* 48, a series that has been rearranged.)

LAW OFFICERS' OPINIONS.

188. 1763-1783. Law Officers' Opinions.

Given by the attorneys general and solicitors general, C. Yorke, F. Norton, W. de Grey, E. Willes, J. Dunning, A. Wedderburn, J. Wallace, Ll. Kenyon, J. Lee, and R. P. Arden. Opinions are rendered on the following cases:

Duties levied by Lord Albemarle at Havana, Mar. 3, May 14, 1764.
Government of Quebec. Aug. 6, 1764.
Auditor General Cholmondeley's patent. Aug. 6, 1764.
Collecting revenues at Quebec. Nov. 17, 1764.
Contractors in America. Mar. 24, 1766.
Collecting customs in America. Oct. 17, 1766.
Recovery of debts from agents of the American contractors. Nov. 23, 1766; Sept. 16, 1777.
Seizure of a ship at Boston. July 25, 1768.
Taking security in Great Britain for offices in America. July 21, 1768.
Unlading ships in American ports. Sept. 9, 1768.
What ships or vessels may pass from port to port in America. Sept. 8, 1768.
Granting writs of assistance in America. Aug. 20, 1768.
Tax act passed in Massachusetts Bay. Feb. 13, 1770.
Whether officers of customs were justified in giving clearances to ships carrying coals, necessary articles of clothing, and other stores and provisions to New York and Rhode Island for the use of the inhabitants. Feb. 8, 1779.
Bills of exchange, St. Vincent. Mar. 9, 1779.
Apothecary general's patent. July 27, 1778.
Contracts for forage. June 11, 1779.
Duties on prize goods, New York case. Aug. 21, 1780.
Payment of salaries of the Board of Trade, whether the board was to draw pay to May 2, 1782 (date of Shelburne's letter notifying the board of its dismissal), or to the date of the act of 1782. The first opinion declared that salaries ceased May 2 (pp. 327-329). The board then memorialized the Treasury, requesting that they might receive salaries up to the later date. This memorial, an important statement, is here quoted (pp. 330-335). The matter was submitted a second time to the lawyers and the former opinion was reversed (p. 336). Jan. 9, 1783. (See *Treas.* 1, **586.**)
Harley and Drummond's contracts for supplying the forces in America. Dec. 7, 1782.
Exportation of goods to New York. Mar. 6, 1783.
(Formerly *Miscellaneous, Various,* 59.)

200. 1779-1780. Copies of Letters from the Commissioners of the Navy to the Lords of the Treasury, relative to the Victualling of Transports. Feb. 3, 1779–Sept. 19, 1780.

This correspondence arose out of the proposal to put the transports for victualling the army in America under the management of the Navy Board. Until this time supplies had been sent in armed vessels, but now it was proposed to have them carried under the protection of regular convoys.

201. 1779-1781. Copies of Letters from Secretary Robinson to the Navy Board on the Victualling Service. Jan. 30, 1779–Aug. 21, 1781.

(These two volumes were formerly in *Miscellaneous, Various,* 77.)

PATENT BOOK.

215-216. 1761-1782. Entry Book of Patents.

The patents in these volumes are entered in full. Patents to all the governors in America, Board of Trade, collectors, naval officers, secretaries, etc., in the colonies that received their authority by letters patent.

SCOTLAND.

219. 1771-1775, 1781-1785. Shipping Returns.

(Formerly *Miscellaneous, Various,* 219.)

240. 1722. Report on Tobacco Frauds in the Tobacco Trade.

Sent by Humphrey Brent, one of the commissioners of the customs in Scotland. It contains no specific reference to the colonies, but most if not all of the tobacco must have come from America. The frauds occurred at Glasgow, Port Glasgow, and Greenock. The names of ships are given, with dates, and nine cases are reported. Nov. 15, 1722.

(Formerly *Accounts, Revenue Accounts, Miscellaneous, Scotland and Ireland,* 3.)

252. 1772-1785. Linens Exported from Scotland.

An account of the quantity of British, Irish, and foreign linens exported from Scotland in the years named, distinguishing each year, each colony, to what port exported, etc. Jan. 4, 1786.

(Formerly *Accounts, Revenue Accounts, Miscellaneous, Scotland and Ireland,* 25.)

VARIOUS.

273. 1707-1749. Various Accounts of Imports and Exports.

Two affidavits regarding bonds for entering Maryland tobacco in England. Jan. 31, 1735[?].

An account of the quantity of sugar imported from the British plantations, and afterward exported, 1728-1733. Mar. 15, 1735.

Id., rum, 1728-1733, distinguishing each year, with the duties paid at importation.

An account of a sale of a parcel of brown sugar sent to France from a French plantation, and the charges thereon compared with the sale of a like quantity sold in London. n. d.

An account of the quantity of sugar imported and from what place, Christmas, 1726–Christmas, 1733, and how much was re-exported. Figures for the West Indies, New York, New England, Pennsylvania, Maryland, and Virginia. Apr. 11, 1735.

Id., 1707-1714.

An account of the quantities of iron in bars, pigs, and sows imported into England from the plantations, 1710-1718, distinguishing each plantation and each year. Maryland and Virginia are the only continental colonies noted and they exported for the first time to London in 1718. Mar. 24, 1737.

Id., 1728-1735.

Id., 1735-1736. Feb. 14, 1738. Virginia and Maryland, Pennsylvania, Jamaica. Chiefly pig-iron.

An account of the quantity of iron wrought and iron in bars, exported to the plantations, 1710-1718. Large amounts to New England, New York, Virginia, and Maryland. Mar. 24, 1737.

Id., 1728-1735. Mar. 24, 1737.

Id., 1735-1736. Feb. 14, 1738.

An account of the quantity of rice carried directly from Carolina to foreign lands, to the southward of Cape Finisterre. 1730-1737. (Two copies.)

An account of the quantity of raw sugar exported from England, 1736-1737. Mar. 22, 1738. (*Inter alia,* to Newfoundland, Virginia, Maryland.)

An account of sugars imported into England from St. Christopher, 1736-1737.

An account of the quantity of refined sugars exported from England, 1736-1737. Considerable quantities sent to all the plantations, especially to Carolina, Jamaica, Virginia, Maryland, and Pennsylvania; very little to New England and New York.

An account of the quantity of rice imported into England from Carolina, 1723-1737. Mar., 1739.

An account of what quantities of rum or spirits, molasses or syrups, sugar or paneles, have been imported into any of His Majesty's northern colonies in America from any of the French, Dutch, or other foreign colonies, 1733-1737, with the account of the duties collected thereon by virtue of the act, 6 George II. (1733). Mar. 28, 1739.

An account of what quantity of rum has been imported from any of the British sugar islands into England. 1727-1737. 1735-1738.

An account of the quantity of refined sugar exported from England, 1708-1737, showing the amount sent to each plantation. Apr. 30, 1739.

Id., manufactured silk, 1720-1740.

An account of the quantity of refined sugar exported from England, yearly, 1728-1742, not distinguishing the individual plantations. Dec. 29, 1743.

An account of the quantity of sugar exported from Barbadoes and the Leeward Islands for the last seven years the journals have been received, distinguished under the different denominations it bears in the journals. (A copy, with remarks.)

An account of the quantity of sugar imported into England, 1738-1743, distinguishing each country and each year. Jan. 29, 1745.

Id., exported.

274. 1750-1779. *Id.*

An account of the money paid and charges incurred by supporting and maintaining the settlement of His Majesty's colony of Nova Scotia, 1750-1751.

An account of the duties imposed by 25 Charles II. (plantation duty), collected in Jamaica for seven years to Christmas, 1751, distinguishing each year and showing how much thereof arose by sugar and

how much by other goods; also an account of the species and
quantities of goods exported from Jamaica to North America for
which the duties imposed by 25 Charles II. have been paid for
seven years to Christmas, 1751, distinguishing each year.

An account of the quantities of sugar imported from Jamaica into England for twenty years ending at Christmas, 1751. Mar. 10, 1753.

A group of papers relating to the export of sugar and rum from the
West Indies to the northern colonies and to England, to 1751.
Mar. 22, 24, 1753.

An account of all British and Irish linens exported from England to the
British colonies and plantations in America, 1740-1753, distinguishing the years and species but not the plantations. Jan. 9,
1755.

An account of the quantity of pig- and bar-iron imported from the British
colonies in America, 1749-1756, distinguishing each year and
each colony, and how much in pig and how much in bar. Feb. 18,
1757.

An account of all corn, meal, malt, flour, bread, biscuit, and starch
exported to any place whatsoever by virtue or in pursuance of
any of the liberties or powers thereby given or granted in the act
for that purpose passed 30, 31, George II. Dec. 5, 1757. Similar tables for 1758, 1766, 1768, 1769 (bundle **276**), 1770 (*ibid.*),
and so on, will be found in this and the next bundle. They
include the amounts exported to the plantations.

An account of British plantations brown sugar imported into and exported from the port of London and the outports and to what
places exported for ten years past, distinguishing each year.
May 3, 1758. Mention of Carolina, New York, Virginia, Maryland.

An account of the several prices His Majesty's Muscovado sugars from
Barbadoes and Leeward Islands sold for at each sale on an average in every year at the Custom House, London, 1727-1758. Mar.
6, 1759.

An account of beaver skins imported and exported, not distinguishing
the plantations. Feb. 11, 1763.

Printed certificate (blanks filled in) certifying that Walter Hatton,
appointed " Comptroller of Accomack in Virginia ", hath received
proper instructions. London, Aug. 16, 1764.

Id. in manuscript. Aug. 28, 1764.

An account of the quantity of rice exported from the colonies of North
Carolina, South Carolina, and Georgia to any part of America to
the southward of South Carolina and Georgia since the passing
of the acts by which such exportation was allowed as far as such
account can be made up (brief). Feb. 17, 1766.

An account of the amount of duties paid on molasses imported into the
northern colonies for the last three years ending at Christmas,
1765, distinguishing each year and each colony. Feb. 17, 1766.

An account of the quantities and different species of merchandise imported into England from Guadeloupe, Martinique, and Havana,
1761-1764. July 31, 1766. Detailed and valuable.

An account of the produce of the duties by 4 George III. on goods imported into and exported from the colonies, from the commencement of said duties, so far as the accounts are received. Nov. 12, 1766. Total £41,614.

Id., payable on sugars which were granted and continued from Sept. 29, 1764, to Jan. 5, 1765, to Jan. 5, 1766, and thence to latest period. Nov. 12, 1766.

An account of the gross and net produce of the duty laid upon the importation of molasses in the colonies by an act passed 6 George II., Feb. 10, 1767. The account runs from 1734 to 1764, a period of 31 years. The highest gross receipt is £2100 (1764), the lowest £2 5s. (1735), the average £442. Net figures are not given.

An account of the gross and net produce of the duty laid upon the importation of molasses in the colonies by an act passed 4 George III., so far as the accounts are received. Feb., 1767. Total duty £24,133.

An account of the quantities of rice, sago powder, and vermicelli imported into England from any of His Majesty's colonies in America, May 4, 1767–Nov. 30, 1767. Rice is the only commodity imported from Carolina, Georgia, New York, New England, Virginia, and Maryland.

An account of the quantity of wheat and wheat flour imported into England from the colonies, Jan. 5, 1767–Oct. 10, 1767. Jan. 10, 1768. New York and Pennsylvania, both wheat and wheat flour; New England a little wheat flour, Carolina, very little.

An account of the quantity of whale-fins and oil imported into England from America, 1765-1767. Feb. 8, 1768.

An account of the net produce of the duties of customs and excise upon teas for 5 years preceding July 5, 1767, with the medium thereof, also the net produce of the duties of customs and excise upon teas from July 5, 1768, to July 5, 1769, with the amount of the net produce of the customs paid upon the importation of teas which were exported to Ireland and the British colonies in America, in 5 years ending July 5, 1767. "Difference to be made good by the East India Company for the loss to the revenue in the year ended July 5, 1769 = £147,378..14..2$\frac{7}{10}$."

275. A bundle of Custom House reports or statements, made out pursuant to orders of the Treasury.

The greater number of these reports were drawn up after 1783 and refer in a majority of cases to England, Ireland, or Europe only, or to places not indicated. In the following, America and the West Indies are mentioned.

Account of the imports into England of foreign linens for three years last past, 1780-1783, specifying the quantities and the countries. The items for America are always "Sails foreign made". Jan. 3, 1785.

Id., exports. Jan. 19, 1785.

Account of the quantities of wine imported during the last thirty years, 1754-1784. Nov. 8, 1785.

Account of the value of all goods, wares, and merchandise, exported and imported, 1780-1783. Enclosed in this report is a statement of the amounts of customs paid into the Exchequer, 1736-1741, 1749-1751, 1784.

Account of the quantity of British linens exported from England for the
years 1773, 1774, 1783. Mar. 4, 1785.

Id., foreign linens.

Account of West India produce exported from England in 1773, 1774,
and 1783, distinguishing the countries to which exported. Apr.
12, 1785.

Id., imported, amounts only.

Account of the quantities of mahogany, satin wood, rosewood (not
including dyeing woods) imported, 1777-1783.

Id., leather manufactures exported, 1774-1784.

Id., live cattle imported (New York, two horses in 1780), 1774-1784.

Id., hides imported, 1774-1784.

Id., wrought iron exported, 1774-1784.

Id., wrought leather, exported, 1774-1784.

Id., Mocha and West India coffee imported, 1782-1785 ; rum, sugar, and
coffee imported, 1783-1785 ; manufactured tobacco into Danish
and Prussian ports, 1786-1787.

Account of the value and amount of goods being British produce and
manufactures, entered for exportation at the several ports of
Great Britain for the British sugar colonies, 1787-1788. Also
foreign produce.

Account of ships and tonnage from the British West Indies, 1788-1789,
with value of imports and custom duties.

Account of goods which by law may now be warehoused, including rice
from the United States, also tobacco and sugar. n. d.

276. *Id.*

An account of the quantity of British soap exported to the colonies from
England, 1764-1769. May 8, 1770.

An account of all goods, wares, and merchandise exported from England
to East and West Florida, and *id.* imported into England from the
same, from 1763 to Christmas, 1767. May 11, 1770. (Valuable.)

An account of the quantity of tobacco imported into England for seven
years last past from Christmas, 1762, to Christmas, 1769, distinguishing each year and each colony. Aug. 22, 1770. The greater
part is from Carolina, Virginia, and Maryland. Very little from
New England, New York, and Pennsylvania.

An account of salted beef, pork, and bacon imported from America,
1769-1770. Dec. 6, 1770.

An account of sugar, rum, cotton, and other commodities imported into
England from St. Vincent, Tobago, Grenada, 1762-1770. Oct. 5,
1771.

Id. from Dominica, 1762-1770. Nov. 7, 1771.

An account of the quantities of wheat and wheat flour, rye, rye meal,
and Indian corn, imported into England, 1772. Dec. 18, 1772.
Pennsylvania, wheat and wheat meal ; Virginia and Maryland,
id., and wheat flour and a little Indian corn.

An account of free port duties collected at Dominica, per 6 George III.,
c. 49.

An account of the quantity of raw hides imported from America, 1768-
1769. Feb. 12, 1774.

Two bulky reports giving accounts of exports from England to Jamaica for seven years preceding the late war, 1748-1755. May 6, 1774. Laid before the House of Lords.

An account of the value of all goods, wares, and merchandises exported from that part of Great Britain called England to the colonies in America. Jan. 26, 1775. Total, £2,462,148 15s. 10d.

A group of papers dealing with the export of tobacco and sugar.

An account of the value of the exports and imports to and from the West Indies and England, Christmas, 1737, to Christmas, 1762. Feb. 17, 1775.

An account of the quantity and value of tobacco imported into England from the colonies, distinguishing each year and each plantation, 1769-1773. Feb. 20, 1775.

An account of the quantity and value of the silk, cotton, worsted, linen, and mixed hose of English manufacture exported to North America and the West Indies, 1772-1774.

An account of the quantity of salt imported into the several colonies from Jan. 5, 1755, to Sept. 8, 1768, distinguishing each colony and each year. Apr. 11, 1775.

An account of coffee exported from England, 1773-1774. Apr. 28, 1775. Virginia and Maryland are the only colonies mentioned.

Id., imported into England (from Carolina, New York, Pennsylvania, and West Indies), 1773-1774.

An account of the bounties paid out of customs upon all goods imported into England from the colonies, being of the produce or fisheries thereof for six years ended at Christmas, 1776. *Id.*, 1761-1777, further on.

An account of the duties paid upon goods imported into England from the colonies; *id.*, exclusive of tobacco, for six years ending at Christmas, 1776, distinguishing such part as hath been paid upon goods imported from East and West Florida, Canada, Nova Scotia, Hudson Bay, and Newfoundland. Sept. 4, 1777.

An account of the quantity of plantation tobacco imported into England, and the quantity exported from England, 1760-1776. Dec. 10, 1777.

An account of the quantities of iron, hemp, and wood, imported into England, 1760-1766. The last two accounts were returned by order of Parliament, dated Dec. 10, 1777.

An account of all cotton-wool of the growth of the colonies, imported annually into England, 1767-1777. Feb. 9, 1779.

Id., 1767-1777, distinguishing the foreign from what was the growth of the British plantations.

(This series was formerly *Revenue Accounts, Miscellaneous, England*, 79 (**273**), 80 (**274**), 81 (**276**), 83 (**275**). *Id.*, 77, 82, and 78 are now *Treas.* 38: **362, 363, 364.**)

291. Bundle of King's Warrants.

The following may be noted:

Pension to Gen. Knyphausen, £393. Feb. 3, 1779.

Pension to Margaret Arnold, "wife of our truly and well-beloved Brig.-Gen. Benedict Arnold". Mar., 1782.

Remittance of a fine imposed on Douglass Campbell, clerk of common pleas, South Carolina, July 28, 1766.

Allowance to Benning Wentworth, as surveyor of lands and woods, £200 for himself, and £200 for his deputies in Nova Scotia. Dec. 12, 1743.

Warrant for James Gohier to be collector or receiver of customs, excise, quit-rents, and all other duties, New York, in place of Thomas Byerly. Aug. 20, 1716.

Pension to Francis Fauquier, £300. July 1, 1768.

Allowance to German Protestants settling in South Carolina for laying out lands allotted to them, to be paid out of the quit-rents by George Saxby. Sept. 28, 1764.

Allowances to Peter Randolph and William Byrd for services as commissioners to arrange a treaty with the Cherokees and Catawbas, £700. July 30, 1761.

Sign manual requiring Gov. Cornbury to deliver up Fletcher's bond taken by Lord Bellomont. n. d.

Warrant for a privy seal to discharge Edward Dummer from his contract to provide packet boats between England and the plantations. Jan. 15, 1707. (Valuable.)

Warrant for the appointment of Hulton, Temple, Birch, Paxton, Robinson, American Board of Customs Commissioners. Aug. 20, 1767. (Important.)

Probably all the warrants in this bundle are entered in the books of King's Warrants, *Treas.* 52.

312. 1769. Exports from Ireland to America.

Papers from the Custom House, Dublin, dealing with exports from Ireland to America, from 1769 on, with a paper or two on smuggling (Carolina rice to Holland, tea, linen, liquor, and brandy in return), called out by the request of the Treasury for reports from outside ports regarding vessels entering from and clearing for North America.

314. 1783-1784. An Account of all Ships belonging to the United States which have been cleared out from the Port of London since the Conclusion of the Peace to March 25, 1784.

The lists distinguish the ports of the United States to which they were bound, together with the manifests of their cargoes. Thirty-four ships (with names, captains' names, and destination) bound for Nantucket, Boston, Philadelphia, Virginia, Rhode Island, Savannah, Salem, Newburyport, Maryland, Charleston, and New York. The manifests are often very elaborate. May 14, 1783–Mar. 24, 1784.

315. 1783. Auditor of Imprests: General Certificate, Trinity Term, 1783.

Contains a few items relating to the colonies.

EXPIRED COMMISSIONS.

Under the control of the Treasury were certain offices, since abolished, and certain commissions, since expired, the books and papers of which were formerly open to inspection only by special permission of the Lords of the Treasury. This rule has now been changed, and at the present time all the collections noted below are accessible without special permit.[1] Among the books and papers in general there are four series of interest to students of American history, though but three relate to the colonial period and but two relate directly to the colonies. These series are: Records of the Royal African Company, 1662, 1672-1822, American Loyalist claims, 1784-1812, East Florida claims, 1785-1789, and papers of the commissioners of American ships and cargoes condemned as prize, 1812-1818. Attention may also be called to the records of the commission on courts of justice, 1815-1824, which are of some importance as throwing light on the organization and procedure of the courts held in the hall of Doctors' Commons. As the report of this commission was printed in 1823-1824, an examination of its papers seems hardly worth while. The papers of the commission on American ships do not fall within our period. Those of the Royal African Company, though relating but indirectly to colonial history, furnish valuable information for the history of the slave-trade and of colonial commerce and are here entered in the form of a list without detailed descriptions.

ROYAL AFRICAN COMPANY.[2]

On Jan. 10, 1662, a company was formed known as the " Governor and Company of the Royal Adventurers of England trading into Africa ", which, starting with a distinguished body of members and at first successful in its undertakings, became financially embarrassed before the end of the decade. In 1672 the company was reconstructed by royal charter as the " Royal African Company of England " and began its new career most prosperously. Before the end of the century opposition to its monopoly of trade was sufficiently strong to bring about a Parliamentary inquiry, the result of which was an act of 1697 which continued the company but restricted its monopoly by the recognition of independent traders under certain conditions.

But the new arrangement proved fatal to the prosperity of the company and in 1730 it was compelled to seek assistance from Parliament, amounting to £10,000 a year. This grant, which was continued until 1743, was increased to £20,000 in 1744. Notwithstanding these appropriations, the object of which was to enable the company to support its forts and garrisons on the west coast of Africa, the company maintained its existence as a joint-stock organization with difficulty, and in 1747 (21 George III.) was dissolved, its forts being transferred in 1752 to the crown (House of Lords MSS., nos. 188-190, 193). The management of the corporation, under the name of the " Company of Merchants trading to Africa " (1750-1821), was entrusted to a committee, to which Parliament made the necessary grants for the maintenance of its forts and which was required to give an account of all its transactions to the Board of Trade once a year. In this fashion, the new company did business until July 3, 1821, when by act of Parliament it ceased to exist (1 and 2 George IV., c. 28).

The property of the company having thus become vested in the crown, its records were removed to the Treasury Chambers and placed in a damp vault

---

[1] Since the previous volume of this *Guide* was issued, all the papers of the American Loyalist Claims Commission, both the Treasury series and the Audit Office series, have been thrown open to the public without restriction. The statement made on p. 11 of that volume must therefore be modified in this particular.

[2] In 1708 the office of the Royal African Company (African House) was in Leadenhall Street, later in the century it was in Cooper's Court, Cornhill. For an account of the company in 1708 see Hatton, *New View of London,* II. 593, and for the company in 1761, see Dodsley, *London and its Environs,* I. 135.

in the basement of the building. In 1842, for the inspection of an assistant keeper of the Public Record Office, nearly all of the papers were removed to the top of the building and there left until they were transferred to the Rolls House in 1846-1849. A few of the papers, notably the Cape Coast Castle accounts, were among the documents left in the cellar and damaged by the inflow of sewer water in 1846.

The papers in this collection are mainly of a routine character, relating to the actual business and administration of the company. Among the most interesting volumes in the series are those containing the minutes of the court of the company, the papers relating to the various reorganizations, the copies of the company's charters, and the entries and papers relating to its financial history, capital, stocks, and dividends. Few papers relating to the external or diplomatic relations of the company are to be found in this series. Very large numbers of papers bearing on the history and experiences of the companies will be found among the Colonial Office papers, *C. O.* 388, 389, *Guide,* I. 249-252, 263-265, and among the papers of the *Modern Board of Trade* 6, below, p. 367. The papers in this series have been three times arranged, in 1856, 1892-1894, 1909-1910. For a further account of these papers, see the *Transactions* of the Royal Historical Society, third series, VI. 197-217.

Treas. 70. —	**1-1663.** 1663-1820. Books and Papers of the Royal African Company (1662-1750) and of the Company of Merchants trading to Africa (1750-1821).

Letter-Books.

1-67. 1678-1750. Letters received from Africa and the West Indies.

68-74. 1750-1818. Letters sent: Outward Letter-Books.

Minute Books.

75-99. 1663-1752. Minutes of the Court of Assistants.

100-101. 1671-1720. Minutes of the General Court of the Royal African Company.

100 contains many records of subscription and transfers of stock.

102-150. 1725-1817. Minutes of Various Committees.

151-154. 1750-1818. Acts of Council at Cape Coast Castle, etc.

155-162. 1770-1792. Reports, Examinations, Orders, and Instructions.

163-168. 1685-1738. Books of Orders and Instructions, containing Memoranda for the use of the Secretary in writing to the Various Stations.

169-175. 1681-1745. Petitions.

To the crown, the Lord Treasurer, Lords Commissioners, House of Commons, and other bodies.

176-177. 1756, 1757. Parliamentary Reports.

177 is the printed return from the Board of Trade to the House of Commons relating to the general state of the trade to Africa.

STOCK.

178-184. 1713-1752 and undated. Books concerning Stock.

185-215. 1674-1751. Stock Ledgers, etc., and Stock Transfer Book.

ACCOUNTS.

216-268. 1672-1806. Various Cash Books.

269-283. 1672-1728. Bill Books.

284-308. 1682-1765. Waste Books.

309-598. 1662-1821. Journals and Warrant Books.

599-892. 1663-1821. Ledgers.

646 is a Barbadoes ledger (1662-1664) and **869-872** are Jamaica ledgers (1665-1702).

893-904. 1671-1700. Receipt Books.

905-907. 1751-1819. Balance Sheets. Accounts of the Committee of the Company of Merchants.

908. 1769-1786. Tables for each Year.

909-961. 1663-1816. Invoice Books: Outwards and Homewards.

962-973. 1678-1720. Freight Books. Copy Books of Accounts of Freight.

974-1182. 1750-1821. Day Books of the Forts.

1183-1194. 1702-1750. Various Account Books.

1195-1197. 1698, 1744-1750, 1720-1735. Bond Books: General and Custom House.

1198-1207. 1699-1807. Books concerning Customs.

The connection of these volumes with the Royal African Company is not clear. **1207** is a printed book (not earlier than 1771) filled in in manuscript, giving custom offices, names of holders, salaries, etc., at colonial ports.

1208. 1698 (*circa*). Debts.

1209 A-D. 1675-1749. Lists of Packets sent to Africa.

   1720-1724. Receipt of goods.

1210-1220. 1674-1816. Ships' Books proper; Ships' Accounts, Diaries, Invoices, Day Books.

1221-1228. 1660-1744. Books concerning Ships not otherwise classified.

1240-1249. 1790-1791. Receipt and Expenditures of Goods.

1250-1262. 1703-1790. Ivory and Gold Books.

1263-1269. 1755-1792. Books concerning Slaves.

PERSONAL.

1270-1272. 1681-1704. Soldiers' Ledgers.

1273-1275. 1705-1793. Pay of Men going out to Africa.

1276-1414. 1751-1821. Garrison Ledgers, Cape Coast Castle.

1415-1416. 1763-1765. Senegal.

1417-1421. 1758-1759. Place Unknown.

1422. 1771-1780. Tantumquerry and Elsewhere.

1423-1425. 1719-1749. Indentures, Covenants, and Deeds.

1426-1427. 1712-1730. Agreements: Printed Forms filled in.

1428-1431. 1671-1751. Security Books.

1432. 1712-1731. List of Securities.

1433. 1685-1702. Black Book: Complaints, Information, Reports against Various Persons.

1434. 1698-1712. Copies of Affidavits, Information and Certificates received from Abroad.
    Similar to **1433**.

1435-1437. 1694-1743. Servants of the Company: List Books of Passengers, Ships' Crews, and Particulars of Passengers, Salaries, and Diet while on Board, etc.

1440-1448. 1673-1741. List of Living and Dead at the Company's Forts.

1449. 1730-1735. Letters of Attorney for Payment of Servants' Salaries.

1450-1453. 1730-1746. Castle Charge Books.

1454-1456. 1750-1815. Register of Servants and Officers.

1457-1461. 1751-1816. Cape Coast Castle Pay Bills.

1462. 1785-1791. African Corps, Independent Companies and Convicts' Pay Bills.

1463-1466. 1703-1730. Various Minutes, Diaries, and Copy Books of Diaries at Various Places: Royal African Company.

1467-1473. 1750-1810. Journals, Diaries, etc., of the Company of Merchants.

1474-1487. 1713-1809. Letter-Books of Particular Persons.

1488-1498. 1769-1794. Account Books of Particular Persons.

1499-1504. 1718-1822. Dead Men's Effects. Books concerning Sales.

1505-1507. Charter, Oath Book, and List of Stockholders of the Royal African Company (1720).

1508-1510. 1756-1819. List of Stockholders of Company of Merchants.

PAPERS.

1511-1512. 1706-1735. Receipt Books for Papers.
1513-1514. 1681-1745. *Id.* Bills of Lading.

DETACHED PAPERS.

1515. Prior to 1750.
1516-1606. 1750-1820.
1607-1663. Alphabets or Indices.

AMERICAN LOYALIST CLAIMS.

The large collection of papers relating to the claims of American Loyalists owes its origin to the attempts made in the years 1783-1803 to carry out the terms of the 6th article of the treaty of Paris regarding the Loyalists and their property. The acts of 23 George III., c. 80, 25 George III., c. 76, 26 George III., cc. 61, 68, 28 George III., c. 40, and 29 George III., cc. 61, 62, were passed in favor of such Loyalists and sufferers and were repeated four times between 1788 and 1802, owing to the failure of the individual American states to carry out the terms of the treaty and the inability of the United States to compel them to do so. From 1784 to 1794, during the delays and negotiations occasioned by England's retention of the western posts and the many violations of article 6 of which the states were guilty, the British government paid to the Loyalists various pensions and compensations for losses, and records of such payments are contained in the documents enumerated below. In making these payments consideration was given only to debts due to British subjects which had been confiscated, in opposition to land forfeited, professional services rendered, and matters of a like nature.

By 1794 the relations between the two countries had become so strained that Washington sent John Jay to England to negotiate a new treaty. By article 6 of this treaty, which was signed on Nov. 19, 1794, by Lord Grenville for Great Britain and Jay for the United States, a board of commissioners was to be appointed to adjudicate all the Loyalist claims and to settle permanently all debts contracted prior to the peace of 1783, due to British subjects, chiefly merchants, by persons of every description, the recovery of which was hindered or prevented by legal impediments in America.

Owing to the resentment which America felt because of England's interference with her neutral rights, the discussions of the treaty in Congress, and difficulties respecting its provisions for West Indian commerce, the ratification of the treaty was delayed until 1796. In 1797 commissioners sent from England sat with the commissioners of America at Philadelphia and for two years endeavored without success to adjust the difficulty. In 1800 the British commissioners returned to England. On Jan. 8, 1802, a convention was signed by Lord Hawkesbury and Rufus King, by which England and the United States agreed upon a mutual payment of claims, and commissioners were appointed for carrying such convention into effect.

In the meantime the British board of commissioners, appointed under the Compensation Act of 1783 and continued in office by supplemental acts passed from time to time, was gradually meeting the claims which were presented to them, and under the act of 43 George III., passed in consequence of the convention of 1802, carried their work to completion. Claims to the amount of £5,408,766 6s. were preferred of which the commissioners allowed nearly one-fourth or £1,420,000 to be good. The divisible fund was £659,493, and successful claimants received dividends *pro rata*.[1] Appropriations for American Loyalists or their families continued to appear in the British budget as late as 1850.

The British commissioners were John Eardley-Wilmot, Daniel Parker Coke, Col. Robert Kingston, Col. Thomas Dundas, and John Marsh. Robert Mackenzie was added in 1786. Col. Dundas and Jeremy Pemberton were commissioners for claims in Nova Scotia. Thomas Crafer was principal clerk, and John Pugh, gentleman-assistant. The office of the commission was first in the Cockpit and afterward in Lincoln's Inn Fields. Two sets of records remain to show the work of the commission: one, consisting of the reports and declarations made at the Audit Office, forms a nearly complete body of evidence, preserved in excellent condition; the other, the original series, less complete owing to the circumstances attending its preservation, is among the Treasury papers. After the expiration of the commission these original records were deposited in a vault in Somerset House, where for some years they lay subject to theft and damage from damp.[2] Transferred to the Treasury Chambers they met with a worse fate. Contained in four large deal boxes they were deposited in the cellar where they suffered from excessive dampness and in 1846 were in part saturated with sewer water. When finally, in 1847, they were taken to the Record Office their condition was deplorable. "Many of the papers were much damaged by dirt and damp, many were in a very tender condition, greatly discoloured and the writing nearly obliterated, many documents and portions of documents had been reduced by wet in some cases to tatters and powder and in others by the obliteration of the ink to the state of discoloured and almost blank paper." Fortunately the Reports of the commissioners and a few other documents relating to the same subject had been deposited in the State Paper Office and received no harm. They were transferred to the Rolls House in 1853.

Of the two series of Loyalist records, that known as the Audit Office series is the largest and most important. It consists of volumes and bundles. The volumes are entry books and ledgers containing the memorials, the evidence of witnesses, either given verbally or in writing, the testimonials, the decisions of the board, and the allowances. These volumes must be supplemented by the ledgers of quarterly payments in *Treas.* 50: **6-28, 31-48**, and by other account books in the same class, **29, 30, 49-56**. The bundles consist of the original memorials, certificates, accounts, and vouchers of the various claimants, as presented to the commission. In some cases where the volumes are missing, the bundles supply the desired information. An index to the American Loyalist Records, Audit Office series, was prepared by the late Benjamin Franklin Stevens, and a typewritten copy will be found in the Government

[1] These are the figures given by C. H. Woodruff in his introduction to the manuscript list in the P. R. O. They should be compared with the statements in Commissioner Wilmot's *Historical View of the Commission* (1815); Lecky's *History of England,* IV. 268; and *Pa. Mag.,* XV. 350.

[2] See John E. Eardley-Wilmot's letter, *Audit Office Series,* **134,** below. On Dec. 1, 1790, the Commissioners wrote to the Treasury that their lease expired at Christmas and they wished for directions as to the disposal of their papers which were packed in seven chests. With the letter was sent a detailed inventory of the papers which can be seen in *Treas.* 1: 1790 (formerly bundle 9). *Cf. A. O. Accounts,* **127,** where are given the expenses of the commission.

Search Room of the Public Record Office. In the New York Public Library are transcripts of many of the volumes listed below, which were made by Mr. Stevens. The most convenient index to the transcripts is the volume (**109**) numbered 11 in the New York series.

(NOTE.—The following is the series in the New York Public Library:

I. B. F. Stevens, Manuscript Report on the Loyalist Records and accompanying Letters, Stevens to J. S. Billings, inserted.

II. Transcripts of various papers relating to the Losses, Services, and Support of the American Loyalists and His Majesty's Provincial Forces during the War of American Independence, preserved amongst the American Manuscripts in the Royal Institution of Great Britain, London, 1777-1783. Transcribed, 1903. Eight volumes, folio.

III. Transcripts of the Manuscript Books and Papers of the Commission of Enquiry into the Losses and Services of American Loyalists, held under Acts of Parliament, of 23, 25, 26, 28, and 29 of George III., preserved amongst the Audit Office Records in the Public Record Office, London, 1783-1790. Transcribed, 1898-1903. Sixty volumes, folio.

    1. Information conveyed to the Commissioners.
    2-3. Temporary Support Claims (Old Claims).
    4-8. *Id.* (Fresh Claims).
    9. Minutes of the Commission in London.
    10. Minutes of the Commission in Nova Scotia.
    11. Commissioners' Reports, Claims Liquidated, Acts of Parliament.
    12. Examinations in Nova Scotia, etc. Connecticut Claimants.
    13. *Id.* Delaware, Georgia, Maryland, and Massachusetts Claimants.
    14. *Id.* Massachusetts and New Hampshire Claimants.
    15-16. *Id.* New Jersey Claimants.
    17-24. *Id.* New York Claimants.
    25. *Id.* Pennsylvania Claimants.
    26. *Id.* South Carolina Claimants.
    27. *Id.* North Carolina, Vermont, and Virginia Claimants.
    28. Determinations in Nova Scotia, etc., on claims from various Provinces.
    29-31. *Id.,* from New York.
    32. *Id.,* from various Provinces.
    33. Nova Scotia Claims, Letter Book, London Claims, Index to Evidences, London and American.
    34. Examinations in London. Georgia Claimants.
    35-37. *Id.* Maryland Claimants, and in 37, Delaware Claimants.
    38-40. *Id.* New Jersey Claimants.
    41-46. *Id.* New York Claimants.
    47-48. *Id.* North Carolina Claimants.
    49-51. *Id.* Pennsylvania Claimants.
    52-57. *Id.* South Carolina Claimants.
    58-59. *Id.* Virginia Claimants.
    60. *Id.* East Florida Claimants.
        This volume of 798 pages contains the examinations in London, memorials, schedules of losses, and evidences in regard to East Florida claimants, and furnishes a record of the losses " suffered in their properties in consequence of the cession of the province of East Florida to the King of Spain. These persons, with but few exceptions, had been the loyal inhabitants of Georgia and South Carolina, and on the evacuation of the garrison at Charleston in 1782 had found an asylum in East Florida ".

IV. Calendar of the Original Memorials, Vouchers, and Other Papers deposited with the Commission of Enquiry into the Losses and Services of the American Loyalists held under Acts of Parliament of 23, 25, 26, 28, and 29 of George III., preserved amongst the Audit Office Records in the Public Record Office, London, 1783-1790. Transcribed, 1903. Six volumes, folio.)

AUDIT OFFICE SERIES.

1-56. 1783-1790. Evidence, that is, Memorials of Claimants.

> A. O. Claims.
> American
> Loyalists.
> —

Of this series fourteen volumes are missing. The remainder has been copied for the New York Public Library (vols. 12-27, 34-59). See *Bulletin,* 1899, p. 416; 1900, pp. 7, 388; 1901, p. 315. Vol. **40**, labelled " Maryland ", contains New Hampshire papers relating to Gov. Wentworth's claim and has been copied for the state of New Hampshire. Vol. **53** contains Francis Waldo's memorial.

57-70. 1785-1790. Decisions, that is, Determination of Claims.
(Copied, N. Y. P. Lib., vols. 28-32.)

71-76. 1788-1790. Examinations: Supplies for the Army and Navy.

77. Index to vols. **71-76.** See also **120** and **122.**

78-95. 1783-1790. Letters, information, etc.

96-102. 1782-1790. Minute books and examinations on fresh claims.
(Copied, N. Y. P. Lib., vols. 9, 10, 4-8.)

103-106. 1783-1790. Tabular statements for colonies.
(Copied, N. Y. P. Lib., vols. 2, 3.)

107. 1782-1785. Intelligence.
(Copied, N. Y. P. Lib., vol. 1.)

108. 1783-1790. Debts due to Loyalists.

109. 1784-1789. Reports and Statements.

This volume contains a summary of proceedings and includes names of claimants, amount of claims, and particulars of liquidation, in tabular form from A to Z. Thus it constitutes a kind of alphabetical index, furnishing a list of the names of those whose records of claims will be found somewhere in the other volumes of the series.
(Copied, N. Y. P. Lib., vol. 11.)

110, 111. 1783. Names of Claimants.

112. 1785-1787. Claims Withdrawn.

113. 1786-1787. Secretary's Letters.

114. 1786-1788. Lists of Papers sent to England.

115. 1783-1790. Recapitulation of Claims.

116. 1780-1783. Books of Claimants.

117-118. 1783. Minutes.

119. 1785-1788. Notices issued at Halifax and Montreal.

120, 122. Supplies to Army and Navy. Index to **71-76.**

121. 1788-1790. Losses sustained by supplying the Navy.
(Copied, N. Y. P. Lib., vol. 10.)

123-124. 1789-1790. New Claims.
(Copied, N. Y. P. Lib., forming part of vol. 33.)

125-128. 1785. Minutes on New Claims.
(Copied, N. Y. P. Lib., part of vol. 33.)

129-130. General Index to Evidence Books.
  (Copied, N. Y. P. Lib., parts of vol. 33.)

131. 1786-1788. Contingent Expenses.
132. 1778-1782. Confiscation Laws, etc.
133. 1785-1788. Minute Book.
  (Copied, N. Y. P. Lib., part of vol. 33.)

134-135. 1815-1831. Letters as to Claims.
136-138. Alphabetical List of Claimants.
  (Copied, N. Y. P. Lib., parts of vols. 3 and 8.)

139. 1785-1789. Letter-Book.
  (Copied, N. Y. P. Lib., part of vol. 33.)

140. 1785. Causes unexamined.
141. 1785-1789. Reports.
142. 1781. Rough account books.
143. 1784. Losses of divers persons.
145. 1786-1787. Statements to the House of Commons.
146. 1785-1786. Reports.

The following numbers are bundles.

1-10. Examinations, etc. A-Z. Claims for supplies furnished to the army and navy. They correspond with vols. **71-76.**
11-26. New Claims, arranged by states and under each state alphabetically.
27-49. Claims.
49-51. New Claims.
52-53. Claims.
54-56. Temporary Assistance.
57-59. New Claims.
60-69. Temporary Support (**66**, wanting).
70-72. New Claims.
73-75. Temporary Assistance.
76-77. New Claims.
78-79. Letters, etc.
80. Claims received too late.
81. New Claims.
82-85. Various Claims.
86-89. Letters.
90-107. Various Papers.
108-116. Temporary Assistance.
117-136. Claims.
137-140. Miscellaneous.

  (All these bundles have been listed, calendared, and their contents noted in six manuscript volumes now in the New York Public Library. See note above, p. 261, IV.)

Treasury Series.

Treas. 75.	**1-59, 65, 66.** Claims.
	60, 61, 64. Letters.
	62-63, 67-72. Miscellaneous Documents.

(Of these volumes **70** and **71**, which are really Audit Office volumes, have been copied for the New York Public Library.)

73-123. Entry Books of Special Agents' Reports on Claims.

124-151. Report of the Commissioners.

70. Index of Names.

84. General Index.

(For the declaration of accounts of disbursements to Loyalists see *A. O. Decl.* Acc., **326**, 1291, 1292; **458**, 4, 5; **459**, 7-43; **850**, 1; **1259**, 432; **1300**, 473; **1324**, 627.

Thirty-four volumes of Loyalist testimony, taken by Commrs. Dundas, Pemberton, and Mackenzie, and one volume containing the reports of the commissioners in England and America, are in the Library of Congress (N. Y. P. Library *Bulletin*, 1899, p. 416; *Guide to the Archives at Washington*, 2d ed., p. 267). These volumes, which contain material more valuable than the corresponding transcripts in the Public Record Office, are printed in the *Second Report of the Bureau of Archives for the Province of Ontario* (1904). This report contains a valuable introduction giving a history of these papers (pp. 4-25). The reports of the British commissioners are given on pp. 1336-1351; that of the commissioners in Nova Scotia on pp. 1351-1376.)

EAST FLORIDA CLAIMS.

" By the treaty of peace concluded at Paris in 1763, East Florida was ceded to Great Britain as an equivalent for the island of Cuba. In consequence of this cession many British subjects settled there, obtained grants of land, and cultivated estates. During the troubles in North America prior to the Declaration of Independence by the United States of America, East Florida remained faithful to the English Crown. In 1776 the people rejected the invitation to join in the great confederation, raised a militia, and repulsed the Georgians in 1777, and East Florida became the rallying point and refuge for Loyalists from the revolted provinces. In 1780 a legislature was formed, which granted in perpetuity to the Crown of England an irrevocable duty of $2\frac{1}{2}$ per cent. on certain imports.

" By the 5th article of the Treaty of Peace concluded at Versailles, 1783, this colony was delivered up to the Crown of Spain. In 1785 the British Parliament passed an act (26 George III., c. 75) entitled, ' An Act for appointing commissioners to inquire into the losses of all such persons who have suffered in their properties in consequence of the cession of East Florida to the King of Spain '. A commission was constituted and two commissioners were appointed to inquire into the respective losses of the sufferers by the cession of the above province. A time was limited for the reception of claims, viz.: in the Bahamas, where many East Floridans had taken refuge, March 1, 1787, and in Great Britain, January 1, 1787. A further act was passed (28 George III., c. 40) entitled, ' An Act for giving relief to such persons as have suffered in their rights and properties during the late unhappy dissensions in America in consequence of their loyalty to the British government and for making compensation to such persons as have suffered in their properties in consequence of the cession of East Florida to the King of Spain '. By the second section of this act the East Florida Commissioners were required to make report to the Treasury, prior to January 1, 1789, and by the third section the Lords of the Treasury were empowered to make provisions for payment to claimants entitled to compensation." (From the introduction to the manuscript list.)

The records of the East Florida Claims Commission were transferred to the Rolls House in 1847. They had suffered from sewer water, while lying in the Treasury cellar, only less seriously than had the records of the Loyalist Claims Commission.

1-18. 1787-1789. Claims, alphabetically arranged.

> Treas. 77.
> ——

Many of these papers were much injured in the Treasury vault. Some of the names in the lists do not represent claimants, but may possibly refer to persons through whom the claimants derived their titles.

19. Reports on Claims, Bahama Islands.

20. Miscellaneous Papers.

Allowances on claims, lists of title deeds, etc., of claimants, statements of land laid out, accounts of the inspector general of refugees (*cf. Declared Accounts, A. O.,* **850,** 1), report upon the general state of East Florida and its inhabitants, etc.

21. Rough Drafts of Correspondence, etc.

22. Fragments decayed past recovery.

Supplemental to the bundles noted above is a volume among the Colonial Papers, as follows:

Colonial Office, Class 5: **562.** 1787-1789. Eight Reports of Col. Nisbet Balfour and John Spranger, Esq., commissioners on East Florida Claims, dated from the East Florida Claims Office, Southampton Buildings, Chancery Lane, and transmitted by the secretary of the Commission, H. C. Litchfield, to Lord Sydney.

    I. Report drawn up, Jan. 30, 1787; transmitted, Feb. 5, 1787.

    II. Report transmitted, Mar. 13, 1787.

    III. Report drawn up, May 9, 1787; transmitted, May 12, 1787.

    IV. Report drawn up and transmitted, Nov. 3, 1787.

    V. Report drawn up and transmitted, Mar. 14, 1788.

    VI. Report drawn up, June 7, 1788; transmitted, June 12, 1788.

    VII. Report drawn up, Dec. 20, 1788; transmitted, Dec. 22, 1788.

    VIII. Report drawn up, May 29, 1789; transmitted, June 6, 1789.

These reports are very full and complete, covering the entire work of the commission, giving number and amounts of losses, character of claims, etc. At the end of I. is a preliminary schedule, with the values of the real and personal property lost; at the end of II. are schedules of actual claims and losses, that is, of actual amounts allowed, with " observations "; similar schedules are at the end of III., IV., V.; but only abstracts at the end of VI., VII., VIII.; the last report contains a general summing up. The number of claims was 369; the total amount claimed, £647,405 6s. 9d.; the amount actually allowed, £169,818 18s. 5½d.

In *Decl. Acc., A. O.,* **861,** 4, is the declaration of the account of H. C. Litchfield, secretary to the commission. In *Treas. Solicitor Papers,* **3662,** are important documents relating to the same subject.

18

TREASURY SOLICITOR PAPERS.

All papers from the Department of the Treasury Solicitor, of date earlier than the nineteenth century, are now in the Public Record Office. Originally stored in 10 Whitehall, neglected and in confusion, many of the papers destroyed by damp and others injured and often unreadable, they were finally removed to the Chapter House in 1853 and to Chancery Lane two years later. They filled 230 tin and wooden boxes and chests, the number of bundles as finally arranged reaching 11,000, each bundle containing the documents relating to a single case. The papers always have been and are still kept strictly private, opened to the searcher only with the permission of the solicitor.

After the papers had been sorted and arranged in the Public Record Office, a manuscript calendar was prepared lettered F. **1**, 1584-1753; F. **2**, 1754-1820; F. **3**, 1820-1850, and Index, F. **6**. Each bundle is numbered, but there does not appear to be any connection between the sequence of numbers and the chronological arrangement. Great quantities of papers have been destroyed, as is evident from the gaps in the numbers that remain. The collection is disappointing, as no colonial cases are to be found of date earlier than 1756, and the total number of such cases is but seventeen at most. From the declared accounts of the Treasury solicitor (above, pp. 77, 103) it appears that prosecutions involving colonial interests came before the solicitor of the Treasury as early as 1675. For an account of the papers see the Deputy Keeper's *19th Report*, p. 14; and for a list of the Treasury solicitors, 1698-1851, *ibid.*, 14-15.

3888. 1756. Appeal in Privy Council. Old John Uncas and the greater part of the tribe of Mohegan Indians, by Samuel Mason, their Guardian, *vs.* the Governor and Company of Connecticut and George Richards, Esq., and several other persons intruders on the Land in question.

> Treas. Solicitor.
> Bundle —.

Mason's petition, with (1) a copy of the estimate annexed to the petitioner's former petition in 1741, (2) an account of money disbursed by the petitioner more than was computed in the foregoing estimate ("This exceeding was occasioned by the unexpected length of the proceedings on the last Commission which make a large volume containing 392 pages, close writ in folio"), (3) an account of the charges attending the despatches and execution of the commission of reviews to determine the controversy more than was received in 1741 from the Treasury and of the subsequent expenses on the appeal, as also an estimate of the future expenses necessary for bringing the said appeal to a final conclusion. The account is full of interesting details; the petition was made to the Treasury and referred to the solicitor, Oct. 6, 1752. *Cf. Acts Privy Council, Colonial,* vol. III., § 392.

Additional papers:

Copy of the order in Council. Jan. 29, 1740.
Copy of Sharpe's report on the petitions. June 4, 1756.

Copy of Mason's petition, with Ferdinand John Paris's letter of Mar. 12, 1756.

Copy of the judgment of the commissioners. Aug. 16, 1743.

Mason's memorial, probably of 1755.

Order in Council. Jan. 14, 1752.

The appellant's case giving an historical outline to 1743.

5158. 1763. A printed paper entitled *A Full State of the Dispute betwixt the Governor and the Commons House of Assembly of South Carolina. With the proper Vouchers and Reasons in support of the Proceedings of the House of Assembly, as transmitted to their Agent in Great Britain. Printed in the year MDCCLXIII.*

1210. 1766. In the Exchequer, between the Hon. and Rev. Robert Cholmondeley, Surveyor and Auditor General of his Majesty's Revenues in America: plaintiff, and William Mathew Burt, Esq., late his Majesty's agent for Guadeloupe in America: defendant. Bill filed Trinity Term, 1766.

Copy of Cholmondeley's patent as auditor general, Nov. 20, 1752. The immediate question was whether or not Cholmondeley could audit the revenue accounts of Guadeloupe; the larger question whether or not he could audit the accounts of territories in America or the West Indies either taken from the enemy and held for a short time or acquired and annexed to the crown since the date of patent. Cholmondeley's brief quotes many precedents: Blathwayt's claim, and the order allowing the claim, to audit the accounts of New York, even though in the hands of the Duke of York, June 10, 1686 (order addressed to Lucas Santen, collector in New York); Walpole's claim to audit prizes taken in America during the war with Spain after 1718, and to audit accounts of Carolina, 1730 (both claims allowed by the Treasury); Cholmondeley's own claim to examine and audit accounts of commissioners appointed to take charge of prizes taken from the French previous to the declaration of war (allowed by the Treasury in the order of Aug. 1, 1758); copies of other petitions and arguments supporting his case. Burt's answer bears many corrections. Cause appointed to be heard July 1, 1766. Copies of brief, bill, Cholmondeley's case, Blathwayt's commission, and opinion of the attorney general and solicitor general on Cholmondeley's patent, which was adverse to the first claim and doubtful on the second. Evidently the trial was a feigned issue in order to obtain a judicial opinion.

825. 1767. In the Common Pleas, between a number of plaintiffs and Gov. James Murray, " for payment of duties, levied by Murray as governor of Quebec, on the ground that they were unlawfully levied ". Hilary Term, 8 George III.

4957. 1768. In the King's Bench, Suit of Major Robert Rogers *vs.* Gen. Gage, on the ground of trespass, assault, and imprisonment, with damages at £20,000.

Exhibits:

Copy of the proceedings at a court-martial held at Montreal, Oct., 1768, for the trial of Rogers, when in command at Michilimackinac, for forming designs of deserting to the French, and for holding a correspondence with His Majesty's enemies (the court acquitted Rogers, but asserted that " at the same time it appears to his Majesty that there was good reason to suspect the same Major Rogers entertaining an improper and dangerous correspondence, which suspicion the account afterwards given of his meditating an escape tended to confirm ").

Copy of Rogers's correspondence, 1766, and other papers in evidence against Rogers.

Copy of his commission to Jonathan Carver, Aug. 12, 1766, and to Capt. James Tuke, of the detachment ordered for the discovery of the river " Ourigan " and the northwest passage.

Narrative of Gen. Gage's proceedings against Rogers, with letters from Capt. Spiesmacher, Lieut. Christie, Potter's deposition, letter from Commissioner Roberts, Daniel Claus's letter to Guy Johnson, and other papers connected with the suit, sixteen in all, in duplicate and triplicate.

3321. 1768. In the Exchequer, the Attorney-General *vs.* the East India Company, respecting the duties on Tea. Information filed, Hilary Term, IX. George III.

Deals with the exportation of tea to the colonies and the drawbacks thereon, in reference to the meaning and construction of the act of Parliament, 7 George III., c. 56.

Petition of the company to Parliament, May 20, 1767, with the report of the committee of Parliament.

Brief for the crown.

State of the question between the Treasury and the East India Company respecting the tea duties.

65. 1769. King *vs.* George Robinson, for publishing in *The Independent Chronicle* from Monday, Dec. 18, to Wednesday, Dec. 20, 1769, No. 36, a libel commencing thus, " When the complaints of a brave and powerful people ", etc. (Junius's letter.)

Other similar trials follow, F. **2**, p. 402, notably **765**, King *vs.* John Almon for publishing the same.

4377. 1771. Appeal in Privy Council from Harry Smith, collector of customs, St. Vincent, *vs.* Richard Otley, respondent.

62. 1775. King *vs.* John Horne, clerk, for publishing on June 8, 1775, the following libel: " At a special meeting of the Constitutional Society, June 7, 1775, proposed that a subscription be raised for the relief of the widows, orphans, and aged parents of our beloved American Fellow Subjects, who faithful to the character of Englishmen, preferring death to Slavery, were, for that reason only, inhumanly murdered by the King's troops at or near Lexington and Concord ", etc.

4710. 1776-1778. King *vs.* Ebenezer Platt for high treason at Savannah, Georgia.

Ebenezer Platt was a " committee man " of Georgia, who boarded the *Philippa* at Savannah in 1775, and seized all the gunpowder of the government, carrying it to the rebels. Others, Levi, Shafto, etc., were engaged in the same business by order of the committee. Platt was captured and confined on a ship of war from Mar., 1776, to Jan., 1777, and then taken to England, where he was heavily ironed and imprisoned in Newgate. He petitioned in 1778 for trial or admission to bail. The case is an interesting one.

3620. 1779. *Re* Valentine Morris, governor of St. Vincent.

3662. 1780-1820. East Florida Claims and Claims for Losses on the Mosquito Shore, 1780. Also **3666**.

A mass of papers relating to claims in East Florida, with a few relating to the Mosquito Shore, sent to H. C. Litchfield in 1820, after Florida had been ceded to the United States in 1819. The papers were sent to Litchfield as secretary to the Commissioners on East Florida Claims and are here filed because Litchfield was solicitor of the Treasury at this time.

Among the papers are:

Printed copy of the convention between Great Britain and Spain. July 14, 1786.

Claims of William Turnbull and Mrs. Harvey, children of Dr. Andrew Turnbull who conducted the Greek immigrants to Florida.

Other claims dating back to 1804.

Bills, accounts, etc.

Great numbers of miscellaneous papers.

Among the last are a copy of the *South Carolina and American General Gazette,* Apr. 2, 1778, and a " List of East Florida claimants who emigrated to the Revolted American States "; William Drayton, Dr. Andrew Turnbull, James Penman, Spencer Mason, Andrew Turnbull, jr., are named, and valuable comments are made on their careers.

Also a statement from the Commission on American Loyalist Claims regarding whether or not losses of land claimed under grants from the crown, the conditions of which have not been complied with in respect of cultivation, are an object of inquiry under the act. Answer adverse, Feb. 2, 1784. The papers include, also, great numbers of notes or depositions of claimants taken before the Commissioners on East Florida Claims.

1206. 1781. Chancery proceedings between Jacob Jordan and Lieut.-Gen. John Burgoyne, defendant. Bill filed, May 30, 1781.

Jacob Jordan lived in Montreal and furnished a carriage train and many supplies for Burgoyne's army. He afterward sued Burgoyne for payment and his brief is full of interesting details. Burgoyne's answer, which contains many interlineations and corrections, is given; also the amended bill, Nov. 7, 1782, and Burgoyne's answer to that; copy of the bill; order for the defendant to examine witnesses. The papers are somewhat damaged.

2080. 1786. *Re* St. Eustatius and its dependencies.

954. 1786. In the King's Bench, between George Macbeth, plaintiff, and Frederick Haldimand, Esq., defendant.

Macbeth was a trader in Canada and sued Gov. Haldimand for money due. A similar suit follows.

151. 1792-1793. Suits against the publishers who issued the whole or a part of Paine's *Rights of Man.* Also in bundles **2289, 1893, 2910, 2717, 3335, 3419, 4053, 1657.**

WAR OFFICE PAPERS.

INTRODUCTION.

During the colonial period the British army was a decentralized force, made up of independent, self-containing regiments of infantry and cavalry, locally raised, and in large part disbanded when no longer needed for active service. Before 1689 the only lawfully permanent forces were the guards of the king's person and the garrisons in special fortresses. Even after 1689, when an army under the control of Parliament was annually created by the Mutiny Bill, no central board or staff existed that can rightly be termed a war office. War policy was directed by that particular secretary of state, within whose territory lay the seat of the war—the Northern Secretary if the war was in northern Europe, the Southern Secretary, if in southern Europe or the colonies, and both, if the territory of both was involved. At the head of the army was a general-in-chief, and in addition there was a secretary, variously known as the secretary at war to all the forces, the secretary to the general of the forces, or the secretary for the affairs of the army. There was a similar secretary at war as well as an independent military establishment for Ireland until 1800 and another for Scotland till 1707. Such official had nothing to do with the militia, which was under the Secretary of State for the Southern Department and the lieutenants of the counties, and nothing to do with the guards and garrisons, which were under the direct command of the king. All matters of arms and ammunition were controlled by the Ordnance Board, which took its orders only from the king, while the business of victualling and transport was managed directly by the Treasury. The forces were paid by an independent official, appointed by the Treasury, the paymaster-general of the forces, and the establishment and allowances for the companies in the plantations, New York, Jamaica, Leeward Islands, Bermuda, Nova Scotia, Newfoundland, etc., the earliest of which was sent over about 1679, thus forming the beginning of a permanent imperial garrison, were fixed by the King in Council. The marines, dating from 1672, came eventually under the control of the Admiralty.

The nucleus of the War Office was the office of the Secretary at War, the origin of which can be traced to the period of the Civil War. William Clarke held that position under Cromwell, and, as Sir William Clarke, was commissioned Secretary at War by Charles II. Jan. 28, 1661. He accompanied the lord general of the forces, the Duke of Albemarle, on board the *Royal Charles,* to the battle with the Dutch, June 2, 1666, where he was wounded and died two days after. At Albemarle's request the king commissioned the duke's private secretary, Matthew Lock, June 20, 1666. Lock had been secretary at war for Ireland, 1661-1662, and adjutant of a foot regiment in England. He was succeeded August 18, 1683, by William Blathwayt, auditor general of the plantation revenues.[1] As Secretary at War Blathwayt accompanied Marlborough

---

[1] The commission to Blathwayt reads as follows: " James II. to all to whom these presents shall come, greeting. Know ye that we reposing especial trust and confidence in the care, fidelity, and circumspection of our trusty and well beloved William Blathwayt, do grant the office and place of my secretary at war to all my standing forces

and William III. to Flanders during the war with France, and in his absence George Clarke, son of Sir William Clarke, acted as his deputy at Whitehall.[1] Blathwayt held the office till 1704 and under his direction it assumed considerable prominence and the papers relating to his incumbency are numerous and important. He was succeeded by St. John, Walpole, Granville, Wyndham, Gwyn, Pulteney, Craggs, Pringle, Treby, Pelham, Yonge,[2] Henry Fox, Lord Barrington, Charles Townshend, Welbore Ellis, and Charles Jenkinson, the last secretary of the colonial period.

In the seventeenth century, till after 1689, both the general of the forces and the Secretary at War had as much to do with the navy as with the army. Both concerned themselves with minor naval appointments, such as gunners and boatswains, who were fighting officers, and sent instructions to the Navy Board. The secretary looked after embargoes, impressments, and transports, and the distribution of booty, and inasmuch as the army was designed for service at sea quite as much as for service on land, the affairs of the navy were for a long time intimately bound up with the interests of the army. Later these dual functions tended to separate; the Admiralty took entire charge of the marines and the Treasury of transport, and the Secretary at War confined his activities to matters that were strictly military.

The duties of the secretary concerned the army wherever it might be. He saw to the raising of levies and the filling up of the regiments with new recruits, and he sent the muster-masters to inspect the regiments when filled. He looked after the quartering and billeting of the soldiers and gave marching orders. He had to know the rules and regulations governing the raising of new levies, and with the aid of the paymaster-general, the master-general of ordnance, and the treasurer of the navy, he drew up the army estimates. He prepared the first draft of the establishment conformably to the estimates laid before Parliament, and he obtained from the king triplicates of these establishments which he laid before the Treasury for the signatures of the board, one for the Treasury, one for the War Office, and one for the paymaster general. As a member of the House of Commons, he had to move the army estimates[3] and in conjunction with the judge advocate general to meet every attack of the opposition upon the commander-in-chief or his office. He looked after the commissions of the officers and the payment of their fees, and countersigned the royal sign manual authorizing their appointments.[4]

both horse and foot, which are now raised and of all my forces and armes which at any time hereafter shall be raised in my kingdom of England, Dominion of Wales, and Town of Berwick upon Tweed and other any Dominion and Territories thereunto belonging and him the said William Blathwayt our Secretary at War to all our standing forces both horse and foot . . . We hereby make, ordain, and institute to have, hold, exercise, and enjoy the said place . . . unto the said William Blathwayt during my pleasure, to be executed by himself or such sufficient deputy or deputies as shall be appointed or allowed by us in writing under my royal sign manual, together with all such fees, rights, etc., thereunto belonging . . . to accept orders from us, my general or commander in chief of our said forces for the time being, according to the rules and discipline of war." *Patent Rolls,* 1 James II., pt. XI., no. 17. The form in later times underwent few changes; see the text of the last commission, 1855, Clode, *Military Forces of the Crown,* I. 687.

[1] According to Pennant, *History and Antiquities of London,* II. 83, referring to Reresby's *Memoirs,* p. 346, William III. offered the office, Apr. 12, 1689, to John Temple, son of Sir William Temple, in Blathwayt's place, but two days afterward Temple committed suicide, giving as his reason his " folly in undertaking what he could not perform".

[2] See ante, p. 3.

[3] The army estimates are regularly given in the *Commons Journal.*

[4] A sign manual warrant of James II., appointing the captain of a regiment in England, countersigned by W. Blathwayt, Nov. 9, 1688, a few days before the king fled from London, was sold in 1913 at Sotheby's.

He controlled certain distributions of money, though the paymaster-general made up the accounts of disbanded regiments, paying the arrears to the colonels, who stated the amounts to the captains. He provided the king with soldiers for special guard service, and after 1735 saw to the removal, for three days while the polling was going on, of troops quartered in places of election.[1] In the seventeenth century his pay was twenty shillings a day, with five shillings for his clerk. In 1720 the clerical establishment numbered nine, and cost £580. There were also certain fees and perquisites, and the secretary was able to hold his office by deputy. Under Barrington the office assumed the dignity of a great department and in 1760 contained a deputy secretary, a first clerk, and twelve other clerks, fourteen in all.

During the war period from 1754 to 1783 the powers of the secretary were rapidly and widely extended. The records of the office became voluminous, even though hundreds of papers relating to military affairs found their way into the state papers, notably those of the Southern Department. The office was organized in all respects as were other departments of the British government, except that it had no board and kept no minutes. Barrington and his successors sent important despatches to the commanders-in-chief in America and to the colonial governors, and received letters from them in return. They corresponded with the under officers in the field and with a great variety of other individuals, and to a greater extent than in the earlier period directed the policy and operations of the troops in America. They looked after the despatch and transport of troops, received petitions for pay and half-pay, rewards and compensations, promotions and leaves of absence, and had complete oversight of discharges, captures, military hospitals, courts-martial, prisoners of war, deserters, and leaves of absence. They could compel absent officers to rejoin their regiments, could control exchanges of prisoners and the invaliding of soldiers, could use the troops to put down riots, and in general were expected to look after the troops in any part of the British empire, except Ireland and the Isle of Man. They kept a record of the war establishment, made up the army list, first printed in 1754 and published annually thereafter, watched the careers of the men, and controlled commissions of army officers and military governors, promotions, and all matters that related to appointments, regimental successions, and the like, with which the Secretary of State did not often interfere. They filed headquarters records, engineers' returns, garrison and hospital returns, and furnished statistical information on these points whenever desired. They carried out all details touching foreign troops in the pay of Great Britain, their charges, numbers, transportation, and losses.

Beyond the duties mentioned, the Secretary at War had no authority and assumed no responsibility. At first all plans of campaign were formulated by the Secretary of State or the commander-in-chief, though later, partly because there was no commander-in-chief in England from 1759 to 1766 and from 1769 to 1778, the Secretary at War had considerable influence upon matters of policy. This was particularly true of Barrington, a secretary honest and consistent, with definite ideas regarding the conduct of his office and firmness of attitude in their execution. But at best the secretary's powers were limited. He had nothing to do with discipline, which was exercised by the colonel. He had no control over the Ordnance Office. This important department was under the master-general and Board of Ordnance, which had an office in Westminster on the north side of St. Margaret Street after 1752, hav-

[1] 8 George II., c. 30. *Cf. W. O.* 4: **711-713.**

ing formerly occupied quarters in Westminster Hall. It had charge of the artillery and engineer corps, barracks, fortifications, and works, and all supplies of arms and ammunition. The business end of the Ordnance Department was at the Tower,[1] and the office there, located in what was known as " Cold Harbour ", was directly under the authority of the board. The Secretary at War could not order a pennyworth of provisions, straw, wood, or bedding, for the Ordnance Board took its commands only from the king.

The Secretary at War corresponded with other departments and, of course, at great length, with the Secretary of State, to whom were referred many cases of departmental disagreement. Letters and petitions received were transmitted from the office of the secretary and generally bear the latter's comments. The Secretary at War received also many orders from the Privy Council, the House of Lords, and the House of Commons for information and for statistics regarding the army. In general he took his orders from the King in Council and the Secretary of State only, and not from the commander-in-chief, if we are to accept the argument in Lord Palmerston's well-known memorandum of 1811.[2] Despite the importance of his office, the Secretary at War had no constitutional responsibility and his duties are nowhere defined by statute.[3] Consequently his office became the centre of much political jobbery and manipulation, particularly in regard to commissions, appointments, and regimental inspections. So unsatisfactory had the situation become by the close of the Revolutionary War, that in 1783 an act was passed which transformed the influential official of Barrington's day into a financial administrator, preparing and submitting the army estimates and the annual mutiny bill to Parliament and framing the articles of war.[4] These duties, further regulated by royal warrant in 1812, kept the office alive until its abolition in 1863.[5]

Of the army itself little need be said here.[6] Each regiment was an independent unit under the colonel, who raised it and was responsible for its finance and discipline. The colonel received the money issued for the regiment by the paymaster-general, and out of it provided for the pay, clothing, and maintenance of his men. The pay of the officers was rather an *honorarium* than pay properly so called, while that of the men was nothing more than a retaining fee for purposes of loot.[7] From both, stoppages were made for Chelsea Hospital and the regimental agent, and from the soldiers' pay

[1] For the Ordnance Department in 1708 see Hatton, *New View*, II. 634, in 1761, Dodsley, *London and its Environs*, V. 70-76. The office at the Tower was taken down and rebuilt in 1775 on account of damage done by fire.

[2] Clode, *Military Forces of the Crown*, II. 689-714.

[3] Before 1783 the Secretary at War is mentioned, I believe, in but one statute, that of 1735 requiring him to remove the soldiers at the time of elections.

[4] 23 George III., c. 50, §§ 20, 22, 26, 27, 28, 29, 35, 37, 38.

[5] Clode, *Military Forces of the Crown*, II. 273, 687; Anson, II., *The Crown*, pt. II., 196. Captain Owen Wheeler's *The War Office, Past and Present* (London, 1914) is published too late for use in this book, but, to judge from reviews, is valuable.

[6] Clode, *passim*; Reide, *A Treatise on Military Forces*, 9th ed., 1805. The various acts for the better regulating the forces, including those in America, are: 11 Anne, c. 4; 1 George I., c. 3; 8 George I., c. 3; 18 George II., c. 10; 29 George II., c. 35; 5 George III., c. 33; 6 George III., c. 18; 7 George III., c. 55; 11 George III., c. 11; 12 George III., c. 12; 13 George III., c. 24; 14 George III., cc. 6, 54; 16 George III., c. 11.

[7] The same idea governed the raising of troops in the colonies. In 1744 Massachusetts, wishing to raise a force of 3000 men for the Louisburg expedition, proposed that " each person so enlisting be allowed twenty five shillings per month and that there be delivered to each man a blanket, that one month's pay be advanc'd, and that they be entitul'd to all the plunder ". *Correspondence of William Shirley*, ed. C. H. Lincoln (New York, 1912), I. 170.

certain percentages were deducted for medicines, for the paymaster-general, for specified victuallings,[1] and for clothing. Of actual pay the men received practically nothing. After the regiment had been raised, by recruiting agents under the direction of the nobleman or gentleman of rank to whom a commission as colonel had been granted, the muster was taken by the muster-master and examined by the comptrollers of army accounts. Frauds arose in both connections, the muster-master either passing the regiment as complete when it was not so, or giving his certificate without seeing a single man, and the comptrollers, who were bound by their instructions to inspect all musters and muster-rolls, neglecting to find out whether such rolls had been issued or not.[2] The army had also a judge advocate general to administer military law,[3] and an apothecary general whose business it was to furnish the several regiments " with good and wholesome medicaments ".[4]

The office of the Secretary at War must have been at first in or near the chambers of the Duke of Albemarle at the Cockpit. Lock is mentioned as having an office at the Guards House in 1676, and probably Blathwayt used Little Wallingford House for the same purpose. Clarke dated his letters from the Horse Guards in 1697. We learn that for a time the War Office was located on the south side of Pall Mall, in the old Ordnance Office, built for the Duke of Cumberland, when captain-general. For the greater part of the early eighteenth century, however, the Secretary at War, the deputy secretary and clerks, the paymaster-general of the forces, and the commissary-general of musters had their quarters in a building on the east side of the street leading from Charing Cross to Westminster, about where the War Office is today. This building had a frontage on the street of 55 feet, but was only 46 feet wide at the rear, while the dimensions up one flight of stairs were only 31 feet before and behind.[5] In 1751 the present building of the Horse Guards was begun and completed in 1756, on the site of the old Guards House, the yard, and the stables, and thither the War Office was removed in the latter year. The officers there established were the commander-in-chief,[6] the Secretary at War, the paymaster-general, the quartermaster-general, the commissary-general of musters, and there were quartered later the muster-master general and paymaster-general of marines and the comptrollers of army accounts. The latter had been established earlier in two old houses, worn-out structures supported by buttresses, on the bank of the

[1] In 1747 Shirley wrote to the Duke of Newcastle sending an account " of the late Tumult, which happen'd in the Garrison [at Louisburg] upon his publishing His Majesty's Orders among the soldiers for making a Stoppage out of their pay for their Provisions ". *Correspondence,* I. 397. *Cf.* p. 461. In Nova Scotia a stoppage was made to pay the charges of the chaplain of the garrison. For the deductions, see *Treas.* 64 : **11.**

[2] On this subject see the *Report* of 1746 and the pamphlet *National Oeconomy Recommended*; Clode, *Military Forces of the Crown,* II. 8-10. The original instructions issued in 1703 to the comptroller of army accounts are given in Clode, II. 668-669. The colonels made large profits out of their regiments, even when the mustering was honestly done. Shirley, who with William Pepperrell was commissioned a colonel on the establishment and authorized to raise a regiment in America, estimated that he cleared £1000 a year. Whether this sum included the profits from the off-reckonings or not is uncertain. *Correspondence of William Shirley,* I. 505.

[3] Clode, I. 77.

[4] *Cf. Treas.* 1 : **77** ; 38 : **816.**

[5] *Crown Lease Book,* VI. 1 ; X. 141 ; XIII. 81, 95-97. The building was very irregular in shape, and in 1756 was described as old and ruinous.

[6] Sir John Ligonier, commissioned in 1757, was the first commander-in-chief to occupy the new building. For a plan showing the location of the offices, see Britton, *Public Buildings of London,* II. 67.

Thames behind the Banqueting Hall, at the end of the passage leading from the Privy Garden to the private water stairs. As these buildings were wanted by the Duke of Richmond, the comptrollers removed in 1738 to Surrey Street, but their office was burned down in 1744. Thence they moved to Spring Garden, and in 1759 to the Horse Guards.[1]

The majority of the War Office records are of date later than 1732, the earlier papers being scattered among those of the Secretary of State, the Admiralty, and the Treasury. The Ordnance records date in some instances from Queen Elizabeth's reign (stores, 1571, registers, 1594). Blathwayt's correspondence is in the British Museum, and letters from the other early secretaries are among the State Papers, Domestic, and the Admiralty papers. The earliest War Office books date from 1660 and the correspondence from about 1683. The importance of the papers for colonial history runs chiefly from 1754 to 1783. The great bulk of the books and papers now deposited in the Public Record Office were originally stored in 6 Whitehall Yard, a house across the street from the Horse Guards, usually called the War Office Depot. This house was entirely filled with the papers—floors, attic, kitchen, and even the spaces under the eaves being brought into use. In 1854 and 1855 these premises were needed for the increased business of the army and the Ordnance Medical Board, and in the latter year the entire mass of material was transferred to Chancery Lane. The amount was estimated at over 40,000 bound volumes, bundles, and parcels, filling 113 vans. During the following five years other papers were brought from the War Office, the commissariat branch, the Horse Guards branch, and elsewhere. Work on the papers was begun at once and many tons of matter were destroyed as useless. The records were, in the main, in excellent condition, though some had been damaged from water leaking through the roof of the kitchen at 6 Whitehall Yard.

IN-LETTERS.

W. O. 1.	**1-13.** 1756-1783. Letters and Enclosures, from Officers in America to the Secretary at War.

       1. 1756-1763. Letters and despatches to the secretaries at war, Barrington and Townshend, and Deputy Secretary Walpole from officers in America.

Gen. Loudoun, Gen. Abercrombie, Capt. Aldridge, J. Napier, director of hospitals in America, from St. John's, Albany, New York, Fort Edward, Lake George, London, with enclosures consisting of reports from subordinates, statistics regarding ordnance, regimental returns, schedules of papers, establishment lists, copies of letters referred to, petitions from officers, etc., including " Maj. Gen. Shirley's answer to the Earl of Loudoun's representation of the state of the military chest in North America at the time of Maj. Gen. Abercrombie's entering on the chief command there ".

Letters from Gen. Shirley, May 8, June 25, 1759, Sept. 1, 1760–Jan. 26, 1761, Capt. Warburton (copy of his commission), Gen. Bouquet, July 13, 1757 (South Carolina), Gov. Pownall, Apr. 1, 1758 (Boston), Gen. Amherst to Gen. Murray, 1760 (Quebec), Gen. James Wolfe, June 6, 1759 (*Neptune*, at sea), Gen. Monck-

[1] *Crown Lease Book*, V. 22, *Works* I, III. 7, VI. 115, 130, 130 b.

ton, 1762 (New York), Gov. Dobbs, 1763 (Brunswick), Gov. Belcher, July 6, 1763 (Halifax), and from other officers, dated at Fort Edward, Plymouth, Placentia, Louisburg, Albany, Quebec, Georgia, and on board men of war, chiefly in 1757.

2. 1763-1776. Letters and despatches to Sec. Barrington, the Marquis of Granby, master-general of ordnance, and the commander-in-chief.

Gen. Gage. New York, Boston, London, 1771–July 23, 1776. Thirty-eight letters in all, that of Apr. 22, 1775, containing a description of the battle of Concord, *cf. C. O.* 5: **92**; that of June 25, 1775, battle of Bunker Hill; that of July 21, 1775, distribution of troops in North America; that of Oct. 1, 1775, *id.*; others contain enclosures giving figures and statistics, copies of letters written by Gage to officers of the 18th Regiment and replies thereto; letters from these officers to Barrington; lists of promotions of commissioned officers, Aug. 24, 1765. Many of the letters from Gage have Barrington's comments upon them.

Gen. Howe. Camp, heights of Charlestown, Boston, Oct. 16, 1775–June 9, 1776. Eighteen letters in all, that of Oct. 16, 1775, containing memorials, and those of Dec. 2, 1775, and Jan. 19, 1775, important enclosures.

Gen. Carleton. Chambly, Montreal, Quebec, June 7, 1775–July 11, 1776. Eight letters in all.

Group of letters from Gen. Burgoyne, Gen. Irwine, Col. Pigot, Capts. MacDonald, Macilwaine, Maclean, Christie, Shirreff, Earl Percy, Boston, Quebec, St. Augustine, Halifax, June, 1775–June, 1776, with many enclosures, and comments by Barrington.

3. 1784-1785. Military despatches of Gen. Haldimand and others to Barrington, with a few earlier documents.

4. 1755-1757. Military despatches from Gen. Shirley to Barrington, New York, Dec. 19, 1755–Sept. 4, 1756, together with Shirley's memorial to the king, Jan. 3, 1757. Twelve letters, with many enclosures, copies of letters to and from Shirley and others, proclamations, declarations, minutes of councils of war. Many of the letters are marked " Duplicate " or " Triplicate " and all but those of Jan. 13, July 4, and Aug. 20 are to be found in *C. O.* 5: **47**. None of the letters are in *C. O.* 5: **887**. In addition to the letters from America are others sent by Shirley to Barrington and the Treasury for the purpose of vindicating himself in his controversy with Loudoun, Feb. 8–June 3, 1757 (six in all, and the memorial addressed to the king).

5. 1758-1763. Correspondence of Gen. Amherst with Barrington, the Duke of Devonshire, first lord of the Treasury, Charles Townshend, etc., New York, Albany, Schenectady, Staten Island. Fifty-one letters in all, with many enclosures; also a few copies of letters sent to officers in America and a letter, New York, Dec. 9, 1763, from Gage to Welbore Ellis, secretary at war. Compare with *C. O.* 5: **54-63**, where letters similar in character but not duplicates will be found. Amherst did not often send duplicate letters even when writing upon the same subject on the same date to Barrington and Pitt, therein following a practice unlike that of Shirley.

6. 1764-1765. Letters from Gen. Gage to Ellis and Barrington. Ten letters in all, with enclosures which are often elaborate, such as those containing descriptions of the Floridas and accounts of dealings with the Indians. Compare **2**, above, and *C. O.* 5 : **83-95**. Gage rarely sent duplicates. In his letters to Ellis and Barrington, he deals strictly with military affairs, such as concerned the condition and state of the army, vacancies, promotions, estimates of military expenses, and the like, which did not concern the Secretary of State.

7. 1766, Jan. 8–Oct. 11. *Id.* Concerned largely with Indian affairs along the frontier and with Pontiac's War.

8. 1767, Jan. 15–1769, June 16. *Id.*

9. 1769, July 22–1774, Dec. 25. *Id.*

10. 1776-1780. Letters from Gens. Howe and Clinton. Those of Gen. Howe cover the period Aug. 9, 1776–Apr. 13, 1778 ; those of Gen. Clinton, June 15, 1778–Oct. 31, 1780. They are concerned but little with matters of policy, dealing chiefly with the condition and management of the army—ammunition, clothing, food, housing, sickness—and show a bad state of affairs, regarding which Howe was very outspoken in his comments, presenting evidences of fraud in the furnishing of supplies and medicines. Clinton's letters are briefer and more formal. Enclosures mentioned are frequently missing, but in some cases may be found in *C. O.* 5: **92-105**. In the volume are three letters from Amherst, Whitehall, Dec., 1778–Feb., 1779.

11. 1776-1781. Letters from Gens. Carleton and Haldimand, Quebec and Canada. Those of Carleton cover the period, Aug. 20, 1776–July 17, 1778, those of Haldimand, July 7, 1778–Oct. 22, 1781. Carleton's letters are full of references to colonial affairs and contain comments on current events. Entered between Haldimand's letters of Nov. 1, 1779, and Oct. 25, 1780, are many letters, petitions, and memorials sent to Barrington by officers of the army in America, with the secretary's memorandum in most cases on the dorse. There are also letters from Howe, Jan. 25, 1779, Amherst, Mar. 27, 1779, Phillips, with enclosures, among which are copies of letters from Lord George Germain and a copy of a letter sent to Washington, Dec. 23, 1780.

12. 1781-1782. Letters from Gens. Clinton and Carleton, and other miscellany. Clinton's letters cover the period Jan. 28, 1781–May 4, 1782, those of Carleton, June 14–Dec. 21, 1782. All concern chiefly routine matters, and contain many elaborate statistical returns. The last third of the volume is filled with miscellaneous letters and papers, chiefly from Canada, 1779-1782.

13. 1782-1783. Letters from Gen. Carleton. These letters are chiefly official despatches, of a formal nature, dealing with promotions, appointments, vacancies, leaves of absence, and containing reports and returns, and copies of many memorials received by Carleton and by him sent to the secretary. Entered between the letters of June 16 and 17, 1783, are forty-one enclosures, with schedules of cash and clothing returns. There is also a short account of the King's American Dragoons.

19. 1760-1763. Letters from Governors and Others in Guadeloupe and Martinique to the Secretary at War.

From Lieut.-Gov. Crump, Gov. Dalrymple, Gov. Melville, Gen. Monckton, Maj. Colin Campbell, Gov. Rufane, with enclosures, among which is a copy of court-martial proceedings, 1759. Crump's letters are often long and the secretary's comments upon them elaborate. The letters from Martinique are mainly of local interest. In the volume are also a few letters from Dominica.

49. 1764. Letters and Papers from West Florida and the West Indies.

The first half of the volume contains papers relating to the cession of West Florida after the treaty of 1763. They were sent over by Maj. Robert Farmar of the 34th Regiment in 1764, and narrate the circumstances of the evacuation of the port of Mobile and the country adjoining, beginning Oct. 20, 1763, and extending to Feb., 1764. They consist of the following: verbal process at Mobile of the cession of that port, harangue to the Choctaw nation by Farmar representing England, and by the governor of New Orleans representing France, military appointments, instructions to officers, tables of Indian villages at the post of Alybamous, store returns, cannon returns, embarkation returns, reports on the state of the forts, on presents to the Indians, on the produce of Louisiana (valuable), list of effects and utensils handed over to Farmar, with valuations attached, verbal process of the cession of the post of Tombekbe, copy of a memorial from Capt. John Farmar to Maj.-Gen. Keppel, letter from Maj. Forbes, commandant at Pensacola, letters from Maj. Farmar to Ellis, lists of inhabitants of Mobile who had taken the oath of allegiance, and a few other papers. This portion of the volume has been copied for the state of Mississippi.

The remainder of the volume contains papers relating to Jamaica, Antigua, and Grenada, Dec. 30, 1760–Aug. 14, 1764.

50. 1768-1777. Letters and Papers from the West Indies.

From Antigua, St. Vincent, Grenada, Jamaica, St. Christopher, and Dominica, chiefly about military affairs.

51. 1777-1788. *Id.*

From Tobago, St. Lucia, Barbadoes, and St. Eustatius, as well as from the islands mentioned above.

52. 1781-1783. *Id.*

From the same islands as in **51** and **52**. All of these letters and papers, though relating chiefly to military affairs, are of importance for the history of the naval conflicts in the West Indies during the Revolutionary War.

57. 1772-1773. Letters and Papers relating to the West India Expedition of 1772-1773.

From Maj. Gordon, Gov. Leyborne, Lieut.-Col. Cane, Gen. Dalrymple, dated from St. Vincent and Grenada, with various military returns. In the same volume are a few letters from Hillsborough and Dartmouth to Barrington and three letters from Gen. Gage, New York, June 29, Aug. 5, Nov. 5, 1772.

404. 1763-1767. Note Book of Intelligence and Business that came before the Committee [Plantation Committee] of the Privy Council.

This book was evidently kept by a secretary or clerk of the committee of the whole Council, but no reason for its presence among the War Office papers appears. The volume contains extracts from a Board of Trade representation, dated Nov. 3, 1763, describing Tobago, Grenada, Grenadillas, St. Vincent, Dominica; notes on proceedings in the Council Chamber, May 7, 1764, on boundary disputes between New Hampshire and New York, on coal mines in Cape Breton, on the boundary of Florida, on prize causes, on plantation appeals (Freebody *vs*. Brenton, Rhode Island, Cleeve *vs*. Mills, Virginia, Despay *vs*. Blaneau, Jamaica, Gov. Boone *vs*. the assembly, South Carolina, Perrin *vs*. Witter, Beckford *vs*. Leake, Howlett *vs*. Osborne, Camm *vs*. Hansford, and Fothergill *vs*. Stover), on Mediterranean passes, on the affairs of Florida and Newfoundland, on the ecclesiastical government of Quebec, on the affairs of New York and Massachusetts, with comments on the argument against the Stamp Act.

616. 1778-1780. Letters from Gen. Amherst to Sec. Barrington.

Amherst was at this time commander-in-chief in England, and his letters deal with the army in general, having little to do with the colonies. An enquiry into the failure of Burgoyne's expedition seems to be the most important matter discussed.

678-682, 684. 1756-1784. Letters from the Secretary of State and the Treasury to the Secretary at War.

Original correspondence. The earlier volumes have little to do directly with colonial affairs but are of importance in understanding the conduct of the war. The later volumes contain many letters bearing on American affairs.

683. 1776-1781. Letters from Lord George Germain, Secretary of State for the Colonies, to Secretary Barrington, concerning American Affairs.

Original letters of Lord George Germain, with copies of letters from the Admiralty and many important schedules of papers. The letters supplement the military correspondence, though but few of them deal with matters of general policy. Some of the longest concern West Indian affairs.

823-826. 1763-1784. Letters from the Treasury.
857-868. 1757-1783. Letters from Various Departments, I.
869-877. 1759-1783. Letters from Various Departments, II.

These three series of volumes contain further installments of the Secretary at War's original correspondence. The letters from the Treasury are similar to those in **678-682, 684**, above. The first series of departmental letters concerns the secretary's relations with the Admiralty, the Secretary of State, etc. The second series, while including departmental letters, contains also letters from various correspondents in Germany, Canada, the West Indies, from governors of colonies, and others. They generally bear the comments of the Secretary at War upon them. Some of the documents are transmitted copies or duplicates. All are important.

890. 1776-1783. Statistics.

This volume relates in part to the war in North America and the West Indies. The statistics include:

Lists of camp necessities and equipages, such as wagons, blankets, watch-coats, " sunks for bât horses with wanties and collars complete ",[1] water-decks,[2] round, square, and bell tents, forage, cords, scythes, whetstones, kettles, canteens, water-flasks, clothing, camp-colors, drum-cases, hand-hatchets, haversacks, knapsacks, powder-bags, nose-bags, horse-pickets, picket-ropes, etc.

Names of transports and victualling ships, with times and places of transportation.

Hospital and medical returns, lists of officers, rules and regulations, allowances, some original correspondence (letter from Gage, Boston, Apr. 4, 1776, p. 219). The American statistics come chiefly in the first half of the volume.

891. 1756-1783. Orders.

Orders of the House of Lords and House of Commons, 1777-1781, requesting statistics regarding the army, etc., in various quarters including America. Orders in Council, 1756-1783, not directly concerning American affairs.

972-1020. 1756-1783. Miscellaneous Letters to the Secretary at War.

These volumes of miscellaneous documents supplement those already described and are of considerable importance for the military aspects of the war. The arrangement is chronological and alphabetical as follows:

972, 1756-1757; **973, 974**, 1757; **975**, 1757-1758; **976**, 1758, A-L; **977**, 1758, M-X; **978**, 1759; **979**, 1759, A-M; **980**, 1759, N-W; **981**, **982**, 1763; **983**, 1763, A-C; **984**, 1763, D-H; **985**, 1763, I-W; **986**, 1765; **987**, 1765, A-G; **988**, 1765, K-Z; **989**, 1766-1767; **990**, 1769-1771; **991**, 1776, A-G; **992**, 1776, G-M; **993**, 1776, M-R; **994**, 1776, S-W; **995**, 1778, A-C; **996**, 1778, C-F; **997**, 1778, G-M; **998**, 1778, M-R; **999**, 1778, R-Z; **1000**, militia in England; **1001**, 1778-later; **1002**, *id.*, A-D; **1003**, *id.*, D-H; **1004**, *id.*, H-M; **1005**, *id.*, M-R; **1006**, *id.*, R-W; **1007**, 1780, A-H; **1008**, 1780, H-M; **1009**, 1780, N-W; **1010**, 1781, A-E; **1011**, 1781, F-H; **1012**, 1781, M-R; **1013**, 1781, R-Z; **1014**, 1782, A-D; **1015**, 1782, E-H; **1016**, 1782, I-Q; **1017**, 1782, R-Y; **1018**, 1783, A-E; **1019**, 1783, F-M; **1020**, 1783, M-Y.

Vol. **972** contains a paper regarding the corps at Fort William Henry, some George Clinton letters, papers regarding different accoutrements, Pownall's scheme for quartering troops in America, certain papers regarding transports and subsistence, etc. Similar papers are scattered through the other volumes, which are neither indexed, listed, nor paged. There are many letters from officers of regiments in the colonies: Colquhoun, Cornwallis (**973**), Brown, Devonshire, Dame, Haldane (**974**), Hunt, Preston, Grant,

---

[1] A bât horse was a pack-horse; a sunk was a straw-stuffed pack-saddle; wanties were pack-ropes for binding a load on the back of a pack-horse.

[2] Water-decks were canvas coverings for protecting a load.

More, Russell, Pitcher (**974**), Hopson (**974**), Prevost, Hartman, Pownall, Farrell, Glasbrook, de Peyster (**975**), Barlow (**976**), Ross, Reede, Sackville, Whitmore (**977**), Hessians, Cunningham, Bailey, Dalling, Dalrymple, Duff, Gillespie (who offers the secretary advice regarding the use of planks or fronts of cork so as to prevent the repetition of such a catastrophe as at Bunker Hill), Mitchell, Mackintosh (**991**), Robert Smith (**994**), Adair, Bullock (**995**). There are also papers regarding the despatch and transport of troops, petitions for pay, leave of absence, redress, promotions, and references to service in America, with details of personal experience. Also returns of soldiers discharged (**974**), captured, or invalided. A few letters from colonial agents appear (Partridge, Ellis). In **1001** is Barrington-Amherst-Burgoyne correspondence; in **1002**, Adair and North letters (hospitals); in **1004**, Burgoyne-Irving correspondence (Irving served at Lexington and Bunker Hill); in **1006**, letters regarding Gustavus Cunningham, state prisoner; in **1007**, some New York papers; in **1008**, a Kingston letter regarding American affairs; in **1009**, four papers from Wacks, auditor to Hessian regiments in America; in **1010**, letters regarding Lieut. Bolton and Capt. Shaules; in **1011**, letter from Richard Gardiner regarding John Money killed in South Carolina; in **1012**, Clinton's instructions regarding invalids sent to England; and in **1018**, letters regarding affairs of the troops in America: petitions for pay or pensions, pay and reduction of troops, Hessians and provincial regiments, case of Samuel Cooke, missionary of the S. P. G., Monmouth Co., New Jersey. All the volumes contain many papers concerning hospitals and hospital service.

OUT-LETTERS.

COMMANDER-IN-CHIEF.

1-6. 1767-1778. Commander-in-Chief. Series I.

23-26. 1765-1786. *Id.* Series II.

> W. O. 3.
> —

Letter-books of the commander-in-chief and adjutant-general of the army in Great Britain. Series I. is of little importance, containing chiefly copies of the letters of Adjutant-General Edward Harvey; series II. contains drafts of letters to colonials, but at best they partake of a routine character.

SECRETARY AT WAR.

1-123. 1684-1783. General Letters.

> W. O. 4.
> —

This series of Secretary at War's letter-books begins with Blathwayt's tenure of the office. It is of importance for the colonies only after 1740 and does not become conspicuously important until after 1756. The most valuable entries are of letters, instructions, and warrants to military officers on the establishment serving in America.

273-275. 1775-1784. American Letter-Books. See also **987-988.**

273. Jan. 2, 1775–July 21, 1777.

Sec. Barrington's despatches to Howe (most numerous), Gage, Carleton (many letters), and lesser officers, Percy, Pigot (letter promoting him for bravery at Bunker Hill), Irvine, Macilwaine, Higgins, Clinton, Gordon, Christie, and others in the West Indies. The letters, which were generally sent in duplicate, contain little touching the general policy or progress of the campaign and only occasional references to battles and the losses of troops. They show that the Secretary at War interfered but little in the management of military affairs in America and gave the commanders-in-chief large discretionary powers, even including within certain limits control over promotions.

The despatches concern promotions, transfers, disposal of troops, leaves of absence, warrants for court-martial (see also *W. O.* 30: **17-35**), with the necessary queries and orders based on memorials transmitted directly to the secretary and sometimes copied here in full, distribution of troops (Hessians and other German auxiliaries), lists of vacancies, instructions and observations, hospital fees and salaries, warrants for pay, additional troops, questions of rank, exchange of prisoners, inquiries in cases of defeat, etc.

274. July 31, 1777–Sept. 11, 1780.

Despatches from Barrington and Jenkinson to Carleton, Howe, Clinton (most numerous), Haldimand, Phillips, Tryon, Bruce, Templer, Harcourt, Prescott, Stopford, and Prevost, and deal with detentions, shipment of clothing, sale of commissions, promotions, memorials, with copies of enclosures, returns of camp equipages, officers to be relieved, hospital instructions and appointments, lists of garrison officers. Letters regarding the Saratoga Convention may be found on pp. 153-154.

275. Sept. 6, 1780–Aug. 20, 1784.

Despatches from Jenkinson, Townshend, Yonge, and Fitzpatrick to Clinton, Phillips, and officers in the West Indies, relating to the same general subjects as the prevous volume, with many lists of various kinds. Numbers of despatches (all after Jan. 6, 1784) sent to Canada and the West Indies (there is also a " West India Letter Book "). An occasional cross-reference shows that letters relating to American affairs were entered in the " Common Letter Book ".

333-334. 1775-1785. Entry Books of Letters.

To governors, officers in command, various officials, and private persons in the West Indies, regarding pay, leaves of absence, promotions, discipline, also instructions, lists, invoices (medicines, etc.). Letters quite short and formal.

604. 1781-1783. Letter-Book for Deserters.

Relating chiefly to deserters from regiments stationed in England.

965-967. 1778-1781. Press Act.

These volumes contain the correspondence relating to the operation of the press acts, 18 George III., c. 53, and 19 George III., c. 10, passed for the purpose of raising men for the army in America. They are valuable for anyone studying the system of recruiting in England and Scotland during the later years of the Revolutionary War, whereby men were raised for the American service. They should be supplemented by *W. O.* 1: **995-1005.** An important report on the success of the second act, drawn up by Jenkinson, is to be found in **966.**

981-983. 1751-1798. Private Letter-Book.

This book contains entries of the Secretary at War's letters regarding leaves of absence, promotions, appointments, and the like, some of which are concerned with advancement on the staff of the British army in America. An occasional statement may be found that is not contained in the formal notification (*W. O.* 25: **122-152**).

987-988. 1763-1784. American Letter-Books.

These volumes are supplemental to **273-275,** and the two series contain the War Office despatches to America during the years named. The despatches, which are of the utmost importance as defining the British war policy, are from the secretaries at war to the commanders-in-chief and the governors of the colonies, and relate solely to the army in America and the West Indies. They are often long and detailed. Occasionally letters received from America are entered. The despatches to Gage have a particular interest.

1044. 1763-1767. Miscellaneous.

Of no particular consequence. On pp. 58, 98, and 99 are copies of instructions sent to Gage and officers in the West Indies regarding drilling, etc.

MARCHING ORDERS.

1-64. 1683-1783. Marching Orders.

W. O. 5.
——

These volumes contain embarkation orders for troops going to America and disembarkation orders for invalids, convalescents, and troops returning to England. See *W. O.* 24. There are no marching orders for America in these volumes.

DEPARTMENTAL.

24-28. 1715-1790. Board of General Officers for inspecting and regulating the Clothing of the Army.

W. O. 7.
——

Of no value for colonial history.

96. 1781-1789. Medical Department.

Contains copies of many letters sent to men in the medical service in America.

122-125. 1716-1787. Muster-Master General's or Commissary-General of Musters' Office.

These volumes are chiefly important for the mustering of regiments in England. In **125** are entered a few letters from the plantations and a few orders relating to the embarkation of troops to the plantations.

IRELAND.

1-7. 1709-1787. Ireland.

<table>
<tr><td>W. O. 8.</td><td>Relate entirely to regiments and officers of the establishment in Ireland. Occasionally a reference to America will be found, as when half-pay was stopped to officers, who refused to go to the West Indies, and when</td></tr>
</table>

later, during the American War, regiments were replaced, etc.

MUSTER-ROLLS AND PAY-LISTS.
GENERAL SERIES.

1882-11099. 1757-1783. General Series.

<table>
<tr><td>W. O. 12.</td><td>The following list notes the regiments of regulars serving between the years 1757 and 1783. The particular regiments serving in America at any time during that period can be ascertained from *W. O.* 24, and in part from *C. O.* 5: **173.** When the name or number of such</td></tr>
</table>

regiment is known, data regarding it can be obtained from these rolls and lists. These documents are not included in the printed *War Office List*.

Vol.	Years.	Regiment and Battalion.	Vol.	Years.	Regiment and Battalion.
1882	1768–84	1 Foot, 1	3592	1760–72	19 Foot, 1
1948	1759–77	1 " 2	3593	1773–83	19 " 1
1949	1778–97	1 " 2	3675	1766–71	20 " 1
2020	1768–80	2 " 2	3676	1772–85	20 " 1
2104	1766–75	3 " 1	3778	1760–83	21 " 1
2105	1776–81	3 " 1	3871	1760–71	22 " 1
2194	1764–80	4 " 1	3872	1772–84	22 " 1
2195	1781–85	4 " 1	3959	1760–73	23 " 1
2289	1760–81	4 " 1	3960	1774–85	23 " 1
2290	1782–97	5 " 1	4059	1760–82	24 " 1
2380	1760–70	6 " 1	4158	1760–70	25 " 1
2381	1771–83	6 " 1	4159	1771–81	25 " 1
2474	1760–80	7 " 1	4160	1782–97	25 " 1
2475	1781–98	7 " 1 and 2	4250	1766–81	26 " 1
2566	1760–97	8 " 1	4329	1759–77	27 " 1
2653	1760–77	9 " 1	4330	1778–88	27 " 1
2654	1781–97	9 " 1	4416	1759–76	28 " 1
2750	1767–78	10 " 1	4417	1777–81	28 " 1
2751	1779–89	10 " 1	4493	1765–83	29 " 1
2838	1760–72	11 " 1	4561	1760–74	30 " 1
2839	1773–81	11 " 1	4562	1775–80	30 " 1
2840	1782–97	11 " 1	4563	1781–98	30 " 1
2934	1760–73	12 " 1	4648	1760–73	31 " 1
2935	1774–90	12 " 1	4649	1774–97	31 " 1
3028	1760–72	13 " 1	4725	1760–81	32 " 1
3029	1773–85	13 " 1	4726	1782–97	32 " 1
3117	1760–80	14 " 1	4802	1760–74	33 " 1
3118	1781–98	14 " 1	4803	1775–90	33 " 1
3228	1759–73	15 " 1	4866	1760–87	34 " 1
3229	1774–86	15 " 1	4949	1759–83	35 " 1
3320	1767–86	16 " 1	5025	1760–79	36 " 1
3405	1760–71	17 " 1	5026	1780–98	36 " 1
3406	1772–83	17 " 1	5100	1760–74	37 " 1
3501	1767–80	18 " 1	5101	1775–91	37 " 1

Vol.	Years.	Regiment and Battalion.	Vol.	Years.	Regiment and Battalion.
5171	1760–78	38 Foot, 1	7313	1774–84	64 Foot, 1
5172	1779–88	38 " 1	7371	1768–82	65 " 1
5246	1769–83	39 " 1	7458	1760–78	66 " 1
5317	1754–76	40 " 1	7459	1779–81	66 " 1
5318	1777–88	40 " 1	7536	1760–75	67 " 1
5404	1760–67	41 " 1	7537	1776–79	67 " 1
5405	1768–78	41 " 1	7538	1780–82	67 " 1
5406	1779–98	41 " 1	7620	1760–75	68 " 1
5478	1759–76	42 " 1	7621	1776–79	68 " 1
5479	1777–86	42 " 1	7622	1780–82	68 " 1
5553	1759–83	42 " 2	7693	1760–76	69 " 1
5561	1759–75	43 " 1	7694	1777–87	69 " 1
5562	1776–86	43 " 1	7780	1774–84	70 " 1
5637	1759–83	44 " 1	7847	1764–83	71 " 1 and 2
5718	1759–81	45 " 1	7924	1764–69	72 " 1
5796	1761–76	46 " 1	7925	1778–97	72 " 1
5797	1777–88	46 " 1	7997	1764–86	73 " 1
5871	1759–83	47 " 1	8059	1779–83	73 " 2
5957	1759–85	48 " 1	8063	1763–91	74 " 1
6032	1774–83	49 " 1	8454	1778–84	80 " 1 (old)
6102	1760–81	50 " 1	8519	1760–63	81 " 1
6176	1756–75	51 " 1	8520	1778–80	81 " 1
6177	1776–82	51 " 1	8521	1781–83	81 " 1
6178	1783–86	51 " 1		1760–63	
6240	1765–79	52 " 1	8597	1778–84	82 " 1
6241	1780–97	52 " 1		1793–97	
6316	1760–77	53 " 1	8671	1778–97	83 " 1
6317	1778–98	53 " 1	8741	1780–98	84 " 1
6398	1760–77	54 " 1	8806	1779–96	84 " 2
6399	1778–98	54 " 1	8812	1780–83	85 " 1
6470	1759–73	55 " 1	8884	1781–83	86 " 1
6471	1774–85	55 " 1	9023	1780–83	88 " 1
6543	1760–82	56 " 1	9090	1780–83	89 " 1
6632	1760–74	57 " 1	9170	1779–83	90 " 1
6633	1775–85	57 " 1	9244	1779–83	91 " 1
6710	1759–74	58 " 1	9393	1780–83	93 " 1
6711	1775–86	58 " 1	9591	1780–83	95 " 1
6786	1765–82	59 " 1	9655	1780–83	97 " 1
6871	1763–97	60 " 1	9784	1782–83	99 " 1
6935	1764–83	60 " 2	9945	1782–83	104 " 1
6998	1757–81	60 " 3	9964	1782–84	105 " 1
7033	1757–98	60 " 4	10491	1781–82	Barbadoes Rangers.
7091	1760–75	61 " 1	10821	1783	King's American Regiment.
7092	1776–82	61 " 1			
7164	1772–82	62 " 1	11020	1782–1809	Newfoundland Fencibles.
7241	1771–77	63 " 1			
7242	1778–88	63 " 1	11099	1783	Tarleton's British Legion.
7312	1760–73	64 " 1			

The following lists of regiments in North America and the West Indies in 1781 are given in *C. O.* 5: **173.**

Coast of the Atlantic: 17 Light Dragoons, Footguards, Regiments of Foot, 3, 7, 16, 17, 19, 22, 23, 30, 33, 37, 38, 40, 42 (1st battalion), 43, 54, 57, 60 (3d and 4th battalions), 63, 64, 69, 70, 71, 74, 76, 80, 82, 84.

Canada: Regiments of Foot, 8, 29, 31, 34, 44, 53, 84 (1st battalion), 47 (three companies).

Leeward Islands: 1 (1st battalion), 13, 15, 27, 28, 35, 46, 55, 60 (2d battalion), 86 (five companies), 87.

Jamaica: 60 (1st battalion), 79, 85, 88, 92, 94, 99.

Further information as to the distribution of the regiments can be obtained from Cannon, *Historical Records of the British Army*, some 70 vols., 1846-1852, continued in a few cases to 1907.

MONTHLY RETURNS.

1-254. 1759-1782. Monthly Returns of British Troops.

W. O. 17.

1153-1155. 1764, 1771-1775, 1776-1782. General Returns.

These volumes contain the monthly returns of His Majesty's forces in North America and the West Indies. **1153** (1764) is a large folio, containing on pp. 283-289 returns from Jamaica; on pp. 313-327, from North America under Gage; on p. 362, Grenada; on pp. 338-340, Jamaica; on pp. 496-524, West Indies in general. The other volumes are little books containing returns from North America and the West Indies, 1771-1782.

1373. 1755, 1761, 1806-1807. Returns from Bermuda.

1489-1498. 1758-1786. Returns from North America.

Beginning as early as 1758 and including returns from Havana, Louisiana, etc., with lists of effectives, killed and wounded, garrisons, winter-quarters, and the regular monthly returns.

1570-1577. 1776-1783. Returns of British, Provincial, and German Troops quartered in Canada.

Bundles or small packets containing the monthly returns as indicated. The contents of the several packets vary considerably. **1576** contains no monthly returns, only a " Liste Générale du Corps des Troupes Allemandes Commandés par le Major General ———, pour le 1er de ———, ——— ", blanks filled in. The German returns are generally written in French.

2480. 1759-1773, 1780-1789. West Indies.

Separate papers. No returns for the years 1774-1778.

VOUCHERS FOR AGENTS' DISBURSEMENTS—ARTILLERY.

1-39. 1770-1783. Agents' Disbursements, Artillery.

W. O. 18.

Bound volumes relating to the Royal Regiment of Artillery, containing the accounts or lists of disbursements made by Cox and Drummond, later Cox and Muir, together with hundreds of original receipts from the different officers and men. The volumes indicated in the printed list as " Pensions " contain the accounts of disbursements for half-pay and pensions, along with receipts or other vouchers. Those indicated as " Miscellaneous " always comprise the disbursements to master gunners and gunners in the several garrisons of Great Britain and a few others.

The volumes contain very few references to America. In **6** some of the receipts are dated at New York; and in the same volume is an account of arrears ordered to be paid to the officers of the Royal Regiment of Artillery in America for the year 1771. In **9** is a similar account for 1772. In **17** is a list of names of men at St. John's and Newfoundland under the command of a captain-lieutenant of the Royal Artillery. In **21** is a list of invalids for 1776-1782. In **30** are documents relating to a surgeon's bill for medicines at Grenada.

REGISTERS.

ESTABLISHMENTS.

1-528. 1673-1783. Registers of Military Establishments.

W. O. 24.

—

This collection is made up of three separate series, formerly existing among the records of the Audit Office, Treasury, and War Office. Duplicates and triplicates, therefore, appear of the same return in nearly every bundle. Not all the bundles contain registers of troops serving in America, and the list given below is a selection of such bundles as contain American material. For data regarding the year 1679 see *Cal. Col., 1677-1680*, p. 1038, and *Acts Privy Council, Colonial*, vol. I., § 1288.

5-7. 1680-1684 (**6** is undated). In addition to the registers of forces, this bundle contains one item of payment out of the garrison account to Jamaica, and another item of payment to Lord Culpeper, by virtue of a warrant of June 24, 1684, and " in compensation of his Letters Patent and Grant of the Quit Rents and other profits of Virginia for Thirty One years, bearing date the 25th of February, 1673, and for all other Pretentions during the government of Virginia ". The sum amounted to £1 12s. 10½d. a day or £600 a year. This annuity was charged against the cost of the military establishment and appears to have been paid after Culpeper's death to his executors until 1699. The item appears in the registers for 1686, 1689, 1694, and 1699.[1]

13. 1690. First mention of the four companies in New York; also of the Duke of Bolton's regiment in the West Indies.

15. 1691-1692. *Id.*

20. 1693. Various lists of regulations and dispositions.

21. 1694. Troops in New York, Leeward Islands, and Jamaica.

22. 1699. Twelve companies of foot and one of grenadiers in the West Indies, forty men each; four companies, New York; one company, Leeward Islands; one, Newfoundland.

---

[1] Lord Culpeper relinquished his claim upon the quit-rents of the southern part of Virginia for £700 cash down and £600 to be paid out of the establishment for twenty-one and a half years, Aug. 25, 1683–Feb. 25, 1704. The quit-rents of the northern part went to Lord Fairfax as Lord Culpeper's executor. Blathwayt's Journal, II. 12, report of 1698. " The said fines and forfeitures, having by Letters Patent been granted by King Charles the Second to the Lord Culpeper and others, were Repurchased by the Late King for divers Considerable Summs of money actually paid to the said Lord Culpeper, and a further pension of Six hundred Pounds a yeare, payable for Twenty One yeares, and now Charged upon the Establishment of your Majesty's Army ", etc., *Acts Privy Council, Colonial*, II. 143.

23. 1700. *Id.*

26. 1701-1702. New York, Bermuda, Newfoundland.

28. 1702-1703. *Id.*

33. 1703-1704. *Id.*

37. 1704. Regulations for regiments in the West Indies.

38. 1704-1705. New York, Bermuda, Newfoundland.

42. 1705. Similar to **37.**

45. 1707-1708; **49,** 1708-1709; **55,** 1709-1710. Same as **38.**

69. 1712. Jamaica, New York, Bermuda, Annapolis Royal, Placentia.

72. 1713-1714. *Id.*

73. 1714-1715. Register of troops in Great Britain and the Plantations.

The remaining volumes may be entered as follows. Except when specially noted they contain the usual registers of plantation troops.

80, 1715-1716; **83,** 1716-1717; **85** (Col. Phillips's regiment of foot at Annapolis Royal and Placentia, 1717); **86,** 1717-1718; **88,** 1717-1718; **89** (Providence and Bahamas); **92,** 1718-1719; **93,** 1719-1720; **99,** 1720-1721; **106,** 1721-1722; **111,** 1722-1723; **114,** 1723-1724; **117,** 1724-1725; **123,** 1725-1726; **129,** 1726-1727; **135,** 1727-1728; **142,** 1728-1729; **147,** 1729-1730; **151,** 1730-1731; **155,** 1731-1732; **159,** 1732-1733; **163,** 1733-1734; **165** (eight independent companies of Jamaica, 1734); **169,** 1734-1735; **173,** 1735-1736; **177,** 1736-1737; **180,** 1737-1738; **183,** 1738-1739; **189** (Lord Cathcart's expedition, 1739); **192,** 1739-1740; **194** (officers of hospital for Cathcart's expedition, 1740); **197,** 1740-1741; **199** (regiments of foot raised in America); **206,** 1741-1742; **208** (regiments of foot raised in America); **218,** 1742-1743; **222** (troops for the service of Georgia); **226,** 1743-1744; **236,** 1744-1745; **241** (Cape Breton, 1745); **247** (*id.,* 1745-1746); **249,** 1745-1746; **251** (Georgia rangers, 1745-1746); **260** (Cape Breton, 1746-1747); **263,** 1746-1747; **272** (Cape Breton, 1747-1748); **274,** 1747-1748; **280** (Cape Breton, 1748-1749); **283,** 1748-1749; **284** (garrison of Rattan Island, 1748-1749); **286** (regiments of dragoons and foot, also three independent companies in South Carolina, 1748-1749); **289,** 1749-1750; **293,** 1750-1751; **297,** 1751-1752; **301,** 1752-1753; **305,** 1753-1754; **308** (two regiments of foot for America, 1754); **311,** 1754-1755; **318,** 1755-1756; **330,** 1756-1757; **337** (seven regiments ordered from Ireland to North America); **341,** 1757-1758; **352** (Cape Breton, 1758-1759); **364** (*id.,* 1759-1760); **367,** 1759-1760; **382** (Guadeloupe, 1760-1761); **383,** 1760-1761; **384** (Quebec, 1760-1761); **396** (Guadeloupe, 1761-1762); **397,** 1761-1762; **398** (Quebec, 1760-1761); **409** (Guadeloupe, 1762-1763); **410** (Havana, 1762-1763); **411** (Martinique, 1762-1763); **412,** 1762-1763; **413** (Quebec, 1762-1763); **421,** 1763; **422** (Quebec, 1763); **425,** 1763-1764; **426** (Quebec, 1763-1764); **431,** 1764-1765; **436,** 1765-1766; **441,** 1766-1767; **446,** 1767-1768; **452,** 1768-1769; **457,** 1769-1770; **462,** 1770-1771; **466,** 1771-1772; **470,** 1772-1773; **475,** 1773-1774; **480,** 1774-1775; **484,** 1775-1776; **489,** 1776-1777; **493,** 1777-1778; **498,** 1778-1779; **503,** 1779-1780; **508,** 1780-1781; **516,** 1781-1782; **523,** 1782-1783; **528,** 1783-1784.

For occasional duplicates of the registers see British Museum, *Egerton* **2543**, f. 295 (1698); *Lansdowne* **673** (1694); *Stowe* **484, 485** (1762); *Harleian* **6425** (1679-1680), **7194** (1689-1690), **7436-7444** (1689-1690); *Add. MSS.* **10453**, ff. 106 (1709), 190 (1710), 220 (1711), **10454**, ff. 22 (1712), 217 (1721), 273 (1722), 290 (1723), 318, 320 (1724), etc., **11286** (1733), **21188** (1728), **28323** (1739), **29256** A-**29256** L (1768-1775), **29268** (1727-1728), **33046** ff. 113 (1741), 138 (1743), 319 (1755), **33047**, ff. 215 (1759), 359 (1760), **33048**, ff. 81 (1761?), 89, 182, 315, 317 (1762 *et seq.*), **36862**, ff. 118, 214, 242 (beginning 1690), etc. The returns are usually dated " December 25 ", with a few exceptions.

748. 1783-1789. Half-Pay, British-American Forces.

This large volume contains a copy of the royal ordinance authorizing half-pay to provincial troops, dated Dec. 23, 1783. Also lists of the reduced officers of the British-American forces, entitled to receive half-pay, in columns headed: " Regiments ", " Officers ", " Names and Quality ", " Half-Pay per diem ".

884-885. 1685-1689, 1692-1703. Entry Books of Copies of Establishments General.

These volumes supplement the earlier volumes, **1-528.**

REGISTERS VARIOUS.

W. O. 25.	**1-38.** 1660-1786. Commission Books. Series I.
—	**89-94.** 1728-1783. *Id.* Series II.

The first series contains tabular lists in six columns of the commissions granted, for example:

Name of officer.	Date	By whom granted.	Name of the Secretary of State.	Name of the Regiment.	Fees.
Wm Shirley,[1] etc. to be colonel of a Regiment of Foot to be forthwith raised for our service. (See *W. O.* 4: **41,** and 25: **135,** 56-57, 143, 146, 150.)	31 August 1745	George R	Harrington	Shirleys	1 : 4 : —

It is evident that these volumes contain more information than is to be found in the notification books, for all blank commissions in the latter can be filled in from the commission books, where many of the documents are given in full. The two series contain much the same kind of information, but each furnishes details not to be found in the other. Generally speaking, one may trace in these volumes the career of every commissioned officer that served in the British army in America or elsewhere. Similar commissions can be found in *S. P. Dom.*, Entry Books, **164-203, 332-385**, where are commissions

---

[1] In 1745 Shirley and Pepperrell had the honor to be appointed colonels on the establishment, with instructions to raise companies of foot in America, as would any British colonel in England at the cost of the crown. *Correspondence of Shirley,* I. 294-295, 311; II. 92-93, 97, 108, 165.

of officers serving in America, warrants for grants of officers in America or connected with American affairs, passes, bills for charters, offices, and the like.

112-117. 1760-1805. Commission Books, Generally Regiments.

Ledger books of commissions, arranged in order of regiments, cavalry first and then the foot regiments. At the end of the volumes are the garrisons in Great Britain and the staff in North America. Besides the officers, this staff list gives town majors, commissaries, barrack-masters, apothecaries, chaplains, etc. The indexes are alphabetical lists of names with page references.

122-152. 1708-1783. Notification Books.

Entry books of notifications by the secretaries of state of the granting of commissions. The request was sent by the Secretary at War asking that commissions for officers and others in the army be prepared and laid before the king for signature. The notifications cover not only the usual commission officers but also adjutants-general, commissaries-general, quartermasters-general, surgeons and engineers with army rank, and military governors as of Louisburg and Mobile. No commissions to officers of provincial regiments are included. The commissions cover appointments to new companies and changes in old companies, and all promotions in rank of officers in America (including Canada and the West Indies) from 1708 to 1783, covering, of course, the early companies in New York, South Carolina, etc. The volumes, especially the indexes, show hard usage. They are particularly valuable after 1755 and during the Revolution. To use them one must know either the particular officer's name, or the number (or name) of his regiment, or the name of the commander-in-chief.

209-212. 1754-1788. Regimental Succession Books. Series I.
221-222. 1773-1788. Succession Books. Series II.

The first series contains regimental lists of successions in the army, giving names, with indication of rank, name of predecessor (generally blank), cause (death, retirement, or transfer), and date. The arrangement is chronological, under each regiment according to the following headings: " General and Field Officers ", " Guards ", " Horse ", " Dragoons ", " Foot Guards ", " Foot ". When the name and regiment are known, these volumes can be used to ascertain the details of advancement in rank of all officers in service in America.

The second series contains the same information for the years 1773-1788, but differs from the other series in that the names are entered without regard to the regiments. The data were evidently taken from the commission and notification books. None of the volumes contain entries regarding the officers of the provincial regiments, for which see *W. O.* 17: **1570-1577**, and other volumes of class 17; *W. O.* 24: **748-762**.

705. 1782-1815. Staff Returns.

Chiefly of date later than 1783 and relating to Africa, Bahamas, Bermuda, and Quebec.

1145. 1758-1797. Embarkation Returns.

Returns of embarkation of troops to Guadeloupe, 1759, Louisburg, 1758, North America, 1760; report on the losses in baggage and necessaries in the wreck of the transport *Pitt* in the St. Lawrence, Aug. 6, 1765; embarkation returns of St. Clair's troops, of the 9th, 20th, 24th, 34th, 53d, 62d Regiments of Foot at Cork, Apr., 1776, including women and children ("Many more women embarked with each regiment, but they were all turned on shore except 60 per regiment; many of the children were also turned on shore"); embarkation made or intended, May 1, 1778; embarkation returns of "British recruits of Gen. Howe's army, 500 embarked in the Clyde for Spithead", May 1, 1778.

2979-2983. 1712-1755. Estimate of Half-Pay and Retired Pay (with names).

2984-2989. Lists of Officers.

2990-2991. Registers of Warrants for Half-Pay.

3020-3036. 1735-1736, 1755-1783. Payments of Pensions to Widows of Full-Pay Officers.

3058-3060. 1762-1790. Cash Books.

3180-3194. 1704-1784. Register of Warrants of Commissary-General of Musters for Leaves of Absence, etc.

3206. 1684-1833. Explanation of Changes in the Establishment of Garrisons.

Only a search can determine how far these volumes contain information of importance for the military history of the colonies.

MISCELLANEA.
HEADQUARTERS RECORDS.

1-10. 1746 - 1747, 1775 - 1783. Headquarters Records, America.

W. O. 28.

1. 1746-1747. Muster-Roll of Connecticut Troops. Muster-roll of a regiment of foot raised for service against Canada, 1746, under the command of Col. Elisha Williams, rector of Yale College, 1726-1740. Officers: Lieut.-Col. Samuel Talcott, Israel Hewitt, James Church, Isaiah Starr, Benjamin Lee, Robert Denison, William Whiting, Elihu Hall, Joseph Wooster. Dated, May 30, 1746–Oct. 31, 1747, from New London, Wethersfield, Hartford, Fairfield, Plainfield, Lebanon, Wallingford, Stratford. A copy of these rolls is in the library of the Connecticut Historical Society. *Cf. Law Papers,* II. 271, 344, 345, 350.

2. 1777-1783. Field-Officers' Letters.

8th Regiment. Maj. de Peyster, Michilimackinac, 1778; Col. Bolton, Niagara, 1778.

Id. Maj. de Peyster, Detroit, 1780; Col. Bolton, Niagara, 1779; Col. Dundas, Niagara, Montreal, 1782.

29th Regiment. Maj. Carleton, Canada, 1778-1780, 1781-1783; Maj. Campbell, Canada, 1781-1783; Maj. Monzell, Canada, 1783.

31st Regiment. Lieut.-Col. French, St. John's, 1777-1783; Maj.-Gen. Clarke, Quebec, 1782-1783; C. Tiesdale, aide-de-camp to Gen. Clarke, Quebec, 1782.

34th Regiment. Lieut.-Col. St. Leger, Quebec, Sorel, 1779-1781; Maj. Dundas, Sorel, 1778-1780.

Id. Lieut.-Col. St. Leger, St. John's, Montreal, 1782-1783; Maj. Hughes, Montreal, 1783; Maj. Green, Montreal, 1782-1783; Maj. Hayes, Niagara, 1783.

44th Regiment. Capt. Norton, Quebec, St. Charles, 1781-1782; Ensign Sullivan, New York, 1782; Lieut.-Col. Hope, Quebec, 1783.

For these field-officers see *W. O.* 25: **209-212**.

3. 1777-1783. *Id.*

53d Regiment. Brig.-Gen. Powell, Montreal, 1778-1779; Capt. Shanks, Montreal, 1778; Capt. Graves, Pointe aux Fere, 1778; Paymaster Currie, Chambly, 1778; Brig.-Maj. Mure, Montreal, 1778.

84th Regiment. Brig.-Gen. Maclean, Montreal, Quebec, 1777-1778; Maj. Nairn, Isle aux Noix, Montreal, 1777-1778.

Id. Maj. Nairn. Montreal, 1779.

Id. Maj. Dunbar, Berthier, 1780; Maj. Harris, Canada, many places, 1780; Brig.-Gen. Maclean, Montreal, 1780; Maj. Nairn, Malbury, 1780.

Id. Same officers. Montreal, Sorel, etc., 1781, 1782.

53d Regiment. Maj. Skene, Niagara, 1781; Brig.-Gen. Powell, Niagara, 1781, 1782; Maj. Nairn, Pointe aux Trembles, Isle aux Noix, 1782, 1783; Capt. Scott, Montreal, 1783; Maj. Baird, St. Dennis, 1783.

84th Regiment. Same officers and places as before. 1783.

4. 1775-1783. Provincial Officers, etc.

Butler's Rangers. Butler, La Chine, Niagara, 1782; his captains, lieutenants, and others, Montreal, Niagara, Three Rivers, Quebec, 1781-1783.

Id. Various papers, letters, lists, officers' commissions, monthly returns and pay bills. 1775-1781.

Royal Highland Emigrants. Various papers relating to the raising of the regiment by order of Gen. Gage, with lists of officers, instructions, accounts, equipment, warrants, recruiting orders, musters, and returns.

Jessup's Loyal Rangers. Maj. Jessup, Quebec, River Duchesne, Sorel, 1783, with monthly returns, 1782, 1783; Majs. Nairn and Jessup, 1782, with lists, returns, and letters, 1777, 1782, 1783.

King's Loyal Americans. Rolls of the King's Loyal Regiment of Americans, raised by order of Gen. Carleton and commanded by Capt. Ebenezer Jessup.

Loyal Volunteers, commanded by Capt. Robert Leake.

Peter's Corps.

McAlpine's Volunteers, raised by order of Gen. Howe.

King's Rangers, raised by order of Gen. Clinton and commanded by Maj. Robert Rogers.

Various royalist corps, 1778, and a state of the detail of royalists, 1778.

5. 1776-1783. Various returns and letters.

King's Royal Regiment of New York, commanded by Sir John Johnson, 1776-1777, including commissary-generals' rolls, pay-rolls, call-rolls or officers' return rolls, comptrollers' rolls, etc.

Field-officers' letters, Sir John Johnson, Maj. Gray, and others. 1777-1780.

Id. 2d battalion in Canada and other papers.

Field-officers' letters, as above. 1781-1783.

Rogers's King's Rangers. Field-officers' letters, chiefly from Maj. Rogers. 1781-1783.

Barrack-master General's Department. Papers concerning the barracking of Hessians and Brunswickers at various points in Canada, and other general returns, with lists of barrack-masters and establishments, returns of stores, etc.

6. 1776-1783. *Id.*

Garrison states and returns of the upper ports, including lists of men employed, returns of staffs and officers, schedule of courts, monthly returns, etc. Montreal, Quebec, Oswegatchie, Isle aux Noix, Cataraqui, Niagara, Detroit, Michilimakinac, Oswego, Carleton Isle, Ontario, 1782-1783.

Engineers' Department. Letters and papers. 1777-1783. Returns of artificers employed, engineers, miners, with a few letters from Lieut. Twiss and Capt. Marr.

General hospital returns. 1777-1781. From hospital staffs in Canadian hospitals, with lists, instructions, and proposals.

Lists of the general and staff officers of the army in Canada (British and German staffs). 1776-1782.

7. 1778-1783. *Id.*

Quartermaster-Generals' Department. General returns, with a few letters, chiefly from Canada. 1778-1781.

Ordnance Department. *Id.* 1777-1782.

Letters from Maj. Dunbar, Brig.-Gen. Maclean, Lieut. Maurer, Maj. Nairn, with enclosures. Montreal, 1779-1780.

Letters from Majs. Powell, St. Leger, Nairn, Carleton, Campbell, Skene, and Hayes. St. John's, Chambly, Isle aux Noix, 1779-1783.

Letters from Brig.-Gen. Maclean and Majs. Dunbar, Harris, and Rogers. Montreal, Sorel, 1781-1783.

8. 1776-1783. *Id.*

Returns of the staff of the Royal Artillery and other British regiments after their arrival in Canada; of the brigade of engineers, with a bill of lading of artillery stores (May 30, 1776); and of the British officers, with the dates of their commissions, 1776; together with a letter from Col. Fraser to Col. (afterward Brig.-Gen.) Maclean.

Letters from officers commanding at Sorel, Maj. Lemoine, Col. St. Leger, and Col. Maclean. 1779-1783.

Letters from Maj. Ross, Capts. Ancram and Alexander Fraser. Carleton Isle, Cataraqui, Oswego, 1779-1783.

Hessian letters, Maj. Ritter, Gen. de Loos, Majs. d'Allenbocrum, Riedesel, Papet, Creuzbourg, de Barner, Jonancourt, Rochenplatt, Speth, Schoele, 1781, 1783, together with " Liste du premier battalion de Hesse Hanau ", etc., Jan. 25, 1783, signed " Lentz Colonel ".

Letters from Lieut. Hamilton, Ensigns Arden and McGrath, commanding at Three Rivers. 1779-1782.

9. 1776-1779. Memorials, Petitions, and Order Books.

Military and provincial memorials addressed to Gen. Haldimand, 1776, 1777, 1779-1782, and to Gen. Carleton, 1776, 1778.

Military and naval memorials addressed to Gen. Carleton. 1777. These petitions ask for promotion, assignments, positions, change of duty, re-establishment, employment, arrears of pay, pardon for deserters, many of them without date.

Id. from Canadian and other inhabitants. 1777-1779. The petitioners, large numbers of whom are French, seek positions, financial aid, annuities for services rendered, relief, trade protection, etc.

Id. from Loyalists in Canada, many of whom fled from the region north of Albany and around Lake Champlain after Burgoyne's surrender. They ask for aid, relief, recompense, and pay, and often present vivid accounts of the situation. The letters are in many cases undated.

In this bundle have been placed Gen. Carleton's general order book, in two volumes, found among the Bank of England records and transferred to the Public Record Office in 1907. The first and largest of the volumes begins May 8, 1782, and extends to June 30, 1783. The second, a book three by eight inches in size, begins July 1, 1783, and extends to Nov. 23, 1783, with an " after order " on the details of the evacuation.

The first entry records the appointment of Brook Watson as commissary-general. Further entries in the first volume concern appointments, promotions, courts-martial, disposition of troops, appointment of boards of various kinds, rations, forage, embarkation, hospital instructions, reviews, funerals, garrison orders, proclamations (Apr. 7, 1783, of cessation of arms " to be read at City Hall at 12 o'c on the 8th "), charges (against Lieut.-Col. George Campbell, June, 1783), leaves of absence (Joshua Loring, commissary-general of prisoners, to go to England for six months, Nov., 1782).

The second volume is a continuation of the first and concerns paroles and countersigns, appointments, promotions, subsistence of troops, clothing, returns of arms, many accounts of courts-martial with names, desertion, robbery, carrying off of negroes, disobedience of orders (punishment by lashes or hanging), counterfeiting (case of Lieut. Moncrief), invalids, sailing of troops (Hessian and others), instructions of June 9, 1783, from the king (entered Aug. 17, 1783), reduction and return of the forces, leaves of absence, garrison orders, funerals, pulling down of buildings in New York, claims of citizens against officers, disbanding of troops (British soldiers settling in Nova Scotia), etc. An order of Aug. 2, 1783, reads as follows: " Any person found committing the smallest depredation on the property of the Inhabitants, either by destroying their Fences, Orchards, Cattle, Corn, Gardens, or in any other manner whatsoever will be severely punished. The Provost Marshal has orders to patrole continually and to apprehend and to execute on the spot any Soldier or follower of the army he finds marauding."

10. 1775-1782. Returns, Lists, and Letters.
Returns and papers respecting various provincial corps in Canada. 1779-1781, 1783.
Annual lists of non-commissioned officers (country, age, size, time), drummers and privates of the German, British, and provincial troops in Canada.
Id. of the provincial troops.
Miscellaneous letters, reports, and returns. 1778-1783.
Letters and papers, Indian Department, containing lists of officers, conferences, minutes of meetings, drafts and copies of speeches. 1775-1782.

MISCELLANEA, VARIOUS.

W. O. 30.

1. 1775-1783. Register of Letters of Attorney.
This register concerns the pay of the soldiers.

13. 1754-1794. Register of Papers relating to Clothing.

17-35. 1684-1785. Registers of Royal Warrants for holding Courts-Martial.

Contains copies of all warrants, of which there are many, sent to the colonies, either empowering governors to appoint courts-martial and to confirm sentences of death, or commanding the holding of courts-martial in special cases. In **14** is contained the evidence in the case of Col. Andrew Frazer, tried for disobedience and neglect of orders in the West Indies. 1788-1790.

54. 1756-1793. Papers relating to the Defence of Great Britain and Ireland.

The last paper in the book is headed, " Remarks on that part of the State No 1, which expresses the force in the Leeward Is. and Jamaica towards the close of the year 1781 ". Apparently by Gen. Roy. The " State " referred to is not in the volume.

88-90. 1685-1746. Reports on Petitions and Memorials.

96. 1777-1798. List of Ships.

UNNUMBERED PAPERS.

1-28. 1753-1783. Unnumbered Papers.

W. O. 40.

These bundles, made up of packets separately tied up, are arranged chronologically, and those for each year alphabetically, *viz.*: those from individuals under the writer's names, those from public offices under the name of the office (Ordnance under O, Treasury under T, etc.), those from corporate bodies, councils, etc., under the name of the place or colony (Antigua under A, etc.). They contain sundry petitions and applications sent to the Secretary at War, relating to commissions, resignations, and the like, together with letters relating to the same. Also papers regarding the embarkation of troops, and other matters that came outside the regular routine of the office. These bundles are not entered in the printed list.

ORDNANCE.

OUT-LETTERS.

5-16. 1699-1783. Master General, Board, and Commander-in-Chief.

W. O. 46.

Very few entries relating to America. In **6** there is a report (1709) on a demand for tents for the Palatines going to New York, and others on powder for Virginia and engineers for Newfoundland and the West Indies. In **7** there is a reference to bills of exchange from Louisburg, which among other things necessitated an issue of money. In **8** are entries of letters to the storekeepers at Jamaica, Annapolis Royal, and Placentia. In **9** are references to engineers for Gage's army, powder and ball for Quebec, and a store-keeper for Dominica. In **13** are entries of two letters to Gen. Phillips in Nova Scotia and one to Gov. Haldimand. There are other references in these volumes of a similar character, the later ones of which are interesting as disclosing the machinery of the Ordnance Office during the American War.

Especially valuable are certain letters of Charles Townshend, master general, in vols. **9** and **10**, which comment not on ordnance but on current events and the state of public opinion. **9** furnishes some interesting accounts by Brig. George Townshend,[1] who served under Wolfe, by Cols. Murray and Isaac Barré, who were present and were therefore eye-witnesses of what occurred, of the battle of the Heights of Abraham, with a reference to observations by the historian Hume.

MINUTES.

1-33. 1644-1781. General Minutes and Journal of Proceedings.

W. O. 47.

See the printed list. The minutes of the board contain but few entries relating to the colonies. Except for **26**, 1781, there are no volumes for the period 1727-1780. In conjunction with these minutes, those of the surveyor general should be consulted, which are complete for the years 1749-1783, *W. O.* 47: **34-102**. These volumes are well indexed and can be conveniently used, though they throw little direct light on military operations in America.

LEDGERS OF ACCOUNTS.

1-127. Treasurers' and Paymasters' Ledgers, General.

W. O. 48.

254-262. 1748-1783. Expense Ledgers.
339-343. 1752-1777. Works Ledgers.

These volumes give convenient summaries of expenditure, under various headings, such as " Military Contingencies ", " Stores ", " Barracks ", etc., and are well indexed.

---

[1] "Townshend MSS.", *Eleventh Report* of the Hist. MSS. Com. Brig. Townshend, afterward the Marquess of Townshend, succeeded to the command after the death of Wolfe. Murray was the first civil governor of Canada, and Barré was at Wolfe's side when he fell.

ACCOUNTS, VARIOUS.

W. O. 49.
—

284-285. 1711-1800. Miscellaneous Subsidiary Papers.

Many of these papers relate to operations in America.

BILL BOOKS.   SERIES I.

W. O. 50.
—

2-11. 1694-1752. Quarterly Bills.
12. 1775-1778. Quebec Bill Books.
13-20. 1678-1754. Bill Books, Miscellaneous.

For a statement regarding the bill books see under Series IV.

BILL BOOKS.   SERIES II.

W. O. 51.
—

1-309. 1630-1783. Bill Books.

These volumes contain the quarterly accounts. Those with items regarding America are as follows: **192** (1753-1755), **197** (1755-1757), **204** (1757-1760), **214** (1760-1763), **226** (1763-1765), **234** (1765-1767), **241** (1768-1770), **247** (1770-1772), **255** (1772-1774), **262** (1774-1775), **267** (1776-1777), **274** (1777-1779), **285** (1779-1780), **293** (1780-1782), **303** (1781-1783).

W. O. 53.
—

BILL BOOKS.   SERIES IV.

445. 1700-1701. Newfoundland Bills.

The Public Record Office furnishes the following information for those using the Ordnance Accounts. " For general financial information the sources which should be examined are, firstly, the Declared Accounts (Audit Office) of the Treasurer of Ordnance ; then the expense ledgers, 1748-1832. Details of expenditure will probably be found in the main series of Treasurer's ledgers. For still further detail as to Ordnance finance the Bill Books should be consulted. These are books containing either copies or the originals of various documents, subsidiary to the accounts of the Treasurer of Ordnance and certain paymasters abroad. These documents comprise bills sent in by contractors, storekeepers' receipts, pay-lists, and miscellaneous vouchers of various descriptions. Series I., II., III., of the Bill Books are entry books ; Series IV. consists of original documents bound up in volumes. Of the four series, the first is a small and miscellaneous collection chiefly consisting of quarterly bill books ; series II. and III. form the main body and extend over the whole period from 1630 to 1859; while series IV. is chiefly made up of vouchers and other subsidiary documents sent in by the paymasters and store-keepers at various ordnance stations.

" Apart from their general importance, in relation to the inner working of the Ordnance Accounts, the Bill Books are valuable as supplementing to a certain extent the somewhat defective registers of the Ordnance Office. (a) The Quarterly Bill Books after 1750 contain, in addition to salaries and allowances paid to those officials and artificers whose names appear in the Quarter Books, lists of payments to superannuated officers and also some pension lists; (b) the vouchers and other subsidiary documents, which comprise the greater part of series IV., contain lists of artificers and civil engineers employed abroad as well as partial lists of artillery and engineers to whom the foreign storekeepers sometimes acted as storekeepers."

MISCELLANEA.

W. O. 55.	**283.** 1757-1760. Reports, North America.
	330-375. 1660-1783. Entry Books of Warrants and Orders in Council.

The original documents are in **423-431, 1642-1669, 1759-1763.**

450. 1772-1857. Original Warrants and Orders in Council. Engineers.

469-496. 1670-1810. Entry Books of Warrants from the Master General and Board of Ordnance. Series I.

497-513. 1711-1795. *Id.* Series II.

1537. 1773-1777. Local Letter-Books, Artillery, America.

1550 (8). 1752. Observation Reports, etc., on Defence, Fortifications, etc., Antigua.

1553 (4). 1770. *Id.,* Dominica.

1557 (1-4). 1774, 1776, 1778, 1780. *Id.,* Newfoundland.

1558 (2, 3). 1740, 1783. *Id.,* Nova Scotia.

1617 (1-6). 1770-1780. Lands, Rents, and Buildings. Statements of Rent received; Reports of Encroachments and Perambulations; Returns, Deeds, Plans, and Papers.

> 1. Annapolis Royal; 2. Antigua; 3. Bahamas; 4. Barbadoes; 5. Berbice; 6. Bermuda.

1618. *Id.,* Canada.

1619 (3, 4). *Id.* 3. Demerara; 4. Dominica.

1620 (2, 3, 6). *Id.* 2. Grenada; 3. Halifax; 6. Jamaica.

1621 (5, 7). *Id.* 5. Newfoundland; 7. Nova Scotia.

1622 (1, 3, 4, 7). *Id.* 1. St. Christopher; 3. St. Lucia; 4. St. Vincent; 7. Tobago.

1625-1766. 1571-1754. Accounts of Stores and Arms issued; Surveys of Stores and Arms.

> **1765** is a store ledger for Annapolis Royal. **1714.** Probably but few of these volumes relate to America.

1813. 1745-1750. Entry Book of Letters relating to the Louisburg Expedition.

1814. 1749. Mr. Paul Wibault's answer to Mr. Bastide's Complaints. Placentia, Newfoundland.

1817. 1753-1754. Letter-Book relating to Canada and other Colonies (Africa).

1820. 1758-1772. Letter-Books. Quebec, Halifax, and America.

1821. 1761-1762. Letter-Book. Halifax.

1822. 1768-1772. Quebec: Various Returns and Estimates.

COMMISSARIAT.
IN-LETTERS.

W. O. 57.

10. 1814-1815. In-Letters: America.

ACCOUNTS.

11-33. 1774-1784. Commissariat Accounts.

W. O. 60.

    11. 1774-1782; **12,** 1782-1783. New York, General Account.

    13. 1782-1783. New York, Journal.

    14. 1781-1783. New York, Ledger.

15. 1782-1783. New York, Cash Books, Memoranda, Sale of Stores, etc.

16. 1776-1783. New York, Account of Victualling.

17, 18. 1782. Abstract of Rations for Foreign Troops.

19, 1782; **20,** 1782; **21,** 1782-1783. Tabular Account.

22, 23. 1776-1784. New York, Vouchers relating to Ships Victualled.

24-33. 1776-1784. New York, Miscellaneous, Vouchers.

Among the books and bundles in this group are: the commissariat papers, found among the records of the Bank of England and transferred to the Public Record Office in 1907 (bundle **14**). They form the official papers of Brook Watson, commissary-general for all the colonies from West Florida to Nova Scotia, and are dated May-Dec., 1782. They consist of books, ledgers, papers (books), and folded papers in packets containing the state of account between the commissary-general and the various contractors and officials for services rendered to the government or for goods supplied, as follows:

Memorandum Book of Brook Watson. Large paper folio, containing memoranda of business to be done, New York, June 12–Aug. 20, 1783, drafts of letters to be written, notes regarding refugees and their provisioning on board sundry vessels, regarding general provisioning, relations with subordinates, copies of letters, and accounts.

Journals, Ledgers, Cash Book, Sale Book, of Transports Victualled; Payments to Masters of Transports.

Abstract Books of Foreign Corps, which furnish a very complete establishment of the Hessians and other German auxiliaries, including the train, hospitals, etc. A number of the books and papers are dated as far back as 1777.

Foreign Corps Victualled or Transports.

Warrant Book of Brook Watson.

The report made by the Public Record Office upon these papers contains the following statement: " The papers give much information not found in the books, *e. g.* as to movements of troops, especially isolated units, and the names of civilian officers and American merchants. They also provide an extensive list of merchant vessels then at sea. Special attention is given to the supplies for the German troops, and for the American Loyalists removed to Nova Scotia. These records might also be valuable to historians for the purpose of supplying information as to the problem of transport and its bearing on the fortunes of the war, though these particular accounts have to do rather with the evacuation of the states at the close of the war."

ARMY LISTS.

MANUSCRIPT LISTS.

1-12. 1702-1752. Army Lists.

13. 1755-1816. *Id.,* Alphabetical.

W. O. 64.
___

Beautifully bound volumes, in soft, dark brown undressed calf, with red labels, and bearing on book plate " War Office, Secretary of State's Library ". The series is not annual, as there are but ten volumes for fifty years.

The arrangement is similar to that in the printed volumes, horse, dragoons, foot, showing names of officers and dates of commissions, all alterations and promotions being indicated in red ink. At the end of each volume will be found the officers of the companies in America, as, for example, in 1745 (**10**) the four companies at New York, the eight companies at Jamaica, the one at Bermuda, and Oglethorpe's. Also a list of field-officers with dates of commissions.

7 and **8** are army gradation books. 1705-1736. A page or more is devoted to each year, and is divided into three grades, captains, lieutenants, cornets or ensigns. The lists give the names of the officers, dates of commissions, and the regiment. Alterations are in red ink.

13 is likewise an army gradation book. 1775-1816. Its pages are divided into columns with printed headings, beginning at the left hand with " Cornet " and ending at the right with " Field Marshal ". The entries are alphabetical, under the letters of the alphabet only, but the arrangement constitutes an alphabetical index to the promotion of each officer, as the dates and regiments are entered under the respective columns. Apparently the entries concern the British army only. At the beginning are explanations as to the length of service required for promotion, etc.

PRINTED LISTS.

1-33. 1754-1783. *Annual Army Lists.* Printed.

These are the annual army lists, issued from the War Office under the direction of the Secretary at War. A specimen title-page is as follows: "War Office, 20 July, 1781. A List of all the Officers of the Army, viz. the General and Field Officers; the Officers of the several Troops, Regiments, Independent Companies, and Garrisons; with an alphabetical index to the whole. Also, A List of the Officers of the Royal Regiment of Artillery, the Corps of Engineers, the Irish Artillery and Engineers, and of the Marine Forces; the Officers on Half Pay and a Succession of Colonels. To which are likewise added The Officers of the Militia Forces, and of the Fencible and Provincial Regiments in Great Britain". Under "Garrisons" are included the companies in America, and there is a separate section for "Officers of the Hospitals for the Forces in North America and the West Indies".

164-166. 1770-1783. Annual Army Lists, made up for official use in the War Office.

164. 1778. A printed list of general and staff officers on the establishment of North America, from 1770, covering staff officers, general hospital staff, artillery officers, officers of dragoons, German auxiliaries, and provincial regiments. The lists of officers of the provincial regiments are on pp. 61-84, where will be found the dates of joining the regiment. The lists differ considerably from those in *Treas.* 64 : **23,** and from those in the next volume.

165. 1783. British American Half-Pay Lists. In 1783, Gen. Carleton directed a return to be made of the names, services, and ages up to that time, of the officers belonging to the provincial regiments, including the officers of the British-American staff and others attached to that part of the service. This return was completed, and a copy was retained by Ward Chipman, deputy muster-master of the provincial regiments, 1777-1783, whose name appears among the general staff officers in this volume and in *Treas.* 64 : **23.** A copy of the return was sent by Chipman to the War Office in 1822 for the purpose of meeting the claims made by the families of the officers of the provincial regiments raised prior to 1783.

The lists given should be compared with those in *Treas.* 64 : **23.** The latter, which is of date later than 1783, as internal evidence shows, contains the names of "Broken Corps", with an explanation of why broken, that are not in the War Office volume, while the latter has a list of "Seconded Officers", not in the Treasury volume. The latter contains a few more names, indications of vacancies and why, and a column of remarks on "alterations", *i. e.,* resignations, successions, and half-pay retirements. The War Office volume notes age, service in the British or provincial corps, and the country or nationality, details which are not to be found in the Treasury volume.

The following list contains the names of sixty-four provincial regiments, as derived from these and other records.

New York Volunteers.
British Legion Cavalry.
British Legion Infantry.
Loyal American Regiment.
Fencible Americans.
New Jersey Volunteers.
De Lancey's Volunteers.
Prince of Wales's American Volunteers.
Orange Rangers.
Maryland Loyalists.
Pennsylvania Loyalists.
South Carolina Loyalists.
King's Carolina Loyalists or King's Florida Rangers.
North Carolina Volunteers.
Maj. Rogers's Rangers.
American Legion (Arnold's Regiment).
King's American Dragoons.
Guides and Pioneers.
St. John Pioneers.
North Carolina Independent Company.
Armed Boat Company.
Black Pioneers.
Duke of Cumberland's Regiment.
King's Royal Regiment.
Col. Butler's Rangers.
Maj. Jessup's Rangers.
King's Rangers.
Royal Highland Regiment.
Royal Nova Scotia Volunteers.
Dutchess County Troops.
Maj. William Stark's Corps.

Philadelphia Dragoons.
Rhode Island Loyalists.
Skinner's Brigade.
Volunteers of Ireland.
Bucks County Light Dragoons.
The Batteaux Company.
Royal Georgia Volunteers.
Nassau Blues.
Georgia Light Dragoons.
Gov. Wentworth's Volunteers.
Georgia Loyalists.
United Corps of Pennsylvania and Maryland.
Light Infantry Company.
Wilmington Light Dragoons.
The Ethiopian Regiment.
Queen's Own Loyal Virginia Regiment.
Troops of Light Horse.
North Carolina Highlanders.
North Carolina Provincials.
Emmerick's Chasseurs.
Roman Catholic Volunteers.
Diemar's Troop of Hussars.
Garrison Battalion.
West Jersey Volunteers.
Loyal American Reformees.
Loyal Foresters.
South Carolina Provincials.
Loyal New Englanders.
Independent Companies.
Queen's Rangers.
West Florida Provincials.
West India Provincials.
Canadian Provincials.

Nos. 1-27 are from the War Office and Treasury lists; 28-45 from the *A. O. Declared Accounts,* **325,** 1287, 1288; 46-48 from the same, **1324,** 627; 49-64 are from the list of " Broken Corps " in the Treasury papers. Probably duplicate names for the same regiment have been included in the list. Lists of persons, not in any particular corps but who received commissions in consequence of their personal service as guides, etc., are also given among the " Broken Corps ". Canadian and West Indian Corps will be found in *W. O.* 65 : **166.** The series here given should be compared with that in *Canadian Archives,* 1883, p. 11.

In 1781 the distribution of the provincials was as follows (*C. O.* 5 : **173**) :

New York District.
First American Regiment or Queen's Rangers.
De Lancey's Volunteers, 3d Battalion.
Skinner's Brigade, 1st, 2d, and 4th Battalions.
Loyal American Regiment.
Loyal New Englanders.

Hussars.
Guides and Pioneers.
Gov. Wentworth's Volunteers.
Carolina and Georgia.
Second American Regiment or Volunteers of Ireland.
Third American Regiment or New York Volunteers.
De Lancey's Volunteers, 1st and 2d Battalions.
Prince of Wales's American Volunteers.
King's American Regiment.
Skinner's Brigade, 3d Battalion.
British Legion.
South Carolinians.
North Carolina Volunteers.
Georgia Rangers.
Bucks County Dragoons.
Pensacola.
Maryland Loyalists.
Pennsylvania Loyalists.
New Providence and Bermuda.
Garrison Battalion.
Nova Scotia.
Fencible Americans.
Orange Rangers.
Nova Scotia Volunteers.
Independent Companies.
King's Rangers.
New York.
Black Pioneers.

Other lists and returns will be found here and there among the Secretary at War's correspondence, either in the War Office series or in the Colonial Office series. In 1781 Secretary at War Jenkinson reported that in Sept., 1780, Sir Henry Clinton sent him a general return of all the provincial forces in North America, a copy of which he sent to Lord George Germain, and separate returns of each of the corps, which he kept in his own office for any use to which it might be thought necessary to apply them (*C. O.* 5: **173**). No trace has been found of these returns.

166. Officers of the British-American Forces placed on Half-Pay and Allowances at the Conclusion of the American War. 1783.

This book contains the following lists:

(a). Of officers entitled to half-pay pursuant to the recommendation of Sir Guy Carleton, as belonging to such regiments as were completed and reported fit for service, agreeable to His Majesty's pleasure, signified by Lord Sackville. 1779.

(b). Of others not recommended by the commander-in-chief but who have since stated their claims in England, and as they appear to be within the spirit of the letter [of Aug., 1784] are allowed to receive half-pay.

(c). Of widows of officers of the provincials whose husbands died in actual service.

(d). Of provincial officers who served in the West Indies.

These lists are corrected to 1832 and are well indexed. They contain the names of Canadian and West Indian corps not to be found in any of the other lists.

HIGH COURT OF ADMIRALTY PAPERS.

INTRODUCTION.

The Lord High Admiral had powers of protection and jurisdiction in all marine affairs. He governed the king's navy and determined maritime causes, both civil and criminal, upon the sea, in ports and harbors, and within navigable rivers below the first bridge. His jurisdiction covered "spoil" cases, mercantile and shipping cases, fishermen, wrecks and find-alls, pirate goods, royal fish, interloping, various torts, collision, salvage, negligence of pilots, masters, and seamen, and he was the conservator of harbors and rivers, hostages, and deodands. He granted vice-admiralty commissions and deputed judges to exercise justice in courts of admiralty. He received the droits or perquisites of admiralty, amercements, goods of pirates, prizes, waifs, strays, wrecks, and deodands.[1]

The origin of the Admiralty Court was intimately connected with the claim of Edward III. to the sovereignty of the seas and can be traced back to the period of the naval battle of Sluys (1340). At first the court was not held in any fixed place, but as early as the first half of the sixteenth century, it got established in Southwark, on St. Margaret's Hill, in part of the old parish church of St. Margaret, which formerly stood there. About 1675 it was removed to Doctors' Commons. The enlargement of the court and its powers dates from 1516-1536, and its records begin with 1524. The holding of distinct sessions for Instance and Prize cases does not appear to have been effected until the middle of the seventeenth century.

Doctors' Commons, where the admiralty and ecclesiastical courts were held, was the place of residence, entertainment, and reception of the judges, advocates, proctors, and others, who dispensed and administered the civil law. Before 1570 the civilians had lodged in a mean and contracted house on the north side of Paternoster Row, which had been the residence of one of the canons residentiary of St. Paul's, and afterward in a tavern known as Queen's Head. But in that year, Dr. Henry Harvey, one of their most conspicuous members, leased of the dean and chapter of St. Paul's an old stone building, the London house of the Blounts, Lords Mountjoy, which belonged to the cathedral and lay on St. Bennet's Hill, south of the churchyard in the parish of St. Bennet, near Paul's wharf. This structure Harvey designed as a home for the doctors of civil law. The society or college, thus housed, was a voluntary association until 1768, when it was incorporated under the title of "The College of Doctors of Law exercent in the Ecclesiastical and Admiralty Courts", and in 1783, the dean and chapter conveyed the site, which belonged to the church of St. Paul's, to the civilians, and vested the freehold and fee simple of Doctors' Commons in that body for £105 a year, clear of all taxes. Mountjoy House was burned in 1666, and for eight years the college was settled in Exeter House in the Strand. New buildings were erected in 1674, on the same site, at the expense of the college, and

---

[1] Marsden, *Select Pleas in the Court of Admiralty*, especially II. xiii-xxxix (powers), lxxix (history, seventeenth century). For a general treatment, see Holdsworth, *A History of English Law*, I. 313-332. In *Cal. Dom.*, 1671, p. 555, is a reference to jurisdiction below the first bridge.

remained in use until the demand for improvements about the cathedral led to their dismantling in 1861-1862, and their final demolition in 1867.

The buildings, consisting of the dining-hall, the hall for the hearing of causes, the library, and the doctors' chambers, lay about two quadrangles, hidden from the street by rows of shops and houses, and were approached through two archways, one from Great Knightrider Street, and the other from the thoroughfare known as St. Bennet's Hill. Across St. Bennet's Hill to the east was the Herald's College or College of Arms, the front of which now faces Queen Victoria Street, the roadway of which passes over what was once the garden of Doctors' Commons.[1]

The college consisted of a president and doctors, who had to be doctors of civil law in one of the English universities, Oxford or Cambridge, and were admitted on petition by the fiat of the archbishop.[2] The name Doctors' Commons came from the practice of dining together, and many interesting practices arose, such as the giving of a breakfast by a newly admitted proctor[3] and the surrender of the gown of a deceased member as a perquisite to the beadle. The system of fees was very elaborate, as may be learned from the fee books and from various reports of royal commissions on the courts of justice.[4]

Before the final dissolution of the corporation in 1857, others than doctors had obtained by special license a right to practise in the courts there. Three of these courts were archiepiscopal, the court of delegates, the court of arches, and the prerogative court of Canterbury, and one episcopal, the consistory court of the Bishop of London. The Admiralty Court since 1660 had sat in two capacities, an Instance Court and a Prize Court, the former exercising ordinary civil jurisdiction, concerning wages, salvage, bottomry, and the like, and the latter dealing with all naval captures in time of war.[5] The criminal division of the Instance Court, or as it was called, the session of Oyer and Terminer and Gaol Delivery for the Admiralty of England, sat in Justice Hall in the Old Bailey, and there cases of murder and piracy were tried. Near Doctors' Commons were the Prerogative Office in Dean's Court and the Faculty Office on the east side of Godliman Street, by Carter Lane, where dispensations and special marriage licenses were obtained and where wills were entered and filed.

The holding of the ecclesiastical and Admiralty courts in Doctors' Commons was due to the fact that only doctors with a special knowledge of civil law could practice in them. The doctors of canon law lost their identity

[1] For a good general account, see Hughson, *London*, III., 464-467. Small plans of Doctors' Commons and the Herald's Office are in Maitland's map of Baynards Castle Ward, and in Rocque's map of London, which was drawn in 1737 and published in 1746. There is a large Rocque map in twenty-four sheets in the British Museum (K. I., tab. 23, no. 8), but it is simply the small map enlarged. The frontispiece to *Registers of St. Ben'et and St. Peter, Paul's Wharf*, Harleian Society, IV. (1912), is a facsimile of a part of Rocque's map, with the course of Queen Victoria Street drawn upon it in red lines.

[2] Entries of admissions may be found in the Books of Accounts.

[3] For further information on this point and for descriptions of the table and the food, see *Adm. Court, Miscellanea*, **813.**

[4] For fees, see *Adm. Court, Miscellanea*, **379-438**; and for the report of the commission of 1734, see *id.*, **842.** Later commissions were those of 1823, appointed to inquire into the duties, salaries, and emoluments of the several courts of justice (report printed, 1824), and 1832, two committees, one ecclesiastical and the other a select committee on the Admiralty and other courts of Doctors' Commons.

[5] On the prize jurisdiction of the Admiralty Court, see statutes of 1661, 1670, 1706, 1739, 1744.

early, probably at the time of the Reformation, when by the statute of 27 Henry VIII. the universities were forbidden to grant degrees of canon law. All procedure in the Admiralty Court was by the civil law, without jury or witnesses ; there was no cross examination, except by an examiner in private. The advocates, who corresponded to the barristers at the common law and were employed by the proctors, who corresponded to the solicitors, presented the case and defended it. The court was always held in the afternoon, in the hall of the college, and spectators were rarely if ever present. In criminal cases, tried by commissioners of oyer and terminer in the sessions hall in the Old Bailey, examinations were held in Doctors' Commons, in the chambers of one of the commissioners, and the trial process was, as in the courts of common law, by judge, jury, and witnesses. In fact, the criminal side of the Instance Court was a common-law court. The chief advocate was known as the king's or queen's advocate general and corresponded to the attorney general, and the chief proctor, the king's or queen's proctor or procurator general, corresponded to the solicitor of the Treasury. The court had its marshal and register, both of whom were frequently served by deputy. The vice-admiralty courts in the colonies were organized in the same way, with the same officials, and trial in them, as in the High Court, was according to the civil law. Hence arose the century-long conflict between the civil law and the common law, between the Admiralty Court and the common-law courts, over the question of jurisdiction. This conflict took place in the colonies as well as in England.

Quite apart from their relation to the vice-admiralty courts in America, Doctors' Commons and the Admiralty Court had much to do with colonial affairs, as the papers of the Admiralty and the High Court show. Many letters relating to admiralty concerns in America are dated from Doctors' Commons and among the Admiralty papers are thirty-three volumes of in-letters from the same quarter and seventeen volumes of out-letters.[1] For the arms and dignities of the members see British Museum, *Add. MSS.,* **34694,** where sixty-nine coats of arms and the names of 708 civilians are recorded.[2] For a characteristic account of what had become in the nineteenth century " a lazy old nook near St. Paul's Churchyard ", see Dickens, *David Copperfield,* chs. XXIII., XXVI., XXXIII. (Prerogative Court) and *Pickwick Papers,* ch. x.

The records of the High Court of Admiralty were originally in the office of the register of that court in Paul's Bakehouse Court, Doctors' Commons. A considerable part of these records were transferred in 1811, 1824, 1825, and 1828 to the Tower, including all the older records of the Instance and Prize courts, the Court of Appeals for Prizes, to which appeals were allowed from the vice-admiralty courts, and from which appeals went to the Privy Council, and the High Court of Delegates, to which appeals were allowed from the ecclesiastical courts and the Instance Court. In 1856 these records

---

[1] *Adm.* 1: **3878-3910,** and *Adm.* 2: **1045-1061.** In the Public Record Office are the Treasurer's Book of Doctors' Commons, 1567-1828, and the Library Accounts of Doctors' Commons, 1730-1844.

[2] See *Sketches of the Lives of Eminent English Civilians,* by Charles Coote, LL. D., with an introduction relating to the college of advocates (1804). The number of advocates and proctors varied, but averaged somewhat less than fifty each. In 1694 there were 44 advocates and 43 proctors. Chamberlayne, *Angliae Notitia, passim.* See also Lambert, *History and Survey of London,* III. 106-118; *Microcosm of London*; Shepherd, *Views of London,* II. 117. Saunders in Knight's *London,* V., gives an excellent description of the hall and the court.

were removed from the Tower to houses in Chancery Lane and thence a few years later to the Public Record Office. When in 1862 it became necessary to consider the demolition of Doctors' Commons, the register requested the Public Record Office to receive further installments of the papers. Many, however, still remained till the opening of the Royal Courts of Justice in 1882, when a further portion was transferred. Additional volumes of the courts of appeal, delegates, and prize, now known as " accruing records ", which had been deposited in the Admiralty division of the High Court of Justice in May, 1909, were removed to the Public Record Office in July of the same year. Thus with the exception of the wills, which were sent to Somerset House, and the muniment books, which were taken with the office of register to the Admiralty Registry, Royal Courts of Justice, practically all the papers relating to our period are deposited in the Public Record Office.

INSTANCE AND PRIZE COURTS.

CALENDARS.

Adm. Court. Instance and Prize. Calendars, Various.

1-8. 1633-1744. Catalogus Libellorum.

This calendar gives the name of the parties to the suit and the number of the document. In the same volumes, reversed, will be found the calendars of the Interrogatories.

9. 1682-1685, 1676-1685. Warrants or Exemplifications.
10. 1652-1674. Allegations (prize) and Interrogatories (prize).
11. 1655-1661. Monitions (prize).
12. 1655-1667. Examinations (prize).
13. 1664-1668. Sentences (prize).
14-27. 1654-1744. Prizes taken.
28. 1671-1672. Ships' Papers taken.
30-31. 1653-1658, 1664-1667. Ships restored.
32. 1662-1664. Ships condemned.

These calendars are of little value and relate chiefly to prizes taken in the Dutch War.

LIBEL FILES.

Adm. Court. Instance and Prize. Libels, etc.

70-139. 1603-1739. Allegations, Decrees, Sentences, etc. Instance Court.

The following list, prepared with the co-operation of Mr. R. G. Marsden, includes, it is believed, references to all, or nearly all, the suits of importance for colonial history. It is possible that some appeals from vice-admiralty courts have been passed over. Each file contains a hundred cases or so, and on an average about two cases in a file relate to America. There is no index or guide. The series extends to 1739, after which date the Admiralty Court became of little importance. Even after 1700 it is chiefly concerned with cases of appeal from vice-admiralty courts. When such cases are known the libel can probably be found without great difficulty. In the Exemplifications (p. 314) and Book of Acts (p. 315) entries relating to all these cases can be found, and as these volumes are much easier to use than are the files, a search may well begin there. The Book of Acts extends to 1748, the Exemplifications to 1768.

Date	Parties to the Suit	File	Number
1608	Popham *c.* Havercombe.	73	274, 279
1620	Virginia Company *c.* Wye.	80	118, 121, 122–124, 126, 127, 131
		81	192 (or 340)
1621–1622	Sir Thomas Dale *c.* Owen and Jones.	80	4, 89–91
1623	Rutt *c.* Matthews.	99	78
	Earl of Warwick *c.* Brustar.	81	6
1624	Stevens and Baker *c.* Plymouth Colony.	82	124
1629	Vassall *c.* Greene.	88	220, 221
1633	Vassall, on account of divers parcels of tobacco.	91	168 (or 171)
1633–1634	Vassall *c.* Goodladd.	91	189 (or 147)
1634	Jones *c.* Lord Baltimore.	91	261 (or 78)
	Leonard *c.* Lord Baltimore.	91	270 (or 69)
	Jones *c.* Lord Baltimore.	91	314 (or 29)
			315 (or 28)
	Vassall *c.* Kingswell.	92	34
1634–1635	Vassall, on account of divers parcels of tobacco.	92	124
1635–1636	Orchard *c.* Lord Baltimore.	93	114, 134, 154
1637	Godborne *c.* Baker.[1]	94	206, 208
		95	137, 138
1638–1639	Cloberry *c.* Claiborne.	98	278
	Claiborne *c.* Cloberry.	98	318
1640	Warwick *c.* Grove.	103	9
	Pillaging gold, pearls, etc., from Warwick's privateers in the West Indies.		
1640	Garretson *c.* Page.	103	189
	Admiralty court, Virginia.		
1642	Cloberry *c.* Leonard Calvert. *Cf.* **98**, 278, 313; **100**, 63.	106	252
	Don Alonzo *c.* Capt. William Jackson.	107	233
	Plundering in the West Indies.		
	Mainwaring *c.* Laudethola.	107	262
	Plundering Spanish ships, trading in the West Indies. *Cf.* **105**, 362; **106**, 4, 6, 24, 25.		
1644–1645	Bercklye *c.* Winthrop.	107	344
1645	Copley and Brent *c.* Ingle.	107	265
	Smith and Franklin *c.* Cloberry.	107	342
1646	Bercklye *c.* Winthrop.	108	2
	Bercklye *c.* Winthrop.	108	12, 43
	(Libel for Feb. 14, 1646, *deest.*)		
	Ingle *c.* Cornwallis.[2]	108	21
1649	Hall *c.* Dobbins.	109	335
	Brazil voyage.		
	Maple *c.* Wood.	109	342
	Barbadoes voyage.		
1650	Bowger *c.* Burchell.	110	30
	Virginia voyage.		
1651	Day *c.* Gibbs.	110	284
	New England voyage.		
	Lord Baltimore *c.* Kirk.	110	329
	Avalon.		
1651–1652	Wilson *c.* Hitching.	111	27
	Guinea to Barbadoes.		
	Lord Baltimore *c.* Kirk.	111	119, 120

[1] Among the papers in this suit is the schedule of books and clothing printed in the *Am. Hist. Rev.*, XI. 328-332.

[2] Some of the documents in this case have been printed by the Maryland Historical Society.

Date	Parties to the Suit	File	Number
1652	Brill *c.* Yeo. Barbadoes.	111	224, 231
1653	Potter *c.* Raymond. James River, Virginia.	111	267
	Arthur *c.* Pott. Barbadoes voyage.	111	340
	Wingfield *c.* Abbott. New England.	111	345
	Bale *c.* Wilkinson. For not carrying persons to Virginia.	111	357
1655–1657	Searchfield *c.* Tilghman. Virginia tobacco.	112	130
	Blachler *c.* Watson. Virginia voyage.	112	216
	Brill *c.* Yeo. Barbadoes prize.	112	224
	Vickers *c.* Scott. Barbadoes.	112	249
	Warne *c.* Watson. Virginia voyage.	112	274
1657–1659	Cox *c.* Norbrook. Jamaica.	113	55
	Yeamans *c.* Symons. Barbadoes.	113	92
	Dixon *c.* Pile. Barbadoes.	113	127
	Ex parte Carvailan. New England.	113	144
	Lutton *c.* Tully. Virginia.	113	172
	Wood *c.* Grove. Newfoundland.	113	194
1659–1662	Wheeler *c.* Trott. Virginia.	114	46
	Flora *c.* Hatch. Barbadoes.	114	139
	Proceedings *c.* Selden and Hunt. Jamaica.	114	224
1662–1664	S. D. N. R.[1] *c.* Johnson. Jamaica negroes.	115	102
	Thomas Martyn, condemned for interloping in the West Indies, sentence.	115	111
	Gubernator, etc., Soc. Danicorum ad partes Guinae *c.* the *Graff Enno,* sentence, West Indies mentioned.	115	124
	S. D. N. R. *c.* the *Peter.* Logwood.	115	139, 141
1664–1672	Meering *c.* Derry. Sentence on appeal.	116	131
	Onions *c.* Sowthin. Virginia voyage.	116	215
1672–1676	Crookes *c.* the *Beginning* of New England.	117	3
	Ogle *c.* the *Madras.* Virginia.	117	59
	Lewis *c.* Prime. Virginia.	117	79
	The *Virgin,* West Indies.	117	93

[1] *Serenissimus Dominus Noster Rex.*

Date	Parties to the Suit	File	Number
	Paxton *c.* Hodges.	117	105
	Cole *c.* Gallop.	117	191–194
	Slaves and gold, Jamaica.		
	Golden Phoenix, sentence, illegal trade.	117	205
	Trott *c.* Piper.	117	202
	Surinam.		
	Sentence from Jamaica, signed by Morgan.	117	205–209 (*circa*)
	Piper *c. Henry and Sarah.*	117	215
	Jamaica.		
1676–1678	*Id.*	118	1, 2
	The *Blackamoor,* illegal trade.	118	80–91 (*circa*)
	The *Endeavor, id.*		
1678–1680	S. D. N. R. *c.* various ships for illegal trading.	118	112–114
		119	1, 2, 16, 37, 39, 41, 62, 63, 71, 77–81, 90, 97–99, 146, 167, 173, 185, 188
	Wilkins *c.* Royal African Company.	119	115
	Negroes, West Indies.		
	Chambers *c.* Bathurst.	119	187
	Jamaica voyage.		
1680–1682	S. D. N. R. *c.* various ships for illegal trading.	120	19, 22, 61, 160
	Jenkins *c.* Phillips.	120	118
	Barbadoes. *Cf.* **141**, 12, a, b.		
	Grill *c.* Phillips.	120	124 b
	Barbadoes.		
1682–1685	Potts *c.* Green.	121	97, 105
	Ship blown up by slaves.		
	Boon *c.* the *Diligence.*	121	124, 126
	Interloper on the rights of the Hudson's Bay Company.		
	Briscoe *c.* the *Richard and Mary.*	121	192, 194
	Interloping, Royal African Company.		
1685–1687	Lynch *c.* St. Loe.	122	181, 192
	Carrying people from Barbadoes without a license.		
1687–1689	S. D. N. R. *c.* the *Constant Love.*	123	89
	Pirate ship. Schedule of silver from Bermuda.		
	S. D. N. R. *c.* the *Revenge.*	123	90, 92
	Pirate ship, Bermuda.		
1690–1693	S. D. N. R. *c.* the *Anne Katherine.*	124	134
	Illegal trading contrary to 12 Car. II.		
	The *St. Pierre,* captured in Canada, under commission from Leisler; condemned as prize, vice-admiralty court, New York.	124	162
	Richards *c.* the *Philadelphia.*	124	205
	Question of ownership.		
1693–1697	Exemplification of proceedings in vice-admiralty court, New York.	125	27
	Phillips *c.* Piers de Bayonne.	125	28
	Appeal from vice-admiralty court, New York.		
	Magnell *c.* Johnson.	125	60
	Barbadoes.		
	Poole *c.* Crist.	125	310
	Ship built in New England.		
	Priosick *c.* Russell.	125	398
	Condemnation signed by Gov. Codrington. Leeward Islands (Antigua) court of vice-admiralty.		

Date	Parties to the Suit	File	Number
1697–1700	Lopez *c.* Moses.	126	24, 89
	Certificate of Jamaica vice-admiralty court.		
	Illegal trade, pass signed by Benjamin Fletcher		
	(Connecticut).	126	133, 140, 152
1700–1703	Kidd and other American pirates.	127	3, 16, 57, 81, 87,
			107 110, 120,
			180
	Shippen *c.* Johnson (the *European*).	127	127, 278
	Bottomry case, Boston.		
1703–1706	Lord High Admiral *c.* Breeden Lane (Kidd).	128	129, 140, 141
	Sentence reversed by delegates (30).		
1706–1710	The *Elizabeth*, illegal trade, appeal.	129	76–79 (*circa*)
	Creagh *c.* Regina.	129	77, 194, 212
	Appeal from Antigua.		
	S. D. N. R. *c.* the *Peace*.	129	120
	Pirate ship.		
	The *Hope*, appeal from Nova Scotia.	129	139
	Swyft *c.* Johnson, the *Providence*.	129	194
	Appeal from the Leeward Islands.		
	Galdy *c.* Handasyd.	129	267
	Appeal from Jamaica.		
	Collings *c.* Peatley.	129	313
	Collision at Barbadoes.		
	John Quelch, pirate sentence, executed at Boston.	129	129, 344, 345
1710–1715	Creagh *c.* Regina and Hamilton.	130	247
	Illegal trade, West Indies. *Cf.* **132,** 56.		
	Ball *c.* Bright.	130	239
	Jamaica voyage.		
1717–1720	Hanson *c.* the *Anne*.	132	32
	Rising of slaves.		
	Hutton *c.* Farrant.	132	74
	Appeal.		
	Cox *c.* Lowther.	132	211, 219
	Barbadoes appeal.		
1720–1722	Squire *c.* Shute.	133	53, 179
	Massachusetts appeal.		
	Ward *c.* Hudson's Bay Company.	133	54
	Barbadoes, vice-admiralty court papers.	133	205, 206
1722–1725	Keeter *c.* Worsley.	134	214, 218, 219,
	Barbadoes appeal.		228
	Bell *c.* Farrant.	134	244, 258
	The *Salamander*, appeal, Bermuda. *Cf.* **135,**		
	60–61.		
	The *America*, appeal from Barbadoes.	134	248, 249
	The *Union, id.*	134	252
	Wilson *c.* Worsley.	134	253
	Appeal.		
1725–1728	The *Delicia*, Providence Island voyage.	135	267–269
1728–1731	Vinery *c.* Lea.	136	12
	Protest at Jamaica.		
	Jenkinson *c.* Upton.	136	40–41
	Great seal of Maryland.		
	Perry *c.* Edwards.	136	50, 167
	Ship built in New England; letters.		
	Whipple *c.* Wilson.	136	210
	Appeal, Rhode Island. *Cf.* **137,** 118.		
	Morton *c.* Van Horne.	136	105
	Massachusetts appeal.		
1736–1739	King *c.* Laurence.	139	60
	Expenses of the king's trial for murder in		
	Maryland.		

The libels, Latin or English, contain the plaintiff's and other pleadings, and are accompanied by exhibits in the form of schedules, inventories, commissions of various kinds, etc., generally in English. Sometimes the libel is very brief, as in the case of Ingle *c.* Cornwallis, sometimes very long, as in the case of Cloberry *c.* Claiborne. The appended documents in many cases are interesting and valuable. A few of the suits to which Vassall was a party do not relate to the colonies, but are of importance as showing Vassall's character and career. There are a number of suits to which Cloberry and Claiborne were parties that are not included in the list (**93**, 157, 165, 167, 183, 194, 203, 234, 273 ; **94**, 52, 73, 109, 153, dated 1635-1637). These suits are of interest as showing the extent of Cloberry's trading undertakings in Ireland, Guinea, and elsewhere, and the frequency of his appearance before the High Court. With him were associated De La Barre and Morehead. There are also a few cases connected with the Newfoundland fisheries, with which De La Barre seems to have been connected. Copies of the libels and papers in the suits of Popham *c.* Havercombe, Virginia Company *c.* Wye, and Warwick *c.* Brustar are in the Library of Congress, and are to be printed in the third volume of the *Records of the Virginia Company,* edited by Miss Kingsbury.

141-148. 1640-1677. Allegations, Prize.
Prize court, many years wanting.

INSTANCE PAPERS.

Adm. Court. Instance Papers. Series Early. —	**1-58.** 1629-1778. Instance Papers. Series Early. Beginning with bundle **10** (1671) the papers are arranged alphabetically according to ships' names, as follows:

10-15. A-Y. 1671-1688.
16-18. A-Y. 1690-1699.
29-33. A-Z. 1700-1712.
34-37. A-Z. 1718-1721.
38-41. Alphabetically, each year. 1731-1770.
42-48. *Id.* 1739-1756.
52-58. *Id.* 1757-1778.

Adm. Court. Instance Papers. Series I. —	**1-48.** 1772-1806. Instance Papers. Series I. Arranged according to numbers, 1-4254. There is a manuscript index to this series, list 5.

INTERROGATORIES.

7-25. 1625-1733. File of Interrogatories (Instance).

26-28. 1653-1673. *Id.* (Prize).

Adm. Court.
Instance and Prize.
Interrogatories.

The calendar to these volumes is very helpful, for by knowing the name and date of a suit the interrogatories can generally be found. In some instances, however, interrogatories either never existed or are missing; but when present will be found to be extremely valuable documents. For example, the interrogatories in the suit against Lord Baltimore (**11**, 323) contain an important summing up of the whole case.

EXAMINATIONS.

36-91. 1602-1750. File of Examinations. First Series.

108-143. 1602-1770. Answers, etc.

Adm. Court.
Instance and Prize.
Examinations.

With some exceptions, these files are from former *Miscellany Books,* 831-886. The examinations consist of the depositions of witnesses and the answers to interrogatories, though it is not clear that interrogatories were always administered. The answers are not in every case easy to find, and both series should be searched. Sometimes they are not entered chronologically, as for example, Baltimore's answer to the interrogatories mentioned above is in **115**, under date June 4, 1636, and Matthews's answer to the libel is in **118**, dated June 29, 1639. The calendar of examinations is of little value. In Vassall's case the plan of making a settlement in Florida or Carolina is elucidated by examinations that are important, supplementing the entries in *Cal. Col.,* 1574-1660. See **51**, Dec. 12, 17, 1634, and Apr. 14, 1635.

APPRAISEMENTS.

1-20. 1626-1745. Appraisements.

Adm. Court.
Instance and Prize.
Appraisements.

After sentence was passed, a commission of appraisement was issued to certain appraisors, who, on the adjournment of the court, made an inventory of the ship and its contents. These volumes contain such appraisements, chiefly of French and Dutch ships, taken as prizes. Though no colonial vessels are listed, the inventories are of interest, as showing cargoes, valuations, and the character of the trade.

WARRANTS.

10-55. 1624-1760. Files of Warrants, Decrees, Summonses, etc.

Adm. Court.
Instance and Prize.
Warrants, etc.

Many bundles wanting. These files contain the warrants, decrees, summonses, etc., issued by the Lord High Admiral for the arrest of ships. A Register of Warrants follows: *Adm. Court, Instance and Prize, Register of Warrants,* **12-77.** 1605-1772.

EXEMPLIFICATIONS.

36-79. 1603-1768. Exemplifications.

Adm. Court.
Instance and Prize.
Exemplifications.
—

Exemplifications are copies of a judgment or orders of the highest authorities to carry out or execute the judgment of a court. In these cases they take the form of orders or instructions, at first in Latin, later in English, from the Lord High Admiral (from the king or in his name, after the office of Lord High Admiral was put in commission), issued to some one to do certain things.

1. To the marshal of the High Court, to release ship or goods wrongly seized in case of prize; to summon the owners of a ship or others to attend "before us or our aforesaid judge or his surrogate in the common hall of Doctors' Commons situate in the Parish of St. Benedict near Pauls Wharf, London"; to recover bond in the case of a person indicted for piracy, who had fled, or to cite the bailsmen to appear or to see judgment and expenses paid; to attach and arrest certain parties until they had paid the sums awarded for damages or costs; to cite certain parties to appear in the common hall, then and there to show cause why something should not be done.

2. In case of appeal from a colonial court, the command was addressed to vice-admirals, justices of the peace, mayors, sheriffs, bailiffs, marshals, constables, and all other officers and ministers, within the liberties and franchises and without, to prevent the carrying out of the decree of the colonial court.

3. In prize cases the command was addressed to the captor or those in whose possession the ship might be to release the ship. In such cases elaborate schedules sometimes accompanied the exemplification.

4. To merchants to furnish a schedule or inventory.

5. To all and singular persons of whatsoever dignity, state, degree, or pre-eminence they be, issued in the case of an exemplification of sentence. A common form.

6. To certain persons to act as a commission for answers and examinations.

7. To the marshal to issue monitions in the cases of derelicts claimed by the crown.

These documents are valuable not only for the information that they contain, but also because they carry the evidence regarding appeals from colonial courts to a much later date than do the libel files, which stop with 1739. The last exemplification here filed is dated 1767, a case of appeal from Dominica. The date of the exemplification, however, gives but slight clue as to the actual date of the appeal.

ASSIGNATION BOOKS.

1-141. 1671-1767. Assignation Books.
190-195. 1776-1789. *Id.,* American Prizes.

Adm. Court.
Instance and Prize.
Assignation Books.
—

Vols. **190-195** contain the record of proceedings before a special court of vice-admiralty erected in pursuance of the proclamation issued, May 1, 1776, by George III. (*Patent Rolls,* 16 George III., pt. IV., no. 16), based on the act of Parliament prohibiting trade with the colonies and authorizing the condemnation of all ships, with their cargoes and furniture, evading the act. The court, thus authorized, held its first session, June 1, 1776. The record, which is very formal and technical, contains the names and ladings of the vessels taken and the sentence of the court. It furnishes few details or incidents of the captures. The volumes are indexed by ships' names, alphabetically.

BOOK OF ACTS.

25-74. 1601-1749. Book of Acts.

75-91. Calendar of Volumes **33-51.**

93-215. 1602-1697. Minutes or Drafts of Acts.

216-274. 1643-1786. Book of Prize Acts.

Adm. Court.
Instance and Prize.
Book of Acts.
—

Vols. **25** to **74** furnish a convenient index to the cases that came before the High Court. They contain the records of each meeting of the court and of the business that came before it day by day, thus giving a chronological history of each suit. There are records in these volumes of suits that do not appear in the calendars, and apparently are not to be found in the libel files. Some of the early suits thus omitted are: Wye *et al.,* master and proprietor of the *Garland, c.* Thomas Sheppard and John Farrar, agents of Wye, on board the ship, Apr. 20, 1620; Sheppard and Farrar *c.* Wye; Ballow and Griffith *c.* Wye; Council of New England *c.* Plymouth ships and merchants. In later volumes we meet with many suits by colonists, Joseph Wragg and Richard Lambton of Charleston, Isaac Pemberton of Philadelphia, against certain ships, as Pemberton *c.* the *Westmoreland* (1744), Wragg and Lambton *c.* the *Lovely Mary* (1744), Young and Gilliard, owners of the *Expedition, c.* Matthews (St. Christopher), Moore and others, the *Recovery c.* Gov. Robinson of Barbadoes; Robert Franks of the *Providence c.* Thomas Mitchell, collector (Virginia, 1748), Matthison *c.* the *Westmoreland* (Jamaica, 1748), Combs and Co. of the *Loyal Mac c.* freight due for transporting goods from Jamaica to the Isle of Wight, and others.

The entries are often brief and but few documents are recorded, but the references are helpful and the volumes will repay a careful examination. There are good indices nominum, and if the name of ship, captain, or plaintiff be known the entry can be readily found.

MONITIONS.

1-53. 1664-1787. Monitions.

Adm. Court.
Instance and Prize.
Monitions.
—

Many years wanting. Monitions were issued in the name of the king and signed by the register of the High Court, warning all persons having any claim or interest in the ship seized to appear before the judge of the High Court, and show cause why the ship should not be condemned as lawful prize, and confiscated and forfeited to His Majesty. Such monitions were affixed to the Royal Exchange.

SENTENCES.

1-42. 1643-1766. Sentences (prize).

43-44. 1776-1788. Sentences in American Prize Causes.

Adm. Court.
Instance and Prize.
Sentences.
—

These volumes and bundles contain sentences in prize causes only. **43-44** repeat the sentences in the American causes noted in *Assignation Books,* **190-195.**

1-1341. 1500-1800. Miscellanea.

> Adm. Court.
> Miscellanea.
> —

Among the first nine hundred bundles and volumes of this series are very few that concern the colonies directly, but many that are of importance for the organization and practice of the High Court itself.

Bundles **167-170** contain *inter alia* accounts of the American Droit Commission, in seven cases where the property after condemnation was restored to the claimants. 1819. **171** is a single volume containing the accounts of ships and goods seized and sold at the island of St. Eustatius in 1781. The prize money here referred to realized nearly a million pounds.

178 American prizes; returns of captures in 1812-1813.

There are many volumes of Admiralty Court accounts—receipts, vouchers, etc., the greater number of which are of date later than 1783. As belonging to the earlier period note may be made of the following:

379-438 constitute a registry of court fees for the years 1656-1783; **562-577** are Instance bill books for 1688-1797, and **603** contains other bills, chiefly prize, 1767-1810; **638-642** contain letters of attorney for prize (original and copies), 1700-1760; and **643-647** are registers for 1760-1791.

706-715 contain taxed bills of costs for 1740-1816, covering claimants, captors, and crown, with ships' names arranged alphabetically.

719 is a court book for 1779-1781, and **731** contains drafts of prize minutes for 1746-1779; **747** contains papers relating to jurisdiction, 1660-1800.

752-763 constitute a valuable series of paper packets, containing the original warrant, sent by the Lord High Admiral or the Admiralty Board and signed by the secretary, for appointments in the High Court and in vice-admiralty courts in England and the colonies, 1604-1801. The first colonial vice-admiralty warrant here found is dated Feb. 17, 1691/2 and creates Sir Edmund Andros vice-admiral of Virginia (**754**, no. 299; no. 300 is the warrant for Samuel Allen's commission, no. 448, Nicholas Trott, no. 467, James Smith, judge, Brian Rushworth, register, Thomas Hayne, marshal, of the vice-admiralty court, Newfoundland, Sept. 1, 1708). The bundles contain also the warrants for other officers of the court. In **756**, no. 409, is the warrant for Quary to be judge of the court for Pennsylvania, West Jersey, and the three Lower Counties, John Moore to be advocate, Josiah Rolfe (Rolph) to be register, and Henry Mallass to be marshal, Aug. 31, 1702. This particular warrant bears traces of having been much handled.

800-803 contain a miscellaneous collection of papers that eventually are to be sorted and rearranged. In **803**, a packet bearing the subnumbering 9. oo–9. rr, a classification device still appearing in red ink in the packet but no longer entered in the list, contains letters of marque issued against America in the years 1812-1814, and a copy of the royal commission (Oct. 13, 1812) authorizing the High Court and duly constituted vice-admiralty courts to proceed against American prizes.

804 contains papers relating to fees and other perquisites of the marshal for the period of the Revolution, 1773 and succeeding years.

805. A large bundle of miscellaneous documents, printed and manuscript.

Among the printed instructions relative to captures by privateers, 1803-1812, is a printed paper, 13 a/1, *Instructions for the Commanders of our Ships and Vessels,* dated May 2, 1776, issued in consequence of the Prohibitory Act. Other papers are as follows:

Directions to exempt from seizure vessels coming from certain West India islands (13 b). 1781.

Printed proclamation appointing the distribution of prizes taken " during the continuance of the Rebellion now subsisting in divers parts of the Continent of North America " (13 gg). Dec. 22, 1775.

Instructions to the commanders of the king's ships in the matter of American prizes (13 hh).

Collection of papers relating to the French prizes taken to Jersey and Guernsey (noted on p. 330). The packet is numbered 13 k/4.

Papers regarding the prize powers of the admiralty court of New York (13 o). 1764-1781.

Among the remaining papers are:

Printed proclamation for granting the distribution of prizes during the present hostilities [against Spain]. June 25, 1779.

Id. ordering pilots to share in prizes. Feb. 12, 1746. (Torn.)

Printed order in Council, permitting Dutch ships to return home. Feb. 16, 1781.

Printed additional instructions to ships of war and privateers that have or may have letters of marque against the French King or the King of Spain or any other enemies or rebellious subjects of the crown of Great Britain. Apr. 19, 1780.

Instructions for the receiver of the droits of admiralty, *temp.* Burrington Goldsworthy (*c.* 1730-1740).

In this paper the droits of admiralty are carefully defined as follows:

In Time of War.

1. Vessels and goods of any enemy that may come by accident or stress of weather, etc., into British or colonial ports or harbors, or that may be taken at sea by a non-commissioned vessel.
2. Vessels and goods of those trading with the enemy or corresponding with them in any manner.
3. Prizes taken by a commissioned captain, who changes his ship without taking out a new commission or by any person acting as captain other than the one named in the commission.
4. Any vessel or goods taken by His Majesty's ships of war, within port, harbor, river, or creek, or within gunshot of any port, castle, or fort.
5. A tenth part of any vessel or goods taken by His Majesty's ships of war on the high seas.

   Id. by privateers or holders of letters of marque.

   Id. of salvage allowed to captors of a vessel rescued or retaken from the enemy.

Whole salvage in case such capture be by His Majesty's ships of war, or by any non-commissioned vessel.

In Time of Peace.

1. Goods and effects of traitors, pirates, homicides, and felons, and other delinquents within the jurisdiction of the Admiralty. Also of all persons *felo de se,* and of fugitives, persons convicted, attainted, condemned, outlawed, or against whom writs of exigents are issued within the jurisdiction of the Admiralty.
2. Fines, forfeitures, amercements, and pecuniary penalties laid or inflicted in any court of admiralty.
3. Royal fishes, "sturgeons, whirlpools, porpusses, whales, dolphins, grampuses, and in general all fish whatever remarkable for their largeness and fatness ".
4. All duties relating to anchorages in seaports and public rivers, from all foreign and other vessels.
5. All wrecks of the sea, lost or waifed goods or merchandises, flotsons (flotsams), jetsons (jetsams), lagans, shares,[1] treasure trove, deodands, and all goods whatever, derelict or forsaken within the jurisdiction of the Admiralty.

828. 1679-1696. Copies of original documents delivered out of the registry of the High Court, consisting of letters of attorney, warrants, bonds, orders, bills of sale, answers, bills of lading, promises to pay, indenture and charter parties, articles of agreement, licenses or passes for merchants, certificates and depositions, proclamations, etc. The registry of the High Court, 1660-1815, contains many documents relating to colonial admiralty appointments and other admiralty business.

829-831. 1675-1805. Receipts for original documents delivered out of the registry.

880. Contains an entry book of papers relating to prize proceedings in the vice-admiralty court of New York during the Revolutionary War. It consists of a single volume, bound in vellum, and labelled " An Account of Letters and Papers occasionally sent to the Registrar of the Admiralty, 1784 ". One entry states that four boxes of records of the court held " during the late war " were received Mar. 16, 1784, from David Mathews, late register of the vice-admiralty court, New York, and duly receipted for by the deputy register in London. This volume contains also a " Catalogue of the Papers in the above mentioned Four Boxes ". See p. 330.

891-1389, formerly known as " Unarranged Miscellanea ", 1542-1800, have now been distributed and classified, topically and chronologically, in part according to the nationalities of the ships concerned, English, American, Spanish, French, and Dutch, in part according to the nature of the contents of the papers. This great

---

[1] Flotsams are goods which from any accidents are found floating or swimming on top of the water. Jetsams are goods cast into the sea or overboard in time of danger and afterward found lying on the shore. Lagans are such parcels of goods as by occasion of shipwreck are sunk in the sea or found under water and to which sometimes may be fastened a buoy or cork in order that they may be found again. Shares are **not** defined, but probably refer to shares of prizes, thirds or tenths.

mass of material, which in one way or another came into the
hands of the register of the Admiralty, is of the most miscellaneous description. In general it consists of official authorizations, attestations, depositions, decrees, valuations, and assess-
ments of vessels seized; interrogatories and answers; fragments
of monitions, warrants, allegations, and libels that appear to have
broken away from the original files and therefore supplement the
Instance and Prize Court papers; commissions and warrants for
the examination of witnesses, notary's certificates, letters of
marque, concordats, register's reports, account books of ships
and merchants, ships' logs and journals, bills of sale, accounts of
prize sales, records of disbursements, itemized accounts of merchants, of the expenses of vessels, and the like. Among the most
interesting papers are the intercepted private and business letters,
some of which had never been opened since they were sealed by
their writers until examined for the purpose of this volume.

Large numbers of the papers are of the character of High Court exhibits,
and consequently are often of value. But nothing so interesting
for colonial history has been discovered as was the Bradford letter
found by Mr. Marsden among these papers, and printed in the
Am. Hist. Rev., VIII. 294-301, or the letters of Altham and
Bridge found in the same bundle and printed by the Massachusetts
Historical Society, *Proceedings*, XLIV. 178-189. These letters
were sent over as exhibits in the suit of Stevens and Fell against
the colony in 1624.

As now rearranged the following bundles are of importance for colonial
history.

SHIPS' BOOKS AND PAPERS.

972. 1773-1780.

Commerce, Samuel Williams, master. Mar.–July 6, 1777. From
Virginia.

Carpenter, Samuel Williams, master. Aug.-Oct., 1773. Falmouth
to Philadelphia.

Commerce. May 22–June 23, 1777. Charleston to Amsterdam.
Unless there were two vessels named *Commerce,* the dates seem to
conflict.

Port au Prince, Joseph Heath, master. Oct. 12–Dec. 5, 1776. Cape
Nicholas Mole to Charleston.

Blair, Thomas Periam, master. Mar.-July, 1777. Dartmouth to
Charleston.

Martha, William Gregory, master. Dec. 26, 1777–Jan. 2, 1778.
Boston toward South Carolina. A duplicate carries the log to
Jan. 3, when the vessel was captured, an event noted in the log.

Warren, John Revell, commander. Dec. 7, 1777–Feb. 10, 1778.
Out of Salem harbor, possibly to Glasgow, as last entry mentions
Isle of Man.

Elizabeth, James Babson, master. Aug. 19–Dec. 6, 1776. Bilboa
toward Cadiz, dismasted off Coruña, and put into that port.

Hooper, William Knapp, master. Apr. 4, 1777–Jan. 10, 1778. Newburyport to James River.

Fame, Joseph Castin, master. May–Nov. 23, 1780. Boston to Amsterdam and return, bearing letter from Amsterdam merchants to their correspondents in Boston.

Hooper[?], William Knapp, master. July 8–Aug. 16, 1774. Newburyport to West Indies (Leeward Islands).

George, Archibald Bog, master. Greenock to Skye, June 26–July 14, 1775, Skye to Cape Fear, Aug. 6, 1775, had a fight with a privateer out of Boston and struck, June 16, 1776.

Wolfe (in same book), Simon Elliot, master. Oct. 16–Nov. 1, 1776. Boston to York River.

Aurora (in same book), John Hucheson, master. Dec. 19, 1776–Jan. 29, 1777. York River apparently to Nantes, but the log ends with the vessel somewhere in the Irish Channel. A duplicate adds under date Jan. 29, " At 1 o'clock was safe in Liverpool dock ".

973. 1777.

Betsey, Capt. Bredon, commander. Mar. 20–July 19, 1777. Bound for South Carolina.

Dickinson (mutilated), William Meston, master. 1775. Cadiz to England; also Jan. 16–Apr. 7, 1776, Philadelphia to Nantes. On Saturday, Mar. 30, 1776, appears this note, " The ship's company finding that the vessel on her arrival at Nantz was to load warlike stores for the Continental Congress thought propper to take the charge of her from the captain and run her into England. Accordingly we did take her from the captain in his Majesty's name." The ship was taken to Bristol.

Elizabeth, Jacob Funck, master. May 10–June 5, 1777. French letters from Charleston.

Rising States, James Thompson, master. Feb. 28–Apr. 14, 1777. Privateer; interesting log.

Some of these log books are very human documents, with covers, fly-leaves, and back-pages embellished with a variety of miscellaneous entries, poems, remarks, calculations, and even pictures.

974. 1774–1779.

Neptune, Larkin Dodge, master. Feb. 16–July 17, 1775. Salem to Dominica and Virgin Isles.

Marquis of Rockingham,[1] George Dodge, jr. June 16–Sept. 9, 1776. In an accompanying packet of papers (labelled " of no consequence ") is a letter from Dodge, Salem, Mar. 21, 1776, in which he speaks of having been taken and carried into Boston, vessel and cargo confiscated. Owned by G. Dodge and Co.

True Briton, Daniel Jacobs, master. July 23–Sept. 5, 1774, from Beverly; Oct. 31–Nov. 30, 1774, from St. Eustatius.

Three Brothers, James Babson, master. Oct. 1, 1776. Salem to Cape May. Almost blank. *Id.* Barbuda to Cape Ann. Dec. 26, 1776. *Id.* Apr. 21–May 19, 1777. Brunswick Island to Bilboa.

Peggy, Alexander Hardie, master. Falmouth to Havre de Grace, then to Charleston, evidently by way of Lisbon, Dec. 13, 1774–Mar. 25, 1775 ; Charleston to Cape Fear, June 4, 1775 ; Cape Fear to Bristol, July 21–Aug. 28, 1775 ; Bristol to Charleston, Nov. 25, 1775–Jan. 30, 1776, taken by H. M. S. *Syren* south of Charleston

---

[1] Name not given in the log, but is to be found in certificate in same packet, signed by committee of correspondence, inspection, and safety.

Bar, condemned in court of vice-admiralty, and sold at public auction on Cattre island. Then became transport ship with Adm. Parker's fleet, and by passport from Parker was allowed to return to Cape Fear, July 26, 1776, and thence to England, Aug. 5–Sept. 16, 1776. Now lies in River Thames, Jan. 23, 1777. Interesting and very full. Interrogatory shows that Hardie was a Scotchman trading between Cape Fear and England. Had no home, but lived on board ship. Had another ship, plying between America, England, and Holland in the Palatine trade. Hardie was a subject of Great Britain.

Reprisal, Elias Ford, commander, on a four months' cruise, Dec. 26, 1778–Mar. 19, 1779, as a privateer from Bristol, bearing a Bristol letter of marque.

990. 1776–1777.

Friendship, Cornelius Taylor, master. May 28, 1776–Apr. 15, 1777. Bristol to Barcelona. In Salo Bay–Bay of Roses, to Apr. 25, thence to London, June 24. A mess book and two account books only partly filled.

Wasp. Mar. 19–Apr. 18, 1776. To Philadelphia.

Lexington, Henry Johnson, commander, for a cruise. Sept. 18, 1777. (Mostly blank.)

991. 1776–1782.

Salem, Simon Byrn, master. Oct. 21–Oct. 26, 1781. Salem to Virginia. (Mostly blank.)

Some records of the New York court of vice-admiralty: *Spitfire* taken by the *Fair American,* Mar. 6, 1782; *Salem,* formerly the *Clementina,* taken by the Americans and renamed, retaken by the *Resolution.* Also ship's papers of the *Swan.*

Lorana, James Haden, master. Left Boston Feb. 7, 1781, with a cargo of lumber and fish for Port au Prince, took on molasses and sugar, Mar. 18–Apr. 13, Cape Cod, Boston, May 7, Boston to Port au Prince, July 15, Turks Island, Aug. 24, Cape Nicholas Mole, Aug. 27, Port au Prince, Sept. 28, Boston, Oct. 22, Boston to Virginia, Jan. 12, 1782, Point Comfort, Feb. 7, Fredericksburg, Feb. 25, took on tobacco from the shore, Apr. 24, began to warp down the river, Apr. 25, abreast of Col. Dangerfield's plantation, continued to receive tobacco, left for Holland May 13, taken about four leagues from the Texel, July 3, 1782. "Shifted the hands and was cared one bord the Privattear wear we found very swell ueaseag more like brothers than foes in every respect not bean cold treated but quite the other way for evean the comon men recived the sailors of the brig with the Best of Sivelety." On Apr. 1, 1782, is the entry: "This day being a Holliday amongst the Buckskins all hands obliged to follow the fashions of the Country" (Virginia).

Sukey of Poole, Christopher Whitewood, master. Dec. 15, 1776–Jan. 19, 1777. Newfoundland toward Barbadoes, taken by Rhode Island privateer. This book was used by James Robertson, commander of the *Tann,* voyage from Charleston to Bordeaux, taken June, 1777. Another log records a voyage from Philadelphia to Coruña and return, Sept. 23–Nov. 8, Nov. 10, 1776–Feb. 6, 1777, Philadelphia to Charleston, Mar. 27, 1777, left Charleston, May 2, log ends, June 9. (Mutilated.)

INTERCEPTED LETTERS.

1066. 1756. Letters from Maryland and Virginia.

Z. W. Young to Capt. William Hamilton. London, Oct. 17.

Samuel Howard to " Dear Brother and Sister " (addressed " Mr. Timothy Brent, London "). Oct. 16.

Job Roughton to John Marshall, Schoolmaster, Northhants. Patapsico ferry, Sept. 6.

William Hale, of Elkridge, to Mrs. Mary Giles, London, regarding a supply of hats from London.

Order from the rector, governor, trustees, and visitors of the free school in the city of Annapolis regarding the legacy of Benedict Leonard Calvert to the school. Oct. 6.

Copy of the *Pennsylvania Gazette*, Aug. 12, 1756, containing a plan of education for the college and academy of Philadelphia. The paper is enclosed in a letter from David Bissett, Bush River, Baltimore Co., Oct. 25, 1756, to his brother, Dr. Charles Bissett, Yorks.

Clementina von Grierson. Annapolis, Oct. 30, 31.

William Stevens to Nathaniel Philips, London. Virginia, Nov. 7. " I have seen but one pretty girl since I have been in the country. This morning I went a fox hunting with some gentlemen where we had excellent sport, for after running him four hours we killed him. I thought the country a very odd place at first to see so many negroes about, for if a man keeps his coach, the coachman, postillion, and footman are all blacks. They all drive with six horses, which are very good ones for their size, for there is none exceeds fourteen hands and a half high." Letters were to be directed to Maj. John Snelson's in Hanover Co., Virginia. In another letter, November, Stevens speaks of " my past follies ".

John Skinner to Robert Skinner, London. Nottingham Iron-Works, Maryland, Oct. 23. " What I wrote you last of Oswego being taken proved too true which was a sadd blow for these provinces as it lays them open to the outrages of their enemys to pour in upon them. In short they seem to be always beforehand with us and execute their schemes before we imagine them to be consulted."

Robert Wilkinson, about Indian fights and scalping. Partapsco River, Bear Creek, Sept. 18.

Daniel Parke Custis to Messrs. Tufton, druggists in the Minories, for " Twig bark for my own taking " and other drugs.

Letter regarding the estate of Ann Mills. Hanover Co., Va., Sept. 30.

John Lockey to his father, Berkshire. Forks of the Gunpowder, Oct. 11.

John Kello. Hampton, Va., Oct. 8, 1755. " Dancing is the chief diversion here and hunting and racing."

Elizabeth Sprigs to her father. Sept. 22. She was evidently a servant, " toiling Day and Night, and then tied up and whipped to that degree you would not treat an animal, scarce anything but Indian corn and salt to eat and that even begrudged. Many negroes are better used. Almost naked, no shoes nor stockings to wear, and the comfort after slaving dureing master's pleasure what rest we can get is to rap ourselves up in a blanket and ly upon the ground."

James Moore to his cousin, Mrs. Margaret Palman regarding public
affairs " at present in a very melancholly and deplorable situation ".
Sept. 19. Another letter, Oct. 4.

Thomas Lloyd, an indented servant, to Edmond Hector, surgeon,
Birmingham, with an account of his service against the Indians.
Augusta Court House, Frontier of Virginia, Oct. 10. Speaks of
his " former follies " and wants to be manumitted.

William Randal. Baltimore, Sept. 23. " This is a very bad country
for servants to live in but very good for free people which bless
God that I am of that number."

Stephen West to Dr. William Martin, London. Upper Marlbro,
Petuxt River, Oct. 25. For drugs, with a list.

An account of Capt. Charles Seabrook's estate, " as it stands with
Thomas Reynold's executor ".

Denys Dulany to John Elgar, London. Georgetown, Nov. 1.

Thomas Saunders, a joiner, to his mother, London. Bush River,
Oct. 9. " i boaght an irich Convict servant named Owen desmond
from Cork just as i was married he soon after Rob'd me of the
chief of my cloaths and also my wifes and run away and i never
heard of him since his first cost was twenty pounds."

Alexander McBean, recruiting officer. Annapolis, Oct. 30. " I
am with Governor Sharp to whom I am singularly obliged and
takes every step in his power to forward the good of the service,
tho his patience is greatly try'd by the Damn'd assembly men that
will hardly do anything for their own or the publick's safety with
good will, they mind nothing but contention and complaining
of taxes and grievances of that kind when their all is almost at
stake." McBean was lieutenant of the fourth battalion of the
Royal American Regiment of Foot at Philadelphia, and at this
time was on recruiting service in Annapolis.

John Smith to Hon. Thomas Bladen, Albemarle St., London, wishing
a recommendation to the governor for the post of sheriff of Cecil
County. Oct. 2.

Nicholas Rogers to John Woodhouse, Essex St., London. Balte-
more Town, Oct. 16. " I intend to send you my eldest son over
which I have named after his uncle James Lloyd in about 7 or 8
years which I intend to have edecated for a lawyer." This eldest
son was then " at the latting school and about 8 years old ".

Richard Tuggey to his mother, Tooting, Surrey. Tuggey was footman to the Hon. Colwatt Tasker.

Daniel Sturgis, a servant or apprentice just out of his time (two
letters). Virginia, June 11, Nov. 4. " I am storekeeper for Mr.
Humphry Bell under his factor. Stores here are much like shops
in London, only with this difference, the shops sell but one kind
or species of wares and stores all kinds. These commodities we
sell to planters and receive in return tobacco, a weed of very little
service to mankind as to its use yet as it is the promoter of a great
trade is of infinite advantage to Great Britain. The people [here
are] neither so industrious no so religious as the English, they are
fond of pageantry and grandure."

Alexander Warfield to Capt. Jehosaphat Rawlings. Severn River,
Maryland, Oct. 16.

Graham Frank to the Bishop of London, giving an account of the church in Virginia and urging the appointment of a suffragan bishop there. Virginia, Nov. 11. In this bundle are a number of important letters from this correspondent. " 'Tis customary with the gentlemen here to send to Scotland for tutors to their children, for the sake of cheapness "; " scarce as [ministers] are in some of the colonies I believe they had better continue so than religion should be disgraced by [immoral] men ".

In this bundle is a packet of letters from the firm of George and John Murdoch, tobacco merchants trading with Virginia. The firm was winding up its business and the letters were received by Capt. George Yuille of the snow *Pelham,* plying between Glasgow and Virginia. As a whole the packet consists of such letters as had accumulated in Yuille's hands between 1750 and 1756, and were received by him at various ports, London, Greenock, Alicante, Nansemond Town, Virginia, etc.

1080. 1777-1779.

This bundle contains a mass of bills, letters, and other papers, some in French to Bordeaux and elsewhere, others scattering from Glasgow, Dublin, and America, the most important being the letters from the British fleet in Narragansett Bay.

J. Dunlop to his wife. Near Belfast, from the *Ambuscade,* Newport, Rhode Island, Feb. 18, 1777. " Our troops have been most surprisingly successful. We have taken so many islands, towns, and forts that we have not men to spare from the garrisoning of them to undertake any important blow before that more succour come out. Twenty thousand Russians are expected and five thousd troops from Cork. It is reported here that there is a hot press at London, a rupture with France expected, and that twenty new regiments of marines are a raising." The whole letter is interesting; it contains some information about Hopkins's fleet.

James Rea to his mother in Dundee. Rhode Island, Feb. 28, 1777. Refers to " a smart skirmish at Springfield in New Jersey, between a party of near 4000 rebels under the command of Gen. Sullivan and the 42d regiment, the famous and gallant highlanders under Sir William Erskine. The rebels were attempting to possess a hill which would have given them a considerable advantage. Sir William perceiving there design directed the highlanders to dispute the ground. They advanced with there usual ador and rune in upon the enemy notwithstanding the great disparity of there numbers and came instantly to close quarters with them and killed upon the spot two hundred and fifty."

A. Forbes to his wife, London. Feb. 26, 1777.

J. Rowe to his agent, London. Feb. 24, 1777. " Last Sitterday the Ribbles came over from Providence in two Row Galleys with about 4 or 500 men but got a sufvear drubing and glad to get back again."

Joseph Ingleden to his father and mother in Yorkshire. Feb. 19, 1777. " We have got Very Troubilsom Times of it all this winter. For the Rabbeles Obligeous to keep a very good Lookout for fear of them Sending feair ships Down upon us To Distroy the fleet for they have mad one attempt."

Thomas Hall to Thomas Hall, cooper, in Blackfryers Gate, Hull. Feb. 29, 1777. "It is generally thought that this next campaign will almost put an end to [the war] for the rebels by all accounts that we have here are a weekning every Day both by epidymical distempers, and by them retiring home as being tir'd of their service thereby beginning to feel in what a deluded condition they are in. We have had within this 3 weeks past several cortels com'd down to exchange prisoners, amongst which that came where some captains and mate of vessells which had been taken by their privateers and carried into Boston. They say it is mostly forc'd Spirit that reigns amongst them there and that country is likely for nothing but a famine amongst them, for had it not been for the few vessels they had taken and carried into that port they would have been ready to a starv'd for a mouthful of bread. They have several privateers laying their and cannot get any hands to man them, the noted commodore Hopkins fleet lays still blockt up at Providence by 2 or 3 of our men of war. It is confidently reported here that the congress have devolved all their power upon Mr. Washington and appointed him dictator in example of the Romans. The reason if the fact be true is very apparent, they find themselves in a slippery situation and are glad to throw their burthen upon the first simpleton of consequence that would take it."

Edmund Dixon to William Wakefield, at the Earl of Huntingdon's, St. James Place. Newport, Feb. 20, 1777. "Tell him he is a happy man to get out of Newport for it is a damd place to live in. I have nothing but my allowance same as a soldier for you cannot get a bit of fresh meat in the whole island."

Peter Regan to John Anthony Pucker, merchant, London. Newport, Feb. 21, 1777. "Our British troops as well as Hessians here are in the greatest of spirits and only wish to distinguish themselves against the rebells, but hope a strong reinforcement will be out by the month of May as the rebells are pushing and exerting themselves to the greatest advantage."

P. Seward to Lieut. Seward of the marines about affairs in America. Halifax, June 24, 1776.

Mark Gregory to Messrs. Gregory and Woolsey, congratulating them on their "victory over the Yankee rebels" and saying that he was glad to hear the marines took the part they did in the affair. Quebec, June 21, 1776.

J. Williamson to his brother and mother, Cumberland, England. Newport, Feb., 1777.

S. Thompson to his wife, London. Newport, Feb. 21, 1777. "My Love, I would give you some american news but we are aferd that the rebels should catch our letters as they hav a great many priveters on the coast. Our army are all well and in good sperets and all wis concors what they have atimted. Our grand army is one the Garseys where they have sundry scrumages with the rebels. Last week we tocke abut 600 prisoners after kiling near 300 and every week more or les but nott enay real feald batel we went for sumor. Last week a cartel come down from Providence with 30 captins of ships which had been tacken by the rebel pirets amongst whom was Capt. Ryle of the Polly and Capt. Clarke of the Hiy-ffield an old lodger at Mr. Laughtons. Theos captins that came from Boston Saylem and marbelhead says the reabls wold ben actually sterved for want of clothing had it nott ben for our ships which they have tacken with so much solders cloas and likewise great quantities of linens and wollin cloth. Sundry ships cargos our men of ware brings in a great miny rebil prizes 3 or 4 in a weeke and retacks minay ships from those pirets and minay of themselfs, the are a poor shiff looking sett generly raged and dirty."

George Brown to father and mother, Alnwick. Newport, Feb. 20, 1777. From on board the *Chatham,* with an account of his experiences since arriving at Staten Island, July 4, 1776; a long and interesting letter showing the British soldier's view of the situation.

S. Rowson to Miss Laverack, Yorkshire. From on board the *Three Sisters,* Rhode Island, Feb. 19, 1777. A lover's letter, narrating experiences with the fleet (12 ships, 60 sail of transports, under Adm. Peter Parker, arriving Dec. 9, 1776, with 5000 English and Hessian troops on board under the command of Gen. Clinton). There are two other letters from the same, one, Feb. 24, 1777, to Capt. John Harnies, which is long and detailed; the other, Feb. 19, to his sister in Lincolnshire.

Timothy Leary to his wife. From on board the *Roman Emperor,* Feb. 24, 1777.

Thomas Plumb, soldier of the 22d Regiment, Capt. McDonald's company, to his brother in Cornwall. Newport, Feb. 22, 1777. "I am resolved to relate our present state and situation in this country at the present time. Our duty is very hard upon the accounts as we receve from the rebels daily such as we are not in sight of as we are day and night within musket shot of each other and they are as numerous as motes in the sea. But we still keep them in constant employ but the cowardly rascals will not stand their ground but watching an opportunity of lying in ambush behind some trees which is the cause of us losing so many men, but thank God where we lose ten they loose 100. But as we routed them from so many places so that they are in the greatest consternation possibly they may give us a field day for it early this spring. I do no doubt but they will as they are almost surrounded by our troops and they must fight or die. But had they the heart as we Britons have we should stand no chance with them." There is another letter from Plumb in **1180**, Feb. 22, 1777.

Thomas Roberts to his wife, London. Rhode Island, Feb. 23, 1777. Also letters from J. Williamson and Jo. Reilly, Feb. 18, 21, 1777. Three prisoners "drummed and fifed from Cape Ann to Ipswich Gaol and there confined for six weeks without liberty of fire or candle or straw to lay on". These men, with 108 others, were exchanged, Feb. 18, 1777.

1085. 1777-1781.

1. Letters from American correspondents in Boston, Philadelphia, and elsewhere to England and France.

John Williams to his sons, Nantes. Boston, 1777. " General Bor-
guine and his army are all kept at Cambridge and I was at Worcester when they all came through extending some miles garded
by our soldiers, a grand sight indeed to se such numbers of our
enemes unarmed and in our power who a few days before threatened Death and Dystruction to all that would not submit to their
master's Tiranical Comand ", and more to the same effect.

An " Account of the Army under General Burgoyne which surrendered to General Gates at Saratoga, Oct. 16, 1777 ".

Letter from Barnabas Deane regarding bills amounting to $2492,
drawn by Congress on the commissioners in France and Spain.
Dec. 22, 1780.

Thomas Greenough to Knox and Mercer, London. Boston, Oct. 28,
1777. " I heartily wish peace was settled with Great Britain and
these states on honorable terms."

Mary Bunker, begging her son to come home from London. Nantucket, Jan. 7, 1778.

2. Letters from Bordeaux and elsewhere in France to various correspondents in America. Some of these letters are from representatives of American business houses, others are from French firms,
and still others from French officials. The letters themselves are
chiefly of a business character.

A dozen letters from Robert Chamberlayne to members of his
family and others in Virginia. 1781.

A package of letters from John Frazer, from which we learn more
about Chamberlayne in Bordeaux. Feb., 1781. In the same
packet are letters from J. Mayo to friends in Richmond. Paris,
1780.

Thomas Ridout to John Ridout of Annapolis. Bordeaux, Jan. 27,
1781.

Letters to " Monsieur Meyer, Premier Sécrétaire de Legation dela
Cour de France pres des État Unis de l'Amérique septrionnale, à
l'hôtel de France à Philadelphie ", on matters of business.

3. Letters to French soldiers and officers in America, from fathers,
uncles, wives, children, etc., unopened until examined for the
purpose of this work. Nearly all of these letters are personal,
rarely touching on public concerns. Occasionally comments are
met with of a more general character, such as " M. Burgoyne me
paroit avoir eu beaucoup plus d'adresse en Angleterre pour sauver
sa tête, que de prudence en Amérique pour conduire son armee ",
dated Feb. 23, 1781, unsigned. Among these letters is a short
note to Luzerne at Philadelphia regarding subscriptions to a
French newspaper.

1180. 1781-1790.

Several packets of miscellaneous letters, some of which, in French
and Dutch, do not relate to America. One collection contains
letters from soldiers and sailors belonging to the squadron lying
in Narrangansett Bay and thus supplements the series in **1080.**
The letters are all informing, though at times the writers make
curious blunders. The latter are generally in humble positions,

as, for example, the servant of an officer in the British light
infantry, Newport, who gives an account of his experiences with
the " Dam'd Yankees ". Another correspondent says, " As this
goes by a merchantman it may miscarry. I write by five different
vessels to my friends, so that if any *one letter gets safe* I have
begged that they would be pleased to let the rest of my friends
know."

In this bundle are a great many letters to importing merchants in
Philadelphia, Baltimore, Annapolis, and elsewhere, and from the
addresses given a directory of such merchants could be compiled.
The following lists are an attempt at such a directory.

Philadelphia. John Richards, jr., John Boyle, M. Hamelin, Peter
Whiteside and Co., Joseph Wharton, Cornelius Barnes, T. M.
Nesbitt and Co., Meuse and Caldwell, William Grahame, John
Leary, jr., and Co., John Purviance, John Swanwick, Mordecai
Lewis and Co., Stewart and Totten, John Ross, Ramsey and Cox,
John Barcley and Co., Samuel Inglis and Co., William Turnbull,
John Bogent, James McCrea, Seagrove and Constable, Andrew
and Hugh Hodge, Blair McClenachan, Butler and Mifflin, John
Pringle, Matthias Harrison, Capt. John Robinson.

Baltimore. Richard Curson, McLure and Young, John Sterrett,
Daniel Bowley and Co., John Lloyd Chamberlain (Talbot Court
House), John Lane, jr. (Pigg Point), Col. Samuel Smith, William Hammond, Samuel and Robert Purviance, Stephen Stewart
and Son, Burtins and Van Wyck, Hugh Young, Robert Gilmore,
Benjamin Rumsey (Joppa), William Neill, William Patterson
and Brother, David Moore, William Taylor, Melchior Küner,
William MacCreary, William McLaughlin, Welsh and Eichel-
berger.

Annapolis. Wallace, Johnson, and Muir, Thomas Rutland, William
Weems, John and Samuel Davidson, Capt. Samuel Maynard
(Herring Bay, Anne Arundel Co.), Thomas How Ridgate (Por-
tobacco), Richard B. Lloyd, John Johnson, Dr. John Hindman
(Talbot Co.), William Stevenson (Chester, Kent Co.), Joseph
Williams, John Weems (Calvert Co.), Samuel Lane (same place).

Virginia. William Thomson (Colchester), Robert McCrea (Alex-
andria), James and John Hendriks (same place), James Buchanan
(Richmond), Watson and Tandy (Alexandria), Robert Beverly
Chew (Fredericksburg).

North Carolina. Maj. Robert Smith (Mecklenburg Co.), Josiah
Collins (Edenton), Webb Bryer and Co. (Edenton), Dr. Nathan
Alexander (Mecklenburg Co.), Daniel Dunscomb, jr. (Chatham).

Boston. John R. Livingston and Co.

In the bundle is a letter to the French consul, Philadelphia, and
another from Tench Coxe to Maj. David S. Franks, Philadelphia,
Apr. 8, 1782.

PROCEEDINGS IN VICE-ADMIRALTY AND OTHER COURTS.

<table>
<tr><td>Adm. Court.
Proceedings.
Vice-Adm. and
Other.</td><td>

59. 1747-1748. Jamaica.

This volume contains the complete record of a court of vice-admiralty held in Jamaica for the trial of four cases of prize, 1747. As an example of procedure in a vice-admiralty court it is unusually clear and complete.</td></tr>
</table>

90. 1723-1739. Virginia, South Carolina, Rhode Island, Pennsylvania, and New York.

Procedure in courts held for the trial of pirates under 11 and 12 William III., " for the more effectual suppression of piracy ".

Virginia, Aug. 14, 1729. For the trial of Edmund Williams and others for piracy at Williamsburg, before William Gooch and others, the judges, by virtue of a commission under the seal of the High Court of Admiralty, bearing date Dec. 13, 1728. The testimony is full of important details for the student of piracy in the colonies.

South Carolina, July, 1734. Trial before the governor of Joseph Lostia, suspected of piracy.

Rhode Island, Sept. 9, 1725. *Id.* at Newport before Gov. Cranston and others of Matthew Perry *et al.* for piracy.

Pennsylvania, Oct. 15, 1731, *Id.* at Philadelphia of John Mackferson and four others. Account of the proceedings partly in manuscript and partly in print from the *American Weekly Mercury*.

New York, July 6, 1724. *Id.* at New York before Gov. Burnet and others of Antonio Nuñez *et al.*

South Carolina, June 12, 1733. *Id.* before Gov. Johnson of Edward Little.

Virginia, Aug. 15, 1728. *Id.* before the president of the council of John Vidal *et al.*

Of similar character though listed under a different heading are the following prize cases :

<table>
<tr><td>Adm. Court.
Prize Papers.
—</td><td>

1821, 1823-1825. 1775-1783. Papers from the Court of Vice-Admiralty, New York. Each bundle labelled " Sent from New York ".</td></tr>
</table>

1821. Monitions or summonses, 1781; letters of marque bonds, 1782-1783; bills of exchange, 1775-1777; appraisements, 1777-1783; libel, James Ferguson *c.* the schooner *York,* filed, Oct. 8, 1777, and other papers in the case; libel, advocate general *c.* the schooner *La Zemire* (from French West Indies to Nantucket), Aug. 21, 1778; sundry intercepted private letters, written in French and Spanish, notes, receipts, bills, permits, invoices, some of early dates, but chiefly of 1773 and following years; libel, advocate general *c.* the brigantine *Young Benjamin,* 1778, with ship's papers; additional libels in packets, labelled alphabetically by ships' names; packet of interrogatories, without answers and undated; accounts of sales by order of the New York court of vice-admiralty, 1778-1782 (large

packet) ; printed instructions from Congress regarding letters of
marque, Apr. 7, 1781 ; printed proclamation in French, endorsed,
" Mr. Britman will be pleased to deliver this to his excellency,
Patrick Henry, Esq."

1823. Three paper-covered books, labelled " List of Causes and Fees
and by whom paid ", 1777-1778; packet labelled " Assignation
Books unbound, recd from N. Y. November 29, 1784 ", containing nine books of admiralty court records, 1777–July 10, 1783.
From another source, we learn that Robert Bayard, judge of the
vice-admiralty court, New York, delivered to the deputy register
of the High Court an assignation book on the date named. This
" book " must be the packet here referred to.

1824. Register of the court of vice-admiralty, New York. Sept. 17,
1777–Oct. 9, 1778, and 1778-1780. Two bound volumes containing letters of agency or attorney (complete list of the names of
captains and men belonging to British ships making captures),
authorizing certain lawyers to recover shares of prize money.
The volumes are well filled, some of the letters being dated earlier
than 1777.

1825. Packets of about 300 allegations on stamped paper. Some are
printed blanks filled in, others are written out in full, 1781-1782.

Large numbers of the papers received from New York will be found in
certain bundles of the series *Adm. Court, Prize Papers,* **260-493,** listed on
pp. 334-340. In *Adm. Court, Miscellanea,* **880,** is a vellum-bound book containing a catalogue of the papers in the four bundles noted above. The
arrangement of the papers has been changed and the catalogue is of value only
as showing the nature of the papers. The most useful part of its contents
is the alphabetical list of ships' names, regarding which the original papers
may be found either in the series named above or among the Prize Papers.
These New York admiralty court papers have got scattered and must be
searched for either in the bundles here described, in certain specified bundles
among the Prize Papers, or among other bundles of the latter collection not
specially designated as containing them.

Many records of proceedings in vice-admiralty courts in the colonies may
be found among the papers in *Adm.* 1, and entries relating to vice-admiralty
matters may be found in the volumes of *Adm.* 2. Special proceedings are
contained in *C. O.* 37 : **11, 12,** K. 25-30 (formerly *B. T. Bermuda,* 10, 11) ;
C. O. 5 : **714,** C. 25, 32 (formerly *B. T. Maryland,* 3) ; *C. O.* 37 : **716,** H. 15
(formerly *B. T. Maryland,* 5) ; *C. O.* 5 : **1260,** E. 48 (formerly *B. T. Proprieties,* 5), etc.

Bundles **1822** and **1826** contain papers relating to the seizure of fourteen
vessels from the French West Indies, which were tried before a special court
of commissioners appointed by the Privy Council, Oct. 13, 1779. The vessels
were condemned and their cargoes sold at the islands of Jersey and Guernsey,
to which the captors belonged. In addition to accounts of disbursements,
charges of sales, vouchers of the commissioners, and reports by the register
of the High Court, will be found detailed lists of the cargoes of the vessels—
sugar, snuff, tobacco, coffee, indigo, cotton, cocoa, salt, licorice, oil, rice, etc.

In *Adm. Court, Miscellanea,* **805,** 13 k/4, are four orders in Council and
other papers relating to these French prizes, from which we learn that the
vessels were taken to Jersey and Guernsey by privateers armed but not duly
commissioned, and were ordered to be sold by order of the High Court under

the rule that the ships and goods of enemies casually met at sea and seized by any vessel not commissioned were droits of admiralty. We learn further that the governors of the islands, claiming to share in the proceeds, obtained process from their respective royal courts overriding the order of the High Court for the sale of the property. They subsequently appeared before the High Court, but their claim was rejected. They then appealed, but without success, and their application to be relieved of the costs was refused. The proceeds of the property were condemned as droits of the crown. In the same bundle are vouchers, receipts, and settlement accounts, and the reports of the commissioners to the Privy Council on each of the fourteen ships.

Among the Prize Papers are documents relating to other vessels captured and taken to Guernsey. The whole matter has some interest for colonial trade, as the Channel Islands were a resort for those engaged in colonial smuggling.

PRIZE PAPERS.

This large collection of 493 bundles contains a great mass of papers relating to the trial and condemnation of ships captured in time of war, arranged alphabetically, by the first letter of the ship's name. To use the bundles, therefore, requires that the name of the ship be known. The nature of the contents can be gathered from the descriptions given in the lists below. Among the most valuable of these papers are the intercepted or captured letters which may be found in considerable numbers in the various groups of bundles.

It is doubtful if much material relating to colonial history is to be found in the first 259 bundles; consequently no attempt has been made to examine them, and the descriptions given are taken from the manuscript list of the papers of the High Court of Admiralty. The bundles **260-493,** on the other hand, are of great value for colonial history, and a brief statement of their contents is here given. The groups are arranged by wars and the letters within parentheses in the descriptions of the first 259 bundles indicate the alphabetical order of ships' names running through each individual bundle.

| Adm. Court. Prize Papers. | **1-12.** 1654-1674. Wars with Holland. |

1. Commission for appraisement.

2-5. Commission for examination and taking depositions in prize causes.

7. Exhibits in prize causes. 1672, 1673, 1674. (A-I, K-R, S-Z.)

8. A parcel of examinations in a prize cause *re Abraham-Sacrifice.* Examinations concerning ships taken by the state in the year 1655. Examinations touching prizes. 1672-1673. (A-G.)

9. Examinations touching prizes. 1672-1673. (H-N and O-Z.)

10-12. Depositions and examinations in prize causes. 1664-1667.

13-45. 1689-1698. War with France.

13-14. Commissions of appraisement. 1689-1698. (Arranged alphabetically by the first letter of the ship's name.)

15-20. Claims, attestations, and other exhibits. 1689-1698. **15** (A-D), **16** (F-H), **17** (I, K, L), **18** (M, N), **19** (O, P, Q, R), **20** (S, T, V, W, Y).

21-23. Allegations and exhibits. 1689-1700. **21** (A-G), **22** (H-O), **23** (P-Z).

24-32. Ships' papers. 1689-1700. **24** (A-C), **24**, pt. 2 (D-F), **25** (F-H), **26** (I), **27** (K, L), **28** (M), **29** (N, O), **30** (P), **31** (Q-S), **32** (T-Z).

33-44. Examinations and ships' papers. 1689-1699. **33** (A), **34** (B, C), **35** (C, 1693-1697, D, E), **36** (F, G), **37** (H), **38** (I, K), **39** (L, M), **40** (N, O), **41** (P, 1689-1696), **42** (P, 1697-1699, Q, R), **43** (S), **44** (T-Y).

45. A parcel of various ships' papers, etc., of the same date found loose. Also a parcel labelled " Commissiones ab anno 1692 ad annum 1700 ".

46-93. 1702-1727. War of the Spanish Succession and years immediately following.

46. Claims, attestations, etc. 1702-1717. (A-M, N-Z.)

47. Allegations in prize causes. 1702-1718. (A-M, N-Z.)

48-86. Examinations and ships' papers. 1702-1727. **48** (A, 1702-1704), **49** (A, 1704-1706), **50** (A, 1707-1720), **51** (B, 1702-1704), **52** (B, 1705-1723), **53** (C, 1702-1704), **54** (C, 1704-1705), **55** (C, 1706-1726), **56** (D), **57** (E), **58** (F, 1702-1704), **59** (F, 1705-1709), **60** (F, 1710-1721, G, 1702), **61** (G, 1703-1722), **62** (H, 1702-1705), **63** (H), **64** (I, 1702-1704), **65** (I, 1704), **66** (I, 1705-1706), **67** (I, 1707-1727), **68** (K, 1702-1719, L, 1702-1704), **69** (L, 1705-1706, 1707-1709, 1710-1720), **70** (M, 1702-1703), **71** (M, 1704-1706), **72** (M, 1707-1719), **73** (N, 1702-1708?), **74** (N, 1707?-1711?), **75** (N, 1712-1722, O, 1702-1718), **76** (P, 1702-1703), **77** (P, 1704-1705), **78** (P, 1706 missing, 1707-1709), **79** (P, 1710-1733, Q, 1703-1718), **80** (R, 1703-1707, 1709-1719), **81** (S, 1702-1705), **82** (S, 1706-1719), **83** (T, 1702-1719), **84** (T, 1702-1719), **85** (U, V, 1702-1719), **86** (W, 1702-1719).

87-91. Ships' papers. 1702-1723. **87** (A, C), **88** (D, E, G, H), **89** (I, K, L, M), **90** (P, Q, R, S), **91** (T, U, W, AY, 1712).

92. Miscellaneous ships' papers found loose ; also some depositions relating to prize causes. 1709-1712.

93. Commission returned from Holland with an examination about the recapture of two " East India Dutchmen " ; also another commission and file of examinations, 1710, 1711.

94-160. 1739. End of War with Spain, etc.

94-159. Collection of prize papers. **94-97** (A), **98-99** (B), **100-103** (C), **104-106** (D), **107-110** (E), **111-112** (F), **113-114** (G), **115-117** (H), **118-125** (I), **126** (K), **127** (L), **128-133** (M), **134-139** (N), **140-141** (O), **142-147** (P), **147** (Q), **148-150** (R), **151-153** (S), **154-155** (T), **156** (U, V), **157-158** (V), **159** (W, Y, Z).

160. Various papers found loose.

These volumes are arranged alphabetically by the first letter of the ship's name. In the case of ships' names beginning with " St." the papers are arranged under the name, as under " John " in the case of " St. John ".

161-259. 1756-1763. Seven Years' War.

    61-256. Prize papers. **161-168** (A), **169-172** (B), **173-179** (C), **180-185** (D), **186-190** (E), **191-194** (F), **195-197** (G), **198-201** (H), **202** (I), **203-210** (J), **211** (K), **212-214** (L), **215-224** (M), **225-228** (N), **229** (O), **230-237** (P), **238** (Q), **239-241** (R), **242-246** (S), **247-249** (T), **250** (U), **251-254** (V), **255** (W), **256** (Y, Z).

    257-258. Various Letters and Papers probably found on board ships taken as prize.

    259. A parcel endorsed " Cranbrook Commns retained by Tyndall with examons in 64 ships and papers annexed ".

260-493. 1776-1786. War of the American Revolution.

This series of 234 bundles is especially important for colonial history. Every vessel captured had on board not only the customary ships' papers but also packages of letters which various correspondents had entrusted to the captains for delivery. Under the Prohibitory Act all papers and writings found on board any ships belonging to the rebels taken as a prize were to be delivered into the registry of the High Court of Admiralty. A brief examination of such intercepted letters gives us the following general table of contents :

Acts of assembly sequestrating British property, conditions existing in prize courts in America, reasons of the French king in joining America, provisioning of Bermuda by the Americans, bounties for American seamen, commissions to American officers, various orders of Congress, a large number of American letters of marque, instructions to American privateers from Congress, ships' papers, logs, and articles, depositions and examinations, prize regulations, passes, signals, lighthouse receipts, some of which are in French and Swedish, licenses to trade, articles between the United States and her seamen, names and lists of crews, lists of prisoners, proclamations, papers regarding Spanish affairs in Louisiana, copies of various treaties, many American newspapers, and a very large number of letters from and to America, from and to England, France, and the West Indies, and occasionally from one American port to another. Among these letters, of which there are hundreds, many of which are extremely valuable, may be found a number written to or by the following persons : André, D'Estaing, Silas Deane, Franklin, Paul Jones, Benedict Arnold, Lafayette, Arthur Lee, Washington, Rochambeau, Henry Laurens, Henry Lee, Jonathan Trumbull, De Kalb, Robert Morris, John Adams, and others. One package of papers relates to the Loyalists and others contain letters from merchants, planters, and others engaged in trade, often dealing with merely routine business, but sometimes giving interesting accounts of affairs in America and the progress of the war.

The entire collection, though a difficult one to handle, ought to be listed and indexed. The rapid survey here given, for which in part I am indebted to Mr. Marsden, does not pretend to include all the bundles containing papers relating to colonial affairs, nor does it attempt, except in one instance (B) by way of illustration, to note all such papers in the bundles listed. Generally speaking these papers fall into three groups : vice-admiralty court papers ; ships' papers of all kinds, articles, complements, accounts, and instructions ; and letters entrusted by various correspondents to the captains for carriage. The documents from the New York court of vice-admiralty are as a rule contained in the bundles indicated, but there are exceptions to this statement, as New York admiralty court papers are to be found in other bundles. Such papers concern either American vessels or French vessels captured in American waters.

A.

260-275. Bundles **274-275** contain prize papers from the New York court of vice-admiralty.

274. *Abigail.* Letter from Boston. 1779.

Active. American letter of marque.

D'Argentré. Letter from captain of the 1st Georgia Regiment of Foot in the Continental army to the governor and commandant-in-chief in and over North Carolina.

St. Anne. Letter to Adams, Deane, and Co., Richmond.

276. *Active.* Letters, Nantucket to London. 1778.

B.

277-287. Bundles **284-287** contain prize papers from the New York court of vice-admiralty.

277. *Black Prince,* taken off Barnegat and carried to New York, 1778; two copies of the log and many papers. This vessel was an American privateer captured while cruising against " the enimeis off the United Stades off America ".

Buckskin, taken in Chesapeake Bay and carried to New York, 1778; log.

Brig Elliot, whaler, started from Sandy Hook, Oct., 1775, captured Aug., 1777.

Betsey, from Little Egg Harbor. July-Sept., 1777.

279. *Bretonne.* Letters from Bordeaux to Charleston, offering trade. 1778.

280. *Brunswick,* from Newburyport, owned in Charleston, seized and taken to Guernsey, 1778; letters, interrogatories.

Blair, from Bedford to Charleston and thence to Bordeaux, seized in the Bay of Biscay, July 7, 1777; letters, interrogatories.

Blessing, taken by the American privateer *Black Prince* off Land's End, June 19, 1779, recaptured with crew and taken to Guernsey.

Billy and Mary (otherwise the *Bell and Mary*), bound for Bordeaux, taken off the capes of Virginia, Mar., 1777, and carried first to New York and then to the River Thames; ships' papers.

Betsey, from Boston to Port au Prince with fish, and thence to Bilboa with sugar and cocoa, 1781; letter of marque from Congress, June 16, 1781, letters from Boston merchants to correspondents in Nantes, register countersigned by Gov. John Hancock, articles of agreement and cargo accounts, bundle of French papers accumulated in the West Indies.

Betsey of Dunkirk, interrogatory taken at place to which vessel was brought, first witness William Ripner, born in Hartford, Conn., lived in Martinique, and afterward at Dunkirk.

Betsey, from Boston for Guadeloupe, but taken near Bermuda, Nov., 1782; French letters from Basseterre, Pointpetre, Guadeloupe.

282. *Bolton,* from Philadelphia to Curaçao, taken off Cape Henlopen, May, 1777, carried to New York and thence to River Thames; papers.

Banter, American privateer, taken in the straits of Belle Isle, between Newfoundland and Labrador, July, 1782; interrogatories.

Brothers, formerly the *Sally,* taken by the *Buckskin,* Dec. 5, 1776, retaken Aug. 9, 1777, by the *General Howe*; the owners, Alexander and Hugh Telfair, Scotsmen of Halifax, N. C., claimed that they were escaping Loyalists and that the ship could not be condemned as prize; papers relating to this claim.

283. *Bien Aimée,* papers regarding ship ashore at Portland.

284. *Badin,* French ship, sailing under French colors, taken by the *Amazon* near Cape Charles, Aug. 26, 1778.

Boreas, from Philadelphia to North Carolina, captured by the transport *Richmond,* Nov. 12, 1779.

Beggar's Benison, from the West Indies to North Carolina or Virginia, taken by a Dominican privateer, July 2, 1778.

Black Joke, taken by the *Galatea,* May 15, 1778.

Baltimore, taken off the capes of Virginia by the *Hammond,* Sept. 25, 1778, while going from Baltimore to Martinique and St. Lucia; instructions to the captain from Baltimore merchants, John McLane, McLane and Sterrett, John Crockett.

Bedford, captured by the *Loyal Subject,* Mar. 9, 1778.

Buckskin, bound for Baltimore from Bordeaux, with cargo worth 700,000 livres, uninsured because (as said T. Ridout, *Adm. Court, Miscellanea,* **1085**) " No one here will insure an American vessel "; ships' papers and instructions, a few letters valuable for trade with Bordeaux during the war. At the same time the *Peggy,* Capt. Bradford, was captured.

Boston, formerly the *Glasgow,* taken by the Americans while on a voyage from Georgia to New York, June 29, 1779, renamed the *Boston,* and recaptured by the *Virginia,* Sept. or Oct., 1779.

Burling, taken in Chesapeake Bay by the *Otter,* the *Fincastle,* and the *Lord North,* May 10, 1779, crew ran her on shore at Gwyn's Island.

Betsey, French ship sailing under American colors, taken near Cape Henry, May 23, 1782, by the *Sukey.* Two packets: one containing letters from Baltimore and Alexandria to Nantes, Cadiz, Marseilles, Bordeaux, and Naples (in French and Spanish); from Josiah Watson, Alexandria, regarding sale of Lord Tankerville's estate in Virginia, 1780; from Hare and Harrison, Alexandria, 1780; from Robert H. Harrison, 1780, speaking of the death of his father, Sept. 11, by falling from the roof of his house, and commenting on the war, a valuable letter, referring to André and Arnold's treason. The second packet contains many business letters, of but little importance. In all these bundles the packets of papers and letters are generally separated from the ship's log, so that only an examination will show to which ship the papers belong.

287. *Baron D'Ozelle,* letters.

C.

288-302. Bundles **299-302** contain papers from the New York court of vice-admiralty.

297. *Constant Friend,* papers regarding a South Carolina regiment. 1777.
Charming Betsey, id.

299. *Charity,* letters to and from Arnold.
Charles, letters to Baltimore and Annapolis.

301. *Centurion,* letters from Philadelphia to Curaçao, St. Eustatius, and elsewhere.

D.

303-314. Bundles **311-314** contain papers from the New York court of vice-admiralty.

304. *Dragon,* many American letters and papers.

309. *Dolphin,* French correspondence, one letter from Lafayette.

311. *Delaware,* American letters. 1778.
Defiance, a few American letters. 1778.

312. *Dauphin,* American letters.

313. *Dove, id.*
Dolphin, id.
Delight, id.
Despatch, id.

E.

315-328. Bundles **325-328** contain papers from the New York court of vice-admiralty.

327. *Elizabeth,* American letters.
Esther, id.

F.

329-337. Bundles **335-337** contain papers from the New York court of vice-admiralty.

329. *Freeman,* letter from Henry Laurens.

330. *Fanny,* American letters.

331. *Françoise,* French letters from America.

332. *Fox,* lists of men from the *Boston* and *Hancock,* American frigates, on H. M. S. *Fox* when retaken by H. M. S. *Flora,* July 7, 1777.

334. *Farmer,* American letters.

335. *Friendship,* letter from Gov. Bruère of Bermuda, saying that the United States will sell food to the West Indies, notwithstanding the war.
Flora, American letters.
Fanny, among other American letters, one from Henry Lee.
Freedom, many letters and papers; instructions from war office, Boston; Great Britain declared the enemy of the United States and of the natural rights of mankind—"the cruel and inveterate enemy".

337. *Fanny,* letter from Benedict Arnold; also from Barnabas Deane to the agent for the French army in Virginia, Jeremy Wadsworth.
Fame, many American papers.

G.

338-346. Bundles **345-346** contain papers from the New York court of vice-admiralty.
343. *Grand Terrien,* papers regarding illicit trade.
344, pt. I. *Gardoqui,* American letters and papers.
346. *George,* letters from St. Eustatius.
Greyhound, American letters.
General Gadsden, id.
Grog, id.

H.

347-359. Bundles **356-359** contain papers from the New York court of vice-admiralty.
347. *Hukard,* French naval code, colored, two sheets.
349. *Harmonie,* American letters to St. Eustatius.
Hector, American letters.
354. *Hooper, id.*
356. *Hunter, id.*
358. *Hector, id.*
Hope, id.
359. *Hope,* bills of lading.

I, J.

360-383. Bundles **380-383** contain papers from the New York court of vice-admiralty. No. **379,** in four parts, contains a great many names of saints.
364. *Jason,* British instructions to those bearing letters of marque.
373. *Infanta D^a Maria,* " A Real Declaracion, etc., de la Ordenanza de Corte ", July 1, 1779, " relativo al reconocimiento y detencion de embarciones neutrales ". Madrid, 1780.
375. *Industry,* American letters.
376. *Johanna, id.*
381. *Jeremiah, id.*
382. *Jane,* copy of a translation of French letters, signed Benjamin Franklin, Arthur Lee, John Adams, requesting all to allow Joy Castle and family to pass to Bordeaux and on to the United States.
Jesus Maria, list of cargo to be brought into England, including harpischords, chafing dishes, silk, etc.
383. *Jemima,* French and American letters to Philadelphia.
James, American letters.
Jeune Pauline, French letters to America.
Inconstant, id.

K.

384-385.

L.

386-392. Bundles **391-392** contain papers from the New York court of vice-admiralty.
387. *Laclocheterie,* interesting French and American letters to America.

391. *Little Betsey,* American letters to Bermuda.
Loup, French letters to Baltimore.
392. *Little Sukey,* American letters to Cape François.
Lady Clausen, American letters.
Liberty, American-French letters.

M.

393-404. Bundles **403-404** contain papers from the New York court of vice-admiralty.
395. *Margueritte,* letter from Pouget, Aleran, and Co. to Thomas Cushing of Boston.
398. *Molly,* recapture, John Paul Jones (important).
399. *Mercury,* papers relating to the plantation trade.
401. *Molly,* letters.
Maria, letters from Baltimore. 1783.
403. *Morning Star,* Pennsylvania letters.
Mermaid, Charleston letters.
404. *Delight* als *Maccaroni,* letters.
Magdalene, French letters to members of the French army in America.

N.

405-415. Bundles **413-415** contain papers from the New York court of vice-admiralty.
411. *Neptune,* letter of marque issued by Benjamin Franklin to Capt. Edward Macattery. Oct. 6, 1777.

O.

416. *Oliver Cromwell,* a Connecticut ship, letter of marque issued by Gov. Jonathan Trumbull.

P.

417-434. Bundles **428-434** contain papers from the New York court of vice-admiralty.
428. *Peggy,* English and French letters to America.
Peggy, American letters.
429. *Polly,* French letters to soldiers in Rochambeau's army.
430. *Passive,* American letters, Franklin, De Kalb.
433. *Port au Prince,* a packet, no. 5, of American letters.
Planter, American letters.
Peggy, id.

Q.

435. *Quartier Moren,* colored plan of a sugar plantation.

R.

436-444. Bundles **441-444** contain papers from the New York court of vice-admiralty.
436. *Rambler,* French and American letters.
437. *Rey,* exposé des motifs de la conduite au Roi de France. See also **445.**

439. *Rebecca,* American letters.

440. *Revenge,* American letters to England and Holland from Baltimore and Annapolis.

441. *Provençal,* French and American letters; also one from Robert Morris to William Lee about John Paul Jones.

    Revenge, letter-book of Gustavus Cunningham of letters to Arthur Lee and others.

443. *Race Horse,* letters to Baltimore.

S.

445-459. Bundles **455-459** contain papers from the New York court of vice-admiralty.

447. *Speculation,* Swedish pass, secret signals, two bundles of letters from Charleston to England.

    Sally, American letters to England.

450. *Success,* papers regarding illicit trade with the Americans. Aug., 1778.

453. *Salisbury,* French and American letters to France; log book.

457. *Swift,* American letters.

    Sally, id.

    Seaflower, French letters.

T.

460-467. Bundles **465-467** contain papers from the New York court of vice-admiralty.

463. *Three Sisters,* French letters from Virginia.

466. *Thomas,* American letters.

    Trumbull, American letters and papers.

467. *Three Friends,* American letters.

    Three Brothers, id.

    Tempest, letters to Silas Deane from his brother, partly in cipher.

    Two Rachels, American letters.

U.

468-469. Bundle **469** contains papers from the New York court of vice-admiralty.

468. *Union,* copy of a long letter from the war office, Boston, Oct. 25, 1777, giving an account of the battle of the Brandywine; also French letters.

V.

470-488. Bundles **487-488** contain papers from the New York court of vice-admiralty.

471. *Vidam de Chalons,* important letters to America; letter from John Adams to Henry Laurens. Apr. 1, 1778.

477. *Venus,* letter from Lafayette.

484. *Virginia Paquet,* large numbers of French letters from America to France.

487. *Virginia,* letters regarding Washington at Valley Forge, etc. (interesting).

W.

489-491. Bundle **491** contains papers from the New York court of vice-admiralty.

490. *William,* Jeremiah Hopkins's book.

491. *Willis,* letter from James White, telling of Washington and Lee's engagement with the British near Philadelphia and of the battle of Monmouth Court House.

Washington, certificate of Benedict Arnold and others.

William, letter from Capt. Jonathan Ingersoll of New Haven, giving the writer's views of political independence. Dec. 22, 1776.

Y, Z.

492.

MISCELLANEOUS (FOUND LOOSE).

493. A number of vessels captured off the Coromandel coast; bundle of letters to Philadelphia.

494-498. 1793-1796. Anglo-French War.

1821-1826. Records from the Vice-Admiralty Court of New York.

The contents of these bundles have already been described on pp. 329-330.

PRIZE APPEAL RECORDS.

The Court of Appeals for Prizes, though at first but the High Court sitting for prize appeal business, became a separate court toward the end of the seventeenth century, under commissioners of appeal in prize cases. It heard all appeals from the vice-admiralty courts in England and America.

The series of volumes and bundles here described are supplemental to the prize papers, in that they record the proceedings on appeal in many of the cases of condemnation there contained. These records consist of papers, assignation books, appeal case books, minute books, acts, sentences, and miscellanea. In the appeal papers the bundles are arranged according to wars, and within the bundles and groups of bundles the papers are arranged alphabetically according to the names of the ships. It is necessary, therefore, to know the name of the ship before the bundles can be used.

APPEAL PAPERS.

1-9. 1689-1699. War with France.

> Adm. Court.
> Prize Appeal Rec.
> Appeal Papers.
> Prize.

1 (A, B), 2 (C), 3 (C), 4 (G, H), 5 (I, K, L), 6 (M), 7 (N, O, P, Q, R), 8 (S, T, V), 9 (W, Y).

10-21. 1702-1730. War of the Spanish Succession.

10 (A, B), 11 (C), 12 (D, F), 13 (G, H), 14 (I), 15 (L, M), 16 (N), 17 (N), 18 (O, P, Q, R), 19 (S), 20 (S), 21 (T, V, W, Y).

23-51. 1743-1752. War with Spain, etc. Attestations, " Libels and Claims in Appeals ".

23 (A), 24 (B, C), 25-26 (C), 27 (D, E), 28 (F), 29 (F), 30-34 (F), 35 (G), 36 (H), 37 (I), 38 (I, K, L), 39-40 (M), 41-42 (N), 43 (O, P), 44 (P), 46 (R), 47 (S), 48 (T, V), 49-50 (U), 51 (W, Y, Z).

52-109. 1756-1763. Seven Years' War.

52-55 (A), **56-58** (B), **59-61** (C), **62-63** (D), **64-65** (E), **67** (F), **68-69** (G), **70-71** (H), **72-78** (I), **79** (K, L), **80-82** (M), **83-85** (N), **86** (O), **87-89** (P), **90** (Q), **91-92** (R), **93-96** (S), **97-98** (T), **99-103** (V), **104** (W, X), **105-108** (Y), **109** (Y, Z).

110-165. 1776-1783. War of the American Revolution.

110-113 (A), **114** (B), **115-118** (C), **119-120** (D), **121** (E),[1] **122** (F), **123-124** (G), **125-127** (H), **128-132** (I), **133** (K), **134-135** (L), **136-139** (M), **140-142** (N), **143** (O), **144** (P), **145** (R), **146-153** (S), **154-155** (T), **156-160** (V), **161** (W), **162** (X, Y), **163-165** (Z).

ASSIGNATION BOOKS.

1-18. 1689-1783. Assignation Books.

Adm. Court.
Prize Appeal Rec.
Assignation
Books.
—

Assignments or preliminary proceedings in appeal causes, generally in English vice-admiralty courts. The documents are arranged chronologically.

36-38. 1779-1796. Assignment Books, American Prizes.

These volumes contain entries of assignments in appeal causes from vice-admiralty courts in Halifax, New York, East Florida, Bermuda, Jamaica, St. Christopher, and from a few vice-admiralty courts in England. The volumes contain a number of records of sentences in cases of appeal to the Privy Council, the regular series of which does not begin till 1834, and indexes of the names of ships. These assignments were held and the necessary bonds were taken out before the surrogate of the lords commissioners of appeals in prize cases, sometimes in the dining-room adjoining the common hall of Doctors' Commons, and sometimes in the surrogate's apartments there.

APPEAL CASE BOOKS.

1-6. 1750-1760. Prize.

7-16. 1770-1800. *Id.*

Adm. Court.
Accruing Records.
Appeal Case
Books.
—

Large thick volumes of printed cases, of which the following is an example:

" Before the Right Noble and Right Honourable the Lords Commissioners of Appeals in Prize Cases; an Appeal from the Vice-Admiralty Court of the Island of Jamaica. The 'Sea Flower', Edmund Snow, Master. Saturnine B. Garrick, Supercargo of the said Ship and Claimant thereof as the Property of Thomas Brown of Sandwich, Massachusetts, Appellant; against Boaz Bryan, Commander of the Private Ship of War, the 'King Grey', the Captor of said ship and Cargo, Respondent." 1798. 30 pp.

Each printed document includes both the appellant's case and the respondent's case and usually an appendix. The ship's name is prominently placed in the heading of each case.

[1] For St. Eustatius see S., bundles **149-153.**

1. Cases to be heard. 1758-1761. Vol. **6**, a large and broad manuscript book, but partly filled, is an index to **1**, entering 101 cases, with the " Points " argued (on the lefthand page) and the names of ship and master, the destination, lading, date of sentence, names of proctors, and whether condemned or restored (on the righthand page). The ships concerned are chiefly Spanish and Dutch, many of which were trading to and from the West Indies.
3. Duplicate of the latter half of **1**, with a manuscript index, and three printed pamphlets bound in.
4. Cases to be heard. 1760, 1761, 1763.
5. *Id.* 1760, 1761, 1763-1765.
7-15. *Id.* 1770-1800. In many cases in these volumes the sentence is written in ink at the end of the statement either of the appellant or of the respondent.
16. Manuscript index to **7-15**, in the form of an alphabetical list of ships' names, with volume and page.

MINUTE BOOKS.

| Adm. Court. |
| Accruing Records. |
| Court Minute |
| Book. |
| — |

1-8. 1776-1783. Court Minute Books.

Volumes of considerable interest and value, containing the rough notes of the proceedings of the court, with the sentence. At the top, or elsewhere on the page, are entered in a fair clerkly hand the name of the ship and an epitome of the facts in the case. The ships concerned are Dutch, French, and American.

1. 1776-1779. Only one case is entered for 1776, and two for 1777. The remainder are for the period Dec., 1778–July, 1779.
2. July, 1779–May, 1780.
3. May, 1780–Dec., 1780.
4. Jan.-June, 1781.
5. July-Dec., 1781 (chiefly Dutch ships).
6. Jan.-May, 1782.
7. June-Dec., 1782.
8. Jan.-Dec., 1783.

Each volume contains an alphabetical index to ships. Some of the cases are for subtraction of wages and are marked " Instance Court ".

ACTS.

| Adm. Court. |
| Prize Appeal Rec. |
| Acts. |
| — |

1-18. 1689-1787. Acts.

These volumes contain the original proceedings in prize appeal cases, as well as various drafts, 1747-1763, and act books, 1689-1713.

SENTENCES.

| Adm. Court. |
| Prize Appeal Rec. |
| Sentences. |
| — |

1-7. 1672-1772. Sentences.
8. 1689-1699. Index of Sentences.

MISCELLANEA.

<table>
<tr><td rowspan="4">Adm. Court.
Prize Appeal Rec.
Miscellanea.
—</td><td>**1-6.** 1689-1786. Draft Instruments.</td></tr>
<tr><td>**8.** 1780-1784. Minutes.</td></tr>
<tr><td>**19-26.** 1690-1783. Account Books of Fees.</td></tr>
<tr><td>**42.** 1690-1746. Original Commissions.</td></tr>
</table>

Among the "Accruing Records" are two series of volumes, Assignation Books and Repertory Books, of the Court of Delegates, which had appellate jurisdiction not only in ecclesiastical court cases but in Instance Court cases also. They are of very little value for our purpose, and a search has disclosed no cases of appeal from the Instance Court. In *Adm. Court, Accruing Records, Repertory Books,* **1,** 1619-1739, is this entry: "Laurentius Washington Rector de Stutesbury a̅s Stotesbury in com Northon diocese Petriburge̅n Cant. prox. con[tra] Johannem Richardson introduct. 27 Augusto 1619". These Repertory Books contain entries of the appointment of the *judices delegati,* or special commissioners, by the Lord Chancellor.

LETTERS OF MARQUE.

DECLARATIONS.

<table>
<tr><td rowspan="4">Adm. Court.
Letters of Marque.
Declarations.
—</td><td>**1-12.** 1689-1761. Against France.</td></tr>
<tr><td>**13-16.** 1707-1718. Against France and Other Enemies.</td></tr>
<tr><td>**17-28.** 1702-1762. Against France and Spain.</td></tr>
<tr><td>**29-32.** 1718-1744. Against Spain.</td></tr>
</table>

33-44. 1778-1783. Against France.
45-52. 1779-1783. Against Spain.
53-59. 1780-1783. Against Holland.
60-70. 1777-1782. Against America.

These volumes contain the letters of marque issued to those whose bails are noted in the volumes of "Bonds" listed below. The letters in vols. **60-70** correspond to those in vol. **56,** as far as they chronologically coincide. Vols. **60-70** contain also copies of "Instructions to Commanders" issued Mar. 27, 1777, and recite in the first case the commission issued to each commander. Variations in the commissions are noted. These volumes contain also a very complete record of English privateering from 1689 to 1783, and particularly a record of privateering during the war of the American Revolution.

BONDS.

<table>
<tr><td rowspan="4">Adm. Court.
Letters of Marque.
Bonds.
—</td><td>**1-7.** 1549-1630. Files of Obligations.</td></tr>
<tr><td>**8.** 1630. Files of Warrants.</td></tr>
<tr><td>**11-13.** 1689-1797. Bonds from Privateers.</td></tr>
<tr><td>**14-21.** 1702-1713. Letters of Marque against France and Spain.</td></tr>
</table>

22-25. 1708-1712. Bails for Letters of Marque.
26-31. 1739-1744. Warrants and Bails, War with Spain and France.

32-37. 1744-1748. Warrants and Bails, War with Spain and France.
38-52. 1756-1762. French Bails.
53-55. 1762. French and Spanish Bails.
56. 1777-1780. American Bails.

This bundle contains two packages of papers labelled " American Rebellion, Bails, April 1-13, 1777 ", and " American Bails, April 14-30, 1777 ". In the first package are 54 letters, in the second 40 arranged chronologically.

204. 1812-1813. American Bonds.

Of the same character as the papers in **56**, but relating to the War of 1812. The papers are in two packages chronologically arranged and are rather elaborately drawn. Among the expired commissions, whose reports and papers are to be found in the Treasury Papers, is one of American ships and cargoes condemned as prize, 1812-1818.

OYER AND TERMINER.

The Court of Oyer and Terminer and Gaol Delivery of the Admiralty of England constituted the criminal branch of the Instance Court, and its sessions were held in Justice Hall in the Old Bailey, generally known as the Sessions House, north of Ludgate Hill, just outside the City wall. The Sessions House was on the second floor, Surgeons Hall being below. The court was presided over by commissioners from Doctors' Commons, but the proceedings were according to the rules of the common law. The trials were for piracy or crime committed on the high seas. For an account of the proceedings in this court, reference may be made to a printed pamphlet (London, 1773) containing an account of a session held, Nov. 10, 1773, for the trial of the crew of the *Sea Flower,* who had resisted customs officials near the island of Brehar.

Adm. Court. Oyer and Ter- miner.

5-27. 1604-1797. Indictments.
28. 1537-1782. Calendar of Indictments.
39-54. 1601-1768. Examination of Pirates.

Such examinations were customarily held before one of the commissioners in his chambers in Doctors' Commons, in the presence of the register or his deputy, who was also a notary public.

55. 1759-1824. Minutes of Proceedings.

These bundles and volumes are of value for the trials of many pirates familiar to students of colonial history. Bundle **15** (12 William III., 1700-1 Anne, 1702) contains papers relating to pirates of Virginia, Pennsylvania, New York, and New England; especially indictments and depositions, and other papers relating to Capt. Kidd. Among these papers is Kidd's original letter or marque, and a deposition signed " C. Wolley ",[1] dated Apr., 1701. Bundle **16** (1 Anne, 1702-11 Anne, 1712) contains similar material. Vol. **48**, 1694-1710, is an entry book of examinations supplemental to the indictments,

---

[1] Probably Rev. Charles Wolley, author of *A Two Years' Journal in New York,* a work published in 1701. Wolley was in New York, 1678-1680, and was known to be familiar with the conditions there. If this surmise be correct the spelling of the name is important in view of the dispute on that point.

etc., noted above, and contains depositions signed often with the mark of the deponent. The bundles and volumes for the reigns of William III. and Anne are of chief importance, though earlier and later collections contain scattered material of interest.

57-58 contain miscellaneous papers—warrants for the summons of juries, precepts of various sorts for the removal of prisoners, the directing of sheriffs to attend executions, and the like—that date from about 1760.

59 contains a number of pardons issued in Charles II.'s reign. They are elaborately illuminated with a portrait of the king and bear the great seal. Pardons were frequent in this court in the eighteenth century.

60-72 contain the original commissions of the court. 1660-1800.

SPECIAL COLLECTIONS.

The earliest donation of a private collection of manuscripts was that of the letters of Sir Thomas Roe presented to the Paper Office in 1772 by the Richardsons, one part of which, relating to Constantinople, had been published in 1740 by Samuel Richardson the novelist. The next gift was the Conway papers made by John Wilson Croker about 1856. Since that time a number of other collections have been received, though in general the Public Record Office will not accept such collections unless they are given without restrictions. In the case of the Chatham papers conditions were at first imposed, to the effect that permission to use them should be asked for in advance, but this restriction has now been removed. The Cornwallis papers were given to the Historical Manuscripts Commission to be deposited in the Public Record Office forever. All the other collections were given without reserve. See Scargill-Bird, *Guide,* 3d ed., pp. 403-405.

MANCHESTER PAPERS.

The Manchester papers were deposited in the Public Record Office by the Duke of Manchester in 1880 and have been calendared by the Historical Manuscripts Commission in the *Eighth Report,* app., pt. II., pp. 1-166. The calendar contains an elaborate introduction and an excellent index and presents the documents arranged chronologically under separate headings. The entire collection contains from three to four thousand documents, of which those bearing on colonial history belong to the period from 1605 to 1647. In the calendar they are entered under the title " Reigns of James I. and Charles I. (colonial)", pp. 31-50. See also Miss Kingsbury's introduction to the *Records of the Virginia Company of London,* I. 61-62.

CORNWALLIS PAPERS.

The Cornwallis papers were deposited by Lord Braybrooke in 1880. They are arranged in fifty-nine separate bundles and consist of nearly eight thousand separate documents. They include mainly " the writings (official and personal) that grew upon the hands of Charles, first Marquis Cornwallis during his successive periods of service in the American plantations and in the East Indian dependencies [of Great Britain]. They are valuable chiefly for their letters from Admiral Arbuthnot, Sir Henry Clinton, and Lord Rawdon, the American papers comprising many notable communications to Lord Cornwallis from subordinate actors on either side of the struggle." " The numerous ' paroles' and documents touching prisoners and exchanges of prisoners during the American War of Independence are not unlikely to yield dates and other minute pieces of testimony for which domestic annalists and personal illustrators have hitherto been vainly seeking."

> Cornwallis MSS.
> Bundle —.

The papers have been briefly calendared by the Historical Manuscripts Commission in the *Eighth Report,* app. I., pp. 287-296, and are described in Stevens's *Index.* Only eight of the fifty-nine bundles contain material for

346

American history. The following account is somewhat more elaborate than that given in the *Report*.

1. Dec. 26, 1741–1779. Miscellaneous papers, of which the earliest documents are five letters to Cornwallis from Charles James Fox, Townshend, the Duke, Hardwicke, and G. Cornwallis. The American documents begin July 12, 1778, and consist of letters to Cornwallis from various subordinates, with many tables, copies of letters, proclamations, and other official rules and regulations. They close with Dec. 25, 1779. In this bundle is a book of forty-eight pages entitled "Description de la riviére de Susquehanna, et du pays qui la borde depuis Harris's Ferry jusqua l'embouchure".

2. Jan. 22, 1779–July 31, 1780. American papers, chiefly letters to Cornwallis from military, naval, and civil officers in America. Many letters from Sir Henry Clinton, with returns, tables, extracts of letters, reports, letters from commissioned officers in the South, Lord Rawdon, Maj. Ferguson, Col. Balfour, etc.

3. Aug. 1–Oct. 31, 1780. American papers similar to those in **2**, relating to movements in Virginia, North Carolina, and South Carolina and containing many enclosures.

4. Nov. 2–Dec. 31, 1780. American papers similar to those above, consisting of letters to Cornwallis from his officers, from Sir Henry Clinton, Maj. Tarleton, Lord Rawdon, Col. Balfour, and others from southern camps. On f. 218 are J. Simpson's " Observations on Mr. Elliot's plan " (for restoring peace).

5. Jan. 8–Apr. 12, 1781. American papers, consisting of warrants, recommendations, queries, estimates of damages, petitions, and of letters from the officers named above. Among the papers are a few letters from Gov. Wright of Georgia and copies of letters from Cornwallis to Lord George Germain.

6. May–Dec. 5, 1781. American papers, similar to those above, bearing specially upon the Yorktown campaign.

7. Aug. 15, 1782–1785. American papers in part, relating to the winding up of Cornwallis's affairs in America. The greater part of the documents in this bundle and all the documents in bundles **8-57** relate to East India affairs.

58. 1781-1819. Packet of papers relating chiefly to the capitulation of York and Gloucester in Virginia and to steps taken to rendering due honor in 1806 to Cornwallis's memory.

Many of the documents in this collection are printed in Stevens, *Campaign in Virginia* (two vols., 1888), which concerns chiefly the controversy between Clinton and Cornwallis, and in *The Correspondence of Charles, 1st Marquis Cornwallis,* ed. Ross (three vols., 1859).

SHAFTESBURY PAPERS.

Shaftesbury MSS.
Section —.
No. —.

The Shaftesbury papers were deposited in 1871 by the Earl of Shaftesbury, and have been calendared in the *Reports* of the Deputy Keeper, 33, pp. 211-269; 34, p. 188; 39, pp. 567-568; 43, pp. 606-608. Additions to the original gift were made in 1872, 1873, 1877, and 1881. Only the papers relating to Carolina have been calendared in *Cal. State Papers, Col.*, and printed *in extenso* in the *Collections* of the South Carolina Historical Society, V. Only the portions of the collection calendared in the *33d* and *34th Reports* contain material of importance for American history. In addition to the South Carolina papers there are a number of others that deal with the West Indies and with trade in general.

RODNEY PAPERS.

Rodney MSS.
Bundle —.

This collection, which throws light, not only on naval and military affairs, but also on trade in North American waters, consists of the correspondence of Adm. George Brydges Rodney, 1719-1792. More than two hundred letters and other papers in this series have been printed in *The Life and Correspondence of the Late Admiral Lord Rodney*, by G. B. Mundy (two vols., 1830); while the letters treating of St. Eustatius were published by Rodney himself in his lifetime, and two copies of the volume are in bundle **19**. The papers were presented to the Public Record Office by Harley Rodney, esq., in May, 1906.

The documents (except one map) are contained in nineteen volumes and bundles. The arrangement of the American material is as follows: **1-2,** Order Books; **3,** Journals; **4,** Log Book and Journal; **5, 6, 8-10,** Letter-Books; **11-14,** Detached Letters and a few Papers; **15,** Detached Miscellaneous Papers; **16-19,** Miscellaneous Books and Detached Papers; Map.

1. 1759–Oct., 1761; Apr.–July, 1763; May 27, 1759–Oct. 19, 1761; Apr. 19–July 4, 1763. Order Books.

2. Oct. 9, 1761–Apr. 25, 1763. Order Book.

3. Dec. 9, 1781–Sept. 21, 1782; July 24–Sept. 21, 1782. Journals.

4. Mar. 3, 1748–Apr. 3, 1752; Jan. 1, 1750–Apr. 15, 1752. Journals of the *Rainbow*.

5. Dec. 10, 1781–Sept. 21, 1782. Letter-Book, chiefly official.

6. June 2, 1749–June 11, 1759; Nov. 23, 1781–June 1, 1782. Letter-Books.

Volume **5** contains letters to and from Rodney (Newfoundland, Halifax, Louisburg); volume **6,** letters from the Admiralty to Rodney.

8. 1761-1762. Letter-Book.

Containing letters to and from Rodney, mostly dating from the West Indies, and largely from and to naval and military officers, governors in the West Indies, and the Admiralty.

9. July 6, 1780–Apr. 27, 1781. Letter-Book.

Containing letters to and from Rodney, mostly dating from New York and the West Indies, and containing, among other matters, many particulars relating to St. Eustatius.

10. 1780-1782. Letter-Book.

Four letters from Rodney to George Jackson, secretary to the Admiralty, the originals of which are in the British Museum, *Add. MSS.* **9344**; also copies of letters from Sir Samuel Hood to Jackson, with copies of Rodney letters enclosed, originals in Brit. Mus. *Add. MSS.* **9343**; also copies of eleven letters and a suppressed despatch from Rodney; a letter-book of Rodney letters, and a copy of a letter from Eliphat Fitch to Rodney, Kingston, Jamaica, May 4, 1782.

11. 1761-1780. Letters from the Admiralty.

To Arbuthnot, 1780; Barrington, 1778-1779; Byron, 1778-1779; Gayton, 1774; Hood, 1781; Parker, 1779-1780; Rodney, 1761-1763, 1768, 1771-1774, 1779-1781; Walsingham, 1780.

12. 1764-1782. Letters, Various.

A collection of letters from various persons and boards to the Admiralty, the Navy Board, the commissioners for sick and wounded, etc.

13. 1749, 1750, 1755, 1762, 1763 to 1781, and undated. Letters to and from Rodney.

Including:
"Particulars of a conversation which passed between Gov. Franklin and Mr. Oswald relative to the Treaty of Peace with America."
Dominica and St. Vincent papers.
Papers relating to Pensacola and to the sailing of the Spanish Fleet, 1771.

14. 1761-1782. Letters, Various.

Relating almost entirely to the West Indies, and concerning official orders, military affairs, naval affairs, importation of bullion, naval stores, confiscations, claims, seizures, prisoners of war, intelligence, and the like. Letter from John Steel, Sept. 22, 1780, gives an account of an engagement between his brig and the *Saratoga* of Philadelphia; other letters deal with the English and Spanish in the Caribbean Sea, seizure of American privateers, observations regarding "my late trip to the Mississippi" (unsigned), and the conditions prevailing among the British and French West Indies.

15. 1758-1781. Miscellaneous Papers.

Among others, the following:
"An extract of the transactions at Louisburg, in the time of that siege", 1758, endorsed "Corrected by G. B. Rodney".
Memorandum concerning the French Protestant colony at Cape Sable, Nova Scotia (proposed), July 12, 1767.
"Plan of attack of New Orleans." 1771.
"Plan to attack Mexico", including also an account of the territory near "Oupelousa, a Spanish post on the Western Coast of the Mississippi", etc. 1771.
Paper entitled "The Object of the War of 1779."
An account of the stores at New York, 1780.
Re Benjamin Hallowell. 1780.
"A List of Prizes taken by the King's Ships and libelled in the court of vice-admiralty", New York, from 13 Sept., 1780.
Information of Joseph Gold *re* ships of war at Philadelphia, Nov. 2, 1780.
Copy of "Memorial concerning the State Papers found amongst those of Mr. Laurens . . . presented to the States General (Nov. 10, 1780) by Sir Joseph Yorke".
Remarks "whilst upon the West Florida station [1780?]".

Numerous papers, mostly relating to the West Indies and mostly dating from 1780, or undated, relating to the following matters: orders to captains; intelligence concerning French and Spanish fleets; lists of ships, including prizes, transports, store-ships, and ships of war; disposition of ships; condition and valuation of ships; line of battle of French and English fleets; signals; contracts for hire of vessels; manifest of prize goods; distribution of soldiers and regimental baggage; regulations respecting and subsistence of prisoners of war; returns of prisoners of war; exchange of prisoners; stores of ships and of hospitals; contractors' stores and provisions at various West India islands; contracts for hire of ships; contracts for provisioning ships and hospitals; state of hospital (Barbadoes, 1780, Long Island, 1780); care of sick and wounded; returns of hospitals; returns of sick, wounded, and killed; appointment of chaplains; leave of absence of rector from Jamaica; petitions praying for promotion.

" A Detail of the proceedings of the French Squadron under the Command of the Chevalier Destouches and of the Action that happened on the 16 of March, 1781, between it and the English Squadron, commanded by Adm. Arbuthnot."

Statements of cases of several navy officers engaged in American War, and of Mr. Knox, Secretary of New York and Provost Marshal of Georgia, submitted to the consideration of Parliament. (Printed.)

16. 1762-1763. Miscellaneous.

Account book of various dates.

Memorandum book of orders given to officers under Rodney's command, of letters sent and received, etc.

17. 1778. Miscellaneous.

List of vessels taken by the squadron stationed at the Leeward Islands under Rodney's command.

Memorial in justification of the conduct of Great Britain in the seizure of foreign vessels and warlike stores designed for the service of the rebels in America.

18. 1772-1781. Miscellaneous.

Sailing directions for Port Royal and Kingston harbors, 1772.

Letter from David Hodges treating of the advantages that would accrue to Spaniards in Mexico and Vera Cruz from shipping money to England or France via Pensacola. Pensacola, Sept. 5, 1772.

Letter from Gov. Peter Chester, enclosing minutes of the council of the province, Dec. 15, 1772, treating of the need of vessels to prevent the illicit trade of the French in the Mississippi and to defend the Pensacola station. Pensacola, Feb. 19, 1773.

Contract between Adm. Barrington on behalf of His Majesty and the merchants of Barbadoes. Mar. 16, 1779.

State of the fortifications of Dominica, 1779.

" The Questions and answers in the examination of Lord Rodney and others at the trial of ————." The first two sheets are missing. The charge evidently refers to what took place, Apr. 16, 1781.

Observations on the Caribbean station, treating of St. Eustatius, American prisoners, etc.

Various papers relating to prizes taken by ships under Rodney's command at the time of the capture of St. Eustatius.

19. Two copies of *Letters from Sir George Brydges, now Lord Rodney, to his Majesty's Ministers . . . relative to the Capture of St. Eustatius.* n. d. (Printed.)

Also, a map, showing Florida, the West Indies, and the region of the Gulf and the Caribbean Sea to the mouth of the Orinoco, entitled "Mapa desde al Cabo Mocomoco al Teste del Ro Orinoco, hasta el Confinen del Seno Aremo".

CHATHAM PAPERS.

The Chatham manuscripts, sometimes known from their donor as the Pringle manuscripts, comprise 372 bundles in two series, of which the first series, bundles **1-100**, contains the correspondence and papers of the first Lord and Lady Chatham; the second series, the correspondence and papers of William Pitt the younger (bundles **101-363**) and of John, second earl of Chatham (bundles **364-372**). Letters written by these members of the Pitt family, whether in the form of originals, copies, or drafts, are in bundles by themselves; most of the other letters are arranged according to the alphabetical order of the names of writers. A manuscript catalogue of the Chatham papers, which will be brought by an attendant upon request, indicates the bundle in which the letters from a given correspondent may be found, and describes in very brief and general terms the character of the contents of those bundles which contain miscellaneous and official papers. The papers were deposited in the Public Record Office by Adm. Pringle in 1888.

The papers of the first Earl and Countess of Chatham are arranged as follows: Bundles **1-69** contain their correspondence, bundles **1-4** comprising the letters printed in the four volumes of *Chatham Correspondence* (1838-1840), **70-74** are miscellaneous papers, **75-100** are official papers.

In the second series, bundles **101-194** contain the correspondence of the younger Pitt, **195-363** are miscellaneous papers, including many letters, **364-369** comprise the correspondence of the second Earl of Chatham, and **370-372** his miscellaneous papers. Comparatively few documents in this second series fall within the scope of this work.

1-69. 1756-1761. Chatham Correspondence.

| Chatham MSS.
Bundle —. | The first sixty-nine bundles contain letters, dating from 1756 to 1761, from the following governors and commanders, as well as from other persons connected with American affairs: |

The first sixty-nine bundles contain letters, dating from 1756 to 1761, from the following governors and commanders, as well as from other persons connected with American affairs: Gen. Abercrombie, Gen. Amherst, Gen. Barrington, Adm. Boscawen, Gov. Dinwiddie, Gov. Arthur Dobbs, Gov. Henry Ellis, Lieut.-Gov. Fauquier, Gen. Forbes, Gen. J. Hopson, Lord Loudoun, Gen. Monckton, Commodore Moore, Gov. R. H. Morris, Gov. Murray, Gov. Thomas Pownall, Gen. Stanwix, Gen. Townshend, Gen. John Thomas, and Adm. Saunders.

70. 1758, 1759. Letter-Book containing Letters relating to Louisburg and Quebec.

73. 1747-1767, and undated.

Petitions to William Pitt from the following memorialists:
John Winslow, reciting his services to the crown in the colonies.
Planters and merchants in the sugar colonies.
Marquis Duquesne. Northampton, Sept. 18, 1758.
John Stuart, captain in the South Carolina provincial regiment. July 26, 1761.
Petitions to George II. and George III. from the following memorialists:
" Dutiful and Loyal Subjects " representing " the sentiments and wishes of a faithful and afflicted people ", praying for peace with the American colonies.
John Hale, who had served in America.
Officers of the 78th Regiment for grants of land in the island of St. John and province of Nova Scotia.
William Vaughan (another copy is in bundle **95**).
Petition to the Duke of Bedford, secretary of state, from nine captains " who raised companys in North America on the intended Expedition against Canada ", 1748-1751.
Petition to the Board of Trade from Thomas Bromley praying that he be appointed clerk to the commons house of assembly of South Carolina. South Carolina, May 25, 1761.
Petition to the House of Commons from Jacob Fletcher, Liverpool merchant, whose brig, the *Nelly,* was burned by Americans at Savannah, Georgia, Dec., 1775.
Petitions to the House of Commons of merchants and traders of London trading to North America.
Memorial to Lord Viscount Ligonier, field marshal, from Capt. Joseph Gorham, who in 1744 was lieutenant of an independent company of foot raised in Massachusetts Bay for the relief of Nova Scotia, asking that six independent companies of Nova Scotia be put upon the British establishment and that he be appointed lieutenant-colonel of the same.
Memorial to " Your Lordships " of the paymaster-general, relating to the value of coin in the colonies.
Petition to the House of Commons of Thomas Orby Hunter, son and heir of Maj.-Gen. Robert Hunter, governor of New York, deceased, mentioning expenses incurred by his father in providing for Palatines sent from England to be employed in raising and manufacturing naval stores.

75-100. 1730-1774. Official papers.
75. Army papers, chiefly estimates and accounts, including references to North America. 1739-1756.
76. Army papers, chiefly estimates and accounts. 1757-1774 and undated.
78. Admiralty papers, 1739-1759, including:
Two papers relating to an English slave-ship captured by pirates, 1752.
Papers relating to Louisburg. 1758-1759.
Copy of a journal of a voyage to Halifax on the intended expedition under Lord Loudoun. 1757.
" Narrative of what pass'd from the time the Blandford, man-of-war was taken, untill Gov. Lyttelton's Arrival in England." 1755.

79. Admiralty papers relating to Canada. 1759-1767.

80. Prizes, Admiralty papers, etc., including:

Cases before the commissioners of prizes, etc. (mostly printed papers, of which some relate to ships engaged in American trade).

Précis of papers from Adm. Boscawen.

81. Revenue, papers relating to accounts, exports and imports, etc., including:

" Reasons . . . for continuing the Asiento contract to great Britain." n. d.

" Reasons . . . against any additional duty or any other measure from whence any additional hardship may ensue to the planters of tobacco or the colony of Virginia." n. d.

" Reasons against laying any new Tax upon Sugar—Beaver Hat Trade." n. d.

Copy of a letter from Lord Holdernesse to the Board of Trade, containing instructions as to correspondence with the governors of the colonies and the appointment of colonial officials. Whitehall, Mar. 30, 1752.

State of exports from Great Britain to North America in 1764.

State of fisheries of North America.

Account of bounties on goods exported from England to North America, and of bounties on goods imported from North America, Dec. 25, 1771–Dec. 25, 1774.

Papers relating to tobacco, sugar, molasses, and codfishery.

82. Miscellaneous papers, including:

A Thanksgiving sermon on the Total Repeal of the Stamp-Act preached at Cambridge, New England, May 20th . . . by Nathaniel Appleton, M. A. (Boston, 1766). (Printed.)

Letter signed " Amor Patriae " treating of taxation of colonies and presenting a scheme for admitting to Parliament representatives from the American colonies and from Ireland. Nov. 17, 1770.

" State of Mr. Hunter's Case relating to his claim on account of the Palatines subsisted by his Father."

95. Miscellaneous papers relating to states of North America, 1742-1757, including:

Letter containing a sketch of Ticonderoga from J. A. to James Abercrombie. From on board the *Nightingale,* June 12, 1757.

Extracts of letters on the present state of North America from a general officer in North America [Abercrombie] to a friend in London. New York, Albany, and Fort Edward, 1756.

James Abercrombie to Pitt, " Some Remarks on the Encroachments made by France on our Colonies in North America ". Craven Street, Nov. 25, 1756.

Undated paper on North American trade, by A. B., beginning " It would take up too much time . . . to enter into a minute Detail of the many and valluable Advantages arising to this Mother kingdom from the Produce and Commerce of her Setlements on the mainland of America." Postscript in another hand: " This was laid before the Ministry sometime in August, 1754."

Instructions from Gen. Braddock to Col. Johnson relating to the Indians. Alexandria, Apr. 16, 1755.

Letters from Col. John Bradstreet to Sir Richard Lyttelton. Halifax, Aug. 15, 1757; Albany, Sept. 5, 1757.

Letter to Pitt from James Buchanan and others, on the trade of Virginia and Maryland. London, Jan. 6, 1757.

Paper by Maj. Corry, 1756, headed " Of the English Provinces ", beginning " The English provinces in North America abound with Inhabitants."

Information from George Croghan, justice of the peace for the county of Cumberland in the province of Pennsylvania, relating to a party " of 60 People who had signed a Paper engageing to go to Fort Du Quesne ". Albany, Sept. 20, 1756.

Robert Dinwiddie's " State of His Majesty's Colonys and Plantations in America ", addressed to Peregrine Fury, and containing the number of fighting men in each colony; annual amount of goods shipped from Great Britain and Ireland to the colonies; annual amount of the natural and improved produce of each of the colonies and their trade with the Spaniards, etc., included; ships belonging to Great Britain trading to and from the colonies; vessels belonging to British subjects residing in the colonies; number of negro slaves in the several Sugar Islands. London, Sept., 1743.

Paper containing an extract from Dulany's letter of Nov. 4, 1756, from Maryland, and an extract from a letter from a gentleman in Philadelphia, Nov. 5, 1756, relating to military affairs.

" A short Narrative of the General Conduct of Connecticut Relating to the War In and Since the year 1755 ", endorsed, " Gov. Fitch's brief account of proceedings respecting the War ".

N. Hardinge to Pitt, with instructions to his deputies in North America. Treasury Chambers, Oct. 16, 1755.

Extract from Lieut.-Col. Heron's letter to Calcraft relating to the equipment of his men. July 21, 1750.

Extracts of letters from the Earl of Holdernesse to the Earl of Loudoun. 1757.

Letter from M. G. Hopson to the Earl of Loudoun. Halifax, Oct. 23, 1757.

Letter from Thomas Knox to James Abercrombie relating to Virginia trade. Bristol, Jan. 4, 1757.

Examination of Michael La Chauvegnere, jr., a French prisoner, before justices of the peace of Berks County, Pennsylvania, and Capt. Thomas Oswald at Reading, Oct. 16, 1757.

Examination of the same before the chief justice of Pennsylvania, Oct. 26, 1757.

Copy of the royal commission appointing Lord Loudoun general commander-in-chief in North America. Dated " examined " Mar. 9, 1756; endorsed, Mar. 5, 1756.

Extract of Lord Loudoun's instructions and letters. 1756.

Draught of a general letter to all the governors of North America on Lord Loudoun's arrival, 1756, enclosing " Queries to the Governors ".

Forces under Lord Loudoun's command. n. d.

Letters from Lord Loudoun to Gov. Pownall. Albany, Nov. 17, 1757; New York, Dec. 6 and 26, 1757.

Précis of Lord Loudoun's letters, and enclosures. 1756-1757.

Memoranda from Lord Loudoun's letters. 1757.

Col. Lydius's Declaration of Oswego and Proposal to Gen. Shirley to attack Niagara. Sept. 21, 1756.

Letter on the state of America, signed W. M. London, Nov. 16, 1756.

Two papers by Charles Pinckney: " The strength of the province of South Carolina considered; and a Scheme proposed for the defence and Security thereof against the French during the present War ", dated Dec. 3, 1756; and a representation to Pitt concerning the weak and exposed state of South Carolina, dated Dec. 6, 1756.

Letters from Gov. Pownall to Lord Loudoun. Boston, Nov. 28, 1757; Dec. 15, 1757; Boston, Dec. 19, 1757.

" Intelligence from Col. Peter Schuyler of the New Jersey Regiment, taken at Oswego, and now a Prisoner at Quebec; sent by Joseph Morse, who left that place October 4, 1757."

Account of Shirley's expedition against French posts at Niagara.

Paper beginning " French Forts where Major John Smith, Commander of a Company of Rangers on the frontiers of Virginia was Prisoner . . . for eleven months ". Endorsed, " extract from Major Smith's Journal, 1756/7, in Mr. Abercrombie's letter of Nov. 16, 1757 to Mr. Wood ".

Copy of a memorial to the king from William Vaughan of Damariscotta in Massachusetts Bay, son of the Hon. George Vaughan, late lieutenant governor of the province of New Hampshire and grandson of William Vaughan, late president of the council of the said province, deceased, relating the services rendered by his ancestors and himself to the crown and praying for recompense. Endorsed, Nov., 1745. Another copy is in **73**.

Memorial to the Duke of Bedford, secretary of state, from nine captains (Peter Wraxall *et al.*) who raised companies in North America, on the intended expedition against Canada, requesting that the Secretary at War hear and report on their case. London, Apr. 26, 1749.

Papers relating to the offer from Capt. von Wreden of Hesse Darmstadt to raise a regiment for service in America, and similar proposals from Samuel Waldo of Boston, New England, and from Messrs. Lauchlan and others of Glasgow.

" Extracts of all Letters from my Deputy in America, which . . . seem to relate to the Course of exchange between Jamaica and London ", etc. Charles Hanbury Williams to the Committee of Secrecy, dated Pay-Office, May 8, 1742.

Memoranda about raising troops in America, 1709, 1740, 1746, 1754-1757.

Copy of the treaty with the Three Nations sealed at Albany, Sept. 14, 1726.

" Extracts from the Papers relating to the Coin and Paper Bills of Credit in the British colonies in America laid before the House of Commons the 28th March, 1740, in pursuance of addresses to his Majesty of the 13th of June, 1739, whereby an Account was desired."

Copy of the royal warrant authorizing the paymaster-general to make assignments of the off-reckonings of the three independent companies to be raised for the service of South Carolina. Apr. 13, 1745.

" Copy of the Leaden Plate buried by Mr. Celeron, 1749, at Trois Rivières and Ohio."

" List of offices in the American Colonys the nomination to which was vested in the Board of Trade by Order in Council of the 11th of March, 1752 ", giving the names of officers in each colony; how appointed; salary; and how paid.

" Recencement general du Pais des Ilinois, 1752."

A few unsigned letters and extracts of letters relating to military and political affairs. 1755-1756.

A Brief State of the Province of Pennsylvania, etc. (Printed, 3d ed., London, 1756.)

Extract of a letter from an officer at Fort Edward. Nov. 17, 1756.

Memorandum with regard to the supposed number of regular troops now in North America. Dec. 13, 1756.

Unsigned paper on the proposed military operations in North America, beginning " Having endeavoured to acquire a knowledge in the affairs of America and reflected a good deal upon them, I have hazarded some thoughts upon our operations in that part of the world." [1756?]

Extract from a letter of an officer in Albany. Jan. 6, 1757.

Several papers relating to expeditions against Louisburg and Quebec.

96. Miscellaneous papers relating to states of North America, 1758-1763, including:

Draft of instructions for Maj.-Gen. Amherst. Mar. 3, 1758.

Extract of a letter from Maj.-Gen. Amherst to Gen. Wolfe. Louisburg, Aug. 15, 1758.

Précis of thirty-five papers enclosed in Maj.-Gen. Amherst's letter of Feb. 28, 1759.

Letters from Maj.-Gen. Amherst, dated New York and Ticonderoga, 1759, to the following: Brig.-Gen. Lawrence, Mar. 9, 16, Apr. 14; Col. Williamson, Mar. 15; Brig.-Gen. Whitmore, Mar. 16, Apr. 16, July 27; Brig.-Gen. Stanwix, on affairs to the southward, Apr. 5; also, Mar. 30, 1759, précis of letters from Gen. Amherst, Gen. Whitmore, Gov. De Lancey and Gov. Pownall; and an extract from Maj.-Gen. Amherst's letter dated Crown Point, Oct. 22, 1759, to Brig.-Gen. Murray, Albany, May 26, 1760; to Lord Barrington, Oct. 18, 1760; and to agents, to contractors for victualling forces in North America, Mar. 17, 1761.

Two letters from Capt. Thomas Bell treating of the relations of the French and English in America, pointing out the " mistakes in the present Limits of the Government of Quebeck " and offering " a new Limitation and . . . the benefits that would accrue therefrom ". Kilkenny Barracks, Sept. 2 and Dec. 4, 1763.

Letter from Ephraim Biggs showing how to destroy the power of the French in America. Philadelphia, Apr. 2, 1759.

Extract of a letter from Lieut.-Gov. Bull of South Carolina to the Board of Trade relating to the Spanish at Pensacola and the French at Mobile, enclosed in a letter from Edward Sedgwick, solicitor and clerk of reports, Aug. 21, 1760. June 30, 1760.

Précis of a letter from the Board of Trade, enclosing letters from Lieut.-Gov. Ellis and the governor of St. Augustine. Apr. 11, 1758.

Letter from Lieut.-Gov. Colden to Pitt (printed in Kimball's *Correspondence of William Pitt,* II. 410-411). New York, Apr. 5, 1761.

Two papers from Maj. Corry on the defense of the English possessions in America. Sept. 15 and Oct. 29, 1763. The first paper begins " A Scheme to preserve Our Conquests in America "; the second, " I observe by the treaty of peace The Island of New Orleans is particularly Reserved to the French."

Letter to Pitt from Maj. Craven, of the regiment late Pepperrell's (printed in Kimball's *Correspondence of William Pitt,* I. 172-175). Castle Street, Leicester Fields, Feb. 1, 1758.

Letter from William Davis, enclosing " the examination of an English Sailor that came in a Flag of Truce from New Orleans ". Philadelphia, Sept. 16, 1758.

Letter from Gov. De Lancey to Pitt, with enclosed letters giving an account of Col. Bradstreet's success at Cataraqui. New York, Sept. 11, 1758.

Copy of the Earl of Egremont's letter to the governors in America. July 9, 1763.

Letter from Gov. Ellis to Pitt relating to the Creek Indians. Georgia, July 10, 1760.

Military sketch-map from Philadelphia to Fort Du Quesne in Brig.-Gen. Forbes's letter of July 12, 1758.

Particulars relating to Gen. Forbes's army, for the Hon. Thomas Penn. Signed W. Smith, London, Jan. 3, 1759.

Paper beginning " Mr. Franklin and Mr. Jackson have consider'd the Points propos'd to them, and are of Opinion That In case the Winter Expedition against Fort Duquesne prove effectual ", etc. [1758?]

Letter from Count de Fuentes relating to Newfoundland. Sept. 9, 1760.

An almost illegible paper relating to Georgia. 1758.

Copy of letters from Col. Jeremiah Gridley to Christopher Kilby relating to the trouble of the Massachusetts assembly with the governor, and the arrival of commissioners for the union from Connecticut. Jan. 19 and 28, 1758.

Copy of a letter from the Earl of Halifax to the Board of Trade treating of the office of superintendent of the settlement on the Mosquito Shore. Nov. 12, 1764.

Copy of a letter from the Board of Trade to the Earl of Halifax treating of same. Dec. 2, 1764.

Petition of William Kelly and Samuel Stilwell, merchants at New York, praying for a letter to His Majesty's ambassador at the Spanish court to reclaim a ship and cargo taken out of a Spanish port in Santo Domingo by a French frigate. 1758.

Letter from Capt. Joshua Loring transmitting " a kind of Journall of what has happened in this Army from the 5th of July to this Day ". Camp Lake George, Aug. 19, 1758.

Id. from the same. Isle Royal in the River St. Lawrence, Aug. 26, 1760.

Letter from Lord Loudoun to Gov. Pownall, Jan. 18, 1758; to the Duke of Argyll, New York, Feb. 14, 1758; précis of a letter from Lord Loudoun, Feb. 14, 1758.

Copy of a letter from Gov. Lyttelton to Maj.-Gen. Amherst. Charleston, Mar. 16, 1759.

Letter from Lieut. Arch. McAulay to Capt. Horatio Gates. Oswego, Aug. 30, 1758.

Letter from the governor and council of North Carolina recommending Robert Rogers for superintendent of Southern Indian affairs. Wilmington, Dec. 9, 1761.

" Considerations on a future Peace etc. as it relates to Great Britain only ", beginning " It is more the Interest of Great Britain ", etc., Paterson to Pitt. Oct. 30, 1759.

Letter from Thomas Penn to Pitt enclosing a letter to Penn from Richard Peters, secretary of Pennsylvania, Dec. 8, 1758, " on several Matters of great importance to be settled with the Ohio Indians at a Treaty expected to be held with them in the Spring ", and also " a Message from an Indian Chief in behalf of himself and several nations of Indians on the River Ohio ". Feb. 3, 1759.

Extracts from letters from Pitt to the North American governors. Dec. 6 and 9, 1758.

Letter from Gov. Pownall to Lord Loudoun. Boston, Jan. 9, 1758.

Précis of Gov. Pownall's letters. [1758.]

Messages to the governor of Pennsylvania from the assembly, and to the assembly from the governor. Sept. 5-14, 1758.

Letter from John Robinson, speaker of the house of burgesses, Virginia. June 11, 1758.

Paper to the effect that the South Carolina merchants are greatly alarmed at the accounts they receive of Col. Montgomery's action on the first, and his marching the second of July toward Charleston to embark and return to Gen. Amherst.

Extract of a letter from William Vassall to Drake and Long giving an account of an illicit trade carried on by the northern colonies for French sugars from Monte Christi, Hispaniola. Boston, Mar. 3, 1759.

Representation to the king from the Virginia house of burgesses reciting the hardships suffered from the commencement of the French and Indian War, and beginning " Sheweth That in the Year One Thousand seven hundred and fifty three, your Majesty's Lieutenant Governor of this Colony received Information that the French were erecting a Fort on Your Majesty's Land on our Frontiers." [1758?]

Address of the burgesses of Virginia to the king presenting the above-mentioned representation of their grievances. [1758?]

Letter from the Society of Merchants in London trading to Virginia and Maryland, congratulating Pitt on the acquisition of Fort Duquesne. London, Feb. 7, 1759.

Clause of the act passed in Virginia, Oct. 15, 1760, relative to the forces of the province, endorsed: Delivered to Mr. Wood by Mr. Abercrombie for Wm. Pitt's information.

Letter from Gen. Whitmore to Maj.-Gen. Wolfe. July, 1759.

Demands for money from Massachusetts Bay, New York, and New Hampshire for 1756 and 1758.

Memorandum of provincials raised for the campaigns of 1758, 1759, and 1760.

Divers papers relating to Louisburg—treating of the number and state of the garrison; troops destined for the siege, and those to stay with Lord Loudoun; plans for the expedition against Louisburg, and number of forces needed; possible destination of the troops in America after the surrender; abstract of the defense from a French officer's journal, June 1–July 27, [1758]; letters from Louisburg from Adm. Boscawen's papers; account of stores that may be taken thence for the expedition of 1759.

Papers from Adm. Boscawen relating to his request that Pennsylvania furnish him with sailors, and the action of the Pennsylvania assembly thereupon, Sept., 1758; also including three letters from Louisburg and one from Fort Amherst.

Account of the action near Fort Duquesne between the English and French, Sept. 14. Philadelphia, Sept. 28, 1758.

Abercrombie's letter about the troops from Louisburg. Oct. 30, 1758.

Lists of winter-quarters for the troops in North America transmitted by Gen. Abercrombie and Gen. Amherst. Nov.-Dec., 1758.

List of the late promotions in America. Dec., 1758–Jan., 1759.

Paper beginning " If it be his Majesty's pleasure that an Expedition over Land be attempted by Colony Troops against a French Settlement on the River St. Lawrence "—outlines plan for raising troops in New England, New York, the Jerseys, and Pennsylvania, and for the conduct of the expedition itself [1758?].

Extracts from French letters from Montreal and Quebec. 1758-1759.

List of materials for a hospital. Mar. 17, 1759.

Copy of a letter from Amherst to Brig.-Gen. Whitmore relating to Quebec. Mar. 16, 1759.

Proceedings at Indian conferences at Philadelphia, Apr. 10, 1759.

List of transports taken up at New York in which Fraser's regiment was embarking, of transports at Philadelphia in which Lascelle's regiment was embarking, of transports arrived from England, and [1759] of transports taken up at Boston for the artillery and Webb's regiment. Apr. 26, 1759.

Spanish letter included in Gov. Moore's of Mar. 20, 1760.

Affidavits and other papers relating to two privateers cruising in the West Indies. New York and Jamaica, 1759-1760.

Papers showing the disposition and state of His Majesty's troops in North America. Oct. 4, 1760; Jan. 1, 1761; Mar. 24, 1761.

A Bill to Enable His Majesty to grant Commissions to a certain Number of foreign Protestants, who have served abroad as Offi-

cers or Engineers, to act and rank as Officers or Engineers, in America only, under certain Restrictions and Qualifications (1760). (Printed.)

An estimate for erecting barracks. n. d.

97. Miscellaneous papers relating to states of North America, 1764-1774, and undated, including:

Letter from "An American Farmer", beginning "The present Distresses of my native Country and the Dread of their Increase has induced me to take the freedom of troubling you with this Letter." [1765.]

Letter signed "Amor Patriae", enclosing a printed sheet with the same signature and beginning "As the Stamp Act and the situation of American affairs relative thereto". Grace Church Street, Feb. 2, 1766.

Précis of enclosures in Gen. Amherst's letter of Mar. 29, [no year].

Brief undated précis of letters relative to the French and Indian War received from Amherst and De Lancey (New York), Pownall (Boston), and Ellis (Georgia).

Letter from Gov. Bernard to the Earl of Shelburne. Boston, Dec. 6, 1766.

Letter to the Earl of Chatham from James Bowdoin, Samuel Pemberton, and Joseph Warren, committee appointed to make representation of the Boston Massacre. Boston, Mar. 23, 1770.

Papers from Maj. William Corry relative to the disciplining and provisioning of the army.

Two copies of a letter from Thomas Cushing, speaker of the house, to Pitt. Massachusetts Bay, Feb. 2, 1768.

Letter from John Dickinson. Philadelphia, Dec. 21, 1765. Extract of a letter from D. Dulany of Maryland to Lord Baltimore. Apr., [1766?].

Copy of a letter from Lieut. James Eidingtoun of the 12th (or Royal Highland) Regiment, one of the four officers who with a hundred of that regiment took possession of Fort Chartres. Fort Chartres, Oct. 17, 1765.

Extract of a letter from Gov. Franklin of New Jersey to the Earl of Shelburne. Burlington, Dec. 18, 1766.

Copy of a letter from Gov. Johnstone to Col. William Taylor, acting brigadier-general for the Southern District. Pensacola, Oct. 4, 1766.

Proposals of London merchants trading to North America to import grain from the plantations to relieve distress at home. London, Oct. 31, 1766.

Copy of a letter from the house of representatives of Massachusetts Bay to the Earl of Shelburne. Dec. 4, 1766.

Letter from the speaker of the Massachusetts house of representatives enclosing the resolves of the house of June 20, 1766, thanking Pitt for his efforts for the repeal of the Stamp Act. Boston, June 21, 1766.

Mississippi Company's papers, sent to Pitt on Apr. 2, 1774, including the "Original Articles of Agreement of the Mississippi Company"; "List of the Mississippi Company" and minutes of some meetings of the company in 1763 and 1767. (Printed in *American Historical Review*, XVI. 311-319.)

Thanks to Pitt from chiefs of the Mohecaunnuck and Wappinger tribes for granting an interview. July 25, 1766.

Copy of Gov. Sir Henry Moore's letter to the Board of Trade. Fort George, New York, Dec. 10, 1766.

Copy of a letter from Gov. Sir Henry Moore to the Earl of Shelburne enclosing an address of the general assembly of New York to the governor touching the quartering of troops. New York, Dec. 19, 1766.

Minutes of a conference held at Albany between Lieut.-Gov. John Nanfan and the Five Nations. July 12-21, 1701. Endorsed " Gov. Pownall. From the Indian Records ".

Copy of the governor's message to the general assembly of New York relating to the quartering of troops. Nov. 17, 1766.

Petition of the merchants of New York to the House of Commons touching recent restrictions of the plantation trade. Nov. 28, 1766.

Précis of letters from Gov. Pownall, Boston, Aug. 22, and Lieut.-Gov. De Lancey, New York, Aug. 24 and 26, relating to the surrender of Fort William Henry and Gen. Webb.

Paper endorsed " Mr. Pownall's plan for Quartering in America ", beginning " The Expence that Innholders and Victuallers Sustain ".

Copy of a letter from Capt. Preston to Commodore Hood enclosing a paper entitled " The Case of Captain Thos. Preston ". Boston Gaol, Mar. 17, 1770.

Copy of " The Remonstrance of the Merchants of the City of London interested in and Trading to the British colonies of Virginia and Maryland ", an undated petition to the king for " Protection to these colonies, adequate to the imminent Danger to which they are now exposed ".

" A short reply to a Pamphlet published in 1739, and Intit'd Considerations on the American Trade before and since the establishment of the South Sea Company." n. d.

" *An Act for granting certain Duties in the British Colonies and Plantations in America*", etc. 4 George III., c. 15. [1764.] (Printed.)

Account of the present mutiny act in America, beginning " Till the the last War there were very few Soldiers in North America ". [1765.]

" Observations on the Trade of Great Britain to her American Colonies, and on their Trade to Foreign Plantations with a Plan for retrieving, extending, and securing thereof, delivered to Mr. Secretary Conway the 1st of November, 1765, by Mr. Huske."

" Agreement between the West India and North American Merchants relating to the Trade of those Colonies." Mar. 10, 1766.

Lords' protest against committing the bill to repeal the Stamp Act. Mar. 11, 1766.

Lord's protest against passing the bill to repeal the Stamp Act. Mar. 17, 1766.

" General Distribution of H. M.'s Forces in N. America." Mar. 29, 1766.

Paper discussing the American " outposts " and their value, beginning " In the month of October, 1763 ". May, 1766.

Minute of a cabinet meeting (" a meeting of the King's Servants ") on a letter to be sent to Gov. Moore about the quartering of troops. Aug. 5, 1766.

Part of the American Mutiny Bill, 1766, showing the words omitted by the committee and those inserted.

Copy of the protest of the Lords against the bill entitled " An Act for the better regulating the Government of the Province of Massachusetts Bay in New England ". May 11, 1774.

Copy of an address to the king from the Continental Congress. [Oct. 26, 1774.] Printed in Ford's *Journals of Continental Congress,* I. 115-122.

Unsigned representation touching the offer made to Lord North by merchants trading to Boston to compensate the East India Company for the destroyed tea. [1774.]

Undated report of a committee on duties on imports into the British colonies.

Thirteen proposals, undated, relating to American trade—first proposal: " To reduce the Duty on Melasses to one penny per gallon ".

Paper, undated and unsigned, relating to the molasses trade, and beginning " The North Americans first Proof was that two Millions of People owe Great Britain Four Millions Sterling."

Reasons for allowing the Importation of Bar Iron from America. (Printed.)

Report of a Committee appointed to investigate the sugar question. n. d.

Heads of arguments touching the relation of Parliament to the colonies—a brief, undated paper, beginning " Each Province has an Assembly, Parliament or Estate."

Heads of arguments touching the relation between the colonies and the home government, beginning " 1. That in several of his Majestys Colonies in North America disorders have of late prevailed ". n. d.

" Heads of Arguments on the Principles of *Right* and *Law* with respect to the Stamp Act." n. d.

Paper beginning " Some Facts stated that prove the French to have been the Aggressors in North America ". n. d.

Paper, unsigned and undated, touching the relations between the Five Nations and the English, beginning " The Indian Country is of two kinds. 1. The Dwelling Lands and Castles. 2. And their Hunting Grounds." Refers to the " Instruction . . . dictated by Mr. Pownall when at Alexandria."

Paper beginning " To Judge from the first principles of the American War ", treating of four military operations obviously necessary on the continent of America, endorsed, "Mr. Abbercrombie". n. d.

Papers relating to the disposition and annual charge of the forces in America. n. d.

Invoices of medicines. n. d.

Abstract touching two intercepted treasonable letters from America addressed to the Duc de Mirepoix and signed " Filius Gallicae ". n. d.

Copy of a Provisional Act for settling the Troubles in America and for asserting the Supreme Legislative Authority and Superintending Power of Great Britain over the Colonies. n. d.

Observations on the acts of 6 George II. and 4 George III. (Molasses Act and Sugar Act). n. d.

Account of stores delivered out of the *Ruby* ordnance transport, by Maj.-Gen. Wolfe's order.

Project for the Indian trade in North America.

Paper beginning " As you will doubtless expect from me my opinion of the measures pursued at home relative to the colonies ". n. d. and unsigned.

Plan of campaign against Canada to be undertaken by regular and provincial troops, beginning " As all attempts to remove the French encroachments in N. America have failed of success ".

Memoranda concerning the gulf and part of the river St. Lawrence.

Minutes of proposals for distressing the French in North America and the West Indies. n. d.

Opinion of a committee [not named] relative to the granting of money by the provincial assemblies. n. d.

Paper treating of the way to oppose the French in America, beginning " The Success of the English in any future attempt upon Fort Duquesne, greatly, if not solely depends ", etc. n. d.

Scheme for the better uniting and cementing the mutual interest and peace of Great Britain and her colonies by representation in the Parliament of Great Britain and dominions thereunto belonging (printed in *The English Historical Review*, Oct., 1907, pp. 757, 758). n. d.

Draft of a bill for creating and issuing bills of credit under the denomination of exchequer bills of union for the use of His Majesty's colonies on the continent of America, submitted to Pitt by Henry McCulloh.

Account of money expended in the intended expedition against Canada.

98. Papers relating to Canada, 1755-1761 ; Newfoundland, Cape Breton, Nova Scotia, and Labrador.

Papers relating to West Indies and the Mosquito Shore, mostly dating from 1742-1768, concerning illicit trade, etc.

Report on logwood. 1717.

Copy of a letter from Gen. Abercrombie to James Abercrombie. Lake George, Aug. 9, 1758.

Paper endorsed " Indian intelligence from Sir Wm. Johnson ". Jan. 29, 1758.

Paper endorsed " French Account of Gen. Braddock's defeate near forte Du Quesne July, 1755 ". In English, accompanied by a letter signed Louis Perault, saying the account was given him by Mr. Roucher. A number of papers (five) from this bundle are printed in Kimball's *Correspondence of William Pitt*, I. 337, 396, 426; II. 247, 451.

101-363. Correspondence and Papers of William Pitt, the Younger.

220. Petitions to William Pitt, jr., including many from officers who had served in America and from Loyalists. 1782-1790. The account of losses suffered often throws light on social and economic conditions.

223. Petitions to the king from former civil and military officials in America and from Loyalists, including petitions from Lord Rodney, Lord Amherst, and William Knox, under secretary of state in the American Department to 1782. 1782-1792.

225. Petitions to the Treasury from officers in the army, colonial officials and Loyalists, and loyal planters in East Florida, including the petition of John Montrésor, July 13, 1793. 1781-1793.

226. *Id.*, memorial of Montrésor, with appendix of documents. Jan. 20, 1798.
Memorial from Maj. Bowes with accounts of money received and paid by him, by order of Lieut.-Gen. Leslie, South Carolina.

227. Petitions to Lord Carmarthen and others, including:
Memorials from British soldiers in the Revolutionary War.
Memorial of Peter Chester, late governor of the province of West Florida.
Memorials of proprietors of patent offices in the late British colonies.
Petition of Sir George Collier and of several captains, on the expedition to Penobscot, 1779.

231. Papers relating to government offices, including
Treasury minutes and other papers relating to the salaries and accounts of colonial governors. 1746-1749; 1780-1783.

286. "Abstract of the exports from the Port of Pensacola to Great Britain between the Quarter Ending the 5th day of July, 1778 and the 5th of July 1779."

343. Papers relating to states of North America, 1780-1793, including:
Account of imports and exports of goods by British merchants into the Mississippi. 1776-1779.
"Hints drawn up Anno 1780, when reconcilation with N. America was expected."
Letters from and to American Treaty Commissioners.
Observations on the American treaty.
Paper touching the retention of North American posts by the British. 1782-1784.
"Review of the Statutes necessary to be revised in consequence of the provisional treaty with America. By Mr. Pownall." Feb. 2, 1783.
Paper by the same relative to the future regulation of the commercial intercourse of Great Britain and the United States. Jan. 30, 1783.
Extract of a letter from . . . Gen. Washington to Sir Guy Carleton. Headquarters, Apr. 21, 1783.
Two papers on the contract for victualling forces in North America —cases concerning charges made against contractors by commissioners for auditing public accounts.

Précis of all remitting contracts for payment of troops in North America from 1754 to July 15, 1778, in Mr. Roger's note of Mar. 9, 1784.

Case of the late Brig.-Gen. Montfort Browne, lieutenant-governor of West Florida and governor-in-chief of the Bahama Islands.

344. Bundle labelled " Papers relating to states of N. America, 1794-1804, and undated, including:

Papers relating to imports into and exports from New York, including a printed proclamation of Gen. William Howe, New York, July 17, 1777, regulating imports and exports in relation to New York Island, Long Island, and Staten Island; and a certificate from the mayor of New York, D. Mathews, regarding the regulation of imports into New York, Mar. 21, 1778.

Papers relating to Georgia, Florida, and South Carolina, mostly petitions, etc., subsequent to 1783, asking relief for losses resulting from the war, and including the *Case of the Merchants and others interested in the Lands in the Province of Georgia ceded by the Cherokee and Creek Indian Nations,* etc., May 3, 1782 (printed).

Papers relating to American Loyalists, dated later than 1783 but referring to events prior to that date.

345. Papers relating to South America, Demerara, Brazil, and the Mosquito Shore, mostly later than 1783.

346. Papers relating to Canada, Newfoundland, New Brunswick, and Nova Scotia, mostly later than 1783.

348-351. Papers relating to the West Indies, *c.* 1774-1804, mostly later than 1783.

352. Resolutions, etc., of West India planters and merchants. 1783-1800.

MODERN BOARD OF TRADE PAPERS.

After the abolition of the old Board of Trade in 1782, business was done by the committee of the whole Council and the secretaries of state, until in 1784 a standing committee of the Council was appointed to take charge of all matters relating to trade and foreign plantations. This committee was dissolved in 1786, and another established which concerned itself chiefly with trade and commerce. The papers and books listed below represent the records and accumulations of this committee, except for certain volumes and bundles among the Miscellanea, which have been transferred from other series. Nearly all the records are of date later than 1783, but a few belong to the earlier period.

B. T. 1.
—
1-357. 1791-1839. In-Letters.

B. T. 2.
—
1-11. 1833-1839. In-Letters, Foreign Office.

B. T. 3.
—
1-28. 1786-1839. Out-Letters.

B. T. 4.
—
1-10. 1808-1839. Reference Books to Minutes.
11-12. Indexes.

B. T. 5.
—
1-46. Mar., 1784–July, 1839. Minutes.
This series of minutes is that referred to in the previous volume of this *Guide,* p. 102, note 3 ; p. 103, note 1.

B. T. 6.
—
1-187. Miscellanea.

1-8. 1771-1793. African Question.
9-11. 1788-1790. Questions, vols. 1, 2, 3.
12. 1788-1789. Africa.
13. 1772-1782. Letters.

All of these volumes relate to the affairs of the Company of Merchants trading to Africa. **13** is an entry book of letters written by the old Board of Trade and signed by Pownall, Cumberland, Grey Elliott, and sometimes by members of the board.

14. 1780-1784. Papers.

A volume of orders, regulations, and reports issued from the African House, London; also an original letter from Robert Stubbs, governor of Annamaboe and vice-president of Cape Coast Castle, to the old Board of Trade. At the end is a printed statement of the company dated London, Nov. 10, 1779.

15-18. Accounts of the African Company.

Reports of committees appointed to look into the accounts of the governors in Africa. 1768-1775.

Report of the governor and council appointed as a committee to examine the public accounts of Cape Coast Castle and several outforts. 1770-1776.

In **17**, at the beginning, are five leaves containing entries of Board of Trade business relating to trade with Leghorn, Venice, Lisbon, Sweden, Holland, Spain, Genoa, Flanders, and Africa, 1699-1788, with marginal references to the journal, entry books, and original documents (*C. O.* 388: **8-11**) of the old Board of Trade. The volume itself contains an account of expenses incurred by the committees of the company in defending the forts and settlements on the Gold Coast, 1779-1782, and *id.* in attending the captured forts of Apam and Bescoe, 1782-1784. Other expense accounts are included. Oddly enough, in this volume will be found minutes of the council in assembly of Nevis, Jan. 13, 1784–Jan. 8, 1785, Jan. 12–May 28, 1785, early pages to Apr. 14, 1784, missing.

18 contains an account of money received and expended by the committees for the support and improvement of the forts and settlements (15 papers). 1770-1784. Also a memorial of the company, Apr. 12, 1786, and summary accounts, 1770-1780, with a paper entitled " Case ", Apr. 19, 1780, a statement of the establishment and obligations of the company as reorganized.

20-27. 1784-1820. America, Trade.
35-36. 1787-1807. Cape Breton.
41. 1772-1790. Dominica.
80. 1783-1784. First Committee Papers with Continuations, America, Commercial Intercourse, Correspondence.
81. *Id.* Minutes.
82. 1784-1786. Domestic Business.
83-84. America and West Indies, Commercial Intercourse.
85-86. 1783-1786. American Intercourse with Great Britain.
87. *Id.* With Newfoundland and Nova Scotia.
88. America and West Indies.
83-88 are mentioned in this volume under " Custom House ", p. 115.

111-114. 1782-1786. Commercial Treaty with France.
187. 1783-1784. American Ships cleared from London.

SUPPLEMENTAL LIST OF VOLUMES AND DOCUMENTS IN THE PUBLIC RECORD OFFICE TRANSCRIBED FOR THE LIBRARY OF CONGRESS.[1]

Admiralty 1. **480- 489.**
              3817-3820.

Treasury 64. **88-90,** Blathwayt's Journal.

Admiralty Court, Instance and Prize, Libel Files. Various numbers from bundles **73, 80, 81, 82, 88, 91, 92, 93, 94, 98, 107, 108.**

Audit Office, Declared Accounts. List of Customs Officials from **756,** 792, to **829,** 1086.

Attention may also be called to the fact that since the list in the preceding volume of the *Guide* was printed, the following series of Colonial Office Papers have been copied.

C. O. 5: **1280-1286, 1287-1297, 1299-1300,** constituting the miscellany and entry books of the series formerly known as *B. T. Proprieties.*

C. O. 324: **3-19,** constituting the entry books of the series formerly known as *B. T. Plantations General.*

The original documents belonging to these series were copied some years ago by the Historical Society of Pennsylvania and the transcripts are now in the library of that society.

---

[1] See Andrews and Davenport, *Guide,* etc., pp. 431-445, and vol. I. of the present work, p. 309. Work of transcription has also begun on the documents at Lambeth Palace and at Fulham Palace, and will be extended, if possible, to cover selected portions of the material in the archives of the Society for the Propagation of the Gospel.

INDEX.

Abbott, suit against, 309

Abercorne, ship, 203

Abercrombie, James, colonial agent, correspondence of, 163, 165, 353, 354, 355, 363; memorial of, 158; papers transmitted by, 359, 362

Abercrombie, *Maj.-Gen.* James, accounts of, 133; letters from, 160, 163, 351, 353, 363; papers from, 165, 275, 359

Abigail, ship, 334

Abraham, Heights of, *see* Heights of Abraham

Abraham-Sacrifice, ship, 331

Acadia, neutrals of, 29

Accomac, customs collectors of, 111; exports and imports of, 51; naval office lists of, 187, 188; sixpenny dues in, 64

Accountant General's Department, papers of, 8, 51-55

Accounts, declared, history and administration of, 79-80; papers concerning, 80-106, 368; reference to, 66; registration in, 40

Accounts, Declared, List and Index of, 79

Accounts, Public, Commissioners for Auditing, 79, 241; enrollments of, 79

Active, ship, 334

Acts, Book of, Admiralty Court Papers, 307, 315

Acts of the Privy Council, Colonial, 13, 47, 119, 144 n., 193, 266

Adair, correspondence of, 281

Adams, Deane, and Company, letter to, 334

Adams, John, advocate, 175; correspondence of, 333, 337, 339

Administration, letters of, 134

Admiral, Lord High, 2, 5; duties of, 1, 3, 14, 15, 17, 38, 304; men in the office of, 2; orders from, 314; prizes condemned to, 14; suit of, 311; warrants issued by, 313, 316; *see also* Admiralty

Admirals, accounts of, 51; as governors, 62, 63-64; contingent fund of, 52; court of, 64; despatches, letters, and instructions to, 3, 9-12, 34-35, 36, 44, 46, 53; information for, 44; proclamations of, 53

Admiralty, 1; accounts laid before, 55; action of, 25; advice to, 18; advocate of, 48, 49; appeals in, 197; appointments by, 36, 37, 46, 318; attitude of, toward Revolution, 41; cases, 21, 186; colonial business of, 34; complaint of, 39; control of marines by, 38, 270, 271; co-operation of, 23; correspondence intercepted by, 44; correspondence of, 27, 28, 29, 34, 36, 41, 52, 55, 56, 57, 59, 139, 163, 174, 183, 210, 244, 279, 348, 349; council for, 35; counsellor of, 3; courts-martial provided by, 40; directions from, 40; droits of, 3, 15, 16, 18, 48, 151, 317-318, 331; entry books of, 35; func-

tions of, 2, 3, 3 n., 36, 123; instructions from, 23, 27, 28, 46, 50, 56, 125; instructions to, 29-30; judge of, 37; letters relating to, 25; licenses granted by, 191; location of offices of, 5-6; meetings of, 45; minutes of, 45-46; officials of, 3, 19, 51; orders in Council to, 33; orders of, 43; papers concerning, 36-37, 352; papers of, 1-65, 275, 353; petition to, 20; perquisites of, 15, 16, 35; proceedings in, 18, 195; procedure of, 5; records of, 5; registers of, 42 n., 319; relations of, with the army, 32; reports to, 18; warrants from, 316

Admiralty, Collection of Statutes relating to the, 3 n.

Admiralty, Commissioners of, 1, 3, 37; comments by, 53; commissions to, 16; correspondence of, 19-21, 34; information for, 44; orders from, 33-34, 54; petition to, 35; powers of, 15, 17, 18, 33, 49, 50

Admiralty, High Court of, 3; functions of, 1; history and procedure of, 304-307; instructions for, 4; instructions prepared by, 34; judge of, 14, 36, 37; letters from, 23; officials of, 18, 35, 36; papers of, 24, 304-345; prize cases in, 24; register of, 35; registry of, 333; reports from, 3; seal of, 329; warrant to, 16

Admiralty, Secretary to, 2; correspondence of, 22, 23, 34-35, 43, 45; orders and instructions from, 29-30; papers of, 9-51; request to, 32

Admiralty, Select Pleas in the Court of, by R. G. Marsden, 304 n.

Admiralty, Solicitor of, 35; letters concerning department of, 14-18

Admiralty courts, accounts of, 66; common-law courts and, 14, 15, 16, 18; condemnation of prizes in, 14; in America, 17, 21, 26, 171, 175, 176, 308, 317; in West Indies, 207; jurisdiction of, 3, 4, 14, 15, 16, 17, 27, 48, 207; letters concerning, 35-37; officials of, 35; proceedings of, 26; warrants to, 16

Admiralty Office, Whitehall papers deposited in and taken from, 8, 9

Admiralty Records, List of, 9 n.

Advocate general, suits of, 329

Affleck, *Com. Sir* Edmund, despatches from, 10

Africa, garrisons on the west coast of, 255; imports into, 117; letter-book concerning, 299; letters from, 256; papers concerning, 366; pay of men going to, 258; staff returns from, 290; trade to, 129, 184, 206, 257, 367; troops in, 195; War Office estimates concerning, 170

African Company, *see* Royal African Company

369

Mackenzie, Robert, secretary to Sir Wm. Howe, accounts of, 70, 83, 87-88; appointed commissioner on Loyalist claims, 260; letter from, 199; money paid by, 67; testimony taken by, 264

Mackferson, John, trial of, 329

Mackintosh, letters from, 281

McLane, John, instructions from, 335

McLane and Sterrett, instructions from, 335

McLaughlin, William, letters to, 328

McLean, expense accounts of, 134

Maclean, *Capt.*, letters from, 276

Maclean, *Brig.-Gen.* Allan, correspondence of, 292, 293; petition of, 191

McLure and Young, letters to, 328

MacNaire, Charles, case of, 154; memorial of, 155

Macomb, John, accounts of, 70, 88

Macouchi, chaplain to Maryland, letter to, 207

Madeira, rice from, 158

Madox, Thomas, *History of the Exchequer*, 136 n.

Madras, ship, 309

Madrid, letters from, 27

Magdalene, ship, 338

Magnell, suit of, 310

Mahogany, 130, 181

Mails, for the colonies, 4; forwarding of, 35; interception of, 44, 45, 319, 322-328, 333; official packets, 37; *see also* Postal service; Post office

Maine, timber cutting in, 183

Mainwaring, suit of, 308

Maitland, William, *Hist. of London,* 6 n.; map of, 305 n.; plan of London, 141 n.

Major and Henniker, accounts of, 85

Malaga, 42

Malbury, letters from, 292

Malcolm, Daniel, papers relating to, 169

Malcolm, J. W., letters from, 119-120

Malcolm, John, charges of, 194; petition of, 188

Malden, port books of, 127

Mallass, Henry, warrant for, 316

Mallett, Jonathan, accounts of, 69, 99

Malpas, *Viscount* (Frederick), office willed to, 146

Malt, exports of, 250

Malta, 42

Man, *Adm.* Robert, despatches and letters from, 10, 59

Man, Isle of, 61, 125, 272

Manchester, *Duke* of (William Drogo Montague), 346

Manchester, merchants of, 187

Manchester papers, 346

Mango trees, 32

Manila, affairs in, 168; expedition to, 190

Mann, Edward, accounts of, 81; observations by, 152

Manufactures, English, 116, 117, 130, 152; Irish, 117

Manxmen, 125

Maple, suit of, 308

Maps, bundle of, 234; of country between the Delaware and the Susquehanna, 83; of Lieut.-Col. Harry Gordon, 105; of road from Philadelphia to Fort Duquesne, 357

Marblehead, conditions in, 326; customs collectors of, 51, 111; duties in, 62, 64; exports and imports of, 51; register of, 223

Margaretha Dorothea, ship, 130

Margarett, ship, 129

Margueritte, ship, 338

Maria, ship, 338

Marine Causes, surveyor of, 1

Marine Corps, Hist. Recs. of the, by Cannon, 38 n.

Marine Department, America, bills drawn for, 70

Marine Office, official papers of, 57-58

Marine Pay Office, 2, 39

Marines, *see* Seamen and Marines

Marines, Hist. Recs. of the Royal, by Edge, 38 n.

Marlborough, *Duke* of, 270

Marque, letters of, against America, 125, 316; against France, 125, 317; against Spain, 317; American, 333, 334; bonds for, 329, 343-344; copy of, 24; from Bristol, 321; holders of, 317; instructions and papers concerning, 319, 330, 337; issued by Benjamin Franklin, 338; by Congress, 334; by Jonathan Trumbull, 338; lists of, 36, 50; question concerning, 50; right to issue or use, 15, 17; ships having, 19; warrants for, 3, 33, 35

Marquis of Rockingham, ship, 320

Marr, *Capt.,* letters from, 293

Marriages, 64

Marriott, *Sir* James, advocate general, appointment of, 18; interrogatories by, 26; letter from, 192; opinion of, 49; reports of, 27, 193

Marriott, Thomas, account of, 72, 155; certificate of, 156; memorials of, 149, 151

Marry, John, 57

Marsden, R. G., assistance of, 307, 333; Bradford letter discovered by, 319; quotation from, 128; *Select Pleas in the Court of Admiralty,* 304 n.

Marseilles, letters to and from, 27, 335

Marsh, John, British commissioner, 260

Marshal, fees of the, 317

Marshall, John, letter to, 322

Martha, ship, 198, 319

Martha's Vineyard, trade of, 172

Martin, Joseph, customs collector, 76

Martin, *Gov.* Josiah, N. C., accounts of, 68, 95-96; appointment made by, 144; letters from, 183, 186; Loyalist pension to, 226; paper of, 185

Martin, *Dr.* William, letter to, 323

Martinique, custom house at, 168; expedition against, 90, 166; governors of, 278; merchandise imported from, 250; papers concerning, 181; reduction of, 43; ships captured at, 91; troops in, 133, 288; *see also* West Indies

Naval officers, commissions to, 14; correspondence of, 12, 14, 34-35, 36, 40, 58-59; courts-martial of, 46; information concerning, 34; in Jamaica, 13; instructions to, 29, 30, 34-35, 36, 45, 48; lists of, 10, 23, 47; oaths administered to, 3; reports of and concerning, 10, 12, 195; transportation of, 32, 32 n.; *see also* Admirals; Commodores; Commanders; Captains; etc.

Naval stations, 2, 8, 9-12, 28, 52, 56

Navigation acts, collectors of, 93; enforcement of, 22, 140, 168, 231, 232; goods under, 171; interpretation of, 49; letters concerning, 209; receipts under, 169; surveyor of, 111; violation of, 114, 124

Navy, British, accounts of, 221; affairs of, 1-5, 46, 271, 304; American-born seamen in, 53; bills drawn on, 151; condition of, 1, 2; courts-martial ordered by, 33; dismissals from, 152; engagements and operations of, 2, 10, 11, 12-13, 22, 24-25, 33, 34, 43, 350; interchangeability of, with the army, 38; letters from, 324; location of offices of, 5-9; money for, 39, 163; papers of and relating to, 5-9, 31; payments in, 39; recruiting men for, 14; supplies for, 28, 30, 54, 115, 196, 199, 262, 263; treasurer of, 56; trees for, 171; upkeep of, 3; victualling of, 221; yards, 52; *see also* Admiralty; Navy Board, etc.; and correlated subjects as Naval officers, Seaman, Squadrons, Ships, etc.

Navy, Commissioners of the, *see* Navy Board

Navy, Discourses of the, by John Hollond, 6 n.

Navy, Ships of War, Coll. of Statutes relating to the Admiralty, 3 n.

Navy Board, accounts laid before, 55; accounts with, 51, 52; clothing furnished by, 40; communications with, 3; correspondence of, 13, 34, 35, 40, 53, 55, 56, 139, 247, 248, 349; expenses not allowed by, 52; functions of, 1, 2, 4; instructions to, 34, 271; lieutenants examined by, 56; location of the offices of, 6-7; minutes of, 56; officers of, 1-2, 3, 7; papers of, 55-56; papers sent to, 202, 208; procedure of, 5; supplies transported by, 109; transports under, 247

Navy House, 3

Navy Office, 1, 6, 7, 8

Navy Pay Office, 1, 7

Naylor, *Commissary*, 246

Neal, petition of, 240

Neath, port books of, 128

Neeser, Robert W., *Despatches of Molyneux Shuldham*, 11

Negroes, Antigua laws concerning, 49; carrying off of, 294; clothing purchased for, 68; imported into Barbadoes, 238; in Jamaica, 309; in West Indies, 310; purchase of, 18; ship trading in, 240; *see also* Slaves

Neill, William, letters to, 328

Neilson, Archibald, deputy in North Carolina, 144; Loyalist pension to, 227

Nelly, brig, 352; brigantine, 195

Nelson, *Gov.* William, Va., letters from, 21

Neptune, ship, 17, 275, 320, 338

Nesbit, accounts of, 85

Nesbitt, accounts of, 68

Nesbitt, T. M., and Company, letters to, 328

Netherlands, commission returned from, 332; exports and imports from colonies of, 237, 238, 249; fleet of, 45; importations from, 166; letters of marque against, 343; letters to, 339; naval prisoners of, 237; ships of, 313, 317, 318; supplies from, 45; tea from, 168, 180; tobacco seized by traders of, 229; trade items concerning, 342, 367; transport service to, 4; troops for, 32; vessels belonging to, 21; wars with, 270, 307, 331

Neven, *Mr.*, customs collector, 162

Nevis, council of, 367; customs collectors of, 75, 76; duties collected from, 93, 94; naval office lists of, 181, 182, 183, 185, 187, 188; vice-admiralty courts in, 27 n.; *see also* West Indies; Leeward Islands

New Brunswick, accounts of the deputy paymaster and governors of, 66, 89; papers concerning, 365

Newburgh, *Lord* (George), *see* Cholmondeley *Earl* of

Newbury, 197

Newburyport, ships for, 254

Newcastle, *Duke* of (Thomas Pelham-Holles), letters to, 159, 162, 274 n.

Newcastle, customs records of, 123, 127; exports and imports of, 51; statistics of, 175; vice-admiralty court in, 35

Newell, Thomas, *Diary,* 187

New England, advocate general of, 24, 37; Andros in, 229; bills for, 208; boatmen in, 222; carpenters in, 167; comptroller of the customs in, 103; council of, 315; customs difficulties in, 168; despatches from, 10; expenditures in, 167, 202; exports and imports of, 120, 176, 219, 220, 248, 249, 251, 252; French design upon, 29; governors of, 35, 205; illicit trade in, 172; impressment in, 17; letter from, 208; merchants of, 204; mines in, 204; naval officers to aid, 34; naval supplies for and from, 13, 158; officers in, 229; ordnance to, 242; Parliamentary grant to, 90, 232; perquisites of the admiralty in, 15-16; pirates and pirate goods in, 243, 344; Randolph in, 229; rebellion in, 43; register of, 223; revenue in, 240; ships, 16, 47, 128, 129, 310, 311; survey of, 73; troops, 87, 150, 158, 359; vice-admiralty courts in, 15; voyage to, 308; *see also* Colonies; Plantations; names of individual colonies

New England Chronicle or Essex Gazette, 11

New England Historical and Genealogical Register, 224

Newfoundland, admiralty in, 197; affairs of, 279; agents of, 213; barrack-masters at, 82; commissariat papers of, 75; customs and duties in, 62, 64, 179, 238; customs collectors of, 111; early history of, 63-64; Edwards's contingent fund at, 52; engineers for, 296; exports and imports of, 115, 116,

soldier in, 326; trade of, 365; transports in, 53

State Paper Branch Office, 9

State Paper Office, 260

State Papers, Domestic, Calendar of, 1 n., 6 n.

Staws, *Capt.*, accounts of, 68

Stede, *Gov.* Edwyn, Barbadoes, 75, 76, 203, 204

Stede, John, petition for, 204

Stedman, proposals of, 176

Stedman, Charles, commissary of captures, accounts of, 72, 92; services of, 201

Steel, John, letter from, 349

Stegg, Thomas, jr., auditor in Virginia, 143

Stephens, letters to, 72

Stephens, Thomas, petition of, 157

Stephenson and Blackburn, accounts of, 68, 85

Sterrett, John, letters to, 328

Sterrett, McLane and, 335

Stevens, experiment of, 159

Stevens, B. F., 260, 261, 346; *Campaign in Virginia,* 347

Stevens, Henry, *Facsimiles,* 12

Stevens, Philip, letter to, 210

Stevens, William, letters from, 322

Stevens and Baker, suit of, 308

Stevens and Fell, suit of, 319

Stevenson, William, letters to, 328

Stewart, Alexander, letter from, 26

Stewart, Anthony, memorial of, 196

Stewart, Charles, receiver general of customs, accounts of, 94, 95, 175, 218; letter from, 174; memorials from, 177; patent to, 78; security for, 206; statistics from, 76

Stewart, *Lieut.* Donald, accounts of, 67, 106

Stewart, Duncan, case of, 183; deception of, 182; letter from, 176; paper concerning, 182

Stewart, J., accounts of, 99

Stewart, James, contractor, memorial of, 195

Stewart, *Adm.* James, despatches from, 9

Stewart, Stephen, and Sons, letters to, 328

Stewart and Totten, letters to, 328

Stewart's Dragoons, 88

Stewiac River, map of, 54

Stilwell, Samuel, petition of, 357

Stirling, *Earl* of (Sir William Alexander), case of, 203, 240

Stockton, customs records of, 123

Stokes, *Chief Justice* Anthony, memorial of, 199

Stone, Andrew, charge against, 156

Stopford, despatches to, 282

Store-ships, *see* Ships

Storey, Enoch, accounts of, 68, 83

Stornaway, emigration from, 224

Story, William, of Mass., case of, 26

Story, William, of R. I., letter to, 210

Stover, suit against, 279

Straits, trade with, 48

Stranraer, emigration from, 224

Stratford, 291

Stringer, *Col.* John, customs collector, 75, 76

Strode, J., accounts of, 80

Stuart, *see also* Stewart

Stuart, *Capt.* John, of S. C. regiment, petition of, 352

Stuart, John, of the Southern Indian Department, accounts of, 70; Indian presents sent to, 191; letters from, 194, 196; papers from, 199; presents to Indians by, 199

Stubbs, Robert, governor of Annamaboe, letter from, 367

Sturgis, Daniel, letters from, 323

Subsidies, 93, 116

Success, ship, 149, 339

Suckling, George, memorials from, 181, 187

Sugar, Act, 363; amount of, collected, 215; clay, 195; committee to investigate, 362; duty on, 81, 94, 144, 213, 251, 353; duties paid in, 111, 112 n.; East India goods concealed in, 122; exports and imports of, 25, 151, 203, 219, 220, 231, 237, 238, 248, 249, 250, 252, 253, 321; illicit trade in, 358; Muscovado, 130, 250; papers concerning, 353; plantation, 338; receipts for, 92; refined, 130, 152; seizure of, 330; ship carrying, 334; warehousing of, 252

Sugar colonies, exports and imports of, 151, 152, 219, 237, 249, 252; papers relating to, 150; petitions from and concerning, 152, 352; slaves in, 354; tonnage of ships from, 219

Sukey, ship, 335

Sukey of Poole, ship, 321

Sullivan, *Ensign,* letters from, 292

Sullivan, George, memorial of, 190

Sullivan, *Gen.* John, letter to, 45; troops under 324

Sunbury, Ga., customs collectors of, 111; exports and imports of, 51; sixpenny dues in, 64

Supplies, accounts of, 8, 57, 75, 163, 298; Albany, 161, 166; application for, 205; army, 29, 30, 31, 33, 44, 45, 74, 82, 83, 85, 87, 98, 109, 110, 134, 150, 162, 163, 186, 192, 193, 195, 198, 222, 242, 244, 247, 262, 263, 269, 280, 294; as presents for Indians, 197; capture and confiscation of, 45, 49; commissaries for, 194; contraband, 23, 44; contractors for, 40; contracts for, 4, 13, 84-86, *passim,* 109, 159, 161, 168, 211; cost of, 54, 82, 158, 163, 212, 221; delivered from the *Ruby,* 363; exports and imports of, 194, 220; for Africa, 195; for American commissariat, 74; for American prisoners, 59; for colonies, 30, 86, 160, 164, 190, 196, 197; for Continental Congress, 320; for expedition of 1759, 359; for French-American settlements, 161; for Indians, 99-101, 177; for Rattan, 148; for store-ships, 30; for transports, 30; French, 44, 45; foreign, 55; from Ireland, 166, 197; from Massachusetts, 160; from Rhode Island, 161; letters and papers relating to, 46, 55, 73, 85, 96, 158, 178, 189, 195, 196, 245, 294, 295; license to carry, 191; lists of, 58, 196, 246; loss of, 212; medical, 5, 5 n., 60; monetary, 159; naval, 3, 4, 13, 17, 19, 29, 30, 40, 48, 49, 52, 54, 158, 163, 204, 262, 263, 349, 350, 352; New York,